KU-023-193

Be a Fodor's Correspondent

Your opinion matters. It matters to us. It matters to your fellow Fodor's travelers, too. And we'd like to hear it. In fact, we *need* to hear it.

When you share your experiences and opinions, you become an active member of the Fodor's community. That means we'll not only use your feedback to make our books better, but we'll publish your names and comments whenever possible. Throughout our guides, look for "Word of Mouth," excerpts of your unvarnished feedback.

Here's how you can help improve Fodor's for all of us.

Tell us when we're right. We rely on local writers to give you an insider's perspective. But our writers and staff editors—who are the best in the business—depend on you. Your positive feedback is a vote to renew our recommendations for the next edition.

Tell us when we're wrong. We're proud that we update most of our guides every year. But we're not perfect. Things change. Hotels cut services. Museums change hours. Charming cafés lose charm. If our writer didn't quite capture the essence of a place, tell us how you'd do it differently. If any of our descriptions are inaccurate or inadequate, we'll incorporate your changes in the next edition and will correct factual errors at fodors.com *immediately*.

Tell us what to include. You probably have had fantastic travel experiences that aren't yet in Fodor's. Why not share them with a community of like-minded travelers? Maybe you chanced upon a cozy *hôtel de charme* or food-with-a-view bistro that you don't want to keep to yourself. Tell us why we should include it. And share your discoveries and experiences with everyone directly at fodors.com. Your input may lead us to add a new listing or highlight a place we cover with a "Highly Recommended" star or with our highest rating, "Fodor's Choice."

Give us your opinion instantly at our feedback center at www.fodors.com/feedback. You may also e-mail editors@fodors.com with the subject line "Provence Editor." Or send your nominations, comments, and complaints by mail to Provence Editor, Fodor's, 1745 Broadway, New York, NY 10019.

You and travelers like you are the heart of the Fodor's community. Make our community richer by sharing your experiences. Be a Fodor's correspondent.

Bon voyage!

Tim Jarrell, Publisher

CONTENTS

Fodor's

PROVENCE & THE CÔTE D'AZUR

7th Edition

Where to Stay and Eat for All Budgets

Must-See Sights and Local Secrets

Ratings You Can Trust

Fodor's Travel Publications   New York, Toronto, London, Sydney, Auckland
www.fodors.com

FODOR'S PROVENCE & THE CÔTE D'AZUR
Editor: Robert I. C. Fisher

Editorial Production: Tom Holton
Editorial Contributors: Sarah Fraser, Rosa Jackson, Heather Stimmler-Hall
Maps: David Lindroth, *cartographer;* Rebecca Baer and Bob Blake, *map editors*
Design: Fabrizio La Rocca, *creative director;* Guido Caroti, *art director;* Moon Sun Kim, *cover designer;* Melanie Marin, *senior picture editor*
Production/Manufacturing: Angela L. McLean
Cover Photo (sunflower field, Provence): Bryan F. Peterson/Corbis

SPECIAL SALES
This book is available for special discounts for bulk purchases for sales promotions or premiums. Special editions, including personalized covers, excerpts of existing books, and corporate imprints, can be created in large quantities for special needs. For more information, write to Special Markets/Premium Sales, 1745 Broadway, MD 6-2, New York, New York 10019, or e-mail specialmarkets@randomhouse.com.

AN IMPORTANT TIP & AN INVITATION
Although all prices, opening times, and other details in this book are based on information supplied to us at press time, changes occur all the time in the travel world, and Fodor's cannot accept responsibility for facts that become outdated or for inadvertent errors or omissions. So **always confirm information when it matters,** especially if you're making a detour to visit a specific place. Your experiences—positive and negative—matter to us. If we have missed or misstated something, **please write to us.** We follow up on all suggestions. Contact the Provence editor at editors@fodors.com or c/o Fodor's at 1745 Broadway, New York, NY 10019.

PRINTED IN THE UNITED STATES OF AMERICA

10 9 8 7 6 5 4 3 2 1

CULTURAL CLOSEUPS

MAPS

ABOUT THIS BOOK

Our Ratings

Sometimes you find terrific travel experiences and sometimes they just find you. But usually the burden is on you to select the right combination of experiences. That's where our ratings come in.

As travelers we've all discovered a place so wonderful that its worthiness is obvious. And sometimes that place is so experiential that superlatives don't do it justice: you just have to be there to know. These sights, properties, and experiences get our highest rating, **Fodor's Choice,** indicated by orange stars throughout this book.

Black stars highlight sights and properties we deem **Highly Recommended,** places that our writers, editors, and readers praise again and again for consistency and excellence.

By default, there's another category: any place we include in this book is by definition worth your time, unless we say otherwise. And we will.

Disagree with any of our choices? Care to nominate a place or suggest that we rate one more highly? Visit our feedback center at www.fodors.com/feedback.

Budget Well

Hotel and restaurant price categories from ¢ to $$$$ are defined in the opening pages of each chapter. For attractions, we always give standard adult admission fees; reductions are usually available for children, students, and senior citizens. Want to pay with plastic? **AE, D, DC, MC, V** following restaurant and hotel listings indicate if American Express, Discover, Diners Club, MasterCard, and Visa are accepted.

Restaurants

Unless we state otherwise, restaurants are open for lunch and dinner daily. We mention dress only when there's a specific requirement and reservations only when they're essential or not accepted—it's always best to book ahead.

Hotels

Hotels have private bath, phone, TV, and air-conditioning and operate on the European Plan (a.k.a. EP, meaning without meals), unless we specify that they use the Breakfast Plan (BP, with a full breakfast), or Modified American Plan (MAP, with breakfast and dinner), or Full American Plan (FAP, including all meals). We always list facilities but not whether you'll be charged an extra fee to use them, so when pricing accommodations, find out what's included.

Many Listings
- ★ Fodor's Choice
- ★ Highly recommended
- ✉ Physical address
- ✚ Directions
- ⬛ Mailing address
- ☎ Telephone
- 🖷 Fax
- ⊕ On the Web
- ✐ E-mail
- 🎫 Admission fee
- ☉ Open/closed times
- ► Start of walk/itinerary
- ▭ Credit cards

Hotels & Restaurants
- 🛏 Hotel
- ⇥ Number of rooms
- ⚐ Facilities
- ❍ Meal plans
- ✕ Restaurant
- ⚐ Reservations
- 👔 Dress code
- ↘ Smoking
- 🍸 BYOB
- ✕🛏 Hotel with restaurant that warrants a visit

Outdoors
- 🏌 Golf
- ⛺ Camping

Other
- ☺ Family-friendly
- ♫ Contact information
- ⇨ See also
- ✉ Branch address
- ☞ Take note

Provence & the
Côte d'Azur

WHAT'S WHERE

	On the marshy flatlands of the Rhône River delta and the raw-rock hills of the Alpilles that divert the river west, this region has been a major crossroads since the Romans first profited from the river, the coast, and an Alpine route. Nowhere in France will you find such a concentration of antiquities so superbly preserved: Roman arenas, still in use, at Arles and Nîmes; a complete Greco-Roman village outside St-Rémy; and the spectacular triple-tier aqueduct called the Pont du Gard. It is a region of haunting natural beauty, too, with the Camargue's hypnotic plane of marsh grass stretching to the sea, interrupted only by an explosion of flying flamingos or a modest stampede of stocky bulls led by latter-day cowboys. The craggy Alpilles to the northeast are filled with feathery olive trees (this is one of Provence's main sources of olive oil) and with time-weathered mas, or farmhouses. The scenery is surpassed only by the cities: feisty, tatty, Latin Nîmes; graceful, golden Arles, still resonant with the memory of Van Gogh; and cosmopolitan St-Rémy-de-Provence, a haven for chic urbanites and a mellow retreat dappled with the shade of ancient plane trees.
	Anchored by the former papal stronghold of Avignon, with its mammoth medieval palace and crenellated city walls, the Vaucluse spreads luxuriantly north into the Rhône vineyards of Châteauneuf-du-Pape and east into mountain country quilted with olive and cherry orchards and fields purpling with lavender. There are fields of Roman ruins in Vaison-la-Romaine and a Roman theater in Orange. But thanks in part to the tantalizing descriptions of British author Peter Mayle, the world beats a path to the Luberon, a long, low mountain, patchworked with vineyards and olive groves and punctuated by medieval hilltop villages: Bonnieux, Ménerbes, Roussillon, and Gordes. Like Mayle, others seek the sun-blessed lifestyle of cool stone farmhouses and warm feet. On Sunday they flock to the antiques market at L'Isle-sur-la-Sorgue to bargain for pastis glasses, quilts, and aspiring Old Masters.
	This is inspirational country, both for the austere beauty of its scenery and the rhythm of its cities, including the cosmopolitan shipping port of Marseille—bold, ancient, larger than life. You can actually taste the best of the Mediterranean here captured in a savory bouillabaisse. Sleek, smart Aix-en-Provence burgeons with international students and the arts. Cézanne lived and died in Aix and painted its rugged countryside in rough-

hewn daubs of russet and green, especially his beloved Montagne de Ste-Victoire. Marcel Pagnol, filmmaker and author of *Jean de Florette* and *Manon des Sources,* spent a lifetime capturing the scent of thyme and the roar of the fish market in his native territory around Marseille. In Aubagne, his hometown, Pagnol's characters come to life in sweet, slightly kitschy terra-cotta figurines called santons. The central coast is a well-kept secret, with pockets of natural beauty that could pass for an Aegean island. The rocky Calanques, fjord-like bays between Marseille and the picture-perfect port of Cassis, make for some of the prettiest coastline in France. Also stretched along this quiet underbelly are local beaches and spectacular views from the coastal highway. Farther east lie Bandol, as well known for its beaches as for its pink wine, and the brawny shipyard city of Toulon. And at the end of the world, the Presqu'île de Giens, ferries leave hourly for the car-free paradise of the Iles d'Hyères. The loveliest of these islands is Porquerolles, protected as a national park.

THE WESTERN CÔTE D'AZUR

This is where the legend begins: palm trees, parasol pines, crystalline sun, a sea improbably blue, all framed against the green Massif des Maures and the red-rock Massif de l'Estérel and backed by the wild Haut Var. There's St-Tropez, with its white-sand beaches and its port cafés thick with young gentry hoping for a glimpse of a movie star . . . (or even a wannabe?). Also in the area are family-beach towns such as Ste-Maxime and Fréjus, and sportif resorts like St-Raphaël and Mandelieu. Just an hour's drive inland, Old Provence awaits in Cotignac, Seillans, and Fayence, palpable in crumbling ocher, heavy-leafed plane trees, and the chink of metal balls in a sandlot game of pétanque. Venture even farther and you'll enter the wild and woolly backcountry of Haute Provence, winding on mountain roads until you reach one of France's greatest natural wonders: the Gorges du Verdon, a Grand Canyon–like chasm roaring with milky green water and edged by some of Europe's most hair-raising roads. At its west end, the faïence center of Moustiers-Ste-Marie proffers elegant pottery on either side of a mountain torrent.

WHAT'S WHERE

Cosseted by Mediterranean breezes and sheltered by green cliffs and silver Alps, this part of the Côte d'Azur has charmed the world, and it's easy to see why. Try these names on for sighs: Cap d'Antibes, Monte Carlo, St-Paul-de-Vence, Nice, Beaulieu-sur-Mer—sunbelievable shangri-las that conjure up resorts sophisticated and gaudy, melt-in-your-mouth scenery, and the feeling that you are a million miles away from all cares. The world's most pampered citizens still head to glamour capitals like Cannes, where palatial hotels such as the Carlton spoil the stars during the May film festival, and Monaco, a principality with money to burn. Cross the high rises of Hong Kong with the amusement park feel of Disneyland, add a royal touch, and there you have Monte Carlo—all 473 acres of it.

At the region's heart, Nice is so nice (ooh, pardon us). Draped along the Baie des Anges and rich with local museums and cuisine, the large city harbors an Old Town studded with bon-bon-colored palaces. You don't need to visit the life-spanning collection of the city's Musée Matisse to understand this great artist: Simply stand in the doorway of his former apartment (at 1 Place Charles Félix) and study the Place de l'Ancien Senat 10 feet away—it's a golden Matisse pumped up to the nth power. But all along the coast you'll experience the scenery and light that seduced artists, including Renoir's garden-villa in the enchanting medieval hilltop village of Haut-de-Cagnes and the Musée Picasso in Antibes's imposing seaside castle (wait until you see how extravagantly beautiful Old Antibes is). For many, the Contemporary Art Road includes a drive into the hill country to St-Paul-de-Vence—a medieval bourg graced by both the Fondation Maeght's beautiful museum and La Colombe d'Or, the famous inn where you can dine under priceless Picassos—and on to Vence and Matisse's sublime Chapelle du Rosaire. More art is found in belle-époque Menton, the lemon-scented seaside resort where a Cocteau collection presides over a fort. But natural splendors also abound: beneath the zillion-dollar hotels of Cap d'Antibes and St-Jean-Cap-Ferrat you'll find two of the most spectacular coastal footpaths in the world. And if you want to look down on the likes of Bill Gates (the proud new owner of the famous La Leopolda villa near the pretty fishing port of Villefranche-sur-Mer), just head up to sky-kissing Èze, a *village perché* that seems to hover just below cloud level.

WHEN TO GO

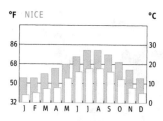

°F NICE **°C**

July and August in Provence and the Côte d'Azur can be stifling, not only because of the intense heat but the crowds of tourists and vacationers. June and September are the best months to be in the region, as both are free of the midsummer crowds and the weather is summer-balmy. June offers the advantage of long daylight hours, although cheaper prices and many warm days, often lasting well into October, make September attractive. Try to avoid the second half of July and all of August, when almost all of France goes on vacation. Huge crowds jam the roads and beaches, and prices are jacked up in resorts. Don't travel on or around July 14 and August 1, 15, and 31, when every French family is either going on vacation or driving home. Watch out for May, riddled with church holidays—one a week—and the museum closings they entail. Anytime between March and November will offer you a good chance to soak up the sun on the Côte d'Azur. After All Saints (November 1) the whole region begins to shutter down for winter, and won't open its main resort hotels until Easter. Still, off-season has its charms—the pétanque games are truly just the town folks' game, the most touristy hill towns are virtually abandoned, and when it's nice out—more often than not—you can bask in direct sun in the cafés.

Climate

Provence has a basically Mediterranean climate, distinguished by winds like the mistral, or "master" wind, which blows down the Rhône up to 150 days a year. This and other winds make the soil here dry and the night sky bright and clear. Temperatures soar on the coast in July and August, and it rains less in summer than at other times of the year.

🎵 Forecasts **Weather Channel Connection** ☎ 900/932–8437, 95¢ per minute from a Touch-Tone phone.

Weather conditions in France can be checked on the Web, at ⊕ www.meteo.fr.

QUINTESSENTIAL PROVENCE

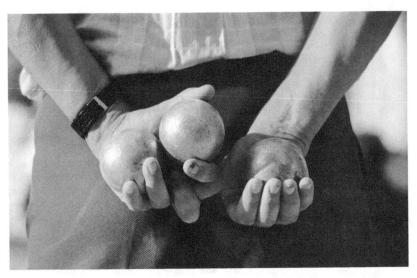

Pastis & Pétanque

In every village from the Rhône Valley to the Italian border, under every deep-shaded *allée* of plane trees, the theater of Provençal life plays itself out slowly, serenely, and sociably. The café is a way of life in Provence, a cool outdoor living room where friends gather like family and share the ritual of the long, slow drink, the discussion of the weather (hot), and an amble over to the *pétanque* (lawn-bowling) court. The players stand, somber and intense, hands folded behind backs, and watch the intricate play of heavy metal balls rolling and clicking. A knot of onlookers gathers, disperses, is reinforced. In this region of the animated debate, the waving gesture, the forefinger punching to chest, it is a surprisingly quiet pastime.

Just as refined a ritual is the drinking of the requisite pastis. The server arrives with a tray loaded with the appropriate props: a carafe of water emblazoned with "Ricard" or "51"; a bowl with an ice cube or two; a bowl of olives, black as jet; and a stubby glass cradling two fingers of amber liquid redolent of anise and licorice. Plop an ice cube into the liquor, then slowly pour a rope of cool water into the glass, watching for the magic moment when the amber transforms itself to milky white. Sip slowly, mop your forehead, and settle in.

Dining à la Midi

You'll eat late in the Midi (south of France), rarely before 1 for lunch, usually after 9 at night. In summer, shops and museums may shut down until 3 or 4, as much to accommodate lazy lunchers as for the crowds taking sun on the beach. But a late lunch works nicely with a late breakfast—and that's another southern luxury. As morning here is the coolest part of the day and the light is at its sweetest, hotels of every

If you want to get a sense of contemporary Provençal culture and indulge in some of its pleasures, start by familiarizing yourself with the rituals of daily life. These are a few highlights—things you can take part in with relative ease—in Provence and the Côte d'Azur.

class take pains to make breakfast memorable and whenever possible served outdoors. There may be tables in the garden with sunny-print cloths and a nosegay of flowers, or even a tray on your private balcony table. Accompanied by birdsong and cool morning sun, it's one of the three loveliest meals of the day.

It's Sunbelievable!

With their worldwide fame as the earth's most glamorous beaches, the real thing often comes as a shock to first-timers: much of the Côte d'Azur is lined with rock and pebble, and the beaches are narrow swaths backed by city streets or roaring highways. Some beaches are reviled for their famous *galets,* round white stones the size of your fist, heaped along the shoreline, just where the sand should be. Sit on them for long, and you'll have to shift; lie on them with a book, and you'll feel like a fakir on a rounded bed of nails, so ma-

tresses are de rigueur. Some resorts ship in truckfuls of sand or shovel in loads from deep water. There are some natural sand beaches on the southern French coast—especially between St-Tropez and Cannes—and some beaches, like La Garoupe on Cap d'Antibes (where folks like Picasso and Cole Porter used to sunbathe) enjoy legendary status. Provence's coastline—between the Camargue and St-Tropez—alternates sandy pockets with rocky inlets called *criques* and *calanques,* where you perch on black rocks and ease yourself into turquoise water. Many beaches are privately operated, renting parasols and mattresses to anyone who pays; if you're a guest at one of the local hotels, you'll get a discount. Fees for private beaches average €6–€15 for a dressing room and mattress, between €2 and €4 for a parasol, and between €10 and €25 for a cabana to call your own. At least the sun is free, yours for the basking.

IF YOU LIKE...

Being Scott & Zelda

Married new money? Made a stock-market killing? Or just remember the old adage "if you don't travel first class, your heirs will"? Well, the Riviera has been a hard place to practice self-denial ever since F. Scott Fitzgerald arrived with the rest of his Jazz Age literati. So drain that glass of Dom. Enough lollygagging! It's time for a power decision: which luxurious pleasure palace will you treat yourself to? Hey, if you can't be self-indulgent on the French Riviera, where can you be?

- **Cap-Eden Roc, Cap d'Antibes.** Where once Hemingway ordered another Pernod and Zelda wore her latest Poiret, this famous hotel is today the rendevous of the film stars. You may find Michael and Catherine in the bar, Harrison behind his *Herald-Tribune,* and Barbra keeping a low profile under her parasol by the cliff-edge pool. Try to be cool and focus on the menu.

- **Château de la Chevre d'Or, Èze.** Seemingly set just below cloud level, this sky-high aerie occupies some of the choicest real estate in Èze, that magical island-in-the-sky perched 1,500 feet over the sea and St-Jean-Cap-Ferrat. Little wonder the views out your window rival those from a NASA space capsule.

- **La Colombe d'Or, St-Paul-de-Vence.** Yes, those are real Picassos, Mirós, Braques, and Bonnards over your dinner table. This legendary hotel and restaurant was once the favored hangout of these artists when you could buy one of their daubs for $5. Today, it is super-stylish, utterly elegant, and you can't move without bumping into a Calder mobile—or an off-duty celebrity dining on the enchanting terrace.

Villages Perchés

Practically defying gravity, the sky-kissing, hilltop-perched villages of Provence and the Riviera are some of the most spectacular sights in France. In the Middle Ages, pirates and Saracens drove village life to put its wagons, as it were, in a circle—and well above the fray. Thus sprouted these villages from the hilltops, Babel-like towers of canted cubes and blunt cylinders seeming to grow out of the rock. Houses mount several levels; thus freed from obstructing neighbors, their windows take in light and wide-open views. The tiniest of streets weave between rakish building blocks, and the houses seem tied together by arching overpasses and rhythmic arcades. Wells spring up in miniature *placettes* (little squares), the trickling sound echoing loud in the stone enclosure. Succumb to their once-upon-a-timeliness and be sure to visit two or three.

- **Èze.** As cute as a Fisher-Price toy village, Èze is so relentlessly picturesque it will practically click your camera for you.

- **Haut-de-Cagnes.** Topped by a Grimaldi castle, once a forgetaway favored by the likes of Renoir, Soutine, and Simone de Beauvoir, this enchanting labyrinth of steep alleys and Renaissance stairways is a magical place where time seems to be holding its breath.

- **Oppède-le-Vieux.** Isolated above the Luberon, this village stands alone in the mist, lovingly cared for by its residents but utterly uncommercial.

- **Peillon.** This perfect example of the eagle's-nest village above the Riviera coast has been voted boutique-free forever by its citizens, and remains marvelously ancient, even primeval, in atmosphere.

Relishing the Riviera

The Côte d'Azur is home to top chefs who are redefining the "new Mediterranean cuisine" in all its costly splendor: "scrambled" sea urchins; herb sausages with chopped truffles and lobster; frogs' legs soup with fresh mint; and poached sea bass flan with crayfish sauce. Grand names like Alain Ducasse still present such delights at showplaces like Monaco's Le Louis XV, but there are any number of young stars on the make. But with access to some of the world's best ingredients, Provençal chefs face a dilemma—do they uphold tradition or go out on a limb? Here are four legends who balance both schools beautifully.

- **Le Louis XV, Monte Carlo.** Crystal, gilt, and period pomp frame the extraordinary cuisine of Alain Ducasse—truffle-sprinkled artichokes, ember-grilled pigeon breast, and salt-seared foie gras, anyone?

- **Moulin des Mougins, Mougins.** Culinary wizard Alain Llorca has given a radical facelift to this Roger Vergé landmark, as you'll discover with one bite of the incredible Mediterranean sea bass steamed with seaweed and white coco beans.

- **Jacques Maximin, Vence.** This temperamental superchef has found peace of mind in a gray-stone farmhouse covered with wisteria where he now whips up dazzling creative country cooking. Who can resist his candied-eggplant sorbet?

- **Le Cagnard, Cagnes-sur-Mer.** While feasting on Jean-Yves Johany's black-truffle lasagna, look up to see the medieval ceiling slide open to reveal the evening sky.

Where Art Comes First

Artists have been drawn to the south of France for generations, awed by its luminous colors and crystal-clear light. Monet, Renoir, Gauguin, and Van Gogh led the way, followed over the years by Léger, Matisse, Picasso, Chagall, and Cocteau. Cézanne had the good fortune to be born in Aix, and he returned to it, and to his beloved country home nearby, throughout his life. The artists left behind them a superb legacy of works, utterly individual but all consistently bathed in Mediterranean color and light. That's why a visit to this region can be as culturally rich as a month in Paris and just as intimately allied to the setting that inspired the work. Art museums abound—but don't forget to pay your respects to Cézanne's studio in Aix and Renoir's garden home in Cagnes.

- **Fondation Maeght, St-Paul-de-Vence.** With its serene setting in a hilltop woods and its light-flooded displays of modern works, this gallery-museum is the best mixed-artist exhibition space in the south of France.

- **Musée de l'Annonciade, St-Tropez.** St-Tropez was the Riviera's first "Greenwich Village" and artists—Signac, Derain, and Matisse, among them—flocked here in the early 20th century. Today, the collection has its share of masterworks.

- **Musée Matisse, Nice.** In a superb Italianate villa above Nice, Matisse's family has amassed a wide-ranging collection of the artist's works.

- **Musée Picasso, Antibes.** In view of the scenes of enchanting Antibes that inspired them, vast paintings by Picasso are mounted in the rooms where they were created.

ON THE CALENDAR

Hundreds of festivals and events are held annually. Here are some of the better-known and better-attended. For complete information, contact the town's tourist information office or log on to the town Web site.

WINTER

February

Around Mardi Gras (Shrove Tuesday), Carnival de Nice is an eye-popping spectacular, when for 28 days the Niçois cut loose in one of Europe's most extravagant celebrations of pre-Lenten joie de vivre. An interactive "flower battle" parade puts the Rose Bowl to shame, and you'll find lots of nighttime parades and floats, with tons of partying musicians and dancers in the streets. Just before Carnival, the tourist office ⊕ www.nice-coteazur.org launches a separate Web site for the event ⊕ www.nicecarnival.com. Other Carnivals are held in Aix-en-Provence, Arles, and Marseille. Menton, that elegant 19th-century resort city sitting on the border of Italy, is famous for its balmy weather year round and flaunts it during its Fête du Citron (International Lemon Festival) ⊕ www.villedementon.com.

SPRING

March

Feria de Pacques ⊕ www.ville-arles.fr is the mother of all Arles bull-fighting festivals, held around Easter weekend. At night, the streets fill up with enormous parties.

April

In Arles, the Fête des Gardians celebrates the unique cowboy culture of the Camargue area with a multiday festival and rodeo usually scheduled to begin the last Sunday in April.

May

Cannes's famous film festival, the Festival International du Film ⊕ www.festival-cannes.org, is geared for film professionals with full accreditation, but try telling that to the mobs in the streets, who hover for 12 days in this resort hoping to rub shoulders with fame and fortune. To maximize stargazing, pick up a schedule for the daily *montée des marches,* when the cast of the featured film being screened runs the press gauntlet up the red carpet into the Palais des Festivals. The Association Française du Festival International du Film oversees the festival. St-Tropez mounts its Bravade de St-Torpes around May 16–17, replete with processions and Provençal costumes. The famous Gypsy festival and religious pilgrimage, the Pélérinage des Gitanes packs the town of Stes-Maries-de-la-Mer every May 24–25 to honor St. Sarah, and the streets ring with flamenco contests, farandoles, horse races, bullfights, and religious processions. In late May, Monte Carlo hosts its roaring Monaco International Grand Prix, ⊕ www3.monaco.mc/monaco/gprix/, where many of the most celebrated race-car drivers try to avoid accidents on the twists and turns of the city avenues.

SUMMER	
June	The Transhumance (transfer of sheep from winter to summer meadows) overuns adorable St-Rémy-de-Provence on Whitmonday. St-Tropez hosts its period-costume Bravade des Espagnols on June 15 to fete the 16th-century Spanish incursion.
July	Juan-les-Pins and Antibes puts on the jazziest International Jazz Festival in July. The nearby town of Hyères also has a jazz festival of note during this month. The play's the thing at the celebrated Avignon Theater Festival ⊕ www.festival-avignon.com held at historic locales throughout the city during the last two weeks of July, notably the courtyard of the majestic Palais des Popes. In the spectacular setting of Orange's ancient Roman amphitheater, the Théâtre Antique, the Chorégies d'Orange ⊕ www.choregies.asso.fr/ is mounted in July and early August, with music, theater, and opera performances. On July 14, Bastille Day is marked by fireworks and merrymaking, with a big celebration always hosted in Avignon. In July, Aix-en-Provence and Vaison-la-Romaine both host month-long festivals of music, theater, and dance.
July–August	Restored by Pierre Cardin's millions, the former château of the Marquis de Sade now hosts a summer-long Festival de Lacoste ⊕ www.easyclassic.com in the town of Lacoste, outside Ménerbes, featuring music and drama. Arles is famous for its Rencontres Internationales de la Photographie ⊕ www.rip-arles.org with many photo events and shows scheduled from July to September.
FALL	
September	The Rice Harvest is celebrated with a festival in Arles in mid-September. Stes-Maries-de-la-Mer hosts a Sea Procession and blessing on the Sunday nearest September 22.
November	A Côtes du Rhône wine festival is held in Avignon in November.

SMART TRAVEL TIPS

Half the fun of traveling is looking forward to your trip—but when you look forward, don't just daydream. There are plans to be made, things to learn about, serious work to be done. The following information will give you helpful pointers on many of the questions that arise when planning your trip and also when you are on the road. In addition, the organizations listed in this section will supplement the information in this guidebook. Note that additional essential information is provided in the Essentials sections found at the end of each regional chapter of this book. Many trips begin by first contacting the French tourist bureau: consult the French Government Tourist Offices listed under Visitor Information, below. Happy landings!

ADDRESSES

Addresses in France are fairly straightforward: there are the number and the street name. However, you may see an address with a number plus "bis," for instance, 20 bis rue Vavin: This indicates the next entrance or door down from 20 rue Vavin. In small towns a street number may not be given, as the site will be the dominant (or only) building on the block or square. In rural areas, however, a site may list only a route name, a number near the site, or sometimes just the name of the small village in which it is located.

Note that in France you enter a building on the *rez-de-chaussée* (RC or 0), as the ground floor is known, and you have to go up one floor to reach the first floor, or *premier étage*.

AIR TRAVEL

BOOKING

When you book, look for nonstop flights and remember that "direct" flights stop at least once. Try to avoid connecting flights, which require a change of plane. Two airlines may operate a connecting flight jointly, so ask whether your airline operates every segment of the trip; you may find that the carrier you prefer flies you only part of the way. To find more booking tips and to check prices and make online flight reservations, log on to www.fodors.com.

CARRIERS

Most major airlines fly to Paris and have connecting flights to the south of France on domestic airlines. The one exception is Delta, which flies nonstop to Nice from New York. From the United Kingdom, EasyJet offers inexpensive nonstop service to Nice and Marseille; BMI British Midland and BMI Baby have direct flights to Nice; low-cost Ryanair flies to Nîmes and Montpellier.

Within France, Air France flies frequently from Paris to Avignon, Marseille, Nice, Montpellier, and Toulon. EasyJet has flights from both Paris airports to Nice.

✈ Domestic Airlines **Air France** ☎ 800/237-2747 in the U.S., 0870/142-4343 in the U.K., 08-20-82-08-20 in France ⊕ www.airfrance.com.
✈ Major Airlines **American Airlines** ☎ 800/433-7300 in the U.S., 08-10-87-28-72 in France ⊕ www.aa.com. **Continental** ☎ 800/231-0856 in the U.S., 01-71-23-03-35 in France ⊕ www.continental.com. **Delta** ☎ 800/241-4141 in the U.S., 08-00-30-13-01 in France ⊕ www.delta.com. **Northwest** ☎ 800/447-4747 in the U.S., 08-90-71-07-10 in France ⊕ www.klm.com. **United** ☎ 800/538-2929 in the U.S., 08-10-72-72-72 in France ⊕ www.united.com. **US Airways** ☎ 800/622-1015 in the U.S., 08-10-63-22-22 in France ⊕ www.usairways.com.
✈ From the U.K. **BMI British Midland** ☎ 0870/607-0222 in the U.K., 01-55-69-83-06 in France ⊕ www.flybmi.com. **British Airways** ☎ 0870/850-9850 in the U.K., 08-25-82-50-40 in France ⊕ www.ba.com. **BMI Baby** ☎ 0870/264-2229 in the U.K., 08-90-71-00-81 in France ⊕ www.bmibaby.com. **EasyJet** ☎ 0990/292-929 in the U.K., 08-25-08-25-08 in France ⊕ www.easyjet.com. **Ryanair** ☎ 0870/156-9569 in the U.K., 08-92-55-56-66 in France ⊕ www.ryanair.com.

CHECK-IN AND BOARDING

To enter France, you need to **carry your passport.** You will be asked to show it when you check in. For more information, *see* Passports & Visas, *below.*

Always **find out your carrier's check-in policy.** Plan to arrive at the airport about two hours before your scheduled departure time for domestic flights and 2½ to 3 hours before international flights. You may need to arrive earlier if you're flying from one of the busier airports or during peak air-traffic times. To avoid delays at airport-security checkpoints, try not to wear any metal. Jewelry, belt and other buckles, steel-toe shoes, barrettes, and underwire bras are among the items that can set off detectors.

Assuming that not everyone with a ticket will show up, airlines routinely overbook planes. When everyone does, airlines ask for volunteers to give up their seats. In return, these volunteers usually get a several-hundred-dollar flight voucher, which can be used toward the purchase of another ticket, and are rebooked on the next available flight out. If there are not enough volunteers, the airline must choose who will be denied boarding. The first to get bumped are passengers who checked in late and those flying on discounted tickets, so get to the gate and check in as early as possible, especially during peak periods.

Always **bring a government-issued photo ID** to the airport; even when it's not required, a passport is best.

CUTTING COSTS

The least expensive airfares to France are often priced for round-trip travel and must usually be purchased in advance. Airlines generally allow you to change your return date for a fee; most low-fare tickets, however, are nonrefundable. It's smart to call a number of airlines and check the Internet; when you are quoted a good price, book it on the spot—the same fare may not be available the next day, or even the next hour. Always check different routings and look into using alternate airports. Also, price off-peak flights and red-eye, which may be significantly less expensive than others. Travel agents, especially low-fare specialists (⇨ Discounts & Deals), are helpful.

Consolidators are another good source. They buy tickets for scheduled flights at reduced rates from the airlines, then sell them at prices that beat the best fare available directly from the airlines. (Many also offer reduced car-rental and hotel rates.) Sometimes you can even get your money back if you need to return the ticket. Carefully read the fine print detailing penalties for changes and cancellations, purchase the ticket with a credit card, and confirm your consolidator reservation with the airline.

When you fly as a courier, you trade your checked-luggage space for a ticket deeply subsidized by a courier service. There are restrictions on when you can book and how long you can stay. Some courier companies list with membership organizations, such as the Air Courier Association and the International Association of Air Travel Couriers; these require you to become a member before you can book a flight.

Many airlines, singly or in collaboration, offer discount air passes that allow foreigners to travel economically in a particular country or region. These visitor passes usually must be reserved and purchased before you leave home. Information about passes often can be found on most airlines' international Web pages, which tend to be aimed at travelers from outside the carrier's home country. Also, try typing the name of the pass into a search engine, or search for "pass" within the carrier's Web site.

If you plan on traveling to and from Paris aboard Air France, you can save on air travel within Europe. As part of their Euro Flyer program, you can buy between three and nine flight coupons, valid on flights to more than 100 European cities, including many French cities. At $120 each (April–September) and $99 each (October–March), these coupons are a good deal, and the fine print still allows you plenty of freedom.

Europe by Air offers a similar program, which functions like Eurail. Their Flight-Passes are available for $99 per flight to non-European customers, and can be exchanged for one-way nonstop flights between any of 30-plus European cities. Their list includes Toulon, Nice, and Marseille, but the minimum purchase is three passes.

🚩 Consolidators AirlineConsolidator.com ☎ 888/468-5385 ⊕ www.airlineconsolidator.com; for international tickets. **Best Fares** ☎ 800/880-1234 ⊕ www.bestfares.com; $59.90 annual membership. **Cheap Tickets** ☎ 800/377-1000 or 800/652-4327 ⊕ www.cheaptickets.com. **Expedia** ☎ 800/397-3342 or 404/728-8787 ⊕ www.expedia.com. **Hotwire** ☎ 866/468-9473 or 920/330-9418

⊕ www.hotwire.com. **Now Voyager Travel** ☎ 212/459-1616 ⊕ www.nowvoyagertravel.com. **Onetravel.com** ⊕ www.onetravel.com. **Orbitz** ☎ 888/656-4546 ⊕ www.orbitz.com. **Priceline. com** ⊕ www.priceline.com. **Travelocity** ☎ 888/709-5983, 877/282-2925 in Canada, 0870/111-7061 in the U.K. ⊕ www.travelocity.com.

🚩 Courier Resources Air Courier Association/ Cheaptrips.com ☎ 800/211-5119 ⊕ www.aircourier. org or www.cheaptrips.com; $20 annual membership. **Courier Travel** ☎ 303/570-7586 ⊟ 313/625-6106 ⊕ www.couriertravel.org; $50 annual membership. **International Association of Air Travel Couriers** ☎ 308/632-3273 ⊟ 308/632-8267 ⊕ www.courier.org; $45 annual membership. **Now Voyager Travel** ✉ 1717 Avenue M, Brooklyn, NY 11230 ☎ 212/459-1616 ⊟ 718/504-4762 ⊕ www. nowvoyagertravel.com.

🚩 Discount Passes FlightPass, EuropebyAir, ☎ 888/387-2479 ⊕ www.europebyair.com. **SAS Air Passes,** Scandinavian Airlines, ☎ 800/221-2350, 0870/6072-7727 in the U.K., 1300/727-707 in Australia ⊕ www.scandinavian.net.

ENJOYING THE FLIGHT

State your seat preference when purchasing your ticket, and then repeat it when you confirm and when you check in. For more legroom, you can request one of the few emergency-aisle seats at check-in, if you're capable of moving obstacles comparable in weight to an airplane exit door (usually between 35 pounds and 60 pounds)—a Federal Aviation Administration requirement of passengers in these seats. Seats behind a bulkhead also offer more legroom, but they don't have underseat storage. Don't sit in the row in front of the emergency aisle or in front of a bulkhead, where seats may not recline. SeatGuru.com has more information about specific seat configurations, which vary by aircraft.

Ask the airline whether a snack or meal is served on the flight. If you have dietary concerns, request special meals when booking. These can be vegetarian, low-cholesterol, or kosher, for example. It's a good idea to pack some healthful snacks and a small (plastic) bottle of water in your carry-on bag. On long flights, try to maintain a normal routine, to help fight jet lag. At night, get some sleep. By day, eat light meals, drink water (not alcohol), and **move around the cabin** to stretch your legs. For additional jet-lag tips consult *Fodor's FYI: Travel Fit & Healthy* (available at bookstores everywhere).

Smoking policies vary from carrier to carrier. Most airlines prohibit smoking on all of their flights; others allow smoking only on certain routes or certain departures. Ask your carrier about its policy.

FLYING TIMES

Flying time to Paris is an hour from London, 7½ hours from New York, 9 hours from Chicago, and 11 hours from Los Angeles. A direct flight from New York to Nice is 7 hours and 50 minutes. Scheduled flying time between Paris and Nice is approximately 1 hour and 35 minutes; between Paris and Marseille approximately 1 hour and 25 minutes.

HOW TO COMPLAIN

If your baggage goes astray or your flight goes awry, complain right away. Most carriers require that you **file a claim immediately.** The Aviation Consumer Protection Division of the Department of Transportation publishes *Fly-Rights,* which discusses airlines and consumer issues and is available online. You can also find articles and information on mytravelrights.com, the Web site of the nonprofit Consumer Travel Rights Center.

Airline Complaints Aviation Consumer Protection Division ⊠ U.S. Department of Transportation, Office of Aviation Enforcement and Proceedings, C-75, Room 4107, 400 7th St. SW, Washington, DC 20590 ☎ 202/366-2220 ⊕ airconsumer.ost.dot.gov. **Federal Aviation Administration Consumer Hotline** ⊠ for inquiries: FAA, 800 Independence Ave. SW, Washington, DC 20591 ☎ 800/322-7873 ⊕ www.faa.gov.

RECONFIRMING

It is wise, given the number of strikes in France, to call the day before your flight to reconfirm.

Check the status of your flight before you leave for the airport. You can do this on your carrier's Web site, by linking to a flight-status checker (many Web booking services offer these), or by calling your carrier or travel agent. Always confirm international flights at least 72 hours ahead of the scheduled departure time.

AIRPORTS

The major gateways to France are Paris's Orly and Charles de Gaulle airports. Nice, Marseille, and Montpellier's airports are also served by frequent flights from Paris and London, and daily connections from Paris arrive at the smaller airports in Avignon and Nîmes.

Airport Information Avignon ☎ 04-90-81-51-51 ⊕ www.avignon.aeroport.fr. **Paris Charles de Gaulle** ☎ 01-48-62-12-12 ⊕ www.adp.fr. **Marseilles-Provence** ☎ 04-42-14-14-14 ⊕ www.marseille.aeroport.fr. **Montpellier-Meditérranée** ☎ 04-67-20-85-85, 04-67-20-85-00 for flight information ⊕ www.montpellier.aeroport.fr. **Nice-Côte d'Azur** ☎ 04-89-88-98-28, 08-20-42-33-33 for flight information ⊕ www.nice.aeroport.fr. **Nîmes-Arles-Camargue** ☎ 04-66-70-49-49. **Toulon Hyères** ☎ 08-25-01-83-87. **Paris Orly** ☎ 01-49-75-15-15 ⊕ www.adp.fr.

BEACHES

The beaches in Provence can vary from fine sand to small pebble to rocky, the latter being the least crowded but requiring mattresses for comfortable sunbathing.

If you're planning to devote a lot of time to beaches and haven't tackled the French coast before, get to **know the distinction between private and public.** All along the coast, the waterfront is carved up into private frontage, roped off and advertised by coordinated color awnings, parasols, and mattresses. These private beaches usually offer full restaurant and bar service, and rent mattresses, umbrellas, and lounge chairs by the day and half-day. Dressing rooms and showers are included; some even rent private cabanas. Prices can run from €10 to €18 or more a day. Private beaches compete with each other not only via fashionable cuisine and flashy colors, but by offering entertainment—children's wading pools, waterskiing, or parasailing.

But interspliced between these commercial beaches is plenty of public space, with open access and (usually) the necessary comforts of toilets and cold rinse "showers" for washing off the salt. At these you must provide your own mattress or mat (indispensable on the rocks) and you can profit from the democratic bar service provided by enterprising vendors who cruise the waterfront with drinks and snacks. Or better yet, have lunch at one of the many shaded snack bars that line the beach, serving fresh salads and sandwiches.

BIKE TRAVEL

The French are great bicycling enthusiasts—witness the Tour de France—and there are tremendous opportunities to practice this Gallic sport in the south. From the Vaucluse, where cyclists pedal through the Luberon, to the Côte d'Azur, where they crisscross the Esterel over the sea, Provence and the coast provide good biking conditions and multiple options for rental and transport. For €15 a day (€23 for a lightweight touring bike) you can rent bikes from many train stations; you need to show your passport and leave a deposit of €150 or a Visa or MasterCard. Mountain bikes (known as VTT or *vélo touts-terrains*) can be rented from many shops, as well as from some train stations. Bikes may be taken as accompanied luggage from any station in France; some trains in rural areas don't even charge for this. Tourist offices supply details on the more than 200 local shops that rent bikes, or you can get the SNCF brochure "Guide du Train et du Vélo" from any station. Contact the Fédération Française de Cyclotourisme for information on bicycling routes in Provence and the Côte d'Azur. For more bicycling trips, *see* Theme Trips *in* Tour Operators, *below.*

🚲 Bicycling Information **Fédération Française de Cyclotourisme** ⊠ 12 rue Louis Bertrand, 94207 Ivry-sur-Seine Cedex ☎ 01-44-16-88-88 ⊕ www.ffct.org. **Comité Départemental de Cyclisme des Bouches du Rhône** ⊠ 14 rue de la Farandole La Grande Conque, 13800 Istres ☎ 04-42-55-31-31 ⊕ http://codep13.ffct.free.fr.

BIKE MAPS

The yellow Michelin maps (1:200,000 scale) are fine for roads, but for off-road bicycling you may want to get one of the Institut Géographique National's detailed, large-scale maps. Try their blue series (1:25,000) or orange series (1:50,000). They also publish a wonderful map of France's major cycling routes.

🚲 Bicycling Information **Institut Géographique National (IGN)** ⊠ 107 rue La Boétie, 75008 Paris ☎ 01-43-98-80-00 ⊕ www.ign.fr.

BOAT & FERRY TRAVEL

Ferries leave various Provence ports for the island of Corsica daily. Ferries to the island of Porquerolles (and the other Hyères islands) leave from the port of Hyères.

FARES & SCHEDULES

Departure times and fares vary daily for Corsica. **It is important to book ahead,** which can now be done via the Internet or through a travel agent. SNCM Ferryterranée boats depart up to five times daily (on summer weekends) from Nice and Toulon; the crossing takes approximately 4½ hours. There are up to three departures from Marseille, all in the evening. Corsica Ferries run up to three times daily from Nice and Toulon to Ajaccio and Bastia. Fares vary depending on the day of travel and the length of your vehicle. Travel at nonpeak times can save up to 50% if you can decipher the schedule and tariff booklet; you'll often find promotional offers online.

TLV ferries servicing the Îles d'Hyères (Porquerolles, Port-Cros, and Le Levant) leave from Port d'Hyères several times daily, depending on the season. Some ferries make the crossing only in the summer, so be sure to check the latest schedule—or consult a travel agent.

🚲 Boat & Ferry Information **Corsica Ferries** ☎ 04-95-32-95-95 or 08-25-09-50-95 ⊕ www.corsicaferries.com. **SNCM Ferryterranée** ☎ 04-93-01-47-56 or 08-25-88-80-88 ⊕ www.sncm.fr. **TLV** ☎ 04-94-58-21-81 ⊕ www.tlv-tvm.com.

BUSINESS HOURS

BANKS & OFFICES

Bank hours vary from branch to branch, but are generally weekdays 8:30 to 4. Most take a one-hour, or even a 90-minute, lunch break around noon.

See Mail & Shipping, *below,* for post-office hours.

GAS STATIONS

Gas stations on the autoroutes are generally open 24 hours. In towns, gas stations close at 8 PM, with the occasional station staying open until 10 PM. Outside the city centers, most stations are closed on Sunday.

MUSEUMS & SIGHTS

Museum hours are somewhat lax in the south, with seasonal variations and a tendency to change slightly and often. Usual opening times are from 9:30 or 10 to 5 or 6, but many close for lunch (noon–2). To allow for long terrace lunches and an afternoon lag in business due to beach time, the lunch hour may be even longer in summer, with some later evening hours to compensate. Most museums are closed one day a week (generally Monday or Tuesday) and on national holidays: **check museum hours before you go.**

SHOPS & MARKETS

Large stores in big towns are open from 9 or 9:30 AM until 7 or 8 PM. Smaller shops often open earlier (8 AM) and close later (8 PM) but take a lengthy lunch break (1 to 4 or 4:30) in the south of France. Corner groceries frequently stay open until around 10 PM. Market days vary from town to town, but stalls generally close by about 1 PM.

BUS TRAVEL

France's excellent train service means that long-distance buses are rare; regional buses are found mainly where train service is spotty. The weakest rail links in the south lie in the Luberon region of the Vaucluse, in the Alpilles, and in the backcountry of the Haut Var, Haute Provence, and the pre-Alpes behind Nice. To explore these lovely regions, you must **work closely with a bus schedule** (available at most train stations) and plan connections carefully. Don't plan on too much multi-stop sightseeing if you're limited to bus connections, as they rarely dovetail with your plans. To visit the popular hill towns just behind the Côte d'Azur—Grasse, St-Paul, Vence, and Biot—you can catch a regional bus or watch for commercial bus excursions advertised in the bigger coastal resorts. Tourist offices provide information on accompanied excursions. Excursions and bus holidays are organized by the SNCF and a plethora of private tour companies. Ask for a brochure at any major travel agent or contact France-Tourisme.

Buses from the U.K. generally depart from London, traveling via hovercraft or ferry from London to Paris. The most direct bus route to the south is from London to Avignon; Eurolines' weekly nonstop service takes 17½ hours and costs £89 round-trip.

🚌 From the U.K. **Eurolines/National Express** ✉ 52 Grosvenor Gardens, London SW1W 0AU ☎ 0870/580-8080 in the U.K., 08-92-89-90-91 in France ⊕ www.eurolines.co.uk. 🚌 Within France **SNCF** ✉ 88 rue St-Lazare, 75009 Paris ☎ 08-20-87-94-79 ⊕ www.voyages-sncf.com.

CUTTING COSTS

If you're planning to travel extensively through Europe, you may wish to purchase a Eurolines Europass, valid for unlimited bus travel between 46 European cities (London, Paris, and Marseille included) for up to 60 days.

🚌 Discount Passes **Eurolines/National Express** ✉ 52 Grosvenor Gardens, London SW1W 0AU ☎ 0870/580-8080 in the U.K., 08-92-89-90-91 in France ⊕ www.eurolines.co.uk.

CAMERAS & PHOTOGRAPHY

As you come upon view after gorgeous view in these regions, reaching for your camera may become a knee-jerk reaction. A few general ideas can help you capture some stunning shots. **Consider the light**—that famous Provençal light which mesmerized so many artists. Pay attention to the light's direction and quality, and try to match your subject with it. Strong sunlight makes for sharp contrast while sidelight accentuates surface textures. So, for instance, a photo of a Roman ruin at bright noon could emphasize its graphic shape while softer, late-afternoon light could pick up the texture of the stone. **Look for detail,** whether you're taking a close-up or trying to find an interesting way to snap a monument. Markets are a terrific place to get an evocative picture; look for bright colors and special wares, like unusual produce or local crafts.

The *Kodak Guide to Shooting Great Travel Pictures* (available at bookstores everywhere) is loaded with tips.

🖪 Photo Help **Kodak Information Center** ☎ 800/242-2424 ⊕ www.kodak.com.

EQUIPMENT PRECAUTIONS

Don't pack film or equipment in checked luggage, where it is much more susceptible to damage. X-ray machines used to view checked luggage are extremely powerful and therefore are likely to ruin your film. Try to ask for hand inspection of film, which becomes clouded after repeated exposure to airport X-ray machines, and keep videotapes and computer disks away from metal detectors. Always keep film, tape, and computer disks out of the sun. Carry an extra supply of batteries, and be prepared to turn on your camera, camcorder, or laptop to prove to airport security personnel that the device is real.

FILM & DEVELOPING

APS and 35-millimeter film are easy to find in Provence. For fast, professional film developing and service, use the FNAC stores, which can be found in any large Provençal town.

CAR RENTAL

Though renting a car in France is expensive—up to twice as much as in the United States—as is gas (about €1.10 per liter at press time), it may pay off if you are traveling with two or more people. In addition, renting a car gives you the freedom to move around at your own pace that the train does not. Rates begin at about $50 a day and $265 per week for an economy car with a manual transmission (an automatic transmission will cost more). Mileage is extra, but there are often multiday packages or weekly rates including some number of kilometers. Be careful to check whether the price includes the 20.6% V.A.T. tax or, if you pick it up from the airport, the airport tax.

🖪 Major Agencies **Alamo** ☎ 800/522-9696 ⊕ www.alamo.com. **Avis** ☎ 800/331-1084, 800/

879-2847 in Canada, 0870/606-0100 in the U.K., 02/9353-9000 in Australia, 09/526-2847 in New Zealand ⊕ www.avis.com. **Budget** ☎ 800/472-3325, 800/268-8900 in Canada, 1300/794-344 in Australia, 0800/283-438 in New Zealand ⊕ www.budget.com. **Dollar** ☎ 800/800-6000, 0800/085-4578 in the U.K. ⊕ www.dollar.com. **Hertz** ☎ 800/654-3001, 800/263-0600 in Canada, 0870/844-8844 in the U.K., 02/9669-2444 in Australia, 09/256-8690 in New Zealand ⊕ www.hertz.com. **National Car Rental** ☎ 800/227-7368 ⊕ www.nationalcar.com.

CUTTING COSTS

For a good deal, book through a travel agent who will shop around. Also, price local car-rental companies—whose prices may be lower still, although their service and maintenance may not be as good as those of major rental agencies—and research rates on the Internet. ADA, a French-owned rental company, has offices in towns, train stations, and airports throughout Provence. The Renault Eurodrive program avoids usual car-rental taxes by offering short-term leases to customers. Offices are in Marseille, Montpellier, and Nice; cars must be rented for at least 17 days.

Remember to ask about required deposits, cancellation penalties, and drop-off charges if you're planning to pick up the car in one city and leave it in another. If you're traveling during a holiday period, also make sure that a confirmed reservation guarantees you a car.

Do look into wholesalers, companies that do not own fleets but rent in bulk from those that do and often offer better rates than traditional car-rental operations. Prices are best during off-peak periods. Rentals booked through wholesalers often must be paid for before you leave home.

🖪 Local Agencies **ADA** ☎ 08-25-16-91-69 ⊕ www.ada-sa.fr.

🖪 Short-Term Leasing **Renault Eurodrive** ☎ 800/221-1052 ⊕ www.eurodrive.renault.com.

🖪 Wholesalers **Auto Europe** ☎ 207/842-2000 or 800/223-5555 🖷 207/842-2222 ⊕ www.autoeurope.com. **Destination Europe Resources** (DER) ✉ 9501 W. Devon Ave., Rosemont, IL 60018 ☎ 800/782-2424 🖷 800/282-7474. **Kemwel** ☎ 877/820-0668 or 800/678-0678 🖷 207/842-2124 or 866/726-6726 ⊕ www.kemwel.com.

INSURANCE

When driving a rented car you are generally responsible for any damage to or loss of the vehicle. Collision policies that car-rental companies sell for European rentals typically do not cover stolen vehicles. Before you rent—and purchase collision or theft coverage—see what coverage you already have under the terms of your personal auto-insurance policy and credit cards.

REQUIREMENTS & RESTRICTIONS

In France your own driver's license is acceptable. You don't need an International Driver's Permit, unless you are planning on a long-term stay; you can get one from the American or Canadian automobile association, and, in the United Kingdom, from the Automobile Association or Royal Automobile Club.

SURCHARGES

Before you pick up a car in one city and leave it in another, ask about drop-off charges or one-way service fees, which can be substantial. Also inquire about early-return policies; some rental agencies charge extra if you return the car before the time specified in your contract while others give you a refund for the days not used. Most agencies note the tank's fuel level on your contract; to avoid a hefty refueling fee, return the car with the same tank level. If the tank was full, refill it just before you turn in the car, but be aware that gas stations near the rental outlet may overcharge. It's almost never a deal to buy a tank of gas with the car when you rent it; the understanding is that you'll return it empty, but some fuel usually remains.

CAR TRAVEL

Your driver's license may not be recognized outside your home country. International driving permits (IDPs) are available from the American and Canadian automobile associations and, in the United Kingdom, from the Automobile Association and Royal Automobile Club. These international permits, valid only in conjunction with your regular driver's license, are universally recognized; having one may save you a problem with local authorities.

Car travel is the best way to see Provence, especially since the famous hilltop villages see a bus only once a day. However, a car may not be the fastest or most economical way to get to Provence: consider flying into Paris, connecting via a smaller airline to Nice or Marseille, and then renting your car in the south. Or purchase a rail-drive pass, available from the SNCF (French national rail company) or one of the larger car-rental companies. This will allow a few days' rail travel—say, from Paris to Nice—and a block of car-rental time. By using the train to cover the long distances, then exploring the region in depth by car, you can make the most of both modes of transit.

France's roads are classified into three types, numbered and prefixed A, N, or D. For the fastest roads between two points, **look for roads marked A for *autoroutes*.** A *péage* (toll) must be paid on most expressways: the rate varies but can be steep. Sample toll charges are €61.70 from Paris to Nice; €14.30 from Nice to Aix-en-Provence. At your first toll stop you will simply retrieve a ticket, and at the next toll you will pay. You may pay by credit card; Visa and American Express are accepted at most toll booths. The main toll roads through Provence are the A6 and A7, which connect Paris to Marseille via Lyon, Avignon, and Aix; and the east–west A8, which traverses the region from the Italian border to Aix via Nice.

The N (Route Nationale) roads, which are sometimes divided highways, are the route of choice for heavy freight trucks, and are often lined with industry and large chain stores. More scenic, though less trafficked than the Ns are the D (Route Départementale) roads, often also wide and fast.

Though routes are numbered, the French generally guide themselves from city to city and town to town by destination name. When reading a map, keep one eye on the next big city toward your destination as well as the next small town; most snap decisions will have to be based on town names, not road numbers.

Negotiating the back roads requires a careful mix of map and sign reading, often at high speeds around suburban *giratoires* (rotaries). But by the time you head out into the hills and the tiny roads—one of the best parts of Provence and the Côte d'Azur—give yourself over to road signs and pure faith: as is the case throughout France, directions are indicated by village name only, with route numbers given as a small-print afterthought. Of course, this means you have to recognize the names of minor villages en route.

To leave Paris by car, figure out which of the *portes* (gates) corresponds to the direction you are going. Major highways connect to Paris at these points, and directions are indicated by major cities. For instance, heading south out of the city, look for Porte d'Orléans (direction Lyons and Bordeaux); after Lyons, follow Avignon, and after Avignon follow Nice and/or Marseille. It's best to **steer clear of rush hours** (7–9:30 AM and 4:30–7:30 PM), although this is only a real concern between Aix and Marseille and around Nice.

EMERGENCY SERVICES
If your car breaks down on an expressway, **go to a roadside emergency telephone (yellow boxes)**, which you'll find every two kilometers, and call for assistance. If you have a breakdown anywhere else, find the nearest garage or contact the police. If there is an injury, call the SAMU (ambulance service) or fire brigade.
🚑 Ambulance (SAMU) 📞 15. Fire Department 📞 18. Police 📞 17.

GASOLINE
Gas is expensive, especially on expressways and in rural areas. When possible, **buy gas before you get on the expressway** and keep an eye on pump prices as you go. These vary from €.90 to €1.30 per liter. The cheapest gas can be found at *hypermarchés* (very large supermarkets) but expect long lines. It is possible to go for many miles in the country without passing a gas station—**don't let your tank get too low in rural areas.** Many gas stations are closed on Sunday. If you are worried about your budget, ask for a diesel car; diesel fuel at gas pumps can be labeled as *diesel, gasoil,* or *gazole.* Unleaded gas will

be labeled as *sans plomb* (SP95 for regular unleaded and SP98 for super unleaded). Be careful, as many gas stations still sell leaded gas, called *super.*

PARKING
Parking can be difficult in large towns; your best option (especially in a metropolis like Nice or Marseille) is to duck into the parking garage nearest the neighborhood you want to visit. Carry the ticket with you, and pay at the vending-machine-style ticket dispenser before you go back to your car. On the street, meters and ticket machines (pay and display) are common and work with parking cards (*cartes de stationnements*). Parking cards work like credit cards in the parking meters and come in three denominations: €10, €20, and €30. Parking cards are available at any café posting the red TABAC sign. Insert your card into the nearest meter, choose the approximate amount of time you expect to stay, and you'll receive a green receipt, which must be clearly visible to the meter patrol; place it on the dashboard on the inside of the front window on the passenger side. **Be sure to check the signs before you park, as rules vary.**

Be careful when parking your car overnight, especially in town and village squares; if your car is still there in the early morning on a market day, it will be towed. In smaller towns, parking may be permitted on one side of the street only—alternating every two weeks—so pay attention to signs.

The coastal area of Provence—especially the Camargue and the Calanques—as well as overlooks along the Côte d'Azur are extremely vulnerable to car break-ins, and the parking lots are often littered with broken windshield glass. It's important that you **never leave valuables visible in the car,** and think twice about leaving them in the trunk. Any theft should be reported formally to the police.

ROAD CONDITIONS
Road conditions in Provence are above average and potholes are rare, especially on highways. Check with the regional information center and the autoroutes hotline

to find out whether there's anything you should know before setting off.

⑦ Autoroute Information ☎ 01-47-53-37-00 ⊕ www.autoroutes.fr.

ROAD MAPS

If you plan to drive through France, **buy a yellow Michelin map or a red IGN map** for each region you'll be visiting. These are available from most bookshops, news-stands, and at highway rest stops. Alternatively, get your hands on one of Michelin's spiral-bound driving atlases. These are easier to handle on the road, but make sure you purchase one with enough detail; the small-scale pocket atlases leave off many village names.

RULES OF THE ROAD

In France, **you may use your own driver's license,** but you must be able to prove you have third-party insurance. Drive on the right and **yield to drivers coming from streets to the right.** However, this rule does not necessarily apply at round-abouts, where you are obligated to yield to those already within (to your left)—but should watch out for just about everyone. You must **wear your seat belt,** and children under 10 may not travel in the front seat. Speed limits are 130 kph (80 mph) on expressways, 110 kph (70 mph) on divided highways, 90 kph (55 mph) on other roads, 50 kph (30 mph) in towns. French drivers break these limits and police dish out hefty on-the-spot fines with equal abandon.

CHILDREN IN PROVENCE & THE CÔTE D'AZUR

If you are renting a car, don't forget to arrange for a car seat when you reserve. For general advice about traveling with children, consult *Fodor's FYI: Travel with Your Baby* (available in bookstores everywhere).

FOOD

The best restaurants in France do not welcome small children; except for the traditional family Sunday-noon dinner, fine dining is considered an adult pastime. Aim for more modest *auberges* (country inns), and if there's a choice, **consider having your meal in the café or bar** rather than in the linen-and-goblet-filled dining room. In cities, brasseries offer a casual option and the flexible meal times that children often require. Many mainstream restaurants have highchairs and serve children's portions *(menu enfant),* usually pizza, spaghetti, or the ubiquitous *steak-frites,* a mountain of fries with a thin steak or fat patty of ground beef, usually extremely rare. If you're queasy about this, ask for it *bien cuit* (well done). Also popular with kids is the *croque monsieur,* a buttery, rich grilled ham-and-cheese sandwich.

If your children go to bed early, opt for your hot meal at noon (there are cheaper prix-fixe menus, too) and consider having a sandwich, quiche, or omelet at a café or brasserie in the early evening; full-service restaurants usually do not serve before 7 PM.

LODGING

Most hotels in Provence and the Côte d'Azur allow children under a certain age to stay in their parents' room at no extra charge, but others charge for them as extra adults; be sure to find out the cutoff age for children's discounts.

If you're planning to stay in hotels, be sure to book ahead. Many small hotels have only one or two rooms that sleep four (triples are much more common); if there are more of you, you'll have to book two neighboring rooms or a suite. If you want a family-size room or a pair of adjoining rooms, book ahead. Larger hotels will often provide cribs free, which is not usually the case at inns and smaller hotels.

Another option: **consider a gîte, a short-term apartment or house rental,** or a home exchange. *See* Lodging, *below,* for information about rental and home exchange organizations.

SIGHTS AND ATTRACTIONS

There are plenty of diversions for the young, and almost all museums and movie theaters offer discounted rates to children. Playgrounds can be found off many toll roads. Kid-friendly activities in the region might include renting bikes for a ride through the Camargue, or exploring the food and flower markets in Aix, Grasse, and Avignon. There are large, classic carousels in downtown Marseille, Nice, and Antibes.

Places that are especially appealing to children are indicated by a rubber-duckie icon (🦆) in the margin.

SUPPLIES AND EQUIPMENT

Supermarkets carry several major brands of diapers (*couches à jeter*), universally referred to as Pampers (pawm-*paires*). Junior sizes are hard to come by, as the French toilet-train early. There's always plenty of baby food, and pharmacies provide the essentials.

TRAIN TRAVEL

The SNCF allows children under 4 to travel free (provided they don't occupy a seat) and children 4 to 11 to travel at half fare. The SNCF's Carte Enfant+ entitles the cardholder and up to four adult companions to deeply discounted rail travel. Teens and young adults can benefit from the Carte 12–25, which allows travelers in that age range reduced fares on train, TGV, and Eurostar travel (⇨ Train Travel, *below*).

Changing compartments for infants are available in most rail stations and on all TGVs, although not on all local trains.

COMPUTERS ON THE ROAD

If you use a major Internet provider, getting online in major cities in the south of France shouldn't be difficult. Call your Internet provider to get local access numbers. Some hotels even have in-room modem lines. Most laptops are dual-voltage, but you will need an adapter.

Think twice before packing your computer, though; it's easy to get online almost anywhere in France. Many hotels have Internet access in their lobbies or business centers, and Internet cafés are easy to find in any Provençal city. Ask at your hotel, or a computer store, for the nearest one.

CONSUMER PROTECTION

Whether you're shopping for gifts or purchasing travel services, **pay with a major credit card** whenever possible, so you can cancel payment or get reimbursed if there's

a problem (and you can provide documentation). If you're doing business with a particular company for the first time, contact your local Better Business Bureau and the attorney general's offices in your state and (for U.S. businesses) the company's home state as well. Have any complaints been filed? Finally, if you're buying a package or tour, always consider travel insurance that includes default coverage (⇨ Insurance).

🔢 BBBs **Council of Better Business Bureaus** ✉ 4200 Wilson Blvd., Suite 800, Arlington, VA 22203 ☎ 703/276-0100 🖷 703/525-8277 ⊕ www.bbb.org.

CRUISE TRAVEL

Many cruise lines offer trips that include a stop in the south of France—in Marseille, Cannes, or St-Tropez, for example—as part of a longer Mediterranean itinerary. To learn how to plan, choose, and book a cruise-ship voyage, consult *Fodor's FYI: Plan & Enjoy Your Cruise* (available in bookstores everywhere).

🔢 Cruise Lines **Celebrity Cruises** ✉ 1050 Caribbean Way, Miami, FL 33122 ☎ 305/539-6000 or 800/437-3111 ⊕ www.celebrity-cruises.com. **Clipper Cruise Line** ✉ 7711 Bonhomme Ave., St. Louis, MO 63105 ☎ 314/727-2929 or 800/325-0010 ⊕ www.clippercruise.com. **Crystal Cruises** ✉ 2049 Century Park E., Suite 1400, Los Angeles, CA 90067 ☎ 310/783-9300 or 800/446-6620 ⊕ www.crystalcruises.com. **Cunard Line** ✉ 6100 Blue Lagoon Dr., Suite 400, Miami, FL 33126 ☎ 305/463-3000 or 800/7-CUNARD ⊕ www.cunardline.com. **easyCruise** ⊕ www.easycruise.com. **Holland America Line** ✉ 300 Elliott Ave. W, Seattle, WA 98119 ☎ 206/281-3535 or 800/426-6593 ⊕ www.hollandamerica.com. **Radisson Seven Seas Cruises** ✉ 600 Corporate Dr., Suite 410, Fort Lauderdale, FL 33334 ☎ 954/776-6123 or 800/477-7500 ⊕ www.rssc.com. **Royal Caribbean Cruise Line** ✉ 1050 Caribbean Way, Miami, FL 33132 ☎ 305/539-6000 or 800/327-6700 ⊕ www.royalcaribbean.com. **Seabourn Cruise Line** ✉ 6100 Blue Lagoon Dr., Suite 400, Miami, FL 33126 ☎ 305/463-3000 or 800/929-9391 ⊕ www.seabourn.com. **Silversea Cruises** ✉ 110 E. Broward Blvd., Fort Lauderdale, FL 33301 ☎ 954/522-4477 or 800/722-9055 ⊕ www.silverseacruises.com. **Star Clippers** ✉ 4101 Salzedo St., Coral Gables, FL 33146 ☎ 305/442-0550 or 800/442-0551 ⊕ www.star-clippers.com. **Windstar**

Cruises ✉ 300 Elliott Ave. W, Seattle, WA 98119 ☎ 206/281-3535 or 800/258-7245 ⊕ www. windstarcruises.com.

CUSTOMS AND DUTIES

When shopping abroad, keep receipts for all purchases. Upon reentering the country, **be ready to show customs officials what you've bought.** Pack purchases together in an easily accessible place. If you think a duty is incorrect, appeal the assessment. If you object to the way your clearance was handled, note the inspector's badge number. In either case, first ask to see a supervisor. If the problem isn't resolved, write to the appropriate authorities, beginning with the port director at your point of entry.

IN AUSTRALIA

Australian residents who are 18 or older may bring home A$900 worth of souvenirs and gifts (including jewelry), 250 cigarettes or 250 grams of cigars or other tobacco products, and 2.25 liters of alcohol (including wine, beer, and spirits). Residents under 18 may bring back A$450 worth of goods. If any of these individual allowances are exceeded, you must pay duty for the entire amount (of the group of products in which the allowance was exceeded). Members of the same family traveling together may pool their allowances. Prohibited items include meat products. Seeds, plants, and fruits need to be declared upon arrival.

🛂 **Australian Customs Service** ⌂ Customs House, 10 Cooks River Dr., Sydney International Airport, Sydney, NSW 2020 ☎ 02/6275-6666 or 1300/363263, 02/ 8334-7444 or 1800/020-504 quarantine-inquiry line 🖶 02/8339-6714 ⊕ www.customs.gov.au.

IN CANADA

Canadian residents who have been out of Canada for at least seven days may bring in C$750 worth of goods duty-free. If you've been away fewer than seven days but more than 48 hours, the duty-free allowance drops to C$200. If your trip lasts 24 to 48 hours, the allowance is C$50; if the goods are worth more than C$50, you must pay full duty on all of the goods. You may not pool allowances with family members. Goods claimed under the C$750 exemption may follow

you by mail; those claimed under the lesser exemptions must accompany you. Alcohol and tobacco products may be included in the seven-day and 48-hour exemptions but not in the 24-hour exemption. If you meet the age requirements of the province or territory through which you reenter Canada, you may bring in, duty-free, 1.5 liters of wine *or* 1.14 liters (40 imperial ounces) of liquor *or* 24 12-ounce cans or bottles of beer or ale. Also, if you meet the local age requirement for tobacco products, you may bring in, duty-free, 200 cigarettes, 50 cigars or cigarillos, and 200 grams of tobacco. You may have to pay a minimum duty on tobacco products, regardless of whether or not you exceed your personal exemption. Check ahead of time with the Canada Border Services Agency or the Department of Agriculture for policies regarding meat products, seeds, plants, and fruits.

You may send an unlimited number of gifts (only one gift per recipient, however) worth up to C$60 each duty-free to Canada. Label the package UNSOLICITED GIFT—VALUE UNDER $60. Alcohol and tobacco are excluded.

🛂 **Canada Border Services Agency** ✉ Customs Information Services, 191 Laurier Ave. W, 15th floor, Ottawa, Ontario K1A 0L5 ☎ 800/461-9999 in Canada, 204/983-3500, 506/636-5064 ⊕ www. cbsa.gc.ca.

IN FRANCE

There is no restriction on goods brought in to France by EU nationals, as long as those goods are for personal use and not for resale. The duty-free allowance for non-EU residents visiting France is: 50 cigarettes or 25 cigarillos or 10 cigars or 50 grams of tobacco; 2 liters of table wine and (1) 1 liter of alcohol over 22% volume (most spirits) or (2) 1 liter of alcohol under 22% by volume (fortified or sparkling wine); 50 grams of perfume; 250 milliliters of toilet water; and other goods to the value of €175 (€90 for those under 15).

🛂 **Regional Customs and Excise Office–Provence** ✉ Hôtel des Douanes, Bd. du Château Double, Aix-en-Provence Cedex 02 13098 ☎ 04-42-95-27-50 🖶 04-42-59-46-58. **French Customs Office–U.S.**

✉ 4104 Reservoir Rd. NW, Washington, D.C. 20007 ☎ 202/944-6375 🖷 202/944-6517 ⊕ www. ambafrance-us.org/customs.

IN NEW ZEALAND

All homeward-bound residents may bring back NZ$700 worth of souvenirs and gifts; passengers may not pool their allowances, and children can claim only the concession on goods intended for their own use. For those 17 or older, the duty-free allowance also includes 4.5 liters of wine or beer; one 1,125-ml bottle of spirits; and either 200 cigarettes, 250 grams of tobacco, 50 cigars, *or* a combination of the three up to 250 grams. Meat products, seeds, plants, and fruits must be declared upon arrival to the Agricultural Services Department.

🎜 **New Zealand Customs** ✉ Head office: The Customhouse, 17–21 Whitmore St., Box 2218, Wellington ☎ 09/300-5399 or 0800/428-786 ⊕ www.customs. govt.nz.

IN THE U.K.

If you are a U.K. resident and your journey was wholly within the European Union, you probably won't have to pass through customs when you return to the United Kingdom. If you plan to bring back large quantities of alcohol or tobacco, check EU limits beforehand. In most cases, if you bring back more than 200 cigars, 3,200 cigarettes, 400 cigarillos, 3 kilograms of tobacco, 10 liters of spirits, 110 liters of beer, 20 liters of fortified wine, and/or 90 liters of wine, you have to declare the goods upon return.

🎜 **HM Customs and Excise** ✉ Portcullis House, 21 Cowbridge Rd. E, Cardiff CF11 9SS ☎ 0845/010-9000 or 0208/929-0152 advice service, 0208/929-6731 or 0208/910-3602 complaints ⊕ www.hmce. gov.uk.

IN THE U.S.

U.S. residents who have been out of the country for at least 48 hours may bring home, for personal use, $800 worth of foreign goods duty-free, as long as they haven't used the $800 allowance or any part of it in the past 30 days. This exemption may include 1 liter of alcohol (for travelers 21 and older), 200 cigarettes, and 100 non-Cuban cigars. Family members from the same household who are traveling together may pool their $800 personal exemptions. For fewer than 48 hours, the duty-free allowance drops to $200, which may include 50 cigarettes, 10 non-Cuban cigars, and 150 ml of alcohol (or 150 ml of perfume containing alcohol). The $200 allowance cannot be combined with other individuals' exemptions, and if you exceed it, the full value of all the goods will be taxed. Antiques, which U.S. Customs and Border Protection defines as objects more than 100 years old, enter duty-free, as do original works of art done entirely by hand, including paintings, drawings, and sculptures. This doesn't apply to folk art or handicrafts, which are in general dutiable.

You may also send packages home duty-free, with a limit of one parcel per addressee per day (except alcohol or tobacco products or perfume worth more than $5). You can mail up to $200 worth of goods for personal use; label the package PERSONAL USE and attach a list of its contents and their retail value. If the package contains your used personal belongings, mark it AMERICAN GOODS RETURNED to avoid paying duties. You may send up to $100 worth of goods as a gift; mark the package UNSOLICITED GIFT. Mailed items do not affect your duty-free allowance on your return.

To avoid paying duty on foreign-made high-ticket items you already own and will take on your trip, register them with a local customs office before you leave the country. Consider filing a Certificate of Registration for laptops, cameras, watches, and other digital devices identified with serial numbers or other permanent markings; you can keep the certificate for other trips. Otherwise, bring a sales receipt or insurance form to show that you owned the item before you left the United States.

For more about duties, restricted items, and other information about international travel, check out U.S. Customs and Border Protection's online brochure, *Know Before You Go.* You can also file complaints on the U.S. Customs and Border Protection Web site, listed below.

🎜 **U.S. Customs and Border Protection** ✉ for inquiries and complaints, 1300 Pennsylvania Ave. NW,

Washington, DC 20229 ⊕ www.cbp.gov ☎ 877/227-5551, 202/354-1000.

DISABILITIES & ACCESSIBILITY

Although the French government is doing much to ensure that public facilities provide for visitors with disabilities, it still has a long way to go. A number of monuments, hotels, and museums—especially those constructed within the past decade—are equipped with ramps, elevators, and special toilet facilities.

The Association des Paralysés de France can provide you with a list of accessible facilities in any region. Many tourist offices publish their own local guides for people with disabilities as well. These list accessible restaurants and hotels, and some even mark reserved parking spaces in town. Beware, however, that drivers in Provence have little respect for handicapped-designated parking spots, especially those in the center of town, so you may find them taken. Bring your own handicapped sticker with you from home since there is a fair amount of red tape to obtain one in France.

If you have a hearing aid, bring batteries with you, as battery types are not coded in the same way. When buying replacements, carry the dead battery with you for a perfect match.

🚩 Local Resources **Association des Paralysés de France** ⊠ 3 av. Antoine Véran, 06100 Nice ☎ 04-92-07-98-00 ⊕ ww.apf.asso.fr. **Comité Nationale Français de Liaison pour la Réadaptation des Handicapés** ⊠ 236 bis rue de Tolbiac, 75013 Paris ☎ 01-53-80-66-66.

LODGING

Tourist offices will have lists of hotels that cater to handicapped persons. Lists of regional hotels include a symbol to indicate which hotels have rooms that are accessible to people using wheelchairs. However quaint, auberges in historic buildings will probably not have special-needs facilities, many don't have elevators, and often the bathrooms are about the size of a postage stamp, difficult for those with mobility problems to negotiate. If you prefer to rent an apartment or villa, Gîtes de France publishes a guide to *Gîtes Accessibles aux*

Personnes Handicapées. See Lodging, *below,* for contact details.

RESERVATIONS

When discussing accessibility with an operator or reservations agent, ask hard questions. Are there any stairs, inside *or* out? Are there grab bars next to the toilet *and* in the shower/tub? How wide is the doorway to the room? To the bathroom? For the most extensive facilities meeting the latest legal specifications, opt for newer accommodations. If you reserve through a toll-free number, consider also calling the hotel's local number to confirm the information from the central reservations office. Get confirmation in writing when you can.

DISCOUNTS & DEALS

Be a smart shopper and compare all your options before making decisions. A plane ticket bought with a promotional coupon from travel clubs, coupon books, and direct-mail offers or purchased on the Internet may not be cheaper than the least expensive fare from a discount ticket agency. And always keep in mind that what you get is just as important as what you save.

DISCOUNT RESERVATIONS

To save money, look into discount reservations services with Web sites and toll-free numbers, which use their buying power to get a better price on hotels, airline tickets (⇨ Air Travel), even car rentals. When booking a room, always **call the hotel's local toll-free number** (if one is available) rather than the central reservations number—you'll often get a better price. Always ask about special packages or corporate rates.

When shopping for the best deal on hotels and car rentals, look for guaranteed exchange rates, which protect you against a falling dollar. With your rate locked in, you won't pay more, even if the price goes up in the local currency.

🚩 Hotel Rooms **Accommodations Express** ☎ 800/444-7666 or 800/277-1064. **Hotels.com** ☎ 800/246-8357 ⊕ www.hotels.com. **Steigenberger Reservation Service** ☎ 800/223-5652 ⊕ www.srs-worldhotels.com. **Turbotrip.com** ☎ 800/473-7829 ⊕ w3.turbotrip.com.

PACKAGE DEALS

Don't confuse packages and guided tours. When you buy a package, you travel on your own, just as though you had planned the trip yourself. Fly/drive packages, which combine airfare and car rental, are often a good deal. In cities, ask the local visitor's bureau about hotel and local transportation packages that include tickets to major museum exhibits or other special events. If you **buy a rail/drive pass,** you may save on train tickets and car rentals. All Eurailpass holders get a discount on Eurostar fares through the Channel Tunnel and often receive reduced rates for buses, hotels, ferries, sightseeing cruises, and car rentals.

EATING & DRINKING

The sooner you relax and go with the French flow, the more you'll enjoy your stay. Expect to spend at least two hours for lunch in a restaurant, savoring three courses and talking over the wine; dinner lasts even longer. If you keep one eye on your watch and the other on the waiter, you'll miss the point and spoil your own fun.

You may benefit from a few pointers on French dining etiquette. Diners in France don't negotiate their orders much, so don't expect serene smiles when you ask for sauce on the side. Order your coffee after dessert, not with it. When you're ready for the check, ask for it. No professional waiter would dare put a bill on your table while you're still enjoying the last sip of coffee. And don't ask for a doggy bag; it's just not done.

Also a word on the great mineral-water war: the French usually drink wine or mineral water—not soda or coffee—with their food. You may ask for a carafe of tap water, *une carafe d'eau,* but not always. In general, diners order mineral water if they don't order wine. It's not that the tap water is unsafe; it's usually fine—just not as tasty as Evian or slightly fizzy Badoit. To order flat mineral water ask for *eau naturelle;* fizzy is *eau gazeuse.*

Restaurants along the coast are generally more expensive than those inland; basic regional fixed-price menus average about €17 to €22, though the high end of this figure represents the usual cost of seafood so often featured on restaurant menus. In high summer reserve at popular restaurants, especially if you want a coveted outdoor table.

The restaurants we list in this guide are the cream of the crop in each price category. Properties indicated by a ✕🏨 are lodging establishments whose restaurant warrants a special trip.

MEALS AND SPECIALTIES

If you're antsy to get to the next museum, or if you plan to spend the evening dining in grand style, consider lunching in a brasserie, where quick, one-plate lunches and full salads are available. Cafés often serve *casse croûtes* (snacks), including sandwiches, which are simply baguettes lightly filled with ham or cheese; or *croques monsieurs,* grilled ham and cheese open-face sandwiches with a rich layer of béchamel. Bakeries and *traiteurs* (delis) often sell savory items like quiches, tiny pizzas, or pastries filled with pâté. On the Côte d'Azur, you can profit from a wealth of street food, from the chickpea-based crepes called *socca* to *pissaladière* (onion-olive pizza) and *pan bagnat* (a tuna-and-egg-stuffed pita-style bun).

One of the wonderful aspects of breakfast in Provence and on the Côte d'Azur is eating outdoors, whether on the restaurant terrace or on your own tiny balcony. Breakfasts are light, consisting of croissants and bread, jam and butter, and wonderful coffee. Many hotels also serve yogurt, fruit juice, cereal, cheese, and even eggs upon request.

MEALTIMES

You'll notice here more than anywhere in France that the lunch hour begins after 1; some places don't even open before that. If you don't mind being a gauche foreigner, eating at noon is one way to get into those sought-after restaurants that do open at noon. If you want to really do as the Romans do, reserve for a lunch at 1 or 1:30.

Breakfast is usually served from 8:30 to 10:30; if you want it earlier, arrange a time the night before. Dinner is usually eaten after 8.

Unless otherwise noted, the restaurants listed in this guide are open daily for lunch and dinner.

PAYING
Credit cards are accepted in most restaurants, cafés, and brasseries, though there's often a minimum charge of €10 or €15. If you plan to eat at a small, off-the-beaten-path place, call ahead to confirm that credit cards are accepted.

RESERVATIONS & DRESS
Reservations are always a good idea; we mention them only when they're essential or not accepted. Book as far ahead as you can, and reconfirm as soon as you arrive. (Large parties should always call ahead to check the reservations policy.) We mention dress only when men are required to wear a jacket or a jacket and tie.

For more on what to wear in the south of France, *see* Packing, *below.*

WINE AND SPIRITS
Provence has several wine appellations (AOCs) that vary in size from the vast AOC Côtes de Provence (which covers most of eastern Provence), to the tiny AOC Palette, which has only one major estate. The hearty red and white wines of AOC Châteauneuf-du-Pape have been famous since Pope Clement V sought them out in the early 14th century. Many Provençals prefer to drink light, dry rosé wines, which they buy in five- or ten-liter jugs at the local wine cooperative. The fresh white wines that are made in the hills surrounding the coastal resort of Cassis (not to be confused with the black-currant syrup of the same name) are also very fine. Apéritif time is extremely popular, the preferred drink being *pastis* (an amber-colored liquor distilled with anise and secret herbs) or a glass of champagne (*une coupe de champagne*).

ELECTRICITY
To use electric-powered equipment purchased in the U.S. or Canada, **bring a converter and adapter.** The electrical current in France is 220 volts, 50 cycles alternating current (AC). French electrical outlets have two round holes ("female") and a "male" ground; your appliances must either have a slender, two-prong plug that bypasses that ground, or a plug with two round prongs and a hole.

If your appliances are dual-voltage, you'll need only an adapter. Don't use 110-volt outlets marked FOR SHAVERS ONLY for high-wattage appliances such as blow-dryers. Most laptops operate equally well on 110 and 220 volts and so require only an adapter.

EMBASSIES & CONSULATES
If you need assistance in an emergency, you can go to your country's embassy or consulate. Proof of identity and citizenship are generally required to enter. If your passport has been stolen, get a police report then contact your embassy for assistance.

🇦🇺 Australia **Australian Embassy** ✉ 4 rue Jean-Rey, Paris, 15ᵉ ☎ 01-40-59-33-00 ⊕ www.austgov.fr Ⓜ Bir Hakeim ⏱ Weekdays 9:15-12:15 PM.

🇨🇦 Canada **Canadian Embassy** ✉ 35 av. Montaigne, Paris, 8ᵉ ☎ 01-44-43-29-02 ⊕ www.amb-canada.fr Ⓜ Franklin-D.-Roosevelt ⏱ Weekdays 8:30 AM-11 AM. **Canadian Consulate** ✉ 10 rue Lamartine, Nice ☎ 04-93-92-93-22 ⏱ Weekdays 8:30 AM-11 AM.

🇳🇿 New Zealand **New Zealand Embassy** ✉ 7 ter rue Léonardo da Vinci, Paris, 16ᵉ ☎ 01-45-01-43-43 ⊕ www.nzembassy.com Ⓜ Victor Hugo ⏱ Mon.-Thurs. 9 AM-1 PM and 2 PM-5.30 PM; Fri. 9 AM-1 PM and 2 PM-4 PM (early closing hours in July and Aug.).

🇬🇧 United Kingdom **British Consulate Paris** ✉ 18 bis rue d'Anjou, Paris, 8ᵉ ☎ 01-44-51-31-00 ⊕ www.amb-grandebretagne.fr Ⓜ Madeleine ⏱ Weekdays 9:30 AM-12:30 PM and 2:30 PM-5 PM. **British Consulate Marseille** ✉ 24 av. du Prado, Marseille ☎ 04-91-15-72-10 ⏱ Weekdays 9 AM-noon and 2 PM-5 PM.

🇺🇸 United States **U.S. Consulate Paris** ✉ 2 rue St-Florentin, Paris, 1ᵉʳ ☎ 01-43-12-22-22 in English, 01-43-12-23-47 in emergencies ⊕ www.amb-usa.fr Ⓜ Concorde ⏱ Weekdays 9 AM-1 PM. **U.S. Consulates** ✉ 12 bd. Paul Peytral, Marseille ☎ 04-91-54-92-00 ⏱ Weekdays 9 AM-noon and 2-5 PM ✉ 7 av. Gustave V, 3rd fl., Nice ☎ 04-93-88-89-55 ⏱ Weekdays 9 AM-noon and 2-5 PM.

EMERGENCIES

France's emergency services are conveniently streamlined and universal, so no matter where you are in the country, you can dial the same phone numbers, listed below. Every town and village has a *médecin de garde* (on-duty doctor) for flus, sprains, tetanus shots, etc. To find out who's on any given evening, call any *généraliste* (general practitioner) and a recording will refer you. If you need an x-ray or emergency treatment, call the ambulance number and you'll be whisked to the hospital of your choice—or the nearest one. Note that outside of Paris it may be difficult to find English-speaking doctors.

In case of fire, hotels are required to post emergency exit maps inside every room door and multilingual instructions.

🚩 **General Emergency** ☎112. **Ambulance (SAMU)** ☎15. **Fire Department** ☎18. **Police** ☎17.

ENGLISH-LANGUAGE MEDIA

NEWSPAPERS & MAGAZINES

The daily English-language *International Herald Tribune* can be found at most newsstands, even in small villages. The *Financial Times* is often available on the day of publication as well. Train stations and airports are the best bets for finding foreign-language magazines and newspapers.

RADIO & TELEVISION

The Côte d'Azur area has a few English-language radio stations. Tune into the long-established Radio Riviera on 106.5 FM. Radio International Côte d'Azur, mostly music with periodic BBC World News broadcasts, can be found at 100.5 or 100.9 FM, depending on where along the Mediterranean coast you are. The Breeze broadcasts jazz and some BBC programs at 88.4 FM.

GAY & LESBIAN TRAVEL

In Provence and the Côte d'Azur, the gay and lesbian communities are low-key and reserved in public, although active and easily accessible to visitors. Discos and nightclubs are numerous and popular. To find out where they are, look for the *Guide Gay Grand Sud* for men and the *Guide Lesbien* for women, available in most gay and lesbian bars and clubs.

Many French cities host pride parades at some point during the year. Montpellier's celebration is usually the first Saturday in June; Marseille's the last Saturday in June or the first Saturday in July. Découvertes Aix-en-Provence offers group and independent packages with specific cultural themes, including contemporary art, gardens, or culinary arts.

🚩 Gay- and Lesbian-Friendly Travel Agencies in France Découvertes Aix-en-Provence ✉ 5 bd. de la Libération, 13840 Rognes ☎ 04-42-50-14-41 ⊕ www.decouvertes.fr. **Gay Provence** ⊕ www.gay-provence.org is a bilingual portal site to promote gay and lesbian-friendly travel in Provence.

🚩 Gay- & Lesbian-Friendly Travel Agencies Different Roads Travel ✉ 1017 N. LaCienega Blvd., Suite 308, West Hollywood, CA 90069 ☎ 310/289-6000 or 800/429-8747 (Ext. 14 for both) 🖷 310/855-0323 ✉ lgernert@tzell.com. **Kennedy Travel** ✉ 130 W. 42nd St., Suite 401, New York, NY 10036 ☎ 800/237-7433 or 212/840-8659 🖷 212/730-2269 ⊕ www.kennedytravel.com. **Now, Voyager** ✉ 4406 18th St., San Francisco, CA 94114 ☎ 415/626-1169 or 800/255-6951 🖷 415/626-8626 ⊕ www.nowvoyager.com. **Skylink Travel and Tour/Flying Dutchmen Travel** ✉ 1455 N. Dutton Ave., Suite A, Santa Rosa, CA 95401 ☎ 707/546-9888 or 800/225-5759 🖷 707/636-0951; serving lesbian travelers.

HEALTH

See Emergencies, *above.*

DOCTORS AND HOSPITALS

For information on doctors and hospitals throughout Provence and the Côte d'Azur, *see* Essentials sections *in* individual chapters.

OVER-THE-COUNTER REMEDIES

For a headache *(mal à la tête)* ask the pharmacist for *aspirine* (aspirin) or *doliprane* (Tylenol). For gas pains, ask for *smecta,* and for menstrual cramps you will be given *spasfon.* For car and boat sickness, *primperan.* For cuts, scrapes, and other minor "ouchies," which the French call "bobos," you will be given a disinfectant spray called *Bétadine. Gel d'Apis* treats mosquito bites (you may need this if you are traveling in the Carmargue). Sore throats are treated with lozenges called *pastilles,* and cough syrup is *sirop.* Diarrhea *(diarrhée)* is treated with *Immodium.*

HIKING

There are many good places to hike in Provence and the Côte d'Azur, especially along the extensive network of mapped-out Grands Randonnées (GRs or Long Trails) that range from easy to challenging. For details on hiking in France and guides to GRs in specific areas, contact the Club Alpin Français or the Fédération Française de la Randonnée Pédestre, which also publishes good topographical maps. The IGN maps sold in many bookshops are also invaluable (⇨ Bicycling, *above*).

Note that some of the best hiking wilderness along the coast—especially around the Calanques between Marseille and Cassis and the Esterel between Fréjus and Cannes—are closed in July and August because of wildfire danger. Before you plan a summer of seaside hikes, **check with local tourist offices to confirm that trails are open.**

🗗 Hiking Organizations **Club Alpin Français** ✉ 24 av. Laumière, 75019 Paris ☎ 01-53-72-88-00 ⊕ www.ffcam.fr. **Fédération Française de la Randonnée Pédestre** ✉ 14 rue Riquet, 75019 Paris ☎ 01-44-89-93-90 🖶 01-40-35-85-48 ⊕ www.ffrandonnee.fr.

HOLIDAYS

With 11 national *jours feriés* (holidays) and 5 weeks of paid vacation, the French have their share of repose. In May, there is a holiday nearly every week, so be prepared for stores, banks, and museums to shut their doors for days at a time. Be sure to **call museums, restaurants, and hotels in advance to make sure they will be open.**

Some holidays to keep in mind: January 1, New Year's Day; mid-April, Easter Monday; May 1, Labor Day; May 8, VE Day; mid- to late May, Ascension; late May to early June, Pentecost Monday; July 14, Bastille Day; August 15, Assumption; November 1, All Saints; November 11, Armistice; December 25, Christmas.

It's also useful to bear in mind France's school vacations, which tend to unleash hordes of families and *classes de mer* (school trips to the coast) on museums, castles, and family hotels. School vacations are divided by region and are spread out over about three weeks in late October–November, Christmas–New Year's, again in February, and finally in April. Provence and the Côte d'Azur are the most crowded during the summer holidays, usually the last week of July and all of August.

LANGUAGE

Although many French people, especially in major tourist areas, speak some English, it's important to remember that you are going to France and that people speak French. However, generally at least one person in most hotels can explain things to you in English (unless you are in a very rural area). Be patient, and speak English slowly.

The French may appear prickly at first to English-speaking visitors. But it usually helps if you **make an effort to speak a little French.** So even if your own French is terrible, try to master a few words. A simple, friendly "bonjour" (hello) will do, as will asking if the person you are greeting speaks English ("Parlez-vous anglais?").

LANGUAGES FOR TRAVELERS

A phrase book and language-tape set can help get you started. *Fodor's French for Travelers* (available at bookstores everywhere) is excellent.

LODGING

Provence and the Côte d'Azur may be the most accommodating region in France, with every kind of hotel, country inn, converted *mas* (Provençal farmhouse), luxury palace, bed-and-breakfast, and vacation rental imaginable. Consider the kind of vacation you want to spend—going native in a country *gîte* (rental house), being pampered in a luxury penthouse over the Mediterranean in Cannes, or getting to know the locals in a cozy B&B. Then check the Fodor's recommendations in each chapter, or contact the local tourist offices for more specific information.

The lodgings we list are the cream of the crop in each price category. We always list the facilities that are available, but we don't specify whether they cost extra; when pricing accommodations, always ask what's included and what costs extra. Properties are assigned price categories based on the range from their least-expensive standard double room at high season (excluding holidays) to the most expensive. Properties marked ✕🍽 are lodging establishments whose restaurants warrant a special trip.

Assume that hotels operate on the European Plan (EP, with no meals) unless we specify that they use either the Breakfast Plan (BP, with a breakfast included in the room rate), or the Modified American Plan (MAP, with breakfast and dinner) or the Full American Plan (FAP, including all meals).

APARTMENT & VILLA (OR HOUSE) RENTALS

If you want a home base that's roomy enough for a family and comes with cooking facilities, consider a furnished rental. These can save you money, especially if you're traveling with a group. Home-exchange directories sometimes list rentals as well as exchanges.

The national rental network, the Fédération Nationale des Gîtes de France, rents rural homes with regional flavor, often restored farmhouses or village row houses in pretty country settings (⇨ Close-Up: "The Gîte Way," *in* Chapter 2). In fact, the system grew out of a subsidized movement to salvage wonderful old houses falling to ruin. Gîtes-de-France are nearly always maintained by on-site owners, who greet you on your arrival and provide information on groceries, doctors, and nearby attractions.

A nationwide catalogue (€22) is available from the Fédération Nationale des Gîtes de France listing gîtes for rent. Called "Nouveaux Gîtes Ruraux," the catalogue only lists the newest additions to the network, because a comprehensive nationwide listing of all gîtes wouldn't fit between two covers. If you know you want to stay in Provence, you can order a regional catalogue (€4.57). Gîtes can also be searched and booked online. ⇨ Vacation Rentals *in* Essentials sections of each chapter for how to contact regional offices.

Individual tourist offices often publish lists of *locations meublés* (furnished rentals); these are often inspected by the tourist office and rated by comfort standards. Usually they are booked directly through the individual owner, which generally requires some knowledge of French. Rentals that are not classified or rated by the tourist office should be undertaken with trepidation, and can fall well below your minimum standard of comfort.

Vacation rentals in France always book from Saturday to Saturday (with some offering weekend rates off-season). Most do not include bed linens and towels, but make them available for an additional fee. Always check on policies on pets and children, and specify if you need an enclosed garden for toddlers, a washing machine, a fireplace, etc. If you plan to have overnight guests during your stay, let the owner know; there may be additional charges. Insurance restrictions prohibit occupation beyond the specified capacity.

The French Government Tourist Office is another source for information about vacation rentals.

🖪 International Agents **At Home Abroad** ⌂ 163 Third Ave., No. 319, New York, NY 10003 ☎ 212/421–9165 🖷 212/533–0095 ⊕ www.athomeabroadinc.com. **Drawbridge to Europe** ✉ 98 Granite St., Ashland, OR 97520 ☎ 541/482–7778 or 888/268–1148 🖷 541/482–7779 ⊕ www.drawbridgetoeurope.com. **Hideaways International** ✉ 767 Islington St., Portsmouth, NH 03801 ☎ 603/430–4433 or 800/843–4433 🖷 603/430–4444 ⊕ www.hideaways.com, annual membership $185. **Villanet** ✉ 1251 N.W. 116th St., Seattle, WA 98177 ☎ 206/417–3444 or 800/964–1891 🖷 206/417–1832 ⊕ www.rentavilla.com. **Villas International** ✉ 4340 Redwood Hwy., Suite D309, San Rafael, CA 94903 ☎ 415/499–9490 or 800/221–2260 🖷 415/499–9491 ⊕ www.villasintl.com.

🖪 Local Agent **Gîtes de France** ✉ 59 rue St-Lazare, 75009 Paris Cedex 09 ☎ 01-49-70-75-75 🖷 01-42-81-28-53 ⊕ www.gites-de-france.fr.

BED & BREAKFASTS

Bed-and-breakfasts, known in France as *chambres d'hôte*, are common in rural Provence, and less so along the Côte d'Azur. Check local tourist offices for details or contact Gîtes de France, the national vacation-lodging organization that lists B&Bs all over the country, from rustic to more luxurious. Often *table d'hôte* dinners (meals cooked by and eaten with the owners) can be arranged for an extra, fairly nominal fee. Note that in B&Bs, unlike hotels, it is more likely that the owners will only speak French. Staying in one may, however, give you more of an opportunity to meet French people.

For B&B listings, Karen Brown's *France: Charming Bed & Breakfasts* and *Rivages Bed & Breakfasts of Character and Charm in France* are available in bookstores or from Fodor's Travel Publications.

🎦 B&B Guides **Fodor's Travel Publications** ☎ 800/533-6478.

CAMPING

French campsites have a good reputation for organization and amenities but are crowded in July and August. Many campsites welcome reservations, and in summer, it makes sense to book in advance. Most parks are closed from November 1 until April 1, but it depends on the park, so make enquiries before setting out. The Fédération Française de Camping et de Caravaning publishes a guide to France's campsites (in French only); they'll send it to you for €12.

🎦 Camping Information **Fédération Française de Camping et de Caravaning** ⊠ 78 rue de Rivoli, 75004 Paris ☎ 01-42-72-84-08 ⊕ www.campingfrance.com.

GÎTES (VACATION RENTALS)

Gîtes de France is a nationwide organization that rents vacation housing by the week, in the countryside, by the sea, or in the mountains. Houses and apartments are classified on a scale of one to five, according to comfort. Housing is strictly supervised, with an on-site welcome from either a representative or the owners of the gîtes themselves. Some gîtes can be quite posh, with swimming pool and all the amenities—these go quickly, so be sure to reserve well in advance if this is the type of accommodation you want. Gîtes de France also has a list of regional bed-and-breakfast sites, and regional farms that open their doors and their dining rooms, where amazing dinners can be arranged. Just

about everything served at these tables d'hôte comes from the farm itself; these dinners are growing in popularity and run from the simple to the gastronomique. Gîtes de France also organizes a variety of tours; hiking tours, canyoning with certified instructors, biking tours with all-terrain bikes, tours for the wine lover with a certified oenologue. Note that if you plan on traveling in July or August, you must do as the French do and **organize well in advance.** (For more information about renting gîtes, *see* Close-Up: The Gîte Way *in* Chapter 2.) Each town's tourist office usually publishes lists of independent rentals (*locations meublés*), many of them inspected and classified by the tourist office itself.

The region west of Nîmes, including some parts of the Camargue, lies in the département of Hérault. Gîtes de France offices for this department are based in Montpellier. Nîmes itself and environs are processed by the gard office. Arles and the Alpilles gîtes are handled by the Bouches-du-Rhône departmental office. In Nice you can rent a furnished Old Town apartment for a few days or up to several weeks from the English-speaking **Nice Time** ☎ 06–81–67–41–22 ⊕ landry.ph@free.fr.

🎦 Gîtes Information–Chapter 1 **La Maison des Gîtes de France et du Tourisme Vert** Paris–head office ⊠ 59 rue Saint-Lazare, Cedex 09, 75439 ☎ 01-49-70-75-75 🖷 01-42-81-28-53 ⊕ info@gites-de-france.fr ⊕ www.gites-de-france.fr/eng. **Montpelier** ⊠ B.P. 3070, Cedex 1, 34034 Montpelier ☎ 04-67-67-62-62 🖷 04-67-67-71-69. **Gard** ⊠ 3 pl. des Aregnes, B.P. 59, Cedex 4, 30007. **Nîmes** ☎ 04-66-27-94-94 🖷 04-66-27-94-95. **Bouches-du-Rhône** ⊠ Domaine du Vergon, B.P. 26, 13370. **Mallemort** ☎ 04-90-59-49-39 🖷 04-90-59-16-75.

🎦 Gîtes Information–Chapter 2 **Gîtes de France de Vaucluse** ⊠ pl. Campana, by the Papal Palace in Avignon ⊠ B.P. 164, Cedex 1 84008. **Avignon City** ☎ 04-90-85-88-49 🖷 04-90-85-88-49 ⊕ www.gites-de-france-84.com.

🎦 Gîtes Information–Chapter 3 **Gîtes de France Bouches-du-Rhône** ⊠ Domaine du Vergon, 13370 Mallemort ☎ 04-90-59-49-39 🖷 04-90-59-16-75. **Gîtes de France du Var** ⊠ BP 215, Rond-Point du 04/12/1974 ☎ 04-94-50-93-93 🖷 04-94-50-93-90.

Gîtes Information–Chapter 4 **Gîtes de France du Var** ✉ Rond-point du 3 Décembre 1974, B.P. 215, Draguignan Cedex 83006 ☎ 04-94-50-93-93 🖷 04-94-50-93-90 ⊕ www.gites-de-france-var.fr. **Gîtes de France des Alpes-Maritimes** ✉ 55 promenade des Anglais, B.P. 1602, Cedex 01 06011 Nice ☎ 04-92-15-21-30 🖷 04-93-86-01-06 ⊕ www.gites-de-france-alpes-maritimes.com. **Gîtes de France des Alpes de Haute Provence** ✉ B.P. 201, 04001 Dignes-les-Bains ☎ 04-92-31-52-39 🖷 04-92-32-32-63 ⊕ www.gites-de-france-04.fr. Gîtes Information–Chapter 5 **Gîtes de France des Alpes-Maritimes** ✉ 57 Promenade des Anglais, B.P. 1602, Cedex 01 06011 Nice ☎ 04-92-15-21-30 🖷 04-93-37-48-00 ⊕ www.gites-de-france-alpes-maritimes.fr. **Gîtes de France du Var** ✉ Rond-Point du 4 Décembre, B.P. 215, Draguignan Cedex 83006 ☎ 04-94-50-93-93 🖷 04-94-50-93-90 ⊕ www.gites-de-france-var.fr.

HOSTELS

No matter what your age, you can save on lodging costs by staying at hostels. In some 4,500 locations in more than 70 countries around the world, Hostelling International (HI), the umbrella group for a number of national youth-hostel associations, offers single-sex, dorm-style beds and, at many hostels, rooms for couples and family accommodations. Membership in any HI national hostel association, open to travelers of all ages, allows you to stay in HI-affiliated hostels at member rates; one-year membership is about $28 for adults (C$35 for a two-year minimum membership in Canada, £15 in the U.K., A$52 in Australia, and NZ$40 in New Zealand); hostels charge about $10–$30 per night. Members have priority if the hostel is full; they're also eligible for discounts around the world, even on rail and bus travel in some countries.

Best Options **Relais International de la Jeunesse** ✉ Bd. de la Garoupe, 06600 Cap d'Antibes ☎ 04-93-61-71-53 🖷 04-93-42-72-57. **Auberge de Jeunesse** ✉ 3 av. Marcel-Pagnol, 13100 Aix-en-Provence ☎ 04-42-20-15-99 🖷 04-42-59-36-12 ⊕ www.fuaj.org. **Auberge de Jeunesse Les Calanques** ✉ RN 559, La Fontasse, 13260 Cassis ☎ 04-42-01-02-72. **Clairvallon Relais International de la Jeunesse** ✉ 26 av. Scudéri, 06000 Nice ☎ 04-93-81-27-63 🖷 04-93-53-35-88. Organizations **Fédération Unie des Auberges de Jeunesse** ✉ 27 rue Pajol, Paris 75018

☎ 08-36-68-86-98 or 01-44-89-87-27 🖷 01-44-89-87-10 ⊕ www.fuaj.org. **Hostelling International–USA** ✉ 8401 Colesville Rd., Suite 600, Silver Spring, MD 20910 ☎ 301/495-1240 🖷 301/495-6697 ⊕ www.hiusa.org. **Hostelling International–Canada** ✉ 205 Catherine St., Suite 400, Ottawa, Ontario K2P 1C3 ☎ 613/237-7884 or 800/663-5777 🖷 613/237-7868 ⊕ www.hihostels.ca. **YHA England and Wales** ✉ Trevelyan House, Dimple Rd., Matlock, Derbyshire DE4 3YH, U.K. ☎ 0870/870-8808, 0870/770-8868, 0162/959-2600 🖷 0870/770-6127 ⊕ www.yha.org.uk. **YHA Australia** ✉ 422 Kent St., Sydney, NSW 2001 ☎ 02/9261-1111 🖷 02/9261-1969 ⊕ www.yha.com.au. **YHA New Zealand** ✉ Level 1, Moorhouse City, 166 Moorhouse Ave., Box 436, Christchurch ☎ 03/379-9970 or 0800/278-299 🖷 03/365-4476 ⊕ www.yha.org.nz.

HOTELS

Hotels are officially classified by the French government from one star to four-star deluxe. Prices must, by law, be posted at the hotel entrance and should include taxes and service. Rates are always by room, not per person. Remember that in France the first floor is one floor up (our second floor), and the higher up you go the quieter the street noise will be.

You should always **check what bathroom facilities the price includes,** if any. Because replumbing drains is often prohibitive, if not impossible, old hotels may have added bathrooms—often with *douches* (showers), not *baignoires* (tubs)—to the guest rooms, but not toilets. If you want a private bathroom, state your preference for shower or tub—the latter always costs more. Unless otherwise noted, lodging listings in this book include a private bathroom with a shower *or* tub.

When making your reservation, **ask for a grand lit if you want a double bed.** The quality of accommodations, particularly in older properties and even in luxury hotels, can vary greatly from room to room, as hotels are often renovated floor by floor; **if you don't like the room you're given, ask to see another.**

If you're counting on air-conditioning, you should **make sure, in advance, that your hotel room is *climatisé*** (air-conditioned). As the French generally haven't fallen in step with American tastes for cold air in a heat wave, air-conditioning is not a given, even at hotels in inland Provence, far from sea breezes. And when you throw open the windows, **don't expect screens** *(moustiquaires)*. Nowhere in Europe are they standard equipment, and the only exceptions are found occasionally in the Camargue marshlands, where mosquitoes are actually a problem.

Breakfast is not always included in the price, but you are sometimes expected to have it and are occasionally charged for it regardless. Make sure to inform the hotel if you are not going to be breakfasting there. In smaller rural hotels you may be expected to have your evening meal at the hotel, too.

Logis de France hotels are small and inexpensive and can be relied on for comfort, character, and regional cuisine. Look for its distinctive yellow and green sign. The Logis de France paperback guide is available from Logis de France (€4.88) or at the French Government Tourist Office. *See* Visitor Information, *below.*

Relais & Châteaux, Small Luxury Hotels of the World, and Leading Hotels of the World are three prestigious international groups with numerous converted châteaux and manor houses among their members. Not as luxurious, but strong on charm, is the Châteaux et Hôtels Independents group, which publishes its own catalog.

It's always a good idea to **make hotel reservations as far in advance as possible,** especially in late spring, summer, or fall. If you arrive without a reservation, however, the tourist office may be able to help.

🗐 Hotel Directories **Châteaux et Hôtels Independents** ✉ 12 rue Auber, 75009 Paris ☎ 01-40-07-00-20 🖷 01-40-07-00-30. **Leading Hotels of the World** ✉ 99 Park Ave., New York, NY 10016 ☎ 212/515-5600 🖷 212/515-5899 ⊕ www.lhw.com. **Logis de France** ✉ 83 av. d'Italie, 75013 Paris ☎ 01-45-84-83-84 🖷 01-45-83-59-66 ⊕ www.logis-de-france.fr. **Relais & Châteaux** ✉ 33 bd. Malesherbes, 75008 Paris ☎ 01-45-72-96-50 or 08-25-32-32-32 🖷 01-45-72-96-69 ✉ 11 E. 44th St., Suite 707, New York, NY 10017 ☎ 212/856-0115 or 800-735-2478 🖷 212/856-0193 ⊕ www.relaischateaux.fr. **Small**

Luxury Hotels of the World ✉ 14673 Midway Rd., Suite 201, Addison, TX 75001 ☎ 800/525-4800 for reservations or 972/866-8010 🖷 972/866-8025 ✉ James House, Bridge St., Leatherhead, Surrey KT22 7EP, U.K. ☎ 44/01372-361873 🖷 44/01372-361874 ⊕ www.slh.com.

🗐 Toll-Free Numbers **Best Western** ☎ 800/528-1234 ⊕ www.bestwestern.com. **Choice** ☎ 800/424-6423 ⊕ www.choicehotels.com. **Comfort Inn** ☎ 800/424-6423 ⊕ www.choicehotels.com. **Hilton** ☎ 800/445-8667 ⊕ www.hilton.com. **Holiday Inn** ☎ 800/465-4329 ⊕ www.ichotelsgroup.com. **Radisson** ☎ 800/333-3333 ⊕ www.radisson.com.

RESERVING A ROOM

Here is a sample letter you can use when making a written reservation.

Cher (Dear) *Madame, Monsieur:*

Nous voudrions réserver une chambre pour (We wish to reserve a room for) (number of) *nuit(s)* (nights), *du* (from) (arrival date) *au* ___ (departure date), *à deux lits* (with twin beds), or *à lit-double* (with a double bed), or *une chambre pour une seule personne* (a room for a single person), *avec salle de bains et toilettes privées* (with a bathroom and private toilet). *Si possible, nous voudrions une salle de bains avec une baignoire et aussi une douche.* (If possible, we would prefer a bathroom with a tub as well as a shower— note that a bathroom with a tub can be more expensive than one with just a shower.) *Veuillez confirmer la réservation en nous communicant le prix de la chambre, et le dépot forfaitaire que vous exigez. Dans l'attente de votre lettre, nous vous prions d'agréer, Madame, Monsieur, l'expression de nos sentiments amicales.* (Can you please inform us about availabilties, the rate of room, and if any deposit is needed? With our friendliest greetings, we will wait for your confirmation.)

MAIL & SHIPPING

In this book, the postal code precedes the city or town in French mailing addresses, in keeping with the way envelopes are addressed in France.

POSTAL RATES

Letters and postcards to the United States and Canada cost €.90 (about $1.05) for 20 grams. Letters and postcards within France and the rest of Europe (including the United Kingdom) cost €.55 (about 36p) for up to 20 grams. Stamps can be bought in post offices (*bureaux de poste*) and cafés displaying a red TABAC sign outside.

RECEIVING MAIL
If you're uncertain where you'll be staying, **have mail sent to the local post office**, addressed as "poste restante," or to American Express, but remember that during peak seasons, American Express may refuse to accept mail. Bring your passport along to collect your mail.

MONEY MATTERS
The following prices are to give you an idea of costs. Note that it is less expensive to eat or drink standing at a café or bar counter than it is to sit at a table. Two prices are listed, *au comptoir* (at the counter) and *à salle* (at a table). Coffee in a bar: €1 to €1.50 (standing), €1.50 to €5 (seated); beer in a bar: €2 (standing), €3 to €6 (seated); Coca-Cola: €2 to €4 a can; ham sandwich: €3.50; one-mile taxi ride: €5.50; movie: €7.50 to €9.50 (sometimes less expensive for screenings before noon); foreign newspaper: €1.50 to €4; museum admission: €1.50 to €9.

Prices throughout this guide are given for adults. Substantially reduced fees are almost always available for children, students, and senior citizens. For information on taxes, *see* Taxes.

ATMS
ATMs (*distributeurs de billets*) are very common in major cities and larger towns and are one of the easiest ways to get cash; you'll find one in almost any but the very smallest towns. Banks usually offer excellent, wholesale exchange rates through ATMs.

To get cash at ATMs in France, **your PIN must be four digits long.** You may have more luck with ATMs if you are using a credit card or a debit card that is also a Visa or MasterCard, rather than just your bank card. Note, too, that you may be charged by your bank for using ATMs overseas; inquire at your bank about charges.

Using a debit card (with a Visa or MasterCard symbol on it) makes it easier to find ATMs that you can use.

Before you go, it's a good idea to **get a list of ATM locations that you can use** in France from your bank. Failing that, you can always ask a passerby on the street for the nearest *distributeur de billets*.

CREDIT CARDS
Many restaurants and stores take both credit and debit cards, though there is often a €10 or €15 minimum. Visa is more widely accepted than American Express, especially in smaller restaurants and hotels.

Throughout this guide, the following abbreviations are used: **AE,** American Express; **DC,** Diners Club; **MC,** MasterCard; and **V,** Visa.

🔢 Reporting Lost Cards **American Express** ☎ 336/393-1111, collect. **Diners Club** ☎ 303/799-1504, collect. **MasterCard** ☎ 0800/90-1387. **Visa** ☎ 0800/90-1179, 410/581-9994 collect.

CURRENCY
On January 1, 2002, the French said *au revoir* to the franc and *bienvenue* to the euro. It was one of 12 European Union members—now known as the "euro-zone"—to introduce the European single currency in place of its national currency.

Although prices in shops and on receipts are still displayed in both French francs and euros—and many locals still refer to prices in francs—only euros are accepted as valid currency. Old franc notes can be exchanged at the central Banque de France until 2012, but the coins are now only good for souvenirs.

Under the euro system, there are seven notes: 5, 10, 20, 50, 100, 200, and 500 euros. Notes are the same for all countries. There are eight coins: 1 and 2 euros, plus 1, 2, 5, 10, 20, and 50 cents. On all coins, one side has the value of the euro on it and the other side has the national symbol of one of the countries participating in monetary union.

At press time, the exchange rate was approximately €.82 to the US dollar; €.67 to the Canadian dollar; €.63 to the Australian dollar; €.58 to the New Zealand dollar; and €1.50 to the British pound sterling.

CURRENCY EXCHANGE

For the most favorable rates, **change money through banks.** Although ATM transaction fees may be higher abroad than at home, ATM rates are excellent because they're based on wholesale rates offered only by major banks. You won't do as well at exchange booths in airports or rail and bus stations, in hotels, in restaurants, or in stores. To avoid lines at airport exchange booths, get a bit of local currency before you leave home.

Exchange Services International Currency Express ✉ 427 N. Camden Dr., Suite F, Beverly Hills, CA 90210 ☎ 888/278-6628 orders ⊟ 310/278-6410 ⊕ www.foreignmoney.com. **Travel Ex Currency Services** ☎ 800/287-7362 orders and retail locations ⊕ www.travelex.com.

TRAVELER'S CHECKS

With the presence of banking machines in even the smallest Provençal towns, traveler's checks are fast becoming obsolete. Store clerks are often unwilling to deal with them, and even some banks now refuse to cash them. Add to this that you will be given a better exchange rate at an ATM, and you might want to consider other options.

PACKING

Although you'll usually have no trouble finding a baggage cart at the airport, luggage restrictions on international flights are tight and baggage carts at railroad stations are not always available, so **pack light.** Even hotel staffs are becoming less and less tolerant of heavy suitcases and heaps of luggage worthy of a *Queen Mary* crossing.

Over the years, casual dress has become more acceptable, although the resorts along the Côte d'Azur and in the Luberon and Aix-en-Provence are still synonymous with smart dressers and fashion plates.

Jeans are very common, though they, too, are worn stylishly, with a nice button-down shirt, polo, or T-shirt without writing. Shorts, though longish per current trends, are a popular item for the younger

crowd in most cities. More and more people are wearing sneakers, although you may still stand out as a tourist with them on, especially if you wear them when you go out at night.

There is no need to wear a tie and jacket at most restaurants (unless specified), even fancy ones, though you should still try to look nice. Most casinos and upscale nightclubs along the Côte d'Azur, however, require jackets and ties.

For beach resorts, take a decent cover-up; wearing your bathing suit on the street is frowned upon.

Most of France is hot in the summer, cool in the winter. Since it rains all year round, **bring a raincoat and umbrella.** You'll need a sweater or warm jacket for the Mediterranean in winter, and you should also bring hats, scarves, and gloves.

If you are staying in budget hotels, **take along soap.** Many hotels either do not provide it or give you a very limited amount. You might also want to bring a washcloth.

In your carry-on luggage, pack an extra pair of eyeglasses or contact lenses and enough of any medication you take to last a few days longer than the entire trip. You may also ask your doctor to write a spare prescription using the drug's generic name, as brand names may vary from country to country. In luggage to be checked, **never pack prescription drugs, valuables, or undeveloped film.** And don't forget to carry with you the addresses of offices that handle refunds of lost traveler's checks. Check *Fodor's How to Pack* (available at online retailers and bookstores everywhere) for more tips.

To avoid customs and security delays, carry medications in their original packaging. Don't pack any sharp objects in your carry-on luggage, including knives of any size or material, scissors, nail clippers, and corkscrews, or anything else that might arouse suspicion.

To avoid having your checked luggage chosen for hand inspection, don't cram bags full. The U.S. Transportation Security Administration suggests packing shoes on top and placing personal items you don't want touched in clear plastic bags.

Lighters, even empty ones, may also be confiscated at check-in.

CHECKING LUGGAGE

You're allowed to carry aboard one bag and one personal article, such as a purse or a laptop computer. Make sure what you carry on fits under your seat or in the overhead bin. Get to the gate early, so you can board as soon as possible, before the overhead bins fill up.

Baggage allowances vary by carrier, destination, and ticket class. On international flights, you're usually allowed to check two bags weighing up to 70 pounds (32 kilograms) each, although a few airlines allow checked bags of up to 88 pounds (40 kilograms) in first class. Some international carriers don't allow more than 66 pounds (30 kilograms) per bag in business class and 44 pounds (20 kilograms) in economy. If you're flying to or through the United Kingdom, your luggage cannot exceed 70 pounds (32 kilograms) per bag. On domestic flights, the limit is usually 50 to 70 pounds (23 to 32 kilograms) per bag. In general, carry-on bags shouldn't exceed 40 pounds (18 kilograms). Most airlines won't accept bags that weigh more than 100 pounds (45 kilograms) on domestic or international flights. Expect to pay a fee for baggage that exceeds weight limits. Check baggage restrictions with your carrier before you pack.

Airline liability for baggage is limited to $2,500 per person on flights within the United States. On international flights it amounts to $9.07 per pound or $20 per kilogram for checked baggage (roughly $640 per 70-pound bag), with a maximum of $634.90 per piece, and $400 per passenger for unchecked baggage. You can buy additional coverage at check-in for about $10 per $1,000 of coverage, but it often excludes a rather extensive list of items, shown on your airline ticket.

Before departure, itemize your bags' contents and their worth, and label the bags with your name, address, and phone number. (If you use your home address, cover it so potential thieves can't see it readily.) Include a label inside each bag and **pack a copy of your itinerary.** At check-in, make sure each bag is correctly tagged with the destination airport's three-letter code. Because some checked bags will be opened for hand inspection, the U.S. Transportation Security Administration recommends that you leave luggage unlocked or use the plastic locks offered at check-in. TSA screeners place an inspection notice inside searched bags, which are re-sealed with a special lock.

If your bag has been searched and contents are missing or damaged, file a claim with the TSA Consumer Response Center as soon as possible. If your bags arrive damaged or fail to arrive at all, file a written report with the airline before leaving the airport.

🔁 **Complaints U.S. Transportation Security Administration Contact Center** ☎ 866/289-9673 ⊕ www.tsa.gov.

PASSPORTS & VISAS

When traveling internationally, carry your passport even if you don't need one. Not only is it the best form of ID, but it's also being required more and more. As of December 31, 2005, for instance, Americans need a passport to re-enter the country from Bermuda, the Caribbean, and Panama. Such requirements also affect re-entry from Canada and Mexico by air and sea (as of December 31, 2006) and land (as of December 31, 2007). **Make two photocopies of the data page** (one for someone at home and another for you, carried separately from your passport). If you lose your passport, promptly call the nearest embassy or consulate and the local police.

U.S. passport applications for children under age 14 require consent from both parents or legal guardians; both parents must appear together to sign the application. If only one parent appears, he or she must submit a written statement from the other parent authorizing passport issuance for the child. A parent with sole authority must present evidence of it when applying; acceptable documentation includes the child's certified birth certificate listing only the applying parent, a court order specifically permitting this parent's travel with the child, or a death certificate for the nonapplying parent. Application forms and instructions are available on the Web site of the U.S. State Department's Bureau of Consular Affairs (⊕ travel.state.gov).

ENTERING FRANCE

All Australian, Canadian, New Zealand, U.K, and U.S. citizens, even infants, need only a valid passport to enter France for stays of up to 90 days.

PASSPORT OFFICES

The best time to apply for a passport or to renew is in fall and winter. Before any trip, check your passport's expiration date, and, if necessary, renew it as soon as possible.

🗃 Australian Citizens **Passports Australia** Australian Department of Foreign Affairs and Trade ☎ 131-232 ⊕ www.passports.gov.au.

🗃 Canadian Citizens **Passport Office** ⊠ to mail in applications: 70 Cremazie St., Gatineau, Québec]8Y 3P2 ☎ 819/994-3500 or 800/567-6868 ⊕ www. ppt.gc.ca.

🗃 New Zealand Citizens **New Zealand Passports Office** ☎ 0800/22-5050 or 04/474-8100 ⊕ www. passports.govt.nz.

🗃 U.K. Citizens **U.K. Passport Service** ☎ 0870/ 521-0410 ⊕ www.passport.gov.uk.

🗃 U.S. Citizens **National Passport Information Center** ☎ 877/487-2778, 888/874-7793 TDD/TTY ⊕ travel.state.gov.

RESTROOMS

Finding a *toilette* in Provence is not difficult—even the smallest bar will have a tiny, and usually clean, toilet. But you must be a paying customer to use the facilities. In larger towns and cities there are often public toilets with an attendant busily cleaning the restroom. The charge is between €.20 and €.50, and is well worth it. Small villages have public toilets, usually next to the boules court, but one must be very brave to enter.

SAFETY

Don't wear a money belt or a waist pack, both of which peg you as a tourist. Distribute your cash and any valuables (including your credit cards and passport) between a deep front pocket, an inside jacket or vest pocket, and a hidden money pouch. Do not reach for the money pouch once you're in public.

Car break-ins have become part of daily life in the south, especially in the isolated parking lots where hikers set off to explore for the day. Be especially careful around the marshes of the Camargue, the departure point for the Iles d'Hyères ferries, the rocky Esterel between Fréjus and Cannes, and the coastal path around St-Tropez: **take valuables with you** and, if possible, **leave your luggage at your hotel.**

Also beware of petty theft—purse snatching and pickpocketing. **Use common sense**: avoid pulling out a lot of money in public, and wear a handbag with long straps that you can sling across your body, bandolier-style, with a zippered compartment for your money and passport. It's also a good idea to wear a money belt. Men should keep their wallets up front, as safely tucked away as possible.

Although cities in Provence are safe during the day, one should take caution at night, especially in port towns such as Marseille, Nice, and Toulon. Avignon also has a high crime rate, and tourists should be alert and walk purposefully through town at night.

SENIOR-CITIZEN TRAVEL

Older travelers to France can take advantage of many discounts, such as reduced admissions of 20%–50% to museums and movie theaters. Seniors 60 and older should **buy the SNCF's Carte Sénior** for discounts on rail travel (⇨ Train Travel, *below*).

To qualify for age-related discounts, mention your senior-citizen status up front when booking hotel reservations (not when checking out) and before you're seated in restaurants (not when paying the bill). Be sure to have identification on hand. When renting a car, ask about promotional car-rental discounts, which can be cheaper than senior-citizen rates.

🗃 Educational Programs **Elderhostel** ⊠ 11 Ave. de Lafayette, Boston, MA 02111 ☎ 877/426-8056, 978/323-4141 international callers, 877/426-2167 TTY 🖷 877/426-2166 ⊕ www.elderhostel.org.

SHOPPING

Don't bargain in shops where prices are clearly marked; but at outdoor and flea markets and in antiques stores bargaining is a way of life. If you're thinking of buying several items, you've nothing to lose by cheerfully suggesting to the proprietor, "*Vous me faites un prix?*" ("How about a discount?").

A number of shops offer V.A.T. tax refunds to foreign shoppers (⇨ Taxes, *below*).

CLOTHING SIZES

To figure out the French equivalent of U.S. clothing and shoe sizes, do the following, simple calculations.

To change U.S. men's suit sizes to French suit sizes, add 10 to the U.S. suit size. For example, a U.S. size 42 is a French size 52.

French men's collar sizes vary in their relation to U.S. collar sizes. But you can get the approximate size by multiplying the U.S. collar size by 2 and adding 8. For example, a U.S. size 15 is a French size 38. A U.S. size 15½ is a French size 39 or 40.

French men's shoe sizes vary in their relation to U.S. shoe sizes. A U.S. men's size 7½ is a French size 40; an 8½ is a 41; a 9½ is a 42.

To change U.S. dress/coat/blouse sizes to French sizes, add 30 to the U.S. size. For example, a U.S. women's size 8 is a French size 38 and a U.S. size 10 is a French size 40.

To change U.S. women's shoe sizes to French shoe sizes, add approximately 31 to the U.S. shoe size. For example, a U.S. size 7 is a French size 38.

KEY DESTINATIONS

Markets in Provence are fabulous, the best markets days being Wednesday in St-Rémy; Tuesday through Sunday morning in Nice; Tuesday, Thursday, and Saturday in Aix-en-Provence; Friday in Carpentras; Wednesday and Friday in Sisteron; Tuesday through Sunday in Apt; and, for antiques, Sunday in l'Isle-sur-la-Sorgue. Make sure you get an early start: markets are usually in full swing by nine in the morning, and most stalls are closing up shortly after one. Many artisanal items can be found in the markets, such as olive oil soaps and soaps of varying fragrances, as well as mass-produced items such as fabrics which come in a multitude of colors and patterns inspired by the light and color of Provence. Upscale

shopping is concentrated in the towns along the Côte d'Azur. Cannes' main street, La Croisette, is full of designer boutiques, as are smaller towns such as St-Tropez and Aix-en-Provence.

SMOKING

No-smoking signs and designated areas are slowly coming to Provence. Some upscale restaurants and brasseries now have no-smoking rooms, but often these postings are ignored by your fellow Provençal diners. Cafés are, and probably always will be, havens for smokers. Cigarettes cost from €3.20 a pack.

STUDENTS IN PROVENCE & THE CÔTE D'AZUR

There are a number of universities in Provence, but the two cities where the college-age population really stands out are Aix-en-Provence and Montpellier.

There are bargains for students holding a valid college or international student ID almost everywhere in the south of France, on train and plane fares, and for movie and museum tickets. If you're under 26, you'll automatically be eligible for a 25% discount on all rail travel (⇨ Train Travel, *below*). **Carry your valid university or international ID card with you at all times** so you can get discounts.

7 **IDs & Services STA Travel** ⊠ 10 Downing St., New York, NY 10014 ☎ 212/627-3111, 800/777-0112 24-hr service center 🖷 212/627-3387 ⊕ www.sta. com. **Travel Cuts** ⊠ 187 College St., Toronto, Ontario M5T 1P7, Canada ☎ 800/592-2887 in the U.S., 416/979-2406 or 866/246-9762 in Canada 🖷 416/979-8167 ⊕ www.travelcuts.com.

TAXES

All taxes must be included in posted prices in France. The initials TTC (*toutes taxes comprises*—taxes included) sometimes appear on price lists but, strictly speaking, are superfluous. By law, restaurant and hotel prices must include 20.6% taxes and a service charge. If they show up as extra charges on your bill, complain.

VALUE-ADDED TAX

A number of shops participating in the Tax-Free Shopping program (you'll see a sticker in the shop window) offer V.A.T.

refunds to foreign shoppers. To qualify for the refund, you must be a national of a non-EU country, at least 15 years old at the time of purchase, and visiting France for less than six months. If you qualify, you are entitled to an Export Discount of 20.6%, depending on the item purchased, and only on purchases of at least €175 in a single store. Remember to **ask for the refund,** as some stores—especially larger ones—offer the service only upon request.

When making a purchase, **ask for a V.A.T. refund form** and find out whether the merchant gives refunds—not all stores do, nor are they required to. Have the form stamped like any customs form by customs officials when you leave the country or, if you're visiting several European Union countries, when you leave the EU. Be ready to show customs officials what you've bought (pack purchases together, in your carry-on luggage); budget extra time for this. After you're through passport control, take the form to a refund-service counter for an on-the-spot refund (which is usually the quickest and easiest option), or mail it to the address on the form (or the envelope with it) after you arrive home.

A service processes refunds for most shops. You receive the total refund stated on the form. Global Refund is a Europe-wide service with 210,000 affiliated stores and more than 700 refund counters—located at major airports and border crossings. Its refund form is called a Tax Free Check. The service issues refunds in the form of cash, check, or credit-card adjustment. If you don't have time to wait at the refund counter, you can mail in the form to an office in Europe or Canada instead.
🚩 V.A.T. Refunds **Global Refund Canada** 🗇 Box 2020, Station Main Brampton, Ontario L6T 3S3 ☎ 800/993–4313 🖷 905/791–9078 ⊕ www.globalrefund.com.

TELEPHONES

AREA AND COUNTRY CODES
The country code for France is 33. All phone numbers in France have a two-digit prefix determined by zone: Paris and the Ile-de-France, 01; the northwest, 02; the northeast, 03; the southeast, 04; and the southwest, 05. Numbers beginning with 08 are either toll-free or toll calls (with an additional charge on top of making the call). Numbers beginning with 06 are mobile phones.

CALLING FRANCE
Note that **when dialing France from abroad, drop the initial 0 from the number.** For instance, to call a telephone number in Paris from the United States, dial 011–33 plus the phone number minus the initial 0 (phone numbers in this book are listed with the full 10 digits, which you use to make local calls). To call France from the United Kingdom, dial 00–33, then dial the number in France minus the initial 0.

DIRECTORY & OPERATOR ASSISTANCE
To find a number in France, **dial 3912 for information.** For international inquiries, dial 00–33–12 (–11 for the U.S., –44 for the U.K.).

INTERNATIONAL CALLS FROM FRANCE
To call out of France, dial 00 and wait for the tone, then dial the country code (1 for the United States and Canada, 44 for the United Kingdom, 61 for Australia, 64 for New Zealand) and the area code (minus any initial 0) and number. Expect to be overcharged if you call from your hotel.

LOCAL AND LONG-DISTANCE CALLS
To call anywhere in France while in France, dial the full 10-digit number, including the initial zero.

LONG-DISTANCE SERVICES
AT&T, MCI, and Sprint access codes make calling long-distance relatively convenient, but you may find the local access number blocked in many hotel rooms. First ask the hotel operator to connect you. If the hotel operator balks, ask for an international operator, or dial the international operator yourself. One way to improve your odds of getting connected to your long-distance carrier is to travel with more than one company's calling card (a hotel may block Sprint, for example, but not MCI). If all else fails, call from a pay

phone. If you are travelling for a longer period of time, consider renting a cellphone from a local company.

📶 Access Codes AT&T Direct ☎ 08-00-99-00-11, 800/874-4000 for information. **MCI WorldPhone** ☎ 08-00-99-00-19, 800/444-4444 for information. **Sprint International Access** ☎ 08-00-99-00-87, 800/793-1153 for information.

PHONE CARDS

Most French pay phones are operated by *télécartes* (phone cards), which you can buy from post offices, métro stations, and some tabacs (tobacco shops) for a cost of €9 for 50 units and €16.25 for 120. Coin-operated pay phones are scarce, found only in cafés (who can set their own rates) and post offices. Phone cards are accepted everywhere else. The easiest but most expensive way to phone is to use your own Visa card, which is accepted in all phone booths and works like a télécarte.

PUBLIC PHONES

Telephone booths can almost always be found at post offices, and often in cafés. A local call costs €.11 for every three minutes; half-price rates apply weekdays between 9:30 PM and 8 AM, from 1:30 PM Saturday, and all day Sunday.

TIME

The time difference between New York and France is 6 hours; when it's 1 PM in New York, it's 7 PM in France. France is 7 hours ahead of Chicago and 9 hours ahead of Los Angeles. France is 1 hour ahead of London. The time difference between France and Sydney is 8 to 9 hours, depending on when daylight savings time is or is not in effect.

TIPPING

The French have a clear idea of when they should be tipped. Bills in bars and restaurants include 15% service, but it is customary to **round out your bill with some small change** unless you're dissatisfied. The amount of this varies: anywhere from €.10 if you've merely bought a beer, to €2 after a meal. Tip taxi drivers and hairdressers 10%–15%. In some theaters and hotels, coat check attendants may expect nothing (if there is a sign saying POURBOIRE

INTERDIT—tips forbidden); otherwise give them €1. Same goes for washroom attendants, unless another sum is posted.

If you stay in a hotel for more than two or three days, it is customary to leave something for the chambermaid—about €1.50 per day. In expensive hotels you may well call on the services of a baggage porter (bell boy) and hotel porter and possibly the telephone receptionist. All expect a tip: plan on about €1.50 per item for the baggage boy, but the other tips will depend on how much you've used their services—common sense must guide you here. In hotels that provide room service, give €1 to the waiter (this does not apply to breakfast served in your room). If the chambermaid does some pressing or laundering for you, give her €1 on top of the charge made.

Gas-station attendants get nothing for gas or oil, but about €1 for checking tires. Train and airport porters get a fixed €1 to €1.50 per bag, but you're better off getting your own baggage cart if you can. Museum guides should get €1 to €1.50 after a guided tour, and it is standard practice to tip tour guides (and bus drivers) €1.50 to €3 after an excursion, depending on its length and your level of satisfaction.

TOURS & PACKAGES

Because everything is prearranged on a prepackaged tour or independent vacation, you spend less time planning—and often get it all at a good price.

BOOKING WITH AN AGENT

Travel agents are excellent resources. But it's a good idea to collect brochures from several agencies, as some agents' suggestions may be influenced by relationships with tour and package firms that reward them for volume sales. If you have a special interest, find an agent with expertise in that area. The American Society of Travel Agents (ASTA) has a database of specialists worldwide; you can log on to the group's Web site to find one near you.

Make sure your travel agent knows the accommodations and other services of the place being recommended. Ask about the hotel's location, room size, beds, and whether it has a pool, room service, or programs for children, if you care about these. Has your agent been there in person or sent others whom you can contact?

Do some homework on your own, too: local tourism boards can provide information about lesser-known and small-niche operators, some of which may sell only direct.

Maison de la France (⇨ Visitor Information, *below*) publishes many brochures on theme trips in France including "In the Footsteps of the Painters of Light in Provence" and "France for the Jewish Traveler."

🛈 Tour-Operator Recommendations **American Society of Travel Agents** (⇨ Travel Agencies). **CrossSphere–The Global Association for Packaged Travel** ⊠ 546 E. Main St., Lexington, KY 40508 ☎ 859/226–4444 or 800/682–8886 🖷 859/226–4414 ⊕ www.CrossSphere.com. **United States Tour Operators Association** (USTOA) ⊠ 275 Madison Ave., Suite 2014, New York, NY 10016 ☎ 212/599–6599 🖷 212/599–6744 ⊕ www.ustoa.com.

GROUP TOURS

Among companies that sell tours to Provence and the Riviera, the following are nationally known, have a proven reputation, and offer plenty of options.

🛈 Super-Deluxe **Abercrombie & Kent** ⊠ 1520 Kensington Rd., Oak Brook, IL 60521-2141 ☎ 800/323–7308, 020/7559–4777 in the U.K. 🖷 630/954–3324 ⊕ www.abercrombiekent.com. **Travcoa** ⊠ 2350 S.E. Bristol St., Newport Beach, CA 92660 ☎ 800/992–2003, 61/2962–3366 in Australia, 416/927–9610 in Canada 🖷 949/476–2538 ⊕ www.travcoa.com.

🛈 Deluxe **Maupintour** ⊠ 10650 W. Charleston Blvd., Summerlin, NV 89135 ☎ 800/255–4266 🖷 702/260–3787 ⊕ www.maupintour.com. **Tauck Tours** ⊠ 276 Post Rd. W, Westport, CT 06880 ☎ 203/226–6911 or 800/788–7885 in the U.S., 1800/122–048 in Australia, 0800/961–834 in the U.K. 🖷 203/221–6866 ⊕ www.tauck.com.

🛈 First-Class **Caravan Tours** ⊠ 401 N. Michigan Ave., Chicago, IL 60611 ☎ 312/321–9800 or 888/227–2826 🖷 312/321–9845 ⊕ www.caravantours.com. **Collette Tours** ⊠ 162 Middle St., Pawtucket, RI 02860 ☎ 401/728–3805 or 800/340–5158 🖷 401/728–4745 ⊕ www.collettetours.com.

🛈 Budget **Tours of Provence** ⊠ 1700 Glen Bar Sq., Denver, CO 80215 ☎ 303/275–9899 ⊕ www.toursofprovence.com.

TRAIN TRAVEL

The SNCF is recognized as Europe's best national rail service: it's fast, punctual, comfortable, and comprehensive. You can get to Provence and the coast from all points west, north, and east, though lines out of Paris are by far the most direct. There are various options: local trains, overnight trains with sleeping accommodations, and the high-speed TGV, the *Trains à Grande Vitesse* (high-speed trains).

The SNCF's TGV Méditerranée, the high-speed rail line connecting Paris to Avignon and Aix-en-Provence, zooms along at 255 kph (160 mph). With the hassles of airport check-in and transfer, you may find train travel the most efficient way to get from Paris to Provence.

All trains to Provence leave from Paris's Gare de Lyon. Travel time from Paris is 2 hours and 40 minutes to Avignon; 3 hours to Nîmes, Marseille, and Aix-en-Provence; 3 hours and 15 minutes to Montpellier; 4 hours to Toulon; and 5½ hours to Nice.

Certain models of the TGV, called a "train duplex," offer luxurious, state-of-the-art comfort, with double-decker seating and panoramic views. When one of these passes along the coast—especially from Nice to Menton—it makes for a dramatic sightseeing excursion, though it pokes along at a local-train snail's pace. Ask about duplex trains when you're connecting from one coastal city to another (Marseille–Toulon–Fréjus–Cannes–Nice–Menton).

Once you're in the south, though, choose your home base carefully. Places in hill country and the mountains—the Luberon, the Alpilles, and the backcountry hills behind Nice—are not accessible by train, and you'll have to get around by bus or rental car.

If you are traveling from Paris or any other terminus, **get to the station half an hour before departure** to ensure that you'll have a good seat.

Before boarding, you must **punch your ticket (but not EurailPass) in one of the orange machines** at the entrance to the platforms, or else the ticket collector will fine you €15 on the spot.

For overnight accommodations, you have the choice between high-priced *wagons-lits* (sleeping cars) and affordable *couchettes* (bunks, six to a compartment in second class, four to a compartment in first, with sheets and pillow provided, priced at €15–€18).

CLASSES

Traveling first class can cost about 50% more than second class, but, with the exception of wider seats, you won't get many more amenities. You'll still need to purchase food, although in first class you can order a hot meal, served on china, if you're willing to pay quite a high price for it.

CUTTING COSTS

To save money, **look into rail passes.** But be aware that if you don't plan to cover many miles, you may come out ahead by buying individual tickets. If you plan to travel outside of Paris by train, **consider purchasing a France Rail Pass,** which allows four days of unlimited train travel (and a discount on Eurostar) in a one-month period. Prices begin at $195 each for two adults traveling together in second class and $229 second class for a solo traveler. First-class rates are $225 for two adults and $263 for a solo traveler. Additional days may be added for $30 a day in either class. Other options include the France Rail 'n Drive Pass (combining rail and rental car), France Rail 'n Fly Pass (rail travel and one air travel journey within France), and the France Fly Rail 'n Drive Pass (a rail, air, and rental car program all in one).

France is one of 17 countries in which you can **use Eurail Passes,** which provide unlimited first-class rail travel, in all of the participating countries, for the duration of the pass. If you plan to rack up the miles, get a standard pass. These are available for 15 days ($588), 21 days ($762), one month ($946), two months ($1,338), and three months ($1,654). If your plans call for only limited train travel, **consider a two-country pass** which costs less money than a EurailPass. With the two-country pass you'll get four flexible travel days between France and Italy, France and Spain, or France and Switzerland for $299. In addition to standard EurailPasses, **ask about special rail-pass plans.** Among these are the Eurail Selectpass Youth (for those under age 26) and the Eurail Selectpass Saver (which gives a discount for two or more people traveling together).

Whichever of the above you choose, remember that you must **purchase your pass at home before leaving for Europe.** Eurail and Europasses are available through travel agents and a few authorized outlets.

Don't assume that your rail pass guarantees you a seat on the train you wish to ride. You need to **book seats ahead even if you are using a rail pass;** seat reservations are required on high-speed trains, and are a good idea on trains that may be crowded—particularly in summer on popular routes. You will also need a reservation for sleeping accommodations.

🚆 Ticket Agents CIT Tours Corp. ✉ 15 West 44th St., 10th floor, New York, NY 10036 ☎ 800/248-7245 for rail, 800/248-8687 for tours and hotels ⊕ www.cit-tours.com. **DER Travel Services** ✉ 9501 W. Devon Ave., Rosemont, IL 60018 ☎ 800/782-2424 ⊕ www.dertravel.com. **Rail Europe** ✉ 226-230 Westchester Ave., White Plains, NY 10604 ☎ 800/438-7245 📠 800/432-1329 ✉ 2087 Dundas E, Suite 105, Mississauga, Ontario L4X 1M2 ☎ 905/602-4195 ⊕ www.raileurope.com.

FARES & SCHEDULES

If you know what station you'll depart from, you can get a free train schedule there (while supplies last), or you can access the multilingual computerized schedule information network at any Paris station and at larger regional stations (Marseille and Nice). You can also make reservations and buy your ticket while at the computer.

FRENCH RAIL CARDS

SNCF offers a number of discount rail passes available only for purchase in France. When traveling together, **two people can save money with the Prix Découverte à Deux.** You'll get a 25% discount during "périodes bleus" (blue periods; weekdays and not on or near any holidays). Note that tickets are non-transferable; and you have to be with the person you said you would be traveling with.

You can **get a reduced fare if you are over 60** with the SNCF's Carte Sénior, which costs €50 and entitles the bearer to deep discounts on rail and TGV travel for a year.

With the Carte Enfant+, **children under 12 can get 25%–50% off** of a full year of travel for €65. There's a wonderful bonus, too: up to four accompanying passengers, whether blood relatives or not, get the discount, too.

If you purchase an individual ticket from SNCF in France and you're under 26, you will automatically get a 25% reduction (a valid ID, such as an ISIC card or your passport, is necessary). If you're going to be using the train quite a bit during your stay in France and **if you're under 26, consider buying the Carte 12–25** (€49), which offers unlimited 50% reductions for one year (provided that there's space available at that price, otherwise you'll just get the standard 25% discount).

If you don't benefit from any of these reductions and **if you plan on traveling at least 1,000 km (620 mi) round-trip (including several stops), look into purchasing a Billet Séjour.** This ticket gives you a 25% reduction if you stay over a Sunday and if you travel only during blue periods. It may be a major organizational feat, but you can save a lot of cash this way.

See the Essentials at the end of each chapter for information about local stations.

RESERVATIONS

You must **always make a seat reservation for the TGV**—easily obtained at the ticket window or from an automatic machine. Seat reservations are reassuring but seldom necessary on other main-line French trains, except at busy holiday times.

🖅 Fares and Schedules **SNCF**
☎ 08-36-35-35-35.
🖅 Web Sites **Eurail** ⊕ www.eurail.com. **Eurostar** ⊕ www.eurostar.com. **SNCF** ☎ 08-36-35-35-35 ⊕ www.ter-sncf.com/uk/paca. **TGV** ☎ 877/ 2TGVMED ⊕ www.tgv.com. **www.beyond.fr** ⊕ www.beyond.fr.

TRANSPORTATION AROUND PROVENCE & THE CÔTE D'AZUR

See the Essentials sections in individual chapters for detailed information about using trains and buses throughout the regions covered in this book. It's possible to have a satisfying initiation to this broad region by train alone. There are sweeping, comprehensive connections all the way from Montpellier to Avignon to Marseille and on to the full length of the Italian coast. There are good regional bus networks, too, that connect out of train stations, but they're not very efficient for village-hopping and multistop sightseeing, as their schedules rarely intersect with yours. And sooner or later you may feel restless and want to burrow inland a bit, and here the trains are much more limited. A rental car is an obvious solution, but if you've flown into Paris, it's a long drive south (7 hours). For an extended vacation in the region, a rail-drive pass allows you to cover a few direct rail trajectories between bases, then take a rental car onto the back roads and byways. Or, you could fly to the south of France and rent a car from the airport. If you really want to sit back and let someone else do the work, consider a holiday bus excursion, where the tour company books all lodging and meals and guides you from sight to sight.

TRAVEL AGENCIES

A good travel agent puts your needs first. Look for an agency that has been in business at least five years, emphasizes customer service, and has someone on staff who specializes in your destination. In addition, **make sure the agency belongs to a professional trade organization.** The American Society of Travel Agents (ASTA) has more than 10,000 members in some 140 countries, enforces a strict code of ethics, and will step in to mediate agent-client disputes involving ASTA members. ASTA also maintains a directory of agents on its Web site; ASTA's TravelSense.org, a trip planning and travel advice site, can also help to locate a travel agent who caters to your needs.

🛅 Local Agent Referrals **American Society of Travel Agents** (ASTA) ✉ 1101 King St., Suite 200, Alexandria, VA 22314 ☎ 703/739-2782 or 800/965-2782 24-hr hotline 📠 703/684-8319 ⊕ www.astanet.com and www.travelsense.org. **Association of British Travel Agents** ✉ 68-71 Newman St., London W1T 3AH ☎ 020/7637-2444 📠 020/7637-0713 ⊕ www.abta.com. **Association of Canadian Travel Agencies** ✉ 130 Albert St., Suite 1705, Ottawa, Ontario K1P 5G4 ☎ 613/237-3657 📠 613/237-7052 ⊕ www.acta.ca. **Australian Federation of Travel Agents** ✉ Level 3, 309 Pitt St., Sydney, NSW 2000 ☎ 02/9264-3299 or 1300/363-416 📠 02/9264-1085 ⊕ www.afta.com.au. **Travel Agents' Association of New Zealand** ✉ Level 5, Tourism and Travel House, 79 Boulcott St., Box 1888, Wellington 6001 ☎ 04/499-0104 📠 04/499-0786 ⊕ www.taanz.org.nz.

VISITOR INFORMATION

Learn more about foreign destinations by checking government-issued travel advisories and country information. For a broader picture, consider information from more than one country.

See the Essentials sections *in* individual chapters for local tourist office telephone numbers and addresses.

🛅 Tourist Information **France On-Call** ☎ 202/659-7779 ☯ Weekdays 9–9. **Chicago** ✉ 676 N. Michigan Ave., Chicago, IL 60611 ☎ 312/751-7800 📠 312/337-6339. **Los Angeles** ✉ 9454 Wilshire Blvd., Suite 715, Beverly Hills, CA 90212 ☎ 310/271-6665 📠 310/276-2835. **New York City** ✉ 444 Madison Ave., 16th floor, New York, NY 10022 ☎ 410/286-8310 📠 212/838-7855. **Australia** ✉ Level 20, 25 Bligh St., Sydney, NSW 2000 ☎ 02/9231-5244 📠 02/9221-8682. **Canada** ✉ 1981 Ave. McGill College, Suite 490, Montréal, Québec H3A 2W9 ☎ 514/876-9881 📠 514/845-4868. **U.K.** ✉ 178 Piccadilly, London W1J 9AL ☎ 09068/244-123 📠 020/7493-6594.

🛅 Regional Tourist Office **Comité Régional du Tourisme de Provence-Alpes-Côtes d'Azur** (PACA, Regional Committee on Tourism in Provence, the Alps, and the Côte d'Azur) ✉ 12 pl. de la Joliette, 13002 Marseilles ☎ 04-91-56-47-00 📠 04-91-56-66-61 ⊕ www.crt-paca.fr.

🛅 Government Advisories **U.S. Department of State** ✉ Bureau of Consular Affairs, Overseas Citizens Services Office, 2201 C St. NW Washington, DC 20520 ☎ 202/647-5225, 888/407-4747 or 317/472-2328 for interactive hotline ⊕ www.travel.state.gov. **Consular Affairs Bureau of Canada** ☎ 800/267-6788 or 613/944-6788 ⊕ www.voyage.gc.ca. **U.K. Foreign and Commonwealth Office** ✉ Travel Advice Unit, Consular Directorate, Old Admiralty Building, London SW1A 2PA ☎ 0870/606-0290 or 020/7008-1500 ⊕ www.fco.gov.uk/travel. **Australian Department of Foreign Affairs and Trade** ☎ 300/139-281 travel advisories, 02/6261-1299 Consular Travel Advice ⊕ www.smartraveller.gov.au or www.dfat.gov.au. **New Zealand Ministry of Foreign Affairs and Trade** ☎ 04/439-8000 ⊕ www.mft.govt.nz.

WEB SITES

Do check out the World Wide Web when planning your trip. You'll find everything from weather forecasts to virtual tours of famous cities. Be sure to visit Fodors.com (⊕ www.fodors.com), a complete travel-planning site. You can research prices and book plane tickets, hotel rooms, rental cars, vacation packages, and more. In addition, you can post your pressing questions in the Travel Talk section. Other planning tools include a currency converter and weather reports, and there are loads of links to travel resources.

For more information specifically on Provence and the Côte d'Azur, visit: Eurail (⊕ www.eurail.com); Eurostar (⊕ www.eurostar.com); French Youth Hostel Federation (⊕ ww.fuaj.org); French Government Tourist Office/Maison de la France (⊕ www.francetourism.com or www.franceguide.com); French Embassy in the U.S. (⊕ www.info-france-usa.org); Provence Tourist Office (⊕ www.visitprovence.com); Riviera Tourist Office (⊕ www.guideriviera.com); and SNCF (⊕ www.sncf.fr/indexe.htm).

The Alpilles, Arles & the Camargue

THE PONT DU GARD, NÎMES, THE RHÔNE DELTA & THE LANGUEDOC FRONTIER

Roman amphitheater, Arles

WORD OF MOUTH

"But, oh to be able to once again ramble amongst the stalls of braided purple garlic, piles of bright green artichokes, *saucisson* wagons, an indescribably vast selection of *chèvres*, and the chicken rotisserie redolent with the aroma of roasting poultry and vegetables. Those are the sights and smells that activate our memories (and salivary glands!) in the famous Wednesday market of St-Remy."

—Lavende

WELCOME TO THE ALPILLES, ARLES & THE CAMARGUE

Wild horses of the Camargue

TOP 5
Reasons to Go

① **Vincent van Gogh's Arles:** Ever since the fiery Dutchman immortalized Arles in all its chromatic drama, this town has had a starring role in museums around the world.

② **A dip in the Middle Ages:** Wander the ghostly ruins of the Château des Baux in Les Baux-de-Provence: a tour de force of medieval ambience.

③ **Provence unplugged:** The famous lagoons of the Camargue will swamp you with their charms once you catch sight of their white horses, pink flamingos, and black bulls.

④ **St-Rémy's relentless charm:** Find inspired gourmet cooking, meditate quietly on Greco-Roman antiquity, or browse bustling markets, basket in hand, at this fashionable village enclave.

⑤ **The Pont du Gard:** This aqueduct of the ancient Roman era is also a spectacular work of art.

Languedoc frontier. The westernmost edge of Provence is highlighted by **Nîmes,** which competes with Arles and Orange as "the Rome of France" and is home to the Maison Carrée, the best-preserved ancient temple in Provence (Thomas Jefferson admired it so much he used it as a model for the Virginia state capitol). To the north is the **Pont du Gard,** most awe-inspiring in the early morning light.

Pont du Gard

Hiking in the Alpilles, Bouches du Rhône

Getting Oriented

Rugged and beautiful, this is landscape that is different from everywhere else in the South. Nowhere else will you find the Camargue's hypnotic plane of marshland stretching out to the sea, or the rocky Alpilles that jut upward hiding medieval fortress towns. Yet city folk find joy here too, in Van Gogh's colorful Arles or in feisty, fiercely independent Nîmes. And if it all gets just a bit too dusty, there is a plethora of options for some pampered R&R.

Uzès

N86

N580

Pont Du Gard ◆

N100

A9

D942

A7

Remoulins

N100

The Alpilles. These spiky mountains guard treasures like **Les Baux-de-Provence**—be bewitched by both its ville morte (dead town) and its luxurious L'Oustau de la Baumanière inn. Nearby is ritzy **St-Rémy-de-Provence**, Van Gogh's famous retreat.

Rhône

N570

D571

N7

Avignon

Cavaillon

D22

D999

Beaucaire

Tarascon

St-Rémy-de-Provence

N113

D99

D5

A54

Grand

N570

D17

Les Baux-de-Provence

N538

Fontvieille

D17

THE ALPILLES

Rhône

Arles

D17

Arles. While little is left of the town that Van Gogh once painted, there are spots where you can still channel his spirit. Today, **Arles** remains fiercely Provençal and is famed for its folklore events.

St-Gilles

D42

D570

Salon-de-Provence

A54

D5

CAMARGUE

Villeneuve

BOUCHES DU RHÔNE

D10

Petit

Etang du Vaccarès

D36

D36

N568

N1569

Etang de Berre

D570

Parc Régional de Camargue

N268

Stes-Maries-de-la-Mer

Golfe de Fos

Port St Louis

Maison Carrée, Nîmes

The Camargue. A bus ride away from Arles and bracketed by the towns of Aigues-Mortes and Stes-Maries-de-la-Mer, the vast **Camargue nature park** is one of France's most fascinating areas. Horseback ride across its mysterious marshland, then enjoy home-style cooking at one of the exclusive *mas* (converted-farmhouse) hotels.

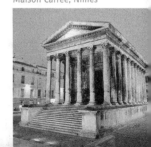

Updated by
Sarah Fraser

SCOURED BY THE MISTRAL and leveled to prairie flatlands by aeons of earth deposits carried south by the Rhône, this region is Provence in its rawest form. At first glance it is endless space broken only by the occasional gully lined with wildflowers, yet after a few moments it starts to take form as one of the most beautiful and intriguing regions in France. It is big-sky country here: mysterious, romantic, and colored with a kaleidoscope of lavenders, wheat-yellows, vibrant greens, and burnt reds. Only the giant rock outcrops of the Alpilles interrupt the horizon, dusted with silvery olives and bristling with somber cypress spears. To the west, where the Provençal dialect gives way to Languedoc, the ancient language of the southwest, vineyards swathe the countryside in rows of green and black. Along the southern coast, the Camargue's savage landscape of reeds and cane secrets exotic wildlife—rich-plumed egrets, rare black storks, clownish flamingos—as well as domestic oddities: dappled white horses and lyre-horned bulls descended from ancient, indigenous species.

The scenery is surpassed only by the genuine warmth of the populace and the fiesty energy of the cities. In-your-face, tatty Nîmes has a raffish urban lifestyle that surges obliviously through a ramshackle, grittychic Old Town and a plethora of Roman architectural marvels. Graceful, artsy Arles, harmonious in Van Gogh hues, mixes culture with a healthy dose of late-night café street life. Chic, luxurious St-Rémy is a gracious retreat for cosmopolitan regulars. Often misleadingly dubbed the Hamptons of Provence, it's not all about luxe, for St-Rémy has an amazingly steady infusion of style, art, and street sass mixed with a love of all things Provençal.

Each of these cities would be fascinating to explore even without its trump card: classical antiquities, superbly preserved, unsurpassed in northern Europe. The Colosseum-like arenas in Nîmes and Arles are virtually intact, solid enough to serve their original purpose as stadiums; they date from the time of Christ. The mausoleum and *arc de triomphe* outside St-Rémy are still so richly detailed they look like reproductions, but they're signed by the children of Caesar Augustus. And across the street, the vivid high-relief ruins of Glanum trace back to the Hellenism of the 3rd century BC.

Rich in history and legends, the region is as varied as the people who inhabit it. There are precise and perfect miniature fortress towns, like Aigues Mortes and Les Baux de Provence—where it is sometimes difficult to distinguish between bedrock and building—or the wide open marshlands of the Camargue, dotted with hidden natural treasures. Add to these attractions Romanesque châteaux and abbeys, seaside fortresses that launched crusades, and sun-sharpened landscapes seen through the perceptive eyes of Van Gogh and Gauguin, and you have a region not only worth exploring in depth, but worth savoring every minute.

Exploring the Alpilles, Arles & the Camargue

This is the kind of country that inspires a Latin latitude (if not lassitude), so with all the ruins and châteaux to visit, allow yourself time to wander through food markets and to sit on a shady terrace watching

PLEASURES & PASTIMES

LAND OF PINK FLAMINGOS. Just south of Arles, the Camargue is one of France's most distinctive and unforgettable landscapes—half water, half marsh, the vast nature preserve is trod by its famous longhorn cattle and dappled-white horses, riddden herd by its unique *gardian* cowboys, and watched over by its spectacular flocks of flamingos. The best way to tour this Edenic land is on horseback, although the wild glamour of the ancient race of Camargue horses becomes downright pedestrian when the now-domesticated beauties are saddled en masse and led single-file through the marsh trails. Rent-a-horse stands proliferate along the marshland highways, and trails are thick with gringos plodding along in subservient lines. But since much of the preserve is limited to walkers and riders, a trip on horseback will let you experience the austerity of the landscape without getting your feet wet.

ROMAN TO ROMANESQUE. Although you'll find Roman traces throughout Provence (and indeed France), the most beautifully preserved are concentrated around the Rhône. With two arenas (at Arles and Nîmes), the ancient Hellenistic settlement outside St-Rémy, the miraculously preserved temple in Nîmes (Maison Carrée), and traces of Roman life scattered over the region, this is the place to concentrate on if your taste runs to the classical. Not surprising, this region was one of the hotbeds of the 12th-century Romanesque style, modeled in ethos after the mother lode. Churches, châteaux, and abbeys still sprinkle the countryside of western Provence, a surprising concentration of them purest Romanesque—

that is, built in the solid progression of arches and barrel vaults that marked Roman engineering and was mimicked in the hinterlands by architects through the 12th and 13th centuries. A sign here might point to an ÉGLISE ROMANE—meaning Romanesque. *Romain* refers to Roman remains—just as prolific in the region.

ON THE MENU. If eating is the national pastime in France, it is a true vocation in Provence. And the pleasure of relaxing in a shady square over a pitcher of local rosé, a bowl of olives, and a regional *plat du jour* is only enhanced in western Provence by quirky local specialties. Consider nibbling tiny *tellines*, salty clams the size of your thumbnail, fresh from the Camargue coast. Or try a crockery bowl of steaming bull stew (*gardianne*), a sinewy daube of lean-and-mean beef from the harsh Camargue prairies, ladled over a scoop of chewy red Camargue rice. The mouth-watering oddity called *brandade* (salt cod pestled with olive oil and milk into a creamy spread) has a peculiar history; cod isn't even native to Nîmes, but was traded, in its leathery salt-dried form, by medieval Breton fishermen in exchange for south-coast salt. The Nîmois mixed in local olive oil and created a regional staple.

Though all of Provence is known for its rosés, some wines produced west of the Rhône merit special mention. Lirac and Tavel, world-famous and highly commercial rosés, come from the Rhône Valley just up the road from the Pont du Gard. The robust red *Costières de Nîmes* grows in stony dry vineyards west of its namesake.

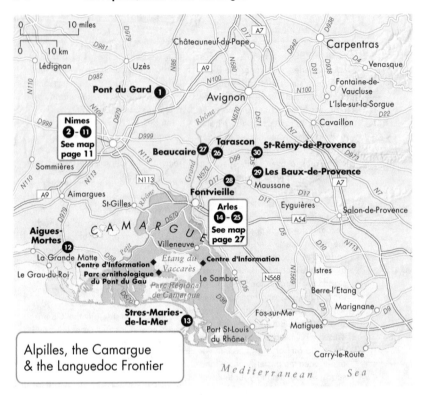

Alpilles, the Camargue
& the Languedoc Frontier

the painterly changes in light. Although Nîmes belongs in spirit to the Languedoc, its proximity to the Camargue and Arles makes it a logical travel package with them. With their rugged hills and rich olive groves, the Alpilles are a world apart, but easily accessible from Arles and environs. You can move from site to site, or choose a central base—say, Arles—and explore them all without driving more than an hour to any one attraction. A couple of days passing through the region allows you to see world-class antiquities; five days allows time to wander the Camargue; a week lets you see the principal sites, enjoy a nature tour, and take a break by the sea. And don't forget that the ravishing old city of Avignon (⇨ Chapter 3) is just an hour's easy run up from Arles.

Numbers in the text correspond to numbers in the margin and on the Alpilles, the Camargue, and the Languedoc Frontier, Nîmes, and Arles maps.

About the Restaurants & Hotels

It's true that every meal is a culinary event here, but during the summer months the local cafés and hotels make a special effort to make breakfast memorable. In turn, breakfast is one of the loveliest meals of the day. It's coolest in the morning—the birds chirp, the air is crisp, and the smell of freshly baked croissants can tempt even the most faithful *avocat* (lawyer) out of his *grace matinée* (sleep-in). Stroll out to the nearest square to sit under shady plane trees and listen to the relaxing bustle of Provence waking up. Tables are adroitly nestled in gardens or sprawled across freshly swept cobblestones, wrapped in flowerprint tableclothes and sprinkled with nosegays made of local flowers. Waiters bustle to and fro calling out friendly greetings while the first cups of gilt-edged espressos are prepared. Of course, "early morning" can be misleading: it could very well be 10 or 11 AM, but another example of southern charm is the option of a late breakfast. Hey, it makes a great excuse for a long late lunch!

Although Arles, Les Baux, and St-Rémy have stylish, competitive hotels with all the requisite comforts and Provençal touches, from wrought iron to *folklorique* cottons, Nîmes doesn't attract—or much merit—the overnight crowds; thus its hotels, with rare exception, have little in the way of charm. But throughout the region and well outside the towns you'll find lovely converted *mas* (farmhouses), blending into the landscape as if they'd been there a thousand years—but offering modern pleasures: gardens, swimming pools, and sophisticated cooking. For information on *gîtes* (houses offered as a vacation rental) and *chambres d'hôtes* (bed-and-breakfasts in private homes), check out the Lodging section in the Smart Travel Tips chapter.

WHAT IT COSTS In euros				
$$$$	**$$$**	**$$**	**$**	**¢**
RESTAURANTS over €30	€23–€29	€18–€22	€12–€17	under €11
HOTELS over €191	€121–€190	€81–€120	€51–€80	under €50

Restaurant prices are per person for a main course at dinner; note that if a restaurant offers only prix-fixe meals, it has been given the price category that reflects the full set-price. Hotel prices are for a standard double room in high season, including tax (19.6%) and service charge. Hotels operate on the European Plan (EP, with no meal provided) unless we note that they use the Breakfast Plan (BP), or also offer such options as Modified American Plan (MAP, with breakfast and dinner daily, known as *demi-pension*), or Full American Plan (FAP, or *pension complète*, with three meals a day). Inquire when booking if these all-inclusive mealplans (which always entail higher rates) are mandatory or optional.

Timing
July and August are very much the high season, especially along the coast, and are best avoided if possible, both because of the crushing crowds and the grilling heat. In winter (from November through February, even into March) you'll find a lot of tourist services closed, including hotels and restaurants, and much of the terrace life driven indoors by rain and wind. Around Easter, the plane trees begin to leaf out and the café tables to sprout. This easy midseason period maintains its lazy, pleasant pace from Easter through June and September to late October.

THE LANGUEDOC FRONTIER

Nîmes and its famous aqueduct hold forth in the département of Gard, considered more a part of the Languedoc culture than that of Provence. Yet because of its proximity to the heart of Provence and its similar climate, terrain, and architecture, it is included as a kindred southern spirit. Center of gaily printed *indienne* cottons, Camargue-style bullfights, and spectacular Roman ruins, it cannot be isolated from its Provençal neighbors. After all, the *langue d'oc* (language of oc) refers to the ancient southern language Occitane, which evolved from Latin; northern parts developed their own *langue d'oïl*. Their names derive from their manner of saying yes: *oc* in the south and *oïl* in the north. By an edict from Paris, the *oïls* had it in the 16th century, and *oui* and its northern dialect became standard French. Languedocien and Provençal merely went underground, however, and still crop up in gesticulating disputes at farmers' markets today.

Pont du Gard

★ ❶ *24 km (15 mi) northeast of Nîmes, 25 km (16 mi) north of Arles, 25 km (16 mi) west of Avignon.*

No other ancient Roman sight in Provence rivals the Pont du Gard, a mighty, three-tiered aqueduct midway between Nîmes and Avignon (⇨ Chapter 3) and the highest bridge the Romans ever built. Erected some 2,000 years ago as part of a 48-km (30-mi) canal supplying water to Roman Nîmes it is astonishingly well preserved. You can't walk across it anymore, but you can get close enough to it to see the amazing gigantic square blocks of stone (some weighing up to six tons) by traversing the 18th-century bridge built alongside it.

If you come to the Pont du Gard very early in the morning—before dawn is ideal—you can discover Provence in its purest blend of natural beauty and antiquity. As the silhouettes of olives emerge from the darkness and the diamond-sharp air wells up slowly with birdsong, you can see the ancient tiers as they were in the days when they carried water to Nîmes. The aqueduct is shockingly noble in its symmetry, the rhythmic repetition of arches resonant with strength, testimony to an engineering concept that was relatively new in the 1st century AD, when the structure was built under Emperor Claudius. And, unsullied by tourists and by the vendors of postcards and Popsicles that dominate the site later in the day, the nature is just as resonant, with the river flowing through its rocky gorge unperturbed by the work of master engineering that straddles it.

> **❝**
>
> Interestingly, the Pont du Gard was built with a slight bend in it to withstand flooding, and it has stood intact when other bridges—Roman and otherwise—collapsed in heavy rain years.
>
> **❞**

In the afternoon, however, crowds become a problem. Even off-season, no one wants to miss this wonder of the world. You can approach the aqueduct from either side of the Gardon River. Whether you choose the Rive Gauche (north side), or the Rive Droite (south side), parking costs the same (€5). However, the Rive Gauche entry is closest to the **Public Information Center** (☎ 04–66–37–50–99 ⊠ €10 ☉ May–Sept., daily 9:30–6:30; Oct.–Dec. and Feb.–Apr., daily 10–5), which contains an interesting multimedia exhibit on the life of Roman cities, their use of water, and the construction of the aqueduct and the Pont du Gard monument itself. There's also a "Ludo"—a space for kids to play—and a film on the history of the monument in English at 3 PM daily. Try to park as close to the attendant's booth as possible, as unfortunately break-ins are a problem. There's also a tourist office on the Rive Gauche with information and postcards. Note that this is also the side that tour buses prefer.

Where to Eat & Stay

$$$$ ✕⊞ **Le Vieux Castillon.** Just up the road from the Rive Gauche of the Pont du Gard, this medieval Relais & Châteaux hotel has sweeping views of the Ventoux valley, rooms tastefully styled with Provençal accents, and spacious modern bathrooms. The honey-color stone terraces and wonderful views further enhance chef Gilles Dauteuil's inventive and rich cooking, one of the highlights of which is local lamb roasted in garlic. The wine list is extensive, especially the Rhône Valley selection, and the cheeses are excellent. ⊠ *Rue Turion Sabatier, 30210 Castillon-du-Gard* ☎ *04–66–37–61–61* 🖷 *04–66–37–28–17* ⊕ *www.relaischateaux. fr/vieuxcastillon* 🛏 *33 rooms* ⚿ *Restaurant, pool, some pets allowed (fee)* ▤ *AE, DC, MC, V* ⊗ *Closed Jan.–mid-Feb. Restaurant closed Mon., no lunch Tues.* ⦿ *EP* ⦿ *MAP.*

Nîmes

24 km (15 mi) southwest of Pont du Gard, 29 km (18 mi) northwest of Arles.

If you have come to the south to seek out Roman treasures, you need look no further than Nîmes (pronounced *neem*), for the Arènes and Maison Carrée are among Continental Europe's best-preserved antiquities. But if you have come to seek out a more modern mythology—of lazy, graceful Provence—give Nîmes a wide berth. It's a feisty, run-down rat race of a town, with jalopies and Vespas roaring irreverently around the ancient temple, and rock bands blasting sound tests into the Arena's wooden stands. Its medieval Old Town has none of the gentrified grace of those in Arles or St-Rémy. Yet its rumpled and rebellious ways trace directly back to its Roman incarnation, when its population swelled with soldiers, arrogant and newly victorious after their conquest of Egypt in 31 BC. Already anchoring a fiefdom of pre-Roman *oppida* (elevated fortresses) before ceding to the empire in the 1st century BC, this ancient city bloomed to formidable proportions under the Pax Romana. A 24,000-seat coliseum, a thriving forum with a magnificent temple patterned after Rome's temple of Apollo, and a public water

> ### FROM NÎMES, WITH LOVE
>
> Blue jeans were first created in Nîmes: The word "denim" is derived from the phrase "de Nîmes" ("from Nîmes"). Originally used by local farmers to make wagon covers and work clothes, denim soon made its way to San Francisco, thanks to Bavarian merchant Levi Strauss. Strauss's durable denim work pants, or jeans (which, incidentally, comes from the American mispronunciation of the Italian port Gênes, from which the fabric was originally shipped), became an instant success with gold miners.

network fed by the Pont du Gard attest to its classical prosperity. Its next golden age bloomed under the Protestants, who established an anti-Catholic stronghold here and violated iconic architectural treasures—not to mention the papist minority. Their massacre of some 200 Catholic citizens is remembered as the Michelade; many of the victims were priests sheltered in the *évêché* (Bishop's Palace), now the Musée du Vieux Nîmes (Museum of Old Nîmes). Chapels throughout the surrounding countryside were damaged by Calvin's righteous rebels.

Perhaps inspired by the influx of architects who studied its antique treasures, Nîmes has opted against becoming a lazy, atmospheric Provençal market town and has invested in progressive modern architecture. Smackdab across from the Maison Carrée stands the city's contemporary answer, the modern-art museum dubbed the Carré d'Art (Art Square) after its ruthlessly modernist four-square form—a pillared, symmetrical glass reflection of its ancient twin. Other investments in contemporary art and architecture confirm Nîmes's commitment to modern ways.

If you want to see everything, or a lot of things in Nîmes, then the **Visite Ensemble** is good value for the money. The ticket costs a mere €10, is valid for three days, and can be purchased at most local monuments and sites.

★ ❷ The **Arènes** (Arena) is considered the world's best-preserved Roman amphitheater. A miniature of the Colosseum in Rome, it stands more than 520 feet long and 330 feet wide, with a seating capacity of 23,000. Bloody gladiator battles and theatrical wild-boar hunts drew crowds to its bleachers. As barbarian invasions closed in on Nîmes, the structure was transformed into a fortress by the Visigoths. Later, medieval residents found comfort and protection for tightly packed thatch-and-timber houses (as well as a small château and chapel). Nowadays the amphitheater has been restored almost to its original look, including exit signs marked VOMITORIUM. An inflatable roof covers it in winter, when various exhibits and shows occupy the space, and concerts and tennis tournaments are held here in summer. Its most colorful event is the *corrida,* the bullfight that transforms the Arena (and all of Nîmes) into a sangria-flushed homage to Spain. ✉ *Bd. Victor-Hugo* ☎ *04–66–76–72–95* 🖳 *€4.55; joint ticket with Tour Magne, €5.50* ⊙ *May–Sept., daily 9–6:30; Oct.–Apr., daily 9–noon and 2–5.*

❸ At the **Musée des Beaux-Arts** (Fine Arts Museum), a few blocks south of the Arènes, is a vast Roman mosaic with an imposing facade. The skylighted central atrium hosts the Roman mosaic, *The Marriage of Admetus,* and provides intriguing insights into the Roman aristocratic lifestyle. Old Master paintings (by Nicolas Poussin, Pieter Brueghel, Peter Paul Rubens) and sculpture (by Auguste Rodin) are among the highlights of the collection. ✉ *Rue de la Cité-Foulc* ☎ *04–66–67–38–21* 🖳 *€4.55* ⊙ *Tues.–Sun. 10–6.*

❹ The **Musée Archéologique et Musée d'Histoire Naturelle** (Museum of Archaeology and Museum of Natural History), a few blocks northeast of the Arènes, occupies a restored Jesuit college. Relics from local digs range from the Iron Age to the Roman period, with a plethora of artifacts from daily life over the ages: coins, dice, earrings, and crockery. There is also

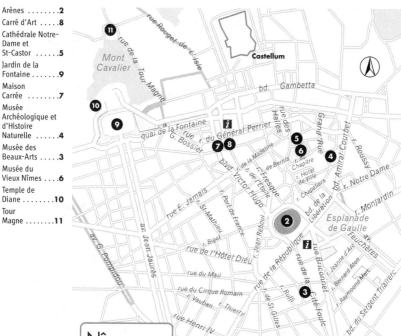

Nîmes

a rich array of Roman artworks, as well as the Marbacum Torso (which goes back to the Celts, before the Roman period), dug up at the foot of the Tour Magne. ✉ *13 bd. de l'Amiral-Courbet* ☎ *04–66–76–74–80* 🖼 *€4.45* ☉ *Apr.–Sept., Tues.–Sun. 10–6; Oct.–Mar., daily 11–6.*

❺ Destroyed and rebuilt in several stages, with particular damage caused by rampaging Protestants who slaughtered eight priests from the neighboring *évêché,* the **Cathédrale Notre-Dame et St-Castor** still shows traces of its construction in 1096. Is that fragment of classically symmetrical pediment an 11th-century reference to the Maison Carrée? Within its walls a miraculously preserved Romanesque frieze dates, for the most part, from the original construction. Its lively Old Testament scenes—reminiscent in style of its contemporary, the Bayeux Tapestry—portray Adam and Eve's cowering shame, the gory slaughter of Abel, a flood-weary Noah. Inside, look for the 4th-century sarcophagus (third chapel on the right) and a magnificent 17th-century chapel (in the apse). ✉ *Pl. aux Herbes* ☉ *Mon.–Sat. 9–10 and 2–6.*

❻ The **Musée du Vieux Nîmes** (Museum of Old Nîmes), opposite the cathedral in the 17th-century Bishop's Palace, has embroidered garments in exotic and vibrant displays, and an exhibit on the history on those blue jeans so popular around the world. Look for the 14th-century jeans jacket made of blue serge "de Nîmes." There are evocative interiors of 17th-century bourgeois homes, complete with painted wood paneling and local pottery. Don't miss the gift shop, where you might find a piece of pottery or fabric copied from period examples, depending on what is being shown. ⊠ *Pl. aux Herbes* ☎ *04–66–76–73–70* 🖾 *€4.45* ☉ *Tues.–Sun. 11–6.*

★ ❼ Lovely and forlorn in the middle of a busy downtown square, the exquisitely preserved **Maison Carrée** (Square House) strikes a timeless balance between symmetry and whimsy, purity of line and richness of decor. Built between AD 3 and 5 and dedicated to Caius Caesar and his grandson Lucius, it has survived subsequent use as a medieval meeting hall, an Augustinian church, a storehouse for Revolutionary archives, and a horse shed. It was modeled on temples to Apollo in Rome and Greece, and so inspired Thomas Jefferson that he had its chaste line of columns copied for the Virginia state capitol in Richmond. Today the building houses Roman statues from the 1st century AD, mosaics from the 1st century BC, and a good background display on the Maison Carrée and its history. ⊠ *Bd. Victor-Hugo* ☎ *04–66–36–26–76* 🖾 *Free* ☉ *May–Oct., daily 9–noon and 2–7; Nov.–Apr., daily 9–7.*

❽ The glass-fronted **Carré d'Art** (it's directly opposite the Maison Carrée) was designed by British architect Sir Norman Foster as its neighbor's stark contemporary mirror. It literally reflects the Maison Carrée's creamy symmetry and figuratively answers it with a featherlight deconstructed colonnade. Homages aside, it looks like an airport terminal. It contains a library, archives, and the **Musée d'Art Contemporain** (Contemporary Art Museum). The permanent collection falls into three categories: French painting and sculpture; English, American, and German works; and Mediterranean styles, all dating from 1960 onward. There are often temporary exhibits of new work. ⊠ *Pl. de la Maison Carrée* ☎ *04–66–76–35–70* 🖾 *€5.55* ☉ *Tues.–Sun. 11–6.*

❾ The **Jardin de la Fontaine** (Fountain Garden), an elaborate formal garden, was landscaped on the site of the Roman baths in the 18th century, when the Source de Nemausus, a once-sacred spring, was channeled into pools and a canal. It's a shady haven of mature trees and graceful stonework, and a testimony to the taste of the Age of Reason. It makes for a lovely approach to the Temple of Diana and the Tour Magne. ⊠ *Corner of Quai de la Fontaine and Av. Jean-Jaurès* ☉ *Mid-Sept.–Mar., daily 7:30–6:30; Apr.–mid-Sept., daily 7:30 AM–10 PM.*

❿ Just northwest of the Jardin de la Fontaine is the shattered Roman ruin known as the **Temple de Diane**, which dates from the 2nd century BC. The temple's original function is unknown, though it is thought to be part of a larger Roman complex that is still unexcavated. In the Middle Ages, Benedictine nuns occupied the building before it was converted into a church. Destruction came during the Wars of Religion.

⓫ At the far end of the Jardin de la Fontaine is the **Tour Magne** (Magne Tower)—the remains of a tower that the emperor Augustus had built on Gallic foundations; it was probably used as a lookout post. Despite having lost 33 feet over time, it still provides fine views of Nîmes for anyone energetic enough to climb the 140 steps. ⊠ *Quai de la Fontaine*

☎ 04–66–67–65–56 🎫 *Tour Magne €3.40; joint ticket with Arènes, €5.50* ☉ *May–Oct., daily 9–7; Nov.–Apr., daily 9–5.*

Where to Eat & Stay

$$–$$$ ✕ **L'Enclos de la Fontaine.** Nîmes's most fashionable post-corrida gathering spot is in the Impérator hotel, with warm-weather dining in an idyllic garden court. The menu offers such dishes as dried cod stuffed in red peppers and roasted lamb cooked in wild mint. Have an after-dinner drink in the bar Hemingway loved; they named it for him. ✉ *15 rue Gaston-Boissier* ☎ 04–66–21–90–30 ☐ AE, DC, MC, V.

★ $$ ✕ **Chez Jacotte.** Duck into an Old Town back alley and into this cross-vaulted grotto that embodies Nîmes's Spanish-bohemian flair. Candle-light flickering on rich tones of oxblood, cobalt, and ocher enhance the warm welcome from the staff. Mouthwatering goat-cheese-and-fig gratin, mullet crisped in olive oil and basil, herb-crusted lamb, and sea-sonal fruit crumbles show off a distinct flair with local ingredients. The homemade cakes and pastries are irresistible. ✉ *15 rue Fresque (Impasse)* ☎ 04–66–21–64–59 ☐ MC, V ☉ *Closed Sun. and Mon.*

$–$$ ✕ **Le Jardin d'Hadrien.** This chic enclave, with its quarried white stone, ancient plank-and-beam ceiling, and open fireplace, would be a culinary haven even without its lovely hidden garden, a shady retreat for sum-mer meals. Generous portions of simple but sophisticated dishes seem like so much gravy when the setting's this nice. Mussel soup with saf-fron and cream, fresh cod fried with olive oil and lemon, or zucchini flowers filled with *brandade* (the creamy, light paste of salt cod and olive oil), and a frozen parfait perfumed with licorice all show Chef Alain Vi-nouze's subtle skills. ✉ *11 rue Enclos Rey* ☎ 04–66–22–07–01 ☐ AE, MC, V ☉ *No lunch Mon.–Wed.*

$–$$ ✕ **Restaurant Nicolas.** You'll hear the noise of this homey place before you open the door. A friendly, frazzled staff serves up delicious *bour-ride* (a thick fish soup) and other local specialties listed on plastic menus at tightly packed tables—at low prices. It's one of the few places in Nîmes open on Sunday. ✉ *1 rue Poise* ☎ 04–66–67–50–47 ☐ AE, MC, V ☉ *Closed Mon. No lunch Sat.*

$–$$ ✕ **Le Wine Bar/Chez Michel.** This classic mahogany-and-brass wine bar, owned and managed by a former sommelier, serves good seafood—in-cluding *brandade de morue* (salt-cod paste)—as well as brasserie clas-sics: foie gras salad, fried calamari, simple steaks. You may opt to dine on the sidewalk terrace, adjacent to the square. Menus start at just €12. ✉ *11 square de la Couronne* ☎ 04–66–76–19–59 ☐ AE, MC, V ☉ *Closed Sun. No lunch Mon. and Sat.*

$–$$ ✕ **Vintage Café.** This popular Old Town wine bar draws a loyal crowd of oenophiles for serious tastings and simple, compatible foods—hot lentil salad with smoked haddock, beef stewed with capers and pickles, and a pressed-goat-cheese terrine. The bar still dominates—all the better for bellying up to a glass of *côstières de Nîmes*—but the dining room has expanded to embrace the neighboring building. Bright ceramics and warm lamplight enhance the warm-ocher Mediterranean interior. Summer nights on the terrace are idyllic. ✉ *7 rue de Bernis* ☎ 04–66–21–04–45 ☐ MC, V ☉ *Closed Sun. and Mon. No lunch Sat.*

$$–$$$ ☐ **Impérator.** Despite its standing as the top hotel in Nîmes, this member of the Concorde group has a bourgeois, businessy feel about it, without the luxurious excesses of more glamorous top hotels. Still, the newest room decors have a pampered, Laura Ashley look, the 1930s elevator is a charming touch, and rooms overlooking the lovely garden court need no further frills. ✉ *Quai de la Fontaine, 30900* ☎ *04–66–21–90–30* 🖷 *04–66–67–70–25* ⊕ *www.hotel-imperator.com* ⤴ *60 rooms* ⚒ *Restaurant, bar, minibars, parking, some pets allowed (fee)* ▭ *AE, DC, MC, V* ⦿ *BP.*

$$ ☐ **La Baume.** In the heart of scruffy Old Nîmes, this noble 17th-century *hôtel particulier* (mansion) has been reincarnated as a chic hotel with an architect's eye for mixing ancient detail with modern design. The balustraded stone staircase is a protected historic monument, and stenciled beam ceilings, cross vaults, and archways counterbalance hot ocher tones, swagged raw cotton, leather, and halogen lights. However, some of the hip interior shows signs of wear and tear. See if one of the wood-ceiling rooms (the largest and prettiest) is available. ✉ *21 rue Nationale, 30000* ☎ *04–66–76–28–42* 🖷 *04–66–76–28–45* ⊕ *www.new-hotel.com* ⤴ *34 rooms* ⚒ *Restaurant, minibars, parking (fee), some pets allowed (fee)* ▭ *AE, DC, MC, V* ⦿ *BP.*

$$ ☐ **L'Orangerie.** A charming hotel situated just beyond the city center, this good value option has a small pool, a gym and its friendly proprietors offer a warm welcome. An added bonus—many of the rooms have private terraces. ✉ *755 rue de la Tour Evêque, 30000* ☎ *04–66–84–50–57* 🖷 *04–66–84–65–99* ⊕ *www.orangerie.fr* ⤴ *31 rooms* ⚒ *Restaurant, minibars, pool, some pets allowed (fee)* ▭ *AE, DC, MC, V* ⦿ *BP.*

★ $–$$ ☐ **Royal Hôtel.** Jazz, Art Deco ironwork, and caged birds set the Latin tone at this bohemian, family-run, shabby-chic urban hotel. Whitewash and scrubbed concrete set off 1930s details and trendy flea-market finds. Bathrooms have newish tiles, and amenities are reasonably up-to-date. Its Spanish restaurant serves tapas on the pedestrian Place d'Assas, but the lobby bar is where you'd expect to run across Picasso slumming over absinthe. ✉ *3 bd. Alphonse Daudet, 30000* ☎ *04–66–58–28–27* 🖷 *04–66–58–28–28* ⤴ *23 rooms* ⚒ *Restaurant, bar, some pets allowed (fee)* ▭ *AE, DC, MC, V.*

$ ☐ **Amphithéâtre.** Just behind the Arena, this big, solid old private home has fortunately fallen into the hands of a loving owner, who has stripped 18th-century double doors and fitted rooms with restored-wood details and antique bedroom sets. A generous breakfast buffet is served in the dining room. Ask for one of the three rooms overlooking the Place du Marché, where you can watch café life from your balcony. ✉ *4 rue des Arènes, 30000* ☎ *04–66–67–28–51* 🖷 *04–66–67–07–79* ⊕ *perso.wanadoo.fr/hotel-amphitheatre* ⤴ *17 rooms* ⚒ *Some pets allowed* ▭ *AE, DC, MC, V* ⦿ *BP.*

Sports & the Outdoors

The *corrida* (bullfight) is a quintessential Nîmes experience, taking place as it does in the ancient Roman Arena. There are usually three bullfighting times a year, always during the carnival-like citywide *férias* (festivals): in early spring (mid-February), at Pentecost (end of May), and during the wine harvest (end of September). These include parades, a running of the bulls, and gentle Camargue-style bullfights (where competitors pluck a ring from the bull's horns). But the focal point, unfortunately, is a twice-daily Spanish-style bullfight, complete with *l'estocade* (the final killing) and the traditional cutting of the ear. Those with delicate nerves will stay away. For tickets and advance information, contact the Arena's **bureau de location** (ticket office ⊠ 4 rue de la Violette, Nîmes 30000 ☎ 04–66–02–80–80 ⊕ www.arenesdenimes.com).

Aquatropic (⊠ 39 chemin de la Hostellerie ☎ 04–66–38–31–00) is a swimming spot with a difference: an indoor and an outdoor pool, wave machines, slides, water cannons, and whirlpools add to the fun for kids and adults. It's open weekdays 10–8 and weekends 11–7 for €4.75 (€1.95 children under 8). Since it's south of the city, it's best to exit the autoroute at Nîmes Ouest.

Shopping

In Nîmes's Old Town you'll find the expected rash of chain stores mixed with fabulous interior-design boutiques and fabric shops selling the Provençal cottons that used to be produced here en masse (Les Indiennes de Nîmes, Les Olivades, Souleiado). Antiques and collectibles are found in tiny shops throughout the city's backstreets, but there is a concentration of them in the Old Town. Anywhere near the arena abounds with bullfighting memorabilia, but if you want to really get into the spirit, you can find your complete toreador outfit at **Maria Sara Création** (⊠ 40 bis rue de la Madeleine ☎ 04–66–21–18–40). She was famous in her day as a female bullfighter. Fashionable shoppers check out the celebrated Nîmes-founded house of **Cacharel** (⊠ 2 pl. de la Maison Carée ☎ 04–66–21–82–82).

The Monday-morning *marché* (market; ⊠ Bd. Jean-Jaurès) stretches the length of the Boulevard Jean-Jaurès and highlights bright regional fabrics, linens, pottery, and *brocante* (collectibles). The permanent covered market called **Les Halles** is at the heart of the city and puts on a mouthwatering show of olives, fresh fish, cheeses, and produce. The colorful *marché aux fleurs* (flower market; parking in the Stades des Costières), though far from the center, is worth seeking out by car. **FNadal** (⊠ 7 rue St-Castor ☎ 04–66–67–35–42) is a tiny shop selling a wonderland of olive oil from vats, herbed soaps, honey, coffee, and spices. The longtime local favorite *boulangerie/patisserie* **Villaret** (⊠ 13 rue de la Madeleine ☎ 04–66–67–41–79) is

> ### NÎMES IN A JAR
>
> The only authentic commercial maker of *brandade*, Nîmes's signature salt-cod-and-olive-oil paste, is **Raymond** (⊠ 24 rue Nationale ☎ 04–66–27–11–98). It's paddled fresh into a plastic carton or sold in sealed jars so you can take it home. Brush toast points with olive oil, and spread it on.

the best place to buy Nîmes's other specialty: jaw-breaking *croquants* (roasted almonds in caramelized sugar).

THE CAMARGUE

For 150,000 hectares, the vast alluvial delta of the Rhône River known as the Camargue stretches to the horizon, an austere marshland unrelievedly flat, scoured by the mistral, swarmed over by mosquitoes. Between the endless flow of sediment from the Rhône and the erosive force of the sea, its shape is constantly changing. Even the Provençal poet Frédéric Mistral described it in bleak terms: *"Ni arbre, ni ombre, ni âme"* ("Neither tree, nor shade, nor soul"). Yet its harsh landscape harbors a concentration of exotic wildlife unique in Europe, and its isolation has given birth to an ascetic and ancient way of life that transcends national stereotype. It is a strange region, one worth discovering slowly, either on foot or on horseback—especially as its wildest reaches are inaccessible by car. If people find the Camargue interesting, birds find it irresistible. Its protected marshes lure some 400 species, including more than 160 in migration—little egrets, gray herons, spoonbills, bitterns, cormorants, redshanks, and grebes, and the famous flamingos. All this nature surrounds a few far-flung villages, rich in the region's odd history and all good launching points for forays into the marshlands.

> **THINK PINK**
>
> In the Camargue, ivory-pink flamingos are as common as pigeons on a city square. Their gangly height, dodolike bill, and stilty legs give them a cartoonish air, and their flight style seems comic up close. But the sight of a few thousand of these creatures taking flight in unison is one you won't forget.

Aigues-Mortes

★ ⓬ *39 km (24 mi) south of Nîmes, 45 km (28 mi) southwest of Arles.*

Like a tiny illumination in a medieval manuscript, Aigues-Mortes (pronounced ay-guh-*mort*-uh) is a precise and perfect miniature fortress-town, contained within perfectly symmetrical castellated walls, with streets laid out in geometric grids. Now awash in a flat wasteland of sand, salt, and monotonous marsh, it once was a major port town from whence no less than St-Louis himself (Louis IX) set sail to conquer Jerusalem in the 13th century. In 1248 some 35,000 zealous men launched 1,500 ships for Cyprus, engaging the infidel on his own turf and suffering swift defeat; Louis himself was briefly taken prisoner. A second launching in 1270 led to more crushing losses, and then Louis succumbed to typhus in Tunis.

Despite his lack of success in the crusades, Louis's **fortress-port** flourished and grew stronger still, its massive stone walls rising double-thick. Completed in 1300, they remain intact and astonishingly well preserved in salt sea winds. Within them now lies a small Provençal village milling with tourists, but the visit is more than justified by the impressive scale of the original structure.

If you're driving, park in one of the lots outside the formidable walls and enter by the main **Porte de la Gardette**; the tourist office is to the left of the entrance. The monumental ramparts, punctuated by massive towers, make for a great walk. To your right, you'll see the town's stronghold, called the **Tour de Constance.** Its 20-foot-thick walls date from 1241–44, when it was built to protect a larger building lost to history. Enter via the 17th-century **Logis du Gouverneur** (Governor's Lodging), itself a conglomerate of several centuries' construction. The tower still contains a small votive chapel dedicated to St-Louis and an upper hall that served as prison to generations of political outcasts. (One Protestant, the heroic Marie Durand, survived 38 years in the tower without relinquishing her faith; she carved the word *résister*—resist—on her cell wall. Her endurance and courage so impressed the Languedoc governor that he had her released along with a handful of her colleagues.) You can climb all the way to the top of the steepled tower, which once served as a lighthouse lantern. From here you can appreciate the rigorous geometry of the fortifications and imagine medieval fleets surging out to sea. ✉ *Porte de la Gardette* ☎ *04–66–53–61–55* 💶 *€6.10* ☉ *Easter–late May, daily 9:30–1 and 2–6; late May–mid-Sept., daily 9:30–8; mid-Sept.–Easter, daily 10–1 and 2–5.*

It's not surprising that the town within the rampart walls has become tourist oriented, with the usual plethora of gift shops and postcard stands. But **Place St-Louis,** where a 19th-century statue of the father of the fleur-de-lis reigns under shady pollards, has a mellow village feel, and the pretty bare-bones **Église Notre-Dame des Sablons** that corners it has a timeless air (it dates from the 13th century, but the stained glass is ultramodern).

Where to Eat & Stay

★ **$$$$** ✕ **Chez Bob.** In a smoky, isolated stone farmhouse chockablock with old posters, you'll taste Camargue cooking at its rustic best. One daily menu includes *anchoïade* (whole crudités with hard-cooked egg—still in the shell—and anchovy vinaigrette), homemade duck pâté thick with peppercorns, and the pièce de résistance: a thick, sizzling slab of bull steak grilled in the roaring fireplace. Sprinkle on hand-skimmed sea salt and dig in. ✉ *At Villeneuve/Romieu intersection of D37 and D36 (watch for tiny sign)* ☎ *04–90–97–00–29* ▤ *MC, V* ☉ *Closed Mon. and Tues.*

★ **$$** ✕▥ **Les Arcades.** Long a success as an upscale seafood restaurant, this beautifully preserved 16th-century house now offers big, airy rooms, some with tall windows overlooking a green courtyard. Pristine white-stone walls, color-stained woodwork, and rubbed-ocher walls frame antiques and lush fabrics, and bathrooms are all new, in white tile. There's even a little courtyard terrace with a small pool. Classic cooking highlights lotte (monkfish) in saffron and poached turbot in hollandaise, and the set menu at €34 is a steal. ✉ *23 bd. Gambetta, 30220* ☎ *04–66–53–81–13* 🖷 *04–66–53–75–46* 🌐 *www.les-arcades.fr* ➥ *9 rooms* ⚐ *Restaurant, pool, some pets allowed (fee)* ▤ *AE, DC, MC, V* ☉ *Closed 1st 2 wks in Mar., 1st 2 wks in Oct.* ⦿❙ *BP.*

$$–$$$ ▥ **Les Templiers.** In a 17th-century residence within the ramparts, this delightful hotel sets the stage with stone, stucco, and terra-cotta floors. Furnishings are classically simple and softened with antiques. On the ground floor are two small, cozy sitting areas; breakfast, weather permitting, is

Continued on page 24

DON'T FENCE ME IN:
FRANCE'S "WILD WEST"

Time: 7:30 AM. Place: The Camargue reserve, Provence's extraordinary nature park. A flock of flamingos suddenly erupts from a stand of black-green parasol pines. To your left, a group of herons mince one-legged through rice paddies. Ahead, a bandanna-wrapped *gardian*—a kind of open-range cowboy—roams the field on a sturdy dappled-white horse, prodding a flock of prong-horned bulls whose bloodlines predate the cave paintings of Lascaux. Atop your pony, you turn your binoculars to watch the rising sun turn the sky rosy red over the endless savannas. This is why you got up so early: to see the Camargue at dawn, primeval and virgin-pure, the last gasp of the Rhône as it seeps over the delta into the Mediterranean sea. This Edenic preserve, where exotic fauna and flora live in splendor in lagoons and salt marshes, remains France's most distinctive nature wonderland.

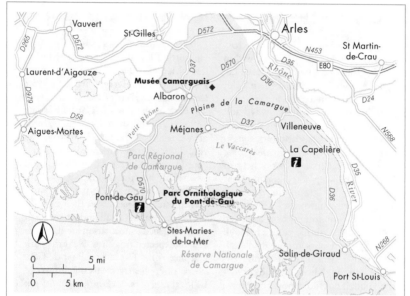

A land of haunting natural beauty, the Camargue was one of the *oubliettes* (forgotten areas) of France only a few decades ago. Today, it is *à la mode.* No matter that the mosquitoes are large and hungry in the summer, or that the mistral wind whistles furiously over sand and sea in the early spring, when thousands of tenderfeet begin to head here to discover a peculiar ecosystem all its own and a culture—wild, quirky, isolated—just as unique.

With its hypnotic plane of marsh grass stretching to the sea, the Camargue is what the French call a *désert d'eau,* a watery desert. Expanses of saltwort, canals, reedbeds, marshy plains, and *è'tangs* (saltwater lagoons) alternate with vast salt-marsh islands called *sansourire.* Little wonder you can appear to be standing in a body of water—beware: there are treacherous pits of quicksand in places—and sink on flat land. The Camargue is formed by the alluvial deposits of the two arms of the Rhône flowing south to the Mediterranean, and the sea does its best to fight back. So much so that an enormous system of dikes, known as the Digue à la Mer, has been built along a 15-mi stretch of the coast near Stes-Maries-de-la-Mer and is now one of France's most spectacular seaside promenades (and best biking routes).

At the Camargue's heart is the Réserve Nationale Zoologique et Botanique de Camargue, a 30,000-acre area set around the Étang de Vaccarès lagoon—a bird-watcher's paradise famed for its rich sightings of egrets, bee-eaters, avocets, cranes, sandpipers, flamingos, and hundreds of other species. Nature has been left blissfully untouched—almost. Man has only squatters' rights to these eternal tidal flats, yet here and there you'll find isolated *mas* (farmhouses, now sometimes converted to luxurious dude ranches); *manades,* the French style of ranches, where the famous bulls are often corralled; and *cabanes,* whitewashed houses with plaited straw roofs used as residences by the gardians. Horses are for rent everywhere, and a gallop across this wide, lonely prairie country will set you apart from the ordinary run of tourists.

A TOUR OF THE PARC RÉGIONAL DE CAMARGUE

As you drive the few roads that crisscross the Camargue, you'll usually be within the boundaries of the **Parc Régional de Camargue** (⊕ www.parc-camargue.fr). Unlike state and national parks in the United States, this area is privately owned and utilized within rules imposed by the state. The principal owners, the famous *manadiers* (the Camargue equivalent of a small-scale ranchers), with the help of their gardians, keep it for grazing their wide-horned bulls and their broad-bellied, dappled-white horses. The strong, heavy-tailed Camargue horse has been traced to the Paleolithic period (though some claim the Moors imported an Arab strain) and is prized for its stolid endurance and tough hooves. The curved-horned bull, if not indigenous, may have been imported by Attila the Hun. When it's not participating in a bloodless bull-fight, a bull may well end up in the wine-rich regional stew called *gardianne de taureau*, an acquired taste.

WHERE TO FIND THE BIRDS

Up north a few miles from Stes-Maries-de-la-Mer, the main town in the Camargue, is a private reserve called the ☾ **Parc Ornithologique du Pont-de-Gau** (Ornithological Park of the Pont-de-Gau). On some 150 acres of marsh and salt lands, birds are welcomed and protected (but in no way confined); injured birds are treated and kept in large pens, to be released if and when ready. Boardwalks (including a short, child-friendly inner loop past the easy-viewing stands) snake over the wetlands, the longest leading to a blind where a half hour of silence, binoculars in hand, can reveal unexpected treasures. Near the park entrance is the Hostellerie Pont-de-Gau, which offers hearty meals much favored by local ranchers. ⊠ *Pont-de-Gau, 5 km (3 mi) north of Stes-Maries-de-la-Mer on D570* ☎ *04–90–97–82–62* ⊕ *www.parcornithologique.com* ✉ *€9* ⊙ *Oct.–Mar., daily 10–sunset; Apr.–Sept., daily 9–sunset.*

DEEP IN THE HEART OF . . . PROVENCE?

While the thought might give pause to some Texas residents, historians now tell us that the American cowboy is actually descended from the French gardian, the Provençal cowboy. "Go West," Horace Greeley once advised, and in the early 19th century, these Camargue ranchers did exactly that: shipping out to the French colony of New Orleans, they then fanned out across America as the first bronc-stompers and horse-wranglers. Although they traded in their iron *trident* pole for a lariat, they brought along their black felt hats, string ties, and—to the later gratification of Levi Strauss—*bleus de travail*, or "jeans" (invented in the Provence city of Nîmes). Their festival wear, including traditional velvet vests—seen in full glory during the Fête des Gardians in Arles in May—inspired a local homeboy, couturier Christian Lacroix. Today, les gardians are a unique breed, proud of their centuries-old traditions and disdainful of the Hollywood "cowboy" poseur. Insular, Byronic, and taciturn, they love to kid you when they first meet you. If you don't take offense, they'll warm up quickly; if you do, they'll kid you even more!

The unique Camargue saddle

1

Heading out on a *Ballade* tour

WHERE TO FIND THE NATURE TRAILS
If you're an even more committed nature lover, venture into the inner sanctum of the Camargue, the **Réserve Nationale de Camargue.** This intensely protected area contains the central pond called **Le Vaccarès,** mostly used for approved scientific research. The wildlife—birds, nutria, fish—is virtually undisturbed here, and you won't come across the cabins and herds of bulls and horses that most people expect from the Camargue. Pick up maps and information at the **Centre d'Information du Parc Naturel Régional du Camargue** (☎ 04–90–97–86–32 🖷 04–90–97–70–82, ☉ Apr.–Sept., daily 10–6; Oct.–Mar., Sat.–Thurs. 9:30–5). It's just up the D570 from the Parc Ornithologique at Pont-de-Gau. To explore this area, you'll

ON THE HORNS OF A DILEMMA

Car, bus, boat, bike, or foot? When you're out to learn about the birds and the bulls of the Camargue, the best way to tour their territory is by horse. Some 30 places rent them for a *promenade équestre* (horseback tour). The **Association Camarguaise de Tourisme Équestre** publishes a list of names and numbers, available at the **Centre d'Information du Parc Naturel Régional du Camargue** at Pont-du-Gau or at the **Stes-Maries tourist office** (5 av. van Gogh). Stables line the roads throughout the Camargue, so they're easy to find; several are concentrated along D570 north of Stes-Maries as well as along the eastern loop D85. An hour's ride averages between €15 and €30, and a whole day €60 to €90 (with *pique-nique* thrown in).

While a *promenade à cheval* can last all day, but most are two hours long; accompanied by commentary on such topics as folklore and ecology, these are called *ballades.* They are occasionally led by gardian cowboys, some—ironically—leading their horses on foot (have to give those legs a stretch). As you wend your way over cattle tracks and wooden footbridges, you'll realize this is the way to get out into those marshy fields yet avoid getting your feet wet. The gardian rides a typical short-stepping Camarguaise horse, small enough to be considered a pony. Most tourists, however, will wind up on an "Arab," a larger, dappled white horse. Tip for tenderfeet: If a horse knows you are afraid of him, he'll press his advantage—so don't let your steed get your goat.

Don't wear red.

have to strike out on foot, bicycle, or horseback paths. Note that you are not allowed to diverge from marked trails.

If you continue north past the village of Albaron, you'll come across the converted sheep-ranch-now-museum, the **Musée Camarguais** (✉ Mas du Pont de Rousty, D570 ☎ 04–90–97–10–82 ☷ €4.60 ⊙ Apr.–Sept., daily 9:15–5:45; Oct.–Mar., daily 10:15–4:45). Lying between Arles and Stes-Maries-de-la-Mer, it explains the region's history, produce, and people. It's also a good place to pick up information on nature trails.

WHERE TO FIND THE BULLS
Near the northern shore of the Étang de Vaccarès, one of the larger ranches in the Camargue has been turned into a showplace for all things taurine. Bullfights, ferrades, horse rides, and *spectacles taurine* (bull-baiting) are just some of the activities offered at the **Domaine de Méjanes Paul Ricard**, 4 km (2½ mi) north of Albaron

on D37). You'll learn about the history of the unique regional species of bullfight, the *cours camarguaise,* in which bulls are not killed in the arena but simply taunted by *raseteurs* (runners) who try to pluck off a red cockade and two white tassels mounted on the bull's horns. Bulls live to enter the arena again and again, and some become such celebrities they have appeared on the covers of French magazines. At the Domaine, you can also ride a *petit train* for a fun 20-minute tour of the marshlands. ✉ *D37, on edge of Étang de Vaccarès* ☎ *04–90–97–10–10* ⊕ *www.mejanes.camargue.fr.*

At the easternmost point of the Étang du Vaccarès, another good visitor center is found at La Capelière. The **Centre d'Information de la Réserve Nationale de Camargue** has maps, exhibits on wildlife, and three *sentiers de découverte* (discovery trails). ✉ *5 km (3 mi) south of Villeneuve/ Romieu, off D37* ☎ *04–90–97–00–97.*

IN THE PINK

Les fleurs qui volent ("the flowers that fly"), flamingos are the most spectacular residents of the Camargue. Proving the preserve's success, the indigenous population of the *flamants roses* (pink flamingos) is now a healthy 50,000.

Flamingos, Camargue, ornithological park

HOME ON THE RANGE

When it comes to the Camargue, you can merely visit it or you can *live* it. A number of renovated *mas* (farmhouses) and *manades* (ranches) now offer a luxurious counterbalance to the region's hard gothic landscapes: fashionable dude ranches *à la provençale,* replete with firelit interiors, regional antiques, and creature comforts. You can spend the day roughing it on a *ballade* horseback tour. At dusk, however, silt-splashed and leather-stained, enjoy a spell in a canopy-draped bathtub and then a candlelit dinner in a grand old ranch-house kitchen. Here are some hotels and restaurants with authentic bull-in-a-china-shop ambience.

★ **$$$$** ✕▣ **Le Mas de Peint.** This may be the ultimate mas experience, set as it is in a 17th-century farmhouse on some 1,250 acres of Camargue ranchland. Luxurious Provençal fabrics and antiques grace the old stone floors, and burnished beams warm the firelit salon and library. Rooms are lavished with brass beds, monogrammed linens, even canopied bathtubs. At dinnertime, guests gather in the kitchen to chat with the cook and settle in for sophisticated specialties using home-grown products (ratatouille and lamb dishes as well as Camargue rice and bull). Diners not staying in the hotel are welcome too, for lunch or dinner; the restaurant is closed Wednesday, and advance reservations are required. In summer (mid-June–mid-September) a light lunch is served by the pool. You're only 20 km (12 mi) south of Arles here, but you should plan on a relaxing immersion in the country rather than a heavy sightseeing itinerary, as other towns are well out of the way. But who would want to leave when you can ride the private grounds on Camargue horses, or take a tour in a four-wheel-drive?

✉ *Le Sambuc, 13200 Arles* ☏ *04–90–97–20–62* 🖷 *04–90–97–22–20* ⊕ *www.masdepeint.com* 🛏 *8 rooms, 3 suites* ⚒ *Restaurant, pool, horseback riding, some pets permitted (fee)* ▭ *AE, DC, MC, V* ⊘ *Closed mid-Nov.–mid-Dec. and mid-Jan.–mid-Mar.* ⦿ *MAP.*

★ **$$$$** ▣ **Mas de la Fouque.** With stylish rooms and luxurious balconies that look out over a beautiful lagoon, this upscale converted farmhouse is a perfect escape from the rigors of horseback riding and bird-watching. Outside are acres of sculpted land, inside is comfort personified—cool elegance, plush carpets, large baths, and prompt service. Every Saturday night Gypsy musicians play flamenco in the lovely bar area. Sprawl out in front of the large stone fireplace and drink in the splendid views over the Camargue. The food doesn't disappoint, either: dive into a mean leg of roasted lamb or savor the tender catch of the day after a refreshing dip in the large pool. ✉ *Rte. du Petit Rhone, 13460* ☏ *04–90–97–81–02* 🖷 *04–90–97–96–84* ⊕ *www.masdelafouque.com* 🛏 *3 rooms* ⚒ *Restaurant, minibars, pool, some pets permitted (fee)* ▭ *AE, DC, MC, V* ⊘ *Closed 3 wks. Dec.–Jan.* ⦿ *MAP.*

Mas de la Fouque

served in the small flower-filled courtyard. ✉ *23 rue de la République, 30220* ☎ *04–66–53–66–56* 🖨 *04–66–53–69–61* 📞 *11 rooms* 🛆 *Pool, parking (fee), some pets allowed (fee)* ☰*MC, V* ⊗ *Closed Nov.–Feb.* ⑩*BP.*

$$ 🏨 **St-Louis.** Within the rampart walls, close to the Tour de Constance and just off Place St-Louis, this homey little hotel warms its medieval construction of cool stone with Provençal charm and comfort. Rooms, which are pleasantly decorated if not stylish, look out on the garden below the ramparts or onto the sunny street. In winter, dinner is served in the beamed restaurant, and in summer, in the shady garden. ✉ *10 rue Amiral Courbet, 30220* ☎ *04–66–53–72–68* 🖨 *04–66–53–75–92* ⊕ *www.lesaintlouis.fr* 📞 *22 rooms* 🛆 *Restaurant, some pets allowed (fee)* ☰ *AE, MC, V* ⊗ *Closed late Nov.–mid-Mar.* ⑩ *BP.*

Festivals

In early October, the **Fêtes Votive d'Aigues-Mortes** (town festival) has bull races, parades, and dancing in the main square.

Stes-Maries-de-la-Mer

⑬ *31 km (19 mi) southeast of Aigues-Mortes, 40 km (25 mi) southwest of Arles.*

The principal town within the confines of the Parc Régional de Camargue, Stes-Maries is a beach resort with a fascinating history. Provençal legend has it that around AD 45 a band of the very first Christians was rounded up and set adrift at sea in a boat without a sail and without provisions. Their stellar ranks included Mary Magdalene, Martha, and Mary Salome, mother of apostles James and John; Mary Jacoby, sister of the Virgin; and Lazarus, risen from the dead (or another Lazarus, depending on whom you ask). Joining them in their fate: a dark-skinned servant girl named Sarah. Miraculously, their boat washed ashore at this ancient site, and the grateful Marys built a chapel in thanks. Martha moved on to Tarascon to tackle dragons, and Lazarus founded the church in Marseille. But Mary Jacoby and Mary Salome remained in their old age, and Sarah stayed with them, begging in the streets to support them in their ministry. The three women died at the same time and were buried together at the site of their chapel.

A cult grew up around this legendary spot, and a church was built around it. When in the 15th century a stone memorial and two female bodies were found under the original chapel, the miracle was for all practical purposes confirmed, and the

THE DA VINCI CODE, PROVENÇAL-STYLE

Ever since Dan Brown's *The Da Vinci Code* popularized the notion that Mary Magdalene—one of the Marys who arrived in Stes-Maries by boat back when—was the consort of Jesus Christ (and mother of his child), buses of photo-snapping, Bermuda-shorts wearing visitors arrive daily here. True believers can check out the two-week expedition Magdalene Tours (www.magdalenetours.com) conducts from the shores of Marseille to the Basilica at St. Maximin-Ste. Baume, where her enshrined skull is purportedly held.

Romanesque church expanded to receive a new influx of pilgrims. But the pilgrims attracted to Stes-Maries aren't all lighting candles to the two St. Marys: the servant girl Sarah has been adopted as an honorary saint by the Gypsies of the world, who blacken the crypt's domed ceiling with the soot of their votive candles lighted in her honor. Two extraordinary festivals take place every year in Stes-Maries, one May 24–25 and the other on the Sunday nearest to October 22. On May 24 Gypsy pilgrims gather from across Europe and carry the wooden statue of Sarah from her crypt, through the streets of the village, and down to the sea to be washed. The next day they carry a wooden statue of the two St. Marys, kneeling in their wooden boat, to the sea for their own holy bath. The same ritual is repeated by a less colorful crowd of non-Gypsy pilgrims in October, who carry the two Marys back to the sea.

★ On entering the damp, dark, and forbidding fortress-church, **Église des Stes-Maries** (Church of the St. Marys), what is most striking is its novel character. Almost devoid of windows, its tall, barren single-aisle nave is cluttered with florid and sentimental ex-votos (tokens of blessings, prayers, and thanks) and primitive and sentimental artworks of the famous trio. On the wall to your left, you'll see the wooden statue of the Marys in their boat; in the crypt below, Sarah glows in the light of dozens of candles. Another oddity brings you back to this century: a sign on the door forbids visitors to come *torse nu* (topless). For outside its otherworldly role, Stes-Maries is first and foremost a beach resort, dead-flat, whitewashed, and more than a little tacky. Unless you've made a pilgrimage to the sun and sand, don't spend much time in the town center; if you've chosen Stes-Maries as a base for viewing the Camargue, stay in one of the discreet mas (country inns) outside its city limits.

ARLES

31 km (19 mi) southeast of Nîmes, 40 km (25 mi) northwest of Stes-Maries.

Seated in the shade of Arles's plane trees on the Place du Forum, sunning at the foot of the obelisk on the Place de la République, meditating in the cloister of St-Trophime, or strolling the rampart walkway along the sparkling Rhône, you'll see what enchanted Gauguin and drove Van Gogh mad with inspiration. It's the light: intense, vivid, crystalline, setting off planes of color and shadow with prismatic concentration. As a foil to this famous light, multihued Arles—with its red and gold ocher, cool gray stone, and blue-black shade—is unsurpassed.

Reigning over the bleak but evocative landscape of the marshlands of the Camargue, the small city of Arles is fiercely Provençal, nurturing its heritage and parading its culture at every colorful opportunity. Warming the wetlands with its atmosphere, animation, and culture, it is a patch of hot color in a sepia landscape—and an excellent home base for sorties into the raw natural beauty and eccentric villages of the Rhône delta.

If you were obliged to choose just one city to visit in Provence, lovely little Arles would give Avignon and Aix a run for their money. It's too chic to become museumlike yet has a wealth of classical antiquities and Romanesque stonework; quarried-stone edifices and shuttered town houses shading graceful Old Town streets and squares; and pageantry, festivals, and cutting-edge arts events. Its atmospheric restaurants and picturesque small hotels make it the ideal headquarters for forays into the Alpilles and the Camargue.

Yet compared to Avignon and Aix, it's a small town. You can zip into the center in five minutes without crossing a half hour's worth of urban sprawl. And its monuments and pretty old neighborhoods are conveniently concentrated between the main artery Boulevard des Lices and the broad, lazy Rhône.

> ## WHISPERS ABOUT VAN GOGH'S EAR
>
> Ill-received and ostracized in Arles, Van Gogh was packed off to an asylum in nearby St-Remy after he cut off the lobe of his left ear on December 23, 1888. Theories abound but historians believe he made the desperate gesture in homage to Gauguin, who had arrived to set up a "Studio of the South." Following the fashion in Provençal bullrings for a matador to present his lady love with an ear from a dispatched bull, Vincent wielded the knife after arguing with Gauguin, whom he had come to idolize.

It wasn't always such a mellow site. A Greek colony since the 6th century BC, little Arles took a giant step forward when Julius Caesar defeated Marseille in the 1st century BC. The emperor-to-be designated Arles a Roman colony and lavished funds and engineering know-how on it, transforming it into a formidable civilization—by some accounts, the Rome of the north. Fed by aqueducts, canals, and solid roads, it profited from all the Romans' modern conveniences: straight paved streets and sidewalks, sewers and latrines, thermal baths, a forum, a stadium, a theater, and an arena. It became an international crossroads by sea and land and a market to the world, with goods from Africa, Arabia, and the Far East. The emperor Constantine himself moved to Arles and brought with him Christianity.

The remains of this golden age are reason enough to visit Arles today. Yet its character nowadays is as gracious and low-key as it once was cutting-edge.

Note: If you plan to visit many of the monuments and museums in Arles, you can purchase a *visite generale* ticket for €12 at most of the town sites and monuments. This covers the €5.50 entry fee to the Musée de l'Arles Antique and any and all of the other museums and monuments (except the independent Museon Arlaten), which normally charge €4 each per visit. It's good for the length of your stay.

A GOOD WALK

The best of Arles is enclosed in the inner maze of streets and alleyways known as the Old Town, nestled along the Rhône, where you'll find noble 18th-century architecture cheek-by-jowl with antiquities. Only the museum of antiquities lies across the Rhône, easily accessed by shuttle bus.

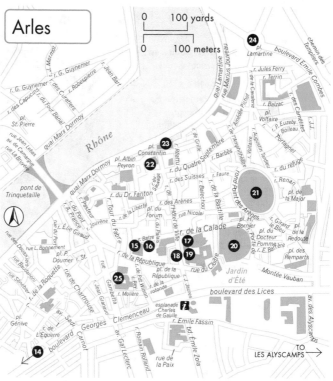

★ Though it's a hike from the center, a good place to set the tone and context for your exploration of Arles is at the state-of-the-art **Musée de l'Arles Antique** ⓮. From here, take advantage of the free museum shuttle; there's an adjacent parking lot if you're day-tripping by car. Get off at the Boulevard Clemenceau and arm yourself with literature at the **tourist information center** just up the road, on Boulevard des Lices. Then walk up Rue Gambetta, right on Rue Molière, and left up Rue Rey to the **Espace Van Gogh** ㉕, the hospital where Van Gogh repaired for his decline into insanity. Continue up Rue du President Wilson to the Rue de la République and the intensely local **Museon Arlaten** ⓯. Just behind, on Rue Balze, explore the underground Roman galleries called the **Crypto-portiques** ⓰.

★
★ Follow Rue Balze to the broad **Place de la République** ⓲, where you'll study the extraordinary Romanesque facade of the **Église St-Trophime** ⓱. Next door, enter the hidden oasis of the **Cloître St-Trophime** ⓳. Continue up Rue du Cloître to the **Théâtre Antique** ⓴, now in Byronesque ruins. Just above
★ rears the **Arènes** ㉑, site of gladiator battles and modern bullfights.

Now wander down evocative backstreets to the river and the **Thermes Constantin** ㉒, the ruins of Roman baths. On Rue du Grand Prieuré, stop into the **Musée Réattu** ㉓, which glorifies native-son painter Jacques

Van Gogh in Arles & St-Rémy

". . . What a lovely country, and what lovely blue and what a sun!"

IT WAS THE LIGHT that drew Vincent van Gogh to Arles. For a man raised under the iron-gray skies of the Netherlands and the gaslight pall of Paris, Provence's clean, clear sun was a revelation. In his last years he turned his frenzied efforts to capture the resonance of ". . . golden tones of every hue: green gold, yellow gold, pink gold, bronze or copper colored gold, and even from the yellow of lemons to the matte, lusterless yellow of threshed grain."

Vincent van Gogh, *Self-Portrait*, 1887, Musée d'Orsay, Paris, France.

Arles, however, was not drawn to Van Gogh. Though it makes every effort today to make up for its misjudgment, Arles treated the artist very badly during the time he passed here near the end of his life—a time when his creativity, productivity, and madness all reached a climax. It was 1888 when he settled in to work in Arles with an intensity and tempestuousness that first drew, then drove away his companion Paul Gauguin, with whom he had dreamed of founding an artists' colony. Frenziedly productive—he applied a pigment-loaded palette knife to some 200 canvases in that year alone—he nonetheless lived within intense isolation, counting his sous, and writing his visions in lengthy letters to his long-suffering, infinitely patient brother Theo. Often heavy-drinking, occasionally whoring, Vincent alienated his neighbors, goading them to action. In 1889 the people of Arles circulated a petition to have him evicted, a shock that left him more and more at a loss to cope with life and led to his eventual self-commitment to an asylum in nearby St-Rémy. The houses he lived in are

no longer standing, though many of his subjects remain as he saw them. The paintings he daubed and splashed with such passion have been auctioned elsewhere.

Thus you have to go to Amsterdam or Moscow to view Van Gogh's work. But with a little imagination, you can glean something of Van Gogh's Arles from a tour of the modern town. In fact, the city has provided helpful markers and a numbered itinerary to guide you between landmarks. You can stand on the Place Lamartine, where his famous Maison Jaune stood until it was destroyed by World War II bombs. *Starry Night* may have been painted from the Quai du Rhône just off Place Lamartine, though another was completed at St-Rémy. The Café La Nuit on Place Forum is an exact match for the terrace platform, scattered with tables and bathed in gaslight under the stars, from the painting *Terrace de café le Soir*; Gauguin and Van Gogh used to drink here. (Current owners

Vincent van Gogh, *Sunflowers*, 1888, National Gallery, London, England.

have determinedly maintained the Fauve color scheme to keep the atmosphere.) Both the Arènes and Les Alyscamps were featured in paintings, and the hospital where he broke down and cut off his ear is now a kind of shrine, its garden reconstructed exactly as it figured in *Le Jardin de l'Hôtel-Dieu*. The drawbridge in *Le pont de Langlois aux Lavandières* has been reconstructed outside of town, at Port-de-Bouc, 3 km (2 mi) south on D35.

About 25 km (15½ mi) away is St-Rémy-de-Provence, where Van Gogh retreated to the asylum St-Paul-de-Mausolée. Here he spent hours in silence, painting the cloisters. On his ventures into town, he painted the dappled lime trees at the intersection of Boulevard Mirabeau and Boulevard Gambetta. And on route between the towns, you'll see the orchards whose spring blooms ignited his joyous explosions of yellow, green, and pink.

Réattu and 20th-century peers. Not Van Gogh, alas. Pay homage to that painter by walking up Rue du Quatre Septembre and Rue Amédée Pichot to **Place Lamartine** ㉔, where the star-crossed artist lived in his famous Maison Jaune, destroyed in the second World War.

TIMING This is an easy day's tour, including time to browse through the Museon Arlaten and trace a few Van Gogh landmarks. If there's an event in the Arena, go and experience Arles's modern and Roman history all in one. But don't "do" Arles. Take the time to laze in a café, wander through the Alyscamps, sit on a park bench, and absorb the city's sweetly winning combination of warm light, cool shade, and Provençal textures.

Sights to See

★ ㉑ **Arènes** (Arena). Rivaled only by the even better-preserved version in Nîmes, this amazingly functional Roman arena dominates Old Arles. Its four medieval towers are testimony to its transformation from classical sports arena to feudal fortification in the Middle Ages—at the sacrifice of a full row of arches and much of the original structure. Younger than Arles's theater, it dates from the 1st century AD and, unlike the theater, seats 20,000 to this day. Its primary function: as a venue for the traditional spectacle of the corridas, or bullfights, which take place annually during the *feria pascale*, or Easter festival. Climb to the top of the tallest medieval tower, by the entry, to see the arena as a whole and take in Old Arles. ⊠ *Rond Point des Arènes* ☎ 04–90–49–36–86 ☜ €4 ⊙ *May–Sept., daily 9–7; Oct., daily 9–noon and 2–6; Nov. and Dec., daily 10–noon and 2–5; Mar. and Apr., daily 9–noon and 2–5.*

★ ⑲ **Cloître St-Trophime** (St-Trophime Cloister). Tucked discreetly behind St-Trophime, this pillared enclosure is a peaceful haven, a Romanesque treasure worthy of the church and one of the loveliest cloisters in Provence. Next to the church portals, enter via broad wooden doors that open onto the Place de la République and cross a peaceful courtyard to the entrance. The slender elegance of its pillars contrasts gracefully with the florid decorations of the capitals, each carved with fine detail and a painterly hand. Even drapery and feathers pop into high relief. The clear dichotomy of Gothic and Romanesque styles—curving vaults versus delicate cross vaults—harmonizes beautifully, as does the cloister as a whole: you wouldn't be surprised to come upon Cyrano's Roxanne embroidering quietly in the light dappling through the oleander. ⊠ *Off Place de la République* ☎ *04–90–49–36–74* ☜ *€3.50* ⊙ *May–Sept., daily 9–7; Oct., Mar., and Apr., daily 9–6; Nov.–Feb., daily 10–5.*

⑯ **Cryptoportiques.** At the entrance to a 17th-century Jesuit college, you can access these ancient and evocative underground galleries. Dating from 30 to 20 BC, this horseshoe of vaults and pillars buttressed the ancient forum from underneath. Yet openings let in natural daylight, and artworks of considerable merit and worth were unearthed here, including the extraordinary bust long thought to be a portrait of the young Octavius wearing the whiskers of mourning for the murdered Julius Caesar. (Current research, alas, identifies it as his grandson Caius.) ⊠ *Rue Balze* ☎ *04–90–49–32–82* ☜ *€3.50* ⊙ *May–Sept., daily 9–noon and 2–7; Oct., Mar.–Apr., daily 9–noon and 2–6; Nov.–Feb., daily 10–noon and 2–5.*

★ ⑰ **Église St-Trophime** (St-Trophime Church). Classed as a world treasure by UNESCO, this extraordinary Romanesque church alone would justify a visit to Arles, though it's continually upstaged by the antiquities around it. Its transepts date from the 11th century and its nave from the 12th; the church's austere symmetry and ancient artworks (including a stunningly Roman-style 4th-century sarcophagus) are fascinating in themselves. But it is the church's 12th-century **portal**—its entry facade—that earns it international respect. Superbly preserved and restored sculptures with high-relief modeling, complex layers of drapery, and a detail of expression that are nearly classical embellish every inch of the portal's surface. Indeed, it is that classicism that marks it as late Romanesque; Chartres Cathedral, of the same era, had long since ventured into fluid Gothicism. The **tympanum** (the half-moon over the door) tells the story of the Last Judgment, inherently symmetrical, with its separation of the blessed who surge toward Christ and the damned who skulk, naked and in chains, toward hell. Christ is flanked by his chroniclers, the evangelists: the eagle (John), the bull (Luke), the angel (Matthew), and the lion (Mark). ✉ *Pl. de la République.*

The most strikingly resonant site, impeccably restored and landscaped to match one of Van Gogh's paintings, is the courtyard garden of what ㉕ is now the **Espace Van Gogh**, featured in *Le Jardin de l'Hôtel-Dieu.* This was the hospital to which the tortured artist repaired after cutting off his earlobe. Its cloistered grounds have become something of a shrine for visitors and there are photo plaques comparing the renovation to some of the master's paintings, including *Le Jardin de la Maison de Santé.* The exhibition hall here is open for temporary exhibitions; the garden is always on view, and in spring and summer blooming flowers decorate the live canvas. Check out shows of contemporary art inspired by "Vince" at the nearby Fondation Vincent van Gogh, located at 24 bis Rond-point des Arènes. For more information about Van Gogh, see the Close-Up Box, "Van Gogh in Arles and St-Rémy" and Place Lamartine, *below.* ✉ *Pl. Dr. Félix Rey* ☎ *04–90–49–39–39* ⊕ *www.ville-arles.fr* ✆ *Free.*

★ ⑭ **Musée de l'Arles Antique** (Museum of Ancient Arles). This is the place to steep yourself in Arles's spectacular classical history. The building was erected on the site of an enormous Roman *cirque* (chariot-racing stadium). It hides its prehistoric collections in a womblike interior but bathes displays of the Roman renaissance in wall-to-wall daylight. Natural materials and earth colors provide counterpoint to the high culture on display, and a preconceived viewing plan enhances the narrative flow of history (ask for the English-language guidebook). And there's more here than glass cases full of toga buckles. You'll learn about all aspects of Arles in its heyday, from the development of its monuments to details of daily life in Roman times. Perhaps the most instructive and fascinating aspect of this museum is its collection of tiny, precise models: a miniature cirque shows tiny chariots charging around its track, with an unfinished cross section that demonstrates building techniques; the amphitheater, forum, and theater as they were used; and a sophisticated 16-wheel water mill used to grind grain. The quantity of art treasures gives an idea of the extent of Arles's importance. Seven superb floor mosaics can be viewed from an elevated platform, and you exit via a hall packed tight with magnificently detailed paleo-Christian sarcophagi. As you leave you will see the belt of St-Césaire, the last bishop of Arles, who died in 542 AD as the countryside was overwhelmed by the Franks and the Roman era met its end. ✉ *Presqu'île du Cirque Romain (follow Bd. Clemenceau to N113 and cross over)* ☎ *04–90–18–88–88* ⊕ *www.arles-antique.org* ⚑ *€5.50* ☉ *Apr.–Oct., daily 9–7; Nov.–Mar., daily 10–5.*

YOU OUGHTA BE IN PICTURES

In July the famous **Rencontres Internationales de la Photographie** (Photography Festival ✉ 10 Rond-point des Arènes, BP 96, Arles Cedex 13632 ☎ 04-90-96-76-06) brings movers and shakers in international photography into the Théâtre Antique for five days of highly specialized colloquiums and homages. Ordinary folks can profit, too, by attending the photography exhibits displayed in some 17 venues in Arles, open to the public throughout July and August.

㉓ **Musée Réattu** (Réattu Museum). Arles can't boast a single Van Gogh painting—excusable, given that his works sell for $20 million today—but did they have to name their art museum after Jacques Réattu, a local painter of dazzling mediocrity? This very local art museum lavishes three rooms on his turn-of-the-19th-century ephemera but it also houses a collection of contemporary art (including paintings by the Belgian Alechinsky), photography, and a gathering of bits and pieces by Picasso, including a delightful tongue-in-cheek depiction of noted muse and writer Lee Miller in full Arles dress. The best thing about the Réattu may be the building, a Knights of Malta priory dating from the 15th century, with its fortress-facade overlooking the Rhône. ✉ *Rue Grand Prieuré* ☎ *04–90–49–37–58* ⚑ *€4* ☉ *Apr.–Sept., daily 10–12:30 and 2–7:30; Oct.–Mar., daily 1–5.*

⓯ **Museon Arlaten** (Arles Museum). Take the time to comb leisurely through the quirky old collection of local paraphernalia housed in this grand 16th-century town house. Created by the father of the Provençal revival, turn-of-the-century poet Frédéric Mistral (he paid for it with his Nobel Prize winnings), it enshrines a seemingly bottomless collection of regional treasures. There are spindled-oak bread boxes (mounted high on the wall like bird cages); the signature Arlésienne costumes, with their pretty shoulder scarves crossed at the waist; dolls and miniatures; an entire Camargue gardian hut, with reconstructed interior; and dioramas with mannequins—tiny tableaux of Provençal life. Following Mistral's wishes, women in full Arlésienne costume oversee the labyrinth of lovely 16th-century halls. ✉ *29 rue de la République* ☎ *04–90–93–58–11* ⚑ *€4, free 1st Sun. of every month* ☉ *Apr., May, Sept., daily 9:30–12:30 and 2–6; June–Aug., daily 9–1 and 2–6; Oct.–Mar., Tues.–Sun. 9:30–12:30 and 2–5.*

You'll have to go to Amsterdam to view Van Goghs. But the city has provided helpful markers and a numbered itinerary to guide you from one landmark to another—many of them recognizable from his beloved canvases. Van Gogh resided in Arles from February 1888 to May 1889 and did about 300 drawings and paintings while here. You can stand ㉔ on **Place Lamartine** (between the rail station and the ramparts), which is the site of his residence here, the now-famous Maison Jaune (Yellow House); it was destroyed by bombs in 1944. The artist may have set up his easel on the Quai du Rhône, just off Place Lamartine, to capture the view that he transformed into his legendary *Starry Night*.

❶❽ **Place de la République.** The slender, expressive saints of St-Trophime overlook the wide steps that attract sunners and foot-weary travelers who enjoy the modern perspective over this broad urban square, flanked by the classical symmetry of the 17th-century **Hôtel de Ville**. This

> " Eight other sites are included on the city's "Promenade Vincent van Gogh" (⊕int.tourisme.ville-arles.fr/UK/a4/a4.htm), linking sight to canvas, including the Place du Forum; the Trinquetaille bridge; Rue Mireille; the Summer Garden on the Boulevard des Lices; and the road along the Arles à Bouc canal. "

noble Italianate landmark is the work of the great 17th-century Parisian architect François Mansart (as in mansard roofs); a passageway allows you to cut through its graceful vestibule from Rue Balze. The **obelisk**, of Turkish marble, used to stand in the Gallo-Roman cirque and was hauled here in the 18th century.

❷⓿ **Théâtre Antique** (Amphitheater). Between the Place de la République and the Arena, you'll come across the picturesque ruins of the amphitheater built by the Romans under Augustus in the 1st century BC. Now overgrown and a pleasant, parklike retreat, it once served as an entertainment venue to some 20,000 spectators. None of its stage walls and only one row of arches remain of its once high-curved back (it was not a natural amphitheater); its fine local stone was borrowed to build early Christian churches. Nonetheless, it serves today as a concert stage for the Festival d'Arles (in July and August) and a venue for the Recontres Internationales de la Photographie (Photography Festival). ⊠ *Rue du Cloître* ☎ *04–90–49–36–25* ✉ *€3* ⊘ *May–Sept., daily 9–noon and 2–7; Oct., daily 9–noon and 2–6; Nov. and Dec., daily 10–noon and 2–5; Mar. and Apr., daily, 9–noon and 2–5.*

❷❷ **Thermes Constantin** (Constantine Baths). Along the riverfront stand the remains of vast and sophisticated Roman baths, luxurious social centers that once included sports facilities and a library—the Barnes & Noble of the 4th century. ⊠ *Pl. Constantin at the corner of Rue de l'Hôtel de Ville* ☎ *04–90–49–36–74* ✉ *€3* ⊘ *Apr.–Sept., daily 9–7; Oct.–Mar., daily 10–6:30.*

OFF THE BEATEN PATH

Though **LES ALYSCAMPS,** the romantically melancholy Roman cemetery, lie away from the Old Town, it's worth the hike if you're in a reflective mood. Follow the Boulevard des Lices past the Jardin d'Été, the post office, and the *gendarmerie* (police station), then cut right. This long necropolis amassed the remains of the dead from antiquity to the Middle Ages; bodies were shipped up the Rhône to this prestigious resting place. Greek, Roman, and Christian tombs line the long shady road that was once the entry to Arles—the Aurelian Way—and the ruins of chapels and churches are scattered among the sarcophagi. The finest of these stone coffins were offered as gifts in feudal times, and tombstones were mined for building stone. Thus no one work of surpassing beauty remains, but the ensemble has an aura of eternity. ☏ *04–90–49–36–74* 🎫 *€3.50* ⊙ *May–Sept., daily 9–noon and 2–7; Oct., Mar., Apr., daily 9–noon and 2–6; Nov.–Feb., daily 10–noon and 2–5.*

Where to Eat & Stay

\$\$\$ ✕ **La Chassagnette.** Set in a sophisticated farmhouse, this restaurant is the latest fashionable address and continues to garner rave reviews. With stone walls, burnt-sienna tiles, and comfortable settees brightened by colorful pillows, the setting is fetching; better yet, the dining area extends outdoors to include large family-style picnic tables under a wooden canopy overlooking extensive gardens. Innovative chef Luc Rabanel serves up melt-in-your-mouth open-rotisserie style prix-fixe menus that use ingredients grown right on the property and are certified organic. ⊠ *Rte. du Sambuc, 13 km (8 mi) south of Arles on D36* ☏ *04–90–97–26–96* ⌂ *Reservations essential* ▭ *MC, V* ⊙ *Closed Tues. and Nov.–mid-Dec. No lunch Wed.*

\$\$\$ ✕ **Lou Marquès.** Whether you dine indoors, surrounded by glowing woodwork and rich Provençal fabrics, or amid the greenery of this former Carmelite cloister, atmosphere figures large in your evening at this Arles institution in the Jules César Hotel. Chefs Pascal Renaud and Joseph Kriz mix classical grandeur with Provençal rusticity: lobster risotto, roast pigeon with cèpes, salsify with veal and tomato polenta, and strawberries in a pastry shell with fresh cream. The wine list is as ambitious as Caesar himself. ⊠ *Jules César Hotel, Bd. des Lices* ☏ *04–90–52–52–52* ⊕ *www.hotel-julescesar.com* ⌂ *Reservations essential* ▭ *AE, DC, MC, V* ⊙ *Closed Nov. and Dec.*

\$\$–\$\$\$ ✕ **Brasserie Nord-Pinus.** With its tile-and-ironwork interior straight out of a design magazine and its Place du Forum terrace packed with all the right people, this cozy-chic retro brasserie highlights light, simple, and purely Provençal cooking in dishes such as roast rack of lamb au jus and panfried fillet of beef in a morel and cream sauce. Discreet service and a nicely balanced wine list only add to its charm. And wasn't that Christian Lacroix (or Kate Moss or Juliette Binoche) under those Ray-Bans? ⊠ *Pl. du Forum* ☏ *04–90–93–02–32* ⌂ *Reservations essential* ▭ *AE, DC, MC, V* ⊙ *Closed Feb. and Wed. in Nov.–Mar.*

\$\$ ✕ **La Gueule du Loup.** Serving as hosts, waiters, and chefs, the ambitious couple that owns this restaurant tackles serious cooking—Provençal specialties such as *rouget* (red mullet) with puréed potatoes, *caillette d'agneau* (lamb baked in herbs), and crème brûlée with anise—and maintains a supercool vibe. Jazz music and vintage magic posters bring the old Arles stone-and-beam interior up-to-date. ⊠ *39 rue des Arènes* ☏ *04–90–96–96–69* ▭ *MC, V* ⊙ *Closed Sun.; Oct.–Mar., closed Mon.; Apr.–Sept., no lunch Mon.*

★ \$ ✕ **L'Affenage.** A vast smorgasbord of Provençal hors d'oeuvres draws loyal locals to this former fire-horse shed. They come here for heaping plates of fried eggplant, green tapenade, chickpeas in cumin, and a slab of ham carved off the bone—followed by roasted potatoes and lamb chops grilled in the great stone fireplace. In summer you can opt for just the first-course buffet and go back for thirds; reserve a terrace table out front. ✉ *4 rue Molière* ☎ *04–90–96–07–67* ▤ *AE, MC, V* ⊘ *Closed Sun. and 3 wks in Aug. No dinner Mon.*

¢–$ ✕ **Lou Caleu.** In a charming 16th-century building behind the Amphitheater, this popular, unpretentious place serves regional specialties cooked by the genial owner and chef Christian Gimenez—homemade salt-cod brandade, *jarret d'agneau* (lamb roasted with black olives), and bourride (Provençal soup)—at good prices. Make sure to order the excellent 1999 Domaine de la Solitude with the fish and to avail yourself of the terrific lunch deals. ✉ *27 rue Porte de Laure* ☎ *04–90–49–71–77* ▤ *AE, DC, MC, V* ⊘ *Closed Mon. and Jan.–Feb.*

¢–$ ✕ **Vitamine.** If you're unaccustomed to French-scale eating (even the lighter southern cuisine), you'll be relieved to find this pretty, Provençal-looking eatery that puts all its energy into fresh, crisp, full-meal salads—50 varieties for under €10 each. There are 15 pasta options, too, a good pear crumble, and a friendly, laid-back staff. ✉ *16 rue du Docteur Fanton* ☎ *04–90–93–77–36* ▤ *MC, V* ⊘ *Closed Sun. in Sept.–June.*

$$$$ ✕▥ **L'Hotel Particulier.** Once owned by the Baron of Chartrouse, this extraordinary 18th-century *hôtel particulier* (mansion) is delightfully intimate and carefully discreet behind a wrought-iron gate. Decor is sophisticated yet charmingly simple: stunning gold-leaf mirrors, white-brocaded chairs, marble writing desks, artfully hung curtains, and hand-painted wallpaper. Rooms look out onto beautifully sculpted lawns; even if you take the five-minute walk to the center of town you can come back, stretch out in front of the pool, and listen to the birds chirp. ✉ *4 rue de la Monnaie, 13200* ☎ *04–90–52–51–40* ▤ *04–90–96–16–70* ⊕ *www.hotel-particulier.com* ⬳ *8 rooms* ♿ *Minibars, pool, some pets allowed (fee)* ▤ *AE, DC, MC, V* ⑂ *BP.*

$$$–$$$$ ▥ **Jules César.** This elegant landmark, once a Carmelite convent but styled like a Roman palace, anchors the lively Boulevard des Lices. Low-slung, with spacious rooms, it's an intimate, traditional hotel, conservatively decorated with richly printed fabrics and burnished woodwork. Rooms are pure Souleiado, from the flower-sprigged fabrics on the wall to the bathroom tiles; the antiques are classic, curvy Provençal. Some windows look over the pool and some over the pretty cloister, where breakfast is served under a vaulted stone arcade. The hotel also owns the beautiful *ancienne baroque* chapel next door, with its statue of St. Thérèse d'Avila. ✉ *Bd. des Lices, 13631* ☎ *04–90–52–52–52* ▤ *04–90–52–52–53* ⊕ *www.hotel-julescesar.fr* ⬳ *50 rooms, 5 suites* ♿ *Restaurant, minibars, Internet, pool, parking (fee), some pets allowed (fee)* ▤ *AE, DC, MC, V* ⑂ *MAP.*

$$$ ▥ **Chateau de Barbegal.** With sculpted greens, a horse and carriage at your disposal, sweeping fireplaces, and fluffy four-poster beds, this château is a step back in time—yet has all the modern conveniences. Each of the large rooms is named after a famous writer—George Sand, Baudelaire—and when you sit outside breathing in the fresh night air, you may feel inspired to start scribbling away; unless, of course, you prefer the lazy indulgence of another glass of vintage wine. ✉ *D33 Rte. de Fontvieille à Raphéle, 13200* ☎ *04–90–54–75–89* ▤ *04–90–54–73–44*

Those Ubiquitous Provençal Cottons

VIVID MEDALLION PRINTS, soft floral sprigs, assertive paisley borders—they've come to define the Provençal Experience, these bright-patterned fabrics, with their sunny colors, naive prints, and country themes redolent of sunflowers and olive groves. And the southern tourist industry is eager to fulfill that expectation, swagging hotel rooms and restaurant dining rooms with gay Provençal patterns in counterpoint to the cool yellow stucco and burnished terra-cotta tiles. Nowadays, both in Provence and on the coast, it's all about country—back to the land with a vengeance.

These ubiquitous cottons are actually Indian prints *(indiennes)*, first shipped into the ports of Marseille from exotic trade routes in the 16th century. Ancient Chinese wax dyeing techniques—indigo dyes taking hold where the wax wasn't applied—evolved into wood-block stamps, their surfaces painted with mixed colors, then pressed carefully onto bare cotton. The colors were richer, the patterns more varied than any fabrics then available—and, what's more, they were easily reproduced.

They caught on like a wildfire in a mistral, and soon mills in Provence were creating local versions en masse. Too well, it seems. By the end of the 17th century, the popular cottons were competing with royal textile manufacturers. In 1686, under Louis XIV, the manufacture and marketing of Provençal cottons was banned.

All the ban did was contain the industry to Provence, where it developed in Marseille (franchised for local production despite the ban) and in Avignon, where the Papal possessions were above royal law.

Their rarity and their prohibition made them all the sexier, and fashionable Parisians—even insiders in the Versailles court—flaunted the coveted contraband. By 1734, Louis XV cracked down on the hypocrisy, and the ban was sustained across France. The people protested. The cottons were affordable, practical, and brought a glimmer of color into the commoners' daily life. The king relented in 1758, and the peasants were free to swath their windows, tables, and hips with a limitless variety of color and print.

But because of the 72-year ban and that brief burgeoning of the southern countermarket, the tight-printed style and vivid colors remained allied in the public consciousness with the name "Provençal," and the region has embraced them as its own. If once they trimmed the windows of basic stone farmhouses and lined the quilted petticoats of peasants to keep off the chill, nowadays the fabrics drape the beveled-glass French doors of the finest *hôtel particuliers* (private mansions) and grandest Riviera hotels.

Two franchises dominate the market and maintain high-visibility boutiques in all the best southern towns: Souleiado and Les Olivades. Fierce rivals, each claims exclusive authenticity—regional production, original techniques. Yet every tourist thoroughfare presents a hallucinatory array of goods, sewn into every salable form from lavender sachets to place mats to swirling skirts and bolero jackets. There are bread bags and bun warmers, undershorts and toilet kits, even olive-sprigged toilet-paper holders. For their fans around the world, these folklorique cotton fabric prints can't be beat.

⊕ *www.barbegal.com* ⌁ *3 rooms, 1 suite* ⅏ *Minibars, pool, parking, some pets allowed* ▤ *AE, DC, MC, V* ⃥ *BP.*

★ **\$\$\$** ⊡ **Nord-Pinus.** The adventurer and mail-order genius J. Peterman would feel right at home in this quintessentially Mediterranean hotel on the Place du Forum; Picasso certainly did. The salon is dramatic with angular, heavy, wrought-iron furniture, colorful ceramics, and a collection of Peter Beard's black-and-white photographs. Rooms are individually decorated: wood or tile floors, large bathrooms, handwoven rugs, and tasteful (if somewhat exotic) artwork are cleverly set off to stylish art-director chic advantage. All this works together to create a richly atmospheric stage-set for literati (or literary poseurs), decor-magazine shoots, and people who refer to themselves as "travelers." Its scruffy insider-chic is not for everyone—traditionalists should head for the mainstream luxuries of the Jules César—but this is where you might brush past a *Vogue* editor on the way to breakfast, and the brasserie is the *dernier cri* in shoulder-rubbing. ⊠ *Pl. du Forum, 13200* ☎ *04–90–93–44–44* 🖷 *04–90–93–34–00* ⊕ *www.nord-pinus.com* ⌁ *19 rooms, 5 suites* ⅏ *Restaurant, bar, some minibars, some pets allowed (fee)* ▤ *AE, DC, MC, V* ⃥ *BP.*

★ **\$\$–\$\$\$** ⊡ **Hôtel d'Arlatan.** Once home to the counts of Arlatan, this noble 15th-century stone house stands on the site of a 4th-century basilica, and a glass floor reveals the excavated vestiges under the lobby. Digging an excavation in your lobby is just another aristocratic pastime for the friendly owners of this jewel of a hotel, with rows of rooms that horseshoe around a lovely fountain courtyard. Rooms are decorated with a chic, light hand, with quarry tiles and Pierre Frey fabrics. The intimate lobby bar is a cool, quiet haven. Breakfast is served in pretty courtside salons. ⊠ *26 rue du Sauvage, 13200* ☎ *04–90–93–56–66* 🖷 *04–90–49–68–45* ⊕ *www. hotel-arlatan.fr* ⌁ *39 rooms, 7 suites* ⅏ *Pool, parking, some pets allowed* ▤ *AE, DC, MC, V* ⃥ *BP.*

★ **\$** ⊡ **Muette.** With 12th-century exposed stone walls, a 15th-century spiral stair, weathered wood, and an Old Town location, a hotelier wouldn't have to try very hard to please. But the couple that owns this place does: hand-stripped doors, antiques, fresh white-and-blue–tiled baths, hair dryers, good mattresses, Provençal prints, and fresh sunflowers in every room show that they care. ⊠ *15 rue des Suisses, 13200* ☎ *04–90–96–15–39* 🖷 *04–90–49–73–16* ⊕ *www.logis-de-france.fr* ⌁ *18 rooms* ⅏ *Parking (fee), some pets allowed (fee)* ▤ *AE, DC, MC, V* ⊙ *Closed last 2 wks of Feb.* ⃥ *BP.*

¢–\$ ⊡ **Le Calendal.** The cheery Provençal colors of this small hotel next to the Arènes reflect the spirit of the hotel and its staff, most of whom speak English. Rooms overlook the Amphitheater or the idyllic courtyard garden; some sleep four. Light meals are served in either the cozy tearoom or the lovely garden. ⊠ *5 rue Porte de Laure, 13200* ☎ *04–90–96–11–89* 🖷 *04–90–96–05–84* ⊕ *www.lecalendal.com* ⌁ *38 rooms* ⅏ *Restaurant, some pets allowed (fee)* ▤ *AE, MC, V* ⃥ *BP.*

★ **¢–\$** ⊡ **Le Cloître.** Built as the private home for the provost of the Cloisters, this grand old medieval building has luckily fallen into the hands of a friendly, multilingual couple devoted to making the most of its historic details—with their own bare hands. They've chipped away plaster from pristine quarried stone walls, cleaned massive beams, restored tile stairs, and mixed natural chalk and ocher to plaster the walls, which are prettily decorated with stencils. Bargain hunters should opt for the sweet little top-floor rooms, with bath but sans WC, with views over the ancient rooftops. ⊠ *16 rue du Cloître, 13200* ☎ *04–90–96–29–50* 🖷 *04–90–96–02–88* ⊕ *members.aol.com/hotelcloitre* ↩ *30 rooms, 28 with bath* ⚿ *Parking (fee), some pets allowed (fee)* ⊟ *AE, MC, V.*

¢–$ ▯ **Le Rhône.** Simple and plain, with fresh pastel paint and a few balconies overlooking the Place Voltaire, this small hotel is distinguished by its charming hosts Benedict and Hervé, who make the low prices all the more welcome. They offer student prices in the off-season. ⊠ *11 pl. Voltaire* ☎ *04–90–96–43–70* 🖷 *04–90–93–87–03* ↩ *12 rooms, 5 with bath* ⊟ *AE, MC, V.*

Festivals

Arles is a true festival town, offering a stimulating mix of folklorique and contemporary arts events. The **férias,** with traditional corridas, or bullfights, vie with the **Fêtes du Riz** (with corrida) in September and the **Fêtes d'Arles** from the end of June to the beginning of July. All have traditional games and races in the Arena, parades, folk-dance events, and—their raison d'être—the beautiful traditional costumes of Arles.

Nightlife & the Arts

To find out what's happening in and around Arles (even as far away as Nîmes and Avignon), the free weekly *Le César* lists films, plays, cabaret, jazz, and rock events. It's distributed at the tourist office, in bars, clubs, and cinemas.

Though Arles seems to be one big sidewalk café in warm weather, the place to drink is the hip bar-restaurant **El Patio de Camargue** (⊠ Chemin de Barriol ☎ 04–90–49–51–76 ⊕ www.chico.fr) on the banks of the Rhône. They serve great tapas and you can hear Gypsy guitar, song, and dance from Chico and Las Gypsies, led by a founding member of the Gypsy Kings. In high season the cafés stay lively till the wee hours; in winter the streets empty out by 11. **Le Cargo de Nuit** (⊠ 7 av. Sadi-Carnot ☎ 04–90–49–55–99 ⊕ www.cargodenuit.com) is the main venue for live jazz, reggae, and rock, with a dance floor next to the stage. There are three concerts per week (Thursday, Friday, and Saturday), and the restaurant serves food until 2 AM.

Shopping

Despite being chic and popular, Arles hasn't sprouted the rows of designer shops found in Aix-en-Provence and St-Rémy. Its stores remain small and eccentric and contain an overwhelming variety of Provençal goods. Regional fabric is available at every turn, including a boutique for **Les Olivades** (⊠2 rue Jean Jaurès ☎04–90–96–22–17). Les Olivades' principal rival, **Souleiado** (⊠18 bd. des Lices ☎04–90–96–37–55), has a shop here as well. Though the charming terracotta folk miniatures called *santons* originate from around Marseille, the **Maison Chave** (⊠14 Rond Point des Arènes ☎04–90–96–50–22), across from the Arena, is a good place to find them. There's always someone painting impossibly tiny fingernails or Barbie-scale kerchiefs, and you're welcome to watch without buying. Best buys are local products such as perfumes, incense, soaps, and candles. There is a nice selection at **L'Occitane** (⊠58 rue de la République ☎04–90–96–93–62). If you want to get into the spirit of things before heading out to the Camargue, **L'Arlésienne** (✉12 rue de la République ☎04–90–93–28–05) is the best place to buy Provençal fabrics, waistcoats, frilly skirts, and gardian (cowboy) shirts. Yes, that grand pooh-bah of Parisian chic, **Christian Lacroix** (✉52 rue de la République ☎04–90–96–11–16) is actually an Arles homeboy and his exuberant style fills this, his original shop.

Arles's colorful **markets,** with produce, regional products, clothes, fabrics, wallets, frying pans, and other miscellaneous items, take place every Saturday morning along the Boulevard des Lices, which flows into the Boulevard Clemenceau. On the first Wednesday of the month there's a **brocante market,** where you can find antiques and collectibles, many of them regional.

Abbaye de Montmajour

★ *6 km (4 mi) north of Arles, direction Fontvieille.*

An extraordinary structure looming over the marshlands north of Arles, this magnificent Romanesque abbey stands in partial ruin, with shrieking rooks ducking in and out of its empty stone-framed windows. Begun in the 12th century by a handful of Benedictine monks, it grew according to an ambitious plan of church, crypt, and cloister; under corrupt lay monks in the 17th century it grew more sumptuous; when those lay monks were ejected by the church, they sacked the place. After the Revolution it was sold to a junkman, who tried to pay the mortgage by stripping off and selling its goods. A 19th-century medieval revival spurred its partial restoration, but its 18th-century portions remain in ruins. Ironically, because of this mercenary history, what remains is a spare and beautiful piece of Romanesque architecture, bare of furniture and art—

Van Gogh was drawn to the womblike isolation of Abbaye de Montmajour and came often to the abbey to paint and reflect.

an abstraction of massive stone arches, vaults, and flowing curves that seem to be poured and molded instead of quarried and fitted in chunks. And its cloister rivals that of St-Trophime in Arles for its balance, elegance, and air of mystical peace. ✉ *On D17 northeast of Arles, direction Fontvieille* ☎ *04–90–54–86–45* 🎫 *€6.10* 🕑 *Apr.–Sept., Wed.–Mon. 9–7; Oct.–Mar., Wed.–Mon. 9–noon and 2–5.*

Tarascon

㉖ *18 km (11 mi) north of Arles, 16 km (10 mi) west of St-Rémy.*

Tarascon's claim to fame is the mythical Tarasque, a monster said to emerge from the Rhône to gobble up children and cattle. Luckily, Saint Martha (Ste-Marthe), who washed up at Stes-Maries-de-la-Mer, tamed the beast with a sprinkle of holy water, after which the natives slashed it to pieces. This dramatic event is celebrated on the last weekend in June with a parade and was immortalized by Alphonse Daudet, who lived in nearby Fontvieille, in his tales of a folk hero known to all French schoolchildren as *Tartarin de Tarascon*. Unfortunately, a saint has not yet been born who can vanquish the fumes that emanate from Tarascon's enormous paper mill, and the hotel industry is suffering for it.

★ Despite the town's modern-day drawbacks, with the walls of its formidable **Château** plunging straight into the roaring Rhône, this ancient city on the river presents a daunting challenge to Beaucaire, its traditional enemy across the water. Begun in the 15th century by the noble Anjou family on the site of a Roman *castellum*, the castle grew through the generations into a splendid structure, crowned with both round and square towers and elegantly furnished. René the Good (1409–80) held court here, entertaining luminaries of the age. Nowadays the castle owes its superb preservation to its use, through the ensuing centuries, as a prison. It first served as such in the 17th century, and released its last prisoner in 1926. Complete with a moat, a drawbridge, and a lovely faceted spiral staircase, it retains its beautiful decorative Renaissance stonework and original cross mullioned windows. ⊠ *D970 at the riverfront, direction Beaucaire* ☎ *04–90–91–01–93* 🎫 *€6.10* ☉ *Daily 9–noon and 2–5.*

Beaucaire

➋➐ *15 km (9 mi) north of Arles, 2 km (1 mi) northwest of Tarascon.*

Though Beaucaire's castle glowering across the Rhône at its ancient enemy Tarascon doesn't hold a candle to its neighbor, this riverside town has an ambience all its own. Virtually unvisited by tourists, its labyrinthine Old Town retains an ancient, empty air—with superb old buildings. The town's **Hôtel de Ville** (Town Hall; ⊠ Pl. Clemenceau) is by 17th-century architect François Mansart. The fabulous **Hôtel de Margailler** (⊠ 23 rue de la République), dating from 1675, is graced with a porch supported by telamones (male column sculptures). Pick up a "Guide du Patrimoine" at the **tourist office** (⊠ Quai Général de Gaulle) and wander at will.

Beaucaire's **Château** was built on the site of a Roman camp in the 11th century, but was remodeled 200 years later and then dismantled in the 17th century on the orders of Cardinal Richelieu. What is left are the ramparts, two towers, the restored Romanesque chapel, and the barbican that defended the castle's entrance. The château is a crumbling ruin now and off-limits to the public except during afternoon falconry displays. But you can wander in the peaceful garden, stopping in briefly to tour the **Musée Auguste Jacquet**, a collection of archeological finds from the castle and environs. **Les Aigles de Beaucaire** features birds of prey handled by falconers in Roman costume. ⊠ *Pl. du Château* ☎ *04–66–59–26–72* ⊕ *www.aigles-de-beaucaire.com* 🎫 *Château free; museum €2.20; bird show €7* ☉ *Museum and château grounds: Wed.–Mon. 10–noon and 2–6 (late Mar.–early Nov., Thurs.–Tues.), with bird shows at 2, 3, 4, and 5 (Mar.–Oct. at 3, 4, 5, and 6).*

Where to Stay

$$ **Domaine des Clos.** In this roomy 18th-century farmhouse in the windswept countryside southwest of Beaucaire, Sandrine and David Ausset offer a warm welcome to families. Guests share a communal breakfast and have access as well to the kitchen and barbecue. (Reserve a table-d'hôte meal well in advance.) Rooms have brass beds and homemade white linens, and bathrooms are fresh. ✉ *On D38, 6 km (10 mi) southwest of Beaucaire, Rte. de Bellegarde, 30300* ☎ *04–66–01–14–61* 🖷 *04–66–01–00–47* 🌐 *www.camargue.fr/desclos/desclos.html* *7 rooms, 5 apartments* *Pool, some pets allowed (fee)* *MC, V* *BP.*

Shopping

Beaucaire's picturesque **markets** are held Thursday and Sunday mornings in front of the Hôtel de Ville (produce) and along the Canal du Rhône à Sète (dry goods), with boats bobbing alongside the fabric stands.

THE ALPILLES

Whether approaching from the damp lowlands of Arles and the Camargue or the pebbled vineyards around Avignon, the countryside changes dramatically as you climb into the arid heights of the low mountain range called the Alpilles (pronounced ahl-*pee*-yuh). A rough-hewn, rocky landscape rises into nearly barren limestone hills, the fields silvered with ranks of twisted olive trees and alleys of gnarled *amandiers* (almond trees). It's the heart of Provence, and is appealing not only for the antiquities in St-Rémy and the feudal ruins in Les Baux, but also for its mellow pace when the day's touring is done. Here, as much as anywhere in the south, is the place to slip into espadrilles, nibble from a bowl of olives, and attempt nothing more taxing than a lazy game of *pétanque* (lawn bowling). Hence, the countryside around St-Rémy is peppered with gentrified gîtes and mas, and is one of the most sought-after sites for Parisians' (and Londoners') summer homes.

Fontvieille

28 *19 km (12 mi) northeast of Arles, 20 km (12½ mi) southeast of Tarascon.*

The village of Fontvieille (pronounced fohn-*vyay*-uh), set among the limestone hills, is best known as the home of 19th-century writer Alphonse Daudet. Summering in the Château de Montauban, Daudet frequently climbed the windswept, pine-studded hilltop to the rustic old windmill that ground the local grain from 1814 to 1915. There the sweeping views of the Rhône valley and the Alpilles inspired his famous, folkloric short stories called *Lettres de Mon Moulin*. Today you can visit the well-preserved **Moulin de Daudet** (Daudet's Windmill), where there's a small museum devoted to his writings; you can walk upstairs to see the original milling system. ☎ *04–90–54–60–78* *€2* ⏲ *Apr.–Sept., daily 9–7; Oct.–Mar., daily 10–noon and 2–5.*

Where to Stay

$$$$ **La Regalido.** In an old olive oil mill covered with vines, this modest Relais & Châteaux property overlooks a stone-terraced garden full of

flowering plants, despite its position in the village center. Its status as a landmark luxury inn sustains it despite a somewhat stuffy, faded interior. The best room is the top-floor suite with beams and its own terrace with rooftop views. Aficionados will love the restaurant's concentration on the raw, new olive oil of the region. There's even a summer menu devoted to it. ⊠ *Rue Frederic Mistral, 13990* ☎ *04–90–54–60–22* 📠 *04–90–54–64–29* ⊕ *www.laregalido.com* 🛏 *13 rooms, 3 suites* △ *Restaurant* ⊟ *AE, DC, MC, V* ☺ *Closed Jan. and Feb.* ⦿ *MAP.*

Les Baux-de-Provence

㉙ *9 km (5½ mi) east of Fontvieille, 19 km (12 mi) northeast of Arles.*

Fodor'sChoice
★

When you first search the craggy hilltops for signs of Les Baux-de-Provence (pronounced *boh*), you may not quite be able to distinguish between bedrock and building, so naturally do the ragged skyline of towers and crenellation blend into the sawtooth jags of stone. As dramatic in its perched isolation as Mont-St-Michel and St-Paul-de-Vence, this tiny château-village ranks as one of the most visited tourist sites in France. Its car-free main street (almost its *only* street) is thus jammed with shops and galleries and, by day, overwhelmed with the smell of lavendar-scented souvenirs. But don't deprive yourself for fear of crowds. Stay late in the day, after the tour buses leave; spend the night in one of its modest hotels; or come off-season, and you'll experience its spectacular character—a tour-de-force blend of medieval color and astonishing natural beauty.

From this intimidating vantage point, the lords of Baux ruled throughout the 11th and 12th centuries over one of the largest fiefdoms in the south, commanding some 80 towns and villages. Mistral called them "a race of eagles, never vassals," and their virtually unchallenged power led to the flourishing of a rich medieval culture: courtly love, troubadour songs, and knightly gallantry. By the 13th century the lords of Baux had fallen from power, their stronghold destroyed. Though Les Baux experienced a brief renaissance and reconstruction in the 16th century, the final indignity followed hard upon that. Richelieu decided to eliminate the threatening eagle's nest once and for all and had the castle and walls demolished in 1632. Its citizens were required to pay the cost themselves. Only in the 19th century did Les Baux find new purpose. The mineral bauxite, valued as an alloy in aluminum production, was discovered in its hills and named for its source. A profitable industry sprang up that lasted into the 20th century before fading into history, like the lords of Baux themselves.

Today Les Baux offers two faces to the world: its beautifully preserved Renaissance village and the ghostly ruins of its fortress, once referred to as the *ville morte* (dead town). In the village, lovely 16th-century stone houses, even their window frames still intact, shelter the shops, cafés, and galleries that line the steep cobbled streets.

Vestiges of the Renaissance remain in Les Baux, including the pretty **Hôtel de Manville,** built at the end of the 16th century by a wealthy Protestant family. Step into its inner court to admire the mullioned windows, Renaissance-style stained glass, and vaulted arcades. Today it serves as the *mairie* (town hall). Up and across the street, the striking remains of the 16th-century Protestant temple still bear a quote from Jean Calvin: POST TENEBRAS LUX, or "after the shadows, light."

In the Hôtel des Porcelet, which dates from the 16th century, the **Musée Yves-Brayer** (Yves Brayer Museum) shelters this local 20th-century artist's works. Figurative and accessible to the point of naiveté, his paintings highlight Italy, Spain, even Asia, but demonstrate most of all his love of Provence. Brayer's grave lies in the château cemetery. ⊠ *Pl. Hervain* ☎ *04–90–54–36–99* ✉ *€4* ⊙ *Apr.–Sept., daily 10–12:30 and 2–6:30; Oct.–Mar., Wed.–Mon. 10–12:30 and 2–5:30.*

The main site to visit in town is the 17-acre cliff-top sprawl of ruins contained under the umbrella name **Château des Baux.** Climb the Rue Neuve and continue up Rue Trencat to the Tour du Brau, which contains the **Musée d'Histoire des Baux.** Entry to this small collection of relics and models gives access to the wide and varied grounds, where Romanesque chapels and towers mingle with skeletal ruins. A numbered audio program (available in English) guides you from site to site—the 16th-century hospital, the windmill, the 13th-century donjon—many of which are recognizable only by their names. Kids are especially fascinated by reconstructions of gigantic medieval siege machines. But be sure to stop into the cemetery; a more dramatic resting place would be hard to find. And the tiny **Chapelle St-Blaise** shelters a permanent film, *Van Gogh, Gauguin, Cézanne au Pays de l'Olivier,* of artworks depicting olive orchards in their infinite variety. You can see painterly views of patchwork olive orchards, as well as vineyards, almond orchards, and low-slung farmhouses, from

> " "Readers should be warned that the *ville morte* (dead town) of Les Baux can be one dangerous place—the area is riddled with crevasses, sinkholes, and collapsed floors. Beware: your next step could be your last!"
> —CheyneNY "

every angle of the château—reason enough alone to pay entry. ☎ *04–90–54–55–56* ⊕ *www.chateau-baux-provence.com* ✉ *€7 with audioguide* ⊙ *Mar.–June and Sept.–Oct., daily 9–7:30; July–Aug., daily 9–8:30; Nov. and Feb., daily 9–6; Dec.–Jan., daily 9–5.*

About half a mile north of Les Baux, off D27, you'll find the unusual **Cathédrale d'Images** (Cathedral of Images), in the majestic setting of the old limestone quarries. Towering rock faces and stone pillars are transformed into a series of colossal screens for an evocative audiovisual program. The theme changes each year and you walk through the series of towering halls, following the 30-minute spectacle. Bring a sweater. ⊠ *Rte. de MailLa.* ☎ *04–90–54–38–65* ⊕ *www.cathedrale-images. com* ✉ *€7* ⊙ *Mar.–Dec., daily 10–6.*

Where to Eat & Stay

$–$$ ✕ **Café Cinarca.** The tiny dining room is nice enough, but the garden courtyard of this small, unpretentious restaurant is a shady haven from the steady flow of tourists climbing the hill. A limited blackboard menu includes a simple fixed-price meal, including *tartes* and salads embellishing one or two hearty meat dishes: beef daube (stew), or *caillette aux herbes* (pork meat loaf) served hot or cold. It's also worth coming for afternoon tea, as the cakes and pastries are homemade and delicious. ⊠ *Rue Trencat* ☎ *04–90–54–33–94* ▭ *MC, V* ☺ *Closed Tues.*

$$$$ ✕▥ **L'Oustau de la Baumanière.** Sheltered by rocky cliffs below the village of Les Baux, this long-famous hotel, with its formal landscaped terrace and broad swimming pool, has a guest book studded with names like Winston Churchill, Elizabeth Taylor, and Picasso. The interior is luxe-Provençal chic, thanks to tile floors, arched stone ceilings, and brocaded settees done up in Canovas and Halard fabrics. Guest rooms—breezy, private, and beautifully furnished with antiques—have a contemporary flair, but the basic style remains archetypal Baux. These rooms are set in three buildings on broad landscaped grounds, the best of which are in the enchanting Le Manoir. As for the famed Baumanière restaurant (reservations essential), chef Jean-André Charial's hallowed reputation continues to attract culinary pilgrims (too many, it would appear from the noisy crowds that drive up the nearby road to the hotel). You can't blame them: the Oustau tradition is a veritable museum of Provençal heritage, but one that has been given a nouvelle face-lift—lobster cooked in Châteauneuf-du-Pape and set on a bed of polenta is a typical dazzler. If you're only dining here, be sure to make reservations. Note that from November to December and in March the restaurant is closed Wednesday and doesn't serve lunch Thursday; during January and February both the hotel and restaurant are closed. Meal plans for both hotels are available with a two-night minimum stay. ⊠ *13520* ☎ *04–90–54–33–07* ▭ *04–90–54–40–46* ⊕ *www.oustaudebaumaniere.com* ⇆ *15 rooms, 12 suites* ⚷ *Restaurant, minibars, 2 tennis courts, pool, horseback riding, some pets allowed (fee)* ▭ *AE, DC, MC, V* ☺ *Closed Jan.–Feb.* ❚⚊❙ *MAP.*

> **A BUDGET BAUMANIÈRE**
>
> You can try a less expensive, though still stylish, Oustau experience a kilometer away at **La Cabro d'Or** (☎ 04–90–54–33–21 ▭ 04–90–54–45–98 ⊕ www.lacabrodor.com). Run by the same owners, it's cheaper (€170–€240), more rustic, and more private; and don't be surprised to see a billy goat wander by your guest-room window. The inn is closed November through mid-December.

$–$$ ✕▥ **La Reine Jeanne.** Sartre and de Beauvoir had separate rooms but a shared balcony—and what a balcony. Jacques Brel and Winston Churchill were also happy guests at this modest but majestically placed inn and stood on its balconies looking over rugged views worthy of the châteaux up the street. The inn is located right at the entrance to the village and offers rooms that are small, simple, and—despite the white, vinyl-padded furniture—fondly decorated with terra-cotta tiles and stencil prints. Reserve in advance for one of the two rooms with a balcony, though even one of the tiny interior rooms gives you the right to spend a quiet evening in lovely Les Baux after the tourists have drained away. Good home-style cooking (try *l'aioli*—a garlic mayonaise fish dish) and a fine plat du jour are served in the restaurant, which offers views from both the panoramic dining room and a pretty terrace; it's one of the best settings for a meal in Les Baux. ☒ *13520* ☎ *04–90–54–32–06* 🖷 *04–90–54–32–33* ⊕ *www.la-reinejeanne.com* ➟ *10 rooms* ⚥ *Restaurant, some pets allowed (fee)* ▭ *MC, V* ☽ *Closed Jan.* ⍓ *BP.*

\$\$\$–\$\$\$\$ ▥ **Mas de L'Oulivié.** Another mas built to look ancient, with recycled roof tiles and hand-waxed chalk walls, the Oulivié is clarity itself, with a cool, clean look and a low-key vibe. There's no upscale restaurant—just easy and unpretentious lunches by the pool (grilled meats, salads, and goat cheese seasoned with the house-label olive oil); you can dabble your feet with an aperitif in hand. Eight rooms on the upper floor of the main house are pretty enough, with floral-print curtains and rich carpet, but ask for one with doors opening onto the lavender gardens and olive groves; there's even one with a private terrace and access to the pool. ☒ *Below Les Baux, direction Fontvieille, 13520 Les Arcoules* ☎ *04–90–54–35–78* 🖷 *04–90–54–44–31* ⊕ *www.masdeloulivie.com* ➟ *22 rooms, 1 suite* ⚥ *Restaurant, minibars, tennis court, pool, some pets allowed (fee)* ▭ *AE, DC, MC, V* ☽ *Closed mid-Nov.–mid-Mar.* ⍓ *BP.*

\$\$\$ ▥ **La Benvengudo.** With manicured grounds shaded by tall pines, this graceful shuttered mas feels centuries old but was built to look that way some 30 years ago. Its heavy old beams, stone fireplace, and terra-cotta tiles enhance the homey, old-fashioned interior. The resident dogs greet you just before the friendly owners do. Dinner is served by the olive-shaded pool, or you can have a drink on the stone-tabled terrace. ☒ *Below Les Baux, direction Fontvieille, 13520 Vallon de l'Arcoule* ☎ *04–90–54–32–54* 🖷 *04–90–54–42–58* ➟ *24 rooms* ⚥ *Restaurant, tennis court, pool, some pets allowed* ▭ *AE, MC, V* ☽ *Closed mid-Nov.–Feb.* ⍓ *MAP.*

\$\$–\$\$\$ ▥ **Le Prince Noire.** Each of the three rooms of this unique bed-and-breakfast is carved right out of the stone face but the semi-troglodyte effect is softened by jute carpets, warm woods, and unbeatable views over the Val d'Enfer. It is the highest house in the city, nestled in the heart of the château. It is a truly remarkable experience to wake up in the morning and see the sun rise over the valley below. Book well in advance. ☒ *Rue de Lorme, Cité Haute, 13520* ☎ *04–90–54–39–57* ⊕ *www. leprincenoire.com* ➟ *1 room, 1 suite, 1 studio* ⚥ *Some pets allowed (fee)* ▭ *AE, MC, V* ⍓ *BP.*

\$ ▥ **Mas de la Fontaine.** This 15th-century mas, under gorgeous cliffs and ancient pines, is the poor man's Oustau de la Baumanière. Modest and *familiale* instead of deluxe, it has all the basics, plus exposed beams, a vaulted breakfast room, and a pool. Rooms are spare with dated bathrooms, but have fresh carpet and wallpaper. Ask for the upstairs room with private roof terrace. ☒ *Below Les Baux on D78, direction Fontvieille, 13520 Vallon de la Fontaine* ☎ *04–90–54–34–13* 🖷 *04–90–12–36–76* ⊕ *www.lemasdelafontaine.com* ➟ *7 rooms, 6 with bath* ⚥ *Some pets allowed (fee)* ▭ *No credit cards* ☽ *Closed Nov.–Easter* ⍓ *BP.*

Shopping

An extravagant choice of souvenirs ranging from kitsch (Provençal-print toilet-paper holders) to class (silk challis shawls from Les Olivades) virtually reach out and grab you as you climb the hill lined with tempting (and not-so) shops. But come with cash: only the post office is equipped to change money, and there's no bank.

St-Rémy-de-Provence

⓾ *11 km (7 mi) northeast of Les Baux, 25 km (15½ mi) northeast of Arles, 24 km (15 mi) south of Avignon.*

There are other towns as pretty as St-Rémy-de-Provence, and others in more dramatic or picturesque settings. Ruins can be found throughout the south, and so can authentic village life. Yet something felicitous has happened in this market town in the heart of the Alpilles—a steady infusion of style, of art, of imagination—all brought by people with a respect for local traditions and a love of Provençal ways. Here, more than anywhere, you can meditate quietly on antiquity, browse redolent markets with basket in hand, peer down the very row of plane trees you remember from a Van Gogh, and also enjoy urbane galleries, cosmopolitan shops, and specialty food boutiques. An abundance of chic choices in restaurants, mas, and even châteaux awaits you; the almond and olive groves conceal dozens of stone-and-terra-cotta gîtes, many with pools. In short, St-Rémy has been gentrified through and through, and is now a sort of arid, southern Martha's Vineyard or, perhaps, the Hamptons of Provence.

St-Rémy has always attracted the right sort of people. First established by an indigenous Celtic-Ligurian people who worshiped the god Glan, the village Glanum was adopted and gentrified by the Greeks of Marseille in the 2nd and 3rd centuries before Christ. They brought in sophisticated building techniques—superbly cut stone, fitted without mortar, and classical colonnades. Rome moved in to help ward off Hannibal, and by the 1st century BC Caesar had taken full control. The Via Domitia, linking Italy to Spain, passed by its doors, and the main trans-Alpine pass emptied into its entrance gate. Under the Pax Romana there developed a veritable city, complete with temples and forum, luxurious villas, and baths.

"St-Rémy is one of the most popular Provençal destinations but has surprisingly few hotels. Book WAY ahead!"

–Carr2

The Romans eventually fell, but a town grew up next to their ruins, taking its name from their protectorate abbey St-Remi in Reims. It grew to be an important market town, and wealthy families built fine hôtels (mansions) in its center—among them the family De Sade (whose distant black-sheep relation held forth in the Lubéron at Lacoste). Another famous native son, the eccentric doctor, scholar, and astrologer Michel Nostradamus (1503–66), is credited by some as having predicted much of the modern age; Catherine de Medici consulted him on every life decision.

Perhaps the best known of St-Rémy's visitors was the ill-fated Vincent van Gogh. Shipped unceremoniously out of Arles at the height of his madness (and creativity), he had himself committed to the asylum St-Paul-de-Mausolée and wandered through the ruins of Glanum during the last year of his life. It is his eerily peaceful retreat as well as the ruins that draw visitors by the busload to the outskirts of modern St-Rémy, but the bulk of them snap their pictures and move on to Les Baux for the day, leaving St-Rémy to its serene, sophisticated ways.

★ To approach Glanum, you must park in a dusty roadside lot on D5 south of town (in the direction of Les Baux). Before crossing, you'll be confronted with two of the most miraculously preserved classical monuments in France, simply called **Les Antiques** (The Antiquities). Though dating from the era of the Caesars, they could be taken for Romanesque, so perfectly intact are their carvings and architectural details. The **Mausolée** (Mausoleum), a wedding-cake stack of arches and columns built about 30 BC, lacks nothing but its finial on top, yet it is dedicated to a Julian (as in Julius Caesar), probably Caesar Augustus. Allegorical scenes in bas-relief represent myths of Greek origin but most likely refer to Julius Caesar's military triumphs. Two sculptured figures, framed in its column-ringed crown, must surely be the honorees; the dedication reads SEX. L.M. IVLIEI C.F. PARENTIBUS SUEIS, or "Sextius, Lucius, Carcus son of Caius, of the family of Julii, to their parents." A few yards away stands another marvel: the **Arc Triomphal**, most likely dating from around AD 20. All who crossed the Alps entered Roman Glanum through this gate, decorated with reliefs of battle scenes depicting Caesar's defeat and the capture of the Gauls.

★ Across the street from Les Antiques, a slick visitor center, set back from D5, prepares you for entry into **Glanum** with scale models of the site in its various heydays. A good map and an English brochure guide you stone by stone through the maze of foundations, walls, towers, and columns that spreads across a broad field; Greek sites are helpfully noted by numbers, Roman ones by letters. At the base of rugged white cliffs and shaded with black-green pines, it is an extraordinarily evocative site and inspires contemplation in even the rowdiest busload of schoolchildren. ⊠ *Off D5, direction Les Baux* ☎ *04–90–92–64–04 info phone at Hôtel de Sade* 🎫 *€6* ⊗ *Daily 9–7* ⊗ *Closed mid-Nov.–Jan.*

You can cut across the fields from Glanum to **St-Paul-de-Mausolée**, the lovely, isolated asylum where Van Gogh spent the last year of his life (1889–90), but enter it quietly. It shelters psychiatric patients to this day—all of them women. You're free to walk up the beautifully manicured garden path to the church and its jewel-box Romanesque **cloister**, where the artist found womblike peace. A small boutique shows works of current patients—*art brut* reminiscent of Munch and Basquiat—for sale. You can climb a stairway to a memorial bust of Van Gogh (donated by the American sculptor Klapholz after the original was stolen) and a picture window that frames a garden view he loved and painted. ⊠ *Next to Glanum, off D5 direction Les Baux* ☎ *04–90–92–77–00* 🎫 *€3.40* ⊗ *Apr.–Oct., Mon.–Sat. 9:30–7; Nov.–Mar., Mon.–Sat. 10:30–1 and 1:30–5.*

St-Rémy is wrapped by a lively commercial boulevard, lined with shops and cafés and anchored by its 19th-century church **Collégiale St-Martin.** Step inside to see the magnificent organ, one of the loveliest in Europe. Rebuilt to 18th-century specifications in the early 1980s, it has the flexibility to interpret new and old music with pure French panache; you can listen to it Saturday afternoon at 5:30 from July through September for free. ✉ *Pl. de la République.*

Within St-Rémy's fast-moving traffic loop, a labyrinth of narrow streets leads you away from the action and into the slow-moving inner sanctum of the **Vieille Ville** (Old Town). Here high-end, trendy shops mingle pleasantly with local life, and the buildings, if gentrified, blend unobtrusively.

Make your way to the **Hôtel de Sade,** a 15th- and 16th-century private manor now housing the phenomenal abundance of treasure unearthed with the ruins of Glanum. There are a statue of Hercules and a graceful bas-relief of Hermes, funeral urns and crystal jewelry, and surprisingly sophisticated tools. There are also the remains of Gallo-Roman funeral obelisks and early Christian altars. The De Sade family built the house around remains of 4th-century baths and a 5th-century baptistery, now nestled in its courtyard. ✉ *Rue du Parage* ☎ *04–90–92–64–04* 🎟 *€2.50* 🕐 *Feb.–mid-Nov., daily 10–6.*

The 18th-century Hôtel Estrine is now the **Centre d'Art Présence Van Gogh** and has many reproductions of the artitist's work, along with letters to his brother Theo and exhibitions of contemporary art, much of it inspired by Vincent. ✉ *Hôtel Estrine, 8 rue Estrine* ☎ *04–90–92–34–72* 🎟 *€3.20* 🕐 *Apr.–Dec., Tues.–Sun. 2:30–6:30.*

Where to Eat & Stay

★ **$$$** ✕ **L'Assiette de Marie.** Though life is lived outdoors in St-Rémy, there are rainy days and winter winds, and this is the place to retreat. Marie Ricco is a collector, and she's turned her tiny restaurant into an art-directed bower of attic treasures—unscrubbed, unrestored, as is. Fringed lamp shades are artfully askew, ancient wallpaper curls from a door, the coatrack sags with woolen uniforms, and classic jazz and candlelight complete the scene. Seated at an old school desk, you choose from the day's specials, all made with Marie's Corsican-Italian touch—marinated vegetables with tapenade, a cast-iron casserole of superb pasta. There's a wide choice of St-Rémy wines as well. ✉ *1 rue Jaume Roux* ☎ *04–90–92–32–14* 🍽 *Reservations essential* 🗖 *MC, V* 🕐 *Closed Jan. No lunch Wed.*

$$–$$$ ✕ **La Maison Jaune.** This modern retreat in the Old Town draws crowds of summer people to its pretty roof terrace. The decor of sober stone and lively contemporary furniture, both indoors and out, reflects the cuisine. With vivid flavors and a cool, contained touch, chef François Perraud prepares grilled sardines with crunchy fennel and lemon confit, ham-cured duck on lentils with vinaigrette, and grilled lamb chops carmelized with honey. Prices are high but one bargain lunch menu offers a minimalist smorgasbord of tastes, and wine is included. ✉ *15 rue Carnot* ☎ *04–90–92–56–14* 🍽 *Reservations essential* 🗖 *MC, V* 🕐 *Closed Mon.*

$–$$ ✕ **Le Bistrot des Alpilles.** This popular institution has a broad sidewalk terrace, glassed in brasserie-style in winter, and a feel of easygoing professionalism. Cheap lunch menus and a reasonable evening menu make the good, traditional cooking a bargain. There's a melt-in-your-mouth *agneau à la ficelle* (local roast lamb), a daily fish specialty, a good rum cake in an orange sauce, and a wine list that includes most of the best wines from the south. ☒ *15 bd. Mirabeau* ☎ *04–90–92–09–17* ⊕ *www. bistrodesalpilles.com* ⌂ *Reservations essential* ☰ *AE, MC, V.*

$–$$ ✕ **La Gousse d'Ail.** An intimate, indoor Old Town hideaway, this family-run bistro lives up to its name (The Garlic Clove), serving robust, highly flavored southern dishes in hearty portions: zucchini timbale, rich homemade pasta in powerful pesto with almonds, and homemade ice cream crepes with fresh fruit. A ceramic pitcher of ice water and a thick flask of house wine offer counterbalance, and the bill is delivered with much-needed mints. The cozy interior (dark timbers, niches full of puppets) matches the warm welcome. Aim for Thursday night when there is Gypsy music and jazz. ☒ *25 rue Carnot* ☎ *04–90–92–16–87* ☰ *AE, MC, V* ☺ *Closed mid-Jan.–mid-Mar.*

$$$–$$$$ ✕▥ **Domaine de Valmouriane.** This genteel mas-cum-resort, beautifully isolated on a broad park, offers you a panoply of entertainment, from billiards to a Jacuzzi. Inside, soft, overstuffed English-country furnishings mix cozily with cool Provençal stone and timber, and massive stone fireplaces warm public spaces. The restaurant is run by chef Pascal Volle, who is determined to please with game, seafood, local oils, and truffles; his ravioli foie gras is sheer decadence. But it's the personal welcome from Philippe and Martin Capel that makes you feel like an honored guest. The pool, surrounded by a slate walk and a delightful garden, is most inviting. ☒ *Petite rte. des Baux (D27), 13210* ☎ *04–90–92–44–62* 🖷 *04–90–92–37–32* ⊕ *www.valmouriane.com* ⤶ *14 rooms* ⌂ *Restaurant, minibars, tennis court, pool, some pets allowed* ☰ *AE, DC, MC, V* ¶◉ *MAP.*

$$$–$$$$ ✕▥ **Hostellerie du Vallon de Valrugues.** This luxurious villa, replete with uniformed footmen and canopy beds, makes no bones about its pretensions to aristocracy, but you might like it for its beguiling views into the Alpilles. The restaurant is formal, pampered, and a trifle stuffy; the bill a blow. ☒ *Chemin Canto-Cigalo, 13210* ☎ *04–90–92–04–40* 🖷 *04–90–92–44–01* ⊕ *www.hotelprestige-provence.com* ⤶ *38 rooms, 15 suites* ⌂ *Restaurant, pool, some pets allowed (fee)* ☰ *AE, MC, V* ☺ *Closed Feb.* ¶◉ *BP.*

$$$–$$$$ ✕▥ **Hotel les Ateliers de l'Image.** Young Lyonnais photographer Antoine Godard created this wonderfully eccentric hotel, the latest hot spot in St-Rémy. It harmonizes bits of several countries: the restaurant is run by Japanese chef Maseo Ikeda who serves dishes like leek soup with langoustine gyoza and soy-laquered lamb with Japanese aubergines; the rooms mix Scandinavian simplicity with a Provençal touch; and the ever-changing artwork features photography from around the world. ☒ *36 bd. Victor Hugo, 13210* ☎ *04–90–92–51–50* 🖷 *04–90–92–43–52* ⊕ *www. hotelphoto.com* ⤶ *28 rooms, 4 suites* ⌂ *Restaurant, minibars, pool, some pets allowed (fee)* ☰ *AE, DC, MC, V* ☺ *Closed Jan. and Feb.*

★ $$$ ✕▥ **Bistrot d'Eygalières.** Belgian chef Wout Bru's understated restaurant in nearby Eygalières is quickly gaining a reputation (and Michelin stars) for light and subtly balanced cuisine like sole with goat cheese, lobster salad with candied tomatoes, and foie gras carpaccio with summer truffles. Guest rooms are chic and comfortable. ⊠ *Rue de la République, Eygalières (10 km [6 mi] southeast of St-Rémy on D99 and then on D24), 13810* ☎ *04–90–90–60–34* 🖷 *04–90–90–60–37* ⊕ *www.chezbru.com* ⮡ *2 rooms, 2 suites ⟁ Restaurant, minibars, parking, some pets allowed (no fee)* ▭ *AE, DC, MC, V* ⧈ *MAP.*

$ ✕▣ **Auberge de la Reine Jeanne.** With all the luxurious mas and châteaux to choose from, you don't have to be scared away if you're on a budget: This charming Logis-de-France property, in a 17th-century stone building that surrounds a green courtyard, offers more-conventional lodgings right in the heart of town. Its strong point is its restaurant, where modestly priced, mainstream French cooking is served in the courtyard in summer and in a firelit, dark-timber hall in winter. Room decor isn't up to St-Rémy style (blue carpeting, polyester quilts), but the best rooms overlook the court and are clean and comfortable. ⊠ *12 bd. Mirabeau, 13210* ☎ *04–90–92–15–33* 🖷 *04–90–92–49–65* ⮡ *11 rooms ⟁ Restaurant, some pets allowed (fee)* ▭ *AE, DC, MC, V* ⧈ *BP.*

$$$–$$$$ ▣ **Château des Alpilles.** At the end of an alley of grand old plane trees, this early-19th-century manor house lords over a vast park. If public spaces are cool and spare to the point of sparseness, rooms are warm and fussy, with lush Provençal prints and polished antiques. Outer buildings offer jazzy modern apartments with kitchenettes, and the poolside grill gives you a noble perspective over the park. ⊠ *Ancienne rte. du Grès, 13210* ☎ *04–90–92–03–33* 🖷 *04–90–92–45–17* ⊕ *www. chateaudesalpilles.com* ⮡ *15 rooms, 4 suites ⟁ Restaurant, tennis court, pool, some pets allowed (fee)* ▭ *AE, DC, MC, V* ☉ *Closed mid-Nov.–mid-Dec. and Jan.–mid-Feb.* ⧈ *BP.*

$$$–$$$$ ▣ **Mas de Cornud.** An American mans the wine cellar and an Egyptian runs the professional kitchen (by request only), but the attitude is pure Provence. David and Nito Carpita have turned their farmhouse, just outside St-Rémy, into a bed-and-breakfast filled with French country furniture and objects from around the world. Guests and hosts unwind with a nightly pastis and a pétanque match. Table d'hôte dinners, cooking classes, and tours can be arranged. Breakfast is included and rooms have to be reserved in advance. ⊠ *Rte. de Mas-Blanc, 13210* ☎ *04–90–92–39–32* 🖷 *04–90–92–55–99* ⊕ *www.mascornud.com* ⮡ *5 rooms, 1 suite ⟁ Dining room, parking, pool, some pets allowed (fee)* ▭ *No credit cards* ☉ *Closed Jan. and Feb.* ⧈ *BP.*

★ $–$$ ▣ **Château de Roussan.** In a majestic park shaded by ancient plane trees (themselves protected landmarks), its ponds and canals graced by swans and birdsong, this extraordinary 18th-century château is being valiantly preserved by managers who (without a rich owner to back them) are lovingly restoring it. Glorious period furnishings and details are buttressed by brocante and bric-a-brac, and the bathrooms, toggled into various corners, have an afterthought air. Cats outnumber the staff. Yet if you're the right sort for this place—backpackers, romantic couples on a budget, lovers of atmosphere over luxury—you'll blossom in this three-dimensional costume drama. ⊠ *Rte. de Tarascon, 13210* ☎ *04–90–92–11–63* 🖷 *04–90–92–50–59* ⊕ *www.chateau-de-roussan.com* ⮡ *21 rooms ⟁ Restaurant, some pets allowed (fee)* ▭ *AE, DC, MC, V* ⧈ *BP.*

Festivals

St-Rémy is fond of festivals, borrowing traditions of bull-races and ferias from its lowland neighbors and creating a few of its own. On Pentecost Monday (the end of May), the **Fête de la Transhumance** celebrates the passage of the sheep from Provence into the Alps, and costumed shepherds lead some 4,000 sheep, goats, and donkeys through the streets. The **Grande Feria,** in mid-August, brings the Camargue to the hills, with bull games, fireworks, and flamenco guitar. Three weekends a year (Ascension in May, late June, and mid-September) are devoted to the **Fête de la Route des Peintres de la Lumière en Provence** (Festival of the Route of Painters of Light in Provence), an enormous contemporary-art fair.

Nightlife & the Arts

La Forge des Trinitaires (✉ Av. de la Libération ☎ 04–90–92–31–52) draws the young, the restless, and the trendily dressed for African and Antillaise music every Friday and Saturday night 11 PM–4:30 AM. At **La Haute Galine** (✉ Chemin Cante Perdrix et Galine ☎ 04–90–92–00–03) a very young crowd gathers (on Friday and Saturday nights only) to eat by the pool and dance into the night. On the second Friday of the month in July and August, **Pégomas** (✉ 3 av. Jean Moulin ☎ 04–32–60–01–90) is the site of a live jazz concert.

At 5:30 every Saturday in July, August, and September, you can hear the magnificent **organ of St-Martin Collégiale** (✉ Pl. de la République) in a free recital, often featuring the boy wonder *organiste-titulaire* Jean-Pierre Lecaudey.

Shopping

Every Wednesday morning St-Rémy hosts one of the most popular and picturesque **markets** in Provence, during which the Place de la République and narrow Old Town streets overflow with fresh produce, herbs and spices, olive oil by the vat, and tapenade by the scoop, as well as fabrics and brocante (collectibles). There's a smaller version Saturday morning.

Interior design is a niche market in this region of summer homes, so **decor shops** abound, not only featuring Provençal pottery and fabrics but also a cosmopolitan blend of Asian fabrics, English garden furniture, and Italian high-design items. Individual artisans fill gallery-style boutiques with their photography, picture frames, and wrought-iron furniture. The common denominator is high here, so good taste has stonewalled tourist kitsch. **Souleiado** (✉ Pl. de l'Église, 2 av. de la Résistance ☎ 04–90–92–45–90) has high-end Provençal fabrics and linens. **Les Olivades** (✉ 28 rue Lafayette ☎ 04–90–92–00–80) has beautiful displays of delightful Provençal fabrics. The design shops, fabric shops, and art gallery–cum–gift shops are scattered throughout the Vieille Ville and along the boulevards that surround it. At **La Boutique des Jardins** (✉ 1 bd. Mirabeau ☎ 04–90–92–11–60), Françoise Gérin displays the booty she trolls on her Asian and African travels, from Egyptian cottons to Indian hanging lamps and tooled metal frames. **Le Grand Magasin** (✉ 24 rue Commune ☎ 04–90–92–18–79) mixes handcrafted jewelry, glass sculpture, pottery, and scarves.

With all the summer people, food shops and *traiteurs* (take-out caterers) do big business in St-Rémy. Olive oils are sold like fine old wines, and the breads heaped in boulangerie windows are as knobby and rough-hewn as they should be. The best food shops are concentrated in the Vieille Ville. Local goat cheeses are displayed like jewels and wrapped like fine pastries at **La Cave aux Fromages** (✉ 1 pl. Joseph-Hilaire ☎ 04–90–92–32–45). At **Chocolaterie Joel Durand** (✉ 3 bd. Victor Hugo ☎ 04–90–92–38–25), the chocolates are numbered to indicate the various flavors, from rose petal to Camargue saffron. Pastry chef Hermann Van Beek has resurrected a variety of scrumptious ancient biscuit recipes (including pine nut "pignolats," which local boy Nostradamus commented on in the *Traité des Fardements et des Confitures*) at **Le Petit Duc** (✉ 7 bd. Victor Hugo ☎ 04–90–92–08–31).

THE ALPILLES, ARLES & THE CAMARGUE ESSENTIALS

To research prices, get advice from other travelers, and book travel arrangements, visit www.fodors.com.

Transportation

If traveling extensively by public transportation, be sure to load up on information (schedules, the best taxi-for-call companies, etc.) upon arriving at the ticket counter or help desk of the bigger hub stations in the area, such as Arles and Nîmes.

BY AIR

Marseille (an hour's drive from Arles) is served by frequent flights from Paris and London, and daily flights from Paris arrive at the smaller airport in Nîmes. In summer, Delta Airlines flies direct from New York to Nice, 200 km (124 mi) from Arles.

BY BUS

A moderately good network of private bus services links places not served, or badly served, by trains. Arles is one of the largest hubs, serviced out of the *gare routière* (bus station) on Av. Paulin-Talabot, opposite the train station; within the city, bus stations are mainly on Blvd. G. Clémenceau. You can travel from Arles to such stops as Nîmes (€6, 1 hr, four daily) and Avignon (€7, 45 minutes, 10 daily); four buses daily head out to Aix-en-Provence and Marseille (only two run on weekends). Out of Arles, Les Cars de Camargue and Ceyte Tourisme Mediterranée can take you on round-trip excursions to the Camargue's Stes-Marie-de-la-Mer (€5, one hour, three daily), Mas du Pont de Rousty, Pont de Gau, as well as stops in the Alpilles area, including Les Baux-des-Provence and St-Remy-de-Provence (neither have train stations); you can also reach the latter's bus station at Place de la République by frequent buses from Avignon. From Nîmes's bus station on Rue Ste-Félicité, you can connect to Avignon and Arles, while Cars Fort runs you into the deep country and offers tourist circuits as well. As for Pont du Gard, this is a 40-min-

1

utes ride from Nîmes; you are dropped off 1 km (½ mi) from the bridge at Auberge Blanche.

🚌 Bus Information **Les Cars de Camargue** ✉ 1 rue Jean-Mathieu Artaud, Arles ☎ 04-90-96-36-25 ⊕ www.carsdecamargue.com. **Ceyte Tourisme Méditerranée** ✉ 14 bd. Georges Clemenceau, Arles ☎ 04-90-18-96-33 ⊕ www.autocars-ctm.com. **Cars Fort** ✉ 27 av. Jean Jaurès, Nîmes ☎ 04-66-36-60-80.

BY CAR

The A6/A7 toll expressway (*péage*) channels all traffic from Paris toward the south. It's called the Autoroute du Soleil (Highway of the Sun) and leads directly to Provence. From Orange, A9 (La Languedocienne) heads southwest to Nîmes. Arles is a quick jaunt from Nîmes via A54.

With its swift autoroute network, it's a breeze traveling from city to city by car in this region. But some of the best of Provence is experienced on back roads and byways, including the isolated Camargue and the Alpilles. Navigating the flatlands of the Camargue can feel unearthly, with roads sailing over terrain uninterrupted by hills or forests; despite this, roads don't always run as the crow flies and can wander wide of a clean trajectory, so don't expect to make time. Rocky outcrops and switchbacks keep you a captive audience to the arid scenery in the Alpilles; to hurry—impossible as it is—would be a waste.

🚗 Car-Rental Information Arles: **Avis** ✉ At the train station ☎ 04-90-96-82-42, **Europcar** ✉ 2 bis av. Victor Hugo ☎ 04-90-93-23-24, **Hertz** ✉ 4 av. Victor-Hugo ☎ 04-90-96-75-23. Nîmes: **Avis** ✉ 1800 av. Mar. Juin ☎ 04-66-29-05-33, **Budget** ✉ 2000 av. Mar. Juin ☎ 04-66-38-01-69, **Europcar** ✉ 1 bis rue de la République ☎ 04-66-21-31-35, **Hertz** ✉ 5 bd. Prague ☎ 04-66-76-25-91.

BY TRAIN

There's regular rail service from all points north to Avignon and then to nearby towns, and the TGV (Trains à Grande Vitesse) *Méditerranée* connects Paris to Avignon in 3½ hours. This TGV train makes stops in two towns in this chapter: Nîmes (eight trains daily on the 4-hr trip from Paris) and Arles (only one TGV train from Paris arrives daily)—first class, one-way tickets cost about €90. From these cities you must transfer to local trains to get to Tarascon or Arles, the only other cities served by rail lines. Arles's train station (gare centrale) is located on Av. Paulin Talabot; from here, you can connect to Nîmes (€7, 30 minutes), Marseille (€12, 1 hr), Avignon Centre (€6, 1 hr), and Aix-en-Provence (€24, 2 hrs with connection). Nîmes's train station is on Blvd. Talabot and trains link Avignon Centre (€8, 45 minutes) and Arles (€7, 30 minutes). Overnight trains run daily to Avignon from Paris, Strasbourg, and other cloud-bound cities, allowing soggy travelers to stretch out on a couchette and wake up to indigo skies (⇨ Train Travel *in* Smart Travel Tips A to Z) but no service beats the TGV for speed and ease.

Although good rail service connects Avignon to Nîmes, Tarascon, and Arles, trains don't penetrate the Alpilles; connections to St-Rémy and Les Baux must be made by bus.

🚆 Train Information **SNCF** ☎ 08-36-35-35-35 ⊕ www.ter-sncf.com/uk/paca. **TGV** ☎ 877/2TGVMED ⊕ www.tgv.com.

Contacts & Resources

EMERGENCIES

For basic information, see this section in the Smart Travel Tips chapter. In most cases, contact the town Commissariat de Police.

🚹 Emergencies **Police** ⊠ 1 blvd. des Lices, Arles ☎ 17.

GUIDED TOURS

The Arles tourist office offers individual tours of the town, including visits to the Roman monuments, during the summer season. Dates and times vary depending on demand; check with them regarding English-speaking guides.

To learn more about Nîmes's monuments and Old Town and to arrange a guided tour in English, contact the Service des Guides at the tourist office. For about €23, you can tour the town in a taxi for an hour; when you stop in front of a monument, the driver slips in a cassette with commentary in the language of your choice. For €45, **Taxis T.R.A.N.** can take you on a round-trip ride from Nîmes to the Pont du Gard (ask the taxi to wait while you explore for 30 minutes).

🚹 Guided Tours Information **Taxis T.R.A.N.** ☎ 04–66–29–40–11.

INTERNET & MAIL

In smaller towns, ask your hotel concierge if there are any Internet cafés nearby.

🚹 Internet & Mail Information **Cyber Sal@delle** ⊠ 17 rue de la République, Arles ☎ 04–90–93–13–56. **Point Web** ⊠ 110 rue du 4 Septembre, Arles ☎ 04–90–18–91–54. **La Poste main post office** ⊠ 5 blvd. des Lices, Arles.

VISITOR INFORMATION

Regional tourist offices prefer written queries only. Local tourist offices for major towns covered in this chapter can be phoned, faxed, or reached by mail. The Comité Régional du Tourisme du Languedoc-Roussillon provides information on all towns west of the Rhône. The remainder of towns covered in this chapter are handled by the Comité Regional du Tourisme de Provence-Alpes-Côte d'Azur. For information on the area around Arles and St-Rémy, contact the Comité Départemental du Tourisme des Bouches-du-Rhône.

🚹 Tourist Office Information **Comité Régional du Tourisme du Languedoc-Roussillon** ⊠ 20 rue République, 34000 Montpellier. **Comité Regional du Tourisme de Provence-Alpes-Côte d'Azur** ⊠ 12 pl. Joliette, 13002 Marseille. **Comité Départemental du Tourisme des Bouches-du-Rhône** ⊠ 13 rue Roux de Brignole, 13006 Marseille. **Aigues-Mortes** ⊠ Porte de la Gardette, 30220 ☎ 04–66–53–73–00 🖷 04–66–53–65–94 ⊕ www.ot-aiguesmortes.fr. **Arles** ⊠ 43 bd. de Craponne, 13200 ☎ 04–90–18–41–20 🖷 04–90–18–41–29 ⊕ www.ville-arles.fr. **Les Baux** ⊠ 30 Grand-rue, 13520 ☎ 04–90–54–34–39 🖷 04–90–54–51–15 ⊕ www.lesbauxdeprovence.com. **Nîmes** ⊠ 6 rue Auguste, 30000 ☎ 04–66–58–38–00 🖷 04–66–21–81–04. **Stes-Maries-de-la-Mer** ⊠ 5 av. Van Gogh, 13732 ☎ 04–90–97–82–55 🖷 04–90–97–71–15. **St-Rémy** ⊠ Pl. Jean-Jaurès, 13210 ☎ 04–90–92–05–22 🖷 04–90–92–38–52. **Tarascon** ⊠ 59 rue Halles, 13151 ☎ 04–90–91–03–52 🖷 04–90–91–22–96.

Village of Gordes

WORD OF MOUTH

"A friend of mine told me that she'd been disappointed in Provence. When she explained what she'd seen, her French seat mate said she'd missed the best part—the Luberon!"

—KathyO

"The lavender fields around the Abbaye de Sénanque are truly gorgeous, and because they aren't commercial fields, will be blooming most of July. In May and June, you'll also be treated to fields of red poppies, beautiful as well."

—PB

WELCOME TO THE VAUCLUSE

Lavender

TOP 5
Reasons to Go

1. **The walled city of Avignon:** While most exciting in July, the theater festival at the Palais des Papes, Avignon is surprisingly youthful and vibrant year-round.

2. **Châteauneuf-du-Pape:** Probably the most evocative Côtes du Rhône vineyard but just one of many villages in this area where you can sample exceptional wines.

3. **Lovely lavender:** Get hip-deep in purple by touring the Lavender Route between the Abbaye de Sénanque (near Gordes) and the historic town of Sault.

4. **The high life:** Experience the Luberon's mountaintop villages perchés, set in a patchwork landscape right out of a medieval Book of Hours.

5. **Seeing red in Roussillon:** With its ocher cliffs that change tones—copper, pink, rust—depending on the time of day, this town is a gigantic ruby embedded in the Vaucluse bedrock.

Avignon's most famous bridge—the subject of a French children's song—now stretches only halfway across the river, so don't make the mistake of trying to drive across it. Take the next bridge to **L'Ile de la Barthelasse,** a rural setting minutes from the city where you can ride a bike through vineyards and overnight in lovely auberges.

Avignon

Getting Oriented

The absence of the scantily clad *demoiselles* from Picasso's famous early Cubist painting may dampen your image of Avignon, but this city has plenty to compensate: with medieval streets and crenellated palaces, it is an ideal gateway for exploring the sunscorched vineyards of the Côtes du Rhône and the Roman ruins of Vaison-la-Romaine and Orange; just east are the hilltop villages of the Luberon and Haut Vaucluse.

Haut Vaucluse. Nestled within the shadow of Mont Ventoux, this region is an unending panorama of sights. Ancient Roman ruins are found in **Orange** and **Vaison-la-Romaine**, famous vineyards entice at **Châteauneuf-du-Pape**, and who can resist the gorgeous hilltop villages of **Le Barroux** and **Crillon-le-Brave?**

The Luberon. This is the chic Provence made famous by Peter Mayle—carpeted with lavender fields and once-upon-a-timefied towns like **Gordes, Oppède-le-Vieux, Bonnieux,** and **Lacoste.**

Sorgue Valley. If you're fond of antiques, plan to join the festive hordes trawling for treasures at the famous Sunday flea market in **L'Isle-sur-la-Sorgue.** Enjoy an idyllic lunch by one of the town watermills, then track down the source of the River Sorgue in the famous spring of **Fontaine de Vaucluse.**

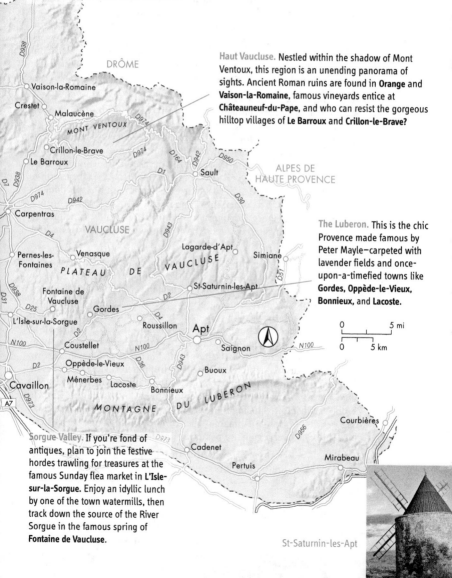

St-Saturnin-les-Apt

Updated by
Rosa Jackson

FOR MANY, THIS IS THE ONLY TRUE PROVENCE: one vast Cézanne masterpiece where sun-bleached hills and fields are tapestries of green-and-black grapevines and silver-gray olives, and rolling rows of lavender harmonize with mountains that loom purple against an indigo sky. It is here, in his beloved Luberon, that British author Peter Mayle discovered and described the simple pleasures of breakfasting on melons still warm from the sun, buying fresh-dug truffles from furtive farmers in smoke-filled bars, and life without socks. The world shared his epiphany, and vacationers now flock here in search of the same sensual way of life, some retreating to lavishly renovated farmhouses with cypress-shaded pools, others heading for the luxurious inns that cater to people fleeing the city's smog. There are budget accommodations, too, in the form of cheerful *chambres d'hôtes* and modest but well-run hotels, which often have very good restaurants. Given the intense summer heat and the distance from the sea, swimming pools and air conditioning are de rigueur, with a few exceptions higher up in the mountains where there is a refreshing breeze.

As if an invisible hand had drawn lines dividing this region into three, the Vaucluse changes character dramatically from north to south, west to east. East of Avignon, you'll find sun-scorched *villages perchés* (perched villages) that lord over the patchwork valleys—Gordes, Bonnieux, Ménerbes, and ocher-tinted Roussillon. Though mass tourism has given them something of a Disney feel, you need only wander off the main shopping drags to get a sense of medieval life in the labryrinthine back alleys and pollard-shaded squares resonant with the splashing of ancient fountains. The otherwise tranquil town of L'Isle-sur-la-Sorgue has become a magnet for international antiques fiends, reaching its peak of activity on Sundays when the entire town turns into a giant *brocante* (antiques fair).

Lying north of Avignon, the Côtes du Rhône produce some of the world's most muscular wines: Châteauneuf-du-Pape and Beaumes-de-Venise are two of the best-known villages, though the names Vacqueyras, Gigondas, and St-Joseph also give wine buffs goose bumps. Despite their renown, this area feels off the beaten track even in midsummer, when it's favored by French rather than foreign tourists. A brisk wind cools things off in summer, as do the broad-leaved plane trees that shade the sidewalk tables at village restaurants and cafés. East of here, the countryside grows increasingly dramatic, first with the jaw-droppingly jagged Dentelles de Montmirail, whose landscape is softened by olive groves and orchards, then the surprisingly lush Mont Ventoux, best known as the Tour de France's most difficult stage. Along the way, you'll find villages such as Séguret and Vaison-la-Romaine where you can sample the slow-paced local lifestyle over a game of pétanque or a lingering apéro.

And all this lies a stone's throw from thriving Avignon, its feudal fortifications sheltering a lively arts scene and a culture determinedly young.

Exploring the Vaucluse

Avignon as well as the Roman centers and papal vineyards to its north lie in arid lowlands, and getting from point to point through these flats can be uninspiring. It's to the east that the real Vaucluse rises up into the green-studded slopes of Mont Ventoux and the Luberon. Here, the back roads are beautiful—the temptation to abandon your rental car in favor of foot travel is often irresistible. Give in; the combination of the smells of wild thyme, lavender, wet stone, and dry pine can be as heady as a Châteauneuf-du-Pape. Anchored by the magnificent papal stronghold of Avignon, the glories of the Vaucluse region spread luxuriantly eastward of the Rhône. Its famous vineyards seduce connoisseurs, and its Roman ruins in Orange and Vaison-la-Romaine draw scholars and arts lovers. Plains dotted with orchards of olives, apricots, and cherries give way, around formidable Mont Ventoux, to a rich and wild mountainous terrain, then flow into the primeval Luberon, made a household name by Peter Mayle.

Avignon is a must, and if you're a wine lover, you'll enjoy exploring the vineyards north of it. If you're a fan of things Roman, you need to see Vaison-la-Romaine and Orange. The antiques market in L'Isle-sur-la-Sorgue makes for a terrific Sunday excursion, as does the nearby Fontaine-de-Vaucluse, a dramatic spring cascade (outside drought season). But the Luberon and its villages perched high up in the hills are a world of their own and worth allowing time for—perhaps even your whole vacation. Note that the Pont du Gard, the superbly preserved Gallo-Roman aqueduct, is just a 30-minute drive west of Avignon, and that Arles, Nîmes, and the windswept Camargue (⇨ Chapter 1) are only a stone's throw to the south and west.

Numbers in the text correspond to numbers in the margin and on the Vaucluse and Avignon maps.

About the Restaurants & Hotels

As the cultural capital of the Vaucluse, Avignon might logically be considered the culinary capital, too. Visit during the July theater festival, however, and you'll have the opposite impression. Sunny sidewalk tables spill out temptingly onto the streets, but nearly all serve the kind of food designed for people on tight schedules: salads, pizzas, and charcuterie plates, often of indifferent quality. For more generous and imaginative Provençal food, you will have to seek out Avignon's few culinary gems or scour the countryside, where delightful meals can be had in roadside restaurants, renovated farmhouses, and restaurants with chefs whose talents are as stunning as hilltop settings they operate in. Be sure to indulge in the sun-drenched local wines from the Luberon, the Côtes du Ventoux, and the Côtes du Rhône (especially its lesser-known vineyards), and if a full bottle seems too much for two people, order one of the 50 cl bottles now popular here (the equivalent of two-thirds of a regular bottle). It pays to do research—too many restaurants, especially in summer, are cynically cashing in on the thriving tourist trade, and prices are generally high.

One of the most popular vacation regions in France, after the seaside, the Vaucluse has a plethora of sleek and fashionable converted *mas* (farmhouses), landscaped in lavender, cypress, and oil jars full of vivid flowers. Given the crushing heat in high summer, the majority have swimming pools and, these days, air-conditioning (but it's wise to check ahead if you're counting on it). However, only a few provide *moustiquaires*, mos-

PLEASURES & PASTIMES

THE SKY'S NO LIMIT! Although there are pretty villages perchés (hilltop villages) throughout the south of France, the Luberon has a surprising concentration of them, some less gentrified (therefore more atmospheric) than others. Gordes, Ménerbes, Roussillon, and Bonnieux have become boomtowns in real estate and tourism but still retain their original honey-gold stone, and the majesty of their extraordinary positions overlooking the countryside is unassailable. Others that are less well known—Seguret, Le Barroux, Mormoiron, Caromb—offer less to buy and eat, but allow you to experience the quiet isolation of these ancient retreats; around Mont Ventoux, it's worth it to turn off toward whatever cluster of hilltop houses catches your eye. Trust your instincts and wander.

GRAPE EXPECTATIONS. The most serious wine center in the south of France is the southern portion of the Côtes du Rhône, home to the muscular reds of Gigondas, Vacqueyras, Rasteau, Cairanne, and of their more famous neighbor Châteauneuf-du-Pape, as well as the fruity Grenache-based rosé of Tavel. Nearby Beaumes-de-Venise famous for its sweet, light muscat. Not to be overlooked are the wines of the Côtes du Ventoux and the Côtes du Luberon, with up-and-coming, often inexpensive reds and rosés and a notable white from Lourmarin. You can visit most vineyards and buy directly from the producer without an appointment. If you find that slightly intimidating or impractical, most wine-making towns have a shop where local wines are sold at the producer's price, with no mark-up.

ON THE MENU. The Vaucluse is the home of the famous Cavaillon melon, that globe of juicy pulchritude that hefts in the hand of marketing matrons, who turn and inspect them with the expertise of an Antwerp jeweler. The right melon, once found and sliced, yields like butter, releases a rich, perfumed nectar onto the cutting board, and melts on the tongue. Half the size of a cantaloupe and twice as flavorful, these melons are labeled, tissue-wrapped, and stacked in market pyramids of acrobatic proportion. Eating them, whether draped with a veil of musky *jambon cru* (cured ham) or cupping a pool of ruby port, is a summer ritual throughout Europe, but especially on the melon's native turf, where they're sold so fresh and unshippably ripe they seem ready to burst.

When the undulating rows of green that spread through the Sorgue Valley's fertile fields aren't yielding melons, they're nurturing prize asparagus, fat stalks of purple-tipped white bound in bands of red, white, and blue. Pampered under mounds of cool earth away from the rays of light that would cause photosynthesis and ruinous traces of green, these albino beauties retain a pure, sweet flavor and enough juice to run down your chin. Unlike the shriveled exports that wither in city supermarkets around the world, the local product is smooth and plump, and once its barky skin is stripped off (time-consuming but indispensable), it's as tender as, well, the local melon. In season (early March–May) restaurants go asparagus-crazy, some offering multicourse menus based entirely on this regional treasure.

Olives, of course, figure large in the Vaucluse culinary scene, from the ubiquitous tapenade (olive and caper spread) on toast to the requisite bowl of the pungent black ovals served with your aperitif. But the real attention-getter here is the truffle, snuffled up beneath Luberon oaks by trained pigs and dogs who are driven wild by their smell. The Vaucluse produces 74% of all truffles sold commercially in France; even more are sold in backroom deals, as though they were smuggled drugs. Vaucluse chefs showcase the truffle in humble ways, the better to highlight its redolent charms. The classic vehicle is a simple *omelette aux truffes.*

MARKETS. Browsing through the *marché couvert* (covered food market) in Avignon is enough to make you renounce dining in the tempting local restaurants; its seafood, free-range poultry, olives, and produce cry out to be gathered in a basket and cooked in their purest form. And the village open-air markets, which are carefully scheduled to cover in turn all the days of the week, including the St-Michel ramparts on Saturday and Sunday and the Place Crillon on Friday, are a visual feast as well.

But food plays second fiddle at one of the most famous markets in Provence. L'Isle-sur-la-Sorgue draws crowds of bargain hunters and collectors to its Sunday antiques and *brocante* (collectibles) fair, strung in picturesque disarray along its water mills and canals. The best pickings in linen sheets, silverware, engravings, pewter, oak furniture, and quirky collectibles can be had if you arrive early, though the after-lunch stroll-and-browse is a fashionable tradition.

VESTIGES OF THE PAST. Though France is full of ancient treasures, there's an extraordinary concentration of them in the Vaucluse. Way back when, dragon's head galleys sailed in from Phocaea, Greece, Rome, and Africa, and the colonizers lost little time in conquering the entire region. The south of France flourished in the glory days of Athens and Alexandria, and by the time Julius Caesar conquered the coast it had been long since well tamed. The best Roman ruins in this region are in Vaison-la-Romaine, where a theater, grand villas, and an entire village complete with boutiques and early toilet systems remain in skeletal form (efficiently constructed; they used fresh water to sweep out raked troughs). In Orange the magnificent theater has retained its great stone stage wall and still serves as an inspiring venue for the summer opera festival.

Avignon's Old Town still stands within the 14th-century wall that protected its rebellious popes from angry skeptics; the popes' luxurious palace crowns the city center. And the magnificently preserved Romanesque Abbaye de Sénanque, outside Roussillon, seems to float in a sea of lavender.

But the most unusual and fascinating antiquities in the Vaucluse are the tiny stone beehive huts called *bories,* of mysterious origin but built in the same, unchanging manner since the Iron Age. Some 3,000 are scattered over the hillsides of the Luberon and environs, and an entire village has been reconstructed outside Gordes.

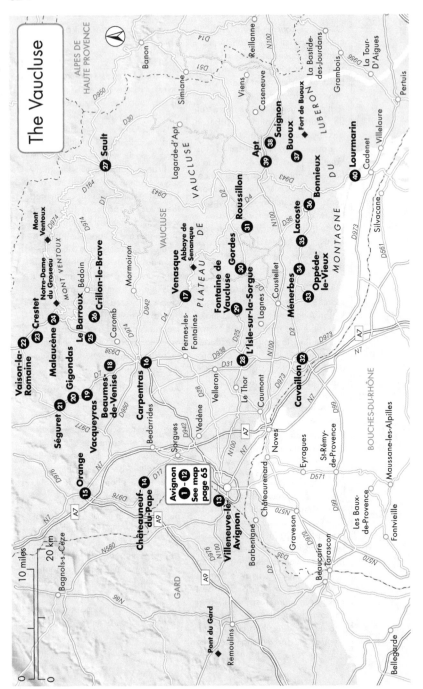

The Vaucluse

ALPES DE HAUTE PROVENCE

Banon

Simiane

Reillanne

La Bastide-des-Jourdans

La Tour-D'Aigues

Grambois

Pertuis

Villelaure

Viens

Caseneuve

Sault **27**

Lagarde-d'Apt

VAUCLUSE

Saignon **38**

Fort de Buoux ◆

LUBERON

Apt **39**

Buoux **37**

Lourmarin **40**

Cadenet

Silvacane

Bonnieux **36**

Mont Ventoux ◆

Notre-Dame du Groseau ◆

Crestet **23**

Malaucène **24**

Bédoin

MONT VENTOUX

Le Barroux **25**

Crillon-le-Brave **26**

Caromb

Mormoiron

PLATEAU DE VAUCLUSE

Roussillon **31**

Lacoste **35**

DU

Gordes **30**

Venasque **17**

Abbaye de Sénanque ◆

Oppède-le-Vieux **33**

Ménerbes **34**

MONTAGNE

Fontaine de Vaucluse **29**

L'Isle-sur-la-Sorgue

Coustellet

Cavaillon **32**

Vaison-la-Romaine **22**

Séguret **21**

Gigondas **20**

Vacqueyras **19**

Beaumes-de-Venise **18**

Carpentras **16**

Bedarrides

Pernes-les-Fontaines

Lagnes

Le Thor

Caumont

Velleron

Vedène

BOUCHES-DU-RHÔNE

Orange **15**

Châteauneuf-du-Pape **14**

Sorgues

Avignon **1–12** See map page 65

Villeneuve-lès-Avignon **13**

Noves

Eyragues

St-Rémy-de-Provence

Maussane-les-Alpilles

Barbentane

Graveson

Les Baux-de-Provence

Fontvieille

GARD

Châteaurenard

Beaucaire

Tarascon

Bagnols-s-Cèze

Pont du Gard ◆

Remoulins

Bellegarde

10 miles

20 km

quito netting put over the bed or window screens to keep out trouble-some flies. Reservations are essential most of the year, and many hotels close down altogether in winter. For information on *gîtes* (houses offered as vacation rentals) and *chambres d'hôtes* (bed-and-breakfasts in private homes), check out the Lodging section in the Smart Travel Tips chapter.

WHAT IT COSTS In euros				
	$$$$	**$$$**	**$$**	**$**	**¢**
RESTAURANTS	over €30	€23–€29	€18–€22	€12–€17	under €11
HOTELS	over €191	€121–€190	€81–€120	€51–€80	under €50

Restaurant prices are per person for a main course at dinner; note that if a restaurant offers only prix-fixe meals, it has been given the price category that reflects the full set-price. Hotel prices are for a standard double room in high season, including tax (19.6%) and service charge. Assume all hotel rooms have air-conditioning, telephones, TV, and private bath, unless otherwise noted. Hotels operate on the European Plan (EP, with no meal provided) unless we note that they use the Breakfast Plan (BP). Some hotels also offer other meal plan options, such as Modified American Plan (MAP, with breakfast and dinner daily, known as *demi-pension*), or Full American Plan (FAP, or *pension complète*, with three meals a day). Inquire when booking if these all-inclusive meal plans (which always entail higher rates) are mandatory or optional during peak season dates.

Timing
High heat and high season hit in July and August with a wallop: this lovely region is anything but undiscovered, thanks in part to Peter Mayle's revelations (he took a break from Provence to avoid the crowds he inspired, then relocated to the quieter south face of the Luberon). June and September are still intense, but better. Low season falls between mid-November and mid-March, when many restaurants and hotels take two or three months off. That leaves spring and fall: if you arrive after Easter, the flowers are in full bloom, the air cool, and the sun warm, and you'll still be able to book a table on the terrace. The same goes for October and early November, when the hills of the Luberon turn rust and gold, and game choices figure on every menu.

AVIGNON

Of all the monuments in France—cathedrals, châteaux, fortresses—the ancient city of Avignon (pronounced ah-veen-*yonh*) is one of the most dramatic. Wrapped in a crenellated wall punctuated by towers and Gothic slit windows, its old center stands distinct from modern extensions, crowned by the Palais des Papes (Popes' Palace), a 14th-century fortress-castle that's nothing short of spectacular. Standing on the Place du Palais under the gaze of the gigantic Virgin that reigns from the cathedral tower, with the palace sprawling to one side, the bishops' Petit Palais to the other, and the long, low bridge of childhood song fame stretching over the river ("Sur le pont d'Avignon on y danse tous en rond . . ."), you can beam yourself briefly into the 14th century, so complete is the context, so evocative the setting.

Yet you'll soon be brought back to the present with a jolt by the skateboarders leaping over the smooth-paved square. Avignon is anything but a museum; it surges with modern ideas and energy and thrives within its ramparts as it did in the heyday of the popes—like those radical church lords, sensual, cultivated, cosmopolitan, with a taste for lay pleasures. For the French, Avignon is almost synonymous with its theater festival in July—thousands pack the city's hotels to bursting for the official festival and "Avignon Off," the fringe festival with some 700

> **TRIP TIP**
>
> Should you make the daring move of showing up without a hotel reservation during the July theater festival, go straight to the tourist office where last-minute vacancies are posted every day (try to arrive in the morning). Keep in mind that hotels raise their prices during the festival; it can be worthwhile to stay outside Avignon, on the lovely Ile de la Barthelasse for instance, and drive (or cycle) into town.

shows. If your French isn't up to a radical take on Molière, look for the English-language productions, or try the circus and mime—there are plenty of shows for children, and street performers abound.

Avignon was transformed into the Vatican of the north when political infighting in the Eternal City drove Pope Clement V to accept Philippe the Good's invitation to start afresh. In 1309 his entourage arrived, preferring digs in nearby priories and châteaux; in 1316 he was replaced by Pope John XXII, who moved into the bishop's palace (today the Petit Palais). It was his successor Pope Benedict XII who undertook construction of the magnificent palace that was to house a series of popes through the 14th century. During this holy reign Avignon evolved into a sophisticated, cosmopolitan capital, attracting artists and thinkers and stylish hangers-on. Founded in 1303, the university burgeoned, with thousands of the faithful from across Europe making the pilgrimage. As the popes' wealth and power expanded, so did their formidable palace. And its sumptuous decor was legendary, inspiring horror and disdain from the poet Petrarch, who wrote of "towers both useless and absurd that our pride may mount skyward, whence it is sure to fall in ruins." The abandoned Italians dubbed Avignon a "second Babylon."

After a dispute with the king, Pope Gregory XI packed up for Rome in 1376, but Avignon held its ground. On his death in 1378, the French elected their own pope, Clement VII, and the Great Schism divided the Christian world. Popes and antipopes abused, insulted, and excommunicated each other to no avail, though the real object of dispute was the vast power and wealth of the papacy. When the king himself turned on the last antipope, Avignon lost out to Rome and the extravagant court dispersed.

Though it is merely the capital of the Vaucluse these days, Avignon's lively street life, active university, and colorful markets present a year-round spectacle far beyond the 800-plus productions on view during the summer Avignon Theater Festival. To take it all in, see the city's steep streets via the tourist train, a type of tram car that resembles a children's party ride (⊕ www.petittrainavignon.com). Two trains, each following

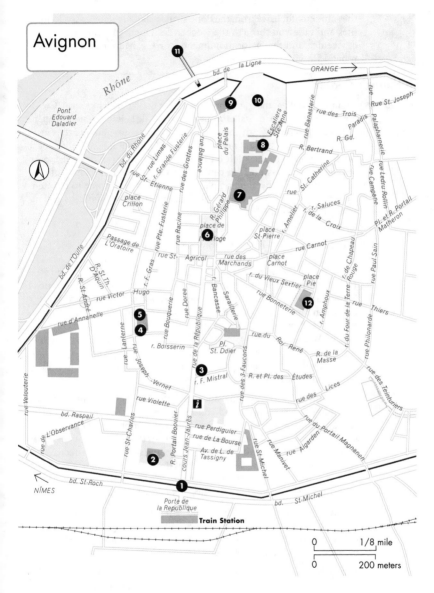

Avignon

the same circuit, leave from the Pope's Palace Square daily every 15 minutes and take you through the Rocher des Doms gardens, the historic city center, and the major monuments, for €7, March 15 through October 15.

The Historic Center

A GOOD
WALK

Begin your walk at the train station (there's a good parking garage). Crossing the busy ring road, walk through the Porte de la République, an opening in **Les Remparts** ❶, the magnificent ramparts surrounding the entire Old Town. Head straight north up Rue de la République. Past the post office on your left, duck left into a backstreet and peek into the **Espace St-Louis** ❷, a 17th- and 18th-century retreat that retains its magnificent courtyard shaded by gigantic plane trees. Today it's home to the Centre National du Théâtre (National Theater Center) and the hotel-restaurant Cloître St-Louis.

At the corner of Rue Joseph-Vernet, stop in at the tourist office for maps and information. A block up from the tourist office, a lovely little 17th-century Jesuit chapel shelters a fascinating jumble of classical stonework in the **Musée Lapidaire** ❸. Double back and turn right (west) onto Rue Joseph-Vernet; two blocks up, you can stop into the tiny, eccentric **Musée Requien** ❹, with its very personal displays on natural history. Next door, don't miss the **Musée Calvet** ❺, a Neoclassical stone mansion housing a collection of 17th- and 18th-century French art, much of it created in Avignon. Continue up Joseph-Vernet to Rue St-Agricol, and follow it right into the animated heart of the city, the **Place de l'Horloge** ❻, anchored by the imposing 19th-century Hôtel de Ville and its Gothic Tour de l'Horloge (Clock Tower).

Tear yourself away from the sidewalk cafés, merry-go-round, jugglers, and mimes on the square and continue north to Place du Palais. Walk straight up the square and bear left until you're opposite the entry gate, so you can take in the full, wide-angle view of the magnificent **Palais des Papes** ❼. After an hour or two touring the awesome interior, recross the square to study the magnificent facade of the Hôtel des Monnaies, a heavily sculpted Baroque masterpiece from the 17th century. Then cut across to the relatively humble but evocative **Cathédrale Notre-Dame-des-Doms** ❽.

At the far end of Place du Palais, the **Petit Palais** ❾—once home to Avignon's bishops and the first of its resident popes—houses a marvelous collection of Italian paintings, much of it (coincidentally) from the era of the popes and antipopes themselves.

Leave the square and climb up Montée du Moulin into the **Rocher des Doms** ❿, a serene hilltop garden park replete with sculptures and black swans a-swimming. From here you can look out over the city, the palace, and the river to the ancient enemy of papal Avignon, the fortified town of Villeneuve. Above all, you'll be able to take in the famous **Pont St-Bénézet** ⓫ in its stunted state and imagine dancers turning *tous en rond* (round and round). From the park, you can climb down past the Tour de Chiens in the ramparts to reach the bridge; or cut behind the Petit Palais.

Follow the scenic Escaliers Ste-Anne down and head right on Rue Ba-
nasterie, but don't let the shops lining the winding backstreets around
Place Carnot keep you from stopping in to salivate over the delicious
goods in **Les Halles** ⑫, the indoor market on Place Pie (pronounced *pee*).

A good investment is the *Avignon Passion*: you pay full price for the
first site/monument you visit and thereafter there are various reductions
on all the other sites, depending on which of them you visit. The 15-
day pass, available at the tourist office, gives discounts of 20%–50%
on visits to every site in Avignon and Villeneuve-lez-Avignon.

TIMING If you spend the morning in the Popes' Palace and visit either the Musée
Calvet or the Petit Palais in the afternoon, you can see these basics in a
day of light sightseeing. (Note that the Petit Palais is closed on Tuesday.) If you're pressed, make a beeline for the Palace, then climb the Rocher
des Doms for an overview that takes in the famous bridge.

Sights to See

❽ **Cathédrale Notre-Dame-des-Doms.** First built in a pure Provençal Romanesque style in the 12th century, then dwarfed by the extravagant
palace beside it, this relatively humble church rallied in the 14th century with a cupola—which promptly collapsed. As rebuilt in 1425, it's
a marvel of stacked arches with a strong Byzantine flavor and is topped
nowadays with a gargantuan Virgin Mary lantern—a 19th-century afterthought—that glows for miles around. The Baroque styling in the nave
dates from 1670. That's the tomb of Pope John XXII in the center-left
chapel—but not his likeness, as his *gisant* (recumbent funeral statue) was
wrecked in the Revolution and replaced with the likeness of a mere bishop,
which he was before he rose to infamy. ⊠ *Pl. du Palais*
☎ *04–90–86–81–01* ☉ *Mid-June–mid Sept., daily 7:30–6; mid-Sept.–mid-
June, daily 7:30–7.*

❷ **Espace St-Louis.** This graceful old 17th-century Jesuit cloister has been
converted for office use by the well-known Avignon Festival—a performing arts event which lasts most of the month of July. The cloister's symmetrical arches (now enclosed as the sleek hotel Cloitre St-Louis) are
shaded by ancient plane trees. You can wander around the courtyard
after you've picked up your festival information. Occasional exhibits
are held inside as well. ⊠ *20 rue du Portail Boquier* ☎ *04–90–14–14–60*
⊕ *www.festival-avignon.com* ☉ *June 13–July 7, weekdays 9–1 and
2–5; July 8–27, daily 9–1 and 2–5.*

⑫ **Les Halles.** By seven every morning (except Monday) the merchants and
artisans have stacked their herbed cheeses and arranged their vine-
ripened tomatoes with surgical precision in pyramids and designs that
please the eye before they tease the salivary glands. This permanent covered market is as far from a farmers' market as you can get, each booth
a designer boutique of *haute de gamme* (top-quality) goods, from jewel-
like olives to silvery mackerel to racks of hanging hares worthy of a Flemish still life. Even if you don't have a kitchen to stock, consider enjoying
a cup of coffee or a glass of (breakfast) wine while you take in the sights
and smells and spectacle. ⊠ *Pl. Pie* ☎ *04–90–27–15–15* ☉ *Tues.–Sun.
6 AM–1 PM.*

⑤ Musée Calvet. Worth a visit for the beauty and balance of its architecture alone, this fine old museum holds a rich collection of art, acquired and donated by an 18th-century Avignon doctor who had a hunger for antiquities and an eye for the classically inspired. Later acquisitions are Neoclassical and Romantic, and almost entirely French, including works by Manet, Daumier, and David, such as *La Mort du Jeune Bara* (*The Death of Young Bara*). The main building itself is a Palladian-style jewel in pale Gard stone dating from the 1740s; the garden is so lovely that it may distract you from the paintings. ✉ *65 rue Joseph-Vernet* ☎ *04–90–86–33–84* ⊕ *www.fondation-calvet.org* 🖅 *€6* ✹ *Wed.–Mon. 10–1 and 2–6.*

③ Musée Lapidaire. Housed indefinitely in a pretty little Jesuit chapel on the main shopping street (it will move eventually to a wing of the Musée Calvet), this collection of classical sculpture and stonework highlights funeral stones and works from Gallo-Roman times (1st and 2nd centuries), as well as samples from the Musée Calvet's collection of Egyptian, Greek, and Etruscan works. They are haphazardly labeled and insouciantly scattered throughout the noble chapel, itself slightly crumbling but awash with light. ✉ *27 rue de la République* ☎ *04–90–86–33–84* ⊕ *www.fondation-calvet.org* 🖅 *€2* ✹ *Wed.–Mon. 10–1 and 2–6.*

④ Musée Requien. Don't bother to rush to this eccentric little natural history museum, but since it's next door to the Calvet Museum, and free, you might want to stop in and check out the petrified palm trunks, the dinosaur skeleton, the handful of local beetles and mammals, and the careful and evocative texts (French only) accompanying them. The museum is named for a local naturalist and functions as an entrance to the massive **library** of natural history upstairs. ✉ *67 rue Joseph-Vernet* ☎ *04–90–82–43–51* ⊕ *www.musee.requiem.fr* 🖅 *Free* ✹ *Tues.–Sat. 9–noon and 2–6.*

⑦ Palais des Papes (Popes' Palace). The Renaissance chronicler Jean Froissart called this palace "the loveliest and strongest house in the world," while Petrarch sneered, "The houses of the apostles crumble as (popes) raise up their palaces of massy gold." Within these magnificent Gothic walls, one of the heydays (or low points) in French history took place, a period of extraordinary sacred and secular power and, to skeptics, outrageous wealth. Once densely decorated in tapestries, frescoes, and sumptuous fabrics, it hosted feasts of Lucullan extravagance and witnessed intrigues of Gothic proportion. The pope ruled within as half god, half prince, eating alone at an elevated table in the crowded dining hall, sleeping in a lavishly decorated bedroom distinctly devoid of sacred reference. His chamberlain's bedroom had eight hiding holes, complete with trapdoors concealed under carpets; who knows to what use they were put?

But don't expect to see eye-boggling luxury today. Resentful Revolutionaries hacked away most traces of excess in the 1780s, and, ironically, what remains has a monastic purity. Most of all you may be struck by the scale; either one of its two wings dwarfs the cathedral beside it, and between them they cover almost 50,000 feet of surface. The grand-scale interiors are evocative as well, with a massive wooden barrel vault arching over the dining hall like a boat belly and a kitchen with fireplaces big enough to house a family. The **Grande Audience** (Grand Audience Hall) and the **Grande Chapelle** are as vast as cathedrals.

From your first exterior view of them, note the difference between the two wings of the palace. The north end, toward the cathedral, is the Palais Vieux (Old Palace), a severe Cistercian bastion built by the sober Pope Benedict XII between 1335 and 1342; the south end was built over the next ten years with slightly airier fantasy by Pope Clement VI, who prized his creature comforts.

An enthusiastic patron of the arts, Clement VI brought in a team of artists from Italy to decorate his

> ## HOW TO PLAY THE PALACE
>
> The Palais des Papes is one of those grand, must-see monuments that can be overwhelmed by shutter-popping groups of travelers at times. But it should be seen nonetheless; aim for visiting during opening time, lunchtime, or evenings if you are there in the middle of summer.

digs. It was led by no less than Simone Martini himself, imported from Siena and Assisi (where he had worked with Giotto). On his death, Mattheo Giovanetti took the lead, and the frescoes that covered every surface must have been one of the wonders of the world. Some of the finest traces remain in Clement's study, called the **Chambre du Cerf** (Stag's Room), where the walls still retain the lovely frescoes he commissioned in 1343. Unlike the Raphael masterpieces that decorate the Vatican chambers in Rome, which use lofty classical themes and powerful Christian images, these paintings depict simple hunting scenes: a stag hunt, bird snaring, and fishing. They're graceful, almost naive in style, and intimate in scale, but the attempts at perspective in the deep window frames remind you that this was an advanced center of culture and learning in the 14th century, and perspective was then downright avant-garde, fresh from the sketchbooks of Giotto. Among many fragments, one other example of Giovanetti's work can be viewed in its entirety in **Chapelle St-Jean** (St. John Chapel), a masterpiece of composition in which the interplay of hands and the implied lines of gazes create a silent dialogue.

Though you may be anxious to see the more famous spaces, take time on entering to study the scale model of the palace in its medieval context. Only then can you take in its enormity, looming like Olympus over the tiny half-timber houses that crowded the Place du Palais—a palace worthy of a royal dynasty and a temple to holy hubris.

For wine lovers, there's a wine cellar devoted to Côtes du Rhônes at the **Bouteillerie** (☎ 04–90–27–50–85) of the Popes' Palace where you can sample and buy regional wines; the selection changes every year and the shop is open daily. Although it's in the Palais, you don't need to pay admission to go to the store. ⊠ *Pl. du Palais* ☎ *04–90–27–50–00* ⊕ *www.palais-des-papes.com* ✒ *€9.50 includes choice of guided tour or individual audioguide; €11.50 for combination ticket with Pont St-Bénezet*

⊘ *Nov.–mid-Mar., daily 9:30–5:45; mid-Mar.–July and Oct., daily 9–7 (until 9 during theater festival in July); Aug.–Sept., daily 9–8.*

★ ❾ **Petit Palais** (Small Palace). This former residence of bishops and cardinals houses a large collection of Old Master paintings, the majority of them Italian works from the Renaissance schools of Siena, Florence, and Venice—styles with which the Avignon popes would have been familiar, but it's a coincidence. The paintings were acquired in the 19th century by the extravagant Italian marquis Campana and bought, on his bankruptcy, by Napoléon III. Divided among provincial museums throughout France, they remained scattered until after World War II; then the 300-some treasures were reunited under this historic roof. But even though the works weren't amassed by the popes, as you move through hall after hall of exquisite 14th-century imagery, you'll get a feel for the elevated tastes of the papal era. A key piece to seek out in the 15th-century rooms is Sandro Botticelli's *Virgin and Child,* a masterpiece of tenderness and lyric beauty created in his youth; 16th-century masterworks include Venetian works by Carpaccio and Giovanni Bellini. ⊠ *Pl. du Palais* ☎ 04–90–86–44–58 ⊠ €6 ⊘ *Oct.–May, Wed.–Mon. 9:30–1 and 2–5:30; June–Sept., Wed.–Mon. 10–1 and 2–6.*

❻ **Place de l'Horloge** (Clock Square). This square is the social nerve center of Avignon, where the concentration of bistros, brasseries, and restaurants draws swarms of locals and tourists to the shade of its plane trees. After a play, the doors of the **Théâtre Municipal** open onto the square and the audience spills into the nearest sidewalk café for a post-performance drink. The **Hôtel de Ville** (Town Hall) on the west side of the square was built in the 19th century around its dominating Gothic clock tower, from which the square gets its name.

★ ⓫ **Pont St-Bénezet** (St. Bénezet Bridge). "Sur le pont d'Avignon on y danse, on y danse . . ." Unlike London Bridge, this other fragment of childhood song (and UNESCO World Heritage site) still stretches its arches across the river, but only part way. After generations of war and flooding, only half remained by the 17th century. Its first stones allegedly laid with the miraculous strength granted St-Bénezet in the 12th century, it once reached all the way to Villeneuve. It's a bit narrow for dancing "tous en rond" (round and round) though the traditional place for dance and play was under the arches. For a fee, you can rent an audioguide and climb along its high platform for broad views of the Old Town ramparts. ⊠ *Port du Rhône* ⊠ *€3; €11.50 for combination ticket with Palais des Papes and audioguide* ⊘ *Apr.–Oct., daily 9–7; Nov.–Mar., daily 9–8.*

❶ **Les Remparts** (The Ramparts). More than 4 km (2½ mi) long, these protective crenellated walls and towers were built by the popes in the 14th century to keep out rampaging brigands and mercenary armies attracted by legends of papal wealth. It's extraordinarily well preserved, thanks in part to the efforts of architect Viollet-le-Duc, who restored the southern portion in the 19th century. Modern-day Avignon roars around its impervious walls on a noisy ring road that replaced a former moat.

⑩ Rocher des Doms (Rock of the Domes). This ravishing hilltop garden, with statuary and swans under grand Mediterranean pines and subtropical greenery, would be a lovely retreat by itself, but its views make it extraordinary. From side to side you can look over the palace, the rooftops of Old Avignon, the St. Bénezet Bridge, and formidable Villeneuve across the Rhône. On the horizon loom Mont Ventoux, the Luberon, and Les Alpilles. ☒ *Montée du Moulin, off Pl. du Palais* ☒ *Free.*

Where to Eat & Stay

$$$$ ✕ **Christian Etienne.** Known as the pope of Avignon cooking, Christian

Fodor'sChoice   Etienne is ensconced in a 12th-century building next to the Palais des

★   Papes with a fabulous terrace overlooking the theatrical square. Eating here is tantamount to a religious experience, especially if you opt for the €60 tomato menu, available only from June–September, whose seven courses range from the apparently simple (tomato tartare) to the extravagant (foie gras with tomato petals and tomato jus with orange). If you're seeking to satisfy sophisticated tastes on a budget, the prix fixe lunch menu for €30 could be the answer to your prayers. ☒ *10 rue de Mons* ☎ *04–90–86–16–50* ⊕ *www.christian-etienne.fr* ⚏ *Reservations essential* ☰ *AE, DC, MC, V* ☺ *Closed Sun. and Mon. (open daily during the theater festival).*

★ $$$$ ✕ **La Mirande.** Whether you dine under the 14th-century coffered ceilings, surrounded by Renaissance tapestries, or in the intimate garden under the Popes' Palace walls, the restaurant of the luxurious Hôtel de la Mirande transports you to another time. Daniel Hebet, the former chef, now runs his own restaurant on L'Isle-sur-la-Sorgue, but chef Sébastien Aminot has kept the standard high with dishes such as red Mediterranean tuna with marinated vegetables, and squab with black olives and gnocchi. Foodies, take note: the restaurant's cooking school, Le Marmiton, invites guest chefs to teach casual, multilingual cooking classes for six to twelve people around the kitchen table, followed by a feast—and there are classes for children, too. ☒ *Pl. de la Mirande* ☎ *04–90–85–93–93* ⊕ *www.la-mirande.fr* ⚏ *Reservations essential* ☰ *AE, DC, MC, V* ☺ *Closed Tues., Wed., and 3 wks in Jan.*

$$$ ✕ **Compagnie des Comptoirs.** Glassed into the white-stone cloister, this chic brasserie sports a theatrical dell'arte decor with a long, narrow fountain down the center of the courtyard terrace, a young, laid-back waitstaff, and a cool bar. The cooking is French fusion with international influences created by twin chefs Laurent and Jacques Pourcel—this is a member of their worldwide chain of bistros dedicated to former French trading posts. The Saint-Jacques (scallops) with Serrano ham on a bed of lettuce hearts is one of their most lauded dishes. ☒ *83 rue Joseph-Vernet* ☎ *04–90–85–99–04* ⊕ *www.lacompagniedescomptoirs.com* ☰ *AE, DC, MC, V* ☺ *Closed Sun. and Mon. (open daily during theater festival).*

$$$ ✕ **La Fourchette.** It doesn't have a terrace, but La Fourchette can be forgiven this small flaw given the quality of the cooking—this is probably Avignon's best-value restaurant, and it's a short walk from the Place de l'Horloge. Philippe Hiely doesn't get too complicated with his €29 prix fixe menu, preferring to perfect the classics of Provençal cooking, such as marinated sardines and a daube *d'agneau* (lamb stew) made in the local style with white wine, anchovies, capers, and gherkins. The high-backed wooden chairs and white tablecloths give the dining room a charming old-fashioned feel. ✉ *17 rue Racine* ☎ *04–90–85–20–93* 🖃 *MC, V* ⊘ *Closed weekends and 3 wks in Aug.*

$$–$$$ ✕ **La Vieille Fontaine.** Summer-evening meals around the old fountain and boxwood-filled oil jars in the courtyard would be wonderful with *steak-frites* alone, but combine this romantic backdrop with stellar southern French cuisine and you have a special event. Give yourself over to rack of lamb in garlic and thyme sauce, morel-stuffed ravioli with truffle sauce, the best regional wines, and an army of urbane servers—and hope for moonlight. It's in the lovely old Hôtel d'Europe. ✉ *12 pl. Crillon* ☎ *04–90–14–76–76* ⊕ *www.heurope.com* ⬥ *Reservations essential* 🖃 *AE, MC, V* ⊘ *Closed Sun.–Mon.; last 2 wks in Aug.; and last wk in Nov.*

$$ ✕ **Restaurant Brunel.** Stylishly decorated in a modern style, this local favorite is helmed by Avignon-born and -bred chef Robert Brunel. Its down-home bistro cooking showcases a sophisticated larder: parchment-wrapped mullet with eggplant and tomatoes, chicken roasted with garlic confit (preserves), and caramelized apples in tender pastry. It's down a quiet street just east of the Popes' Palace. ✉ *46 rue de la Balance* ☎ *04–90–27–16–00* ⬥ *Reservations essential* 🖃 *MC, V* ⊘ *Closed Sun. and Mon. (Sun. only during theater festival).*

$–$$ ✕ **L'Epicerie.** L'Epicerie doesn't have great gastronomic pretensions, but the cheerful food, hip waiters, and perfect terrace in the quiet, cobbled Place St-Pierre make it a local favorite. Order a tapas plate (which might include goat cheese flan, tomato crumble, fougasse (flatbread) with ratatouille, melon with cured ham) or a steak with *vraies frites* (real, chunky French fries), and soak up the atmosphere with the help of some well-chosen local wine. ✉ *10 pl. St-Pierre* ☎ *04–90–82–74–22* 🖃 *MC, V* ⊘ *Closed Sun. and Nov.–Mar. (open daily during theater festival).*

★ $ ✕ **Le Grand Café.** Behind the Popes' Palace, in a massive former factory—a setting of carefully preserved industrial decay—this hip entertainment complex combines an international cinema, a bar, and this popular bistro. Gigantic 19th-century mirrors and dance festival posters hang on crumbling plaster and brick, and votive candles half-light the raw metal framework—an inspiring environment for intense film talk and a late supper of foie gras, goat cheese, or marinated artichokes, with some dishes served in terra-cotta *tajines* (domed stew pots). ✉ *La Manutention, 4 rue des Escaliers Ste-Anne* ☎ *04–90–86–86–77* 🖃 *MC, V* ⊘ *Closed Mon. and Sun. Aug.–June.*

¢ ✕ **Simple Simon.** Since the 1970s, this quaint (there is no other word for it) English tearoom—dark wooden beams, teapots on shelves, a table laden with cakes and pies—has catered to homesick expats and locals, who are intrigued by the pieman's tempting wares and the properly brewed teas served in silver pots. Owned since the beginning by a Frenchwoman whose mother was English, it's a real ode to British tradition, with hot dishes such as shepherd's pie, cheese-and-onion crumble tart, or turkey hotpot at lunch. During the theater festival, it's also open for dinner.

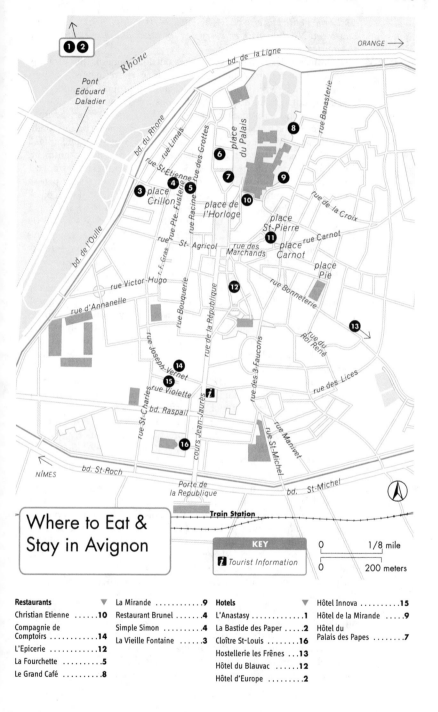

Where to Eat & Stay in Avignon

KEY

i Tourist Information

| 0 | 1/8 mile |
| 0 | 200 meters |

Restaurants ▼

Christian Etienne **10**
Compagnie de
Comptoirs **14**
L'Epicerie **12**
La Fourchette **5**
Le Grand Café **8**
La Mirande **9**
Restaurant Brunel **4**
Simple Simon **4**
La Vieille Fontaine **3**

Hotels ▼

L'Anastasy **1**
La Bastide des Paper **2**
Cloître St-Louis **16**
Hostellerie les Frênes . . .**13**
Hôtel du Blauvac **12**
Hôtel d'Europe **2**
Hôtel Innova **15**
Hôtel de la Mirande **9**
Hôtel du
Palais des Papes **7**

⊠ *29 rue Petite Fusterie* ☎ *04–90–86–62–70* ▭ *MC, V* ⊘ *Closed Sun. and Mon. No dinner (open every day for lunch and dinner during the theater festival).*

★ **$$$$** ✕▦ **Hostellerie les Frênes.** Five minutes outside Avignon, this adorably charming 19th-century country house combines the refinement of Louis XV furnishings with modern touches and all-around elegance. The mansard-roofed main house—which looks like it could have stood in for the Germonts' Provence residence in *La Traviata*—has rooms adorned with antiques and heirlooms; those in the annex are done in bright, south-ern-Provençal style. There are whirlpool baths in every room and a small spa with sauna. Better yet, the manicured park is a total enchantment, studded with one of the prettiest pools in Provence. The restaurant serves innovative twists on regional dishes such as the roasted pigeon cooked in grapes and Châteauneuf-du-Pape, or beef roasted with black olives and chickpeas. ⊠ *645 av. des Vertes-Rives, 84140 Montfavet, 5 km [3 mi] outside Avignon* ☎ *04–90–31–17–93* 🖷 *04–90–23–95–03* ⊕ *www.lesfrenes.com* ⇆ *12 rooms, 4 suites, 2 apartments* ⅄ *Restaurant, pool, sauna, in-room hot tubs, gym, in-room data ports, Wi-Fi in rooms, some pets allowed* ▭ *AE, DC, MC, V* ⊘ *Closed Nov. 15–Mar.*

$$$$ ▦ **Hôtel de la Mirande.** Arguably Avignon's loveliest hotel, this famous
Fodor'sChoice landmark exults Provence in all its 18th-century charm and splendor.
★ A former cardinal's palace (set, in fact, just below the Palais des Papes), it has been superbly restored, with interiors richly decorated with ex-quisite reproduction chintzes and toiles de Jouy and beeswax-buffed an-tiques—the Salon Rouge is a jewel lined with red-and-lime silk and warmed by chandeliers and comfy chairs covered with paisley shawls *à la anglaise*. The enclosed garden is a breakfast and dinner oasis, the central lounge a skylit and jazz-warmed haven. Guest rooms are both beautiful and comfortable and the luxurious marble bathrooms have deep soaking tubs and elegant touches. Half the rooms face the garden, the other half the palace facade; a few even have tiny balconies with rooftop views. If you're driving, get detailed directions; the entrance is tricky to find by car. ⊠ *Pl. de la Mirande, 84000* ☎ *04–90–85–93–93* 🖷 *04–90–86–26–85* ⊕ *www.la-mirande.fr* ⇆ *19 rooms, 1 suite* ⅄ *Restaurant, bar, parking (fee)* ▭ *AE, DC, MC, V.*

★ **$$$–$$$$** ▦ **Cloître St-Louis.** Standing serene and noble within its sturdy 16th-cen-tury walls, this sleek hotel encloses a magnificently cloistered courtyard lined with grand old plane trees. In this cloister setting, you can enjoy meals served in summer, with a market-inspired menu during the week and a popular buffet lunch on Sundays. The early Baroque building, erected by the Jesuits in 1611, was first a theological school for novi-tiates and later a hospital, before it became a hotel. Now interiors are stripped and modernist (especially those in a wing newly designed by Jean Nouvel), playing up the cool old stone. There's a small roof-top pool, and the hotel is a block's walk from the train station. ⊠ *20 rue du Portail-Boquier, 84000* ☎ *04–90–27–55–55* 🖷 *04–90–82–24–01* ⊕ *www.cloitre-saint-louis.com* ⇆ *80 rooms* ⅄ *Restaurant, pool, bar, cable TV, in-room data ports, parking (fee)* ▭ *AE, DC, MC, V.*

$$$–$$$$ ▦ **Hôtel d'Europe.** Napoléon slept here, and so did Robert and Elizabeth Browning, Picasso, and Jacqueline Onassis, and any number of artists and writers, right up to the theater luminaries who stay here today. This 16th-century home, built by the Marquis of Graveson, still has some historic vibes—along with modern amenities such as Wi-Fi internet access. With hyperclassic decor and a seasoned staff, this place will attract festival goers for centuries to come. The pricier guest rooms are vast, with two suites overlooking the Popes' Palace, but there are also smaller rooms for those on tighter budgets. The downside? The room decor is so "18th-century"–generic you might feel you're in any hotel from Paris to Lille. Happily, the restaurant, La Vieille Fontaine, allures with fine wood paneling and remains one of Avignon's finest. Beware, however the startling cost of breakfast (€23). ⊠ *12 pl. Crillon, 84000* ☎ *04–90–14–76–76* 🖷 *04–90–14–76–71* ⊕ *www.heurope.fr* 🛏 *41 rooms, 3 suites* ♻ *Restaurant, Wi-Fi in lobby and in some rooms, some pets allowed* ▭ *AE, DC, MC, V.*

$$ ▦ **La Bastide des Papes.** It's hard to believe that this idyllic island on the Rhône, called the Ile de la Barthelasse, is just a 10-minute drive from the center of Avignon. At the ocher-hued, gray-shuttered country house of La Bastide des Papes, you can borrow a bike and cycle among the pear orchards and vines, cool off in the pool and whip up your own dinner in the well-equipped kitchen to enjoy on the terrace—you might even be tempted to skip Avignon altogether. The name is not merely for show—a pope's family inhabited the oldest part of the house in the 15th century. Each of the five impeccably decorated rooms (think *Elle Decor* or *Marie Claire Maison*) is named after a pope, and the newest part of the house dates from the 19th century. The pool is lovely. ⊠ *352 chemin des Poiriers, 84000* ☎ *04–90–86–09–42* 🖷 *04–90–82–38–30* ⊕ *www. bastidedespapes.com* 🛏 *5 rooms* ♻ *Pool; no a/c, no room phones* ▭ *AE, DC, MC, V* ⵏ◎⎮ *BP.*

$–$$ ▦ **Hôtel du Palais des Papes.** This third-generation family-run institution is a notably solid and comfortable place—all the better for its location just off the Place du Palais. Rooms pair exposed stone and beams, updated with ironwork furniture and rich fabrics, with modern tile baths. A film-set Louis XIII restaurant downstairs is more for honeymooners than gastronomes, although it has been serving local Provençal food for the past 100 years. ⊠ *3 pl. du Palais, 84000* ☎ *04–90–86–04–13* 🖷 *04–90–27–91–17* ⊕ *www.hotel-avignon.com* 🛏 *27 rooms, 1 suite* ♻ *Restaurant, bar, cable TV, in-room data ports, some pets allowed; no a/c in some rooms* ▭ *AE, MC, V.*

$ ▦ **L'Anastasy.** On the Ile de la Barthelasse (7 km/4 mi from Avignon), this pretty farmhouse inn has country-fresh rooms, home cooking, and an interesting social mix if you care to mingle: Madame Manguin lets guests withdraw or join in as they like, whether during meals, poolside chats, or while having drinks in the cozy kitchen-salon. Modest-priced meals (not included) are prepared on advance request only; cooking lessons can be arranged as well. Breakfast costs €10 extra. ⊠ *Ile de la Barthelasse, 84000, follow signs for "L'Anastasy" (the owners' home is across the road from Manguin)* ☎ *04–90–85–55–94* 🖷 *04–90–82–59–40* ⊕ *www.olga-manguin.com* 🛏 *5 rooms* ♻ *Pool, some pets allowed; no room phones, no room TVs, no a/c in some rooms* ▭ *No credit cards* ⵏ◎⎮ *BP.*

★ $ ⊞ **Hôtel du Blauvac.** Just off Rue de la République and Place de l'Horloge, this 17th-century nobleman's home has been divided into 16 guest rooms, many with pristine exposed stonework, and lovely tall windows that look, alas, onto backstreet walls. Pretty fabrics and a warm, familial welcome more than compensate, however. It's a simple budget hotel (no elevator, no air-conditioning) and utterly charming. ⊠ *11 rue de la Bancasse, 84000* ☎*04–90–86–34–11* 🖷*04–90–86–27–41* ⊕*www.hotelblauvac.com* 🖙 *16 rooms* ♿ *Cable TV; no a/c* ☱ *AE, DC, MC, V.*

¢ ⊞ **Hôtel Innova.** You may feel like a student boarder in this modest budget lodging; but rooms are big and clean and freshly decorated, all have a phone and most have a TV. All have their own miniature bathroom fit neatly into a closet; and friendly owner Ghislain is on hand to welcome and look after you. It's just up the street from the Musée Calvet. ⊠ *100 rue Joseph-Vernet, 84000* ☎ *04–90–82–54–10* 🖷 *04–90–82–52–39* ✍*hotel.innova@wanadoo.fr* 🖙 *11 rooms, 9 with shower only* ♿ *Cable TV; no a/c* ☱ *MC, V.*

Nightlife & the Arts

Small though Avignon is, its inspiring art museums, strong university, and 60-some years of saturation in world-class theater have made the city an antenna for the arts south of Paris. Held annually in July, the Avignon festival, known officially as the **Festival d'Avignon** (☎ 04–90–14–14–14 ⊕ www.festival-avignon.com), has been bringing the best of world theater to this ancient city since 1947. Some 800 productions—some official, others "off" and "off-off"—take place every year; the prestigious, big-budget showpiece every year is held in the *cour d'honneur,* the courtyard of the Palais des Papes. You can get information about the unofficial performances at the Web site for **le festival OFF** (⊕ www.avignon-off. org)—tickets go on sale in May (and don't delay in placing your order).

> Overflowing with traveling players and audiences of every kind, the city takes on the look of a medieval fête or a grand party thrown by Clement VII during the July theater festival.

A winter festival, **Les Hivernales** (☎04–90–82–33–12 ⊕ www.hivernales-avignon.com), celebrates French contemporary dance every January and February. Its central venue is **La Manutenation** (⊠ Rue Escalier Ste-Anne ☎ 04–90–82–33–12).

For information on events and tickets, too, stop into the massive book-and-record chain **FNAC** (⊠ 19 rue de la République ☎04–90–14–35–35).

La Manutenation is a cultural complex on Rue Escalier Ste-Anne. It includes the cinema **Utopia, La Grande Café,** the contemporary dance association **Les Hivernales,** and the jazz club **Ajme** (☎ 04–90–86–08–61).

NIGHTLIFE Within its fusty old medieval walls, Avignon teems with modern nightlife well into the wee hours. The **Bistrot du Cinéma** (⊠ 4 rue Escalier Ste-Anne ☎ No phone) serves drinks in a dark, intimate space just outside the cinema in La Manutention. **Pub Z** (⊠ 58 rue Bonneterie ☎04–90–85–42–84) is the hot spot for rock, sometimes live; the black-and-white interior incorporates a zebra theme. **Le Rouge Gorge** (✉ 10 bis rue Peyrollerie ☎ 04–90–14–02–54) presents a dinner show with singers, dancers, and comedians and after-dinner dancing every Friday and Saturday night. On other nights other comedy and music groups perform.

THE ARTS Two cinema complexes show first-run, mainstream movies in *v.o.* (*version originale,* meaning in the original language with French subtitles). **Cinéma Utopia** (✉ 4 rue Escalier Ste-Anne ☎ 04–90–82–65–36) shows hard-to-find international independent works. **République** (✉ 5 rue Figuière ☎ 04–90–82–65–36) is a popular cinema.

At **AJMI** (Association Pour le Jazz et la Musique Improvisée; ✉ 4 rue Escaliers Ste-Anne ☎ 04–90–86–08–61), in La Manutention entertainment complex, you can hear jazz performed by artists of some renown.

Shopping

Avignon is too big and too resident-oriented to be full of tourist-aimed boutiques; instead, it has a cosmopolitan mix of French chains, youthful clothing shops (it's a college town), and a few plummy dress shops. **Rue des Marchands,** off Place Carnot, is one shopping stretch, but **Rue de la République** is the main artery. Dominating the main drag is trendy, cheap-chic clothing store **Zara** (✉ 25 rue de la République ☎ 04–90–80–64–40).

If you're hungry for books in English, find **Shakespeare** (✉ 155 rue Carreterie ☎ 04–90–27–38–50); in addition to new and used books in English, it has a tearoom, café, and terrace.

If you're a fan of fine French cookware, head to **Jaffier-Parsi** (✉ 42 rue des Fourbisseurs ☎ 04–90–86–08–85), a professional cooking supply store that has been stocking heavy copper pots, stainless-steel ladles, mortar-and-pestle sets, and great knives since 1902. Among the myriad vendors of Provençal pottery throughout the region, **Terre et Provence** (✉ 26 rue République ☎ 04–90–85–56–45) maintains a high esthetic standard, with lovely pitchers, platters, and tureens.

All those famous, gorgeous Provençal fabrics can be found at **Souleïado** (✉ 5 rue Joseph-Vernet ☎ 04–90–86–47–67). More goods made from the signature printed fabrics can be found at Souleïado's competitor **Les Olivades** (✉ 28 rue Marchands ☎ 04–90–86–13–42).

Mouret Chapelier (✉ 20 rue Marchands ☎ 04–90–85–39–38) has a cornucopia of old-fashioned, old-world, and marvelously eccentric hats in a jewel-box setting.

HAUT VAUCLUSE

Situated north and northeast of Avignon, this land of rolling orchards and vineyards spreads lazily at the foot of Mont Ventoux, redolent of truffles, lavender, and fine wine. Perhaps that's why the Romans so firmly established themselves here, erecting grand arenas and luxurious villas that still in part remain. From Avignon head north into the vineyards, making a brief tour of Châteauneuf-du-Pape, even if you don't stop to

CLOSE UP

Du Bon Vaing pour Votre Sangté

AS MUCH AS IT IS IDENTIFIED with olives and cypress trees, the Provençal landscape is defined by the retreating perspective of row on rocky row of gnarled grapevines, their green shoots growing heavy through the summer and by fall sagging under the weight of ripe fruit. Although Provence has a few fine wines—notably the lower Rhône greats such as Châteauneuf-du-Pape and Beaumes-de-Venise and a few excellent whites from Cassis, Bandol, and Palette—the majority of wine drunk here is unpretentious, sunny stuff, with the most by far being rosé. Red or rosé, it is usually drunk icy-cold, whether to quench arid thirsts or to hide a less than rounded finish.

There are several subregions of southern wines. In the eastern Languedoc, above the Camargue, spreads the region known as Costières-de-Nîmes, and a straightforward table wine from the Côtes-du-Luberon appears on every Vaucluse table, alongside the equally unpretentious Côtes-du-Ventoux. But generally from the Rhône eastward—most heavily focused in the Haut Var behind Saint-Tropez—the wines fall under the undemanding umbrella title of Côtes de Provence. Remember that in these parts the word *vin* (wine) twangs through the nose like a broken banjo string and sounds more like *vaing*. *Santé* (to your health)!

drink and buy wine. Orange is just up the highway; though the town isn't the most picturesque, its Roman theater is a must-see. Between Orange and Mont Ventoux are wine centers (Beaumes-de-Venise, Gigondas, Vacqueyras) and picturesque villages such as Crestet, Séguret, Le Barroux, and Malaucène, which the first French pope preferred to Avignon. Visit Vaison-la-Romaine for a strong concentration of Roman ruins.

Villeneuve-lez-Avignon

★ ⑬ *2 km (1 mi) west of Avignon.*

Just across the Rhône from Avignon, this medieval town glowers at its powerful neighbor to the east. Its abbey, fortress, and quiet streets offer a pleasant contrast to Avignon's bustle.

In the 14th century Villeneuve benefited enormously from the migration of the popes into Avignon, as an accompanying flood of wealthy and influential cardinals poured over the river. No fewer than 15 of the status-seeking princes of the church built magnificent homes on this neighboring hilltop—in truth, some simply requisitioned mansions from other owners, giving these "freed" town palaces the unfortunate moniker *livrées cardinalices*. In addition, kings Philip the Fair and Louis VIII built up formidable defenses on the site to keep an eye on the papal territories.

However, it was the bounty and extravagant lifestyles of the cardinals that nourished the abbey here, known as **Chartreuse du Val-de-Bénédiction** or, literally, the Charterhouse of the Valley of Blessings. Inside the abbey are spare cells with panels illuminating monastic life, the vast 14th-century **cloître de cimetière** (cemetery cloister), a smaller Romanesque cloister, and, within the remains of the abbey church, the Gothic tomb of Pope Innocent VI. Theatrical events are staged here during Avignon's annual theater festival. ☎ *04–90–15–24–24* ✉ *€6.10* ⊘ *Apr.–Sept., daily 9–6:30; Oct.–Mar., daily 9:30–5:30.*

At the top of the village is the **Fort St-André,** which once ostensibly protected the town of St-André, now absorbed into Villeneuve. The fortress's true importance was as a show of power for the kingdom of France in the face of the all-too-close Avignon popes. You can explore the fortress grounds and the bare ruined walls of inner chambers for free (there's a good view from the Notre Dame de Belvézet church within the fort walls); you can also climb (for a fee) into the twin towers for broad views over Avignon, the Luberon, and Mont Ventoux. Don't miss the fortress's formal Italianate **gardens** (☎ *04–90–25–55–95*), littered with remains of the abbey that preceded the fortifications. Admission to the gardens, which are privately owned, is €4. They are open Tuesday through Sunday 10–12:30 and 2–6. ☎ *04–90–25–45–35* ⊕ *www. monum.fr* ✉ *Towers: €4* ⊘ *Apr.–Sept., daily 10–12:30 and 2–6; Oct.–Mar., daily 10–12 and 2–5.*

★ Below the abbey, the **Musée Pierre de Luxembourg** gives you access to one of the luxurious, 14th-century cardinals' manors. Here you'll find a notable collection of art, including the spectacularly colorful and richly detailed *Couronnement de la Vierge (Coronation of the Virgin)*, an altarpiece painted in 1453 by Enguerrand Quarton. One of the greatest paintings of the 15th century, it shows rows and rows of Avignonnais hieratically sitting around the figures of God the Father and God the Son. Depicted by Quarton—the leading painter of the Avignon School—as identical twins, they bless Mary and hover over a surreal landscape that places Montagne St-Victoire in between Heaven and Hell. ☎ *04–90–27–49–66* ⊕ *www. gard-provencal.com/musees/pdluxem.htm* ✉ *€3* ⊘ *Apr.–Sept., Tues.–Sun. 10–12:30 and 3–7; Oct.–Mar., Tues.–Sun. 10–12 and 2–5:30.*

Châteauneuf-du-Pape

⑭ *18 km (11 mi) north of Avignon, 22 km (13½ mi) west of Carpentras.*

The countryside around this famous wine center is a patchwork of rolling vineyards, of green and black furrows striping the landscape in endless, retreating perspective. Great gates and grand houses punctuate the scene, as symmetrical and finely detailed as the etching on a wine label, and signs—discreet but insistent—beckon you to follow the omnipresent smell of fermenting grapes to their source. Behind barn doors, under cellar traps, and in chilly caves beneath châteaux, colossal oak vats nurture this noble Rhône red to maturity. The pebbly soil here is particularly suited to the growth of vines: The small stones act like a wool sweater, retaining the heat of the sun's rays and keeping the vines warm and cozy during the night.

Once the source of the table wine of the Avignon popes, who kept a fortified summer house here (hence the name of the town, which means "new castle of the pope"), the vineyards of Châteauneuf-du-Pape had the good fortune to be wiped out by phylloxera in the 19th century. The wine's revival as a muscular and resilient mix of up to thirteen varietals moved it to the forefront of French wines, with an almost porklike intensity (it can reach 15% alcohol content). The whites, though less significant, are also to be reckoned with. To learn more about local wine production, stop in at the **Musée du Vin Caveau Brotte Père Anselme,** a private collection of tools and equipment displayed in the *caveau* (wine cellar) of the Brotte family. ⊠ *Rte. d'Avignon* ☎ *04–90–83–70–07* ⊕*www.brotte.com* 🖅*Free* ☉ *Daily 9–noon and 2–6.*

There are *caves de dégustation* (wine-tasting cellars) on nearly every street; get a free map of the caves from the tourist office on Place du Portail. Also head to the discreet *vignobles* (vineyards) on the edge of town. Some of the top Châteauneufs (and the oldest) come from Domaine de la Nerthe, Château de Vaudieu, and Château Fortia, and are priced accordingly. If you're not armed with the names of a few great houses, look for *medaille d'or* (gold medal) ratings from prestigious wine fairs; these are usually indicated by a gold sticker on the bottle. If you're disinclined to spend your holiday sniffing and sipping, climb the hill to the ruins of the **Château.** Though it was destroyed in the Wars of Religion and its remaining donjon (keep) blasted by the Germans in World War II, it still commands a magnificent position. From this rise in the rolling vineyards, you can enjoy wraparound views of Avignon, the Luberon, and Mont Ventoux.

Where to Eat & Stay

$–$$ ✕ **Le Verger des Papes.** It's well worth the slog up the hill to the château simply to linger on the terrace of this long-established restaurant and savor the view over Mont Ventoux, Avignon, the Luberon, and the Rhône. The Estenevins have lived in Châteauneuf-du-Pape for three generations and Philippe and Jean-Pierre took over the restaurant from their parents a few years ago. Dishes such as cod with saffron-scented vegetables and grilled leg of lamb with eggplant and tomato reveal their love for the region's cuisine, and you can visit the restaurant's well-stocked wine cellar on your way to the top. ⊠ *Rue Montée du Château* ☎ *04–90–83–50–40* ⊕ *www.vergerdespapes.com* 🖃 *MC, V* ☉ *Closed Dec. 20–Mar. 1. No dinner from Nov.–May and Sun. June–Sept.*

$ ✕ **Le Pistou.** Study the blackboard menu here for satisfying Provençal specialties, such as whole herb-roasted dorade (a small Mediterranean fish), baked basil lamb wrapped in zucchini with a light white wine sauce, or the pistou (a thick Provençal vegetable-pesto soup). The welcome is warm, the interior has been recently dressed up with colorful tablecloths, fresh paint, and pictures, and the prix-fixe menus start cheap. ⊠ *15 rue Joseph-Ducos* ☎ *04–90–83–71–75* 🖃 *AE, MC, V* ☉ *Closed Mon. No dinner Sun.*

$ ✕⊞ **La Garbure.** With four modest rooms decked in jewel tones upstairs and a tiny formal dining room downstairs, this intimate hotel offers a romantic, slightly old-fashioned stopover. The cooking aims for the haute rather than the hearty, with dishes like red mullet fillets with olives, coq au vin made with Châteauneuf-du-Pape, and a heady sorbet of Marc de Châteauneuf-du-Pape, the eau-de-vie made of local grapes. You can dine here without staying over, but make sure to reserve in advance, since seating is limited. ✉ *3 rue Joseph-Ducos, 84230* ☎ *04–90–83–75–08* 🖷 *04–90–83–52–34* ⊕ *www.la-garbure.com* ⇄ *8 rooms* ⌂ *Restaurant, cable TV, some pets allowed; no room phones* ▤ *AE, MC, V* ⊗ *Closed mid-Nov.–mid-Dec.*

Orange

⑮ *12 km (7 mi) north of Châteauneuf-du-Pape, 31 km (19 mi) north of Avignon.*

Even less touristy than Nîmes (⇨ Chapter 1) and just as eccentric, the city of Orange (pronounced oh-*rawnzh*) sprawls somewhat gracelessly over the Rhône flatlands. Its hotels and restaurants have a vaguely bohemian air—eclectic decors, patchwork menus—and its insular attitude offers little of the easy grace of the rest of the Vaucluse. The air of neglect may be due in part to efforts to boycott the city since the election of a far-right-leaning government. Nonetheless it draws thousands every year to its ★ spectacular **Théâtre Antique,** a colossal Roman theater built in the time of Caesar Augustus. The vast stone stage facade, bouncing sound off the facing hillside, climbs four stories high—Louis XIV famously called it "the greatest wall in my kingdom"—and the niche at center stage contains the original statue of Augustus, just as it reigned over centuries of productions of classical plays. The theater has a seating capacity of 9,000; from its last row

UNDER THE STARS

To witness the torches of *Nabucco* or *Aïda* flickering against the 2,000-year-old Roman wall of the Théâtre Antique and to hear the extraordinary sound play around its semicircle of ancient seats is one of the great summer festival experiences in Europe. Every July and the first week in August, **Les Chorégies d'Orange** (☎ 04–90–34–24–24 ⊕ www.choregies.asso.fr ✉ Chorégies, B.P. 205, Orange Cedex 84107) echo tradition and amass operatic and classical music spectacles under the summer stars in Orange. Be sure to book tickets well in advance; they go on sale the previous October. In addition, Orange hosts a jazz festival, **Orange Se Met au Jazz,** from June 27–July 1 and a classical music festival, **VIe Recontres Classiques d'Orange,** in the second half of July.

atop **Colline St-Eutrope** you can see the ruins of the château of Orange's princes, razed by Louis when he annexed the principality of Orange for France. Today this setting inspires and shelters world-class theater, as well as concerts of dance, classical music, poetry readings, and even rock concerts. Orange's summer opera festival is one of Europe's best, and one of its best-known. ✉ *Pl. des Frères-Mounet* ☎ *04–90–51–17–60*

✍ €7.50 (audio tour included), joint ticket with Musée d'Orange ⊘ Apr., May, and Sept., daily 9–6; Mar. and Oct., daily 9:30–5:30; June–Aug., daily 9–7; Nov.–Feb., daily 9:30–4:30.

Across the street from the theater, the small **Musée d'Orange** displays antiquities unearthed around Orange, including fragments of three detailed marble *cadastres* (land survey maps) dating from the 1st century. Upstairs a vivid series of 18th-century canvases shows local mills producing Provençal fabrics, each aspect illustrated in careful detail. There are also personal objects from local aristocrats and a collection of faïence pharmacy jars. ⊠ *Pl. des Frères-Mounet* ☎ *04–90–51–17–60* ✍ *€7.50, joint ticket with Théâtre Antique* ⊘ *Apr., May, and Sept., daily 9–6; Mar. and Oct., daily 9:30–5:30; June–Aug., daily 9–7; Nov.–Feb., daily 9:30–4:30.*

★ North of the city center and in the middle of modern-day traffic stands the magnificent **Arc de Triomphe** that once straddled the Via Agrippa between Lyon and Arles. Three arches support a heavy double attic (horizontal top) floridly decorated with battle scenes and marine symbols (notably a ship's prow, referring to Augustus's victories at Actium, where he defeated Mark Anthony). The arch commemorates Caesar's triumph over the Gauls, a fact of which the Romans were inordinately proud. The arch, which dates from about 20 BC, is superbly preserved, particularly the north side, but to view it on foot you'll have to cross a roundabout seething with traffic. ⊠ *North of the center on Av. de l'Arc, direction Gap.*

Vieil Orange, the Old Town neighborhood you must cross to hike from one Roman monument to the other, carries on peacefully when there's not a blockbuster spectacle in the theater. Lining its broad squares, under heavy-leaved plane trees, are a handful of shops and a few sidewalk cafés.

Where to Eat & Stay

$–$$ ✕ **Le Yaca.** At this intimate, unpretentious bistro you are greeted by the beaming owner/host/waiter, then pampered with an embarrassment of riches in bargain menu choices (from €13 to €23 for a full meal). The home cooking draws local regulars. Specialties are emphatically *style grandmère*—slow cooked and heavily seasoned—and include rabbit stew, *caillette* (pork-liver meat loaf), and *faux-filet* (steak) with pepper sauce. It's all in a charming stone-and-beam interior, complete with a Gothic archway. ⊠ *24 pl. Sylvian* ☎ *04–90–34–70–03* 🖶 *AE, MC, V* ⊘ *Closed Wed. and Nov. No dinner Tues.*

$$–$$$ 🏨 **Arène.** On a quiet square in the old center, this comfortable hotel is filled with a labyrinth of rooms densely decorated in rich colors and heavy fabrics. The nicest ones look out over the square. As it's been constructed of several fine old houses cobbled together, there's no elevator, but a multitude of stairways instead. ⊠ *Pl. de Langues, 84100* ☎ *04–90–11–40–40* 🖶 *04–90–11–40–45* ⊕ *www.hotel-arene.com* 🛏 *35 rooms* ♻ *Restaurant, in-room data ports, some pets allowed* 🖶 *AE, DC, MC, V.*

★ **$$** ◫ **L'Orangerie.** Hosts Micky and Gérard pour creative energy into this auberge, just 4 km (2½ mi) north of Orange. His artwork, her flamboyant taste, and their mutual world travels have resulted in an eclectic decor. The restaurant's menu reflects their wide-ranging interests as well, as influences from Asia and the Caribbean show up among the Provençal dishes. An annex, **La Mandarine** (☏ 04–90–29–69–69), is just up the road in the open country; the five-room stone mas has a fireplace, a pool, and a library. ✉ *4 rue de l'Ormeau, 84420 Piolenc* ☏ *04–90–29–59–88* 🖷 *04–90–29–67–74* ⊕ *www.orangerie.net* ⬎ *5 rooms* ⚄ *Restaurant, in-room data ports, some pets allowed; no a/c* ▭ *AE, MC, V* ⊘ *Closed 2 wks in Jan.–Feb.* ¡◎¡ *BP.*

$–$$ ◫ **Hôtel Lou Cigaloun.** After a short-lived stint as part of a chain, this central hotel was undergoing transformations at press time under a new owner, intent on brightening each room with Provençal fabrics and sponge paint. The service has warmed up, too, and the rooms have modern comforts such as air-conditioning and wireless Internet access. ✉ *4 rue Caristie, 84100* ☏ *04–90–34–10–07* 🖷 *04–90–34–89–76* ⊕ *www.hotel-loucigaloun.com* ⬎ *27 rooms* ⚄ *Room service, cable TV, in-room data ports, Wi-Fi, some pets allowed* ▭ *AE, DC, MC, V.*

Carpentras

⑯ *24 km (15 mi) northeast of Avignon, 24 km (15 mi) southeast of Orange.*

Though its name figures in most highway directions and it serves as a major market crossroads, Carpentras is often bypassed by tourists en route to the Vaucluse's less prominent byways. Yet at its core lies an atmospheric **Centre Historique** (Old Quarter) that bursts into activity every Friday, when the sizable market takes over the narrow, circuitous inner streets. And on winter Fridays, Carpentras draws a steady stream of serious gastronomes in search of the perfect truffle.

> **THE NOSE KNOWS**
>
> Sniff deep, scratch with your thumbnail, and flash your cash—discreetly, of course. Subtle and deliciously dubious, Carpentras's truffle market flourishes on intrigue. Watch out for shady deals, including truffles weighted with buckshot, caked with mud, or painted black.

Once the seat of the bishopric and blessed with gifts from the Avignon popes, old Carpentras tightly encircles the **Cathédrale St-Siffrein,** whose expressive gargoyles loom halfway across the tiny streets around it. Construction on the cathedral began in 1405; the building included a high gallery where the bishop could slip in and out unobserved. The structure's pure Gothic style frames a startlingly Baroque altar, which in turn surrounds a modern stained-glass window. The 15th-century south portal, in a heavy and bombastic Flamboyant Gothic style, is known as the **porte Juive** (Jewish door), through which converted Jews were said to pass on their way to their baptism.

There was, in fact, a sizable Jewish population in Carpentras from the Middle Ages until the Revolution, when the population was 1,500 strong. Banished from the Kingdom of France, the Jews of Provence were protected by the Avignon popes and thrived in relative liberty in Avignon, Cavaillon, and Carpentras. Relative indeed: they were constrained to live within a ghetto, called a *carrière,* whose portals were closed at night. That neighborhood was razed in the 19th century to create the ★ Place de l'Hôtel de Ville. Yet one treasure remains—the **synagogue**. Built in 1367, it's one of the oldest in France. Bathed in light from its clear arched windows, the second-story sanctuary exudes a cool simplicity, a strong contrast to the dark mysticism of its Christian contemporaries. In the basement are spring-fed pools for purification bathing; on the ground floor, there's an oven for baking unleavened bread. ⊠ *Pl. de l'Hotel-de-Ville* ☺ *Mon.–Thurs. 10–noon and 3–5; Fri. 10–noon and 3–4; closed to visitors during Jewish holidays.*

Carpentras has a headily secular draw, too—its **truffle market.** From the last week of November to the end of March, these perfumed black mushrooms, cultivated and dug in the surrounding oak woods, are brought to the Place Aristide Briand and the Café l'Univers and sold in a tense, quiet street exchange, directly from the dealers' baskets. If you're ready to invest the €600 or more per kilo they cost in high season, look for an honest face and pay in cash. But remember, you're not allowed to take them out of the country. A number of restaurants in Carpentras cook up truffle-dominated menus during the season.

Where to Eat & Stay

$ ✕ **Chez Serge.** The setting couldn't be more inviting: an ancient lime tree reigns over a courtyard terrace made colorful with purple parasols, red-painted folding chairs, and cheerful flowerpots. Zinc-topped tables and contemporary art indoors add to the funky feel, as do the young and efficient if not terribly cordial staff. The food drifts from the Mediterranean to the Middle East, with puffy-crusted pizzas and Armenian stuffed vegetables among the specialties. Chef Serge, who is a bit of a personality, hosts a summer truffle fair on Friday mornings from June to August. ⊠ *90 rue Cottier* ☎ *04–90–63–21–24* ▤ *MC, V* ☺ *Closed Sun. and Mon.*

$ ✕ **Le Marijo.** This friendly little Old Quarter bistro with mismatched wooden tables and Provençal tablecloths has become renowned in the area for its local specialties, such as *aïoli* (salt cod with eggs, carrot, zucchini, potato, cauliflower, and garlicky mayonnaise), served only on Fridays, by reservation; saddle of lamb filled with tapenade; truffle dishes in season; and the *tian de Carpentras* (a vegetable flan). Saturday lunch is by reservation only. ⊠ *73 rue Raspail* ☎ *04–90–60–42–65* ▤ *MC, V.*

★ $–$$ ▥ **Hôtel du Fiacre.** Graced with tapestries, period furnishings, and a lovely garden courtyard, this 18th-century hôtel particulier is a grand place for an atmospheric overnight. There are sweet attic rooms with rooftop views across the Old Town maze, plus a grand suite with high molded ceilings and French windows opening over the greenery. Though the plasterwork and bathrooms could use a face-lift, the welcome is warm, the feeling distinctly regional, and the location for sorties into the Vaucluse ideal. ⊠ *153 rue Vigne, 84210* ☎ *04–90–63–03–15* 📠 *04–90–60–49–73* ⊕ *www.hotel-du-fiacre.com* ⇘ *18 rooms* ⌂ *Some in-room data ports, cable TV in some rooms* ☰ *MC, V.*

Venasque

⑰ *12 km (7 mi) southeast of Carpentras, 35 km (22 mi) northeast of Avignon.*

Once the bishopric and capital of Comtat Venaissin, the large agricultural region east of Avignon, Venasque now has a population of only about 675 inhabitants. The village, tucked inside fortified walls, stands proudly on a hill overlooking the Carpentras Plain. With its sweeping views, stonework, and masses of flowers, it's pretty enough to visit for atmosphere alone.

★ But if you're interested in early churches, head straight for the stunning Merovingian **baptistery** behind the Église de Notre-Dame; it dates from the 6th century and is thus one of the oldest religious structures in France. Thought to have been built on the site of a Roman temple, of which you can see columns recycled into chapel form, it retains its Greek-cross shape despite reconstruction in the 11th century. The pure curves of its arches and the simplicity of the decoration perfectly match the serenity of the cliff-top setting, and the ensemble as a whole surpasses its peers in Fréjus, Aix, and Riez. ⊠ €3 ⊙ *Jan.–Mar., daily 9:15–5; Apr.–mid-Oct., daily 9–6; mid-Oct.–mid-Dec., daily 9–5; also Sun. morning mass.*

Where to Eat & Stay

★ $$ ✕🏠 **Auberge de la Fontaine.** You'll climb winding stone stairs to reach this graceful 18th-century house. It's been converted into a clever complex of stylish apartments, each with a bedroom, kitchenette, and fireplace salon. Don't cook in every night, though—the pretty, rustic restaurant merits your full attention, and you can even sign up for three-day cooking classes that include visits to local markets. Chef-owner Christian Soehlke adds sunny Provençal flavors (truffles, thyme flowers) to local lamb and pigeon, and even knows by name the goats that provide his tiny cabri cheeses. There's a ground-floor bistro, too, for lighter meals (salads, airy pâtés, pastries) or the morning papers. ⊠ *84210* ☎ *04–90–66–02–96* 📠 *04–90–66–13–14* ⊕ *www.auberge-lafontaine.com* ⇘ *5 apartments* ⌂ *2 restaurants, kitchenettes, some pets allowed* ☰ *MC, V.*

Beaumes-de-Venise

⑱ *23 km (14 mi) east of Orange, 9 km (5½ mi) north of Carpentras.*

Just west of the great mass of Mont Ventoux, surrounded by farmland and vineyards, is Beaumes-de-Venise, where streets of shuttered bourgeois homes slope steeply into a market center. This is the renowned source of a delicately sweet muscat wine, but if you're tasting, don't overlook the local red wine. Look for **Domaine des Bernardins** (⊠ Av. Castaud ☎ 04–90–62–94–13), a vineyard with a tasting cave, for both.

In the town center you can also buy fruity, unfiltered olive oil produced in the area; it's made in such small quantities that you're unlikely to see it anywhere else. In the sleepy backstreets of the historic center, **Largisoleil** (⊠ Place Pierre Curie ☎ 04–90–65–02–29) sells unusual hand-painted pottery with floral or face motifs.

Beaumes lies at the foot of the **Dentelles de Montmirail,** a small range of rocky chalk cliffs eroded to lacy pinnacles—whence their name *dentelles* (lace). From tiny D21, east of town, you'll find dramatic views north to the ragged peaks and south over lush orchards and vineyards interspersed with olive groves, pine and yew trees. It's a splendid drive, and if you love nature it would be well worth staying in this area—many of the stone houses have been converted into bed-and-breakfasts.

Where to Stay

★ **$–$$** 🏠 **La Treille.** Looking like it's straight out of the pages of a chic shelter magazine, this 18th-century house is the most stylish of the B&Bs in the area, with textured gray walls and an eclectic decor—a four-poster bed in one room, a weathered Moroccan tray serving as a headboard in another. Windows open onto a breathtaking view of the Dentelles de Montmirail, and the stone swimming pool is simply sublime. If you enjoy your independence, opt for one of the three apartments. ⊠ *Route de Malaucène, 84190 Suzette (7 km/4 mi northeast of Beaumes-de-Venise)* ☎ *04–90–65–03–77* 🛏 *3 rooms, 3 apartments* ⚲ *Pool; no a/c, minibars, room phones* ▭ *MC, V* ⚲⚲ *BP.*

Vacqueyras

⓳ *5 km (3 mi) northwest of Beaumes-de-Venise, 16 km (10 mi) northwest of Carpentras.*

Smaller and more picturesque than Beaumes, with stone houses scattered along its gentle slopes, Vacqueyras gives its name to a robust, tannic red wine worthy of its more famous neighbors around Châteauneuf-du-Pape or Gigondas. Wine domaines beckon from the outskirts of town, and the center strikes a mellow balance of plane trees and cascading wisteria, punctuated by discreet tasting shops. Thanks to its consistently rising quality, Vacqueyras was the latest of the Côtes du Rhônes to earn its own appellation—the right to put its village name on the bottle instead of the less prestigious, more generic Côtes-du-Rhône label.

Gigondas

★ **⓴** *3 km (2 mi) north of Vacqueyras, 19 km (12 mi) northwest of Carpentras.*

The prettiest of all the Mont Ventoux Côtes-du-Rhône wine villages, Gigondas is little more than a cluster of stone houses stacked gracefully up a hillside overlooking the broad sweep of the valley below. At the top, a false-front Baroque church anchors a ring of medieval ramparts; from here you can take in views as far as the Cévennes.

Its few residents share one vocation: the production of the vigorous Grenache-based red that bears the village name. At the 41 *caveaux* (tasting caves) scattered through the village and the surrounding country, you're welcome to visit, taste, and buy without ceremony. Pick up a contact list from the tourist office at the village entrance.

Where to Eat & Stay

$$ ✕▦ **Les Florêts.** Winter or summer, Les Florêts makes a romantic hideaway with its full-on view of the Dentelles de Montmirail and a salon centered around a giant white fireplace and body-hugging red armchairs. Guest rooms are equally warm, dressed up with bright colors and antique furniture, and the restaurant is one of the best in the area—try the saddle of lamb roasted with lavender or the red mullet and *brandade de morue* (salt cod paste) with olive oil. À la carte meals are pricey, but set menus start at €24.50. ✉ *Rte. des Dentelles, 84190* ☎ *04–90–65–85–01* 🖷 *04–90–65–83–80* ⊕ *www.hotel-lesflorets.com* 🔿 *15 rooms* ♨ *Restaurant, cable TV, in-room data ports, some pets allowed; no a/c* ⊟ *AE, DC, MC, V.*

Séguret

❷ *8 km (5 mi) northeast of Gigondas, 23 km (14 mi) north of Carpentras.*

Nestled into the sharp rake of a rocky hillside and crowned with a ruined medieval castle, Séguret is a picture-book hill village that is only moderately commercialized. Its 14th-century clock tower, Romanesque St-Denis Church, and bubbling Renaissance fountain highlight steep little stone streets and lovely views of the Dentelles de Montmirail cliffs. Here, too, you'll find peppery Côtes du Rhône for the tasting.

Where to Eat & Stay

$–$$$ ✕▦ **La Table du Comtat.** Clinging to the top of the village and enjoying breathtaking valley views, this 14th-century former hospice now functions as a simple hotel and serious restaurant. Flamboyant chef Franck Gomez may present you with julienned truffle and scrambled eggs served in an eggshell, foie gras poached in anise consommé, or roast pigeon with licorice sauce. Upstairs, eight plain, stucco rooms look over the valley or the pretty garden. The kidney-shaped pool melts into a hillside terrace. ✉ *Just after Pl. de l'Église, 84110* ☎ *04–90–46–91–49* 🖷 *04–90–46–94–27* ⊕ *www.table-comtat.com* 🔿 *8 rooms* ♨ *Restaurant, pool* ⊟ *AE, DC, MC, V* ⊗ *Hotel closed Feb.; restaurant closed Tues. dinner and Wed. Oct.–June.*

★ $ ✕▦ **La Bastide Bleue.** An idyllic youth hostel until a few years ago, this old stone farmhouse is now an unpretentious but enchanting country inn. It's set in a pine-shaded garden court, and its blue-shuttered windows conceal pretty rooms done in stone, pine, and stucco, with bright, artisanal-tiled baths. Downstairs is a low-slung dining room with plank tables by a stone fireplace. Look for fluffy chicken-liver terrine, garlic-roasted lamb, duck breast with honey and rosemary, and lavender-scented crème brûlée. ✉ *La Bastide Bleue, 1 km (½ mi) south of Séguret on D23, 84110* ☎ *04–90–46–83–43* ⊕ *perso.wanadoo.fr/labastide-bleue* 🔿 *7 rooms* ♨ *Restaurant, pool* ⊟ *MC, V* ⊗ *Closed Jan.*

Vaison-la-Romaine

㉒ *10 km (6 mi) northeast of Séguret, 27 km (17 mi) northeast of Orange.*

Fodor'sChoice
★

In a river valley green with orchards of almonds and apricots, this ancient town thrives as a modern market center. The Provençal market on Tuesdays is a major tourist draw (there is also a smaller organic farmers' market on Tuesday and Saturday mornings), as is the five-day food festival in early November. Yet it retains an irresistible Provençal charm, with medieval backstreets, lively squares lined with cafés and, as its name implies, remains of its Roman past. Vaison's well-established Celtic colony joined forces with Rome in the 2nd century BC and grew to powerful status in the empire's glory days. No gargantuan monuments were raised, yet the luxurious villas surpassed those of Pompeii.

There are two broad fields of **Roman ruins,** both in the center of town: before you pay entry at either of the ticket booths, pick up a map (with English explanations) at the **Office de Tourisme** (☎ 04–90–36–02–11), which sits between them. It's open daily 9–12:30 and 2–6:45 from July through August, and Monday through Saturday 9–noon and 2–5:45 from September through June.

> **FAST FORWARD TO THE 1300s**
>
> Take the time to climb up into Vaison's **Haute Ville,** a medieval neighborhood perched high above the river valley. Its 13th- and 14th-century houses owe some of their beauty to stone pillaged from the Roman ruins below, but their charm is from the Middle Ages: a trickling stone fountain, a bell tower with wrought-iron campanile, soft-color shutters, and blooming vines create the feel of a film set of an old town.

★ Like a tiny Roman forum, the **Quartier de Puymin** spreads over the field and hillside in the heart of town, visible in passing from the city streets. Its skeletal ruins of villas, landscaped gardens, and museum lie below the ancient Theater, all of which are accessed by the booth across from the tourist office. Closest to the entrance, the foundations of the **Maison des Messii** (Messii House) retain the outlines of its sumptuous design, complete with a vast gentleman's library, reception rooms, an atrium with a rain-fed pool, a large kitchen (the enormous stone vats are still there), and baths with hot, cold, and warm water. It requires imagination to reconstruct the rooms in your mind (remember all those toga movies from the '50s), but a tiny detail is enough to trigger a vivid image—the thresholds still show the hinge holds and scrape marks of swinging doors. A formal garden echoes a similar landscape of the time; wander under its cypresses and flowering shrubs to the **Musée Archéologique Théo-Desplans.** In this streamlined venue, the accoutrements of Roman life have been amassed and displayed by theme: pottery, weapons, gods and goddesses, jewelry, and, of course, sculpture, including full portraits of the emperor Claudius (1st century) and a strikingly noble nude Hadrian (2nd century). Cross the park behind the museum to climb into the bleachers of the 1st-century **Theater,** which is smaller than Orange's but is still used today for concerts and plays. Across the parking lot is the **Quartier de la Villasse,** where the remains of a lively market town evoke images of main-street shops, public gardens, and grand private homes, complete with floor mosaics. The most evocative image of all is in the *thermes* (baths): a neat row of marble-seat toilets lined up over a raked trough that rinsed waste instantly away. ⊠ *Av. Gén. de Gaulle at Pl. du 11 Novembre* ☎ *04–90–36–02–11* 🖭 *Ruins, museum, and cloister, €7* ⊗ *June–Sept., daily 9:30–6; Mar.–May and Oct., daily 10–12:30 and 2–6; Nov.–Feb., daily 10–noon and 2–4:30. Museum: June–Sept., daily 9:30–6; Mar.–May and Oct., daily 10–12:30 and 2:30–6; Nov.–Feb., daily 10–11:30 and 2–4. Quartier de la Villasse: June–Sept., daily 9:30–6; Mar.–May and Oct., daily 10–12:30 and 2–6; Nov.–Feb., daily 10–noon and 2–4:30.*

In the medieval Haute Ville, stop into the sober Romanesque **Cathédrale Notre-Dame-de-Nazareth,** based on recycled fragments and foundations of a Gallo-Roman basilica. Its **cloister** is the key attraction. Created in the 12th and 13th centuries, it remains virtually unscarred, and its pairs of columns retain their deeply sculpted, richly varied capitals. ⊠ *Av. Jules-Ferry* ⊗ *June–Sept., daily 9:30–6:15; Mar.–May, daily 10–12:30 and 2–6; Oct.–Feb., daily 10–noon and 2–4:30.*

The remarkable single-arch **Pont Romain** (Roman Bridge), built in the 1st century, stands firm across the River Ouvèze; it was one of the few structures to survive the devastating flood that roared through Vaison in 1992, destroying 150 homes and killing 37 people. It's a living testimony to Roman engineering and provokes reflection: had it not been "quarried" for medieval projects, how much of Roman Vaison would still be standing today?

While Vaison has centuries-old attractions, the most popular for Americans may well now be **Patricia Wells's Cooking Classes.** A living monument of Provence, the celebrated food critic first made her name known through posh food columns and *The Food Lover's Guide to France.* Firsthand, she now introduces people to the splendors of French cooking in her lovely farmhouse near Vaison through week-long cooking seminars—luxe ($3,000 a student), eight students only, and set over Madame Wells's own Chanteduc vineyards. The truffle workshop is usually sold out, so book early. ⊕ *www.patriciawells.com.*

FodorśChoice
★

Where to Stay

★ **$$–$$$** 🖭 **Le Beffroi.** Perched on a cliff top in the Old Town, this gracious grouping of 16th-century mansions comes together as a fine hotel. The extravagant period salon leads to curving stone stairs and up to sizable rooms with beamed ceilings and antiques. The corner rooms have wonderful views. By day you can take a dip in the courtyard pool. In season, have dinner on the walled-in terrace, where the sweeping view takes precedence over the decent if unexciting food. The restaurant is a good spot for children thanks to the adjoining garden equipped with a swing set. ⊠ *Rue de l'Évêché, 84110* ☎ *04–90–36–04–71* 🖷 *04–90–36–24–78* ⊕ *www.le-beffroi.com* ➴ *22 rooms* ♨ *Restaurant, pool, some pets allowed; no a/c* ▭ *AE, DC, MC, V* ⊘ *Closed Jan. 20–Feb.*

$$ ⊡ **L'Évêché.** If you want to base yourself in the medieval part of town, stay in one of the four small rooms in this turreted 17th-century former bishop's palace, owned by the friendly Verdiers. The warm welcome and rustic charm—delicate fabrics, exposed beams, wooden bedsteads—have garnered a loyal following among travelers who prefer B&B character to modern luxury. In summer, breakfast is served in a bower of greenery overlooking the Ouvèze Valley. Make sure to look into the groin-vaulted art gallery across the street. ⊠ *Rue de l'Évêché, 84110* ☎ *04–90–36–13–46* 🖷 *04–90–36–32–43* ⊕ *www. eveche.com* ➴ *5 rooms* ♨ *No a/c, no room phones* ▭ *No credit cards* ⵔ⊙⵿ *BP.*

Crestet

㉓ *7 km (4½ mi) south of Vaison-la Romaine.*

Another irresistible, souvenir-free aerie perched on a hilltop at the feet of the Dentelles de Montmirail cliffs and of Mont Ventoux, Crestet has it all—tinkling fountains, shuttered 15th-century houses, an arcaded *place* at the village's center, and a 12th-century castle crowning the lot. Views from its château terrace take in the concentric rings of tiled rooftops below, then the forest greenery and cultivated valleys below that.

Malaucène

㉔ *9 km (5½ mi) southeast of Crestet, 10 km (6 mi) southeast of Vaison-la-Romaine.*

Yet another attractive composition of plane trees, fountains, and *lavoirs* (public laundry fountains), crowned by a church tower with campanile, this sizeable market town began as a fortified church-village. Its 14th-century church follows classic Provence Romanesque form (a broad, vaulted nave, a semicircle apse) and houses an ornate carved-oak organ from the 18th century. The town's nerve center is the Cours des Isnards, where butchers, bakers, and cafés draw commerce from the tiny near-ghost-towns scattered through the countryside. Since Internet cafés are not exactly thick on the ground in these parts, it's good to know about **Net & Cie** (⊠ Av. de Verdun), open Monday–Saturday 9:30–12:30 and 3–6:30.

Just east of town, the **Chapelle Notre-Dame-du Groseau** is all that remains of the mighty 12th-century Benedictine abbey that Pope Clement V preferred as lodging before he settled into Avignon. The cliffs and woodlands are just as wild and wonderful today. This is also a good place to launch a scenic circle drive over the crest of Mont Ventoux (⇨ *below*). ⊠ *Off D974 direction Col des Tempêtes.*

Perched Villages

This region has a bevy of *villages perchés* (perched villages). Each is often often wrapped in a wall and crowned with the two strongest assurances of protection, sacred and secular: a steeple and a watchtower. Nowadays many of the hill towns are nearly ghost towns, though more and more are tapping into the tourist boom. Those closest to the coast and to urban centers—in the Luberon and in Nice's backcountry, in particular—

have become souvenir malls choked with galleries of dubious quality. Yet as the tourist packs rove on in search of authenticity, the other hill towns develop their commerce and find new life. In these, you can still wander aimlessly through the maze of tunnel-like *ruelles* (alleys) and feel the isolation—often idyllic, sometimes harsh—of these eagle's-nest enclaves, high above the world.

Where to Eat & Stay

$ ✕▯ **L'Origan.** Directly on the tree-lined main commercial street, this family-run hotel/restaurant offers simple, comfortable rooms and straightforward, homey cooking. Crisp mesclun with hot goat-cheese toasts, daubes bristling with wild herbs, and homemade fruit tarts are what you should expect. ⊠ *Cours des Isnards, 84334* ☎ *04–90–65–27–08* ☎ *04–90–65–12–92* ⚡ *23 rooms* ⚐ *Restaurant* ▭ *MC, V* ☻ *Restaurant closed mid-Oct.–Mar.*

Le Barroux

㉕ *6 km (4 mi) southwest of Malaucène, 16 km (10 mi) south of Vaison-la-Romaine.*

Fodor'sChoice ★

Of all the marvelous hilltop villages stretching across the south of France, this tiny ziggurat of a town has a special charm. A labyrinth to the past, Le Barroux has more than a whiff of fairy tale in the air, lording over a patchwork landscape as finely drawn as a medieval illumination, luminous as an illustration in a children's book. This aerie has just one small church, one post office, and one tiny old *épicerie* (small grocery) selling canned goods, yellowed postcards, and today's *Le Provençal*. You are forced, therefore, to look around you and listen to the trickle of the ancient fountains at every labyrinthine turn. Houses, cereal-box slim, seem to grow out of the bedrock, closing in around your suddenly unwieldy car.

Its **Château** is its main draw, though its Disney-perfect condition reflects a complete restoration after a World War II fire. Grand vaulted rooms and a chapel date from the 12th century; other halls serve as venues for contemporary art exhibits. Even if you don't go in, climb up to its terrace, where you can gaze across farmlands toward competing châteaux at Crillon and Caromb. ☎ *04–90–62–35–21* ▯ *€3* ☻ *June and Sept., weekends 10–7; July–Aug., daily 10–7.*

Where to Eat & Stay

$ ×⊞ **Les Géraniums.** The owner of this family-run auberge also wears the chef's toque. At the restaurant, take a seat on the broad garden terrace stretching along the cliff side and sample herb-roasted rabbit, a truffle omelet, quail pâté, local cheeses, and a good foie gras in Beaumes-de-Venise muscat (a sweet white wine). Demi-pension is strongly encouraged and highly recommended. Spend the day sightseeing and come back to a modest, peaceful room. New rooms in the annex across the street take in panoramic views. ⊠ *Pl. de la Croix, 84330* ☎ *04–90–62–41–08* 🖷 *04–90–62–56–48* ⤵ *22 rooms* ⌂ *Restaurant, bar; no a/c, no room TVs* ⊟ *AE, DC, MC, V* ⊗ *Closed Jan.–mid-Mar.*

Crillon-le-Brave

㉖ *12 km (7 mi) south of Malaucène (via Caromb), 21 km (13 mi) southeast of Vaison-la-Romaine.*

The main reason to come to this minuscule hamlet, named after France's most notable soldier hero of the 16th century, is to stay or dine at its hotel, the Hostellerie de Crillon-le-Brave. But it's also pleasant—perched on a knoll in a valley shielded by Mont Ventoux, with the craggy hills of the Dentelles in one direction and the hills of the Luberon in another. Today the village still doesn't have even a *boulangerie* (bakery), let alone a souvenir boutique. The village makes a good base camp for exploring the region if you can afford to stay at the hotel; with no other commercial establishments in the village, and little more to visit than a tiny music-box museum and an ocher quarry, you're a captive audience.

Where to Eat & Stay

★ $$$$ ×⊞ **Hostellerie de Crillon-le-Brave.** The views from these interconnected Relais & Châteaux hilltop houses are as elevated as their prices, but for this you get a rarefied atmosphere of medieval luxury. Set on a series of terraces *à l'italienne,* the stone facades—-oh-so-prettily decked out with baby-blue shutters—look out over vineyards and Mont Ventoux. Inside, a cozy-chic southern decor runs throughout, from the book-filled salons to the brocante-trimmed guest rooms. Some rooms have terraces looking out over the surrounding hills and plains. Fountains splash in the garden overlooking the pool. The showpiece of the complex is the Maison Roche—a wonderfully vaulted stone two-story space (once the village school)—where you can sample Philippe Monti's superstylish Mediterranean cooking—smoked dorade (sea bream) with stuffed zucchini flowers, monkfish with wild savory morel mushrooms and eggplant caviar, lamb with green anise. ⊠ *Pl. de l'Église, 84410* ☎ *04–90–65–61–61* 🖷 *04–90–65–62–86* ⊕ *www.crillonlebrave.com* ⤵ *32 rooms* ⌂ *Restaurant, pool, Wi-Fi in lobby; no a/c in some rooms, TV on request only* ⊟ *AE, DC, MC, V* ⊗ *Closed Nov.–Apr.*

Mont Ventoux

In addition to all the beautiful views *of* Mont Ventoux, there are equally spectacular views *from* Mont Ventoux. From Malaucène or any of the

Continued on page 101

Just exactly where does Provence's famous Lavender Route begin? Any number of towns have fields gloriously carpeted with the purple flower, but chances are this particular journey starts back home with your first sight of a travel poster showing hills corduroyed with rows of lilac, amethyst, and mauve. Or when that vial of essence of *Lavandula vera* is passed under your nose and

BLUE GOLD: THE LAVENDER ROUTE

you inhale the wild, pure-blood ancestor of the incense-intense aroma that characterizes all those little folkloric potpourris. Sated with the strong scent of gift-shop soaps and sachets, you develop a longing for the real thing: the fragrance of meadow-soft, mountain-fresh lavender. Well, let your nostrils flare, for your lavender lust is about to be requited.

OUR LAVENDER MAGICAL MYSTERY TOUR

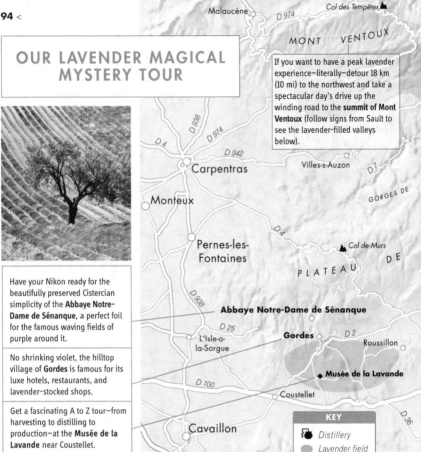

If you want to have a peak lavender experience—literally—detour 18 km (10 mi) to the northwest and take a spectacular day's drive up the winding road to the **summit of Mont Ventoux** (follow signs from Sault to see the lavender-filled valleys below).

Have your Nikon ready for the beautifully preserved Cistercian simplicity of the **Abbaye Notre-Dame de Sénanque**, a perfect foil for the famous waving fields of purple around it.

No shrinking violet, the hilltop village of **Gordes** is famous for its luxe hotels, restaurants, and lavender-stocked shops.

Get a fascinating A to Z tour—from harvesting to distilling to production—at the **Musée de la Lavande** near Coustellet.

KEY
- Distillery
- Lavender field

Provence is threaded by the "Routes de la Lavande" (the Lavender Routes), a wide blue-purple swath that connects over 2,000 producers across the Drôme, the plateau du Vaucluse, and the Alpes-de-Haute-Provence, but our itinerary is lined with some of the prettiest sights—and smells—of the region. Whether you're shopping for artisanal bottles of the stuff (as with wine, the finest lavender carries its own Appellation d'Origine Contrôlée), spending a session at a lavender spa, or simply wearing hip-deep purple as you walk the fields, the most essential aspect on this trip is savoring a magical world of blue, one we usually only encounter on picture postcards.

To join the lavender-happy crowds, you have to go in season, which runs from

Purple haze

Gordes

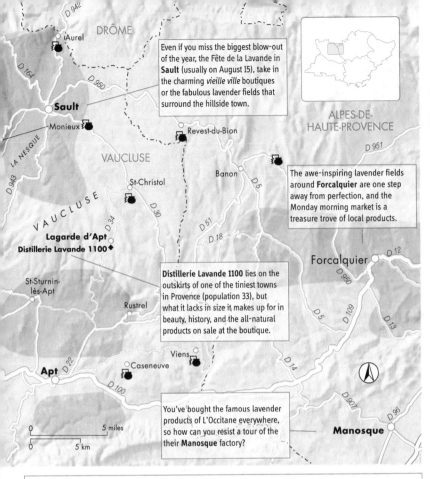

Even if you miss the biggest blow-out of the year, the Fête de la Lavande in **Sault** (usually on August 15), take in the charming *vieille ville* boutiques or the fabulous lavender fields that surround the hillside town.

The awe-inspiring lavender fields around **Forcalquier** are one step away from perfection, and the Monday morning market is a treasure trove of local products.

Distillerie Lavande 1100 lies on the outskirts of one of the tiniest towns in Provence (population 33), but what it lacks in size it makes up for in beauty, history, and the all-natural products on sale at the boutique.

You've bought the famous lavender products of L'Occitane everywhere, so how can you resist a tour of the their **Manosque** factory?

June to early September. Like Holland's May tulips, the lavender of Haute-Provence is in its true glory only once a year: the last two weeks of July, when the harvesting begins—but fields bloom throughout the summer months for the most part. Below, we wind through the most generous patches of lavender. Drive the colorful gambit southeastward (Coustellet, Gordes, Sault, Forcalquier, and Manosque), which will give you good visiting (and shopping) time in a number of the villages that are *fou de la lavande* (crazy for lavender). And for the complete scoop on the hundreds of sights to see in lavender land, contact: **Les Routes de la Lavande** ✉ *2 av. de Venterol, 26111 Nyons* ☎ *04-75-26-65-91* 🖷 *04-75-26-32-67* ⊕ *www.routes-lavande.com.*

Lavender Harvest Festival, Sault

Monday Morning Market, Forcalquier

Abbaye Notre-Dame de Sénanque

DAY 1

SÉNANQUE:
A Picture-Perfect Abbey

An invisible Master of Ceremonies for the Lavender Route would surely send you first to the greatest spot for lavender worship in the world: the 12th-century Cistercian **Abbaye Notre-Dame de Sénanque**, which in July and August seems to float above a sea of lavender, a setting immortalized in a thousand travel posters. Happily, you'll find it via the D177 only 4 km (2½ mi) north of Gordes, among the most beautiful of Provence's celebrated perched villages. An architecture student's dream of neat cubes, cylinders, and pyramids, its pure Romanesque form alone is worth contemplating in any context. But in this arid, rocky setting the gray stone building seems to have special resonance—ancient, organic, with a bit of the *borie* about it. Along with the abbeys of Le Thornet and Silvacane, this is one of the trio of "Three Sisters" built by the Cistercian order in this area. Sénanque's **church** is a model of symmetry and balance. Begun in 1150 and completed at the start of the 13th century, it has no decoration but still touches the soul with its chaste beauty. The adjoining **cloister**, from the 12th century, is almost as pure, with barrel-vaulted galleries framing double rows of discreet, abstract pillars (you'll find no child-devouring demons or lurid biblical tales here). Next door, the enormous vaulted **dormitory** and the **refectory** shelter a display on the history of Cistercian abbeys. The few remaining monks here now preside over a cultural center that presents concerts and exhibitions. The bookshop is one of the best in Provence, with a huge collection of Provençaliana (lots in English). ☎ *04–90–72–05–72* ⊠ *€5* ⊙ *1-hour guided tours of the abbey (in French only) by reservation. Bookshop open Feb.–Oct., Mon.–Sat. 10–6, Sun. 2–6; Nov.–Feb., daily 2–6.*

THE ESSENCE OF THE MATTER

Provence and lavender go hand in hand—but why? The flower is native to the Mediterranean, and grows so well because the pH balance in the soil is naturally perfect for it (pH 6–8). But lavender was really put on the map here when ancient Romans arrived to colonize Provence and used the flower to disinfect their baths and perfume their laundry (the word comes from Latin *lavare*, "to wash"). From a small grass-roots industry, lavender proliferated over the centuries until the first professional distillery opened in Provence in the 1880s to supply oils for southern French apothecaries. After World War I, production boomed to meet the demand of the perfumers of Grasse (the perfume center of the world). Once described as the "soul of Haute-Provence," lavender is now farmed in England, India, and the States, but the harvest in the South of France remains the world's largest.

After spending the morning getting acquainted with the little purple flower at Sénanque, drive south along the D2 (or D177) back to **Gordes**, through a dry, rocky region mixed with deep valleys and far-reaching plains. Wild lavender is already omnipresent, growing in large tracts as you reach the entrance of the small, unspoiled hilltop village, making for a patchwork landscape as finely drawn as a medieval illumination. A cluster of houses rises above the valley in painterly hues of honey gold, with cobbled streets winding up to the village's picturesque Renaissance château, making it one of the most beautiful towns in Provence. Gordes has a great selection of hotels, restaurants, and B&Bs to choose from (see our listings under Gordes, *above*). Spend the early afternoon among tasteful shops that sell lovely Provençal crafts and produce, much of it lavender-based, and then after lunch, head out to Coustellet.

COUSTELLET:
A Great Lavender Museum

Set 2 mi south of Gordes, Coustellet is noted for its **Musée de la Lavande** (take the D2 southeast to the outskirts of Coustellet). Owned by one of the original lavender families, who have cultivated and distilled the flower here for over five generations, this museum lies

If you plan to be at the Musée de la Lavande between July 1 and August 25 you can work up a sweat cutting your own swath of lavender with a copper scythe, then make your own distillation in the museum's lab.

on the outskirts of more than 80 acres of prime lavender-cultivated land.

Not only can you visit the well-organized and interesting museum (note the impressive collection of scythes and distilling apparatus), you can buy up a storm in the boutique, which offers a great selection of lavender-based products at very reasonable prices. ☎ *04–90–76–91–23* ⊕ *www.museedelalavande.co* ✉ *€5* ⊙ *Daily July–Aug., daily 9–7; Sept.–Dec., Mar.–June, daily 9–noon, 2–6.*

There are four main species. True lavender (*Lavandula angustifolia*) produces the most subtle essential oil and is often used by perfume makers and laboratories. Spike lavender (*Lavandula latifolia*) has wide leaves and long floral stems with several flower spikes. Hybrid lavender (*lavandin*) is obtained from pollination of true lavender and spike lavender, making a hybrid that forms a highly developed large round cluster. French lavender (*Lavandula stoechas*) is wild lavender that grows throughout the region and is collected for the perfume industry. True lavender thrives in the chalky soils and hot, dry climate of higher altitudes of Provence. It was picked systematically until the end of the 19th century and used for most lavender-based products. But as the demand for this remarkable flower grew, so did the need for a larger production base. By the beginning of the 20th century, the demand for the flower was so great that producers planted fields of lavender at lower altitudes, creating the need for a tougher, more resistant plant: the hybrid *lavandin*.

Lavender Harvest Festival, Sault

DAY 2

LAGARDE D'APT:
A Top Distillerie

On the second day of your lavender adventure, begin by enjoying the winding drive 34 km (21 mi) east to the town of **Apt**. Aside from its Provençal market, busy with all the finest food products of the Luberon and Haute Provence, Apt itself is unremarkable (even actively ugly from a distance) but is a perfect place from which to organize your visits to the lavender fields of Caseneuve, Viens, and Lagarde d'Apt. Caseneuve (east exit from Apt onto the N100 and then northwest on the D35) and Viens (12 km/7 mi east from Apt on the D209) are small but charming places to stop for a quick bite along the magnificent drive through the rows upon rows of lavender, but if you have to choose between the three, go to the minuscule village of Lagarde d'Apt (12 km/7 mi east from Apt on the D209) and visit the **Distillerie Lavande 1100** (follow signs on the D34). As one of the most important distilleries in the region, this heavenly domain, planted by Maurice Fra

at 1,100 meters altitude, produces primarily lavender but also delves into the realms of other aromatic plants. The picture-perfect stone building rises up like a lighthouse, surrounded by waves of color; aside from admiring the views, you can tour the distillery, learn more about how to cultivate lavender and take your time to browse among the all-natural products that line the shelves of the shop. ☎ 04–90–75–01–42 ✉ Free July 25–Aug. 25 ⊗ Daily 9AM–7PM.

SAULT:
The Biggest Festival

To enjoy a festive overnight, continue northwest from Lagarde d'Apt to the village of **Sault**, 16 km (10 mi) to the northeast. Beautifully perched on a rocky outcrop overlooking the valley that bears its name, Sault is one of the key stops along the Lavender Route. There are any number of individual distilleries, producers, and fields to visit—to make the most of your visit, ask the Office du Tourisme (☎ 04–90–64–01–21, ⊕www.tourism.fr/office-du-tourisme/sault.html) for a list of events. Make sure to pop into the **Cen-**

tre de Découverte de la Nature et du Patrimoine Cynégétique (✉ Av. de l'Oratoire ☎ 04–90–64–13–96 💶 €8) to see the exhibitions on the natural history of the region, including some on lavender. Aim to be in Sault for the not-to-be-missed **Fête de la Lavande** (✉ along the D950 at the Hippodrome le Defends ⊕ www.fetedelalavande.com), a day-long festival entirely dedicated to lavender, the best in the region, and usually held around August 15. Village folk dress in traditional Provençal garb and parade on bicycles, horses leap over barrels of fragrant bundles of hay, and local producers display their wares at the market—all of which culminates in a communal Provençal dinner (€17) served with lavender-based products.

DAY 3

FORCALQUIER:
The Liveliest Market

On your third day, the drive from Sault over 35 km (23 mi) east to Forcalquier is truly spectacular. As you approach the village in late July, you will see endless fields of *Lavandula vera* (true wild lavender) broken only by charming stone farmhouses or discreet distilleries. The epicenter of Haute-Provence's lavender cultivation, **Forcalquier** boasts a lively Monday morning market with a large emphasis on lavender-based products, and it is a great departure point for walks, bike rides, horse rides, or drives into the lavender world that surrounds the town. In the 12th century, Forcalquier was known as the capital city of Haute-Provence and was called the *Cité des Quatre Reines* (City of the Four Queens) because the four daughters (Eleanor of Aquitaine among them) of the ruler of this region, Raimond Béranger V, all married royals. Relics of this former glory can be glimpsed in the Vieille Ville of Forcalquier, notably its Cathédrale Notre-Dame and the Couvent des Corde-

MAKING SCENTS

BLOOMING:

Lavender fields begin blooming in late June, depending on the area and the weather, with fields reaching their peak from the first of July to mid-October. The last two weeks in July are considered the best time to catch the fields in all their glory.

HARVESTING:

Lavender is harvested from July to September, when the hot summer sun brings the essence up into the flower. Harvesting is becoming more and more automated; make an effort to visit some of the older fields with narrow rows—these are still picked by hand. Lavender is then dried for two to three days before being transported to the distillery.

DISTILLING:

Distillation is done in a steam alembic, with the dry lavender steamed in a double boiler. Essential oils are extracted from the lavender by water vapor, which is then passed through the cooling coils of a retort.

liers. However, everyone heads here to marvel at the lavender fields outside town. Contact Forcalquier's Office du Tourisme (✉ 13 pl. Bourguet ☎04–92–75–25–30 ⊕www.forcalquier. com) for information on the lavender calendar, then get saddled up on a bicycle for a trip into the countryside at the town's Moulin de Sarret. Plan on enjoying a fine meal and an overnight stay (reserve way in advance) at the town's most historic inn, the **Hostellerie des Deux Lions** (✉ 11 pl. du Bourguet ☎ 04–92–75–25–30). For a workshop on lavender, meet **Monique Claessens** (☎ 04–92–73–06–76) in the village of Mane but found often at her stand in Forcalquier's Monday market (8 AM–noon).

MANOSQUE:
Love That L'Occitane

Fifteen mi (9 km) south of Forcalquier is Manosque, home to the **L'Occitane** factory. You can get a glimpse of what the Luberon was like before it became so hip—Manosque is certainly not a tourist epicenter—but a trip here is worth it for a visit to the phenomenally successful cosmetics and skin care company that is now the town's main employer. Once you make a reservation, you can take a two-hour tour of the production site, view a documentary film, get a massage with oils, then rush into the shop where you can stock up on L'Occitane products for very reasonable prices. From Manosque you can head back to Apt and the Grand Luberon area or turn south about 52 km (30 mi) to Aix-en-Provence. ✉ *Z. I. St-Maurice* ☎*04–92–70–19–00* ⊕*www. loccitane.com* ☉ *Weekdays 10–noon and 2:30–4:30.*

BRINGING IT HOME

Yes, you've already walked in the pungent-sweet fields, breathing in the ephemeral scent that is uniquely a part of Provence. Visually, there is nothing like the waving fields rising up in a haze of bees. But now it's time to shop! Here are some top places to head to stop and smell the lavender element in local wines, honey, vinegar, soaps, and creams. A fine place to start is the **Ferme Lavanicole Château du Bois** (✉ Les Espanols, Lagarde d'Apt ☎04–90–76–91–23). The **Distillerie Lavande 1100** (✉ follow signs on the D34, Lagarde d'Apt ☎ 04–90–75–01–42), open daily from July 25 to August 25, offers a nice selection of natural products, skin care, and creams. In Gordes and Sault there are lovely Provençal markets that have a wide range of lavender-based products, from honey to vinegar to creams. A great selection of the finest essential oils is available at **Distillerie du Vallon** (✉ Rte. des Michouilles, Sault ☎ 04–90–64–14–83). **L'Occitane** (✉ Z.I. St-Maurice, Manosque ☎ 04–92–70–19–00) is the mother store. In nearby Volx you can hit the **Maison aux Huiles Essentiels** (✉ Z.I. La Carretière, Volx ☎ 04–92–78–46–77) for aromatherapy in all its glory.

SCENT-SATIONAL

2

surrounding hill towns you can take an inspiring circle drive along the base and over the crest of the mountain, following the D974. This road winds through the extraordinarily lush south-facing greenery that Mont Ventoux protects from vicious mistral winds. Abundant orchards and olive groves peppered with stone farmhouses make this one of Provence's loveliest landscapes. Stop for a drink in busy **Bédoin,** with its 18th-century Jesuit church at the top of the Old Town maze.

Mont Ventoux was the site of the first recorded attempt at *l'escalade* (mountain climbing), when Italian poet-philosopher Petrarch grunted his way up in 1336. Although people had climbed mountains before, this was the first "do it because it's there" feat. Reaching the summit itself (at 6,263 feet) requires a bit of legwork. From either Chalet Reynard or the tiny ski center Mont Serein you can leave your car and hike up to the peak's tall observatory tower. The climb is not overly taxing, and when you reach the top you are rewarded with gorgeous panoramic views of the Alps. And to the south, barring the possibility of high-summer haze, you'll take in views of the Rhône Valley, the Luberon, and even Marseille. Hiking maps are available at tabacs (tobacco shops) and tourist offices. Town-to-town treks are also a great way to explore the area; one of the most beautiful trails is from Malalucène to Séguret. In the off-season, lonely Mont Ventoux is plagued with an ungodly reputation due to destructive winds. Attempts at saving its soul are evidenced by the chapels lining its slopes. Whether it's possessed by the devil or not, don't attempt to climb it in inclement weather. From late fall to early spring, in fact, the summit is closed by snow.

Where to Eat

$ ╳ **Le Chalet Reynard.** This is the spot for lunch and a bask in the sun (or on the covered terrace) on your way up the eastern slope of Mont Ventoux. Bikers, hikers, and car-trekkers alike gather at plank tables on the wooden deck or warm themselves in the chalet-style dining area. The food is far beyond the merely acceptable, from simple dishes such as omelets (with truffles in season) to *civet de lapin* (rabbit cooked in wine) or even spit-roasted bull for groups of 15 or more. ⊠ *At the easternmost elbow of D974* ☎ *04–90–61–84–55* ⊕ *www.chalet-reynard. com* ☰ *MC, V* ☺ *Closed Tues. Oct.–June.*

Sault

★ ㉗ *41 km (25½ mi) southeast of Malaucène, 41 km (25½ mi) northeast of Carpentras.*

Though at the hub of no fewer than six *routes départementales,* Sault remains an utterly isolated market town floating on a stony hilltop in a valley of lavender. Accessed only by circuitous country roads, it remains virtually untouched by tourism. The landscape is traditional Provence at its best—wind-scoured, oak-forested hills and long, deep valleys purpled with the curving arcs of lavender. In the town itself, old painted storefronts exude the scent of honey and lavender. The damp church, Église St-Sauveur, dates from the 12th century; the long, lovely barrel nave was doubled in 1450.

From Sault all routes are scenic. You may head eastward into Haute Provence, visiting (via D950) tiny **Banon,** source of the famed goat cheese. Wind up D942 to see pretty hilltop Aurel or down D30 to reach perched **Simiane-la-Rotonde.** Or head back toward Carpentras through the spectacular **Gorges de la Nesque,** snaking along narrow cliff-edge roads through dramatic canyons carpeted with wild boxwood and pine. If you're exploring the Lavender Route, head eastward some 48 km (27 mi) to discover the epicenter of Haute-Provence's fabled lavender in the sleepy, dusty town of **Forcalquier.**

Where to Eat & Stay

$$$ ✕🏠 **Hostellerie du Val de Sault.** A holiday feel infiltrates this quiet retreat, once a summer camp. Five modern buildings range over the casually land-scaped grounds, separated by low drystone walls and shaded by pines. Rooms are small and modular, with pine plank floors and private decks looking over the valley. Suites offer tiny sitting rooms (which can dou-ble as children's bedrooms) and whirlpool baths, and four new "Provence-Asie" rooms depart from Provençal clichés. Head to the main lodge for the rich regional cooking of owner-chef Yves Gattechaut, with dishes such as asparagus and mountain ham served in a foie gras sauce, Sault lamb roasted in cassis and lavender, and Carpentras strawberries in pastry with candied chestnuts. Work it all off in the fitness center, which is equipped with a sauna and a whirlpool perfumed with lavender essence. ⊠ *An-cien-Chemin-d'Aurel, 84390* 🕾 *04–90–64–01–41* 🖷 *04–90–64–12–74* ⊕ *www.valdesault.com* 🛏 *15 rooms, 5 suites* ⚘ *Restaurant, 2 tennis courts, pool, bicycles, gym, bar, in-room data ports, cable TV, some pets allowed; no a/c* ⊟ *AE, DC, MC, V* ⊘ *Closed Nov.–Mar.*

THE SORGUE VALLEY

This gentle, rolling valley east of Avignon follows the course of the River Sorgue, which wells up from caverns below the arid hills of the Vau-cluse plateau, gushes to the surface at Fontaine de Vaucluse, and rolls down to turn the mossy waterwheels in picturesque L'Isle-sur-la-Sorgue. It is a region of transition between the urban outskirts of Avignon and the wilds of the Luberon to the east.

L'Isle-sur-la-Sorgue

28 *23 km (14 mi) east of Avignon.*

Fodor'sChoice
★

Crisscrossed with lazy canals and alive with moss-covered waterwheels that once drove its silk, wool, and paper mills, this charming valley town retains its gentle appeal . . . except on Sunday. Then this easygoing old town transforms itself into a Marrakech of marketeers, "the most charming flea market in the world," its streets crammed with antiques and brocante, its cafés swelling with crowds of chic bargain browsers making a day of it. Yves St-Laurent bigwig Pierre Bergé, Viscount Lin-ley (the noted furniture designer and son of Princess Margaret), and in-terior decorator Jacques Grange all flock here. Even hard-core modernists inured to treasure hunts enjoy the show as urbane couples with sweaters over shoulders squint discerningly through half lenses at mono- grammed linen sheets, zinc wash- stands, *barbotine* ware, china spice sets, Art Deco perfume bottles, tinted engravings, and the paintings of modern almost-masters. For high- style big purchases—furniture, $5,000 quilts, and the like—head to the town's noted antiques shops (*see* Shopping, *below*). There are also street musicians, food stands

BEST TIME TO GO "FLEA"-ING

L'Isle's antiques market ratchets up to high speed twice a year when the town hosts a big an- tiques show, usually four days around Easter and another in mid-August, nicknamed the *Grand Déballage*—the "Great Unpacking."

groaning under rustic breads, vats of tapenade, cloth-lined baskets of spices, and miles of café tables offering ringside seats to the spectacle. After London's Portobello district and the flea market at St-Ouen out- side Paris, L'Isle-sur-la-Sorgue is reputedly Europe's third-largest antiques market. Prices can be high but remember that in many cases, dealers expect to bargain.

On a non-market day, life returns to its mellow pace. There are plenty of antiques dealers doing business year-round, but also fabric and inte- rior design shops, bookstores, and food stores to explore. People curl up with paperbacks on park benches by shaded fountains and read in- ternational papers in cafés. While the food stands and arts and crafts shops hold forth along the Avenue de la Libération, the antiquaires hold Sunday squatters' rights from the Place Gambetta up the length of Av- enue des 4 Otages. Dealers and clients catch up on gossip at the Place Gambetta fountain and at the Café de France, opposite the church of Notre-Dame-des-Anges. Most of the clusters of antiques dealers, known as the Villages d'Antiquaires, lie just outside the ring formed by the canals of La Sorgue. Wander the maze inside the ring to admire a range of ar- chitectural styles, from Gothic to Renaissance, with the occasional burst of color where an owner has broken from local tradition to paint an archway indigo blue or a pair of shutters lemon yellow.

The Provençal Venice, L'Isle is dotted with watermills and canals, which once drove the wheels of silk, paper, oil, grain, and leather mills. Today, these wheels—eight of them—turn idly, heavy with moss, adding to the charm of the winding streets. If you want to explore the vestiges of L'Isle's 18th-century heyday, stop in the tourist office and pick up a brochure called "Vagabondages L'Isle-sur-la-Sorgue." This map and commentary (in French only) will guide you to some of the town's grand old hôtels particuliers. One of the finest of L'Isle's mansions, the **Hôtel de Campre- don–Maison René Char,** has been restored and reinvented as a modern- art gallery, mounting temporary exhibitions of modern masters. ⊠ *20 rue du Docteur Tallet* ☎ *04-90-38-17-41* ⊕ *www.campredon-expos. com* ⊘ *Tues.–Sun. 9:30–12:30 and 3–5:30.*

L'Isle's 17th-century church, the **Collégiale Notre-Dame-des-Anges,** is ex- travagantly decorated with gilt, faux marble, and sentimental frescoes. Its double-colonnaded facade commands the center of the Old Town. ⊠ *Pl. de l'Église.*

The Gîte Way

YOU COME HOME from a hard day's sightseeing, slip off your shoes, pull a pitcher of cold water from the fridge, pour a pastis and carry it out to the terrace. There's a basket heavy with goodies from the village market—a fresh rabbit, three different tubs of olives, a cup of fresh-scooped tapenade, apricots and melons warm from the sun. After your drink, you'll sort it all out and fix supper, French pop music playing gently on the radio. You'll eat as long and as late as you like, and carry the children to their twin beds in the back room before you take a stroll through the almond grove or crunch through the wild thyme to look at the city lights strung far below. Even doing the dishes in the sink seems okay in this faraway, summer-cottage mode, far from the minibars, lobby lounges, and snooty waiters of the beaten tourist track.

This is the gîte way, the alternative to hotels and restaurants and even to the anonymous seaside vacation flats farmed out by agencies abroad. The national network known as Gîtes de France has organized and catalogued a vast assortment of rural houses, many of them restored farmhouses and old village bastides, most of them rich in regional character and set in the picturesque countryside. The participating houses are inspected and categorized by comfort level (for example, three stars includes a washing machine), with standardized lists of minimum furnishings (from corkscrews to salad spinners to vegetable peelers).

But the key to the charm is the personal touch: Gîtes de France owners greet their guests on arrival, and may pop by (discreetly, rarely) during the week with lettuce from their garden, a bottle from their vineyard, holiday candy for the kids. There's a cupboard full of maps and brochures on local museums, and often the name of a nearby restaurant if you're too sunburned to cook. And they'll come to collect the key a week later and wish you a bon voyage.

There are drawbacks, of course. You'll have to bring towels and linens, and make up the beds yourself (you can often rent linens from the host if you prefer), and you are requested to leave the house in the same condition in which you found it—which usually means impeccable, and requires some mopping and scrubbing.

But the privacy and independence counterbalance any drudgery, and you'll meet people far different from the tourists and supercilious concierges of standardized hotels: farmers, teachers, winemakers, artists, anyone with the time to care for a cottage, a neighboring farmhouse, a converted stone barn.

Contact the headquarters of the département you plan to visit and request a catalogue of properties, then make a reservation by phone or fax. You must give them a 25% down payment with your reservation, then the rest when you return the contract, one month before your visit. For more information on the gîte way, *see* Lodging *in* Smart Travel Tips A to Z.

Where to Eat & Stay

★ **$$$–$$$$** ✕ **Le Jardin du Quai.** Daniel Hébet made his name at La Mirande in Avignon and Le Domaine des Andéols in St-Saturnin-lès-Apt before opening this bistro in his own image—young, jovial, and uncompromising when it comes to quality. Off a noisy street near the train station is the gate to this garden haven, with metal tables under the trees and an airy interior with a vintage tile floor. Hébet offers a single set menu at lunch and another at dinner, and the food is so good that no one is complaining at the lack of choice (though he has been known to substitute meat for fish on request): local white asparagus with fava beans, chanterelle mushrooms, shaved Parmesan and a frothy little sauce, cod crusted with quinoa and served on ratatouille, fresh cherries and melon in verbena-infused syrup are all yumptious. This is where the local antiques dealers come to eat, and the place feels so welcoming that it would be easy to linger for hours. ⊠ *91 av. Julien Guigue* ☎ *04–90–20–14–98* ▭ *MC, V* ⊗ *Closed Tues. and Wed.*

$ ✕ **Lou Nego Chin.** In winter you'll sit shoulder to shoulder in the cramped but atmospheric dining room (chinoiserie linens, brightly hued tiles), but in summer tables are strewn across the quiet street, on a wooden deck along the river. Ask for a spot at the edge so you can watch the ducks play, and order the house wine and the inexpensive three-course (€18) menu du jour, often a hot salad and a steak or a good and garlicky stew. ⊠ *12 quai Jean Jaurès* ☎ *04–90–20–88–03* ▭ *MC, V* ⊗ *Closed Mon. No dinner Sun.*

★ **$$–$$$** ✕▤ **Le Prévôté.** With all the money you saved bargaining on that chipped Quimper vase, splurge on lunch at this discreet, pristine convent hidden off a backstreet courtyard. An indigo-blue archway (not belonging to the hotel) draws your eye down a quiet street to this place, which shares a wall with the neighboring church. The newly added guest rooms are decorated with the fine local materials; they are spacious and fairly simple in decor. In the restaurant, Jean-Marie Alloin works with local flavors—try his *tatin d'agneau* (caramelized lamb) with tapenade and confit garlic, or royal sea bream with potatoes cooked in local white wine. The wine list is succinct and favors reasonably priced local reds. But evening and à la carte meals are an investment best suited to buyers of antiques rather than brocante. ⊠ *4 rue Jean-Jacques-Rousseau, 84800* ☎ *04–90–38–57–29* ▣ *04–90–38–52–31* ⊕ *laprevote.site.voila. fr* ☞ *5 rooms* ⬩ *Restaurant* ▭ *MC, V.*

★ **$–$$** ✕▤ **Le Mas de Cure-Bourse.** For a real taste of the countryside, base yourself at this graceful yet casual 18th-century postal-coach inn well outside the fray, snugly hedge-bound in the countryside amid fruit trees and fields southwest of the town. Here you can relax on six acres of green landscape, read by the large pool, and sleep in rooms freshly decked out in Provençal prints and painted country furniture. Meals are memorable, whether taken by the grand old fireplace or on the terrace. The sophisticated cooking keeps a local touch with dishes such as stuffed zucchini flowers, pumpkin gnocchi, goat cheese with *pistou* (pesto) or tapenade, and deliciously gooey chocolate cake with cherries. Sunday dinner is a tradition here, served on rustic ceramic platters under vaulted ceilings and daubed beams, with the massive family hound standing guard.

✉ *Rte. de Caumont, 84800* ☎ *04–90–38–16–58* 🖷 *04–90–38–52–31* ⊕ *www.masdecurebourse.com* ⇆ *13 rooms* ⚏ *Restaurant, pool, some pets allowed; no a/c* ▭ *MC, V* ☺ *Restaurant closed Nov. and 3 wks in Jan.*

$ 🏠 **La Gueulardière.** After a Sunday glut of antiquing along the canals, you can dine and sleep amidst a cache of collectible finds, from the school posters in the restaurant to the oak armoires and brass beds that furnish the simple lodgings just up the street. Each room has French windows that open onto the enclosed garden courtyard, where you can enjoy a private breakfast in the shade. ✉ *1 rue d'Apt, 84800* ☎ *04–90–38–10–52* 🖷 *04–90–20–83–70* ⇆ *5 rooms* ⚏ *Restaurant, some pets allowed; no a/c* ▭ *MC, V.*

Shopping

Throughout the pretty backstreets of L'Isle's Old Town (especially between Place de l'Église and Avenue de la Libération), there are boutiques spilling baskets full of tempting goods onto the sidewalk to lure you inside; most concentrate on home design and Provençal goods. **Sous l'Olivier** (✉ 16 rue de la République ☎ 04–90–20–68–90) is a food boutique crammed to the ceiling with bottles and jars of tapenade, fancy mustards, candies shaped like olives, and the house olive oil.

Of the dozens of antiques shops in L'Isle, one conglomerate concentrates some 40 dealers under the same roof: **L'Isle aux Brocantes** (✉ 7 av. des Quatre Otages ☎ 04–90–20–69–93). It's open Saturday through Monday. The high-style crowd adores the higher-end antiques concentrated at the twinned shops of **Xavier Nicod and Gérard Nicod** (✉ 9 av. des Quatre Otages ☎ 04–90–38–35–50 or 04–90–38–07–20), which are open weekends and by appointment. Many collectors make a beeline for the treasures found at **La Maison Biehn** (✉ 7 av. des Quatre Etages ☎ 04–90–20–89–04) which are crammed into a lovely ivy-covered town house. Doyenne of dealers is **Nathalie Légier** (✉ Av. des Quatre Otages ☎ 04–90–38–03–30), as her ancestor Joseph Légier opened the town's first antiques shop in 1890. **Espace Béchard** (✉ 1 av. Jean-Charmasson ☎ 04–90–38–25–40) throws 11 different dealers together, all with fabulously overscaled objects too big to carry home on the plane, every Saturday, Sunday, and festival day from 9:30 to 7. **Maria Giancatarina** (✉ across from the train station, 4 av. Julien Guigue ☎ 04–90–38–58–02) has beautifully restored linens, including monogrammed linen sheets, lacy pillowcases, piqué throws, and *boutis* (Provençal quilts).

Fontaine de Vaucluse

㉙ *7 km (4½ mi) east of L'Isle sur la Sorgue, 30 km (19 mi) east of Avignon.*

Like the natural attraction for which it is named, this village has welled up and spilled over as a Niagara Falls–type tourist center; the rustic, pretty, and slightly tacky riverside town is full of shops, cafés, and restaurants, all built to serve the pilgrims who flock to its namesake. And neither town nor fountain should be missed if you're either a connoisseur of rushing water or a fan of foreign kitsch.

★ There's no exaggerating the magnificence of the **Fontaine de Vaucluse,** a mysterious spring that gushes from a deep underground source that has been explored to a depth of 1,010 feet . . . so far. Framed by towering cliffs, a broad, pure pool wells up and spews dramatically over massive rocks down a gorge to the village, where its roar soothes and cools the visitors who crowd the riverfront cafés.

You must pay to park, then run a gauntlet of souvenir shops and tourist traps on your way to the top. But even if you plan to make a beeline past the kitsch, do stop in at the legitimate and informative **Moulin Vallis-Clausa.** A working paper mill, it demonstrates a reconstruction of a 15th-century waterwheel that drives timber crankshafts to mix rag pulp, while artisans roll and dry thick paper *à l'ancienne* (in the old manner). The process is fascinating and free to watch (the guided tour lasts an hour), though it's almost impossible to resist buying note cards, posters, even lamp shades fashioned from the pretty stuff. Fontaine was once a great industrial mill center, but its seven factories were closed by strikes in 1968 and never recovered. All the better for you today, since now you can enjoy this marvelous natural spot in peace. ⊠ *On the riverbank walk up to the spring* ☎ *04–90–20–34–14* ⊙ *Open year-round with variable hours depending on the month. July–Aug., Mon.–Sat. 9–7:20; Sun. 10–7:20.*

Fontaine has its own ruined **Château,** perched romantically on a forested hilltop over the town and illuminated at night. First built around the year 1000 and embellished in the 14th century by the bishops of Cavaillon, it was destroyed in the 15th century and forms little more than a sawtooth silhouette against the sky.

The great Renaissance poet Petrarch, driven mad with unrequited love for a beautiful married woman named Laura, retreated to this valley to nurse his passion in a cabin with "one dog and only two servants." He had met her in the heady social scene at the papal court in Avignon, where she was to die years later of the plague. Sixteen years in this wild isolation didn't ease the pain, but the serene environment inspired him to poetry, and the lyrics of his *Canzoniere* were dedicated to Laura's memory. The small **Musée-Bibliothèque Pétrarque** (Petrarch Museum-Library), built on the site of his residence, displays prints and engravings of the virtuous lovers, both in Avignon and Fontaine de Vaucluse. ⊠ *On the left bank, direction Gordes* ☎ *04–90–20–37–20* 🖾 *€3.50* ⊙ *Apr. and May, Wed.–Mon. 10–noon and 2–6; June–Sept., Wed.–Mon. 10–12:30 and 1:30–6; Oct. 1–15, Wed.–Mon. 10–noon and 2–6; Oct. 15–Nov. 7, Wed.–Mon. 10–noon and 2–5. Group visits by reservation only Nov. 8–Mar.*

Where to Eat & Stay

$ ✕🖾 **Le Parc.** In a spectacular riverside setting in the shadow of the ruined château, this solid old hotel has basic, comfortable rooms (whitewashed stucco, all-weather carpet) with clean baths and no creaks. Five take in river views. The restaurant (closed Wednesday) spreads along the river in a pretty park with tables shaded by trellises heavy with grapes and trumpet vine. Moderately priced daily menus include river-fresh salmon, de rigueur in this locale. ⊠ *Rue de Bourgades, 84800*

☎ 04–90–20–31–57 📠 04–90–20–27–03 🛏 *12 rooms* ⛅ *Restaurant* ▭ *AE, DC, MC, V* 𐫱 *Closed Jan.–mid-Feb.*

$–$$ 🖼 **La Maison aux Fruits.** Even before you enter, you know an artist lives here and that this small B&B is no ordinary lodging. The carved front door and the painted woodwork set the tone for the faux marble, murals, painted ceilings, and the owner's art collection inside. An oval staircase takes you up to a sitting and dining room and a terrace. There are also two little apartments that you may rent by the week; some rooms overlook the roaring river. Some of the artworks are for sale; aficionados may even be seduced to sign up for an art class here. ✉ *Rue de l'Isle de Sorgue, 84800* ☎ *04–90–20–39–15* 📠 *04–90–20–27–08* 🛏 *2 rooms, 2 apartments* ▭ *No credit cards* 🍽 *BP.*

THE LUBERON

"'Have you ever been to the Luberon? Between Avignon and Aix. It's getting a little chichi, specially in August, but it's beautiful—old villages, mountains, no crowds, fantastic light . . . Leave the autoroute at Cavaillon, and go towards Apt.' . . . Murat poured the red wine and raised his glass. '*Bonnes vacances,* my friend. I'm serious about the Luberon; it's a little special. You should try it.'"

After Peter Mayle, no doubt barefoot by the pool, typed these words in his first novel *Hotel Pastis,* the world took a map in hand. They had already taken note when his chronicles *A Year in Provence* and *Toujours Provence* painted a delicious picture of backcountry sunshine, copious feasts, and cartoonishly droll local rustics; now they had directions to get there.

They came. They climbed over Mayle's hedges for autographs. They built pink and yellow houses, booked his favorite restaurant tables, traced his footsteps with the book in hand. And not only the English. *A Year in Provence* sold 4 million copies and was translated into 20 languages, including French (where its sequel corrected his grammar to *Provence Toujours*). His name is a household word here (Peet-aire May-eel) and doesn't always bring the oft-described grin and shrug from the locals. Perhaps that's why Mayle took a sabbatical from Provence, relinquishing the home with the famously immovable stone table. He has since returned, putting down roots on the south face of the Luberon, in Lourmarin.

> **“** The locals may hate Peter Mayle's books for bringing carloads of visitors to their erstwhile sleepy area but they can't complain about the skyrocketing prices they now can command for their houses. **”**

The dust has settled a bit, and despite the occasional Mayle Country bus tour rattling through from Cavaillon, the Luberon has returned to its former way of life. There were always Lacoste shirts here, and converted mas with pools (after all, Mayle's mas was already gentrified when they installed central heating), and sophisticated restaurants catering to seekers of the Simple Life. They're all still here, but so are the extraordinarily beautiful countryside, the golden perched villages, the blue-black forests, and the sun-bleached rocks.

The broad mountain called the Luberon is protected nowadays by the Parc Naturel Régional du Luberon, but that doesn't mean you should expect rangers, campsites, and his-and-hers outhouses. It has always been and remains private land, though building and forestry are allowed in moderation and hiking trails have been cleared.

The N100, anchored to the west by the market town of Cavaillon and to the east by industrial Apt, parallels the long, looming north face of the Luberon, and from it you can explore the hill towns and valley villages on either side. To its north, the red-ocher terrain around Roussillon, the Romanesque symmetry of the Abbaye de Sénanque, and the fashionable charms of Gordes punctuate a rugged countryside peppered with ancient stone *bories*. To its south lie Oppède-le-Vieux, Ménerbes, Lacoste, and pretty perched Bonnieux. From Bonnieux you can drive over the rugged crest through Lourmarin and explore the less gentrified south flank of the mountain. Although the Luberon is made up of two distinct regions, only the more civilized Petit Luberon, up to Apt, is covered in this chapter. If you're a nature lover, you may want to venture into the wilder Grand Luberon, especially to the summit called Mourre Nègre.

Gordes

★ ③⓪ *10 km (6 mi) east of Fontaine de Vaucluse, 39 km (24 mi) east of Avignon.*

The famous village perché of Gordes is only a short distance from Fontaine de Vaucluse, but you need to wind your way south, east, and then north on D100A, D100, D2, and D15 to skirt the impassable hillside. It's a lovely drive through dry, rocky country covered with wild lavender and scrub oak and may tempt you to a picnic or a walk. How surprising, then, to leave such wildness behind and enter resort country. Once a summer retreat favored by modern artists such as Andre Lhôte, Marc Chagall, and Victor Vasarely, Gordes used to be a famous, unspoiled hilltop village; it has now become a famous, unspoiled hilltop village surrounded by luxury vacation homes, modern hotels, restaurants, and B&Bs, much patronized by chic Parisians. No matter. The ancient stone village still rises above the valley in painterly hues of honey gold, and its mosaiclike cobbled streets—lined with boutiques, galleries, and real-estate offices—still wind steep and narrow to its Renaissance château.

The town **Château** was built by the d'Agoult-Gordes family in the 13th century, then made over in Renaissance style by the Lords of Simiane. The only way to see its interior is to pay to see its collection of mind-stretching photo paintings by Pop artist Pol Mara, who spent his last years in Gordes. It's worth the price to look at the fabulously decorated stone fireplace, created in 1541; it covers an entire wall with Neoclassic designs and stretches to frame two doors. ⊠ *Pl. du Château* ☎ *04–90–72–02–75* ✆ *€4* ☉ *Daily 10–noon and 2–6.*

Head downhill from the château and follow signs to the **belvédère** overlooking the miniature fields and farms below. From this height all those modern vacation homes blend in with the ancient mas—except for the aqua blue pools. Before leaving town be sure to pay a call on the village's church of **St-Fermin,** whose interior is overblown Rococo—all pink and gold.

★ Just outside Gordes, on a lane heading north from D2, follow signs to the **Village des Bories.** Found throughout this region of Provence, the bizarre and fascinating little stone hovels called *bories* are concentrated some 20 strong in an ancient community. Their origins are provocatively vague. Built as shepherds' shelters with tight-fitting, mortarless stone in a hivelike form, they may date back to the Celts, the Ligurians, even the Iron Age—and were inhabited or used for sheep through the 18th century. This village was reconstructed from remains. From Gordes, take D15, turning right to D2. ☎ *04–90–72–03–48* ✉ *€5.50* ☉ *Daily 9–sunset or 8, whichever comes first.*

Gordes is surrounded by beautiful lavender fields and one of the most beautiful is found at the celebrated 12th-century **Abbaye de Sénanque,** a great place to start off exploring the region's famous Lavender Route.

Abbaye de Sénanque   **See Page 96**

Where to Eat & Stay

\$\$ ✕ **Le Comptoir des Arts.** Directly across from the château, this tiny but deluxe bistro serves an international clientele without a trace of condescension. At lunch time, when tables spill out onto the square, the menu highlights a daily aïoli, a smorgasbord of fresh cod and lightly steamed vegetables crowned with pestled garlic mayonnaise. Evenings are reserved for intimate, formal indoor meals à la carte—roast Luberon lamb, beef with truffle sauce, or a salty-sweet raspberry-sauced *pintade* (guinea fowl). Leave room for the chocolate cake, and take the owner's advice on lesser-known, local finds in wine. The '30s-style bistro tables and architectural lines are a relief from Gordes's ubiquitous rustic-chic. ⊠ *Pl. du Château* ☎ *04–90–72–01–31* ♙ *Reservations essential* ▤ *MC, V* ☉ *Closed Nov. 15–Dec. 15, Jan. 15–Mar. 15. No dinner Tues. Sept.–May. No lunch Fri. and Sat.*

\$ ✕ **Le Jardin du Levant.** In a town that relies so much on its history, it's a surprise to find this Thai restaurant, its terrace brightened with tropical plants and parasols and its vaulted stone dining room cheerfully furnished with Formica and wooden tables and mismatched chairs. The menu keeps it simple, sticking to a short list of classics such as yellow chicken curry, beef with Thai basil, and squid saté, and the staff is welcoming. ⊠ *Rte. de la Combe* ☎ *04–90–72–12–43* ▤ *MC, V* ☉ *Closed Thurs.*

\$\$–\$\$\$ ✕▥ **La Ferme de la Huppe.** Want to be sprinkled by magical Provençal FodorśChoice pixie dust? Head to this 18th-century stone farmhouse standing all ★ alone in the lavender-scented countryside outside Gordes. Past the well in the courtyard and the swimming pool in the garden, down cobbled walkways, set into adorable nooks (one was the goats' stable—its

Old as the Hills

SINCE THE CAVE PAINTINGS OF LASCAUX, man has extracted ocher from the earth, using its extraordinary palette of colors to make the most of nature's play between earth and light. Grounded in these earth-based pigments, the frescoes of Giotto and Michelangelo glow from within, and the houses of Tuscany and Provence seem to draw color from the land itself—and to drink light from the sky. Says Barbara Barrois of the Conservatoire des Ocres et Pigments Appliqués at Roussillon, "Ça vibre à l'oeil!" (literally, "It vibrates to your eyes.")

The rusty hues of iron hydroxide are the source of all this luminosity,

intimately allied with the purest of clays. Extracted from the ground in chunks and washed to separate it from its quartz-sand base, it is ground to fine powder and mixed as a binder with chalk and sand. Applied to the stone walls of Provençal houses, this ancient blend gives the region its quintessential repertoire of warm yellows and golds, brick, sienna, and umber.

In answer to the acrylic imitations slathered on new constructions in garish shades of hot pink and canary yellow (following a Côte d'Azur trend), there is an ocher revival under way, thank goodness.

hayloft is now on view in the dining room), you'll find the guest rooms, each with its own private entrance. Some have lovely accents, such as the large medieval fireplace in the room called La Cuisine. A few have wood-beam ceilings; decor runs to modern wood beds, pretty prints, and secondhand finds. What more could you want? How about roast guinea fowl in saffron and ginger and an icy bottle of local rosé? The family chef will be glad to serve you by the poolside terrace, but reserve ahead; the restaurant (closed Thursday) is as popular as the hotel. ✉ *84220 Les Pourquiers, 3 km (2 mi) east of Gordes* ☎ *04–90–72–12–25* 🖷 *04–90–72–01–83* ⊕ *www.lafermedelahuppe.com* ⤳ *10 rooms* ⚐ *Restaurant, pool, cable TV, in-room data ports* ▭ *AE, MC, V* ☉ *Closed Nov.–Mar.* ⟦◯⟧ *BP.*

$$$–$$$$ 🏨 **La Bastide de Gordes & Spa.** There is no shortage of luxury accommodation in this region, but this hotel in the center of Gordes stands out for its vast, three-level spa by Daniel Jouvance and two swimming pools (indoor and outdoor). The rather old-fashioned rooms have all the comforts you could dream of and, to complement the restaurant with its panoramic view of the area, there is a wine shop and cellar. ✉ *Le Village, 84220* ☎ *04–90–72–12–12* 🖷 *04–90–72–05–20* ⊕ *www. bastide-de-gordes.com* ⚐ *2 pools (1 indoors), sauna, gym, cable TV, some pets allowed* ▭ *AE, MC, V.*

$$–$$$$ 🏨 **Domaine de l'Enclos.** Though this cluster of private stone cottages has had a major face-lift (eradicating much patina), antique tiles and faux patinas keep it looking fashionably old. There are panoramic views and a pool, babysitting services and swing sets, and a welcome that is surprisingly warm and familial for an inn of this sophistication. Half-board arrangements (even for one-night stays) keep costs down; in winter, the demipension visitors are treated like house guests. ⊠ *Rte. de Sénanque, 84220* ☎ *04–90–72–71–00* 🖷 *04–90–72–03–03* ⊕ *www. avignon-et-provence.com/domaine-enclos* ⇗ *12 rooms, 5 apartments* ⚘ *Pool, cable TV, some pets allowed* 🚳 *AE, MC, V.*

$$–$$$ 🏨 **Hôtel le Mas des Romarins.** At this 18th-century farmhouse on a hilltop crossroads on the outskirts of town you can gaze across the valley at Gordes while you breakfast on a sheltered terrace. Newly renovated guest rooms are clean, well lit, and feel spacious. Be sure to ask for a room with a valley view, especially No. 1, in the main building, from whose white-curtained windows you can see forever. Another good pick is the atelier room with a terrace; front rooms overlook a busy road. Warm rugs, antique furniture around the fireplace in the sitting room, and a pool surrounded by borie-like stone add to your contentment. There is no restaurant, but meals are available to guests on Monday, Wednesday, and Friday. ⊠ *Rte. de Sénanque, 84220* ☎ *04–90–72–12–13* 🖷 *04–90–72–13–13* ⊕ *www.hoteldesromarins.com* ⇗ *14 rooms* ⚘ *Pool, cable TV, Internet access in lounge, some pets allowed* 🚳 *MC, V* ⊗ *Closed Jan. 5–mid-Mar.*

Shopping

If you're shopping for a gift or souvenirs you'll find tasteful Provençal tableware at **Le Jardin** (⊠ Rte. des Murs ☎ 04–90–72–12–34) which also has a charming tearoom in its leafy courtyard garden. **Sud** (⊠ Pl. du Château ☎ 06–75–05–72–19) has an unusually good selection of AOC (Appellation d'Origine Contrôlée) Provençal olive oils, most of which are difficult if not impossible to find outside France.

Roussillon

★ ㉛ *14 km (9 mi) southeast of Gordes, 43 km (27 mi) southeast of Avignon.*

A rich vein of ocher runs through the earth of Roussillon, occasionally breaking the surface in Technicolor displays of russet, deep rose, garnet, and flaming orange. Roussillon is a mineral showcase, perched above a pocket of red-rock canyonlands that are magically reflected in the stuccoes applied on every building in town, where the hilltop cluster of houses blends into the red-ocher cliffs from which their stones were first quarried. The ensemble of buildings and jagged, hand-cut slopes are equally dramatic, and views from the top look over a landscape of artfully eroded bluffs that Georgia O'Keeffe would have loved.

Unlike neighboring hill villages, there's little of historic architectural detail here; the pleasure of a visit lies in the richly varied colors that change with the light of day, and in the views of the contrasting countryside, where dense-shadowed greenery sets off the red stone with Cézannesque severity. There are pleasant *placettes* (tiny squares) to linger in nonetheless, and a Renaissance fortress tower crowned with a clock in the 19th century; just past it, you can take in expansive panoramas of forest and ocher cliffs.

2

Choose from local flavors such as *calisson d'Aix* (almond candy), *pain d'épice,* and melon at the ice-cream shop and café of **L'Ocrier** (⊠ Les Ocres, av. Burlière ☎ 04–90–05–79–53) before wandering through the village or taking the *sentier* (hiking path) to explore the cliffs.

This famous vein of natural ocher, which spreads some 25 km (15½ mi) along the foot of the Vaucluse plateau, has been mined for centuries. You can visit the old **Usine Mathieu de Roussillon** (Roussillon's Mathieu Ocher Works) to learn more about ocher's extraction and its modern uses; though it has long since been closed as a mine, it functions today as the Conservatoire des Ocres et Pigments Appliqués (Conservatory of Ochers and Applied Pigments). There are explanatory exhibits, ocher powders for sale, and guided tours in English with advance request. ⊠ *On D104 southeast of town* ☎ *04–90–05–66–69* ۞ *Closed 2 wks in Jan. Hours vary depending on the season. July–Aug., exhibits daily 9–7, 50–60 min guided tours (in English by reservation only) 10–12 and 2–6.*

Where to Eat & Stay

$$$ ✕▦ **Le Clos de la Glycine.** This new hotel combines modern comforts (an elevator, air-conditioning) with Provençal tradition, though the decor is still too fresh to have acquired the patina found in more established places. The most desirable rooms have terraces with views of the ocher cliffs, a panorama shared by the terrace of Restaurant David, which plays to a full house in summer with dishes such as spelt risotto with sea bream and fish soup, and rabbit leg with vegetables and aïoli. ⊠ *Pl. de la Poste, 84220* ☎ *04–90–05–60–13* 🖶 *04–90–05–75–80* ⊕ *www. luberon-hotel.com* ☜ *9 rooms* ♨ *Restaurant, cable TV, Internet access* ▭ *AE, DC, MC, V.*

★ $$ ▦ **Ma Maison.** The artist-owners have infused this isolated 1850 mas in the valley below Roussillon with a laid-back, barefoot, cosmopolitan style acquired, in part, in California. Their personality and imagination show in every corner, from the big saltwater pool that's surrounded with brass beds (instead of lounge chairs) to the mosquito netting draped over the beds to the artworks—mostly their own—hanging on every surface. Rooms are big and private, some with fireplaces and separate entrances onto the grounds. Breakfast, with homegrown, homemade marmalade, is served from a massive blue-and-white-tile country kitchen. The idyllic, all organic garden spans 7½ acres, much of it in shade in the afternoon, with views toward Bonnieux and the Luberon. ⊠ *Quartier Les Devens, 4 km (2½ mi) south of Roussillon, 84220* ☎ *04–90–05–74–17* 🖶 *04–90–05–74–63* ⊕ *www.mamaison-provence.com* ☜ *4 rooms, 2 suites* ♨ *Pool, Internet access in lounge; no a/c, no room TVs* ▭ *MC, V* ۞ *Closed Nov.–Feb.* ⭗ *BP.*

Cavaillon

32 *15 km (9½ mi) north of Salon de Provence, 16 km (10 mi) southeast of Avignon.*

Geographically, Cavaillon is a great place to use as a base of operations—this is a good spot for bus and train connections. It's also known as one of the biggest agricultural market towns in France and is famous for its honey-scented melons. At one point in history, Cavaillon had the largest Jewish population in the papal enclave, but after the Revolution the majority of Cavaillon's Jews moved to the bigger cities of Provence. What does remain of the Jewish legacy is a beautiful **synagogue** with its own museum on Rue Hébraïque. Tours can be booked through the Cavaillon tourist office. ⊠ *Rue Hébraïque* ☎ *04–90–66–00–34* ⊕ *Apr.–Oct., Wed.–Mon. 9:30–12:30 and 2:30–6:30* 🖾 *€3; €1 to take pictures.*

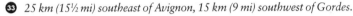

Oppède-le-Vieux

🟤 *25 km (15½ mi) southeast of Avignon, 15 km (9 mi) southwest of Gordes.*

Heading toward Apt on D22 out of Avignon, follow signs right into the vineyards, toward Oppède. You'll occasionally be required to follow signs for Oppède-le-Village, but your goal will be marked with the symbol of *monuments historiques*: Oppède-le-Vieux. A Byronesque tumble of ruins arranged against an overgrown rocky hillside, Oppède's charm— or part of it—lies in its preservation. Taken over by writers and artists who choose to live here and restore but not develop it, the village offers a café or two but little more.

Cross the village square, pass through the old city gate, and climb up steep trails (beware hidden holes and precarious stairs) past restored houses to the church known as **Notre-Dame-d'Alydon.** First built in the 13th century, its blunt buttresses were framed into side chapels in the 16th century; you can still see the points of stoned-in Gothic windows above. The marvelous hexagonal bell tower sprouts a lean, mean gargoyle from each angle. It once served as part of the village's fortifications; the views from the plateau it dominates overlook the broad valley toward Ménerbes.

You can also clamber up to the ruins of the **Château,** first built in the 13th century, then lorded over by Baron d'Oppède, who laid waste to the Waldensians, and then transformed in the 15th century. From the left side of its great square tower, look down into the dense fir forests of the Luberon's north face. Just outside town is the **Sentier Vigneron d'Oppède,** a long hiking trail through vineyards and olive groves and lined with descriptive plaques.

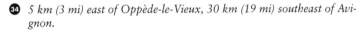

Ménerbes

🟤 *5 km (3 mi) east of Oppède-le-Vieux, 30 km (19 mi) southeast of Avignon.*

As you drive along D188 between Oppède and Ménerbes, the rolling rows of grapevines are punctuated by stone farmhouses. But something is different. These farmhouses have electric gates, tall arborvitae hedges, and swimming pools. Peter Mayle isn't the only outsider to have vacationed here and contrived to stay.

The town of Ménerbes itself clings to a long, thin hilltop over this sought-after valley, looming over the surrounding forests like a great stone ship. At its prow juts the **Castellet,** a 15th-century fortress. At its stern rears up the 13th-century **citadelle.** These redoubtable fortifications served the Protestants well during the War of Religions—until the Catholics wore them down with a 15-month siege. A campanile tops the Hôtel de Ville (Town Hall) on pretty **Place de l'Horloge** (Clock Square), where you can admire the delicate stonework on the arched portal and mullioned windows of a Renaissance house. Just past the tower on the right you'll reach an overlook taking in views towards Gordes, Roussillon, and Mont Ventoux.

But what you really came to see is **Peter Mayle's house,** right? Do its current owners a favor and give it a wide berth. After years of tour buses spilling the curious into the private driveway to crane their necks and snap pictures, the heirs to the stone picnic table, the pool, and Faustin's grapevines wish the books had never been written. And besides, Peter Mayle has moved now, to the other side of the mountain.

Where to Eat & Stay

★ $$–$$$ ✕🏨 **Le Roy Soleil.** In the imposing shadow of the Luberon and the hilltop village of Ménerbes, this luxurious country inn has pulled out all stops on comfort and furnishings. (Think wrought-iron beds and marble and granite bathrooms.) But the integrity of its 17th-century building, with thick stone walls and groin vaults and beams, redeems it just short of pretentiousness (unlike the much more expensive La Bastide de Marie across town) and makes it a wonderful place to escape to. Sophisticated meals are served in the vaulted dining room but, in summer, no one can resist dining on the picture-perfect roofed patio facing the trees. ⊠ *Rte. des Beaumettes, 84560* ☎ *04–90–72–25–61* 🖷 *04–90–72–36–55* ⊕ *www.roy-soleil.com* ⇨ *21 rooms* ⚐ *Restaurant, pool, bar, cable TV, Wi-Fi in lobby, some pets allowed* ⊟ *AE, DC, MC, V* ☉ *Hotel closed Dec. 15–Easter. Restaurant closed Oct. 15–Easter.*

Lacoste

③⑤ *7 km (4½ mi) east of Ménerbes, 37 km (23 mi) southeast of Avignon.*

Like Ménerbes, gentrified hilltop Lacoste owes its fame to an infamous literary resident. Little but jagged ruins remain of the once magnificent **Château de Sade,** where the Marquis de Sade (1740–1814) spent some 30 years of his life, mostly hiding out. Exploits both literary and real, judged obscene by various European courts, kept him in and out of prison despite a series of escapes. His mother-in-law finally turned him in to authorities, and he was locked away in the Paris Bastille, where he passed the time writing stories and plays. Written during his time in the Bastille, *120 journées de Sodome* (*120 Days of Sodom*) featured a Black Forest château suspiciously similar in form and design to his Lacoste home. The once-sumptuous château was destroyed with particular relish in the Revolution but for some years, the wealthy Paris couturier Pierre Cardin has been restoring the castle wall by wall. Under his generous patronage the **Festival Lacoste** takes place here throughout the months of July and August. A lyric, musical, and theatrical extravaganza, events (and their dates) change yearly, ranging from outdoor poetry recitals to ballet to colorful operettas. Lacoste has a few lodging options, the best of which is the Hôtel de France. ⊠ *Carrières du Château* ☎ *04–90–75–93–12* ⊕ *www.easyclassic.com/festival-lacoste/19juillet. php* ✉ *Festival performances: €20–€140.*

Bonnieux

★ ❸❻ *5 km (3 mi) southeast of Lacoste, 42 km (26 mi) southeast of Avignon.*

The most impressive of the Luberon's hilltop villages, Bonnieux (pronounced Bun-*yer*) rises out of the arid hills in a jumble of honey-color cubes that change color subtly as the day progresses. Strewn along D36, the village is wrapped in crumbling ramparts and dug into bedrock and cliff. Most of its sharply raked streets take in wide-angle valley views, though you'll get the best view from the pine-shaded grounds of the 12th-century **Église Vieille du Haut,** reached by stone steps that wind past tiny niche houses. Shops, galleries, cafés, and fashionable restaurants abound here, but they don't dominate. It's possible to lose yourself in a back *ruelle* (small street) most of the year. If you have a car, you're in luck—to every point of the compass, there are lovely drives from Bonnieux threading out through Le Petit Luberon. Of the four, the best is the eastward course, along the D943 and D113, which leads to the Romanesque ruins of the Prieuré de St-Symphorien.

Where to Eat & Stay

$$ ✕ **Le Fournil.** In a natural grotto deep in stone, lighted by candles and arty torchères, this restaurant would be memorable even without its trendy decor touches (jade and gold cement tiles, mix-and-match jacquard linens) and stylishly presented Provençal cuisine. But add adventurous dishes such as tomato-crisped pigs'-feet *galette* (patty), subtle seafood, an informed wine list, and the option of sitting on the terrace by the fountain, and you have an experience to note in your travel diary. ⊠ *5 pl. Carnot* ☎ *04–90–75–83–62* ▤ *MC, V* ☺ *Closed Mon., and Dec.–Jan., and Tues. in Oct.–Apr. No lunch Sat. and Tues., July–Aug.*

★ $$–$$$ 🖼 **Hostellerie du Prieuré.** Not every hotel has its own chapel, but this gracious inn occupies an 18th-century abbey and has kept its noble details. The interior is vivid and warm, from the saffron-color bar to the leather chairs in the firelit salon to the dining room glowing with Roussillon ocher. Summer meals and breakfasts are served in the enclosed garden, which makes you feel like you're no longer in the village center. Rooms have plush carpets and antiques; one has a very small, sheltered terrace overlooking the chapel bell. Ask about the tiny, low-priced room with a toilet down the hall. Its double windows open over the garden. At press time, a pool was in the works. ⊠ *In center of village, 84480* ☎ *04–90–75–80–78* 🖶 *04–90–75–96–00* ⊕ *www.hotelprieure.com* 🗗 *11 rooms* ♨ *Restaurant, bar, pool, cable TV; no a/c in some rooms* ▤ *MC, V* ☺ *Closed Nov. 10–Mar.*

★ $–$$ 🖼 **Le Clos du Buis.** At this Gîtes de France B&B, whitewash and quarry tiles, lovely tiled baths, and carefully juxtaposed antiques create a regional look in the guest rooms. Relaxed, homey public spaces, with scrubbed floorboards, a fireplace, and exposed stone, invite you to hang around barefoot, like lodgers or weekend guests. It even has a pool

2

and a pretty garden, and it overlooks the valley from the village center. ⊠ *Rue Victor Hugo, 84480* ☎ *04–90–75–88–48* 🖶 *04–90–75-88-57* ⊕ *www.leclosdubuis.com* 🗬 *7 rooms* ⚇ *Pool; no room TVs, no room phones* ☰ *MC, V* ⊗ *Closed Nov. 15–Dec. 20, Jan. 5–Feb. 20* ⦿| *BP.*

Buoux

㊲ *8 km (5 mi) northeast of Bonnieux, 9 km (5½ mi) south of Apt.*

To really get into backcountry Luberon, crawl along serpentine single-lane roads below Apt, past orchards and lavender fields studded with bories. Deeply ensconced in the countryside, the tiny hamlet of Buoux (pronounced Bu-*ooks*) offers little more than a hotel and a café, sheltered by white brush-carpeted cliffs. If you squint you can just make out the dozens of rock-climbers dangling, spiderlike, from slender cables along the cliff face.

An even tinier road can take you to the **Fort de Buoux,** the ruins of an ancient village and a fortification that has defended the valley since Ligurian and Roman times. Several houses and an entire staircase were chiseled directly into the stone; it's uncertain whether they're prehistoric or medieval. Louis XIV dismantled the ancient fortifications in the 17th century, leaving Turneresque ruins to become overgrown with wild box and ivy. ☎ *04–90–74–25–75* 🎫 €3 ⊗ *Daily sunrise–sunset, except when weather is bad.*

Where to Eat & Stay

★ $ ✕🏠 **Auberge des Seguins.** Delve deep into this romantic valley to find this fabulous hideaway, at the foot of an imposing white-rock cliff. The *dortoires* (shared public bunk rooms) and simple tile-and-stucco rooms make it a terrific retreat for families, hikers, and rock-climbers. Better yet, meals at the restaurant are several cuts above summer-camp chow. The owner is passionately Provençal and insists on wonderful regional food: aïoli, tapenade, curried chickpeas, lamb stews, delicate goat cheese, and local wines. This is where the French come for reunions and weekends with friends, to lounge in lawn chairs or dip in the stream-fed swimming pool. In high season, make a dining reservation ahead of time. Half-board is mandatory for overnight stays. ⊠ *3 km (2 mi) below downtown Buoux, 84480* ☎ *04–90–74–16–37* 🖶 *04–90–74–03–26* 🗬 *29 rooms, 21 bunks* ⚇ *Restaurant, pool* ☰ *MC, V.*

Saignon

㊳ *15 km (9 mi) northeast of Buoux, 5 km (3 mi) southeast of Apt.*

Set on the Plateau de Claparédes and draped just below the crest of an arid hillside covered with olive groves, lavender, and stone farms, Saignon is an appealing hill town anchored by a heavyset Romanesque church. Neat cobbled streets wind between flower-festooned stone houses and surround a central *placette* (small square) with a burbling fountain. Yes, it's been gentrified with a few boutiques and restaurants, but the escapist feel hasn't been erased.

Where to Eat & Stay

$–$$ ✕⊡ **Auberge du Presbytère.** Three stone houses on the village's central *place* join to make this graceful inn. Their country roots show in the exposed rafters, vaulted ceilings, weathered quarry tiles, and blue-shuttered windows. One bargain room has a bathroom down the hall; another offers spectacular valley views from a private terrace. Generally, the rooms are pretty, cool, and accented with lovely bursts of color. The restaurant (closed Wednesday) aims high with a pair of regional menus. Look for delicate goat cheese mousse in a tomato-basil coulis, milk-fed lamb with thyme flowers, and a summery watermelon sorbet. ⊠ *Pl. de la Fontaine, 84400* ☎ *04–90–74–11–50* 🖷 *04–90–04–68–51* 🌐 *www. auberge-presbytere.com* ↩ *16 rooms* ♿ *Restaurant, bar, in-room data ports, some pets allowed; no a/c in some rooms, no room TVs* ▭ *MC, V* ☉ *Closed mid-Nov.–mid-Feb.*

Apt

③⑨ *40 km (25 mi) east of Avignon.*

Actively ugly from a distance, with a rash of modern apartment blocks and industrial buildings, Apt doesn't attract the tourism it deserves. Its central Old Town, with tight, narrow streets shaded with noble stone houses and strings of fluttering laundry, seethes with activity. The best time to visit is Saturday, when the town buzzes with a vibrant Provençal market, selling crafts, clothing, carpets, jewelry, and—not incidentally— all the finest food products of the Luberon and Haut Provence.

| EN ROUTE | Between Apt and Lourmarin, the *départemental* road D943 winds dramatically through deep backcountry, offering the only passage over the spine of the Luberon. Bone-dry and bristling with scrub oak, pine, coarse broom, and wild lavender, it's a landscape reminiscent of Greece or Sicily. If you climb into the hills, you won't get views; this is landlocked, isolated terrain, but it's wildly beautiful. |

Where to Eat & Stay

$$$$ ✕⊡ **Le Domaine des Andéols.** In a complete departure from Provençal chic, this collection of cubic houses, which recently joined the Alain Ducasse group, immerses guests in a contemporary environment—each individually decorated house contains works by top designers and artists. Wildest is the Maison du Voyageur, with its stuffed tiger, zebra skin, and antler sculpture, while the Maison des Lointains has a barbed-wire chandelier, suggestive black-and-white photos, and a stone bath in each room. You can sip an aperitif accompanied by delicious house nibbles on your own terrace before venturing down to the restaurant, where a young Ducasse-trained chef concocts a set menu that changes daily. From the swimming pool and the dramatic stepped garden patios, admire dramatic views of the countryside; there is also an indoor pool should the mistral (fierce wind) strike. What really makes this place special, though, is the staff in their flowing white clothes, who seem to anticipate your every need. ⊠ *84490 St-Saturnin-lés-Apt* ☎ *04–90–75–50–63*

🚗 04–90–75–43–22 ⊕ *www.domainedesandeols.com* 📞 *9 houses*
🍴 *Restaurant, 1 indoor pool, 1 outdoor pool, steam room, spa, kitch-enettes, in-room data ports* ▤ *AE, DC, MC, V.*

Lourmarin

2

🔟 *12 km (7 mi) southeast of Bonnieux, 54 km (33 mi) southeast of Avi-gnon.*

The highly gentrified village of Lourmarin lies low-slung in the hollow of the Luberon's south face, a sprawl of manicured green. Albert Camus loved this place from the moment he discovered it in the 1930s. After he won his Nobel prize in 1957 he bought a house here and lived in it until his death in 1960 (he is buried in the village cemetery). Loumarin's Renaissance-era **Château** is its main draw, privately restored in the 1920s to appealing near-perfection. Of the old wing (15th century) and the new (begun in 1526 and completed in 1540), the latter is prettiest, with a broad-ranging art collection, rare old furniture, and ornate stone fire-places—including one with exotic *vases canopes* (ancient Egyptian fig-ure vases). In summer, the château hosts concerts. ☎ *04–90–68–15–23* 🎟 *€5* ⊙ *Guided tours (in French; 45 mins long) daily 11, 2:30, 3:30, and 4:30; July–Aug. every half hour.*

Where to Stay

$ 🏨 **Villa Saint Louis.** In a town as gentrified as Lourmarin, it's surprising
Fodor'sChoice to find such a bargain as this B&B set in a 17th-century house replete
★ with antiques and enclosed garden. Mme Lassalette bought this former post house 16 years ago, and her decorator husband made the interior look as though it hadn't changed in centuries—the house has been fea-tured in decorating magazines worldwide. Rabbits run free in the grassy garden, where breakfast (included in the price) is sometimes served. There is no pool, but guests have been known to cool off their feet in the foun-tain. ✉ *35 rue Henri de Savornin, 84160* ☎ *04–90–68–39–18* 🚗 *04–90–68–10–07* ⊕ *www.villasaintlouis.com* 📞 *5 rooms* 🍴 *In-room data ports; no a/c* ▤ *AE, DC, MC, V* 🍽 *BP.*

VAUCLUSE ESSENTIALS

To research prices, get advice from other travelers, and book travel arrange-ments, visit www.fodors.com.

Transportation

If traveling extensively by public transportation, be sure to load up on information (schedules, the best taxi-for-call companies, etc.) upon ar-riving at the ticket counter or help desk of the bigger hub stations in the area, such as Avignon and Orange.

BY AIR

Marseille's Marignane airport is served by frequent flights from Paris and London; it's about an hour's drive from Avignon. The smaller Avi-

gnon Caumont airport has frequent daily flights from Paris and Cler-
mont Ferrand.

⚑ Air Travel Information **Marignane airport** ☎ 04-42-14-14-14 ⊕ www.marseille.
aeroport.fr. **Avignon Caumont airport** ⊠ Chemin Felmons Montfavet, southeast of Avignon ☎ 04-90-81-51-51 ⊕ www.avignon.aeroport.fr.

BY BOAT

There are four boat tour companies operating out of Avignon (all of which
have the same contact information) that offer various outings to such
local sites as Arles and Châteauneuf-du-Pape. Trips cost anywhere from
€7 to €33.50, and can include lunch, dinner, and dancing.

⚑ Boat Travel Information **Les Grand Bateaux de Provence** ⊠ Allée de L'Oulle, 84000
Avignon ☎ 04-90-85-62-25 🖷 04-90-85-61-14 ⊕ www.mireio.net.

BY BUS

Major bus transport companies carry travelers from surrounding cities
into towns not accessible by rail; bus and rail services usually dovetail. Avignon's gare routière (bus station) has the heaviest interre-
gional traffic.

A reasonable network of private bus services (called, confusingly enough,
cars) links places not served or poorly served by trains. Ask for bus schedules at train stations and tourist offices, or head for Avignon's gare routière,
next to the train station. Avignon has a sizable station, with posted schedules; buses branch out into every corner of the Vaucluse from here. Cars
Lieutaud has a booth just outside the Avignon train station, offering daily
bus excursions into different regions—for instance, the Luberon, Vaison, and the Alpilles. Some of them are one-way runs, useful as simple
transport; others are round-trip guided tours.

The main destinations serviced to/from the Avignon bus station (10 to
20 buses daily) are Orange (€6, 45 minutes) and Carpentras (€4, 45
minutes). Five or less buses daily connect with: Aix-en-Provence (€12,
1½ hrs); Apt (€8, 1 hr); Arles (€9, 1½ hrs); Cavaillon (€4, 1 hr); Vaison-la-Romaine (€8, 1 hr); Nîmes (€9, 1½ hrs); and Pont du Gard (€7,
1 hr). As for the Luberon villages, a bewildering number of bus companies feature routes with (infrequent) buses; the bus station in Cavaillon has routes to L'Isle-sur-la-Sorge, Aix-en-Provence, and Avignon, and
some of the hard-to-get hilltop villages. You can get to Gordes on the
two-to-four buses daily run by Les Express de la Durance. Autocars Sumian has routes that service Loumarin, Bonnieux, and Apt. Voyages Arnaud has routes that include L'Isle-sur-la-Sorgue, Fontaine-de-Vaucluse,
and Bonnieux. Autocars Barlatier runs buses that stop in Bonnieux and
rarely Oppède-le-Vieux. Rubans Bleu connects Avignon with Cavaillon
and Lourmarin.

⚑ Bus Travel Information **Gare routière** (bus station) ⊠ 58 blvd. St-Roch
☎ 04-90-82-07-35. **Autocars Barlatier** ☎ 04-90-38-15-58. **Autocars Sumian**
☎ 04-90-71-03-00. **Cars Lieutaud** ☎ 04-90-86-36-75 ⊕ www.cars-lieutaud.fr. **Les
Express de la Durance** ☎ 04-90-71-03-00. **Rubans Bleu** ☎ 04-90-79-19-25. **Voyages Arnaud** ☎ 04-90-38-15-58.

BY CAR

The A6/A7 toll (*péage*) expressway channels all traffic from Paris to the south. At Orange A7 splits to the southeast and leads directly to Avignon and N100 (in the direction of Apt), which dives straight east into the Luberon. To reach Vaison and the Mont Ventoux region from Avignon, head northeast toward Carpentras on D942. D36 jags south from N100 and leads you on a gorgeous chase over the backbone of the Luberon, via Bonnieux and Lourmarin; from there it's a straight shot to Aix and Marseille or to the Côte d'Azur. Or you can shoot back west up D973 to Cavaillon and Avignon.

With spokes shooting out in every direction from Avignon and A7, you'll have no problem accessing the Vaucluse. The main *routes nationales* (national routes, or secondary highways) offer fairly direct links via D942 toward Orange and Mont Ventoux and via N100 into the Luberon. Negotiating the roads to L'Isle-sur-la-Sorgue and Fontaine de la Vaucluse requires a careful mix of map and sign reading, often at high speeds around suburban *giratoires* (rotaries). But by the time you strike out into the hills and the tiny roads—one of the best parts of the Vaucluse—give yourself over to road signs and pure faith. As is the case throughout France, directions are indicated by village name only, with route numbers given as a small-print afterthought. Of course, this means you have to recognize the minor villages en route.

BY TRAIN

Trains arrive from all points north—Paris, Strasbourg, Nantes, and Bordeaux—in Marseille. Those from Paris and Strasbourg pass through Orange and Avignon. Many of these routes have overnight runs, with *couchettes* (sleeper bunks) and, sometimes, *wagons-lit* (minicabins with hotel-like service). The quickest train link, of course, is the high-speed TGV (Trains à Grande Vitesse) *Méditerranée* line that connects Paris and Avignon (2 hrs 40 mins) and then goes on to Orange, another 40 minutes away. Keep in mind that the Gare Avignon TGV is located a few miles southwest of the city in the district of Courtine (a *navette* shuttle bus connects with the train station in town); other trains (and a few TGV) use the Gare Avignon Centre station located at 42 blvd. St-Roch. You can hop on one of the TGV trains to make a connection to Nîmes (€14, 45 minutes), Marseille (€22, 1 hr), and Nice (€47, 2½ hrs). From Gare Avignon Centre, to/from destinations in the region include: Orange (€5, 20 minutes) and Arles (€6, 20 minutes), L'Isle-sur-la-Sorgue, and Cavaillon. The center city of Orange is a 15-minute walk from the train station—walk from Avenue F. Mistral to Rue de la République, then follow signs. For the most part, secondary train connections in this area are slim to nonexistent, so you'll have to use buses to get into the Luberon villages.

◪ Train Information **SNCF** ☎ 08-36-35-35-35 ⊕ www.ter-sncf.com/uk/paca. **TGV** ☎ 877/2TGVMED ⊕ www.tgv.com.

Contacts & Resources

CAR RENTAL

Avignon, as a major rail crossroads and springboard for the Vaucluse, has plenty of car-rental agencies, and it's fairly easy to get out of town toward other destinations. Avis has an office at the Avignon rail station, Budget is to your left just as you leave the train station, and Hertz is on the station's right, by the bus station. You can penetrate as far as L'Isle-sur-la-Sorgue by train and then rent from Avis or Budget. In Orange, Avis has a location by the train station; cars must be reserved in advance. And if you telephone Budget, they'll pick you up at the station and transport you to their office about 3.5 km (2 mi) away.

🚗 Car-Rental Information Avignon: **Avis** ✉ 34 bd. St-Roche ☎ 04-90-27-96-10. **Budget** ✉ 20 bd. St-Roch ☎ 04-90-27-94-95. **Hertz** ✉ 2A av. Monclar ☎ 04-90-14-26-90. L'Isle-sur-la-Sorgue: **Avis** ✉ 58 Zone Industrielle Grande Marine ☎ 04-90-38-03-60. **Budget** ✉ Rue André Autheman ☎ 04-90-20-64-13. Orange: **Avis** ✉ 19 av. Charles de Gaulle ☎ 04-90-34-11-00. **Budget** ✉ 42 bd. Edouard Daladier ☎ 04-90-34-00-34.

EMERGENCIES

For basic information, see this section in the Smart Travel Tips chapter. In most cases, contact the town Comissariat de Police.

🚨 Emergencies **Police** ✉ Blvd. St-Roch Avignon ☎ 17.

GUIDED TOURS

An accompanied tour of Avignon's Old Town is given by the tourist office from April through October, leaving from its headquarters Tuesday, Thursday, and Saturday at 10 AM (English on request; ⇨ Visitor Information, *below*); the jaunt takes 2 hours and costs €8.

Daily bus excursions into different regions, with commentary, are offered by Cars Lieutaud; there's a booth just outside the Avignon train station. Some offer English commentary; ask in advance.

INTERNET & MAIL

In smaller towns, ask your hotel concierge if there are any Internet cafés nearby.

📧 Internet & Mail Information **Ad'Art Informative** ✉ 32 rue de la Balance, Avignon ☎ 04-90-86-68-70. **Chez WM** ✉ 41 rue du Vieux Sextier, Avignon ☎ 04-90-86-19-03. **La Poste main post office** ✉ Cours Président Kennedy, Avignon.

VISITOR INFORMATION

The Comité Départemental de Tourisme en Vaucluse accepts written queries only; streamline your request and specify your needs by category (lodging, restaurants, general sights, biking). ⊕ www.provenceguide.com is useful, too.

🏛 Tourist Office Information **Comité Départemental de Tourisme en Vaucluse** 📮 B. P. 147, Cedex 1 84008 Avignon ⊕ www.vaucluse.fr. **Apt** ✉ Av. Ph.-de-Girard, 84400 ☎ 04-90-74-03-18 🖶 04-90-04-64-30. **Avignon** ✉ 41 cours Jean-Jaurès, 84008 ☎ 04-32-74-32-74 🖶 04-90-82-95-03 ⊕ www.avignon-tourisme.com. **Bonnieux** ✉ 7 pl. Carnot, 84480 ☎ 04-90-75-91-90 🖶 04-90-75-92-94 ⊕ www.bonnieux.com. **Carpentras** ✉ Hôtel de Dieu, Pl. Aristde Ariand 84200 ☎ 04-90-63-00-78 🖶 04-90-60-41-02 ⊕ www.tourisme.fr/carpentras. **Cavaillon** ✉ Pl. François Tourel, 84305 ☎ 04-90-71-32-01 🖶 04-90-71-42-99 ⊕ www.cavaillon.com. **Châteauneuf-du-Pape** ✉ Pl. du Portail, 84230 ☎ 04-90-83-71-08 🖶 04-90-83-50-34. **Fontaine de Vaucluse** ✉ Chemin du Gouffre, 84800 ☎ 04-90-20-32-22 🖶 04-90-20-21-37. **Gigondas** ✉ Pl. du Portail, 84190 ☎ 04-90-65-85-46 🖶 04-90-65-88-42 ⊕ www.hautvaucluse.com. **Gordes** ✉ Salle des Gardes du Château, 84220 ☎ 04-90-72-02-75

🖶 04-90-72-02-26 ⊕ www.gordes-village.com. **L'Isle-sur-la-Sorgue** ✉ Pl. de l'Église, 84800 ☎04-90-38-04-78 🖶04-90-38-35-43 ⊕www.oti-delasorgue.fr. **Lourmarin** ✉ 9 av. Philippe de Girard 84160 ☎ 04-90-68-10-77 🖶 04-90-68-10-77 ⊕ www.lourmarin.com. **Orange** ✉ 5 cours A. Briand, 84100 ☎04-90-34-70-88 🖶 04-90-34-99-62 ⊕ www.ville-orange.fr. **Roussillon** ✉ Pl. de la Poste, 84220 ☎ 04-90-05-60-25 🖶 04-90-05-63-31 ⊕ www.roussillon-provence.com. **Sault** ✉ Av. de la Promenade, 84390 ☎ 04-90-64-01-21 🖶 04-90-64-15-03 ⊕ www. saultenprovence.com. **Vacqueyras** ✉ Pl. de la Mairie 84190 ☎ 04-90-12-39-02 🖶04-90-65-83-28 ⊕www.vacqueyras.tm.fr. **Vaison-la-Romaine** ✉Pl. du Chamoine Sautel, 84110 ☎ 04-90-36-02-11 🖶 04-90-28-76-04 ⊕ www.vaison-la-romaine. com. **Venasque** ✉ Grand Rue, 84210 ☎🖶 04-90-66-11-66. **Villeneuve-lez-Avignon** ✉ 1 pl. Charles David, 30400 ☎ 04-90-25-61-33 🖶 04-90-25-91-55 ⊕ www. villeneuvelezavignon.fr.

De-Coding Da Vinci in Provence

QUESTIONS, QUESTIONS, QUESTIONS. Did Mary Magdalene die in a grotto high above Marseille? Why, in fact, are so many statues of the Madonna in France "black"? And was the "Da Vinci Code" handed down through the centuries through the gypsies in France? These are just some of the mysteries you'll find addressed on the www. magdalentours.com web site. And answers can be found on their utterly fascinating "In Search of the Magdalene, the Black Madonna, and the Lost Goddess" tours, which begin in Marseille and thread through Provence to the Massif Central.

Thanks to the staggering success of Dan Brown's 2003 novel, *The Da Vinci Code*, interest in Mary Magdalene has intensified to a large degree, and so has her connections with Provence. Of course, some critics say the book should have been called *The Da Vinci Crock*—but Provence itself may hold the key. Medieval lore holds that following Jesus' crucifixion, Mary Magdalene and a small entourage of other Marys (Mary Salomé and Mary Jacobé), were chased out of Jerusalem and condemned to die—thrown unmercifully into a boat without sail or pilot. But the intrepid Marys miraculously landed safely on the shores of Les Baux in Provence.

The area was promptly christened Stes-Maries-de-la-Mer (*see* Chapter 1). And, although no official documentation of their arrival exists today, Provençal culture is now saturated with tales about them—especially predominant are ones about Mary Magdalene and, surprisingly, the young servant Sara Kali, otherwise known as Saint Sara

the Egyptian or the Black Queen, who is still revered today by gypsies. There are yearly festivals in their honor and pilgrimages dedicated to their beauty, wisdom, and saintliness.

The Da Vinci Code exploded onto the literary scene with the controversial thought that Mary Magdalene was the consort of Jesus Christ. In all fairness, this is not a totally new concept: earlier literary works like the 1983 book *Holy Blood, Holy Grail* already made this claim, and the Nag Hammadi texts, a series of early Christian gospels discovered in Egypt in 1945, suggest the same. Some believe she was a pagan priestess, and bore Jesus a child. Highbrow intellectuals call the attraction to "the Magdalene" a profound awakening to the idea that the Christian idea of God (and his human incarnation, Jesus) can no longer be separated from their female counterparts.

There are now official pilgrimages, where travelers can retrace the steps of those who worshiped the "divine feminine" in pagan and Christian times; you can do your own with a bit of research or check out the two-week expedition of Magdalene Tours. One of its many highlights—literally—is a visit to a holy cave high above Marseille where Mary Magdalene is said to have ended her life in a state of meditative prayer. Today, some scholars feel that the Da Vinci "proposition" was actually a right-wing con job begun by Provençal aristocracy and used by them for centuries to exaggerate their noble lineage. The goal? To further subjugate the lower classes they ruled over. The jury is still out.

Aix, Marseille & the Central Coast

AUBAGNE, CASSIS & THE ILES D'HYÈRES

Outdoor fish market, Old Port, Marseille

WORD OF MOUTH

"Ah, complicated Marseille—its reputation was already a bit fishy for me, and movies like the *French Connection* didn't exactly help. But what about the restoration of some seriously stunning architecture, the welcoming smiles of the people, and the TGV from Paris? Marseille is a study in contrasts. So maybe, then, it's best to be surprised—kind of like when you eat that first steaming spoonful of savory bouillabaisse."

—Cheyne

WELCOME TO AIX, MARSEILLE & THE CENTRAL COAST

Produce market, Aix-en-Provence

Aix-en-Provence. For one day, join all those fashionable folk for whom café-squatting, people-watching, and boutique-shopping are a way of life. Track the spirit of the town's most famous son, Paul Cézanne, by visiting the Jas de Bouffon, his newly opened family estate, and Mont Ste-Victoire, the main motif of this founder of modern art.

Marseille, France's second largest city, is the place to head to enjoy the colorful sights and smells of a Mediterranean melting pot—cultures have mingled here ever since the Greeks invaded, in about 600 BC. Tour the cathedrals and museums, visit the Vieux Port, famous haunt of Marcel Pagnol's Fanny, then head east to Aubagne to walk the Circuit Pagnol.

A51

E80

Aix-en-Provence

MONT STE-VICTOIRE

A7

D543

A51   D7   D6

N96

Gardanne   A52

D9   D6   D8   D908

N368

N8   BOUCHES-DU-RHONE

A55

A55

N568   A7   D908   A52

Marseille   A50   Aubagne   N396

D2

N8   N8

D559   D3

Cassis   A50

Les Calanques

Mediterranean Sea

Central Cassis. From **Cassis**—a lovely harbor town that conjures up the St-Tropez of 1920s—take an excursion boat to the famously beautiful Calanques coves: enjoy a picnic and a chilled bottle of Cassis white and clamber down the steep sides to the hidden beaches and fjord-like finger bays that probe the coast. To the east are **Toulon** and **Iles d'Hyères,** the realization of a film producer's idea of the Garden of Eden.

Marseille

Getting Oriented

Rough-hewn and fiercely beautiful, this is the sculpted land of Cézanne and Pagnol: bordered by a coastline of lonely pine-studded cliffs and fjord-like Calanques. Posh and proper Aix-en-Provence stands carefully aloof from Marseille, tough, vibrant, and larger than life. The backcountry between them ambles along at a 19th-century pace of *boules, pastis,* and country markets.

3

TOP 5 Reasons to Go

1 Aix's extraordinary Cours Mirabeau: The Champs-Élysées of posh Aix-en-Provence, this boulevard is lined with lovely cafés like Les Deux Garçons, where Cézanne and Zola used to hang out.

2 Go fishing for Marseille's best bouillabaisse: Order ahead at Chez FonFon's and indulge in classic bouillabaisse—this version will make your tastebuds stand up and sing *La Marseillaise.*

3 Become a Calanques castaway: Near Cassis, these picturesque coves make you feel like you've stumbled onto the set of *The Blue Lagoon.*

4 Paul Cézanne, superstar: Tour Cézanne country in the area around Mont Ste-Victoire, near the artist's hometown of Aix-en-Provence.

5 Iles d'Hyères, nature's paradise: A sense of pure escape can still be enjoyed on these islands covered with pine forests and sandy beaches.

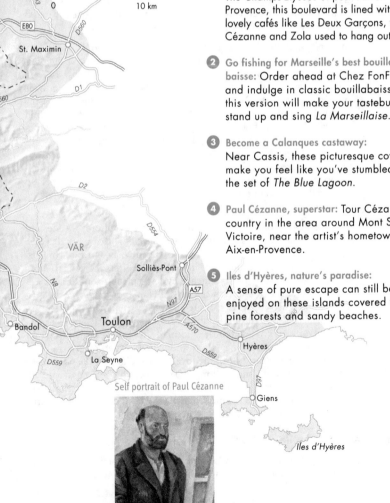

Self portrait of Paul Cézanne

Updated by
Sarah Fraser

WHEN YOU CROSS THE IMAGINARY BORDER INTO PROVENCE for the first time, you may experience a niggling sense of déjà vu. The sun-drenched angular red rooftops, the dagger-narrow cypresses, the picture-perfect port towns, and the brooding massifs fire the imagination in a deep, soul-stirring way. And it's no wonder: Some of the world's greatest artists were inspired by the unforgettable landscapes found here. Cézanne colored his canvases in daubs of russet and black-green, the rough-cut structure of bluff and twisted pine inspiring a building-block approach to painting that for others jelled into Cubism. Marcel Pagnol painted pictures with words: the smells of thyme and rosemary crunching underfoot, the sounds of thunder rumbling behind rain-starved hills, the quiet joy of opening shutters at dawn to a chorus of blackbirds in the olive grove. Both Cézanne and Pagnol were native sons of this region east of the Rhône who were inspired to eloquence by the primordial landscape and its echoes of antiquity. And yet, like most who visit the region, they were equally fascinated with the modern Provençal world and its complex melding of the ancient with the new.

For here you'll find that the stylish, charming, 200-year-old village hotel will more often than not have Internet access. In the midst of the prettiest lavender field, you'll hear the chirp of cell phones almost as often as of cicadas. And, increasingly, the influx of *bon chic, bon genre* crowds looking for the newest Michelin-starred restaurant will eclipse the pastis-drinking knot of *pépés* at the local bar. Yet it will still be possible to find the idyllic Provence of old mixed in with all this newness—the local Monday morning market where sheep bells tonk behind ancient stone walls and rosy-cheeked *paysannes* proffer homemade cheese; the narrow, cobblestone streets riddled with local cafés and tinkling fountains and historic monuments; and some of the finest Roman ruins in Europe. No wonder the world continues beat a path here to seek out its understated wonders.

A visit to this region encompasses the best of urban culture, seaside, and arid backcountry. Aix is a small, manageable city with a leisurely pace, studded with stunning architecture and a lively concentration of arts, due in part to its active university life. Marseille offers the yang to Aix's yin. Its brash style, bold monuments, and spectacular sun-washed waterfront center are reminiscent of those of Naples or modern Athens; it is much maligned for its crime rate and big-city energy, and often unfairly neglected by visitors. Up in the dry inland hills, Pagnol's hometown of Aubagne gives a glimpse of local life, with a big farmers' market in the plane tree–lined town center and makers of *santons* (terra-cotta figurines) at every turn. Both the lovely port-village of Cassis and the busy beach town of Bandol allow time to watch the tides come and go, though for the ultimate retreat, take the boat that leaves for the almost tropical Iles d'Hyères. Like most of this region, these islands are a true idyll, but even more so since they are car-free.

Exploring Aix, Marseille & the Central Coast

Aix lies at a major crossroads of autoroutes: one coming in from Bordeaux and Toulouse, then leading up into the Alps toward Grenoble;

the other a direct line from Lyons and Paris. Aix is extremely well placed for trips to the Luberon, Avignon, and Arles, and it's a quick half hour from Marseille. All the coastal towns line up for easy access between Marseille and Toulon, so you can cruise along A50, which follows the coastline, and take in all the sights. Although Marseille is one of the biggest cities in France, it's a matter of minutes before you're lost in deep backcountry on winding, picturesque roads that lead to Cassis or Aubagne and beyond.

To make the most of your time in this region, plan to divide your days between big-city culture, backcountry tours, and waterfront leisure. You can "do" Marseille in an impressive day trip, but its backstreets and tiny ports reward a more leisurely approach. Aix is as much a way of life as a city charged with tourist must-sees; allow time to hang out in a cours Mirabeau café and shop the backstreets. Aubagne must be seen on a market day (Tuesday, Saturday, or Sunday) to make the most of its charms. Cassis merits a whole day if you want to explore the calanques and enjoy a seaside lunch; Bandol is less appealing unless you're committed to beach time. The complete seaside experience, with rocky shoreline, isolated beaches, a picturesque port, and luxurious near-tropical greenery, can be found on the island of Porquerolles, one of the Iles d'Hyères; if your budget and schedule allow, spend a night or two in one of its few hotels and have much of the island to yourself.

About the Restaurants & Hotels

One eats late in Provence: rarely before 1 PM for lunch (and you can happily find yourself still at the table at 4 PM) and 8 to 9 PM for dinner: Be prepared for somewhat disdainful looks—"tourists!"—and slow responses if you try to come any earlier. Most restaurants close between lunch and dinner, even in the summer, and no matter how much you are willing to spend or how well dressed you are, you will be firmly turned away. If you are craving an afternoon glass of rosé *bien frais* and a light snack, head to one of the smaller beach or roadside sandwich kiosks, and/or the local *boulangerie* (bakery), which usually has a selection of fresh treats. The more intrepid sort can try a slice of Provençal life and brave one of the smoky, lottery playing, coffee-and-pastis drinking *tabacs* that line every main street in the South. You'll find they also often have basic fare for a reasonable price.

Accommodations in the area range from luxury villas to modest city-center hotels. This is no longer just converted *mas* (farmhouse) country. Nonetheless, hotels in this region favor Provençal flavor and aim to provide outdoor space at its loveliest, from gardens where breakfast is served to parasol pine–shaded pools. As in all of France, hotels book up well in advance for July and August. For information on *gîtes* (houses offered as a vacation rental) and *chambres d'hôtes* (bed-and-breakfasts in private homes), check out the Lodging section in the Smart Travel Tips chapter.

PLEASURES & PASTIMES

YOURS FOR THE BASKING. Wherever there's water in France, *les plages* (beaches) of every shape and substance fill up with sun lovers from June to September. The most popular beach resort is Bandol, but for a quieter retreat, head for genteel Cassis, where you can perch on rocky promontories along the *calanques* (coves). The shipbuilding port town of La Ciotat has the most sandy beach surface at the Clos des Plages, situated just beyond the pleasure-boat port.

LES SPÉCIALITÉS. Aix is one of the capitals of olive oil production in Provence, and its market tables groan with the weight of industrial-scale jugs of the stuff. Far more than a medium here, it takes center stage at the table: a pool of liquid chartreuse encircles goat cheese, a fillet of sea bass shimmers on a mirror of green-gold. The olives themselves—gleaming beads of briny salt fruit—figure everywhere, in every degree of ripeness and marinade imaginable, scooped from vats into tiny bowls to accompany the aperitif. Ground into a caviar-like spread called tapenade, made even more pungent with the addition of capers, anchovies, and garlic, the local olives appear on toast and add zip to a rosy leg of lamb.

But it's in leaving the highlands that you come upon the star cuisine of this region. Marseille and its environs have some of the finest seafood dishes in France, cooked robustly with garlic and flush with the fruits of the adjacent sea. It's here, more than anywhere else along the southern coast, that you find authentic bouillabaisse, the quintessential fish stew of Provence. In it, chunks of Mediterranean fish otherwise too small and, frankly, too ugly to market—*rascasse, congre, grondin*—float with shellfish in a powerful broth of tomato-red fish stock, perfumed with garlic, onion, fennel, herbs, and—a must—orange peel and saffron. The simmered concoction (*bouillir*, for boiled, and *abaisser*, for reduced) is served in two courses: First the broth is poured over bread slices; it is then followed by a parade of tender fish. A dollop of *rouille* (chili peppers and garlic whipped into olive oil paste) gives an extra jolt to the broth. Because of the price of fresh seafood, an authentic bouillabaisse will set you back from €31 to €40; order a bottle of chilled Cassis and enjoy the ritual.

If bouillabaisse is too rich for your blood, the ubiquitous *soupe de poisson* (fish soup) is an affordable alternative: less subtly seasoned and stirred to a thick velouté, it appears as a first-course option on just about every regional menu. Spread the oil-brushed croutons with rouille and float them in the soup along with a sprinkle of ground cheese.

Where you eat in this region is often as wonderful as what you eat: outdoor tables pepper the sidewalks of Marseille and Aix nearly year-round, and coastal restaurants vie to give you the best sea views.

SEA FOR YOURSELF. If you find yourself without a yacht on this wild and lovely coastline, it's easy to jump on a tourist cruiser, whether you putter from calanque to calanque between Marseille and Cassis or commute to the car-free Iles d'Hyères. Many boats are glass-bottomed for underwater viewing, and most allow you

3

to climb onto the top deck and face the bracing wind as the cruiser bucks the waves.

ROSÉS & REDS. The heart of the **Côtes de Provence** region is summer wine country, where its fresh, unpretentious rosés will be found chilling in buckets at every table. There are also reds, rather Italian in their hearty, fruity strength, and negligible whites, too, but the category always conjures rosés first and foremost. The smaller **Côteaux d'Aix** region, surrounding Aix-en-Provence, produces unsensational but very drinkable rosés, as well as minor reds and whites. Yet this region concentrates the very best of Provence, indeed its only fine wines, labeled by their place name rather than the umbrella title of Côtes de Provence. **Bandol,** famous as the best-rounded and most viable of all the rosés, makes a crisp white and a strong red, too. **Cassis** (not to be confused with the black-currant liqueur produced in Burgundy) creates marvelous whites with distinct shades of almond; it's the wine of choice with a spicy bouillabaisse, and it won't overwhelm a simple fillet. But the lone contender for the title of Great Wine comes from a tiny region around Aix, called **Palette.** Here Château Simone produces a magnificent red redolent of *garrigue,* the wild thyme, rosemary, and pine that flavor its soil, as well as a wonderful, substantial white; by all means, splurge.

CALLING ALL HIKE-A-HOLICS. The walk from Cassis to the Calanques is one of the most dramatic in France, with cliff-top views over the ocean and clambering descents to intimate inlet beaches. In the hills above Marseille, so beloved by Pagnol, you can still follow his childhood trails and stand on the spot from which

Ugolin screamed, *"Manon, je t'aime!"* ("Manon, I love you!") in *Manon des Sources* (*Manon of the Springs*). The mountain called Ste-Victoire, often painted by Cézanne, has wonderful hikes and beautiful views. Contact the Bouches-du-Rhône departmental tourist office (⇨ Aix, Marseille, and the Central Coast A to Z, *below*) for information about hikes in the area.

SHOPPING À LA FOLKLORIQUE. Some of the smallest villages have their predatory claws unfurled these days, with every house a storefront overflowing with doodads and gewgaws on Provençal themes. Pottery mugs with good-luck cicadas and coasters of the famous sunflowers are the bastard children of legitimate crafts and products that are intrinsically Provence—marvelously mild and natural *savon de Marseille* (Marseille soap); *boutis,* intricately quilted cotton throws; richly textured Provençal fabrics in 18th-century reproduction paisley prints, put to legitimate use as skirts, curtains, and tablecloths; artisanal olive oils from the Alpilles; and if you acquire the taste, the sometimes exquisitely rendered *santons,* tiny terra-cotta figurines first made for Provençal Christmas crèches. The best *santonniers* have studios in Aubagne, but you'll find gift stores with them throughout the region, including Marseille.

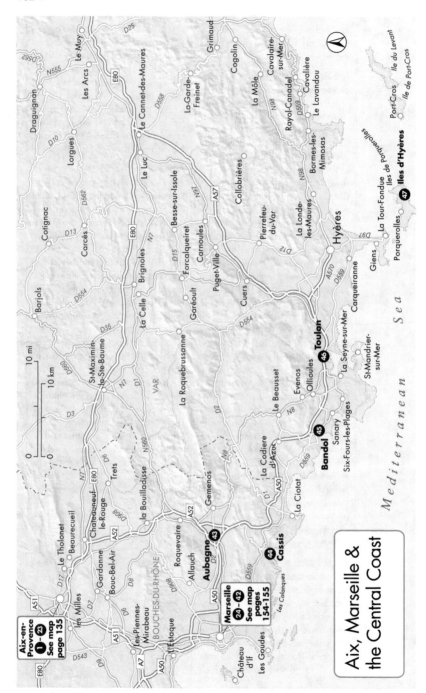

Aix, Marseille & the Central Coast

D25

D566

N555

Draguignan

Le Muy

Les Arcs

Le Cannet-des-Maures

Grimaud

Cogolin

La Môle

Cavalaire-sur-Mer

Cavalière

Rayol-Canadel

Le Lavandou

La Garde-Freinet

D559

D10

Lorgues

Le Luc

D562

D13

Cotignac

Carcés

Besse-sur-Issole

N97

Collobrières

Pierrefeu-du-Var

Bormes-les-Mimosas

N98

D559

Port-Cros   Île du Levant

Île de Port-Cros

Îles d'Hyères

Iles de Porquerolles

La Tour-Fondue

47 Îles d'Hyères

D97

Porquerolles

Forcalqueiret

Carnoules

Puget-Ville

La Londe-les-Maures

Hyères

Borjols

D554

Brignoles

E80

N7

La Celle

Garéoult

Cuers

D554

A570

D559

Giens

Carqueiranne

La Roquebrussanne

VAR

Toulon

La Seyne-sur-Mer

St-Mandrier-sur-Mer

46

St-Maximin-la-Ste-Baume

D80

N7

D1

Evenos

Ollioules

Le Beausset

N8

D2

D3

D35

Trets

N560

D6

N7

E80

Châteauneuf-le-Rouge

A52

Bandol

45

Sanary

La Cadière-d'Azur

D559

Six-Fours-les-Plages

Mediterranean   Sea

Mediterranean Sea

Gardanne

Bouc-Bel-Air

D8

D7

A51

A52

La Bouilladisse

Roquevaire

Gemenos

A50

La Ciotat

D1

Aubagne

43

Cassis

44

D559

Les Calanques

Allauch

D908

BOUCHES-DU-RHÔNE

D543

Les Pennes-Mirabeau

A51

L'Estaque

A7

A50

Château d'If

Les Goudes

Aix-en-Provence

1 – **23**

See map
page 135

D17

Le Tholonet

Beaurecueil

A51

D17

Les Milles

D9

E80

Marseille

24 – **42**

See map
pages 154-155

10 mi

10 km

0

	\$\$\$\$	**\$\$\$**	**\$\$**	**\$**	**¢**
WHAT IT COSTS In euros					
RESTAURANTS	over €30	€23–€29	€18–€22	€12–€17	under €11
HOTELS	over €191	€121–€190	€81–€120	€51–€80	under €50

Restaurant prices are per person for a main course at dinner; note that if a restaurant offers only prix-fixe meals, it has been given the price category that reflects the full set-price. Hotel prices are for a standard double room in high season, including tax (19.6%) and service charge. Assume all hotel rooms have air-conditioning, telephones, TV, and private bath, unless otherwise noted. Hotels operate on the European Plan (EP, with no meal provided) unless we note that they use the Breakfast Plan (BP), the Modified American Plan (MAP, with breakfast and dinner daily, known as *demi-pension*), or Full American Plan (FAP, or *pension complète*, with three meals a day). Inquire when booking if these all-inclusive mealplans (which always entail higher rates) are mandatory or optional during peak season dates.

Timing

High season falls between Easter and October, but if you come in the winter you may be pampered with warm sun and cool breezes. When the mistral attacks (and it can happen year-round), it channels all its forces down the Rhône Valley and blasts into Marseille like a one-way tornado. But, happily, the assault may last only one day. This is not the day, however, to opt for a boat ride from Cassis or Porquerolles; aim instead for the sheltered streets of Aix.

AIX-EN-PROVENCE: CITY OF CÉZANNE

Longtime rival of edgier, more exotic Marseille, the lovely town of Aix-en-Provence (pronounced *ex*) is gracious, cultivated, and made all the more cosmopolitan by the presence of some 40,000 university students. In keeping with its aristocratic heritage, Aix quietly exudes well-bred suavity and elegance—indeed, it is now one of the ten richest townships in France. The influence and power it once had as the old capital of Provence—fine art, noble architecture, and graceful urban design—remain equally important to the city today. And, although it is true that Aix owns up to a few modern-day eyesores, the overall impression is one of beautifully preserved stone monuments, quietly sophisticated nightlife, leafy plane trees, and gently splashing fountains. With its thriving market, vibrant café life, spectacularly chic shops, and superlative music festival, it's one of the towns in Provence that really should not be missed.

The Romans were first drawn here by mild thermal baths, naming the town Aquae Sextiae (Waters of Sextius) in honor of Roman consul Sextius who defeated the Celto-Ligurians at Entremont in 122 BC; the remains of his camp lie just outside the city. In 142 BC the great Roman general Marius flanked and pinned 200,000 invading Germans against the mountain known ever since as Ste-Victoire. The name Marius is still popular in Provence today.

The fall of the Roman Empire saw a corresponding decline in Aix, although it remained significant enough to have its first cathedral built in the 5th century. Under the wise and generous guidance of Good King René in the 15th century, it became a center of Renaissance arts and letters. A poet himself and patron of the arts, the king encouraged a veritable army of artists to flourish here. The artists in turn gratefully left a handful of masterpieces, including Nicolas Froment's *Triptyque du Buisson Ardent (Burning Bush Triptych)* in the Cathédrale St-Sauveur. At the height of its political, judicial, and ecclesiastical power in the 17th and 18th centuries, Aix profited from a surge of private building, each *grand hôtel particulier* (mansion) meant to outdo its neighbor. The ring of boulevards, the *cours,* punctuated by great fountains and intriguing passageways, date from this time.

It was into this exalted elegance that artist Paul Cézanne (1839–1906) was born, though he drew much of his inspiration not from the city itself but from the raw countryside around it, often painting scenes of Montagne Ste-Victoire. A schoolmate of Cézanne's made equal inroads on modern society: the journalist and novelist Emile Zola (1840–1902) attended the Collège Bourbon with Cézanne and described their friendship as well as Aix itself in several of his works. You can sense something of the vibrancy that nurtured these two geniuses in the streets of modern Aix, not only charged by its large university population but continually injected with new blood from exchange programs: Vanderbilt, California State, Michigan, and Wisconsin all send students to this stimulating city. Aix is also home to a high-tech industry nexus that rivals Sophia Antipolis on the Côte d'Azur, with numerous research institutes and France's biggest appeals court outside Paris. There's also a British-American Institute and an American Center—

> ## IT'S AN ILL WIND THAT BLOWS
>
> If you come to Provence in late autumn or early spring, bring your windbreaker. The infamous mistral is a bitterly cold, dry wind that comes sweeping down from the north whenever a low pressure weather system develops over the Mediterranean. The temperature can drop dramatically in just a matter of minutes. Many roads, fields, and towns have wind-breaks of closely planted trees or stone walls to give some shelter from these fierce winds, which, some say, often bring out irritable "mistral nerves" in the locals—one reason the Aixois have a reputation for being snappy.

in short, enough students and intellectuals to keep the crêperies and cafés crowded into the wee hours and to sustain a branch of The Gap. It's not just the universities that keep Aix young: its famous Festival International d'Art Lyrique (International Opera Festival) has imported and created world-class opera productions as well as related concerts and recitals since 1948. Most of the performances take place in elegant, old Aix settings, and during this time the cafés, restaurants, and hotels spill over with the *beau monde* who've come to Aix especially for the July event.

The Historic Heart

The famous Cours Mirabeau, a broad, shady avenue that stretches from one grand fountain to another, bisects old Aix into two distinct neighborhoods. Below the Cours, the carefully planned Quartier Mazarin

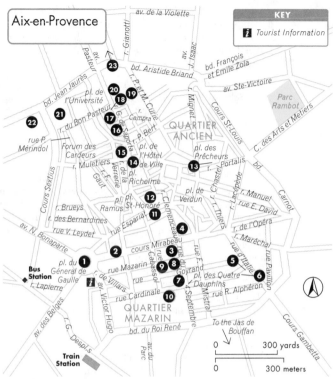

is lined with fine 17th- and 18th-century mansions. Above, the Old Town twists and turns from square to fountain square, each turn leading to another row of urban boutiques and another buzzing cluster of café tables. If you turn a blind eye to these enticing distractions, you can see the best of Aix in a day's tour—but you'll be missing the point. The music of the fountains, the theater of the café crowds, and the painterly shade of the plane trees are what Aix is all about.

**A GOOD
WALK**

Begin at the tourist office, which anchors the Cours Mirabeau at Place du Général de Gaulle. The spiraling traffic, kiosks, newsstands, events posters, and crowds of students contrast sharply with **La Rotonde ❶**, the monumental sculpture-fountain in black and white marble that towers above the swirl of modernity. Walk up the **Cours Mirabeau ❷**, which is both the physical and social heart of the city. With vibrant café life to your left and grand old mansions to your right, you pass a series of fountains, including the magnificently mossy **Fontaine d'Eau Chaude ❸** (which actually steams with thermal-spring water). At No. 55 are traces of the hat shop founded by Cézanne's father, now worn away by time: the sign still reads CHAPELLERIE DU COURS MIRABEAU, GROS ET DÉTAIL (Hat shop of the Cours Mirabeau, wholesale and retail). Cézanne himself hung out at the **Café les Deux Garçons ❹**, the landmark café-restaurant that still serves gold-rimmed cups of espresso to artists and dreamers, all nowadays armed with mobile phones. If you want to explore Cézanne sites in-depth, be sure to pick up the fabulous pamphlet, "In Cézanne's Footsteps" at the tourist office: it has all the details on the sites, linked together by the **Circuit Cézanne**, a series of brass plaques right on the sidewalks that mark the itinerary.

Now cut right down the lively market street Rue d'Italie and turn left at the **Église St-Jean-de-Malte** ❺, once the chapel for a Knights of Malta priory and one of the earliest Gothic structures in France. Just across the way, the **Musée Granet** ❻, to reopen in summer 2006 with a block-buster show, "Cézanne in Provence," co-curated with the National Gallery of Art in Washington, D.C. Beyond its beautiful exterior, the museum houses a quite formidable collection of French art and archaeology. Follow Rue Cardinale to the heart of the elegant Quartier Mazarin, the city's 18th-century district: the **Fontaine des Quatre Dauphins** ❼, a graceful obelisk framed by curving dolphins, which set off the patrician symmetry of the regal homes around it. Turn right up Rue du 4 Septembre (home to several spiffy antique shops) to the **Musée Paul Arbaud** ❽, with its highly personal collection of faïence and regional books. Then continue west down Rue Goyrand to Rue Cabassol; No. 3 is the imposing **Hôtel de Caumont** ❾, now home to the Conservatoire de Musique Darius-Milhaud. Head down Rue Cabassol (away from Cours Mirabeau) to Rue Cardinale, and you may see students of the Lycée Mignet crossing the courtyard of the former **Collège Royal-Bourbon** ❿, just as alumni Cézanne and Zola once did.

Now head back up Rue Cabassol and cross Cours Mirabeau to enter the lovely labyrinth above it. Plunge straight in and veer left; on your right is the graceful **Place d'Albertas** ⓫, lined with fine old shuttered mansions. The **Muséum d'Histoire Naturelle** ⓬, with its collection of dinosaur fossils (including hundreds of eggs found on Ste-Victoire), is just behind you in the Hôtel Boyer d'Eguilles. Follow Rue Espariat to Place de Verdun, where the Palais de Justice looms over an antiques market held three times a week. Walk the length of the square and the adjoining Place des Prêcheurs to the **Église de la Madeleine** ⓭, where you'll find Barthélemy Van Eyck's *Annunciation,* a landmark in art history texts and one of the most famous paintings of the Franco-Netherlandish 15th-century school. Next wind your way back via Rue de Montigny to Place Richelme and the **Ancienne Halle aux Grains** ⓮, these days a post office. Walk around to the front and admire its allegorical frieze of the rivers Rhône and Durance. You're now on the gorgeous Place de l'Hôtel de Ville, often the setting for a flower market. Up and to the left stands the **Hôtel de Ville** ⓯, with its soaring, 15th-century clock tower.

Continue up Rue Gaston de Saporta to the **Musée du Vieil Aix** ⓰, which houses eclectic memorabilia from Aix's past, including a wonderfully fragile line of mechanical puppets that depict the Corpus Christi procession that was a staple of Aix's life every June until the 20th century. Just beyond it on the left is the **Hôtel de Châteaurenard** ⓱, where interesting trompe-l'oeil murals are concealed around a grand staircase; peek in, as it's a public building. Next door in the **Hôtel Maynier d'Oppède** ⓲ is a French-language school; its courtyard is where concerts are held during the July opera festival. Across the street, the luxurious Palais de l'Archevêché (Bishop's Palace) houses the **Musée des Tapisseries** ⑲, containing a rich collection of Beauvais tapestries including a particularly lively series of scenes from *Don Quixote*; an open-air theater occupies its majestic courtyard during the summer. Next to it, the **Cathédrale St-Sauveur** ⑳ provides a survey course in architectural history, from its 5th-century baptistery to its Gothic-Romanesque double nave, and shelters the magnificent *Triptyque du Buisson Ardent.*

You're not far now from the very last traces of the medieval ramparts that once surrounded this ancient city; they're just up from the cathedral and to the left. Continue past this old stone wall, and you'll reach an even older landmark: the **Thermes Sextius** ㉑, now a high-tech treatment center. Just behind, turn left along the busy Boulevard Jean-Jaurès and continue to the **Pavillon de Vendôme** ㉒, an extremely elegant 17th-century country house displaying regional furniture and art. From here, you may want to make a pilgrimage across the busy boulevard to the **Atelier Cézanne** ㉓, built by the artist when the beloved country house in which he worked was sold. Heading to the south of the city, the family estate of Cézanne, the **Jas de Bouffan** recently opened to the public as part of the 2006 commemoration of the 100th anniversary of the painter's death. It is a quintessentially beautiful (and melancholy) Provençal house and park, immortalized in numerous canvases by Cézanne who spent his formative years here.

TIMING If you want to only take in the big picture, you can easily stroll this broad circuit in a half day, browsing through shops and morning markets in the Old Town, then crossing Cours Mirabeau to the Quartier Mazarin to admire the fine old architecture. If you want to visit one of the Mazarin's museums, spend a half day in this neighborhood, then devote the afternoon to the Old Town and the cathedral north of Cours Mirabeau. A visit to Cézanne's Atelier requires extra walking time beyond the town center.

What to See

⑭ **Ancienne Halle aux Grains** (Old Grain Market). Built in 1761, this former grain market serves as a post office today—a rather spectacular building for a prosaic service. The frieze, portraying an allegory of the Rhône and Durance rivers, is the work of Aix sculptor Jean Chaste (1726–93); he also created the fountain out in front. That's a real Roman column at the fountain's top. ⌂ *Pl. Richelme.*

⑳ **Atelier Cézanne** (Cézanne's Studio). After the death of his mother forced
Fodor'sChoice the sale of Paul Cézanne's beloved country retreat known as Jas de Bouf-
★ fan, he had this studio built just above the town center. In the upstairs work space, the artist created some of his finest paintings, including *Les Grandes Baigneuses* (*The Large Bathers*). The latter was so large, in fact, that the artist had a special slot built into the studio wall, as the canvas was too broad to carry down the stairs. But what is most striking is the collection of simple objects that once featured prominently in the still lifes he created: the tin milk can, the ginger jar, the flowered crockery, bottles and glasses from *La Nature Morte aux Oignons* (*Still Life with Onions*),

and a tin coffee pot from *La Femme à la Cafétière* (*The Woman with the Coffee Pot*). Also here are Cézanne's redingote and bowler hat, hanging from pegs just as he left them; brushes, paint tubes, and the engravings with which he surrounded himself—works by Courbet, Delacroix, and Poussin. The atelier is behind an obscure garden gate on the left as you climb the Avenue Paul-Cézanne. For more on Cézanne's art and the 2006 events honoring the centenary of his death, see "Paul Cézanne, Superstar" in this chapter. ✉ *9 av. Paul-Cézanne* ☎ *04–42–21–06–53* ⊕ *www. atelier-cezanne.com* 🖃 *€5.50* ⊗ *Apr.–June and Sept., daily 10–noon and 2–6; July–Aug., daily 10–6; Oct.–Mar., daily 10–noon and 2–5.*

❹ **Café-Brasserie les Deux Garçons.** Cézanne enjoyed his coffee and papers
Fodor'sChoice here, as have generations of *beau monde,* intellectuals, and neighbor-
★ hood *habitués* since its founding in 1792. The gilt-and-muraled interior is original, so be sure to take a look. The locals often prefer to take a table on the boulevard terrace of the Cours Mirabeau, considering it to be *the* place to sit to see and be seen. But if you want to travel back in time to the *époque consulaire,* sit inside. ✉ *53 cours Mirabeau* ☎ *04–42–26–00–51* ⊕ *www.les2garcons.com.*

★ ❷⓿ **Cathédrale St-Sauveur.** Built, according to legend, on the site of an ancient temple of Apollo, this marvelous cathedral was originally built in the 5th century but had ongoing construction up until the 18th century. The resulting architectural hodgepodge is quite spectacular, and is immediately obvious as soon as you look at the facade. To the south, a 12th-century Romanesque gate tucks into a Roman wall; to the north a richly sculpted Gothic gate leads to a tower erected in the 13th century. Although the interior may pale by first comparison, closer inspection reveals a remarkable double nave, Romanesque and Gothic side by side. The right-hand nave has an extraordinary Merovingian (5th-century) **baptistery,** its colonnade mostly salvaged from old Roman temples. Shutters hide the ornate **portals,** opened by a guide on request, and the hole in the ground is a curious testament to the old days of baptism by total immersion.

At the very end of the left-hand nave is a 17th-century **Corpus Domini chapel** with a painting by Jean Daret. But by far the most remarkable element is the 15th-century altarpiece painted by Nicolas Froment, the *Triptyque du Buisson Ardent* (Burning Bush Triptych). It depicts the generous art patrons King René and Queen Jeanne kneeling on either side of the Virgin, who is poised above a burning bush. An artist himself (his illuminated *Book of the Broken Heart* is one of the most beautiful works of art of the Late Gothic), René founded one of Europe's most refined courts in nearby Tarascon. The extraordinary details of Froment's painting are charged with biblical references—for example, the imperfect mirror in the Virgin's hand (St. Paul to the Corinthians: "For now we see through a glass, darkly") and Moses barefoot in the thorns and thistles (the burning bush to Moses: "Put off thy shoes from off thy feet, for the place whereon thou standest is holy ground"). There's even a complete trio of Adam, Eve, and a serpent in an angel's cameo. Froment was eager to show off his newly acquired perspective technique in the rippling planes of red drapery and the juxtaposition of the king and queen: if you imagine the side panels fitted together at a 45-degree angle, the background detail falls into one plane—and the king and queen kneel side by side before the Virgin. The painting owes its extraordinary condition to having been hidden away in a Carmelite convent for centuries and opened only once a year. It's just as delicate today, and there's the rub—now it's kept closed indefinitely to prevent its oil and tempera mix from being damaged. If you care passionately about seeing it (as you should), you can view it on Tuesday from 3 to 4, or make your wish known to the porters and administration and even the tourist office. An impassioned plea could open doors—or protective shutters. ⊠ *Rue Gaston de Saporta* ☎ *04–42–23–45–65* ☉ *Mon.–Sat., 7:30–noon and 2–6 (except during services); Sun. 9:30–noon and 2–6 (except during services).*

🔟 **Collège Royal-Bourbon.** It's within these walls, which now belong to the Lycée Mignet, that Cézanne and his schoolmate Emile Zola discussed their ideas. Cézanne received his baccalauréat *cum laude* here in 1858 and went on to attend a year of law school to please his father. ⊠ *Rue Cardinale at Rue Joseph-Cabassol.*

NEED A BREAK? For an excellent cup of inexpensive, fresh-roast coffee, wander into **La Brûlerie Richelme** (⊠ Pl. Richelme). Comfy chairs and lively student patronage add to the casual ambience and the light snacks are just the thing.

★ ❷ **Cours Mirabeau.** At the heart of the city, with its deep shade of tall plane trees interlacing their heavy leaves over the street, Cours Mirabeau is the social nerve center of Aix. One side of the street—the northern border of the Quartier Mazarin—is lined with dignified 18th-century mansions that house mostly banks or businesses; you can view them from a seat in one of the dozen or so cafés and restaurants that spill onto the sidewalk on the opposite, sunnier, side. The street is named after the radical, not to mention hypnotically ugly, Count of Mirabeau. A rake in his youth, he scandalized society by leaving his carriage—*all night*—outside the home of his fiancée before their wedding. He went on, despite this extraordinary lapse in judgment, to be elected to the quasi-noble Third Estate in Aix in 1789.

⓭ **Église de la Madeleine.** Though the facade now bears 19th-century touches, this small 17th-century church still contains the center panel of the fine 15th-century *Annunciation Triptych,* attributed to the father of Jan Van Eyck, the greatest painter of the Early Netherlandish school. Some say the massive painting on the left side of the transept is a Rubens. The church is used regularly for classical concerts. ⊠ *Pl. des Prêcheurs* ☎ *04–42–38–02–81* ☉ *Daily 8–11:30 and 3–5:30.*

❺ **Église St-Jean-de-Malte.** This 12th-century chapel of the Knights of Malta, a medieval order of friars devoted to hospital care, was Aix's first attempt at the Gothic style, and its delicate groin-vaulted ceilings and tall windows have a touching purity of line. It was here that the counts of Provence were buried throughout the 18th century; their tombs (in the upper left) were attacked during the Revolution and only partially repaired. ⊠ *Intersection of Rue Cardinale and Rue d'Italie.*

③ Fontaine d'Eau Chaude (Hot Water Fountain). Deliciously thick with dripping moss, this 18th-century fountain is fed by Sextius's own thermal source. It seems representative of Aix at its artfully negligent best. In sunny Provence, Aix was famous for its shade and its fountains; apropos, James Pope-Hennessy, in his *Aspects of Provence,* compares living in Aix to being at the bottom of an aquarium, thanks to all the fountains' bubbling water and the city's shady streets and boulevards. ⊠ *Cours Mirabeau.*

⑦ Fontaine des Quatre Dauphins (Four Dolphins Fountain). Within a tiny square at a symmetrical crossroads in the Quartier Mazarin, this lovely 17th-century fountain has four graceful dolphins at the foot of a pine cone–topped obelisk. Under the shade of a chestnut tree and framed by broad, shuttered mansions, it makes an elegant ensemble worth contemplating from the park bench. ⊠ *Pl. des Quatre Dauphins.*

⑨ Hôtel de Caumont. This elegant mansion built in 1720 contains the **Conservatoire de Musique Darius-Milhaud** (Darius-Milhaud Music Conservatory). A native of Marseille, the composer Milhaud (1892–1974) spent several years of his childhood in Aix and returned here to die. He was a member of the group of French composers known as Les Six, and created fine-boned, transparent works influenced by jazz and Hebrew chant. Aix has yet to make a museum of his memorabilia. ⊠ *3 rue Joseph-Cabassol* ☎ *04–42–26–38–70* ☜ *Free.*

⑰ Hôtel de Châteaurenard. Across from a commercial gallery that calls itself the Petit Musée Cézanne (actually more of a tourist trap), this 17th-century mansion once hosted Louis XIV—and now houses government offices. This means that during business hours you can slip in and peek at the fabulous 18th-century stairwell, decorated in flamboyant trompe l'oeil. Pseudo-stone putti and caryatids pop into three dimensions—as does the false balustrade that mirrors the real one in stone. ⊠ *19 rue Gaston de Saporta* ☽ *Weekdays 9–4.*

⑱ Hôtel Maynier d'Oppède. This ornately decorated mansion houses the **Institut d'Etudes Françaises** (Institute of French Studies), where foreign students take French classes. During the July opera festival its courtyard is used for a series of classical concerts. ⊠ *23 rue Gaston de Saporta* ☎ *04–42–21–70–92.*

⑮ Hôtel de Ville (City Hall). Built between 1655 and 1678 by Pierre Pavillon, the City Hall is fronted by a pebble-encrusted courtyard set off by a wrought-iron gateway. At the back, a double stairway leads to the Salle des Etats de Provences, the old regional assembly room (where taxes were voted on) that is hung with interesting portraits and pictures of mythological characters. From the window, look for the unmistakable 16th-century clock tower with an open ironwork belfry. The tree-lined square in front—where cafés set up tables right into the center of the space—is a popular gathering place. ⊠ *Pl. de Hotel-de-Ville* ☎ *04–42–91–90–00.*

⑥ Musée Granet. In the graceful Quartier Mazarin and set below the Cours Mirabeau, this museum was once the town's École de Dessin (Art School). Its entry in the history books is a bit inglorious, as it once granted

Cézanne a *second* prize in 1856. The academic teacher in charge poopooed the young Paul and, in fact, wouldn't allow any Cézannes to enter the museum collection while he was alive (surprisingly, this philistine attitude is still shared by a large number of Aixois). Once the former priory of the Église St-Jean-de-Malte, the museum has recently completed a massive renovation which should triple the exhibition area. By summer 2006, the doors will open again, first to showcase the "Cézanne in Provence" show, co-organized by Philip Conisbee and Denis Coutagne, curators, respectively from Washington, D.C.'s National Gallery and the Musée Granet. By fall 2006, the Granet's important collection of Provençal and Flemish painters will once again be on view, now housed in some rather disconcertingly modern rooms. Happily, the sculpture collection still resides in grandeur in its 19th-century hall. Collection highlights include paintings by Rubens, a collection of works by the museum's founder, François Granet, and eight of Cézanne's paintings, as well as a nice collection of his watercolors and drawings (interesting enough, bestowed on the museum by the national government, since the locals still have mixed feelings about their resident master). ⊠ *Pl. St-Jean-de-Malte* ☎ *04–42–38–14–70* ☒ *€2* ⊙ *Wed.–Mon., 10–noon and 2–6.*

⑧ Musée Paul Arbaud. A rich and varied collection of Provençal faïence is displayed in this grand mansion in the Mazarin quarter. It also contains a library full of books on Provençal culture. ⊠ *2 rue du 4-Septembre* ☎ *04–42–38–38–95* ☒ *€2.50* ⊙ *Musée Mon.–Sat. 2–5; library Tues. and Thurs. 2–5.*

★ ⑲ Musée des Tapisseries (Tapestries Museum). Housed in the hyper-elegant 17th-century **Palais de l'Archevêché** (Archbishop's Palace), this sumptuous collection of tapestries actually decorated the walls of the bishops' quarters. Their taste was excellent: there are 17 magnificent hangings from Beauvais, including a lush series on the life of Don Quixote from Compiègne. The main opera productions of the Festival International d'Art Lyrique are presented in the spacious courtyard. ⊠ *28 pl. Martyrs de la Résistance* ☎ *04–42–23–09–91* ☒ *€2.50* ⊙ *Wed.–Mon., 10–12:30 and 1:30–5.*

⑯ Musée du Vieil Aix (Museum of Old Aix). An eclectic assortment of local treasures resides in this 17th-century mansion, from faïence to santons (terra-cotta figurines). There are 19th-century puppets displayed in historic tableaux, and ornately painted furniture. The building itself is lovely, too, from the dramatic stairwell to the painted beams and frescoes. The lovely boudoir is capped with a cupola decked with garlands of flowers, painted by artists who worked on the trompe l'oeil in the Châteaurenard. ⊠ *17 rue Gaston de Saporta* ☎ *04–42–21–43–55* ☒ *€4* ⊙ *Apr.–Oct., Tues.–Sun. 10–noon and 2:30–6; Nov.–Mar., Tues.–Sun. 10–noon and 2–5.*

⑫ Muséum d'Histoire Naturelle (Natural History Museum). An unusual collection of dinosaur eggs is this museum's claim to fame. Even if these don't interest you, the 17th-century Hôtel Boyer d'Eguilles's interiors are magnificent, with ornate woodwork and sculpture scattered among the fossilized bones. ⊠ *6 rue Espariat* ☎ *04–42–26–23–67* ☒ *€2* ⊙ *June–Oct., daily 10–6; Nov.–May, daily 10–noon and 1–5.*

Paul Cézanne, Superstar

MATISSE CALLED HIM "the father of us all." He helped catapult Picasso into Cubism. And nearly every artist working today owes a huge debt to the man who finally kicked over the traces of traditional art—Paul Cézanne (1839–1906), Aix-en-Provence's most famous native son. His images of Mont Ste-Victoire and his timeless still-lifes are the founding icons of 20th-century painting. With them, he not only invented a new pictorial language but immortalized his Provençal homeland. So it it is only proper that Provence is returning due honor in 2006 by marking the centenary of his death with a packed calendar of special events. The "Saison Cézanne" is spearheaded by a blockbuster show first seen at Washington, D.C.'s National Gallery of Art—"Cézanne in Provence" on view at Aix-en-Provence's Musée Granet, June 9–Sept. 17, 2006. For all the festivities, log on to www.cezanne-2006.com.

A Cézanne self-portrait seen on an Aix street.

Great Cézannes may hang in museums (or appear for sale—one brought $50,000,000 in 2003) but you can't really understand the artist without experiencing his Provence firsthand. As it turns out, he is everywhere: Aix even has a Cézanne trail (marked with "C" copper studs) to mark sites within town. The two most moving locales, however, are set just outside the city. Cézanne's father bought the Jas de Bouffon estate in 1859 to celebrate his rise from hatmaker to banker. The budding artist lived here until 1899. Today, its salons are empty but the grounds are full of his spirit, especially the Allée des Marronniers out front. Opening April 2006 for the first time to the

public, the Jas is a mile south of town and can only be visited on tour by booking a minibus seat through the town's central tourist office (www. aixenprovencetourism.com—hours and prices were not fixed at press time). One mile north of Aix's center is "Les Lauves," the studio the artist built in 1901 (see Atelier Cézanne in What to See), set in a magically overgrown olive grove. The high point here lies a mile further along the Chemin de la Marguerite: the belvedere spot from which the artist painted his last views of Mont Ste-Victoire (indeed,

The Allée des Marronniers, Jas de Bouffon.

3

Mont Ste-Victoire.

he died shortly after being caught in a storm here).

The Mona Lisa of modern art, Cézanne painted self-portraits that were inscrutable and hiding many secrets. He was illegitimate; he wound up having an 17-year-long affair with Hortense Piquet; and he hid his own illegitimate son from his father to inherit the family fortune.

Indeed, this "painter of peasants" never worked a day in his life. Unless, that is, you consider revolutionizing the art of painting "work."

When he abandoned Aix's art academy for the dramatic landscapes of the surrounding hills, he became smitten with the stark, high-noon light of Provence, rejecting the sugar-almond hues of Impressionism. Instead of mixing colors to create shadows like Monet, he simply used black. Instead of using translucent haze to create an effect of distance,

he focused on ruler-straight Provençal streets (laid out by ancient Romans) to hurtle the eye from fore to background.

In the end, Cézanne wanted to impose himself on the landscape, not vice versa. So why not do the same? With brochures from the Aix tourist office, head out into Cézanne country—the roads leading to Le Tholonet and Mont Ste-Victoire. Walk these shady trails and you'll learn just how Cézanne became the trailblazer of modern art.

At the Les Lauves studio.

㉒ Pavillon de Vendôme. This extravagant Baroque villa was first built in
FodorsChoice 1665 as a "country" house for the Duke of Vendome; its position just
★ outside the city's inner circle allowed the duke to commute discreetly
from his official home on the Cours Mirabeau to this love nest, where
his mistress, La Belle du Canet, was comfortably installed. Though
never officially inhabited, it was expanded and heightened in the 18th
century to showcase the classical orders—Ionic, Doric, and Corinthian—
in its parade of neo-Grecian columns. Inside its cool, broad chambers
you'll find a collection of Provençal furniture and artworks. ✉ *13 rue
de la Molle* ☎ *04-42-21-05-78* 🎟 *€2* ☉ *Mar.-Sept., Wed.-Mon.
10-noon and 2-6; Oct.-Feb., Wed.-Mon. 10-12:30 and 1:30-5:30.*

⑪ Place d'Albertas. Of all the elegant squares in Aix, this one is the most
evocative and otherworldly. Set back from the city's fashionable shopping streets, it forms a horseshoe of shuttered mansions, with cobbles
radiating from a simple turn-of-the-20th-century fountain. No wonder
chamber music concerts are held here in summer. ✉ *Intersection of Rue
Espariat and Rue Aude.*

★ ❶ **La Rotonde.** If you've just arrived in Aix's center, this sculpture-fountain
is a spectacular introduction to the town's rare mix of elegance and urban
bustle. It's a towering mass of 19th-century attitude. That's Agriculture
yearning toward Marseille, Art leaning toward Avignon, and Justice looking down on the Cours Mirabeau. But don't study it too intently—you'll
likely be sideswiped by a speeding Vespa. ✉ *Pl. de Gaulle.*

㉑ Thermes Sextius (Thermal Baths of Sextius). Warm natural springs first
discovered under the leadership of Sextius, the Thermes now house the
glass walls of an ultramodern health spa. The small fountain in the interior marks the warm spring of the original 18th-century establishment;
today the facility's offerings include a great gym, pressure showers,
mud treatments, and underwater massages. ✉ *55 cours Sextius*
☎ *04-42-23-81-82* ⊕ *www.thermes-sextius.com* ☉ *Weekdays
8:30-7:30, Sat. 8:30-1:30 and 2:30-6:30; gym also open Sun. 8:30-7:30.*

Where to Eat & Stay

★ **$$$$** ✕ **Le Clos de la Violette.** Whether you dine in the shade of the broad chestnut trees or in the airy, pastel dining room of this noble old house, you'll
experience the Mediterranean cuisine of top chef Jean-Marc Banzo,
whose Spanish father and Italian mother influenced his famously colorful cooking. Banzo spins tradition into gold, from panfried tuna with
crushed basil, smoked bacon, and crystallized shallots to rack of herb-
encrusted lamb served with roasted goat cheese and rosemary potatoes.
The wine list is devoted to the best of the region, too. The restaurant is
not far from the Atelier Cézanne, outside the Old Town ring. ✉ *10 av.
de la Violette* ☎ *04-42-23-30-71* ⊕ *www.closdelaviolette.fr* ⌚ *Reservations essential* 🏛 *Jacket required* 🖃 *AE, MC, V* ☉ *Closed Sun. No
lunch Mon. and Wed.*

$$$-$$$$ ✕ **L'Amphitryon.** For years now, this restaurant has led the pack of soigné
FodorsChoice and refined *cuisine moderne* spots in Aix. Now, with chef Bruno Ungaro
★ at the helm, elegance triumphs yet so does utter, utter deliciousness. You
may have to go way back in your memory-book to remember such mem-

orably raffinée and scrumptious creations: Portobello mushrooms are given a newer-than-now nouvelle spin, salmon is a dazzling fusion of Provence and Asia, and desserts are pretty-as-a-picture. ⊠ *2-4 rue Paul Doumer* ☎ *04–42–26–54–10* 🖃 *AE, MC, V* ☉ *Closed Sun.–Mon.*

$$$–$$$$ ✕ **Les Bacchanales.** Despite a position on a tourist-trap street off Cours Mirabeau, this is a pleasant, intimate restaurant with an inviting interior of daub-filled beams, yellow-ocher stucco, and Louis XIII chairs. The broad range of fixed-price menus may include a delicate smoked salmon with rosemary and green onion cream, a classic garlic-roasted lamb, or a *rouget* (red mullet) perfumed with sage and a dessert of crushed almonds flavored with marinated cherries. As the name implies, wine figures large here, and the list is extensive. ⊠ *10 rue de la Couronne* ☎ *04–42–27–21–06* 🖃 *AE, MC, V* ☉ *Closed Tues.; no lunch Wed. and Sat.*

$$–$$$ ✕ **Antoine Coté Court.** Trendy insiders and fashion-conscious Aixois fill this lively Italian restaurant. It has floor-to-ceiling windows that give almost every table a view of the plant-filled courtyard. Delicious smells wafting out from the open kitchen make the patrons practically hum in hungry anticipation. Pastas are superb; try the mushroom and prosciutto fettuccine or the gnocchi à la Provençal. ⊠ *19 cours Mirabeau* ☎ *04–42–93–12–51* 🖃 *DC, MC, V* ☉ *Closed Sun. No lunch Mon.*

★ **$$–$$$** ✕ **Le Passage.** Noted chef Riene Sammut has created an edgy, urban brasserie, wildly popular as a spot for good, affordable food. Located in a sleekly converted former candy factory in the center of town, the three-story complex also includes a bookstore, cooking workshop, and a small wine and épicerie all arranged around a sunny atrium. Its New York appeal runs from the Andy Warhol reproductions in the main dining room to the menu: roasted beef fillet with thick-cut fries and a terrific raspberry crème brûlée with fig chutney. ⊠ *10 rue Villars* ☎ *04–42–37–09–00* ◿ *Reservations essential* 🖃 *AE, MC, V.*

$$–$$$ ✕ **La Vieille Auberge.** A large fireplace reaching up to the wood-beamed ceiling, lightly painted pink walls hung with clusters of dried flowers and herbs, and sparkling white tablecloths only enhance the small-town country Provençal feel of this charming restaurant. Chef Jean-Marie Merly's refined cooking and creative cuisine is high in regional color and flavor, seen in dishes such as red mullet stuffed with eggplant and Parmesan on a red pepper *pain perdu,* and is nicely presented on delicate rose-rimmed tableware. ⊠ *63 rue Esparia* ☎ *04–42–27–17–41* 🖃 *MC, V* ☉ *Closed Mon. lunch and Jan.*

$$ ✕ **Café-Brasserie Les Deux Garçons.** Dating back to 1792, this fabled café
Fodor'sChoice has wined and dined everyone: Cézanne, Zola, Churchill, Picasso, Sartre,
★ Mistinguett, Piaf, Belmondo, and Truffaut are just a few of the Livre d'Or names. Too bad the food is rather ordinary—stick to the copious hot salads—but eating isn't what you come here for. It's the linen-decked sidewalk tables looking out to the Cours Mirabeau, the fresh flowers, the white-swathed waiters snaking between chairs, and the little gilt-edged,

espresso-filled cup at the end of the meal. Dining inside may be less festive, but if you're into period decor you won't be able to resist the sumptuous *epoque consulaire* (early 19th-century) decor, all mirrors, gold-ivory boiseries, neoclassical reliefs, and elegantly painted ceilings. At night, the upstairs turns into a cozy, dimly lit piano bar buzzing with an interesting mix of local jazz lovers and students. Call it 2G (pronounced *zhay*) and everyone will think you're a regular, too. ⊠ *53 cours Mirabeau* ☎ *04–42–26–00–51* ⊕ *www.les2garcons.com* ⊟ *AE, MC, V.*

$$ ✕ **Chez Thomé.** At a crossroads deep in Cézanne country east of Aix, near the Château Noir and in the shadow of Montagne de Ste-Victoire, this ramshackle, fashionably bohemian hunting lodge conceals a series of intimate dining rooms and a broad terrace shaded by massive chestnut trees. Service is young and laid-back, the prix-fixe menu a steal at €24, and portions are more than generous: lamb roasted in tangy tapenade, zucchini carpaccio with market vegetables and goat-cheese terrine, and crème brûlée perfumed with lavender. ⊠ *D12, 5 km (3 mi) east of Aix, La Plantation, Le Tholonet* ☎ *04–42–66–90–43* ⊟ *MC, V* ⊙ *Closed Mon.*

$–$$ ✕ **Le Bistro Latin.** With soft tones of orange and yellow and wood-backed chairs, this unpretentious little restaurant has only two menus with lots of choice, each combining fresh ingredients and equally fresh ideas. Doing honor to southern cooking, olive oil figures large, as do typical Provençal herbs and spices. Consider mussels and spinach in a saffron sauce, roasted pork loin with honey and garlic, lamb stew, or a subtle terrine of chickpeas and fresh goat cheese with balsamic vinegar. ⊠ *18 rue de la Couronne* ☎ *04–42–38–22–88* ▭ *MC, V* ☉ *Closed Sun.; no lunch Sat. and Mon.*

$–$$ ✕ **Chez Maxime.** Delightfully eclectic and much sought-after, this buzzing and atmospheric restaurant specializes in meat. Maxime himself carves up great hunks of beef and lamb, slapping it on to a large charcoal grill and serving it out in big hungry-man portions. Ignore the rather lack-luster vegetables—you're not here for fancy fixin's—what interests you is the most succulent, mouthwateringly good steak in Aix. ⊠ *12 pl. Ramus* ☎ *04–42–26–28–51* 🖷 *04–42–26–74–70* ▭ *DC, MC, V* ☉ *Closed Sun. No lunch Mon.*

$–$$ ✕ **Le Grillon.** Another contender for the mobile-phone set on the lively stretch of Cours Mirabeau, this brasserie terrace gives sun baskers and hair tossers a place to preen and be seen. Not just for tourists, many of the Aixois eat here, too. It has waiters in black and white, crisp linens, and a simple but proficient menu that's especially strong at lunch. ⊠ *49 cours Mirabeau* ☎ *04–42–27–58–81* ▭ *MC, V.*

¢–$ ✕ **La Pizza.** The perfect setting for a romantic rendezvous, this little pizze-ria comes alive every night with tables spilling out onto the cobblestones. The pizzas are fresh from the wood-fired oven, and the pastas and risot-tos are served with genial Italian hospitality. ⊠ *3 rue Aude* ☎ *04–42–26–22–17* ▭ *AE, MC, V.*

$$$$ ✕🖾 **Le Pigonnet.** If you close your eyes and think of the perfect Provençal

Fodor's Choice hotel, the chances are you'll conjure up Le Pigonnet. A picture-perfect

★ mas-mansion, this Shangri-la comes replete with a typically and elegantly French estate park and vistas that would please any artist—Cézanne him-self painted Ste-Victoire from the garden terrace here. What he would have made of all the suave luxury now on view one can only wonder, for this is the sort of place now patronized by the likes of Princess Car-oline, Iggy Pop, and Clint Eastwood. If you don't mind your Provence glossed up, you'll love the spacious light-filled rooms adorned with plush rugs, beautifully preserved antique furniture, and impressive mar-ble bathrooms; Small, artfully placed balconies look out over the ex-tensive formal gardens. The restaurant's terrace spills out onto this sculpted green; inside, the main dining room—lined with picture win-dows and topped by a series of filigreed chandeliers—is a glittering, gilded concoction almost more delicious than the inspired creations of chef Philippe Sorrel: duck roasted with a pepper and honey sauce, regional lamb with creamed garlic, or the simply grilled sea bass with fresh herbs (deftly complemented with a great Provençal wine list). So if you want to see the beauty of Provence distilled in one magical retreat, save your pennies for this one. ⊠ *5 av. du Pigonnet, 13090* ☎ *04–42–59–02–90* 🖷 *04–42–59–47–77* ⊕ *www.hotelpigonnet.com* ⤴ *52 rooms, 1 apart-ment* ⚒ *Restaurant, minibars, cable TV, pool, parking, some pets al-lowed (fee)* ▭ *AE, MC, V* ❑ *MAP.*

★ **$$** ✕🖾 **Relais Ste-Victoire.** In this isolated country inn nestled at the foot of Ste-Victoire, you can lose yourself in Chef René Judy-Bergés's impec-cably fresh Provençal cuisine: endive stuffed with lobster in celery butter and hazelnuts, and monkfish sautéed in Parmesan butter served with tomato and country ham ravioli. The intimate, formal atmosphere captures the essence of country-auberge dining, and Judy-Bergés is a charming host, cheerfully gliding from one table to the next. You can spend the night in rooms that are sizable, but that seem something of an afterthought in '70s-style beige with catalog furniture. To reach the restaurant from Aix, it's only a 10-km (6-mi) taxi ride, or, if you have a car, take the scenic D17 toward Le Tholonet and Cézanne country; turn right on D46 into Beaurecueil. ⊠ *53 av. Sylvain Gautier, 13100 Beaurecueil* ☎ *04–42–66–94–98* 🖷 *04–42–66–85–96* ⊕ *www.relais-sainte-victoire.com* 🛏 *12 rooms* ♤ *Restaurant, minibars, cable TV, pool, parking, some pets allowed (fee)* ☰ *AE, MC, V* ☉ *Restaurant closed Mon.; no dinner Sun., no lunch Fri. Hotel closed 1st wk Jan., 2 wks in Feb., and 1st wk Nov.* ◯ *BP.*

★ $$$$ 🖫 **Villa Gallici.** One of the most beautiful hotels in Provence, this high-style retreat made the editors of decorating magazines mad with joy when it opened its doors in 1994. A former archbishop's palace perched on a hill overlooking the pink roofs of Aix, the Gallici was transformed into a homage to *le style Provençaux* thanks to the wizardry of three designers, Gilles Dez, Charles de Montemarco, and Daniel Jouvre. But don't come here for sunbaked walls, white tiles, and urns with cactus— this is the Provence that Parisian aristocrats enjoyed back in the 19th century. Hued in the lavenders and blues, ochres and oranges of Aix, rooms swim in the most gorgeous Souleiado and Rubelli fabrics and trim. If a Louis Seize chair covered in gingham check gets to be a bit much, just step outside to the Florentine-style garden, shaded by ancient cypress and plane trees and landscaped with jars of laurel and topiary boxwood. A pool beckons, as does Marcel, the cat. Happily, this luxurious hilltop garden retreat stands serenely apart from the city center on the outskirts of town (offering great views), but the shops of Cours Mirabeau are only a 15-minute walk away. Now, however, that the original owners have sold out and moved on, readers say the bloom is off this gilded lily. Time will tell. ⊠ *Av. de la Violette, 13100* ☎ *04–42–23–29–23* 🖷 *04–42–96–30–45* ⊕ *www.villagallici.com* 🛏 *18 rooms, 4 suites, 3 duplexes* ♤ *Restaurant, cable TV, pool, in-room data ports, some pets allowed (fee)* ☰ *AE, DC, MC, V* ◯ *MAP.*

$$$–$$$$ 🖫 **Hôtel des Augustins.** The best aspect of this Old Town hotel, just a half block back from Cours Mirabeau, is its reception area. The groin-vaulted stone, stained glass, and ironwork banister date from the 15th century, when the house was an Augustinian convent (Martin Luther was once a guest). The rooms are perfectly nice but a bit of a letdown. Instead of monastic oak and pristine linens, you get heavy carpeting and fabric-covered walls. Bathrooms are all-white tile and marble, and a few rooms have private balcony-terraces with views of the steeple of St-Esprit. The staff is efficient and eager to please. ⊠ *3 rue de la Masse, 13100* ☎ *04–42–27–28–59* 🖷 *04–42–26–74–87* 🛏 *29 rooms* ♤ *Minibars, cable TV* ☰ *MC, V* ◯ *MAP.*

★ $$$–$$$$ 🖫 **Hôtel Cézanne.** Three blocks from Cours Mirabeau and the train station, this smart, very spiffy, and cozily stylish hotel is a great option. Just a minute's stroll away is the Quartier Mazarin, the 18th-century district lined with some of Aix's most beautiful buildings and antiques

3

shops. While the hotel is set on a busy avenue, all noise and distractions disappear with just one foot inside the glowing red lobby, mightily warmed by the friendliness of the staff (who are quick to point out the gratis eats and drinks in the seating-area bar). Upstairs, the guest rooms are classic Provençal—modern in comfort yet with old armoires, elegant chandeliers, patterned historic wallpapers, and very comfy beds (ooh, those pillows). Out back is an Aix garden-courtyard with looming trees that would tempt Cézanne's own paintbrush, so try to book a room in the back. Final plus: the breakfast buffet is one of the very best around— a bevy of cheeses, hams, juices, and jams will reboot you delightfully. ⊠ *40 av. Victor-Hugo, 13100* ☎ *04–42–37–61–00* 📠 *04–42–37–61–11* ⊕ *www.hotelaix.com* 🛏 *34 rooms* 🛆 *Minibars, cable TV, in-room data ports, bar, some pets allowed (fee)* ⊟ *AE, DC, MC, V.*

$$ 🏨 **Nègre-Coste.** "You are about to enter a time machine," states the hotel Web site, and they aren't entirely off the mark. Legend says Louis XIV once stayed here, while the guest book proves such V.I.P.s as 19th-century chanteuse Yvette Guilbert opted for this hotel. Its lavish public areas and great central location make this 18th-century town house still a popular hotel, especially with musicians during the summer festivals. If people-watching is your thing, you may cotton to the hotel's prominent perch on the very bustling Cours Mirabeau throughfare. If not, be sure to request a quieter room at the back of the hotel where the view extends to the cathedral. With period furniture, marble busts, and lots of old-fashioned style, guest rooms are bright with Provençal gold fabric, antique tables, and small chandeliers. ⊠ *33 cours Mirabeau, 13100* ☎ *04–42–27–74–22* 📠 *04–42–26–80–93* ⊕ *www.hotelnegrecoste.com* 🛏 *37 rooms, 1 suite* 🛆 *Minibars, cable TV, parking (fee)* ⊟ *AE, MC, V.*

★ **$–$$** 🏨 **Quatre Dauphins.** In the gorgeously elegant Mazarin neighborhood below the Cours Mirabeau, this modest but impeccable lodging inhabits a noble hôtel particulier. Its pretty, comfortable little rooms have been spruced up with *boutis* (Provençal quilts), Les Olivades fabrics, quarry tiles, jute carpets, and hand-painted furniture. The tiny top-floor rooms are even more charming. The house-proud but unassuming owner-host bends over backward to please. ⊠ *55 rue Roux Alphéran, 13100* ☎ *04–42–38–16–39* 📠 *04–42–38–60–19* 🛏 *13 rooms* 🛆 *Some pets allowed (fee)* ⊟ *MC, V* 🍽 *BP.*

$–$$ 🏨 **Saint Christophe.** With so few mid-price *hôtels de charme* in Aix, you might as well opt for this glossy art deco–style hotel, where the comfort and services are remarkable for the price. The Roaring '20s look dates from 1994, but the Cézannesque murals, burled-wood curves, and Constructivist leather chairs carry you back to the Jazz Age. Rooms are slickly done in deep jewel tones, and the top-floor rooms have artisanal tiles in the bathrooms. For a pittance more, you can have a junior suite with a sleeping loft. ⊠ *2 av. Victor-Hugo, 13100* ☎ *04–42–26–01–24* 📠 *04–42–38–53–17* ⊕ *www.hotel-saintchristophe.com* 🛏 *58 rooms, 7 suites* 🛆 *Restaurant, minibars, cable TV, parking (fee), some pets allowed (fee)* ⊟ *AE, MC, V* 🍽 *MAP.*

$ 🏨 **Cardinal.** In a lovely 18th-century house in the Quartier Mazarin, this
Fodor'sChoice eccentric and slightly threadbare inn is the antithesis of slick. Its large
★ rooms are furnished gracefully enough with secondhand finds, and some rooms have original 18th-century painted door panels. If you like

charm, you'll notice the novel furniture, the elegance of the structure, and the music of the bells of St-Jean-de-Malte. A favorite among writers, artists, and musicians on hand for the festival, it also has kitchenette suites; the two that are across from the Musée Granet and the ground-floor one with a private garden are the best. ✉ *24 rue Cardinale, 13100* ☎ *04-42-38-32-30* 🖷 *04-42-26-39-05* 📻 *24 rooms, 6 suites* ♿ *Minibars, cable TV, parking (fee), some pets allowed (fee)* 🟰 *MC, V.*

Nightlife & the Arts

To find out what's going on in town, pick up a copy of the events calendar *Le Mois à Aix* or the bilingual city guide *Aix la Vivante* at the tourist office.

Every July during the **Festival International d'Art Lyrique** (International Opera Festival; ☎ 04-42-17-34-00 for information ⊕ www.aixenprovencetourism.com/aix-festival-lyrique.htm), you can see world-class opera productions in the courtyard of the Palais de l'Archevêché. It is one of the most important opera festivals in Europe, and cutting-edge productions involve the best artists available—guests in the past have included director Peter Brook, choreographers Trisha Brown and Pina Bausch, and conductor Claudio Abbado. The repertoire is varied and often offbeat, featuring works like Britten's *Curlew River* and Bartók's *Bluebeard's Castle* as well as the usual Mozart, Puccini, and Verdi. Most of the singers, however, are not celebrities, but rather an elite group of students who spend the summer with the Academie Européenne de Musique, training and performing under the tutelage of stars like Robert Tear and Yo-Yo Ma. Tickets can be purchased as early as November for the following summer, but it's usually possible to find seats a month in advance. After that, seats are scarce.

As for nightspots, **Hot Brass** (✉Rte. d'Eguilles, Celony ☎04-42-21-05-57) draws an older, car-owning crowd to the suburbs for live concerts of funk, soul, rock, blues, and Latin bands, mainly local. **Le Scat Club** (✉ 11 rue de la Verrerie ☎ 04-42-23-00-23) is the place for live soul, funk, reggae, rock, blues, and jazz. **Le Mistral** (✉ 3 rue Frédéric-Mistral ☎ 04-42-38-16-49) is an established student club with big-name DJs and a strict door policy, so get dressed up and get there early. **Le Divino** (✉ Mas des Auberes, Rte. de Venelles [5 km from town] ☎04-42-99-37-08) is New York–stylish and draws the hip, young, and beautiful people. **Bistrot Aixois** (✉ 37 cours Sextius ☎04-42-27-50-10) is newly renovated and still the hottest student nightspot in town, with young BCBG's lining up to get in. **IPN** (✉ 23 cours Sextius ☎04-42-26-25-17) has great ambience, good music, and reasonable prices. **The Red Clover** (✉ 30 rue de la Verrerie ☎ 04-42-23-44-61) is a friendly, boisterous Irish pub. Don't expect to speak any French here.

For a night of playing roulette and the slot machines, head for the **Casino Municipal** (✉ 2 bis av. N.-Bonaparte ☎ 04-42-26-30-33).

The **Cézanne** (✉ Rue Marcel Guillaume ☎ 08-36-68-72-70) and **Renoir** (✉ 24 cours Mirabeau ☎ 08-36-68-72-70) cinemas both show some films in *v.o.* (*version originale,* i.e., not dubbed).

The stunningly inventive choreography of **Le Ballet Preljocaj** (⊠ Rue Allumettes ☎ 04–42–93–48–00) can be seen September to May in Aix, their home base.

The Outdoors

Because it's there, in part, and because it looms in striking isolation above the plain east of Aix, its heights catching the sun long after the valley lies in shadow, Cézanne's beloved **Montagne Ste-Victoire** inspires climbers to conquest. The Grande Randonée stretches along its long, rocky crest from the village of Le Bouquet at its western end all the way east to Puyloubier. Its alternate route climbs the milder north slope from Les Cabassols. Along the way it peaks at 3,316 feet at Pic des Mouches, from where the view stretches around the compass. But the real draw lies to the east at the **Croix de Provence** (3,100 feet), a gargantuan cross rising 92 feet above the mountaintop. You'll have sweeping views over the whole of Provence from the Luberon to the Alps. From Les Cabassols to the Cross, allow 3½ hours round-trip for this fairly strenuous hike. A bus from Aix's *gare routière* (bus station) carries hikers toward Vauvenargues and Les Cabassols departure point. Pick up detailed maps at the tourist office.

Shopping

Aix is a very snazzy market town, and unlike the straightforward, country-fair atmosphere of nearby Aubagne, a trip to the market here is a foodie's delight, with rarefied, high-end delicacies shoulder to shoulder with garlic braids. You'll find fine olive oils from the Pays d'Aix (Aix region), barrels glistening with olives of every hue and blend, and vats of tapenade (crushed olive, caper, and anchovy paste). Melons, asparagus, and mesclun salad are piled high, and dried sausages bristling with Provençal herbs hang from stands. A **food and produce market** takes place every morning on Place Richelme; just up the street on Place Verdun is a good, high-end *brocante* (collectibles) market Tuesday, Thursday, and Saturday mornings.

In addition to its old-style markets and jewel-box candy shops, Aix is a dazzlingly sophisticated modern shopping town—perhaps the best in Provence. The winding streets of the Vieille Ville above Cours Mirabeau—focused around **Rue Clemenceau, Rue Marius Reinaud, Rue Espariat, Rue Aude, Rue Fabrot,** and **Rue Maréchal Foch**—have a plethora of goods, from high-end designer clothes such as Sonia Rykiel, Escada, and Yves Saint Laurent, to Max Mara, Laura Ashley, and The Gap. On the fashion front, particularly noteworthy is **Gago** (⊠18–21 rue Fabrot ☎04–42–27–60–19), a fashion leader with stylish designer wear for men and women including Prada, Helmut Lang, and Gucci. You'll also find **Max Mara** and **Yohji Yamamoto** on the same street (no. 12 and no. 3). **Gérard Darel** (⊠ 13 rue Fabrot ☎04–42–26–38–45) is the shop for classic French tailoring. **Tehen** (⊠ 6 rue Clemenceau ☎ 04–42–26–85–50) sells soft, draped knits. **Mephisto** (⊠16 bis pl. Verdun ☎04–42–38–23–23) sells its signature walking shoes and boots to a mostly foreign clientele, as French women find them unaesthetic. **Catimini** (⊠ 9 pl. Chapeliers ☎ 04–42–27–51–14) offers an imaginative, jazzy stock of kids' sweaters, jackets, and dresses. Toddlers will love the traditional wooden toys at **Le Nain Rouge** (✉ 47 rue Espariat ☎ 04–42–93–50–05). Fabrics, pottery, and decorative arts for the home also figure large. **Les Olivades** (✉ 15 rue Marius Reinaud ☎ 04–42–38–33–66) is one of the last *maisons* that print Provençal fabrics in the traditonal Marseille style. Sophisticated Provençal pottery can be found at **Scènes de Vie** (✉ 3 rue Granet ☎ 04–42–21–13–90). Splurge for your one-of-a-kind made-to-order embroidered chair cover at **Arts Vivendi** (✉ 2 av. Villemus ☎ 04–42–21–22–83). Aix's most celebrated santon, or miniature statue, maker is **Santon Fouque** (✉ 65 cours Gambetta ☎ 04–42–26–33–38). The **Book in Bar** (✉ 1 bis rue Joseph Cabassol ☎ 04–42–26–60–07) is a cozy English bookshop near the Cours Mirabeau and is not only a great place to buy and read English-language books, but also to meet other English speakers.

> **TOUT SWEET**
>
> A great Aixois delicacy is *calissons*. A blend of almond paste and glazed melon, they are cut into geometric almond shapes and stacked high in *confiserie* windows. The most picturesque shop specializing in calisson candies is Bechard (✉ 12 cours Mirabeau ☎ 04–42–26–06–78). Leonard Parli (✉ 35 av. Victor-Hugo ☎ 04–42–26–05–71), housed in a sugar-sweet, 19th-century emporium, also offers a lovely selection of calissons.

MARSEILLE

Popular myths and a fishy reputation have led Marseille to be unfairly maligned as a dirty urban sprawl plagued with impoverished immigrant neighborhoods and slightly louche politics. It is often given wide berth by travelers in search of a Provençal idyll. What a shame. As so often is the case here, there is no simple truth: Marseille, even its earliest history, has maintained its contradictions with a kind of fierce and independent pride. Yes, there are scary, even dangerous neighborhoods, some modern eyesores, even a high crime rate—but there is also tremendous beauty. Cubist jumbles of white stone rise up over a picture-book seaport, bathed in light of blinding clarity, crowned by larger-than-life neo-Byzantine churches, and framed by massive fortifications; neighborhoods teem with multiethnic life; souklike African markets reek deliciously of spices and coffees, and the labyrinthine Old Town radiates bright shades of saffron, cinnamon, and robin's-egg blue.

And now the TGV (fast train) phenomenon that makes Marseille a mere three hours from Paris has also brought in an influx of "weekend tourists" who are snapping up more and more pieds-à-terre and throwing themselves into renovation projects. The government is also in the spirit and is in the process of completing an ambitious project to clean up and revitalize the Vieux Port. The second largest city in France, Marseille remains a vibrant city. Fiesty and fond of broad gestures, it is also as complicated and as cosmopolitan now as it was when the Phoenicians first founded it as an international shipping port 2,600 years ago.

In 600 BC a band of Phoenician Greeks sailed into the well-placed natural harbor that is today's Vieux Port. Legend has it that on that same day a local chieftain's daughter, Gyptis, needed to choose a husband, and her wandering eyes settled on the Greeks' handsome commander Protis. Her dowry brought land near the mouth of the Rhône, where the Greeks founded Massalia, the most important Continental shipping port in antiquity. The port flourished for some 500 years as a typical Greek city, enjoying the full flush of classical culture, its gods, its democratic political system, its sports and theater, and its naval prowess. Caesar changed all that, besieging the city in 49 BC and seizing most of its colonies. Massalia's Greeks were left only their famous university and their highly valued independence. They struggled until the 12th century when Marseille finally reactivated its port and started making money embarking and maintaining supply lines to the Crusaders.

In 1214 Marseille was seized by Charles d'Anjou and was later annexed to France by Henri IV in 1481, but it was not until Louis XIV took the throne that the biggest transformations of the port began; he pulled down the city walls in 1666 and expanded the port to the *Rive Neuve* (New Riverbank). The city was devastated by plague in 1720, losing more than half its population. By the time of the Revolution, Marseille was on the rebound once again, with industries of soap manufacturing and oil processing flourishing, encouraging a wave of immigration from Provence and Italy.

> **TRIP TIP**
>
> If you plan on visiting many of the museums in Marseille, buy a museum *passport* (city pass) for €16 (2 days €23) at the tourism office. It covers the entry fee for all the museums in Marseille.

With the opening of the Suez Canal in 1869, Marseille became the greatest boomtown in 19th-century Europe. With a large influx of immigrants from areas as exotic as Tangiers, the city quickly acquired the multicultural population it maintains to this day. By 1964 the population had outgrown available space, and housing shortages demanded rapid, and unfortunately somewhat careless, construction of new neighborhoods. By the mid-1970s these areas often had high unemployment and serious problems with drugs and crime. Thrown into the volatile mix was a series of political scandals centered around corruption and extortion, cementing Marseille's unsavory reputation. Since then, "reform" has become the new buzzword, with the conservative right-wing mayor introducing new plans that have both revitalized the economy and started the clean-up process for the badly tattered Marseillais image. And so, with the enthusiastic support of its very cosmopolitan population, it seems that one of France's oldest cities is finally rising up (again) from the proverbial ashes.

The Quai du Port and Le Panier

Though Marseille is the second-largest city in France, it functions as a conglomerate of distinct neighborhoods—almost little villages. One of these microcosms—the Neapolitan-style maze of laundry-lined lanes called Le Panier—merits intimate exploration and the will to wander. There

Marseille

Rade
de
Marseille

Bassin
de la
Grande
Joliette

Avant-Port
de la
Joliette

Fort
St-Jean

rue de Forbin

Av. C. rue Pelle...

rue Fachier

rue Montolieu

rue Duverger

rue de la Joliette

bd. des Dames

rue de
Lorette

rue de L'Asquin

Passage de
Lorette

rue de
Lorette

pl. des
13 cantons

rue du petit.

rue du Panier

rue St-Antoine

pl. Sadi
Carnot

rue Ch...

rue

29

30

rue des Repenties

LE PANIER

Montée des Accoules

pl.
Daviel Grand'Rue

rue Caisserie

rue de
Lacydon

pl. Victor
Gelu

31

Av. de St-Jean

rue de la
Loge

rue Coutellerie

32

quai du Port

33

Ferry
Boat

Vieux
Port

Pl. aux
Huiles

Pl.
Thiars

Neu...

3

Jardin
du Pharo

41

Tunnel du Vieux Port

quai de Rive
Nueve
rue des
Sainte Catherine

Pl.
Huiles

35

36

bd. Charles Livon

40

Rampe Saint-Maurice

rue
Croix

rue de la
Croix

rue
Sainte

37

39

bd. de la Corderie

rue
des Lices

Jardin
P. Puget

cours Pierre

rue Re...

Av. Pasteur

Av. de la Course

bd. de la Corderie

rue du
Combaud Tadrei

rue d'Endoume

rue
E. D

corniche J.F. -Kennedy

Bd. Ch. Creusse

rue du
Olive

rue
H. Valéry

Four A. Chaut

rue
Jouve

rue
Samatan

rue
Fénelon et R.Guidicelli

rue
Charras

rue de
Chataigner

rue
Decores

rue Joël Recher

rue Chiras

rue du Coteau

rue
Sauveur

bd. André Aune

bd. Notre-Da...

Chemin d'Endoume

Boulevard
d'Endoume

rue de la Gorge

rue
Vauvenargues

Montée de l'Oratoire

rue du Vallon

Bd. des
Dardanelles

rue du Vallon

pl.
St-Eugène

bd. Marius Thomas

rue Perlet

Av.
J.-Etienne

rue
Léon-Seyssaud

bd. Michel Gachet

Ch. Y. Dollo

Vallon Jourdan

rue
Rigaud

Av.
David

38

rue Fort du
Sanctuaire

rue
Bompard

rue E'ndoume

bd. Bensa

rue Papon

Trav. Targinsi

Trav.
du Frioul

rue
Pont

corniche J.F. Kennedy

Trav.
de la
Cascade

Chemin d

rue des Flots Bleus

bd. Bompard

rue E. Mein

Ch. du Roucas

bd. Amédée Autran

rue
Martin Brignoudy

rue
du Terrail

avenue des Roches

Av. du Bois Scare

Av. St-François

TO ANSES,
PLAGE DU PRADO
↓

rue du Docteur Frédéric Gramer

are also myriad museums tied into Marseille's nautical history, and the striking museum complex of the Vieille Charité, all worth a browse.

A GOOD
WALK

Begin at the tourist office at the base of the Vieux Port, known as the Quai des Belges. Be sure to start early because this is the stage for the first of a series of theatrical scenes that are part of Marseille's daily life: the **Marché aux Poissons** ㉔. The port behind them is a show in itself, with its colorful mix of gleaming white pleasure boats, scruffy blue and green fishing boats, and even a couple of restored schooners, all bobbing together in the vast horseshoe of water. Don't bother to come if the mistral has been roaring over the water; then the fishermen keep their boats safely tied in port.

Walk up La Canebière to the **Musée de la Marine et de l'Economie de Marseille** ㉕, where you can learn about the port's history through miniatures, paintings, and engravings. Just past the port is the unusual **Musée de la Mode** ㉖, where high-fashion clothes from the 1930s to today are on display. Head a half block over into the mall to enter the **Musée d'Histoire de Marseille** ㉗, which illustrates the classical history of this ancient city. Then wander into the adjoining **Jardin des Vestiges** ㉘ to see the foundations of Greek fortifications.

Next, head up broad Rue de la République, past grand old apartment buildings and Place Sadi Carnot. Just past the square, on the left, the elegant Passage de Lorette leads you into a claustrophobic courtyard with laundry fluttering like medieval banners overhead, typical of Marseille. From here, climb the steep stairs that lead into the famous neighborhood known as **Le Panier.** The anchor of the revitalization of this decaying but appealing neighborhood is the **Centre de la Vieille Charité** ㉙, once a hospice, now the home of two museums.

Follow Rue du Petit Puits to Place des 13 Cantons, head left on Rue Ste-Françoise, then cross Avenue Robert Schumann to the neo-Byzantine **Cathédrale de la Nouvelle Major** ㉚. Then wind back down the Montée des Accoules to Place Daviel, turn right and double back right down Rue du Lacydon to the **Musée du Vieux Marseille** ㉛. Housed in the Maison Diamantée, it highlights collections of pottery, furniture, costumes, and santons (terra-cotta figurines). Just a block up from the port, the **Musée des Docks Romains** ㉜ displays the remains of 1st-century waterfront warehouses that lined this busy port.

Go down to the Quai du Port and past the Baroque-era Hôtel de Ville (City Hall). At the water's edge wait for the picturesque **Ferry Boat** ㉝ (pronounced *fay*-ree *bow*-aht) and ride across the port in style.

TIMING

Allow at least a half day to explore the backstreets of Le Panier, a whole day if you intend to visit any of the fascinating museums at the foot of its hill; you could easily spend a morning appreciating the wonders (both architectural and archeological) of the Vieille Charité museum complex. Wear good walking shoes and be prepared to climb: Much of this district is spread over steep slopes.

What to See

㉚ **Cathédrale de la Nouvelle Major** (The Major Cathedral). A neo-Byzantine church, the largest built in France since the Middle Ages, that was started in 1852 and completed in 1893, it's remarkable for its marble and rich red porphyry inlay. Napoléon III ordered the 11th-century original chapel, the Ancienne Major (parts of which date back to Roman times), torn apart to make way for its flashy new replacement. All that remains of the old church are the choir and the transept: restoration continues, but it is in a bad state of disrepair. ☒ *Pl. de la Major, Le Panier* ☎ *04–91–90–53–57* ☉ *Daily 10–noon and 2–5:30.*

★ ㉙ **Centre de la Vieille Charité** (Center of the Old Charity). Built between 1671 and 1749 and designed by Pierre and Jean Puget, this delightful complex, originally constructed as a shelter for the poor, has beautiful open balconies on three stories nestled around a courtyard. Dominated by a magnificent Baroque chapel with a novel oval-shaped dome, the inner court offers an interesting retreating perspective of the triple arcades. The *salon de thé* (tearoom) serves drinks and light meals alfresco under the lovely arches.

Renovated and reopened as a cultural center in 1986, the former chapel houses temporary exhibitions. Further along are two excellent museums. The larger is the **Musée d'Archéologie Méditerranéenne** (Museum of Mediterranean Archaeology), with a superb collection of archaeological finds from the Mediterranean and Provence, including a sizable collection of ceramics, bronzes, funeral stelae, statues from ancient Greece, and Roman glassware. It also has the most important Egyptian collection in France outside of Paris. Along with mummified people, cats, and flowers, there are plenty of hieroglyphics and gorgeous sarcophagi in evocative tomb-like surroundings. The **Musée d'Arts Africains, Océaniens et Amérindiens** (Museum of African, Oceanian, and American Indian Art) has artifacts from Africa, the Pacific, and the Americas. The spectacular masks and sculptures—including some rather tastefully engraved human skulls—are mounted along a black wall, eerie with indirect lighting. Labels and explanations are across the aisle. ☒ *2 rue de la Charité, Le Panier* ☎ *04–91–14–58–80* ☒ *€2 for each museum* ☉ *May–Sept., Tues.–Sun. 11–6; Oct.–Apr., Tues.–Sun. 10–5.*

㉝ **Ferry Boat.** To hear the natives say "*fay*-ree *bow*-aht" (they've adopted the English) is one of the joys of a visit to Marseille. For a pittance you can file onto this little wooden barge, which serves as handy mass transit just as it did in Marcel Pagnol's play *Marius*. It chugs between Place des Huiles on the Quai de Rive Neuve side and the Hôtel de Ville on the Quai du Port 8 AM to 6:30 PM daily (round-trip ticket costs €80). ☒ *€1.*

㉘ **Jardin des Vestiges** (Garden of Remains). Discovered in 1967 while the foundations for the Center Bourse shopping center were being dug, the remains of Marseille's Greek walls, a necropolis, 1st-century loading docks, and a corner of the Roman port are all well-preserved here. The gardens are now a part of the **Musée d'Histoire de Marseille** (Marseille History Museum), which also has a remarkably well-preserved 3rd-century ship recovered from the sea in 1974. ☒ *Centre Bourse, Vieux Port* ☎ *04–91–90–42–22* ☒ *€2; includes admission to the Musée d'Histoire de Marseille* ☉ *Mon.–Sat. noon–7.*

★ ㉔ **Marché aux Poissons** (Fish Market). Up and going by 8 AM every day, this market puts on a vivid and aromatic show of waving fists, jostling chefs, and heaps of fish from the night's catch still twitching. You'll hear the thick soup of the Marseillais accent as blue-clad fishermen and silk-clad matrons bicker over prices, and you'll wonder at the rainbow of Mediterranean creatures swimming in plastic vats before you,

> For the perfect bouillabaisse, take a taxi to the Vallon des Auffes, one of Marseille's myriad charming fishing ports—here, Chez Fonfon serves the specialty against a film-set backdrop.

each uglier than the last: the spiny-headed *rascasse* (scorpion fish), dog-nosed *grondin* (red gurnet), the monstrous *baudroie* or *lotte de mer* (monk-fish), and the eel-like *congre*. "Bouillabaisse" as sold here is a mix of fish too tiny to sell otherwise; the only problem with coming for the early morning show is that you have to wait so long for your bouillabaisse lunch. ☒ *Quai des Belges, Vieux Port* ☉ *Daily 8–1.*

㉜ **Musée des Docks Romains** (Roman Docks Museum). Nazis destroyed the neighborhood along the Quai du Port in 1943—a rather brutal act of urban renewal—ironically laying the groundwork for new discoveries. During postwar reconstruction, workers dug up remains of a 1st-century Roman shipping house. The museum created around the site preserves documents, equipment, and techniques used in maritime trade with exhibits of terra-cotta jars and coins. ☒ *Pl. de Vivaux, Vieux Port* ☏ *04–91–91–24–62* ☜ *€2* ☉ *Oct.–May, Tues.–Sun. 10–5; June–Sept., Tues.–Sun. 11–6.*

★ ㉗ **Musée d'Histoire de Marseille** (Marseille History Museum). With the Jardin des Vestiges in its backyard and its front door in a shopping mall, this modern, open-spaced exhibition illuminates Massalia's history by mounting its treasure of archeological finds in didactic displays. You can learn about ancient metallurgy, Gallo-Roman pottery making, and shipbuilding. There's a section on medieval Marseille, and some background on the marks Louis XIV and Vauban left on the city. Best by far is the presentation of Marseille's Classical halcyon days. There's a recovered wreck of a Roman cargo boat, its 3rd-century wood amazingly preserved, and the hull of a Greek boat dating from the 4th century BC. And that model of the Greek city should be authentic—it's based on the eyewitness description of Aristotle. ☒ *Centre Bourse, entrance on Rue de Bir-Hakeim, Vieux Port* ☏ *04–91–90–42–22* ☜ *€2; includes Jardin des Vestiges* ☉ *Mon.–Sat. noon–7.*

㉕ **Musée de la Marine et de l'Economie de Marseille** (Marine and Economy Museum). Inaugurated by Napoléon III in 1860, this impressive building houses both the museum and the city's Chamber of Commerce. The front entrance and hallway to the museum are lined with medallions celebrating the ports of the world with which the city has traded, or trades still. The museum charts the maritime history of Marseille from the 17th century onward with paintings and engravings. It is a model-lover's dream, with hundreds of steamboats and schooners, all in miniature. ✉ *Palais de la Bourse, 7 La Canebière, La Canebière* 🕾 *04–91–39–33–33* ✉ *€3* 🕓 *Daily 10–6.*

㉖ Musée de la Mode (Fashion Museum). Adding a bit of panache and style to the normal museum rounds are these galleries filled with clothes. More than 3,000 dresses and accessories, dating mainly from 1945 onward, form a permanent collection, while temporary exhibits highlight anything from a star designer's collection to the contents of a fashion diva's wardrobe. ✉ *11 La Canebière, La Canebière* 🕾 *04–91–56–59–57* ✉ *€3* 🕓 *Tues.–Sun. 10–6.*

㉛ Musée du Vieux Marseille (Museum of Old Marseille). The 16th-century **Maison Diamantée** (Diamond House), named for its diamond-faceted Renaissance facade, was built in 1570 by a rich merchant and was one of the few buildings in this quarter spared by Hitler. Focusing on the history of Marseille, the museum normally presents santons, crèches, and furniture, but at press time was closed indefinitely for renovations. A small part remains open for an exhibition of old photographs. ✉ *Rue de la Prison, Vieux Port* 🕾 *04–91–13–89–00 for more information.*

★ **Le Panier.** This louche, scruffy *quartier* is the oldest part of the city, slicing between Quai du Port and Rue de la République, and has been a traditional first stop for successive waves of immigrants. A maze of high-shuttered houses looming over narrow cobbled streets, Le Panier is the principal focus of the city's efforts at urban renewal, with plans for the restoration of over 1,500 houses. It's hard to resist the charm of steep stairways, narrow streets, and pastel-painted shops selling pottery and soap. And, with its population gradually changing to hip young artists and students, more and more chic boutiques and stylish restaurants are opening up, changing the area from seedy to atmospheric. Locals warn that Le Panier can still be a bit dubious late at night; it's best to wander during daylight hours only, or in groups.

The Quai de Rive Neuve

If in your exploration of Le Panier and the Quai du Port you examined Marseille's history in miniature via myriad museums, this walk will give you the "big picture." From either the crow's-nest perspective of Notre-Dame-de-la-Garde or the vast green Jardin du Pharo, you'll take in spectacular Cinemascope views of this great city and its ports and monuments. Wear good walking shoes and bring your wide-angle lens.

A GOOD WALK

From the Quai des Belges, head left and up the Quai de Rive Neuve, then head away from the port up Rue Fortia. To your right opens **Place Thiars ㉞**, a lively center with restaurants and cafés. Back on Rue Fortia, continue a block over to Cours d'Estienne d'Orves and **Les Arcenaulx ㉟**, a high-textured, state-of-the-art shop-and-restaurant complex in the old armory and a prime example of Marseille's commitment to renewal. Now head back to the waterfront and stop in for a pastis at the **Bar de la Marine ㊱**, scene of the salty barkeeper's saga in Pagnol's trilogy of plays and films *Marius, Fanny,* and *César.* All along the waterfront there are popular bars, and the alleys are peppered with small theaters.

Continue up the quai to the **Théâtre National de Marseille La Criée** ㊲, where the city's prestigious state theater company performs in a former fish-auction house.

If you're willing and able to tackle the steep (and seemingly endless) climb to the city's sentimental landmark, **Notre-Dame-de-la-Garde** ㊳, you'll be rewarded with one of the best views in Provence, panning over the brilliant white stone of the city, its complex of ports, islands, and neighboring mountains. (Hint: Bus 60 makes the run regularly from the Cours Jean Ballard, between the Quai des Belges and the Parking Estienne d'Orves, and on the descent you can get off at the Abbaye St-Victor if you like.) The church itself, another testimony to Napoléon III's megalomaniacal passion for overscaled kitsch, conceals quirky treasures.

A more modest climb up Rue Robert and Rue Neuve Ste-Catherine brings you to the **Abbaye St-Victor** ㊳, a splendid Romanesque church-fortress. Walk past the looming walls of **Fort St-Nicolas** ㊵ to get across the boulevard and up to the **Jardin du Pharo** ㊶: from this vast green hilltop you can take in dramatic views of the fort and its opposing **Fort St-Jean.**

TIMING   This walk involves about a half-day's worth of heavy hiking, half of it uphill. If you opt for a bus ride, you can make a beeline straight up to Notre-Dame-de-la-Garde and take in the spectacular views, all in a couple of hours.

What to See

★ ㊳ **Abbaye St-Victor.** Founded in the 4th century by St-Cassien, who sailed into Marseille's port full of fresh ideas on monasticism acquired in Palestine and Egypt, this abbey grew to formidable proportions. A spectacular fortified medieval church built on the remains of an ancient necropolis, its severe exterior of crenellated stone and the spare geometry of its Romanesque church would be as much at home in Middle East as its founder. The earlier church, destroyed by invading Saracens, was the city's first basilica and, with its formidable proportions, an impressive seat of religious power. It was rebuilt in the 11th century, then fortified against further attack in the 14th century. Its crudely peaked windows demonstrate the dawning transition from Romanesque arches to Gothic points; in the nave the early attempts at groin vaulting were among the first in Provence.

Chunks of the earlier church remain in what is by far the best reason to come: **the crypt**, St-Cassien's original, which is buried under the new church's medieval structure. In evocative nooks and crannies you'll find early medieval sarcophagi, including a 5th-century one that allegedly holds the martyr's remains. Upstairs look for the tomb of St-Victor, who was ground to death between two millstones, probably by the Romans. There's also a passage into tiny **catacombs** where early Christians worshipped St-Lazarus and Mary Magdalene, said to have washed ashore at Stes-Maries-de-la-Mer. The boat in which they landed is reproduced in canoe-shaped cookies called *navettes,* which are sold during the annual procession for Candelmas in February as well as year-round. ⊠ *3 rue de l'Abbaye, Rive Neuve* ▦ *Crypt entry: €2* ⊗ *Daily 9:30–7.*

③⑤ Les Arcenaulx (The Arsenal). In this broad, elegant stone armory, first built for Louis XIV, a complex of upscale shops and restaurants has given the building—and neighborhood—new life. Its bookstore has a large collection of publications on Marseille, all in French (as well as art, photography, history, and rare books); a boutique sells high-end cooking (and serving) goods with a southern accent; and a book-lined restaurant serves sophisticated cuisine. It's worth a peek to remind yourself that Marseille is not the squalid backwater people continue to expect. ✉ *25 cours d'Estienne d'Orves, Vieux Port* ☎ *04–91–59–80–37* ⊙ *Bookstore Mon.–Sat. 10 AM–midnight; boutique Mon.–Sat., 10:30–6:30; restaurant Mon.–Sat., noon–2:30 PM, 8–10 PM.*

③⑥ Bar de la Marine. Even if you've never read or seen Marcel Pagnol's trilogy of plays and films *Marius, Fanny,* and *César* (think of it as a three-part French *Casablanca*), you can get a feel for its earthy, Old Marseille feeling by stopping into the bar it was set in. The walls are blanketed with murals and comfortable café chairs fill the place, all in an effort to faithfully reproduce the bar as it was in the days when the bartender César, his son Marius, and Fanny, the shellfish girl, lived out their salty drama of love, honor, and the call of the sea. ✉ *15 quai Rive Neuve, Vieux Port* ☎ *04–91–54–95–42.*

④⓪ Fort St-Nicolas and Fort St-Jean. This complex of brawny fortresses encloses the Vieux Port's entry from both sides. In order to keep the feisty, rebellious Marseillais under his thumb, Louis XIV had the fortresses built with the guns pointing *toward the city.* The Marseillais, whose local identity has always been mixed with a healthy dose of irony, are quite proud of this display of the king's (justified) doubts about their allegiance. They're best viewed from the Jardin du Pharo.

④① Jardin du Pharo (Pharo Garden). The Pharo, another larger-than-life edifice built to Napoléon III's epic tastes, was a gift to his wife, Eugénie. It's a conference center now, but its green park has become a magnet for city strollers who want to take in panoramic views of the ports and fortifications. ✉ *Above Bd. Charles-Livon.*

★ ③⑧ Notre-Dame-de-la-Garde. With its hilltop perch, gargantuan gilt statue of Madonna and child (almost 30 feet high), and a Technicolor interior of red-and-beige stripes and glittering mosaics, this neo-Byzantine church, erected in 1853 by Napoléon III, is one of the emblems of Marseille. Deeply loved by locals and visitors alike, the Virgin attracts thousands who give thanks for having spared them from disease, car crashes, and other modern-day plagues. The walls are filled with *ex-votos,* stilted but passionate art offered in genuine gratitude (mostly by fishermen, who recognize Notre-Dame as their patron saint) for each eleventh-hour divine intervention. Venetian floor tiles and marble pillars add charm to the surprisingly intimate chapel, and the esplanade around the basilica offers spectacular views of the city. ✉ *On foot climb up Cours Pierre Puget, cross the Jardin Pierre Puget, cross a bridge to Rue Vauvenargues, and hike up to Pl. Edon. Or catch Bus 60 from Cours Jean-Ballard* ☎ *04–91–13–40–80* ⊙ *May–Sept., daily 7 AM–8 PM; Oct.–Apr., daily 7–7.*

③④ Place Thiars. An ensemble of Italianate 18th-century buildings frames this popular center of activity, where one sidewalk café spills into another, and every kind of bouillabaisse is yours for the asking. At night the neighborhood is a fashionable hangout for young professionals on their way to and from the theaters and clubs on Quai de Rive Neuve. ☒ *Framed by Quai Neuve, Rue Fortia, Rue de la Paix Marcel-Paul, and Cours d'Estienne d'Orves.*

③⑦ Théâtre National de Marseille La Criée (National Theater of Marseille at "The Fish Auction"). Behind the floridly decorated facade of this grand old fish-auction house, a prestigious state theater company performs. Innovative director Jean-Louis Benoit brings an edgy streetwise energy to the season's productions. ☒ *30 quai Rive Neuve, Vieux Port* ☎ *04–91–54–70–54 for reservations* ⊙ *Box office Tues.–Sat. 11–6* ☒ *€10–€25.*

OFF THE
BEATEN
PATH

CHÂTEAU D'IF – This wildly romantic island fortress, its thick towers and crenellated walls looming in the sea spray just off Marseille's coast, is the stuff of history—and legend. François I, in the 16th century, recognized the strategic advantage of an island fortress surveying the mouth of Marseille's vast harbor, so he had one built. Its effect as deterrent was so successful, it never saw combat and was eventually converted to a prison. It was here that Alexandre Dumas locked up his most famous character, the Count of Monte Cristo. Though he was fictional, the hole Dumas had him escape through is real enough, and it's visible in the cell today. (By contrast, the real-life Man in the Iron Mask, whose cell is still being shown, was not actually imprisoned here.) As you walk from cell to cell, each labeled for the noble (or ignoble) prisoner it held, video monitors replay scenes from film versions of the Dumas tale, including the Count's Houdini-like underwater escape from a body bag thrown from the tower. Even the jaded and castle-weary will find themselves playing nightwatch from the ramparts. The boat ride (from the Quai des Belges, €10) and the views from the broad terrace alone are worth the trip. ☎ *04–91–59–02–30* ⊕ *www.monuments-france.fr* ☒ *Château €4.60* ⊙ *Apr.–Sept., daily 9–7; Oct.–Mar., Tues.–Sun. 9:30–5:30.*

La Canebière

In a direct line east from the Vieux Port, this famous avenue used to serve as the dividing line between those Marseillais who had money and those who did not. In the last hundred years it has lost much of its former glory, and is now dominated by shopping malls and fast-food restaurants. It's architecture and 19th-century wedding-cake facades still make for an interesting walk, and it's a great place from which to make forays through the North African neighborhood along Rue Longue-des-Capucins, to the bohemian Cours Julien via Rue d'Aubagne, and on to the Palais Longchamp and its fine-arts and natural-history museums.

**A GOOD
WALK**

The famous **La Canebière** was the louche and lively nerve center of Marseille between the wars. From the Vieux Port, head up La Canebière and turn right on **Rue Longue-des-Capucins,** narrow, lively, and crammed with tiny North African shops opening onto the street. Across from the Noaille métro station, near the intersection with La Canebière, Place du Marché des Capucins concentrates the best of the North African influence in this city. Continue up the street and make a jaunt to the right down Rue Vacon, where miles of Provençal cottons are sold from heavy bolts. Then double back and go right up **Rue d'Aubagne,** cross the Cours Lieutaud, and climb up to the **Cours Julien.** At its upper end, this popular pedestrian thoroughfare opens out into a sea of restaurants, shops, and cafés, with people sunning by the modern fountain and musicians busking from table to table.

To browse through grand old museums of art and natural history in a mega-monumental public building, hike the length of La Canebière to the **Palais de Longchamp** ㊷, which houses the Musée des Beaux Arts and the Musée d'Histoire Naturelle. It's some 3 km (2 mi) slightly uphill, but it's possible to walk it in about 45 minutes; if you wear out, catch Bus 41 from anywhere on La Canebière. It's an easy run on Bus 81 from Quai des Belges.

TIMING Allow an hour to wander through the market and streets around Place du Marché des Capucins. Aim for lunch or a coffee break along Cours Julien. Give yourself about half a day for the Palais de Longchamp—it takes time to get there and back and to visit one of its two museums.

What to See

La Canebière. This wide avenue leading from the port, known affectionately as the "Can o' Beer" by American sailors, was once crammed with cafés, theaters, bars, and tempting stores full of zoot suits and swell hats, and figured in popular songs and operettas. It's noisy but dull today, yet you may take pleasure in studying the grand old 19th-century mansions lining it.

Cours Julien. A center of bohemian *flânerie* (hanging out), this is a lovely place to relax by the fountain, in the shade of plane trees, or under a café umbrella. Its low-key and painterly tableau is framed by graceful 18th-century buildings.

㊷ **Palais de Longchamp.** This extravagant and grandiose 19th-century palace, inaugurated in 1869, was built to celebrate the completion of an 84-km (52-mi) aqueduct bringing the water of the Durance river to the open sea. The massive, classical-style building crowns a hill, and is splayed with impressive symmetrical grace around a series of fountains with a triumphal arch at its center and museums in either wing. In the **Musée des Beaux-Arts** (Fine Arts Museum) are 16th- and 17th-century paintings, including several by Rubens, as well as fine marble sculptures and drawings by the Marseille architect Pierre Puget. There's a delightful group of sculptures by caricaturist Honoré Daumier, and a collection of French 19th-century paintings, including Courbet, Ingres, and David, is strong. In the right wing of the palace is the **Musée d'Histoire Naturelle** (Natural History Museum) with a collection of prehistoric and zoological artifacts,

Continued on page 170

CUISINE OF THE SUN

Why do colors seem more intense in Provence, flavors more vivid? It could be the hot, dry climate, which concentrates the essence of fruit and vegetables, or the sun beaming down on the market stalls. Or perhaps you are just seeing the world through rosé-tinted (wine) glasses. Whatever the reason, the real story of Provençal food is one of triumph over the elements. Here's how to savor its *incroyable* flavor.

From Hot to Haute

As you bite into a honey-ripe Cavaillon melon or a snow-white, fennel-perfumed sea bass fillet, you might think that nature has always been kind to Provence. Not so. On the wind-battered coast of Marseille, fishermen salvaged the boniest rock fish to create a restorative soup—bouillabaisse—that would become legendary worldwide. In the sun-blasted mountains north of Nice, impoverished farmers developed a repertoire of dishes found nowhere else in France, using hardy Swiss chard, chickpea flour, and salt cod (shipped in from Scandinavia to compensate for a scarcity of fresh fish). Camargue cowboys tamed the wild bull to create their own version of *daube*, a long-simmered stew that transforms tough cuts of meat into a gourmet marvel. Olive oil, the very symbol of Provençal food, is only now overcoming a 1950s frost that entirely wiped out France's olive groves— the local production is tiny compared to that of Spain or Italy but of exceptionally high quality. Even the tomato has a relatively short history here, having been introduced in the 1820s and at first used only in cooked dishes.

Fish Tales

If Provençal cooking is united by a common struggle against the very conditions that give its ingredients their intensity— brilliant sunshine, arid soil, fierce wind, infrequent, pounding rain—it is divided by the area's dramatically changing landscapes. In the Vaucluse alone, scorched plains punctuated by ocher cliffs give way to remarkably lush, orchard-lined mountains and gently sloped vineyards. The wild Calanques of Marseille— source of spiky sea urchins and slithering octopuses—ease into the more tranquil waters

AIL DE PROVENCE	OLIVES DE NICE

An indispensable ingredient in Provençal cooking, these garlic bulbs can be white, pink, or purplish; the darker the color, the stronger the flavor.	True Niçois olives are not uniformly black but come in delicate shades of green and deep violet.

of St-Tropez, home to gleaming bream and sea bass. Everywhere you will find sun-ripened fruit dripping provocatively with nectar and vegetables so flavor-packed that meat might seem a mere accessory. The joy of visiting this region lies in discovering these differences, which might be subtle (as in a local version of boullabaisse or fish soup) or unmistakable (as in the powerful scent that signals truffle season in Carpentras).

Pots, Pans & Picks

The best Provençal chefs remain fiercely proud of the dishes that define their region or their village, even while injecting their own identities and ideas into the food. Thanks to its ports, Provence has always been open to outside influences, yet the wealth of readily available ingredients prevents chefs from straying too far from their roots—when the local basil is so headily perfumed, why use lemongrass? If menus at first seem repetitive, go beyond the words (*tapenade, ratatouille, pistou*) to notice how each chef interprets the dish: this is not a land of printed recipes but of spontaneity inspired by the seasons and the markets. Don't expect perfect food every time, but with the help of this book, seek out those who love what they do enough to make *la cuisine de soleil* even more dazzling than the sunshine.

LA VIE EN ROSE

One sip and you'll agree: rosé wine tastes wonderful in the south of France, particularly along the coast. Some experts claim that the sea air enhances the aroma, which might explain why a bottle of Côtes de Provence rosé loses some of its holiday magic at home. French rosés are generally dry, thirst-quenching, and best served chilled. They are considered easy-drinking holiday wines, and quality is constantly improving. Be sure to try a Bandol at least once; the rest of the time, you can't go wrong with a good local rosé.

THE TOP TEN DISHES

Aïoli

The name for both a dragon's-breath mayonnaise made with helpings of garlic and also a complete recipe of salt cod, potatoes, hard-boiled eggs, and vegetables, *aïoli* pops up all over Provence, but seems most beloved of the Marseillais. Not an indigenous food, salt cod arrived on the French coast in the Middle Ages from Scandinavia. In keeping with Catholic practice, some restaurants serve it only on Fridays. And it's a good sign if they ask that you place your order at least a day in advance. A grand aïoli is a traditional component of the Niçois Christmas feast.

Bouillabaisse

Originally a humble fisherman's soup made with the part of the catch that nobody else wanted, bouillabaisse—the famous fish stew—consists of four or five kinds of fish: the villainous-looking *rascasse* (red scorpion fish), *grondin* (sea robin), *baudroie* (monkfish), *congre* (conger eel), and *rouget* (mullet). Snobs add lobster. The whole lot is simmered in a stock of onions, tomatoes, garlic, olive oil, and saffron, which gives the dish its golden color. When presented properly, the broth is served first, with croutons and *rouille*, a creamy garlic sauce that you spoon in to suit your taste. The fish comes separately, and the ritual is to put pieces into the broth after having a go at the soup on its own.

Bourride

Bourride

This poached fish dish owes its anise kick to pastis and its garlic punch to aïoli. The name comes from the Provençal *bourrido*, which translates less poetically as "boiled." Monkfish—known as *baudroie* in Provence and *lotte* in the rest of France—is a must, but chefs occasionally dress up their *bourride* with other species and shellfish.

Daube de boeuf

To distinguish their prized beef stew from boeuf bourguignon, Provençal chefs make a point of not marinating the meat, instead cooking it very slowly in tannic red wine that is often flavored with orange zest. In the Camargue, *daube* is made with the local *taureau* (bull's meat), while the Avignon variation uses lamb. In Nice, try *ravioli à la daube*.

Fougasse

The Provençal answer to Italian focaccia, this soft flatbread is distinguished by holes that give it the appearance of a lacy leaf. It can be made savory—flavored with olives, anchovy, bacon, cheese, or anything else the baker has on hand—or sweet, enriched with olive oil and dusted with icing sugar. When in Menton, don't miss the sugary *fougasse mentonnaise*.

Les petits farcis

The Niçois specialty called *les petits farcis* are prepared with tiny summer vegetables (usually zucchini, tomatoes, peppers, and onions) that are traditionally stuffed with veal or leftover *daube* (beef stew). Enjoy them warm (not hot); this is the best temperature to appreciate their flavors. Like so many Niçois dishes, they make great picnic food.

Fougasse, the Provençal answer to Italian focaccia

Ratatouille

At its best, *ratatouille* is a glorious thing—a riot of eggplant, zucchini, bell peppers, and onions, each sautéed separately in olive oil and then gently combined with sweet summer tomatoes. A well-made *ratatouille*, to which a pinch of saffron has been added to heighten its flavor, is also delicious served chilled.

Socca

You'll find *socca* vendors from Nice to Menton, but this chickpea pancake cooked on a giant iron platter in a wood-fired oven is really a Niçois phenomenon, born of sheer poverty at a time when wheat flour was scarce. After cooking, it is sliced into finger-lickin' portions with an oyster knife. Enjoy it with a glass of *pointu*, chilled rosé.

Soupe au pistou

Provençal's answer to pesto, *pistou* consists of the simplest ingredients—garlic, olive oil, fresh basil, and Parmesan—ideally pounded together by hand in a stone mortar with an olivewood pestle. Most traditionally it brings a potent kick to *soupe au pistou*, a kind of French minestrone made with green beans, white beans, potatoes, and zucchini.

Tian de légumes

A tian is both a beautiful earthenware dish and one of many vegetable gratins that might be cooked in it. Again showing the thrifty use of ingredients in Provençal cooking, the tian makes a complete meal of seasonal vegetables, eggs, and a little cheese. Swiss chard is a favorite ingredient in winter, while eggplant and tomato are best bets in summer.

THE ITALIAN CONNECTION

The most distinctive food on the Riviera comes from Nice. It's a curious mixture of Parisian, Provençal, and Italian cuisine, pungent with garlic, olives, anchovies, and steaming shellfish. Among the specialties here: *pissaladière*, an onion tart laced with black olive puree and anchovies; *pan bagnat*, a French loaf—a baguette—split down the middle, soaked in olive oil, and garnished with tomatoes, radishes, peppers, onions, hard-boiled eggs, black olives, and a sprig of basil; and *l'estocaficada*, a ragout of stockfish (air-dried unsalted fish, often cod), soaked in water before being cooked and served with potatoes, tomatoes, and zucchini.

THE TASTEMAKERS

It is not entirely surprising that some of France's best chefs now work in Provence and on the Riviera. It was here—in Villeneuve-Loubet, outside Cannes—that **Auguste Escoffier**, the legendary founding father of haute cuisine, was born (his villa is now a museum). Today, Escoffier's heirs are forging new paths in the "new Mediterranean cuisine" in all its costly splendor. Everybody knows the name of Alain Ducasse, whose luxurious *cuisine moderne* is on show at Monaco's Le Louis XV. Here are the newer stars that are making gastronomes genuflect today.

Alain Llorca

Former Negresco chef **Alain Llorca**—whose name reveals his Basque roots—has found the perfect setting for his Spanish-influenced style in the freshly renovated, plum-and-white dining room of the Moulin de Mougins, the famous culinary temple put on the map years ago by Roger Vergé. No matter how simple or complex the dish, Llorca makes each ingredient sing—a crisp-skinned farmer's chicken breast proves tender enough to cut with a fork, its accompanying spring vegetables straight from his own *potager* (vegetable garden). Llorca's sense of humor comes through in his *ronde des tapas*—look for such whimsical nibbles as foie gras bonbons, goat cheese croque-monsieur, and bouillabaisse-style octopus.

Antique dealers feel at home at Le Jardin du Quai in L'Isle-sur-la-Sorgue, which jovial young chef **Daniel Hébet** runs like an open house. In summer, regulars linger on the garden patio reading the paper and chatting, while in winter the high-ceiling bistro-style dining room exudes the same welcoming vibe.

Shrugging off the constraints of haute cuisine with a no-choice set menu at lunch and dinner, Hébet still makes clever use of techniques, serving vivid green, individually skinned broad beans in a frothy sauce with barely cooked chanterelles and artfully peeled fat white asparagus. Don't miss his quinoa-crusted cod.

After an illustrious haute cuisine career, **Jacques Maximin** has found contentment in running a convivial country *auberge* near Vence. The name, La Table d'Amis, speaks volumes about his approach—here the chef treats customers like old friends, occasionally even relieving them of decision-making by serving what he has decided they should eat. Even if you're not so lucky, you can hardly go wrong with a menu that reveals his long experience and a renewed joie de vivre—Catalan-style scallops with risotto are just one perfect example of his openness to other southern cooking styles.

The summer tomato menu has become a much-anticipated annual tradition at **Christian Etienne**'s restaurant next to the Palais des Papes in Avignon, where each year he celebrates the versatility of this vegetable with a tasting extravaganza that might include tartare of three varieties with oil from the Bleu Argent olive mill in Provence, foie gras with Roma tomato petals, and tomato macaroon with lime sorbet. Etienne is one of the long-established masters of Provençal cooking, and if his cooking sometimes makes generous use of butter (rather than uniquely olive oil), his customers aren't complaining.

Christian Etienne

TO MARKET, TO MARKET

Marché aux poissons, Marseille

Markets define Provençal living, from the see-and-be-seen Cours Saleya in Nice to villages that spring to life once or twice a week as the trucks bearing goat cheese or sunny-yolked farmers' eggs pull up to the main square. Below are a few of the best; all are open Tuesday through Sunday except Cotignac.

COURS SALEYA, NICE – The coast's most colorful market, as much for the people as for the goods on display (it's liveliest on weekends). Local producers cluster in Place Pierre Gauthier.

MARCHÉ FORVILLE, CANNES – Though not the best-known market on the Côte d'Azur, Forville has an extraordinary selection, from the small producers who line the center aisle to the small fish market, which is usually sold out by late morning.

MARCHÉ RICHELME, AIX-EN-PROVENCE – This market is legendary, and rightly so, for its lovely setting in the Old Town and its eye-popping range of goods. No wonder Cézanne immortalized such apples and pears.

MARCHÉ AUX POISSONS, MARSEILLE – You'll understand the wonder of bouillabaisse once you've visited this market on the Vieux Port: colorful fishing boats pull up to the quay and fill blue plastic tubs with still-leaping fish and lively octopuses.

COTIGNAC MARKET (TUESDAY) – One of dozens of small markets in Provence, Cotignac has retained a real village atmosphere and provides the perfect excuse to visit this seductive town.

TRUFFES DE CARPENTRAS

This town in the Vaucluse is the center of the "black diamond" trade, thanks to its Saturday truffle market, held from November to March.

plus a large aquarium with fish from around the world. ✉ *End of Bd. Longchamp, La Canebière* ☎ *04–91–14–59–30* or *04–91–14–59–50* 💳 *€2, Musée des Beaux-Arts;* €*3, Musée d'Histoire Naturelle* ☉ *May–Sept., Tues.–Sun. 11–6; Oct.–Apr., Tues.–Sun. 10–5.*

Rue Longue-des-Capucins/Rue d'Aubagne. Stepping into this atmospheric neighborhood, you may feel you have suddenly been transported to a Moroccan souk. Shops with open bins of olives and coffee beans and tea and spices and dried beans and chickpeas and couscous and peppers and salted sardines serve the needs of Marseille's large and vibrant North African community. Tiny shoebox cafés proffer exotic sweets.

Anses: East of Town

Along the coastline east of Marseille's center, a series of pretty little *anses* (ports) leads to the more famous and far-flung Calanques. These miniature inlets are really tiny villages, with pretty, balconied, boxy houses (called *cabanons*) clustered around bright-painted fishing boats. Don't even think about buying a cabanon of your own, however; they are part of the fishing community's heritage and are protected from gentrification by the outside world.

A GOOD
DRIVE

Drive up the Quai de Rive Neuve to the Corniche J.-F. Kennedy, which roars along the dramatic cliff top above the Mediterranean. The Art Deco **Monument aux Héros de l'Armée d'Orient et des Terres Lointaines** (Monument to the Heroes of the Army of the East and Faraway Lands) marks your turning point. Head left into the picture-perfect little fishing port called the **Vallon des Auffes.** You could paddle across it in two strokes, but this miniature inlet concentrates all the color (blue, red, and green fishing boats, azure water) of a Rossellini film set.

Continue past the wealthy **Roucas-Blanc** neighborhood and the full-scale 19th-century reproduction of Michelangelo's *David,* standing incongruously at the center of Avenue du Prado. When the Marseillais do something, they do it big. The city's main beaches lie at David's feet in the **Parc Balnéaire** du Prado, including the Plage de David. From the sands, you'll have breathtaking views of the Iles de Frioul (Frioul Islands), which you can visit by boat from Marseille's port.

After David and the beaches, continue up the road to **Port de Plaisance de la Pointe Rouge** and then **La Madrague,** both postcard-pretty anses wedged with bobbing boats and toy-block cabanons in saturated tints. Pursue the road to its dead end at **Les Goudes** and climb over boulders and tidal ★ pools to the extraordinary **Anse Croisette,** a rough inlet paradise of crashing waves and rock. It was near here, known to the Marseillais as the Bout du Monde (End of the World), where the *Grand St-Antoine*—the ship that brought the plague to Marseille in 1720—was sunk, but too late to save the 100,000 who died from its deadly cargo.

TIMING
Allow a half day for this dramatic drive—longer if you succumb to the temptation to clamber around on barnacle-covered rocks, to sip a pastis while watching the fishing boats come in at dusk, or to settle in for a full-out bouillabaisse.

OFF THE
BEATEN
PATH

L'ESTAQUE – At this famous village north of Marseille, Cézanne led an influx of artists eager to capture its cliff-top views over the harbor. Braque, Derain, and Renoir all put its red rooftops, rugged cliffs, and factory smokestacks on canvas. Pick up the English-language itinerary "L'Estaque and the Painters" from the Marseille tourist office and hunt down the sites and views they immortalized. It's a little seedy these days, but there are cafés and a few fish shops making the most of the nearby Criée (fisherman's auction). This is where the real wholesale auction moved from Marseille's Quai de Rive Neuve. A novel way to see Cézanne's famous scenery is to take a standard SNCF train trip from the Gare St-Charles to Martigue; it follows the L'Estaque waterfront and (with the exception of a few tunnels) offers magnificent views.

Where to Eat & Stay

★ $$$$ ✕ **Chez Fonfon.** Tucked into a picturesque waterside spot in the tiny fishing port Vallon des Auffes, this Marseillais landmark has one of the loveliest settings in greater Marseille. Once presided over by cult chef "Fonfon," it used to be a favorite movie-star hangout. Plain, fresh seafood impeccably grilled, steamed, or roasted in salt crust is still served in two pretty pink dining rooms with picture windows that overlook the fishing boats that supply your dinner. The crowds come to indulge in classic bouillabaisse served with all the bells and whistles—decadently rich broth, hot-chili rouille, and flamboyant table-side filleting. ✉ *140 rue du Vallon des Auffes, Vallon des Auffes* ☎ *04-91-52-14-38* ⊕ *www.chez-fonfon.com* ✍ *Reservations essential* ▭ *AE, DC, MC, V* ⊙ *Closed Sun. and 1st 2 wks in Jan. No lunch Mon.*

★ $$$–$$$$ ✕ **L'Epuisette.** Artfully placed on a rocky, fingerlike cliff surrounded by the sea, this seafood restaurant offers gorgeous views of crashing surf on one side and the port of Vallon des Auffes on the other. Chef Guillaume Sourrieu has acquired a big reputation (and Michelin stars) for

> When bouillabasse is presented properly, the broth is served first with croutons and rouille, a creamy garlic sauce that you spoon in to suit your taste. The fish comes separately, and the ritual is to put pieces into the broth after having a go at the soup on its own.

sophisticated cooking—mullet fillets on a bed of peppers and eggplant sauced with peppery rouille, or sea bass baked in a salt crust are some top delights—all matched with a superb wine list. Save room for dessert. ✉ *Anse du Vallon des Auffes, Vallon des Auffes* ☎ *04-91-52-17-82* ▭ *AE, DC, MC, V* ⊙ *Closed Mon. No lunch Sat. No dinner Sun.*

$$$–$$$$ ✕ **Mets de Provence.** Climb the oddly slanted wharf-side stairs and enter a cosseted Provençal world. With boats bobbing outside the window and a landlubbing country decor, this romantic restaurant makes the most of Marseille's split personality. Classic Provençal hors d'oeuvres—tapenade, brandade, aïoli—lead into seafood (dorado roasted with fennel and licorice) and meats (rack of lamb in herb pastry). The four-course

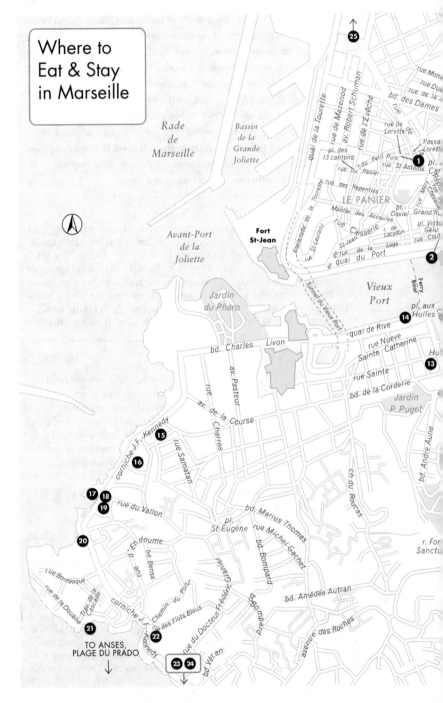

Where to
Eat & Stay
in Marseille

Rade
de
Marseille

Bassin
de la
Grande
Joliette

LE PANIER

Fort
St-Jean

Avant-Port
de la
Joliette

Jardin
du Pharo

Vieux
Port

Fort St-Jean

quai du Port

Tunnel du Vieux Port

pl. aux
Huiles

quai de Rive

bd. Charles Livon

rue Nueve
Sainte Catherine

rue Sainte

bd. de la Corderie

Jardin
P. Puget

av. Pasteur

rue des Charros

av. de la Course

corniche J.F. Kennedy

rue Samatan

rue du Vallon

pl.
St-Eugène

bd. Marius Thomas

rue Michel Gachet

bd. André Aune

ch. du Roucas

bd. Bompard

bd. En doume

bd. Bensa

rue Bouresque

rue de la Douane

T.av. de la Cascade

corniche J.F. Kennedy

Chemin du Port

rue des Flots Bleus

rue du Docteur Frédéric Granet

bd. Bompard

bd. Amédée Autran

avenue des Roches

bd. Véran

TO ANSES,
PLAGE DU PRADO
↓

rue de la Tourette

quai de la Tourette

rue de Mazenod

av. Robert Schuman

rue de l'Évêché

pl. des
13 cantons

r. du Petit Puits

rue St-Antoine

rue du Panier

rue des Repenties

Montée des Accoules

pl.
Daviel

r. de
Lacydon

rue Caisserie

rue St-Jean

av. rue de la Loge

Esplanade de la Tourette

rue St-Laurent

rue de
Lorette

Passa.
Loretti

pl.
Carté.

Grand'Ru.

pl. Victo
Gelu

rue Cout.

rue des Dames

bd. de la

rue Due.

rue Mon.

Ferry
Boat

1
2
13
14
15
16
17
18
19
20
21
22
23
24
25

Restaurants ▼

Hotels ▼

lunch (€38, including wine) is marvelous. ⊠ *18 quai de Rive Neuve, Vieux Port* ☎ *04–91–33–35–38* ☰ *MC, V* ⊘ *Closed Sun. No lunch Sat. No dinner Mon.*

★ **$$$–$$$$** ✕ **Miramar.** A Marseille institution, this restaurant is justifiably famous for its bouillabaisse, and is one of the best places to sample the city's fabled dish. It maintains a '60s style of red-velvet-and-wood-paneling elegance (you almost expect to spot Jackie O in a pillbox hat at the next table) but the portside terrace tables cut through the stuffiness. Unlike many seafood restaurants in town, it always has bouillabaisse on the menu, so you don't have to order in advance. Desserts are spectacular, thanks to an innovative pastry chef, and with a chilled bottle of Cassis it is truly a dining event. ⊠ *12 quai du Port, Vieux Port* ☎ *04–91–91–10–40* ☰ *AE, MC, V* ⊘ *Closed Sun., Mon., and 2 wks in Jan.*

$$$–$$$$ ✕ **Une Table au Sud.** After learning as much as he could from super-chef Alain Ducasse in Paris, Lionel Lévy quickly won his own reputation for modern French cooking when he opened this stylish and contemporary restaurant. The rather stark interior is softened by draping yellow curtains, warm red-toned carpets, and lots of sunlight. Rich desserts like *croquant au chocolate fondant* (chocolate ganache layered inside almond pastry) add a nice finish to an already delightful meal—try the zucchini flowers stuffed with feta cheese followed by grilled tuna steak with teriyaki gelée—and friendly service encourages you to linger over a last glass of wine while gazing out at the port. ⊠ *2 quai du Port, Vieux Port* ☎ *04–91–90–63–53* ☰ *MC, V* ⊘ *Closed Sun. and Mon.*

$$–$$$ ✕ **Les Arcenaulx.** At this book-lined, red-walled haven in the stylish print-and-boutique complex of the renovated arsenal, you can have a delicious and refined Provençal lunch—and read while you're waiting. Seafood figures large on the menu—try the fresh sea bream from the market two blocks away or the garlic-perfumed octopus stew. The fact that diners enter by passing rows of burnished leather-bound antique tomes appeals to Marseille's finer side, and you'll find an interesting mix of politicians, actors, and professors inside. ⊠ *25 cours d'Estienne d'Orves, Vieux Port* ☎ *04–91–59–80–30* ☰ *AE, DC, MC, V* ⊘ *Closed Sun.*

★ **$$–$$$** ✕ **La Baie des Singes.** On a tiny rock-ringed lagoon as isolated from the nearby city as if it were a desert island, this beautiful cinematic spot was once a customs house under Napoléon III. You can rent a mattress and lounge chair (€10), dive into the turquoise water, and shower off for the only kind of meal worthy of such a location: fresh fish. There's bouillabaisse, of course, but also fresh-grilled sardines, mullet, and baudroie; and crabs, lobster, and local *cigales de mer* (shrimplike "sea locusts"). It's all served at terrace tables overlooking the water. The expansive owner, son of a fishmonger and grandson of a fisherman, knows his craft, and boasts—literally—Jacques Chirac and Catherine Deneuve among his loyal clientele. ⊠ *Anse des Croisettes, Les Goudes* ☎ *04–91–73–68–87* ☰ *MC, V* ⊘ *Closed Oct.–Mar.*

$$–$$$ ✕ **L'Escale.** In the sleepy little village of Les Goudes, 20 minutes outside of the center of Marseille, this seaside dining room and terrace has become a village landmark. The catch of the day couldn't be much fresher, and former fisherman and fishmonger Serge Zarokian brings years of experience to a hearty, earthy bouillabaisse (order in advance) or deli-

CLOSE UP

How to Eat a Sea Urchin

" . . . But answer came there none–/ And this was scarcely odd, because/ They'd eaten every one," wrote Lewis Carroll in *Through the Looking Glass.*

Urchins, those spiny little balls, are cracked open and served belly up on a platter of seaweed, usually six or a dozen at a time. To the uninitiated, they're not a pretty sight: Each black demiglobe comes with quills still . . . well, waving, but only slightly. Within this macabre natural bowl floats a dense puddle of (it must be said) muddy brown grit and bile-green slime. Supporting the rim with your left thumb and index finger (taking care not to impale yourself),

scrape said slime to the sides with the point of your spoon. Here lies what the fuss is all about: there are six coral-pink strips of sea-perfumed stuff inside, more foam than flesh (you may have experienced a more substantial version in sushi). Scrape these gently up and spread them on a slice of baguette. Or just slide them into a spoon and bite. An ocean of milky-sweet flavor is concentrated in this rosy streak. Granted, a dozen won't make a meal, but keep the little guys company with oysters, mussels, clams, sea snails, a crock of butter, a basket of bread, and an icy bottle of Cassis.

3

cately sautéed baby squid. It's very popular, especially for Sunday lunch, so book ahead. ✉ *2 bd. Alexandre Delabre, Les Goudes* ☎ *04–91–73–16–78* ⌂ *Reservations essential* ☱ *AE, DC, MC, V* ✆ *Closed Jan. No lunch Mon. and Tues. in May–Sept. Closed Mon. and Tues. in Oct.–Apr.*

$$–$$$ ✕ **Le Peron.** Chic and stylishly modern with a dark-wood interior and large windows overlooking the sea, this restaurant is a magnet for hip, young professionals—you'll need to book ahead. Surprisingly service-oriented and very friendly, the staff are efficient and quietly accommodating. Meals are well presented and tasty—try grilled garlic scallops in a puree of purple potatoes or lobster risotto—and the view is one of the best in the city. ✉ *56 corniche J.-F. Kennedy, Endoume* ☎ *04–91–52–15–22* ☱ *AE, DC, MC, V.*

$–$$ ✕ **Caffè Milano.** With its old mirrors and pictures of famous (mostly French) stars who have stopped by for a meal, this popular spot serves Italian and Provençal dishes in an upscale, busy space. Photographers, models, and fashion wannabes mix and mingle downstairs while the rather imposing mezzanine is a good place to people-watch. Simple fare, the daily pasta special is usually worth a try, and the salad with chicken and ginger makes a nice light lunch. ✉ *43 rue Sainte, Vieux Port* ☎ *04–91–33–14–33* ☱ *MC, V* ✆ *Closed Sun. No lunch Sat.*

$–$$ ✕ **Chez Jeannot.** This is the poor man's Chez Fonfon, around the port from the prestigious restaurant and run by a member of the same family. It's so popular that it's become something of a theme-restaurant version of itself (plastic menus, wedding-banquet-style dining rooms), but it's a wonderful place to get away from town and enjoy a casual meal in an lovely spot. The pizzas are heavy, and there are towering platters of shellfish still twitching—but you're here for the film-set scenery as much as for the food. Terrace tables overlooking the fishing boats justify taxi fare from the center, but reserve in advance or you'll end up in the smoky interior. ⊠ *129 Vallon des Auffes, Vallon des Auffes* 📠 *04–91–52–11–28* 🚍 *AE, V* ☉ *Closed Mon. No lunch Tues.–Fri.*

$–$$ ✕ **Chez Vincent.** Although it's in the mini-red-light district of the Vieux Port, this little Italian restaurant is all it's cracked up to be. The spaghetti with tiny clams is excellent, as is the lasagna, and it is jammed with lively night-owl regulars, including singers from the Opéra around the corner. ⊠ *25 rue Glandèves, Vieux Port* 📠 *04–91–33–96–78* 🚍 *No credit cards* ☉ *Closed Mon. No lunch Sun.*

¢–$ ✕ **Au Petit Naples.** With huge portions, a convivial vibe, and a small, busy beachfront location in the Estaque suburb, this restaurant is jammed with locals and savvy tourists from every walk of life. Some connoisseurs say that the pizza here is even better than at Etienne's. Seafood, especially fried calamari, is another specialty. ⊠ *14 plage de l'Estaque* 📠 *04–91–46–05–11* 🚍 *No credit cards* ☉ *Closed Sun. No lunch Sat.*

★ ¢–$ ✕ **Pizzeria Etienne.** A historic Le Panier hole-in-the-wall, this small pizzeria is filled daily with politicos and young professionals who enjoy the personality of the chef Stéphane Cassero, who was famous at one time for having no printed menu and announcing the price of the meal only after he'd had the chance to look you over. Remarkably little has changed over the years, except now there is a posted menu (with prices). Brace yourself for an epic meal, starting with a large anchovy pizza from the wood-burning oven, then dig into fried squid, eggplant gratin, and a slab of rare grilled beef all served with the background of laughter, rich patois, and abuse from the chef. ⊠ *43 rue de la Lorette, Le Panier* 📠 *No phone* 🚍 *No credit cards* ☉ *Closed Sun.*

¢–$ ✕ **Toinou Dégustation.** You can join the crowd at the outdoor stand and split a few oysters on the hoof. But it's more comfortable settling into a brasserie booth at this landmark shellfish joint where you can get heaps of Cassis urchins, cream-filled *violets* (a kind of monstrous sea slug), clams, mussels, and, of course, oysters. Try the North African hot sauce or opt for the powerful aïoli. ⊠ *Cours St-Louis, Vieux Port* 📠 *04–91–54–08–79* 🚍 *No credit cards* ☉ *Closed Aug.*

★ $$$$ ✕🖼 **Le Petit Nice.** Despite its name, this glamorous hideaway out-Rivieras anything in Nice. On a rocky promontory overlooking the harbor and the Iles de Frioul, this turn-of-the-20th-century Greek-style villa was bought from a countess in 1917 and converted to a hotel/restaurant in anticipation of the Jazz Age rush to the Côte d'Azur. The Passédat family has been getting it right ever since. Most of the modern designer rooms are sleek and minimalist and open onto balconies overlooking the sea. For a more time-burnished ambience, opt for a room in the Marina Wing. Accented with plate-glass windows, the restaurant proffers such delights as truffled brandade, sea anemone beignets, fresh fish cooked whole, and licorice soufflé. In summer, meals are served by the saltwater pool overlooking the crashing surf. (The restaurant is closed Sunday and Monday for lunch in summer, and Sunday and Monday in winter; fixed-price menus are €110 and €139.) All in all, some might consider this a Hollywood set for the South of France of their dreams. ⊠ *Anse de Mal-*

dormé, *Corniche J.-F. Kennedy, Endoume, 13007* ☎ *04–91–59–25–92*
🖷 *04–91–59–28–08* ⊕ *www.petitnice-passedat.com* 🗐 *13 rooms, 3 suites*
⚅ *Restaurant, minibars, cable TV, pool, in-room data ports, free parking, some pets allowed (fee)* ☰ *AE, DC, MC, V* Ⓞ *MAP.*

$$$$ ▣ **Sofitel Palm Beach Marseille.** Sleek with stunning 260-degree views of the bay and the islands, this white-on-white modern hotel offers designs by Starck, Zanotta, and Emu. Service is prompt and unobtrusive, and the huge windows make for a light-filled reception area. The saltwater pool is fed by a natural spring and the rooms are up-to-the-minute in decor. ✉ *200 corniche J.-F. Kennedy, Endoume, 13002* ☎ *04–91–16–19–00* 🖷 *04–91–16–19–39* ⊕ *www.sofitel.com* 🗐 *150 rooms, 10 suites* ⚅ *Restaurant, in-room data ports, minibars, cable TV, pool, parking (fee), some pets allowed (fee)* ☰ *AE, DC, MC, V* Ⓞ *MAP.*

★ **$$$–$$$$** ▣ **Mercure Beauvau Vieux Port.** Chopin spent the night and George Sand kept a suite in this historic hotel overlooking the Vieux Port. Entirely renovated, rooms have kept the gloss of real antiques, burnished woodwork, Provençal-style details, and plush carpets, while having modern touches like Internet access and soundproof windows. It's all part of this intimate urban hotel's genuine charm. Port-view rooms with balconies high over the fish market more than justify the splurge. ✉ *4 rue Beauvau, Vieux Port, 13001* ☎ *04–91–54–91–00, 800/637–2873 for U.S. reservations* 🖷 *04–91–54–15–76* ⊕ *www.mercure.com* 🗐 *72 rooms, 2 suites* Ⓞ *MAP.*

$$$ ▣ **Residence du Vieux Port.** The flat glass-and-concrete facade of this postwar structure grants all the rooms here broad picture-window views all the way to Notre-Dame de la Garde. Lower rooms are classic and pastel-modern, but be aware that unless you have a discerning eye for the subtleties of heavy floral design, the pricier Provençal rooms are not much different. There is a generous breakfast buffet, worth the small supplement. ✉ *18 quai du Port, Vieux Port, 13002* ☎ *04–91–91–91–22* 🖷 *04–91–56–60–88* ⊕ *www.hotelmarseille.com* 🗐 *40 rooms, 6 suites* ⚅ *Restaurant, minibars, cable TV, parking (fee), some pets allowed (fee)* ☰ *AE, DC, MC, V* Ⓞ *BP.*

$$ ▣ **New Hotel Vieux Port.** In the heart of things, at the crossroads of the Quai du Port and the Quai des Belges, this old, urban hotel is being slicked up a little bit more every month with its ongoing, yet amazingly quiet, renovations. The cage elevator and the weathered marble stairs lead up to spare, modern rooms with tile baths. Ask for a corner room overlooking the ports. ✉ *3 bis rue Reine-Elisabeth, Vieux Port, 13001* ☎ *04–91–90–51–42* 🖷 *04–91–90–76–24* ⊕ *www.new-hotel.com* 🗐 *47 rooms* ⚅ *Minibars, bar, cable TV, some pets allowed (fee)* ☰ *AE, DC, MC, V* Ⓞ *BP.*

$$ ▣ **Le Rhul.** This is the Hôtel Le Petit Nice for ordinary people: a broad, '60s-style roadside inn to the *left* of the corniche but still taking in spectacular sea views. Okay, so the stark architecture is cozied up with doilies and overstuffed chairs, and the rooms have beige laminate built-ins. But its restaurant is renowned for its bouillabaisse, and all but three rooms overlook the sea; three others have little balconies from which you can thumb your nose at the more famous inn below. ✉ *269 corniche J.-F. Kennedy, Endoume, 13007* ☎ *04–91–52–01–77* 🖷 *04–91–52–49–82*

⤴ *16 rooms* ⌂ *Restaurant, minibars, cable TV, parking (fee), some pets allowed (fee)* ☰ *AE, MC, V* ⦿ *MAP.*

$$ ▦ **Saint Ferréol.** Set back from the port in the heart of the shopping district, this cozy little hotel offers a warm reception and a homey breakfast room–cum–bar. Rooms are heavily decked out in homage to various artists—Picasso in red, black, and gilt, for example, with jazzy Cubist curtains. ✉ *19 rue Pisançon (at Rue St-Ferréol), Vieux Port, 13001* ☎ *04–91–33–12–21* ⎙ *04–91–54–29–97* ⊕ *www.hotel-stferreol.com* ⤴ *19 rooms* ⌂ *Cable TV, some pets allowed (fee)* ☰ *MC, V* ⦿ *BP.*

$–$$ ▦ **Alizé.** On the Vieux Port, its front rooms taking in postcard views, this straightforward lodging has been modernized to include tight double windows, slick modular baths, and a laminate-and-all-weather-carpet look. Public spaces have exposed stone and preserved details, and a glass elevator whisks you to your floor. It's an excellent value and location for the price range. ✉ *35 quai des Belges, Vieux Port, 13001* ☎ *04–91–33–66–97* ⎙ *04–91–54–80–06* ⊕ *www.alize-hotel.com* ⤴ *39 rooms* ⌂ *Cable TV, some pets allowed (fee)* ☰ *AE, DC, MC, V* ⦿ *BP.*

$–$$ ▦ **Hermès.** Although the rooms are rather snug, this modest city hotel is right around the corner from the Quai du Port and is good value. Ask for one of the fifth-floor rooms with tiny balconies overlooking the port—or the crow's nest "nuptiale" double with private rooftop terrace. ✉ *2 rue Bonneterie, Vieux Port, 13002* ☎ *04–96–11–63–63* ⎙ *04–96–11–63–64* ⊕ *www.hotelmarseille.com* ⤴ *28 rooms* ⌂ *Cable TV, parking (fee), some pets allowed (fee)* ☰ *AE, DC, MC, V* ⦿ *BP.*

★ $ ▦ **Hotel Perron.** A family-run jewel, this eclectic, rather eccentric hotel features rooms with different decorative themes, from delicate, rather austere Japanese to playful Dutch to colorful Moroccan. It was the first hotel in Marseille to install baths in the 1960s, and, yes, the originals are still here—charming but very small. Almost every room has a stunning sea view. The nights are very quiet, and the service is excellent. ✉ *119 corniche J.-F. Kennedy, Endoume, 13007* ☎ *04–91–31–01–41* ⎙ *04–91–59–42–01* ⊕ *www.bestofprovence.com* ⤴ *27 rooms* ⌂ *Bar, parking, some pets allowed (fee); no a/c in some rooms* ☰ *AE, MC, V* ⦿ *BP.*

Nightlife & the Arts

With a population of more than 800,000, Marseille is a big city by French standards, with all the nightlife that entails. Arm yourself with *Marseille Poche,* a glossy monthly events minimagazine; the monthly *In Situ,* a free guide to music, theater and galleries; *Sortir,* a weekly about film, art, and concerts in southern Provence; or *TakTik,* a hip weekly on theater and new art. They're all in French.

Le Trolleybus (✉ 24 quai de Rive Neuve, Bompard ☎ 04–91–54–30–45) is still the hottest disco in town, and the starting—and ending—point of Marseille nightlife. Different dance "grottos" offer techno, salsa, and funk, and a young, hip crowd ranging from bankers to rappers in Nike track suits and gold jewelry. **The New Cancan** (✉ 3 rue Senac-de-Meilhan, Vieux Port ☎ 04–91–48–59–76) is Marseille's largest gay club, with stage shows and great music, as well as a friendly, mixed crowd that livens up a rather dark space. **Dôme-Zénith** (✉ 48 av. St-Just, St-Just ☎ 04–91–47–01–25) is Marseille's big modern venue for international rock acts and various French celebrities.

The Red Lion (✉ 231 av. Pierre Mendès France, Vieux Port ☎ 04–91–25–17–17) is a mecca for English speakers, who pour onto the sidewalk, pints in hand, pub-style. There's happy hour daily (5 to 8) and live music Wednesday.

At **La Part des Anges** (✉ 33 rue Saint, Vieux Port ☎ 04–91–33–55–70), good wines are brought in from all over France and served by the glass or by the bottle. Open until 2 AM daily, it attracts an eclectic crowd, from hip, arty, and trendy to overdressed women and men in bad suits.

Watch out for the local group Gachempega; they play on occasion at **L'Intermediaire** (✉ 63 pl. Jean Jaurès, La Canebière ☎ 04–91–47–01–25), which is the hippest venue in town for jazz, blues, and rock concerts. For rap and techno, try **L'Affranchi** (✉ 212 bd. de St-Marcel, La Canebière ☎ 04–91–35–09–19). The long-standing and very active **Espace Julien** (✉ 39 cours Julien, Notre Dame du Mont ☎ 04–91–24–34–14) has international blues, pop, and local techno. At the vast **Docks des Suds** (✉ Bd. de Paris, Vieux Port ☎ 04–91–99–00–00 ⊕ www.docks-des-suds.org), host to the Fiesta des Suds each autumn, you'll now find world and Latin music year-round. **Le Moulin** (✉ 47 bd. Perrin, St-Just ☎ 04–91–06–33–94) is a converted cinema that has become one of Marseille's best live-music venues for visiting French and international music stars.

> Marseille's vibrant multicultural mix has evolved a genre of music that fuses all the soul of Arabic music with rhythms of Provence, Corsica, and Southern Italy, and douses it with reggae and rap.

In a beautifully restored 1901 building, **Le Café Parisien** (✉ 1 pl. Sadi Carnot, up Rue de la République, Le Panier ☎ 04–91–90–05–77) is a dynamic melting pot where workers take their breakfast and the club crowds come when the clubs close. At night, intellectuals and the BCBG's mingle at night over drinks and Latin music, digging into first-rate tapas (€7 for a large plate) on Thursday and Friday. **La Caravelle** (✉ 34 quai du Port, Vieux Port ☎ 04–91–90–36–64) has a cocktail bar, great live jazz, and a narrow balcony that has a picture-perfect view over the port.

Classical-music concerts are held in the **Abbaye St-Victor** (☎ 04–96–11–20–60 for information). Operas and orchestral concerts take place at the **Opéra Municipal** (✉ 2 rue Molière, Pl. Ernest Reyer, Notre Dame du Mont ☎ 04–91–55–00–70).

At the **Théâtre National de Marseille La Criée** (✉ Quai de Rive Neuve, Vieux Port ☎ 04–91–54–74–54), a strong and solid repertoire of classical and contemporary works is performed. **Théâtre Off** (✉ Quai de Rive Neuve, Vieux Port ☎ 04–91–33–12–92) presents alternative productions of classics. Celebrity-cast road shows and operettas are performed in the

Théâtre Municipal's **Espace Odéon** (⊠ 163 La Canebière, La Canebière ☎ 04–91–92–79–44).

At **Badaboum** (⊠ Quai de Rive Neuve, Vieux Port ☎ 04–91–54–40–71), adventurous, accessible productions for children are performed. The **Théâtre des Marionettes** (⊠ Theatre Massalia, 41 rue Jobin, La Canebière ☎ 04–91–11–45–65) entertains a young audience with puppets, dance, and music—occasionally in English. It's by the Gare St-Charles.

Sports & the Outdoors

Marseille's waterfront position makes it easy to swim and sunbathe within the city sprawl. From the Vieux Port, Bus 83 or Bus 19 takes you to the vast green spread of reclaimed land called the **Parc Balnéaire du Prado.** Its waterfront is divided into beaches, all of them public and well equipped with showers, toilets, and first-aid stations. The beach surface varies between sand and gravel. You can also find your own little beach on the tiny, rocky **Iles de Frioul**; boats leave from the Vieux Port and cost €10.

If you want to venture into wilder coastal country, and have a car, drive it to the end of the world. Head out the coastal road to Les Goudes, then penetrate even farther (up the road marked SANS ISSUE, or dead end) until you reach Callelongue. From here you can strike out on foot, following the GR 98 to the idyllic **Calanque de Marseilleveyvre,** a rocky finger-inlet perfect for an isolated swim. From this point, the famous Calanques continue all the way to Cassis; though most of them lie on Marseille's official turf, they are most often accessed from Cassis. You can visit them by boat from Marseille, too, on a 4-hour minicruise with the **Groupement des Armateurs Cotiers Marseillais** (G.A.C.M.; ⊠ 1 quai des Belges, Vieux Port ☎ 04–91–55–50–09). Tours leave at 2 on Wednesday, Saturday, and Sunday (except in stormy mistrals).

Marseille is a major center for diving (*plongée),* with several organizations offering "baptêmes" ("baptisms," or first dives) to beginners. The coast is lined with rocky inlets, grottos, and ancient shipwrecks, not to mention thronging with aquatic life. For general information, contact the **Association Plongez Marseille** (⊠ 32 rue Antoine Merille, Vieux Port ☎ 06–14–89–17–71). **Océan 4** (⊠ 83 av. de la Pointe-Rouge, Vieux Port ☎ 04–91–73–91–16) is an English-speaking company that offers initiations and day trips, and has equipment, showers, and storage. There are initiations, day trips, equipment rental, and showers and storage at the English-speaking **Palm Beach Plongée** (⊠ 2 promenade de la Plage, Vieux Port ☎ 04–91–22–10–38).

Shopping

The locally famous bakery **Four des Navettes** (⊠ 136 rue Sainte, Notre-Dame ☎ 04–91–33–32–12), up the street from Notre-Dame-de-la-Garde, makes orange-spice, shuttle-shape navettes. These cookies are modeled on the little boat in which Mary Magdalene and Lazarus washed onto Continental shores (⇨ Stes-Maries-de-la-Mer *in* Chapter 1), before Lazarus worked his way over to Aix and Marseille.

Savon de Marseille (Marseille Soap) is a household expression in France, often sold as a satisfyingly crude and hefty block in odorless olive-oil green. There's a world market, though, for the chichi offspring of this earth mother: dainty pastel guest soaps in almond, lemon, vanilla, and other scents. If you're not one for lingering in the odoriferous boutiques that sell these in gilt gift boxes, consider the no-nonsense outlet of **La Compagnie de Provence** (☒ 1 rue Caisserie, Vieux Port ☎ 04–91–56–20–97), at the foot of Le Panier. Here blocks of soap are sold in plain brown boxes, but you can have them gift wrapped on request. For every kind of nautical doodad, from brass fittings for your yacht's bathroom to sturdy pea coats and oilskins, head down the quai to **Castaldi** (☒ 25 quai de Rive Neuve, Vieux Port ☎ 04–91–33–30–49). For exotic food products shipped into this international port, browse in the **Arax** (☒ 24–27 rue d'Aubagne, La Canebière ☎ 04–91–54–11–50), crammed floor to ceiling with Armenian specialties and aromatic goodies from North Africa, China, and the Middle East.

For good old-fashioned big-city shopping, the Rue St-Ferréol (four blocks back from the Vieux Port) is flanked with major department stores: **Nouvelles Galeries** (☒ Centre Bourse/Bir Hakeim, Vieux Port ☎ 04–91–56–82–12), a mid-price department store, anchors the corner one block back from the port and the tourist office. Check out the hip boutique **La Thuberie** (☒ 14–16 rue Thubaneau, Belsunce ☎ 04–91–90–84–55), run by designer Linda Cohen. It's a showcase for local talent, and has some beautiful cutting-edge designs plus furniture and housewares. Offbeat designer clothing created in Marseille can be found on Cours Julien, including the home-base for the trendy, high-texture clothes and jewelry made by **Madame Zaza of Marseille** (☒ 73 cours Julien, Notre Dame ☎ 04–91–48–05–57). At **Diable Noir** (☒ 69 cours Julien, Belsunce ☎ 04–91–42–86–73), next door to Zaza on the Cours Julien, you'll find glamorous, slightly retro evening gowns in extravagant tulles and taffeta. Diable Noir's "downtown" shop anchors the edgy shopping district along **Rue de la Tour,** across from the Centre Bourse off Place du Général de Gaulle; dubbed "Rue de la Mode," it parades the earthy creativity of Marseille's fusion-fashion culture.

> ## QUEL PASTIS!
>
> Specializing in pastis, anisette, and absinthe, the smart litte shop of La Maison du Pastis (☒ 108 quai du Port, Vieux Port, ☎ 04–91–90–86–77) just opened up in 2005. To really savor these unique delights, just head next door to L'Heure Verte, a new "absinthe café."

THE CENTRAL COAST

With the floods of vacationers pouring onto the beaches from St-Tropez to Menton every summer, it's surprising that the coast between Marseille and Hyères is often dismissed. Although there are a few industrial pockets around La Ciotat and Toulon, there are just as many sections of magnificent coastline—white cliffs peppered with ragged, wind-twisted pines.

CLOSE UP

The S Is (Hardly Ever) Silent

(Or, how to brag to your friends about staying in a beautiful mas outside Cassis without mispronouncing a thing.)

The rule of thumb in Provence is to pronounce everything, even to the point of pronouncing letters that aren't there. *Pain*, in the north pronounced through the nose without a final consonant, becomes "peng" in the south. *Vin* becomes "veng," *enfin* "on feng," etc.

But there are words in constant dispute, especially among a people toilet-trained on the Academie Française, that holy arbiter of the French language. One of the words caught in the crossfire: *mas*. This old Provençal word for farmhouse is a "mahss" in the south, but Parisians hold out for a more refined Frenchification: "ma."

Cassis, on the other hand, is a booby trap. For one thing, there are two drinks named Cassis, one a black-currant liqueur made in Burgundy to be blended in white wine *kirs*, the other the famous wine from the coastal country east of Marseille. The liqueur is always called "cass-*eess*," and Northerners (who consume the most kirs) insist on pronouncing the wine "Cass-*eess*" but the village "Cass*ee*." But ask the locals, and they'll snort in disdain. "C'est 'Cass-*EESS*,' " they'll explain, as if all the words in the French language followed the pattern.

There you have it: In Paris, it's cass-ee and mah; in Provence, it's cass-eess and mahss.

Just inland, in the dry white hills, lies the peaceful market town of **Aubagne**; climb to the top of its outlying hills, and you can see the ocean sparkling below. **Cassis** is the jewel of this region, a harbor protected by the formidable Cap Canaille, 1,300 feet high. Between Cassis and Marseille stretch the extraordinary **Calanques,** a series of rocky fjords that probe deep into the coastline. Following the coastal highway, you come to La Ciotat, a gargantuan (but oddly picturesque) naval shipyard, and reach the popular beach resort of **Bandol**—incidentally the source of one of Provence's most famous wines. A popular rainy-day excursion from Bandol leads to the hilltop medieval village of Le Castellet; you may want to stop at some of the wineries along the way. **Toulon** is an enormous naval base and a tough big city with an interesting Old Town for the intrepid; just east of the city is where you catch the ferry to Porquerolles, the best of the wild and beautiful **Iles d'Hyères.**

Aubagne

 15 km (9 mi) east of Marseille, 10 km (6 mi) north of Cassis.

This easygoing, plane-tree-shaded market town (pronounced Oh-*bahn*-yuh) is proud of its native son, the dramatist, filmmaker, and chronicler of all things Provençal, Marcel Pagnol, best known to Anglophones as author of *Jean de Florette* and *Manon des Sources* (*Manon of the Springs*). Here you can spend the morning exploring the animated market or digging through used Pagnol books and collectibles in the Old

Town. Make sure you visit Aubagne on a market day (Tuesday, Saturday, or Sunday), when the sleepy center is transformed into a tableau of Provençal life. The Tuesday market is the biggest.

You can study miniature dioramas of scenes from Pagnol stories at **Le Petit Monde de Marcel Pagnol** (The Small World of Marcel Pagnol). The characters are all santons, and there are superb portraits of a humpback Gerard Départdieu and Yves Montand, resplendent in mustache, fedora, and velvet vest, just as they were featured in *Jean de Florette*. ⊠ *Esplanade de Gaulle* ⊠ *Free* ☉ *Daily 9–noon and 2–6.*

Aubagne claims the title of santon capital of Provence. The craft, originally from Marseille, was focused here at the turn of the 20th century, when artisans moved inland to make the most of local clay. The more than a dozen studios in town are set up for you to observe the production process. Daniel Scaturro is one of the best. He specializes in portraits, mostly of Pagnol's film characters—but you can have one made of yourself for €650. His main display studio, simply called **Daniel Scaturro** (⊠ 20a av. de Verdun ☎ 04–42–84–33–29), is on the edge of town in an industrial quarter. Scaturro's sons demonstrate the family craft on a smaller scale in a shop in the central **Old Town** (⊠ Bd. Jean-Jaurès/Rue Martinot).

The history of the craft of santon-making and other uses to which the local clay was put—faïence and hand-painted tiles—can be studied at the **Ateliers Thérèse Neveu,** named for Aubagne's first master *santonière* (santon maker). Also on display are excellent temporary exhibitions about pottery. ⊠ *Chemin Entrecasteaux, at the top of the Old Town hill* ☎ *04–42–03–43–10* ⊠ *Free* ☉ *Tues.–Sun. 10–noon and 2–6.*

Even if you haven't read Pagnol's works or seen his films, you can enjoy the **Circuit Pagnol,** a hike in the raw-hewn, arid *garrigues* (scrublands) behind Marseille and Aubagne. Here Pagnol spent his idyllic summers, described in his *Souvenirs d'un Enfance* (*Memories of a Childhood*), crunching through the rosemary, thyme, and scrub oak at the foot of his beloved Garlaban. When he grew up to be a famous playwright and filmmaker, he shot some of his best work in these hills, casting his wife, Jacqueline, as the first Manon of the Springs. After Pagnol's death, Claude Berri came back to the Garlaban to find a location for his remake of *Manon des Sources,* but found it so altered by brush fires and power cables that he chose to shoot farther east instead, around Cuges-les-Pine and Riboux. (The lovely village and Manon's well were filmed in Mirabeau, in the Luberon.) Although the trail may no longer shelter the pine-shaded olive orchards of its past, it still gives you the chance to walk through primeval Provençal countryside and rewards you with spectacular views of Marseille and the sea. To access the marked trail by yourself, drive to La Treille northeast of Aubagne and follow the signs. For an accompanied tour with literary commentary, contact the **Office du Tourisme** (☎ 04–42–03–49–98).

Aubagne on a **market** day is a feast, in more ways than one. For sale are fresh local asparagus, plant-ripened tomatoes and melons, and mesclun scooped by the gnarled fingers of blue-aproned ladies in from the farm.

CLOSE UP

Little Saints with Feet of Clay

THEY BECKON FROM SHOP WINDOWS in every hill town, these miniatures called *santons*, from the dialect *santouns* for "little saints." But whatever commercial role they may play today, their roots run deep in Provence.

The Christmas crèche has been a part of Provençal tradition since the Middle Ages, when people reenacted the tableau of the birth of Christ, wise men, shepherds, and all. When the Revolution cracked down on these pastoral plays, a crafty Marseillais decided to substitute clay actors. The tiny terra-cotta figures caught on and soon upstaged their human counterparts for good.

A Marseille tradition that eventually migrated to Aubagne in the hills above (the clay was better), the delicate doll-like figurines spread throughout Provence, and are displayed every Christmas in church crèches that resemble a rustic backcountry hill village as much as they do Bethlehem. Against a miniature background of model stone houses, dried-moss olive groves, and glass creeks, quaint, familiar characters go about their daily tasks—the lumberjack hauling matchstick kindling, the fisherman toting a basket of waxy fish, the red-cheeked town drunk leering drolly at the pretty lavender-cutter whose basket hangs heavy with real dried sprigs. The original cast from Bethlehem gets second billing to a charming crowd of

Gypsies, goatherds, and provincial passersby. And wait—isn't that Gérard Depardieu? And Raimu? And Yves Montand? Even beloved film actors have worked their way into the scene.

It's a highly competitive craft, and while artisans vie for the souvenir trade, some have raised it to an art form: Daniel Scaturro, of Aubagne, was named a Meilleur Ouvrier de France in 1997, one of the highest national honors granted to craftsmen.

Molded, dried, then scraped with sharp tools down to the finest detail—wrinkled foreheads and fingernails—the santons are baked at 1,000°C (1,832°F). Once cool, they are painted with a watchmaker's precision: eyelashes, nostrils, and gnarled knuckles. The larger ones have articulated limbs to allow for dressing; their hand-sewn costumes, Barbie-scaled, are lavished with as much fine detail as the painted features.

Many artisans maintain highly public studios, so you can shop direct. Little ones (about an inch high), without articulated limbs, run about €4; big ones (8 to 10 inches), dressed and painted by the best artists, cost around €40. Or you can splurge and commission a portrait of yourself for the mantel—€650 at Scaturro's.

But the preferred format is the crèche tableau, and it's easy to get hooked on building a collection of Provençal rustics to be lovingly unwrapped and displayed every Christmas season.

The Tuesday market is the biggest, with clothing, purses, tools, and pots and pans spilling onto the esplanade, but the Saturday and Sunday markets make more of regional products; those labeled Pays d'Aubagne must be organically raised. You won't find the social scene you'll see in Aix, but this is a more authentic farmers' market.

Another claim to fame for Aubagne: it's the headquarters for the French Foreign Legion. The legion was created in 1831, and accepts recruits from all nations, no questions asked. The discipline and camaraderie instilled among its motley team of adventurers, criminals, and mercenaries have helped the legion forge a reputation for exceptional valor—a reputation romanticized by songs and films in which sweaty deeds of heroism are performed under the desert sun. The **Musée de la Légion Étrangère** (Museum of the Foreign Legion) does its best to polish the image by way of medals, uniforms, weapons, and photographs. ⊠ *Caserne Viénot (to get there, take a left off D2 onto D44A just before Aubagne)* ☎ *04–42–18–82–41* 🎟 *Free* ☉ *June–Sept., Tues.–Thurs. and weekends 10–noon and 3–7, Fri. 10–noon; Oct.–May, Wed. and weekends 10–noon and 2–6.*

Where to Eat & Stay

$–$$ ✕ **La Farandole.** Cosseted here by rustic Provençal lemon-print cloths, lace curtains, and the region's typical bow-legged chairs, you can enjoy good home cooking with the local regulars who claim the same table every day. They are drawn to the flower-filled terrace with a small fountain, friendly waitresses, and home-baked cakes, all of which enhance the small-town feel. The inexpensive daily menu may contain crisp green salad with foie gras in a raspberry vinaigrette or baked goat cheese; wine is included. ⊠ *6 rue Martino (off Cours Maréchal, on a narrow street leading into the Old Town)* ☎ *04–42–03–26–36* ▭ *MC, V* ☉ *No dinner Sun. and Mon.*

★ **$** ✕ **Le Triskel.** This miniature shoebox of an Old Town restaurant has a living santon for a chef—mustache, toque, and broad gestures worthy of Pagnol. While gesticulating and bantering with the the loyal locals who crowd in elbow to elbow, he hauls heavy daubes from the wood-fire oven and ladles pot-au-feu over duck-leg confit. There are kidneys grilled with thyme, homemade gnocchi, eggplant gratinée, and, almost incidentally, pizzas. ⊠ *12 rue Jean-Jacques Rousseau* ☎ *04–42–03–59–86* ▭ *No credit cards* ☉ *Closed Wed.*

$$$ ▦ **Hostellerie de la Source.** Too bad it's in a suburban location 4 km (2½ mi) outside Aubagne. This 17th-century country house stands in vast boxwood gardens surrounding tennis courts and an indoor-outdoor pool. Inside there's a slick hotel feel well suited to banquets and conferences. Rooms are bright and tidy, entirely rebuilt in the late 1980s. ⊠ *St-Pierre-des-Aubagne, 13400* ☎ *04–42–04–09–19* 🖷 *04–42–04–58–72* ⊕ *www.hostellerie-lasource.com* 🛏 *24 rooms, 1 suite* ⚷ *Restaurant, minibars, pool, parking, some pets allowed* ▭ *MC, V* ⦿ *MAP.*

Cassis

㊹ *22 km (14 mi) southeast of Marseille, 10 km (6 mi) north of Aubagne.*

Fodor'sChoice
★

Surrounded by vineyards, flanked by monumental cliffs, guarded by the ruins of a medieval castle, and nestled around a picture-perfect fishing port, Cassis is the prettiest coastal town in Provence. Best known for its delicate white wines and wild Calanques, it is a quiet fishing village out of season and inundated with sun-worshippers in the summer. The pastel houses at rakish angles framing the port and harbor attracted early-20th-century artists including Dufy and Matisse. Even the mild rash of parking-garage architecture in the outer neighborhoods can't spoil the effect of unadulterated charm. Stylish without being too recherché, Cassis provides shelter to numerous pleasure-boaters, who restock their galleys at its market, replenish their Saint James nautical duds in its boutiques, and relax with a bottle of local wine and a platter of urchins in one of its numerous waterfront cafés. The imposing **Château de Cassis** has loomed over the harbor since the invasions of the Saracens in the 7th century, evolving over time into a walled enclosure crowned with stout watchtowers. It's private property today and best viewed from a sunny port-side terrace.

Touring the **Calanques,** whose fjord-like finger bays probe the rocky coastline, is a must. Either take a sightseeing cruise in a glass-bottom boat that dips into each Calanque in turn (tickets, sold at the eastern end of the port, are €10–€18 depending on how many Calanques you see) or hike across the cliff tops, clambering down the steep sides to these barely accessible retreats. Or do both, going in by boat and hiking back; make arrangements at the port (*see* the Close-Up box, "Touring the Calanques"). Of the Calanques closest to Cassis, **Port Miou** is the least attractive. It is also the only one fully accessible by car. It was a *pierre de Cassis* (Cassis stone) quarry until 1982 when the Calanques became protected sites, and now has an active leisure and fishing port. **Calanque Port Pin** is prettier, with wind-twisted pines growing at angles from white-rock cliffs. But with its tiny beach and jagged cliffs looming overhead, covered with gnarled pine and scrub and its rock spur known to climbers as the "finger of God," it's **Calanque En Vau** that's a small piece of paradise.

> ## CLOS ENCOUNTERS
>
> If you're a wine lover, pick up the brochure "Through the Vineyards" from the tourist office. There are 12 domaines open for tasting and buying, but the most spectacularly sited is the Clos Sainte Magdeleine (✉ Chemin du Revestel ☎ 04-42-01-70-28), set on the slopes of towering Cap Canaille.

Where to Eat & Stay

$$$ ✕ **Chez Nino.** This is the best of the many restaurants lining Cassis's harbor, with top-notch Provençal food and wine and a spectacular terrace view. The owners, Claudie and Bruno, are extremely hospitable as long as you stick to the menu—don't ask for sauce on the side—and you are as passionate about fish and seafood as they are. The sardines in *escabeche* are textbook perfect, as are the grilled fish and the bouillabaisse. ✉ *Quai Barthélémy* ☎ *04–42–01–74–32* ☰ *AE, DC, MC, V* ☾ *Closed Mon. and mid-Dec.–mid-Feb. No dinner Sun. off-peak season.*

★ **$$$** ✕ ▢ **Jardin d'Emile.** Just off the waterfront, tucked under massive cliffs and parasol pines, this stylish but homey rose-colored inn stands in a tropical garden and has views of the cape from the restaurant and some rooms. View or not, the rooms are intimate and welcoming, with rubbed-chalk walls, scrubbed pine, weathered stone, and soft lighting to enhance the romantic surroundings. The restaurant, encircled by a garden ter-

CLOSE UP

Touring the Calanques

To go on a boat ride to Les Calanques, get to the port around 10 AM or 2 PM and look for a boat that's loading passengers. Two of the best choices are the *Moby Dick III* and the *Ville de Cassis*–they have glass-bottom views and full commentary (in French only). But a slew of alternative boats won't leave you stranded. Round-trips should include at least three calanques and average €11. In July and August there is a "Spectacle Son et Lumiere" boat trip that leaves nightly at 10:30 PM (€10). For specific daytime departure times, contact La Visite des Calanques (☎ 04–42–01–90–83.).

You can also visit the Calanques from Marseille's Vieux Port on a four-hour minicruise with the Groupement des Armateurs Cotiers Marseillais ((G.A.C.M) ⊠ *1 quai des Belges* ☎ *04–91–55–50–09* ⊕ *answeb.net/ gacm*). Tours leave at 2 every Wednesday, Saturday, and Sunday (except in stormy mistrals).

To really get up close and personal, remember that the Calanques offer some of the best diving in France.

Weather permitting, there are spectacular cave daily dives to view brightly colored coral and abundant fish. Maestro diver Henri Cosquer (famous for discovering one of the oldest caves in the area) runs Cassis Services Plongée (☎ 04–42–01–89–16 ⊕ www.cassis-services-plongee.fr ☉ Closed mid-Nov.–mid-Mar.).

To hike the Calanques, gauge your skills: the GR98 (marked with red-and-white bands) is the most scenic route, but requires ambitious scrambling to get down the sheer walls of En Vau. The alternative is to follow the green markers and approach En Vau from behind. The faded markers could use revision nonetheless. If you're ambitious, you can hike the length of the GR98 between Marseille and Cassis, following the coastline, a distance of roughly 30 km (18 mi). Arrange in advance for a boat pickup or drop-off at En Vau. For guided nature walks, diving, kayaking, or sailing along the Calanques, contact Massilia Sport Adventure (☎ *06–12–39–59–59* ⊕ *www.massilia-aventure.com*).

---

race and, by night, illuminated cliffs, offers regional specialties with a cosmopolitan twist, such as fresh tuna with zucchini, almonds, and Spanish peppers or sardines with eggplant and cumin. ⊠ *Av. Admiral Ganteaume, Plage du Bestouan, 13260* ☎ *04–42–01–80–55* ⊟ *04–42–01–80–70* ⊕ *www.lejardindemile.fr* ⊅ *7 rooms* ⚘ *Restaurant, minibars, cable TV, parking, some pets allowed (fee)* ⊟ *AE, DC, MC, V* ☉ *Closed mid-Nov.–mid-Dec. and Jan.* ⧆ *BP*.

$$$–$$$$ ⊞ **Les Roches Blanches.** Perched above the sea facing Cap Canaille, this cliff-side villa takes in superb views of Cassis's port. There's a beautifully landscaped terrace shaded by massive pines and an infinity pool that seems to spill into the sea. Rooms, in traditional Provençal style, are airy and light-filled; the bland '60s-style annex just behind the main building compensates for its looks with full-length balconies. The aura is far from snooty or deluxe; it's friendly, low-key, and pleasantly mainstream and the panoramic restaurant is a good sunset-watching spot.

✉ *Rte. des Calanques, 13260* ☎ *04–42–01–09–30* 🖷 *04–42–01–94–23*
⊕ *www.roches-blanches-cassis.com* ⇨ *19 rooms, 5 suites* ⚭ *Restaurant, cable TV, pool, parking, some pets allowed (fee); no a/c* ▭ *AE, MC, V* †◎† *MAP.*

Bandol

④⑤ *25 km (15½ mi) southeast of Cassis, 15 km (9 mi) west of Toulon.*

Although its name means wine to most of the world, Bandol is also a popular and highly developed seaside resort town. In the 1920s, the glamorous social life of the Riviera stretched this far west, and grand seaside mansions rivaled Cap d'Antibes and Juan-les-Pins for high society and literati. Today its old port is a massive gray parking lot and the Old Town that fronts the quays is lined with seafood snack shops, generic brassieres, and palm trees. Yet westward, toward the Baie de Renecros, are some of the belle époque houses that once made Bandol famous. In high season the harbor is filled with yachts, and the waterfront promenade is packed with summer tourist crowds. A port-side stroll up the palm-lined Allée Jean Moulin feels downright Côte d'Azur. If you're not a beach lover, pick up an itinerary from the tourist office and visit a few Bandol vineyards just outside of town.

Several sights around Bandol are worth pursuing. Three kilometers (2 mi) north on the D559 is the **Jardin Exotique et Zoo de Sanary Bandol** (Sanary Bandol's Exotic Garden and Zoo), where cacti and hundreds of exotic tropical plants grow to remarkable sizes. In a small zoo setting, animals such as flamingos, gibbons, and gazelles frolic in shady gardens. ⊹ *Exit Bandol from A8, take first right (direction Route de Beausset) and follow the signs to the Zoo, being careful not to miss the very first right after the autoroute exit* ☎ *04–94–29–40–38* 🔄 *€8.50* ⊙ *June–Aug., Mon.–Sat. 8–noon and 2–7, Sun. 2–7; Sept.–May, Mon.–Sat. 8–noon and 2–6, Sun. 2–6.*

Continuing north on the same D559 is the village of **Le Castellet,** perched high above the Bandol vineyards. Its narrow streets, 17th-century stone houses, and (alas!) touristy shops are designed for beach lovers on a rainy day. **Paul Ricard Boats** (☎ *06–11–05–91–52* 🔄 *€6*) make the 2-km (1.2-mi) sail from the Embarcadéro to the **Ile de Bendor** hourly. The Ile de Bendor was only a large rock until pastis magnate Paul Ricard bought it in the 1950s and turned it into a tourist center with fine beaches, crafts shops, and an *espace culturel* (cultural space) showing Paul Ricard's lifetime works. Although local restaurants offer a surprisingly wide selection, sunny days and scenic views make for a lovely picnic.

Just east of Bandol, still on the D559, past the smaller resort of Sanary, as you turn left onto the D63 you'll see signs pointing to the small stone chapel of **Notre-Dame de Pépiole.** It's hemmed in by pines and cypresses and is one of the oldest Christian buildings in France, dating from the 6th century and modeled on early churches in the Middle East. The simple interior has survived the years in remarkably good shape, although the colorful stained glass that fills the tiny windows is modern—composed mainly of broken bottles. ⊙ *Most afternoons 3–5.*

From Notre-Dame de Pépiole, retrace your route toward Sanary and head south on D616 around the **Cap Sicié** for a tremendous view across the Bay of Toulon. Or head north on D11 to Ollioules; just past the village, follow N8 (in the direction of Le Beausset) through a 5-km (3-mi) route that twists its scenic way beneath the awesome chalky rock faces of the **Gorge d'Ollioules.** Even more spectacular: take a left at Ollioules on D20 and follow the winding road along the crest of **Le Gros Cerveau.** You'll be rewarded first with inland mountain views, then an expansive panorama of the coastline.

OFF THE BEATEN PATH

LA CADIERE D'AZUR (6 km/4 mi north of Bandol) – This is one of Provence's secrets, a beautiful, sleepy medieval town perched on a limestone hill overlooking the majestic vineyards of Bandol. Van Gogh and French painter Favory passed through here, as did several writers and poets. Small, generations-old shops selling local pottery and produce line the main street today. An added attraction is the special trip–worthy Hostellerie Bérard.

Where to Eat & Stay

★ **$$$–$$$$** ✕⊡ **Hostellerie Bérard.** Master Chef René Bérard is as celebrated for his haute cuisine as he is for his elegant country inn. The rooms, decorated in suavely handsome Provençal style, are scattered throughout a cluster of beautifully restored old buildings, including an 11th-century monastery. In the airy and window-filled restaurant, delicious Mediterranean-inspired Provençal meals emphasizing local seafood and fresh produce grace the tables. Try the ravioli stuffed with goat cheese, sorrel, and Parmesan in a lemon chicken broth, then proceed to lightly grilled red mullet wrapped in seaweed and topped with peas and fresh rosemary. If you want to attempt similar gastronomic heights at home, Chef Bérard, cheerfully sympathetic to all cooking woes, has week-long culinary getaways. ⊠ *83740, La Cadiere d'Azur* ☎ *04–94–90–11–43* 🖷 *04–94–90–01–94* ⊕ *www.hotel-berard.com* ⮐ *48 rooms, 5 suites* ♨ *Restaurant, minibars, cable TV, pool, parking, some pets allowed (fee)* ⊟ *AE, DC, MC, V* ⚊⚊⚊ *MAP.*

Toulon

46 *67 km (41½ mi) east of Marseille, 29 km (18 mi) northwest of La Tour Fondue (departure point for the Iles d'Hyères).*

Toulon is a city of big contrasts: ugly with crowded postwar high-rises, yet surprisingly beautiful with its tree-lined littoral; a place with some frankly unappealing nightlife and yet by day, charming and colorful with its restaurant scene. Best known for the day in World War II when 75 French ships sunk themselves rather than fall into the hands of attacking Germans, Toulon has kept its place as France's leading naval port with a kind of dogged determination. Though you may see nothing but endless traffic and graffiti-covered block-style apartments crossing the city, the Vieille Ville (Old Town) and port area have well-kept cafés and a sunny waterfront where yachts and pleasure boats—some available for trips to the Iles D'Hyères or around the bay—add bright splashes of color. Back from the port lies the gritty red-light district Le Petit Chicago, currently undergoing restoration. Once in the heart of the Old Town, the maze of streets is packed with designer shops and quirkily appealing stretches of ruined medieval houses mixed with lurid neon.

Park your car under Place de la Liberté and take Boulevard de Strasbourg, turning right onto Rue Berthelot, which leads into the heart of the pedestrians-only streets of the **Vieille Ville.** Wander through **Place des Trois Dauphins,** with its mossy and fern-lined fountain, or stop in the café-filled **Place Puget**; Victor Hugo lived in No. 5 when he was researching *Les Misérables.* One block east, the **Cours Lafayette** becomes a wonderfully animated, authentic Provençal morning market (daily except Monday), and the **Hôtel de Ville** has evocative Baroque figures, carved by the Marseillais sculptor Pierre Puget.

Behind the port and the Vieille Ville lies the new town. At Place Victor Hugo, the **Opera de Toulon** (⊠ Pl. Victor Hugo ☎ 04–94–92–70–78 ⊘ box office: weekdays 10–12:30 and 2:30–5:30) hosts theater, opera, and dance productions. Farther west is the **Musée des Beaux Arts** showing paintings by Vernet and Fragonard as well as postwar abstract art and the cartoon-influenced Di Rosa brothers. ⊠ *113 bd. Maréchal Leclerc* ☎ *04–94–36–81–00* ⊠ *Free* ⊘ *Daily 1–6.*

Avenue de la République, an ugly arrangement of concrete apartment blocks, runs parallel to the waterfront. At the western edge of the gray is the **Musée National de la Marine** (Naval Museum), with large models of ships, figureheads, paintings, and other items related to Toulon's maritime history. Photographs of the World War II sinking bring the sickening story to life. ⊠ *Pl. Monsenergue* ☎ *04–94–02–02–01* ⊠ *€5* ⊘ *Apr.–Sept., daily 10–6:30; Oct.–Mar., Wed.–Mon. 10–noon and 2–6.*

Mount Faron rises above the town and can be reached by taking the circular Route du Faron in either direction or in six minutes by cable car from Boulevard Admiral Jean-Vence. ☎ *04–94–92–68–25* ⊠ *€6 round-trip* ⊘ *July–Aug., Tues.–Sun. 9:30–7:45, Mon. 2:15–7:45; Sept.–June, Tues.–Sun. 9:30–noon and 2:15–6. Closed on windy days.*

At Mt-Faron's summit are a zoo, a great view, and the **Musée du Débarquement** commemorating the 1944 liberation of Provence. ☎ *04–94–88–08–09* ⊠ *€4* ⊘ *July–Aug., daily 9:45–11:45 and 1:45–5:30; Sept.–June, daily 9:45–11:45 and 1:45–4:30.*

OFF THE BEATEN PATH

BRIGNOLES (45 km/28 mi north of Toulon) – Although known as the market center for the wines of the Var, the largest attraction is still the Abbaye de la Celle, a 12th-century Benedictine abbey that served as a convent until the 17th century. Shut down when young nuns of good family began to run wild, known less for their chastity than "the color of their petticoats and the name of their lover," the abbey was abandoned until Maria Fournier, owner of the Iles of Porquerolles, decided to open it as a hotel in 1945. In spite of its suddenly becoming more upscale with the likes of Charles de Gaulle vacationing here, the town continued to firmly resist change. In fact, the simple Romanesque chapel housing a 14th-century Christ figure largely acclaimed as an anonymous masterpiece still serves today as the parish church. It's here in this historic spot that celebrated chef Alain Ducasse has his culinary hideaway Hostellerie de l'Abbaye de La Celle (*see below*).

Where to Eat & Stay

★ **$$$** ✕ **Le Gros Ventre.** In a cozy and romantic space enhanced by soft lighting, tasteful decorations, and tables set at discreet distances from each other, you can enjoy some of the best Provençal cooking in Toulon. Specializing in seafood and beef, self-taught Chef Audibert brings to the table delights like fillet of beef served with grapes and foie gras, or fish, caught daily by the restaurant's personal fisherman, steamed with fresh Mediterranean garden-grown vegetables. An enormous wine list of more than five thousand bottles can be a little intimidating, but friendly servers help guide you through it. ✉ *297 Littoral F. Mistral le Mourillon* ☎ *04–94–42–15–42* ▤ *AE, MC, V* ☉ *Mid-Sept.–Apr., no lunch Tues.–Thurs.; May–mid-Sept., closed Tues. and no lunch.*

$$$$ ✕▥ **Hostellerie de l'Abbaye de La Celle.** Superchef Alain Ducasse put this
Fodor'sChoice country inn—buried in the unspoiled backcountry north of Toulon and
★ just south of Brignoles—back on the map a decade ago. Up the road from the town's royal abbey, this beautifully restored 18th-century *bastide* (country house)—a dream in ocher-yellow walls, Arles green shutters, and white stone trim—was once part of the convent where future queens of Provence were raised. Guest rooms mix Louis XVI and regional accents; half are split-level with their own gardens, some with views of vineyards, others of a park thick with chestnut and mulberry tress. Beds are enormous—none more so than those of the Charles de Gaulle suite (where the great man once stayed). Wherever you bed down, the scent of fresh thyme and lemon basil waft through the windows from the gardens. Each room is named after an aromatic herb grown in the garden or a famous person who has spent time here. All are spacious, light-filled, simple, and authentic, with a sharp eye for Baroque detail and wonderfully comfortable furnishings. Today, the formidable kitchen is headed up by Chef Benoît Witz, whose seemingly magical creations find a superb balance between taste and texture: velouté of crawfish gently covering a bruschetta topped with tomatoes and garden herbs, or duck breast with polenta and cherries. ✉ *Pl. du Général de Gaulle, 83170 La Celle* ☎ *04–98–05–14–14* ▤ *04–98–05–14–15* ⊕ *www.abbaye-celle.com* ↪ *10 rooms* ⚭ *Restaurant, minibars, cable TV, pool, library, shop, parking* ▤ *AE, DC, MC, V* ▥◊ *BP.*

$$ ▥ **Les Bastidieres.** Through the Louis XVIII wrought-iron gate, a tree-lined entrance leads to a vine-covered 18th-century manor house. The rooms, charmingly named after various Provençal flowers, are decorated in the soft luminous shades of the Midi, carefully accented with oak furniture and rose-colored tiles. Breakfast (fee), brought to your room on an elegant tray with hand-painted china, is lovely taken on your private terrace. The well-cultivated garden offers quiet shaded benches under hundred-year-old fig trees and a large, refreshing pool. ✉ *2371 av. de la Résistance Cap Brun, 83100* ☎ *04–94–36–14–73* ▤ *04–94–42–49–75* ↪ *5 rooms* ⚭ *Pool, parking, some pets allowed (fee)* ▤ *No credit cards* ▥◊ *BP.*

$$ ⬚ **Résidence du Cap Brun.** Tucked away down a side road leading to the sea, this charming hotel has smallish rooms in pastel shades. With acres of strollable garden around it, not to mention the sweet scent of a newly planted orange grove, weddings are a serious summertime business here, and Saturday mornings can be noisy. This picturesque spot is a delightful surprise after the hustle and bustle of Toulon; be sure to ask for a room with a terrace and a view. ✉ *192 chemin de l'Aviateur Gayraud, Cap Brun, 83100* ☎ *04–94–41–29–46* 🖶 *04–94–63–16–16* 🛏 *15 rooms* ♨ *Pool, parking, some pets allowed (fee)* ▤ *V* ☉ *Closed Nov.–Mar.* ❚◉❙ *BP.*

Iles d'Hyères

🚇 *32 km (20 mi) off the coast south of Hyères.*

Strung across the Bay of Hyères and spanning some 32 km (20 mi) is an archipelago of islands reminiscent of a set for a pirate movie. In fact, they have been featured in several, thanks not only to their wild and rocky coastline but also their real pirate history. In the 16th century the islands were seeded with convicts meant to work the land; they promptly ran amok, ambushing and sacking passing ships heading for Toulon.

Today the pirates are long gone, replaced by a thriving local population and tourists. The islands consist of three main bodies: Levant, Port-Cros, and Porquerolles. Eight percent of **Levant** is military property, and is kept strictly guarded with barbed-wire fences. The remaining area, Héliopolis, is a nudist colony, where you're welcome if you want to participate, as opposed to simply being curious. **Port-Cros** is a magnificent national park with no cars, no smoking, and no dogs. You can hike on pine-scented trails with astonishingly spectacular views, or follow the underwater path, snorkeling or diving with fish and aquatic ★ life representative of the Mediterranean. **Porquerolles** (pronounced pork-uh-*rohl*) is the largest and most popular escape from the modern world. The village of Porquerolles was originally used as a retirement colony for Napoleonic officers (the Fort du Petit-Langoustier and the Fort Ste-Agathe, although no longer active, still loom imposingly over the marina), which explains its remarkable resemblance to a military outpost. At the turn of the 20th century a Belgian engineer named François-Joseph Fournier made a killing in the Panama Canal, then bought Porquerolles at auction as a gift for his new bride. It was only in 1970 that France nationalized the island, leaving Fournier's widow with a quarter of her original inheritance; her granddaughter now helps run the luxurious Mas du Langoustier. Off-season it's a castaway idyll of pine forests, sandy beaches, and plunging cliffs over a rocky coastline. Inland, its preserved pine forests and orchards of olives and figs are crisscrossed with dirt roads to be explored on foot or, if you prefer, on bikes rented from one of the numerous rental outfits in both port and village. In high season (April to October), day-trippers pour off the ferries, running for the beaches and soap boutiques, and T-shirt shops appear out of the woodwork to cater to vacationers' whims.

Ferries run from La Tour Fondu in Giens (every 30 minutes in summer and every 60 to 90 minutes in winter for €15 round-trip) for the 20-

minute trip to Porquerolles, and from Hyères at Hyères Plages to Port-Cros and Levant (€19–€24 round-trip). You can also get to all three islands from Port-de-Miramar or Le Lavandou (35–60-minute crossing, €21 round-trip).

Where to Eat & Stay

★ **$$$$** ✕⊡ **Mas du Langoustier.** Amid stunningly lush terrain at the western-most point of the Ile de Porquerolles, 3 km (2 mi) from the harbor, this luxurious hideout is a popular getaway for the yacht-and-helicopter set and a standard day trip from high-season St-Tropez. Madame Richard, the granddaughter of the lucky woman who was given this island as a wedding gift, picks you up at the port. Choose between big California-modern or old-style Provençal rooms. Chef Joël Guillet creates inspired southern French cuisine. Try the tuna tartare with oysters and wasabi vinaigrette, the open ravioli with sautéed artichokes and pesto, or the roasted lobster tail with green apple puree and vanilla. Wash it all down with a rare island rosé. ⊠ *Pointe du Langoustier, 83400 Isle de Por-querolles* ☎ *04–94–58–30–09* 🖷 *04–94–58–36–02* ⊕ *www.langoustier. com* ➟ *50 rooms* ♨ *Restaurant, tennis court, beach, billiards, Inter-net* ☰ *AE, DC, MC, V* ☻ *Closed Nov.–Apr.* ⟦◌⟧ *FAP.*

$$$–$$$$ ✕⊡ **Les Glycines.** In soft shades of yellow-ocher and sky-blue, this sleekly modernized little bastide (country house) has an idyllic enclosed court-yard, verdant with lemon trees, ivy, and an ancient *figuier* (fig tree). Back rooms look over a jungle of mimosa and eucalyptus. Public salons have Provençal chairs and fabrics. The restaurant, with seating on the terrace or in the garden, has port-fresh tuna and sardines. In the summer sea-son (April through September) children stay (and eat) for free. The inn is just back from the port in the village center. ⊠ *Pl. d'Armes, 83400 Ile de Porquerolles* ☎ *04–94–58–30–36* 🖷 *04–94–58–35–22* ⊕ *www. porquerolles.net* ➟ *11 rooms* ♨ *Restaurant, bar* ☰ *AE, MC, V* ⟦◌⟧ *FAP.*

$$$–$$$$ ✕⊡ **Le Manoir.** A mix of southern-coast bourgeois and Provençal touches adds a splash of color to the sunlit, airy rooms of this family-owned colo-nial-style hotel. Private patios look over a large secluded park bordered by eucalyptus, pink oleanders, and palm trees. Thoughtful service and absolute calm firmly encourage relaxation. After a day of hiking through forests, swimming in the pool, or simply sitting on the flower-filled ter-race, you can sample Chef Vincent Cordier's delicious, hearty Provençal fare, such as smoked duck salad garnished with grilled tomatoes, or rack of lamb with island herbs and ratatouille. Diners stop in from all over the island to immerse themselves in the intimate charm of the simply decorated restaurant, murmuring comfortably over a final warmed brandy. With a price that can include both your meals and your accom-modation, this is a gentle touch of civilization in the isolated wilderness. ⊠ *83400 Isle de Port-Cros* ☎ *04–94–05–90–52* 🖷 *04–94–05–90–89* ➟ *23 rooms* ♨ *Restaurant, bar; no a/c in some rooms, no room TVs* ☰ *MC, V* ☻ *Closed late Oct.–mid-Apr.* ⟦◌⟧ *FAP.*

The Outdoors

You can rent a mountain bike (*velo tout-terrain,* or VTT) for a day to pedal the paths and cliff-top trails of Porquerolles at **Cycle Porquerol** (⊠Rue de la Ferme ☎ 04–94–58–30–32) or **L'Indien** (⊠ Pl. d'Armes ☎ 04–94–58–30–39).

If you prefer to explore on foot, pick up a map at the tourist kiosk on the landing docks, or simply follow the arrows. The main road back from the village leads over the island's forested crest to the Cap d'Arme, with dramatic views of the lighthouse. To its right you can strike out toward the Gorges du Loup; the precarious trail breaks out in the open over a spectacular rocky cove with crashing surf. If you head right of town you'll pass through a series of botanical-study orchards, full of hybrid figs and olives, with a series of inlets and rocky coves for picnics and reflection. If you head left you'll follow the broad stretch of beaches, first the popular Courtade, then the isolated, pine-shadowed Notre-Dame. Roads and trails are marked for difficulty, but only a few are narrower than Jeep-width.

Locamarine 75 (✉ at the port ☎ 04–94–58–35–84) rents motorboats to anyone interested, whether or not you have a license. At the **Club de Plongée du Langoustier** (✉ 7 carré du Port ☎ 04–94–58–34–94) you can take a diving class, hire a guide, rent diving equipment, and refill scuba tanks.

AIX, MARSEILLE & THE CENTRAL COAST ESSENTIALS

To research prices, get advice from other travelers, and book travel arrangements, visit www.fodors.com.

Transportation

If traveling extensively by public transportation, be sure to load up on information (schedules, the best taxi-for-call companies, etc.) upon arriving at the ticket counter or help desk of the bigger hub stations in the area, such as Aix-en-Provence, Marseille.

BY AIR

Marseille has one of the largest airports in France, the Aéroport de Marseille Provence in Marignane, about 20 km (12 mi) northwest of the city center. Regular flights come in daily from Paris and London. In summer Delta Airlines flies direct from New York to Nice (about 190 km [118 mi] from Marseille and about 150 km [93 mi] from Toulon).

Airport shuttle buses to Marseille center leave every 20 minutes 5:30 AM–10:50 PM daily (€8). Shuttles to Aix leave hourly 8 AM–11:10 PM (€7.30).

🔢 Air Travel Information **Aéroport de Marseille Provence in Marignane** ☎ 04-42-14-14-14 ⊕ www.marseille.aeroport.fr.

BY BIKE & MOPED

Bikes can be rented from the train stations in Aix-en-Provence, Arles, Avignon, Marseille, Nîmes, and Orange at a cost of about €10 per day. Contact the Comité Départemental de Cyclotourisme for a list of scenic bike routes in Provence.

🔢 Bike Maps **Comité Départemental de Cyclotourisme** ✉ Les Passadoires, 84420 Piolenc ☎ 04-90-29-64-80.

BY BUS

A good network of private bus services (confusingly called *cars*) strikes out from Marseille's *gare routière* (bus station), adjacent to the Metro Gare St-Charles train station, and carries you to points not served by train. Tickets costs €1.60 and multiple ticket carnets are available. From Marseille, buses link many destinations, including Aix-en-Provence (€5, 1 hr, leaving every half hr), Nice (€25, 3 hrs, serviced by Phocéens Cars), Cassis (€4, 1½ hrs), Carpentras (€12, 2 hrs), Cavaillon (€12, 1 hr), and Avignon (€16, 2 hrs). As for Aix-en-Provence, it has a dense network of bus excursions from its station. To/from destinations include Marseille (€5, 1 hr, every half hr), Arles (€10, 1½ hrs, two to five daily), and Avignon (€12, 1½ hrs, two to four daily). C.A.P. (Compagnie Autocars de Provence) makes daily forays from 2 to 7 into Marseille, the Calanques of Cassis, Les Baux, the Luberon, and Arles, departing in front of the tourist office, at the foot of Cours Mirabeau. One Web site that provides in-depth info on bus travel is www.beyond. fr.

Aix-en-Provence has a municipal bus that services the entire town and outlying suburbs (such as Jas de Bouffon). A ticket costs €1.10 and you can get a carnet of 10 or a one-day pass. There is a navette shuttlebus that connects La Rotonde/Cours Mirabeau with the bus and train station, as well as one that heads out to the TGV station (departing from the bus station), which is some 8 km (13 mi) west of town, and the Marseille-Provence airport.

🚌 Bus Information **Aix-en-Bus** ✉ Pl. du Général du Gaulle ☎ 04-42-26-37-28 ⊕ www. aixenbus.com. **Aix-en-Provence's** *gare routière* (bus station) ✉ Av. de la Europe ☎ 04-42-91-26-80. **Marseille's** *gare routière* (bus station) ✉ 3 pl. Victor Hugo ☎ 04-91-08-16-40. **C.A.P.** (Compagnie Autocars de Provence) ☎ 04-42-97-52-10 ⊕ www. beyond.fr. **Phocéens Cars** ☎ 04-93-89-41-45. www.beyond.fr ⊕ www.beyond.fr.

BY CAR

The A6/A7 toll expressway (*péage*) channels all traffic from Paris toward the south. At Orange, A7 splits to the southeast and leads directly to Aix. From there A51 leads to Marseille. Also at Aix, you can take A52 south via Aubagne to Cassis and A50, the coastal autoroute tollway; running parallel but closer to the water is the slow (but occasionally scenic) highway D559. Either of these will give you access to the coastal towns (Bandol, Toulon), inland sights (Le Castellet, Ollioules), and the Giens Peninsula for ferries to the Iles d'Hyères.

Although you can see this region by train, a car allows you greater freedom to visit vineyards, to drive along the vertiginous edge of Cassis's Cap Canaille, and to explore the gorges, hilltop villages, and scenic countryside around Bandol and Toulon.

The Aix-Marseille-Toulon triangle is well served by a network of autoroutes with a confusing profusion of segmented number-names (A50, A51, A52, A55). Hang onto your map and follow the direction signs.

As with any major metropolis, it pays to think hard before driving into Marseille: if you want to visit only the port neighborhoods, it may be easier to make a day trip by train. However, you'll need to drive to visit the smaller ports and bays outside the center. To approach downtown

Marseille, try to aim for the A51 that dovetails down from Aix; it plops you conveniently near the Vieux Port, while A55 crawls through industrial dockside traffic.

The autoroute system collapses inconveniently just at Toulon, forcing you to drive right through downtown; allow time for traffic if you're aiming for a ferry to the Iles d'Hyères.

Beautiful backroads between Aix, Marseille, and Aubagne carry you through Cézanne and Pagnol country; the N96 between Aix and Aubagne is worth skipping the freeway for. The D559 follows the coast, more or less scenically, from Marseille through Cassis to Hyères.

You can drive straight to La Tour-Fondue to take a ferry trip to Porquerolles (pedestrians-only), one of the Iles d'Hyères; you must pay for parking, day and night. But remember, don't even think about leaving luggage in your car.

BY TRAIN

The high-speed TGV *Méditerranée* line ushered in a new era in *Trains à Grande Vitesse* (or "Trains at Great Speed") travel in France; the route (lengthened last year from the old terminus, Valence, in Haute Provence) means that you can travel from Paris's Gare de Lyon to Marseille in a mere three hours. Not only is the idea of Provence as a day trip now possible (though, of course, not advisable), you can even whisk yourself there directly upon arrival at Paris's Charles de Gaulle airport.

After the main line of the TGV divides at Avignon, the southeast-bound link takes in Aix-en-Provence, Marseille, Toulon, and the Côte d'Azur city of Nice. There is also frequent service by daily local trains to other towns in the region from these main TGV stops. With high-speed service now connecting Aix, Nîmes, Avignon, and Marseille, travelers without cars will find a Provence itinerary much easier to pull off. For full information on the TGV *Méditerranée,* log onto the TGV Web site; you can purchase tickets on this Web site or through RailEurope, and you should always buy your TGV tickets in advance.

It's also easy to take a night train from Paris and wake up in Marseille (⇨ Train Travel *in* Smart Travel Tips A to Z). From Marseille it's a brief jaunt up to Aix. The main rail line also continues from Marseille to Toulon.

Aix has train routes to Marseille (€6, 30 minutes, 12 to 20 trains daily), Nice (€28, 3½ hrs, eight trains daily), and Cannes (€26, 3½ hrs, eight trains daily), along with other destinations. Marseille has train routes to Aix-en-Provence (€6, 30 minutes, 12 to 20 trains daily), Avignon (€16, 1 hr, hourly), Nîmes (€22, 1½ hrs), Arles (€12, 1 hr), and Orange (€20, 1½ hr). Once in Marseille, you can link up with the coastal train route with links all the resort towns lining the coast eastward to Monaco and Menton. You can also catch trains to Cassis, Bandol, Aubagne, and Toulon. There are local stops in Bandol, too, and even in Hyères-Plages, where you can catch a boat to the Iles d'Hyères. One Web site that provides in-depth info on train travel is www.beyond.fr.

Marseille boasts a Metro system. Most of the two metro lines service the suburbs, but several stops in the center city can help you get around quickly, including the main stop at Gare St-Charles, Colbert, Vieux Port, and Notre-Dame. A ticket costs €1.60, with multiple carnet tickets available.

🚆 Train Information **Aix-en-Provence's** *Gare SNCF* (train station) ⊠ Av. Victor Hugo ☎ 04-91-08-16-40. **Marseille's** *Gare St-Charles* (train station) ☎ 04-91-08-16-40. **SNCF** ☎ 08-36-35-35-35 ⊕ www.ter-sncf.com/uk/paca. **TGV** ☎ 877/2TGVMED ⊕ www.tgv.com. **www.beyond.fr** ⊕ www.beyond.fr.

Contacts & Resources

CAR RENTALS

🚗 Aix-en-Provence **Avis** ⊠ 11 bd. Gambetta ☎ 04-42-21-64-16. **Budget** ⊠ 16 av. des Belges ☎ 04-42-38-37-36. **Hertz** ⊠ 43 av. Victor Hugo ☎ 04-42-27-91-32.
🚗 Marseille **Avis** ⊠ Central Train Station ☎ 04-91-64-71-00. **Hertz** ⊠ Central Train Station ☎ 04-91-90-14-03.

EMERGENCIES

For basic information, see this section in the Smart Travel Tips chapter. In most cases, contact the town Comissariat de Police, Préfecture, or Gendarmerie.

🚨 Emergencies **Police** ⊠ Pl. B. Niollon Aix-en-Provence ☎ 04-42-91-91-11. **Police** ⊠ Pl. de la Préfecture Marseille ☎ 04-91-39-00-00.

GUIDED TOURS

Two-hour Aix walking tours are organized by the tourist office; tours of the Old Town (in French) leave at 3 on Wednesday and Saturday (€8). A tour of Cézanne landmarks (with an optional finish at his Atelier) leaves from the tourist office at 9:30 Saturday morning (€8); it follows the bronze plaques in the city sidewalks. You can request the tour in English.

Marseille walking tours are organized by the tourist office; these cover various neighborhoods and take place three times a week. In July and August they leave the tourist office on Monday, Wednesday, and Friday at 2 PM. The tours cost €8 per person and you can request them in English.

If you're feeling flush, footsore, or overwhelmed by the city, splurge on a Marseille taxi tour with cassette commentary in English; each taxi holds three adults or two adults and two children under 10. The drivers are selected by the tourist office and the itineraries fixed. In one-and-a-half hours (€32) you'll be whisked up to the hard-to-reach Notre-Dame-de-la-Garde and Palais du Pharo; on the two-hour trip (€54) you'll also cruise the seaside cliff called the Corniche and duck into the picturesque fishing port Vallon des Auffes. Four hours (€96) shows you more ports, more monuments, and more neighborhoods. It's a good introduction to a huge city; reserve at the tourist office.

Even if you don't choose to hike the 12-km (7-mi) or 20-km (12-mi) loop through the garrigues above Aubagne, there's a bus tour of Marcel Pagnol landmarks that leaves from the tourist office. It takes place in July and August on Wednesday and Saturday at 4; the cost is €7. Request an English-speaking guide in advance.

📲 Guided Tour Information **Aix Tourist Office** ⊠ 2 pl. du Général de Gaulle 🖀 04-42-16-11-61 ⊕ www.aixenprovencetourism.com. **Aubagne Tourist Office** ⊠ Av. Antide Boyer 🖀 04-42-03-49-98 ⊕ www.aubagne.com. **Bandol Tourist Office** ⊠ Allée Vivien 🖀 04-94-29-41-35 ⊕ www.bandol.fr. **Cassis Tourist Office** ⊠ Quai des Moulins 🖀 04-42-01-71-17 ⊕ www.cassis.fr. **Marseille Tourist Office** ⊠ 4 La Canebière 🖀 04-91-13-89-00 ⊕ www.marseille-tourisme.com.

INTERNET & MAIL

In smaller towns, ask your hotel concierge if there are any Internet cafés nearby.

📲 Internet & Mail Information **Esc@lia** ⊠ 3 rue Coutelleine, Marseille 🖀 04-91-91-65-10. **Hub Lot Cybercafé** ⊠ 15 rue Paul Bert, Aix-en-Provence 🖀 04-42-21-37-31. **La Poste main post office** ⊠ Sq. Mattéi, Aix-en-Provence. **La Poste main post office** ⊠ 1 Pl. de l'Hôtel des Postes, Marseille.

VISITOR INFORMATION

The regional tourist office, the Comité Départemental du Tourisme du Var, has extensive documentation on lodging, restaurants, rentals, hikes, and attractions in Var. Written requests are preferred, with specific interests detailed. The same is true for the Comité Départemental du Tourisme des Bouches-du-Rhône.

📲 Local Tourism Information **Comité Regional du Tourisme de Provence-Alpes-Côte d'Azur** ⊠ 12 pl. Joliette, 13002 Marseille 🖀 04-91-56-47-00 🖷 04-91-56-47-01 ⊕ www.crt-paca.fr. **Comité Départemental du Tourisme du Var** ⊠ 1 bd. Maréchal Foch, 83300 Draguignan 🖀 04-94-50-55-50 🖷 04-94-50-55-51. **Comité Départemental du Tourisme des Bouches-du-Rhône** ⊠ 13 rue Roux de Brignole, 13006 Marseille 🖀 04-91-13-84-13 🖷 04-91-33-01-82 ⊕ www.visitprovence.com.

Aix ⊠ 2 pl. du Général de Gaulle, B.P. 160, Cedex 1 13605 🖀 04-42-16-11-61 🖷 04-42-16-11-62 ⊕ www.aixenprovencetourism.com. **Aubagne** ⊠ Av. Antide Boyer, 13400 🖀 04-42-03-49-98 🖷 04-42-03-83-62 ⊕ www.aubagne.com. **Bandol** ⊠ Pavillon du Tourisme, on the waterfront, 83150 🖀 04-94-29-41-35 🖷 04-94-32-50-39 ⊕ www.bandol.fr. **Cassis** ⊠ Pl. Baragnon, 13260 🖀 04-42-01-71-17 🖷 04-42-01-28-31 ⊕ www.cassis.fr. **Ile de Porquerolles** ⊠ Carré du Port, 83400 🖀 04-94-58-33-76 🖷 04-94-58-36-39 ⊕ www.porquerolles.com. **Marseille** ⊠ 4 La Canebière, 13001 🖀 04-91-13-89-00 🖷 03-91-13-89-20 ⊕ www.marseille-tourisme.com. **Toulon** ⊠ Sq. William et Catherine Booth, 83000 🖀 04-94-18-53-00 🖷 04-94-18-53-09 ⊕ www.toulontourisme.com.

The Western Côte d'Azur

ST-TROPEZ TO THE ESTÉREL, THE HAUT VAR & THE GORGES DU VERDON

Moustiers-Ste-Marie, Alpes de Haute-Provence

WORD OF MOUTH

"Young happy couple looking for a town to honeymoon in with the best beaches and nightlife with daytime shopping and restaurants? St-Tropez, hands down!"

—Todor

"Be careful of traveling by boat on windy days . . . unless you can cope with the boat in vertical positions. I now understand why we pay as we go onto the boat!"

—AnneMg

www.fodors.com/forums

WELCOME TO THE WESTERN CÔTE D'AZUR

La Napoule Castle

TOP 5
Reasons to Go

① **St-Tropez à go-go:** Brave the world's most outlandish fishing port in high summer and soak up the scene. Just don't forget the fake-tan lotion.

② **Les Gorges du Verdon:** Peer down into its vertiginous green depths and you'll understand why this is one of the most dramatic natural sites in France.

③ **Picture-perfect Moustiers-Ste-Marie:** Best known for its faïence, this town is also worth visiting for the sight of houses clinging to the cliffs—often with entrances on different levels.

④ **A gothic château extravaganza:** In Mandelieu-La Napoule, discover the most bizarrely extravagant house of the coast—the Château de la Napoule, festooned with tapestries, peacocks, and art students.

⑤ **Beguiling Cotignac:** With almost no boutiques but a lively weekly market, this is a place to experience Provençal life in the slow lane.

Haut Var & into Haut Provence. Far from the frenzy of the coast, the backcountry hills called the *arrière-pays* remain deeply Provençal. Here, in the region known as the Haut Var, explore **Aups,** a center of the black truffle trade. Around **Moustiers-Ste-Marie** are faïence workshops where you can discover the art of this brightly painted tableware. Not far away is **La-Palud-sur-Verdon,** gateway to the spectacular **Gorges du Verdon.**

0   4 mi

0   4 km

St-Tropez at sunset

Estérel

Getting Oriented

If it's most often associated with celeb-heavy coastal resorts, particularly St-Tropez, the Western Côte d'Azur is also a nature-lover's paradise. North of the coast, the Massif des Maures and the Massif de l'Estérel remain remarkably wild and unspoiled, while further up, the Gorges du Verdon draws hard-core hikers willing to forego the local rosé to keep their wits about them as they tackle France's answer to the Grand Canyon.

The Estérel Resorts.
To the east of the twin waterfront resorts of **Fréjus** and **St-Raphaël**, the **Massif de l'Estérel** is pure hiking heaven. Made up of red volcanic rocks and softened by patches of lavender and gorse, its shore is lined with calanque coves and the Corniche de l'Estérel, one of the coast's most spectacular drives.

4

Castellane
D952
N85
La-Palud-sur-Verdon
Trigance
D71
D21
CAMP MILITAIRE DE CANJUERS
D563
Mons
N85
N85
ALPES MARITIMES
Grasse
D19
Seillans
D2562
D3
Bargemon
Fayence
Antibes
D955
D562
Cannes
VAR
A8
N98
Golfe Juan
Draguignan
Mandelieu-La Napoule
D25
N7
La Napoule
Théoule-sur-Mer
D10
N7
A8
St-Raphael
MASSIF DE L'ESTÉREL
Corniche de l'Estérel
Sea
D7
Fréjus
N98
Golfe de Fréjus
Mediterranean
MASSIF DES MAURES
D558
D25
Cap des Sardinaux
Ste-Maxime
N98
Cap de St-Tropez
Port-Grimaud
St-Tropez
Grimaud
D93
D559
Gassin
Ramatuelle

St-Tropez is really quite low-key in the off-season, when the giant yachts moored in the port serve as the only reminder of its glamour. In high-season, dodge the paparazzi by going to the nearby hilltop villages of **Gassin** and **Ramatuelle,** where some streets are so steep even goats have difficulty with them.

Updated by
Rosa Jackson

THE SERIES OF PICTURE-BOOK GULFS that scoop into this part of the French Mediterranean coastline is less famous and less exotic than its other half to the east. Above the coastline of the Var *département* (county), the horizon is dominated from all directions by the rugged red-rock heights of the Massif de l'Estérel and the green-black bulk of the Massif des Maures. Blue-green waters lap at the foot of thriving resort towns—St-Tropez, of course, but also Fréjus, St-Raphaël, Mandelieu, and La Napoule. Like France's perennially popular rock star Jonny Hallyday, St-Tropez never fades—it just gets another face-lift and keeps going, brasher than ever. The difficulty reaching this portion of the coast—the train only goes as far as Ste-Maxime—naturally separates the wheat (who swan in by helicopter) from the chaff (who crawl along in midsummer traffic jams, sweaty and miserable). You need to be a little masochistic to visit St-Tropez in August, but the town does have a fair number of budget hotels and sheds most of its pretension in the off-season, becoming simply a small fishing port with very big yachts. Neighboring resorts can't help but feel lower-key, providing stretches of sandy beach and guaranteed balmy temperatures to sun-starved northerners. In high summer, masses flood the beaches, feast on the fish, fill up the marinas, luxuriate in the spa treatments, and crowd the hotels and cafés. Bored, sunburned, or regarding each other in mutual *snobbisme,* they then take to the hills—the glorious vineyard-lined, village-crowned hills that back the coast as the continent climbs gently toward the Alps.

They are a virtual subculture, these *villages perchés* (perched villages) and historic towns, which live in touristic symbiosis with the coast. To the east lie the famous, gentrified tourist towns of Grasse, St-Paul, and Vence; to the north rises Fayence, a definitive 18th-century Provençal town that now lives as much off the renown of its souvenirs as its spectacular views.

These towns make great day trips from the coast, though they're often dominated in high season by busloads of excursion-takers out of Cannes or St-Raphaël. But if you have a car and the time to explore, you can plunge even deeper into the backcountry, past the coastal plateau into the Haut Var. Here the harsh and beautiful countryside—raw rock, pine, and scrub oak—is lightly peppered with little hill villages that are almost boutique-free. You can hear the *pétanque* (lawn bowling) balls thunk, the fountains trickle, and the bells tolling within their wrought-iron campaniles. If you like what you see and press on, you'll be rewarded with one of France's most spectacular natural wonders: the Gorges du Verdon, a Grand Canyon–style chasm roaring with milky-green water and edged by one of Europe's most hair-raising drives. Backpacks, hiking boots, and picnics (or quick café meals) are de rigueur around the Gorges, until you reach lovely Moustiers-Ste-Marie, an atmospheric center for *faïence* where you can treat yourself to a leisurely meal and take in breathtaking views.

Exploring the Western Côte d'Azur

You can visit any spot between St-Tropez and Cannes in an easy day trip, and the hilltop villages and towns on the coastal plateau are just

PLEASURES & PASTIMES

SUN, SAND & SEX. Following upon their worldwide fame as the earth's most glamorous beaches, the real things often come as a shock to first-time visitors. Much of the Côte d'Azur is lined with rock and pebble, and the beaches are narrow swaths backed by city streets or roaring highways. Only St-Tropez, on this stretch of the Mediterranean, has the curving bands of sandy waterfront you've come to expect from all those '50s photographs—and even there, the 3-mi stretch of Pampelonne Beach supports no fewer than 36 restaurants and private businesses, complete with thatched parasols and beach bars. And there's a range of acceptable behaviors on these beaches: some are topless, some feature nudity, some are favored by gays. You won't need a diagram to tell you which is which.

THE GRAPE ESCAPE. Along the coast and into the hills above, vines stripe the fields in patchwork rows, their fruit destined for the unpretentious, all-encompassing wines known as Côtes de Provence. Even St-Tropez has vineyards, and the wild backcountry west of Draguignan bristles with roadside signs luring you into their *caves* (wine cellars) for *dégustations* (tastings). Most wines produced here are rosés, with a few strong red table wines thrown in. Of the region's myriad versions of Côtes de Provence, one in particular gets top billing: the rosé of Domaine des Marchandises, produced outside Roquebrune-sur-Argens, is subtler than the usual coral-pink blends. Even modest rosés, such as the well-known Domaine de Jale produced near St-Tropez, are far more dry and refreshing than most of the rosés known to Americans.

HIKING HEAVEN. Despite the mix of flash and glamour along the coast, the Massif des Maures and the Massif de l'Estérel are crisscrossed with excellent trails leading into rugged backcountry, often with views toward the sea. Several *sentiers du littoral* (waterfront trails) follow the water's edge along the base of the Estérel; another goes around the St-Tropez Peninsula. From the heights of the Estérel, the *grande randonée* (national hiking trail) GR51 heads into the highlands east of Draguignan, and the GR49 strikes off for Fayence, giving wide berth to the crackling crossfire on the *camp militaire* (military camp) of Conjuers. North of the camp, the GR49 continues all the way to the Gorges du Verdon, where it intersects with France's most spectacular grande randonée, the GR4. Its star trail is the precarious Sentier Martel, which goes through the heart of the Gorges du Verdon.

LE SHOPPING. On quaint Old Town streets and up cobbled alleys in hilltop villages, you'll be bathed in the odor of soaps, sachets, and potpourri wafting out of souvenir shops. Provence in general, but the Riviera in particular, makes the most of the flowers—especially lavender—proliferating in its sun-favored climate. The most prestigious makers of Provençal fabrics have prominent spots in the main tourist centers. And Moustiers (by the Gorges du Verdon) still makes and sells its acclaimed faïence (glazed earthenware), as it has done since the 17th century.

Just What Is the Côte d'Azur?

ASK FOUR FRENCHMEN to define the boundaries of the Côte d'Azur, and you'll get four (emphatic) answers. Purists will insist on limiting this stellar title to the subtropical stretch of seaside cliffs between Nice and the Italian border; this the Victorian English first called the French Riviera, and all other resorts are impostors. Another may stretch his definition to embrace palm-studded Cannes and the border of the department of Alpes-Maritimes (literally, Seaside Alps). But where does that leave sultry St-Tropez? *Alors,* expand southwest to include the democratic sandy beaches of St-Raphaël, Fréjus, and Ste-Maxime and reach the elite fishing port whose name everyone loves to drop. But why stop there? After all, the sandy coast east of Toulon has

unsung enclaves and the lovely *calanques* (rocky coves) feather the coastline all the way to Marseille. Keep on going this way and you'll wind up in Barcelona. Suffice it to say that the resonant appellation "Côte d'Azur" is coveted by all the coastal resorts on France's southeastern underbelly. Here, we have split the difference, lumping much of the Var coast into Chapter 4 (The Western Côte d'Azur) and the whole of the Alpes-Maritimes coast (Cannes to Menton) into Chapter 5 (Nice & the Eastern Côte d'Azur). The seductively warm coastline west of St-Tropez we have loosely defined as the Central Coast (⇨ Chapter 3). West of Marseille spans the Rhône delta, and the Languedoc coast lies beyond (⇨ Chapter 1).

as accessible. Thanks to the efficient raceway A8, you can whisk at high speeds to the exit nearest your destination up or down the coast; thus even if you like leisurely exploration, you can zoom back to your home base at day's end. Above the autoroute things slow down considerably, and you'll find the winding roads and overlooks between villages an experience in themselves. Venturing farther north, either by the Route Napoléon or D995, is a bigger commitment and, to be fully enjoyed, should include at least one overnight stop.

Situated between the watercolor port of St-Tropez and the rugged red rock of the Estérel, this captivating stretch of the Riviera has drawn sun lovers and socialites since the days of the Grand Tour. Here the coastal highway hugs the spectacular waterfront, snaking past sophisticated getaway towns as well as a staggering concentration of restaurants, high-rise resorts, gas stations, tourist traps, and beach discos. Proceed just a few miles inland to find picturesque Provençal villages perched above the fray; penetrate farther still and you'll be rewarded with mountain scenery and serene little towns.

Numbers in the text correspond to numbers in the margin and on the Western Côte d'Azur and The Haut Var and into Haute Provence maps.

About the Restaurants & Hotels

Restaurants in the coastal resorts are expensive and often a risky investment, as they cater mostly to crowds *en passage.* St-Tropez prices can

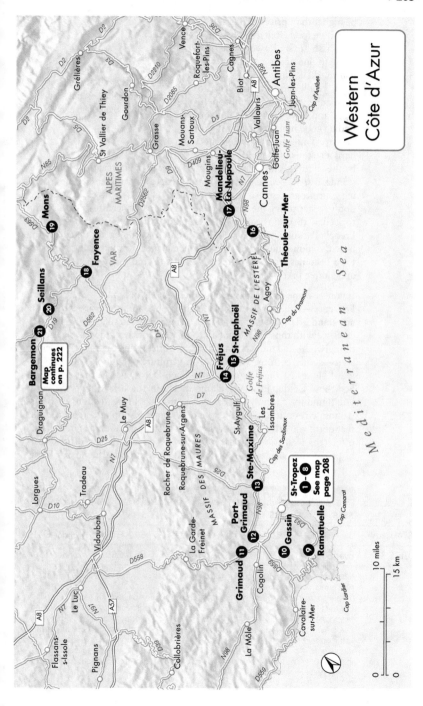

Western
Côte d'Azur

Vence
Roquefort-
les-Pins
Cagnes
Biot
Antibes
Juan-les-Pins
Cap d'Antibes
Grolières
Gourdon
St Vallier de Thiey
Grasse
Mouans-
Sartoux
Vallauris
Golfe-Juan
Golfe Juan
ALPES
MARITIMES
Mougins
**17 Mandelieu-
la-Napoule**
Cannes
Mons 19
Fayence 18
VAR
16 Théoule-sur-Mer
MASSIF DE L'ESTÉREL
Agay
Cap du Dramont
Seillans 20
Bargemon 21

Map
continues
on p. 222

Draguignan
Le Muy
St-Raphaël 15
14 Fréjus
Golfe
de Fréjus
Mediterranean Sea
Rocher de Roquebrune
Roquebrune-sur-Argens
St-Aygulf
Les
Issambres
Cap des Sardinaux
MASSIF DES MAURES
Lorgues
Tradeau
Vidauban
La Garde-
Freinet
Ste-Maxime 13
**Port-
Grimaud 12**

St-Tropez 1–8
See map
page 208

Cogolin
Grimaud 11
Gassin 10
9 Ramatuelle
Cap Camarat
Flassans-
s-Issole
Le Luc
Pignans
Collobrières
La Môle
Cavalaire-
sur-Mer
Cap Lardier

0   10 miles
0   15 km

be higher than prices in Paris. It's a fine town for a (staggeringly expensive) fish feast, however, as it is home to one of the country's finest fish markets, just off the port. Inland, you'll tap into a culture of cozy auberges (inns) in hilltop villages and have a better chance of finding good home cooking for your money. You can also judge how hard a restaurant is trying to please

As a general rule, the curlier the printing on a menu the more pretensions a country auberge has; some of the best post only handwritten chalkboard menus.

by the children's menu, which in the better restaurants goes beyond the standard *steak-haché* (bunless hamburger) and frites, sometimes offering gourmet grub such as roast lamb with scalloped potatoes. In St-Tropez don't forget to try the *tropézienne*, a rich, pastry cream-filled brioche topped with grainy sugar that provides yet another example of the French Paradox when you see the flawless bodies sprawled on the beach. Around the Gorges du Verdon, a magnet for hikers and climbers, food becomes less of a priority—expect to find mostly pizzas, salads, and simple hikers' fare.

If you've come to this area from other regions in France—even western Provence—you'll notice a sudden sharp hike in hotel prices, costly by any standard but skyrocketing to dizzying heights in summer. St-Tropez's rates vie with those in Monaco. You'll also notice a difference in decor: though more and more coastal hotels are attempting to import Provençal style—sunny cottons, wrought-iron furniture—the look still leans toward "le style Côte d'Azur," a slick, neo-Deco pastiche that smacks of Scott-and-Zelda, Jazz-Age glamour. Up in the hills above the coast you'll find the charm you'd expect, both in sophisticated inns with gastronomic restaurants and in friendly mom-and-pop auberges; the farther north you drive, the lower the prices. For information on *gîtes* (houses offered as a vacation rental) and *chambres d'hôtes* (bed-and-breakfasts in private homes), check out the Lodging section in the Smart Travel Tips chapter.

WHAT IT COSTS In euros				
$$$$	$$$	$$	$	¢
RESTAURANTS over €30	€23–€29	€18–€22	€12–€17	under €11
HOTELS over €191	€121–€190	€81–€120	€51–€80	under €50

Restaurant prices are per person for a main course at dinner; note that if a restaurant offers only prix-fixe meals, it has been given the price category that reflects the full set-price. Hotel prices are for a standard double room in high season, including tax (19.6%) and service charge. Assume all hotel rooms have air-conditioning, telephones, TV, and private bath, unless otherwise noted. Hotels operate on the European Plan (EP, with no meal provided) unless we note that they use the Breakfast Plan (BP). Some hotels also offer other meal plan options: *demi-pension* (two meals a day) or *pension complète* (three meals a day); Inquire when booking if these meal plans (which always entail higher rates and are occasionally mandatory in peak season) are available.

Timing

Unless you enjoy jacked-up prices, traffic jams, and sardine-style beach crowds, avoid the coast like the plague in July and August, especially the last week of July and first three weeks of August. Many of the better restaurants simply shut down to avoid the coconut-oil crowd. Another negative about July and August: the Estérel is closed to hikers during this flash-fire season. From Easter through October the café life is in full swing; May is mild and often lovely, but the best restaurants and hotels may be crowded with spillover from the Cannes film festival.

Once you move into the highlands, you won't feel the crush of summer crowds, though the Gorges du Verdon is an attraction for rock climbers and hikers. Be prepared for late-spring and even late-summer snows as altitudes average 3,280 feet and the region is far from the Mediterranean that warms the coast. To see the Gorges du Verdon in full fall color, aim for early October, though the odds of rainy days increase as autumn advances.

ST-TROPEZ & THE MASSIF DES MAURES

Shielded from the mistral by the broad, forested mass of the Massif des Maures, this small expanse of pampered coastline is crowned by the sparkling lights of St-Tropez, itself doubly protected by the hills of the Paillas. A pretty pastel port in winter, in season it becomes glamorous "*St-Trop.*" For day trips you can escape to the simple life in the hill towns of Ramatuelle and Gassin or delve deep into the Maures in La Garde-Freinet. Ordinary mortals, especially vacationing families on a budget, usually aim for Ste-Maxime, across the bay, where the hyperdevelopment typical of the Riviera begins.

St-Tropez

35 km (22 mi) southwest of Fréjus, 66 km (41 mi) northeast of Toulon.

At first glance, it really doesn't look all that lovely. There's a pretty port, but it's crammed with overscale yachts, double parking, and cafés charging €3.80 for a coffee. There's a picturesque old town in sugared-almond hues, but there are many prettier in the hills nearby. There are sandy beaches, rare enough on the Riviera, and old-fashioned squares with plane trees and pétanque players, but these are a dime a dozen throughout Provence. So what made St-Tropez an internationally known locale? Two words: Brigitte Bardot. When this *pulpeuse* (voluptuous) teenager showed up in St-Tropez on the arm of Roger Vadim in 1956 to film *And God Created Woman,* the heads of the world snapped around. Neither the gentle descriptions of writer Guy de Maupassant (1850–93) nor the watercolor tones of Impressionist Paul Signac (1863–1935), nor the stream of painters who followed (including Matisse and Bonnard) could focus the world's attention on this seaside hamlet as did this one voluptuous woman in head-scarf, Ray-Bans, and capris.

With the film world following in Bardot's footsteps, St-Tropez became the hot spot it to some extent remains. Celebrity-spotting remains the

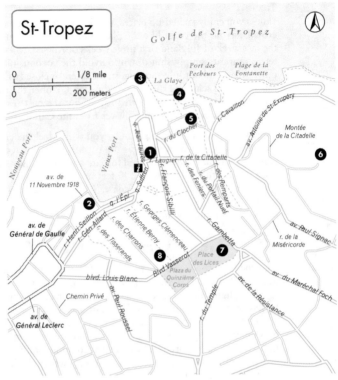

foremost local sport, and largely free (unless Sir Elton John can only be found deep inside an expensive restaurant). In 2004, *Vanity Fair* ran a big article, "Saint Tropez Babylon," detailing the over-the-top petrodollar parties, mega-yachts, and Beyoncé–d paparazzi. But don't be turned off: the next year, Stewart, Tabori & Chang released an elegant coffee-table book, *Houses of St-Tropez,* packed with photos of supremely tasteful and pretty residences, many occupied by fashion designers, artists, and writers (once a hangout for Colette, Anaïs Nin, and Françoise Sagan, the town yet earns its old moniker, the "Montparnasse of the Mediterranean").

> St-Trop ("Saint Too Much," as the French call it) has become such a byword for wealth, sun, and glitter that you might be surprised to find that it's so small and insulated. The lack of train service, casinos, chain hotels keeps it that way.

Fame, in a sense, came too fast for St-Trop. Unlike the chic resorts farther east, it didn't have the decades-old reputation of the sort that would attract visitors all year around. For a good reason: its location on the south side of the gulf puts it at the mercy of the terrible mistral winter

CLOSE UP

The Dogs of St-Tropez

IN AD 68 THE ROMAN EMPEROR NERO had a centurion from Pisa decapitated for his Christian tendencies; to drive the lesson home for witnesses, he had the headless body placed in a boat with a cock and a dog, then set adrift at sea. When the boat washed ashore on St-Tropez's beach, the starving animals still kept their loyal vigil, refusing to touch the holy flesh. Perhaps it's because of this heroic act of self-discipline that dogs are held in such high esteem in modern St-Tropez. They are clearly the companion (and accessory) of choice, as prevalent as mobile phones in the Vieux Port cafés.

If you want to get the right port-front table at Le Gorille, consider borrowing a dog and accessorizing appropriately. Want to look like your yacht's being swabbed down for that lunch-run to Monte Carlo? A Lhasa Apso to match your ascot. Showing those canvases you daubed in the Alps last winter? Hot pants, hip-length hair, Timberlands, and an Afghan hound. Your bistro courting the Festival crowd out of Cannes? Green Lacoste sweater, red toupée, red German shepherd. Just drawn up a marriage contract to cover the London flat and Daddy's domaine in Burgundy? Matching buckskin jackets, separate phones, and a twinned team of golden retrievers.

4

---

winds. So, in summer the crowds descend and the prices rise into the stratosphere. In July and August, you must be carefree about the sordid matter of cash. After all, at the most Dionysian nightclubs in town, Corona beers can go for $30 and when the mojo really gets going, billionaires think nothing of "champagne-spraying" the partying crowds—think World Series celebrations but with $1,000 bottles of Roederer Cristal instead of Gatorade.

Anything associated with the distant past seems almost absurd in St-Tropez. Still, the place has a history that predates the invention of the string bikini, and people have been finding reasons to come here since AD 68, when a Roman soldier from Pisa named Torpes was beheaded for professing his Christian faith in front of Emperor Nero, transforming this spot into a place of pilgrimage. Today, a different sort of celeb is worshipped: Ever since St-Tropez became "hot" again, there have been Elton, Barbra, Oprah, Jack, and Bruce sightings. Most stars, however, stay hidden in villas, so the people you'll see are mere mortals, lots of them, many intent on displaying the best (or at least the most) of their youth, beauty, and wealth. In the heat of summer days tourist crowds are thick, gawking at the golden boys swabbing yacht decks and perusing the art daubed and painted along the port. By night, when the crowds thin and the air softens, stylish couples make for the cafés, where they subtly preen among others who share their creed.

Still, if you take an early-morning stroll (before the 11 AM breakfast rush at Le Gorille Café) along the harbor or down the narrow medieval streets—the rest of the town will still be sleeping off the Night Before—you'll see just how charming St-Tropez is. There's a weekend's worth of boutiques to explore and many cute cafés where you can sit under colored awnings and watch the spectacle that is St-Trop saunter by. Along medieval streets lined with walled gardens and little squares set with dripping fountains you'll be able to discover historic delights like the Chapelle de la Misericorde, topped by its wrought-iron campanile, and Rue Allard, lined with picturesque houses such as the Maison du Maure. In the evening, everyone moves from the cafés on the quais to the cafés on the squares, particularly Place des Lices, where a seat at the Le Café allows you to watch the boules players under the glow of hundreds of electric bulbs (paging Deborah Kerr and David Niven in *Bonjour Tristesse*). In the end, it's not too hard to experience what the artists first found to love and what remain the village's real charms: its soft light, its warm pastels, and the scent of the sea wafting in from the waterfront.

Keep in mind that while St-Tropez can be heaven, getting there can be hell. Out on a limb, scorned by any train route, you can only get to St-Trop by car, bus, or boat (from nearby ports like St-Raphaël). Driving a car is truly hellish, considering the crowds, the narrow roads, and the Parking du Port parking lot (opposite the bus station on Avenue du Général de Gaulle, with shuttle bus into town mid-March to October) or the new Parc des Lices (beneath the Place des Lices) in the center of town and their fees: a staggering €5 an hour in peak season. For bus and boat information, see the Essentials section at the end of this chapter.

Start your St-Trop tour at the *nouveau bassin* (new harbor) for private pleasure boats. There's a large parking lot and the bus station here. With the sea on your left, walk around to the Vieux Port (old harbor), enjoying the life of the quays and the views around the bay as you go. The **Vieux Port**, bordered by the Quai de l'Epi, the Quai Bouchard, the Quai Peri, the Quai Suffren, and the Quai Jean-Jaurès, is the nerve center of this famous yachting spot, a place for strolling and looking over the shoulders of artists daubing their versions of the

> ## YOU CAN NEVER BE TOO RICH, TOO THIN, OR TOO TAN
>
> Along the quais you'll see plenty of B. B. wannabes—not all of them female—who strut along the port side in skintight leopard skin, toting leopard-collared terriers, mixing in with a "BCBG" (bon-chic-bon-genre," or "well-bred yuppie") crowd in nautical togs and Gap shirts. Only golden retrievers or Dalmations, please!

view on easels set up along the water's edge, surreptitiously looking out for any off-duty celebs. For it is here, from folding director's chairs at the famous port-side cafés Le Gorille (named for its late exceptionally hirsute manager), Café de Paris, and Sénéquier's—which line Quai Suffren and Quai Jean-Jaurès—that the cast of St-Tropez's living theater ❶ plays out its colorful roles. **Sénéquier** provides a fine front-row seat from which to observe the multicolored scene. Arrive at breakfast time and you'll find those who danced all night mingling with those who just got up; arrive at sunset, and the glory of the view may distract you from people-watching.

Just inland from the southwest corner of the Vieux Port stands the extraordinary **Musée de l'Annonciade**, where the legacy of the artists who loved St-Tropez has been lovingly preserved. The Annunciation Museum, housed in a 16th-century chapel, traces the evolution of painting from neo-Impressionism to the Fauves—many of whom painted in and around St-Tropez. It was Paul Signac who "discovered" the seductive light of this fishing village, using fine sprays of confetti dots to explore the vacillations of light and color on its pale-ocher houses and rippling water. A rich man, he had been sailing the coast in his yacht (*L'Olympia,* named after Manet's infamous nude), when bad weather forced him to make port. Smitten, he built La Hune (on Rue Paul-Signac) and his house parties transplanted the best from Paris's St-Germain-des-Pres. Before long, fellow artists Bonnard, Matisse, Marquet, Dufy, Derain, Vlaminck, and Van Dongen fell in love with the town. Several of Signac's port views may be on display at any given time, buttressed by those of lesser-known followers. A handful of bold Fauvist paintings includes the moody *L'Estaque* by Braque, painted north of Marseille. Although there are only 50 or so paintings and a handful of sculptures, few small museums achieve such a balance of theme and concentration of quality. ⊠ *Quai de l'Épi/Pl. Georges Grammont* ☎*04–94–17–84–10* 🎫*€5.50* ☉*June–mid-Oct., Wed.–Mon. 10–1 and 3–10; mid-Oct.–May, Wed.–Mon. 10–noon and 2–6.*

Head back past the Quai Suffern—a statue of the Bailli de Suffren, an 18th-century customs official, stands guard—past the famous cafés. If the wind isn't too strong, walk out along the Mole Jean Réveille, the harbor wall, for a good view of Ste-Maxime across the sparkling bay, the hills of Estérel and, on a clear day, the distant Alps. Retrace your steps along the mole and quayside to the 15th-century **Tour du Portalet** and head past it to the old fisherman's quarter, the **Quartier de la Ponche,** just east of the Quai Jean-Jaurès. Here you'll find the **Port des Pécheurs** (Fishermen's Port), on whose beach Bardot did a star-turn in *And God Created Woman.* Twisting, narrow streets, designed to break the impact of the mistral, open to tiny squares with fountains. The main drag here, Rue de la Ponche, leads into Place l'Hôtel de Ville, landmarked by a **mairie** (town hall) marked out in typical Tropezienne hues of pink and green. Head up Rue Guichard to the Baroque **Église de St-Tropez,** to pay your respects to the bust and barque of St. Torpes, every day but May 17th, when they are carried aloft in the Bravade parade honoring the town's namesake saint.

> Complete with gulf-side harbor, this Old Town maze of backstreets and old ramparts is daubed in shades of gold, pink, ocher, and sky-blue. Trellised jasmine and wrought-iron birdcages hang from the shuttered windows, and many of the tiny streets dead-end at the sea.

Continue northward over a few blocks to Rue de la Citadelle, which leads away from the port up to the looming Citadel, set on a hill to the west of town. St-Tropez's 16th-century **Citadelle** stands in a lovely hilltop park. Inside its *donjon* (defense tower), a **Musée Naval** (Naval Museum) displays ship models, cannons, and pictures of St-Tropez from its days as a naval port. The views from its terrace take in the whole of the gulf and the hills behind and are the sort to tempt any artist to set up an easel in a jiffy. ⊠ *Rue de la Citadelle* ☎ *04–94–97–06–53* 🖼 *€4* ☉ *Nov.–Mar., Wed.–Mon. 10–12:30 and 1:30–5:30; Apr.–Oct., Wed.–Mon. 10–12:30 and 1–6:30.*

Leaving the Citadelle, make your way down to the Montée Ringrave, past the 17th-century **Chapelle de la Miséricorde** (on Rue de la Miséricorde) to the social center of the old town, the **Place des Lices** (also called the Place Carnot). Here, you'll hear pétanque balls—a southern version of boules—clicking in the sand square. Lying two blocks inland, straight back from the Quai Suffren, the square's symmetrical forest of plane trees (what's left of them) provides shade to rows of cafés and restaurants, skateboarders, children, and the grandfatherly pétanque players. Enjoy a time-out in the town "living room," Le Café (not be be confused with the nearby Café des Arts). The square becomes a moveable feast (for both eyes and palate) on market days—Tuesday and Saturday. Heading back to the Vieux Port area, take in the boutiques lining rues Sibilli, Clemenceau, or Gambetta to help accessorize your evening look—you never know when that photographer from *Elle* will snapping away at the trendies.

❽ A block west of Rue Clemenceau is the **Musée du Papillon**. In a pretty house at the end of a typically Tropezien lane, the Museum of Butterflies is a delight for children (and their parents). Sweetly aflutter, the 4,500 specimens can be toured with the collector, Dany Lartigue. ⊠ *9 rue Etienne Berny* ☎ *04–94–97–63–45* 🖼 *€3* ☉ *Mon.–Sat., 2:30–6.*

To experience St-Tropez's natural beauty up close, consider walking the *sentier du littoral* (coastal path) around the peninsula. It's 12 km (7 mi) long and takes an average of four hours. Leave from the Tour du Portalet or the Tour Vieille at the edge of the Quartier de la Ponche. Follow the footpath from Plage des Graniers along the beaches and cliffs overlooking the water, often with views toward the Estérel or out to the open sea. From Cavalaire, at the southwest root of the peninsula, you can catch a bus back to St-Tropez.

Where to Eat & Stay

★ $$$$ ✕ **Leï Mouscardins.** Breton-born chef Laurent Tarridec has left the pétanque courts of the Bistrot des Lices for this spectacular seaside spot with 180-degree sea views, just on the edge of the Quartier de la Ponche. Luckily, he's brought with him a sophisticated tradition of upscale Provençal cuisine: watch for a frothy mullet soup, an earthy *galette* (patty) of chestnuts and morel mushrooms, the house *bourride* (a fish, vegetable, and white-wine stew served over bread), and tender, long-simmered veal. ⊠ *Tour du Portalet* ☎ *04–94–97–29–00* ⊕ *www.leimouscardins.com* 🖃 *AE, DC, MC, V* ☉ *Closed Tues. and Wed. Oct.–May. No lunch June 25–Sept. 10.*

★ $$$–$$$$ ✕ **La Table du Marché.** With an afternoon tearoom and a summer sushi bar, this charming bistro, masterminded by celebrity chef Christophe Leroy, offers up a mouthwatering spread of regional specialties. For something

CLOSE UP

C'est Délicieux!

TYPICAL THROUGHOUT PROVENCE is a garlicky mayonnaise called *aïoli*, a staple condiment that's especially at home with a cold serving of fresh coastal fish. In the words of poet Frédéric Mistral, "Aïoli sums up the heat, the strength, and the joy of the Provençal sun. Its other virtue: It drives off flies." Made of mortar-crushed raw garlic whipped with egg yolk and olive oil, aïoli can bring tears to your eyes—and later, to those of your fellow travelers. Never mind: Heap it on hard-boiled eggs, poached salt cod, or raw vegetables. And watch for it as a Friday lunch special, when all of the above appear in a Provençal smorgasbord.

Even more pungent than aïoli is the powerful paste called *anchoïade*. Whether spread on tiny toasts or used as a dip for raw vegetables, its base of Mediterranean anchovies provides an emphatic kick of concentrated salt and fish.

Another staple of the region is *pistou*, the Provençal pesto (which originates from the Italian port of Genoa, nearby). Made of a savory blend of basil, garlic, Parmesan, and olive oil, minus the pine nuts found in Italian pesto, it shows up in *soupe au pistou* (reminiscent of minestrone), *pâtes* (pasta) *au pistou*, and as a sauce for almost anything.

4

---

light, sink into one of the overstuffed armchairs in the upstairs dining room, cozy with warm colors, chic Provençal accents, and antique bookshelves, and try the tomato pistou tart or dive into an €18 or €26 set menu. ⊠ *38 rue Georges Clemenceau* ☎ *04–94–97–85–20* ⊕ *www. christophe-leroy.com* ☱ *AE, MC, V.*

$$–$$$$ ✕ **L'Escale.** Ivana Trump put this new hot spot on the map when she hosted a white tie and tiara party here a few seasons ago. Lined with photos of the real saint of St-Tropez—Brigitte Bardot—this port-side retreat has a menu that focuses on the tastiest denizens of the deep. The real draw, however, is the plate-engulfing pizzas, which are also available to go. ⊠ *9 quai Jean-Jaurès* ☎ *04–94–97–00–63* ☱ *AE, DC, MC, V.*

$$–$$$$ ✕ **Villa Romana.** Bruce Willis, George Clooney, and other lotharios have made this the latest paparazzi favorite. The decor is "Tropezienne"—an over-the-top orgy of neo-Pompeian murals, leopard-skin banquettes, overstuffed chairs, and red-velvet tassels. Food is not quite the raison d'être—along with the usual tuna and veal numbers, you can get everything from caviar to pizzas to a chocolate blow-out called "Halicarnasse"—since the partying crowd seems to be more interested in the luscious bonbons sitting at the next table rather than those on the dessert trolley. Open in the evenings only, this spot closes on certain weeknights in low season, when it also opens for Sunday lunch. ⊠ *Chemin des Conquettes* ☎ *04–94–97–15–50* ⊕ *www.villa-romana.com* ☱ *AE, DC, MC, V.*

$$ ✕ **Le Girelier.** Fish, fish, and more fish—sea bass, salmon, sole, sardines, monkfish, lobster, crayfish, fish eggs spread on a thin slice of toast—they're painted on the walls, sizzling on the grill, trying to jump for their lives as the boats come into the Old Port. Will they make it? Not if chef

Yves Rouet gets to them first, with a little thyme or perhaps a whisper of olive oil and garlic. Like his father before him, chef Yves makes an effort to prepare Mediterranean-only fish for his buffed and bronzed clientele, who enjoy the casual sea-shanty space and the highly visible Vieux Port terrace tables. Grilling is the order of the day, with most fish sold by weight, but this is also a stronghold for bouillabaisse. There's beef on the menu, too, in case you're a fish-phobe. ⊠ *Quai Jean-Jaurès* ☎ *04–94–97–03–87* ⊟ *AE, DC, MC, V* ⊘ *Closed Mon. and Nov.–Feb. No lunch July–Aug.*

$–$$ ✕ **Le Bistrot.** Following the departure of chef Laurent Tarridec, who made this address one of the most celebrated in town, the former Bistrot des Lices has lowered its culinary aspirations. Now a "brasserie-lounge bar," it serves comfort cooking at lunch (think roast chicken with truffled potato mash) and salads or open-faced sandwiches all day long—try the classic Caesar or the Chinese salad with greens, cashews, and chicken. Prices are more than acceptable considering the chic setting—leather chairs, a cushion-strewn banquette and appropriately large mirrors, all lit by a giant chandelier—and amazing people-watching potential of the terrace on the leafy Place des Lices. ⊠ *3 pl. Carnot* ☎ *04–94–97–11–33* ⊕ *www.bistrot-saint-tropez.com* ⊟ *AE, MC, V.*

$–$$ ✕ **Le Café.** A landmark once famed as a hangout for literati and artists, this big, convivial brasserie on the Place des Lices draws regulars for the generous plats du jour of classic bistro fare: *gigot* (leg of lamb) with *gratin dauphinois* (scalloped potatoes), monkfish *bourride* (in a sauce made with garlic mayonnaise), local seafood, and homemade desserts. Tables set up on the square provide courtside seats for the pétanque games. ⊠ *Pl. des Lices* ☎ *04–94–97–44–69* ⊕ *www.lecafe.fr* ⊟ *AE, MC, V.*

$ ✕ **La Boîte à Sardines.** A restaurant named after tinned sardines might not initially sound promising, but this sleek little bistro tucked away in the old town in fact serves the classics of Marseillais cooking, with an ode to this much-maligned fish. Start with the obligatory pastis before tasting one of the sardine specialties—in puff pastry, raw in a tartare, or even in sushi or maki—and follow with a Marseillais classic such as simple grilled fish or *pied et paquets,* which uses unlikely parts of the lamb. ⊠ *3 rue St-Jean* ☎ *04–94–56–48–08* ⊕ *www.laboiteasardines.com* ⊟ *MC, V* ⊘ *Closed Sun.–Tues. and Jan.–Feb. 15.*

★ $$$$ ✕▣ **Le Byblos.** Arranged like a toy Mediterranean village, fronted with stunning red, rust, and yellow facades, and complete with ocher-stucco cottagelike suites grouped around courtyards landscaped with palms, olive trees, and lavender, this longtime fave of the glitterati began life as a "Phoenician-style" resort (the name means Bible) dreamed up by a Lebanese millionaire. Decades later, it has seen the jet set *jet, jet, jet.* This is where "les beautiful people" come to shine in all their gold-and-white Frenchness, lavishly bored, lounging in *the* place to dine, Spoon, über-chef Alain Ducasse's concept restaurant, the height of hip multiethnic Mediterranean cuisine with influences from Italy, Spain, North Africa, and of course, the Riviera. Meals here tend to be light, healthy, and full of flavor; soups, salads, steamed dishes, grilled fish, and spicy *tajines.* If you can't drag yourself away from the pool, try the Mediterranean nosh at the poolside restaurant Bayader. You won't need to leave the hotel to hit one of the hottest nightspots in town either—les Caves du Roy is on-site (expect the old St-Tropez narrow-eyed once-over before they let you in). Recovering from it all is easy with an amazing massage *aux huiles essentielles* and mud soak the next morning. ⊠ *Av. Paul-Signac, 83990* ☎ *04-94-56-68-00* 🖷 *04-94-56-68-01* ⊕ *www. byblos.com* 🛏 *51 rooms, 44 suites* ⟁ *2 restaurants, in-room safes, pool, gym, spa, nightclub, in-room data ports, cable TV, some pets allowed* ⊟ *AE, DC, MC, V* ⊘ *Closed mid-Oct.–Easter.*

$$$$ ✕⊞ **Hôtel Résidence de la Pinède.** Perhaps the most opulent of St-Tropez's luxe hangouts, this balustraded white villa and its broad annex sprawl elegantly along a private waterfront, wrapped around an isolated courtyard and a pool shaded by parasol pines. Louis XVI bergères, a beam here and there, gilt frames, indirect spots, and oh-so-comfy beds make for an alluring if somewhat homogenized interior. Spend a day lounging with a book underneath a parasol by the enormous swimming pool and manicured lawns, or take to the sea where you can scuba dive, sail, windsurf, and jet ski. Pay extra for a seaside room, where you can lean over the balcony and take in broad coastal views over the private beach (and the distant range of grey-blue mountains) and the large seafront restaurant; the chef has a celebrated reputation, and you'll understand why after one taste of his truffled ravioli. Rates including half-board are available. ⊠ *Plage de la Bouillabaisse, 83991* ☎ *04-94-55-91-00* 🖷 *04-94-97-73-64* ⊕ *www.residencepinede.com* 🛏 *35 rooms, 4 suites* ⟁ *Restaurant, cable TV, golf privileges, pool, beach, boating, jet skiing, in-room data ports, Wi-Fi in public areas, some pets allowed* ⊟*AE, MC, V* ⊘ *Closed mid-Oct.–Easter.*

★ **$$-$$$** ⊞ **Ermitage.** Surrounded by mimosas and lemon trees, this big, old-fashioned villa-hotel stands on a hill above town and, from back rooms and garden, commands striking sea views. The fireplace and cozy armchairs in the bar, the light-bathed rooms in soft pastels, and owner Annie Bolloreis's friendly welcome make this a real charmer. ⊠ *Av. Paul-Signac, 83990* ☎ *04-94-97-52-33* 🖷 *04-94-97-10-43* 🛏 *27 rooms* ⟁ *Cable TV, bar* ⊟ *AE, MC, V.*

$$ ⊞ **Hôtel Baron Lodge.** All the small, brocante-furnished rooms overlook the Citadelle's green park, some from tiny balconies. If you're more than two, ask for the pretty loft suite, with its private spiral-stair entrance. Breakfast is served in the cozy "library" bar. ⊠ *23 rue de l'Aïoli, 83990* ☎ *04-94-97-06-57* 🖷 *04-94-97-58-72* ⊕ *www.hotel-le-baron.com* 🛏 *12 rooms, 3 suites* ⟁ *Bar, cable TV, some pets allowed; no a/c in some rooms* ⊟ *MC, V* ⊘ *Closed mid-Nov.–mid-Dec. and 2 wks in Jan.*

$-$$ ⊞ **Lou Cagnard.** Inside a lovely enclosed garden courtyard is this pretty

Fodor'sChoice little hotel owned by an enthusiastic young couple, who have fixed it ★ up room by room and recently added air-conditioning. Five ground-floor rooms open onto the flowered and manicured garden, where breakfast is served in the shade of a fig tree. Most rooms have regional-tile baths, quarry-tile floors, and Provençal fabrics. If you're willing to share a toilet down the hall, five of the rooms are real bargains. ⊠ *18 av. Paul Roussel, 83900* ☎ *04-94-97-04-24* 🖷 *04-94-97-09-44* ⊕ *www. hotel-lou-cagnard.com* 🛏 *19 rooms, 14 with bath* ⟁ *Cable TV, bar* ⊟ *MC, V* ⊘ *Closed Nov.–late Dec.*

Nightlife & the Arts

Costing the devil and often jammed to the scuppers, **Les Caves du Roy** (✉ Av. Paul-Signac ☎ 04–94–56–68–00), a disco in the Byblos Hotel, is *the* place to see and be seen; it's filled with svelte model types and their wealthy, silver-haired fans. There's a horrific door policy during high season; don't worry, it's *not* you. Seeking light, action, and

> You, too, may be doused with Moët during one of those champagne-spraying midnight parties—so many bottles are set off, waiters are given football helmets.

music with giddy determination, teens, twentysomethings, and Hollywood Venuses and Tarzans cram into the vast **Le Papagayo disco** (✉ Résidence du Port ☎ 04–94–54–88–18), which anchors the end of a commercial and residential building called the Résidence du Port. The **VIP Room** (✉ Résidence du Port, just off the main parking lot ☎ 04–94–97–14–70) symbolizes *le saint-tropez attitude*. If you are young, fun, tan, rich, and love to dance, you have just found paradise. The scene peaks only after 2 AM, winding down around 6, and the club is closed off-season (Oct.–Easter). Set in the picturesque La Ponche neighborhood, **Le Pigeonnier** (✉ 13 rue de la Ponche ☎ 04–94–97–84–26) is the leading gay disco.

Every July to September, **classical music concerts** take place in the sultry, palm-studded gardens of the private manor house called the **Château de la Moutte** (✉ Rte. des Salins ⊕ www.music-lamoutte.com). For ticket information about Le Festival des Nuits du Château de La Moutte, inquire at the tourist office.

Sports & the Outdoors

Despite the hip-to-hip commerce and piped-in pop music, the *plages* (beaches) around St-Tropez are the most isolated on the Côte d'Azur, providing one of the rare stretches where your back doesn't lean up against the coastal highway. The closest to town, just at the base of the Citadelle, is the **Plage des Graniers**, easily accessible on foot and the most family-friendly. To the southwest of the port (and the vast expanse of parking lot that precedes it) stretch the beaches of **La Bouillabaisse**, in which you'll find the newly stylish private club Golfe Azur. But the best beaches lie on a long ribbon of white sand that wraps around the peninsula east of the center, reached by the Route des Plages and its parallel fork, the Route de Tahiti. From here you'll find signs pointing to the two principal beaches: the relatively unexploited **Les Salins** and the famous, highly commercialized **Plage de Pampelonne**. The 5-km-long (3-mi-long) sweep of the white Pampelonne is home to some 50 private beachside restaurants, including the dignified, chic **Moorea**, the celebrity hangout **Tahiti**, and the classic **Club 55**—the latter is very Bel-Air, with a moneyed and tasteful crowd. Most notorious of all—famous for A-list debauches and a regular clientele of mega-movie stars and nymphet wannabes—are **La Voile Rouge** and **Nikki Beach**. All these beaches are divided into private turf right up to the waves, and you must pay an average of €10 to €25 per day to access their restaurants, colorful lounge chairs, hot showers, and mattress-side bar service. Be sure to get there early to get a good spot; everybody wants to lounge in the sun on a mattress comfortable enough to take a nap on, definitely worth the small investment. There are, however, a few public-access beaches between the private ones, many equipped with showers and less-than-perfect toilets with a long line of frazzled tourists waiting impatiently. There are cane-shaded parking lots near most of these beaches, though you might consider renting a bike for an easy getaway at sundown. There is a beach for every lifestyle, for families, for gays (**Coco**), and for those who don't mind a parade of exposed aureolae (**Tahiti**). Note that when you head to the beach bars and restaurants, you are expected to cover up a bit.

Bicycles are an ideal way to get to the beaches. **Holiday Bikes** (✉ 14 av. Général-Leclerc ☎ 04–94–97–09–39) rents mountain bikes at an affordable €15 for a full 24 hours. There are also minibuses linking St-Tropez's central Place des Lices and the beaches at Salins and Pampelonne, as well as a bus from the gare routière.

Shopping

There is something about St-Tropez that makes shopping simply irresistible. **Rue Sibilli,** behind the Quai Suffren, is lined with all kinds of trendy boutiques, many carrying those all-important sunglasses. **Zadig & Voltaire** (✉ Rue François-Sibilli ☎ 04–94–79–12–06), open year-round, sells beautifully cut clothes by this popular Parisian designer. To dress like a local, visit the St-Tropez institution **Blabla** (✉ Pl. de la Garonne ☎ 04–94–97–45–09), which sells head-turning clothes by designers scoped out around the world—just don't forget you'll need the tan to match. Prefer more traditional luxe? Don't miss **Le Dépot** (✉ Bd. Louis-Blanc ☎ 04–94–97–80–10), which stocks castoffs by Chanel, Prada, Gucci et al. The **Place des Lices** overflows with produce and regional foods, as well as clothing and *brocantes* (secondhand items), every Tuesday and Saturday morning. The picturesque little **fish market** occupies the Place aux Herbes every morning.

Ramatuelle

❾ *12 km (7 mi) southwest of St-Tropez.*

A typical hilltop whorl of red-clay roofs and dense inner streets topped with arches and lined with arcades, this ancient market town was destroyed in the Wars of Religions and rebuilt as a harmonious whole in 1620. Now its souvenir shops and galleries attract day-trippers out of St-Tropez, who enjoy the pretty drive through the vineyards as much as the village itself. During high season, traffic jams can be spectacular between Ramatuelle and St-Tropez, inflating what should be a short drive into a three-hour crawl. At the top of the village you can visit the Moulin de Paillas, on Route du Moulin de Paillas, a windmill recently restored in the old style with a mechanism made entirely of wood; the site offers a panoramic view of the coastline. Free guided tours of the windmill are held every Tuesday 10–12. The town cemetery is the final resting place of Gérard Phillipe, an aristocratic heartthrob who died in 1959 after making his mark in such films as *Le Diable au Corps.*

EN ROUTE From Ramatuelle, the lovely ride through vineyards and woods full of twisted cork oaks to the hilltop village of Gassin takes you over the highest point of the peninsula (1,070 feet).

Where to Eat & Stay

$$$$ ✕⊡ **Les Moulins.** A satellite of planet St-Tropez, this outpost of show-biz chef Christophe Leroy lures off-duty celebrities and the swank to its lovely perch near Pampelonne beach. Ceiling fans, rattan chairs, and blond-wood accents heighten the pleasure of the scrumptious dishes served here—don't miss out on the vichyssoise with truffles. Upstairs are five cozy, rustic guest rooms. ⊠ *Rte. des Plages, 83350* ☎ *04-94-97-17-22* 🖨 *04-94-97-11-46* ⊕ *www.christophe-leroy.com* ⇨ *5 rooms* ⚹ *Restaurant, cable TV, some pets allowed* ⊟ *AE, MC, V* ⊗ *Closed Nov.–Mar.*

★ $$$$ ✕⊡ **Villa Marie.** It's not quite your own private paradise, but it might feel like it as you are whisked off in a golf cart up the hill, having left your car at the bottom. Jocelyne and Jean-Louis Sibuet, best known for their luxury ski retreats in Megève (notably Les Fermes de Marie), in-fuse each of their hotels with inimitable French style. Here, they play up the location facing the Bay of Pampelonne with pastel colors, four-poster beds, embroidered curtains, baroque bathtubs, and a stunning estate garden. Each of the rooms is individually decorated, and the bar and restaurant focus on fish with seashell motifs and a simple, fresh menu (fritto misto, grilled sea bream). To complete the experience, treat your-self to an outdoor spa treatment using the products developed for Les Fermes de Marie. ⊠ *Rte. des Plages, Chemin Val Rian, 83350* ☎ *04-94-97-40-22* 🖨 *04-94-97-37-55* ⊕ *www.villamarie.fr* ⇨ *42 rooms* ⚹ *Restaurant, bar, pool, spa, cable TV, Wi-Fi in rooms, some pets allowed* ⊟ *AE, DC, MC, V* ⊗ *Closed Nov.–Apr.*

$–$$ ✕⊡ **Ferme Ladouceur.** Not far from the talcum-powder beach of Pampelonne and surrounded by vineyards is this naïf farmhouse, domain of Constance Ladouceur, whose paintings adorn the hallways and whose restaurant is a draw for budget-minded locals. Quirky, simple, afford-able, with breakfast included in the price—little wonder you need to book here far in advance. ⊠ *Quartier la Rouillère, 83350* ☎ *04-94-79-24-95* 🖨 *04-94-79-12-14* ⊕ *http://fermeladouceur.com/index-gb.htm* ⇨ *7 rooms* ⚹ *Restaurant, some pets allowed; no a/c, no room phones, no room TVs* ⊟ *AE, MC, V* ⊗ *Closed Nov.–Mar.* ⦿| *BP.*

Gassin

❿ *7 km (4 mi) northwest of Ramatuelle.*

Though not as picturesque as Ramatuelle, this hilltop village gives you spectacular views over the surrounding vineyards and St-Tropez's bay. In winter, before the summer haze drifts in and after the mistral has given the sky a good scrub, you may be able to make out a brilliant-white chain of Alps looming on the horizon. There's less commerce here to distract you; for shops, head to Ramatuelle.

EN ROUTE

The dramatic forest scenery of D558 winding west and northwest of St-Tropez merits a drive even if you're not heading up to A8. This is the **Massif des Maures,** named for the Moors who retreated here from the Battle of Poitiers in 732 and profited from its strong position over the sea. The forest is dark with thick cork oaks, their ancient trunks girdled for cork only every 10 years or so, leaving exposed a broad band of sienna brown. Looming even darker and thicker above are the chestnut trees cultivated for their thick, sweet nuts, which you are not allowed to gather from the forest floor, as signs from the growers' co-operative warn. Between wine domaines' vineyards, mushroom-shape parasol pines, unique to the Mediterranean, crowd the highway.

4

Where to Eat & Stay

$$$$ ✕⟦⟧ **Villa Belrose.** Perched on the highest point of the peninsula, this Hollywoodesque palace has unrivaled views of the Gulf of St-Tropez and the kind of decadently rich élan that would make Scott and Zelda feel right at home. Public salons have Louis XVI and Florentine accents, while guest rooms are spacious yet cozy, with marble bathrooms and romantic balconies. Besides the 180-degree views, the restaurant, run by Alain Ducasse disciple Thierry Thiercelin, supplies first-rate Mediterranean cuisine, pleasant service, and a top-drawer wine list. Rates including half-board are available. ⊠ *Bd. des Crètes, 83580* ☎ *04–94–55–97–97* 🖷 *04–94–55–97–98* ⊕ *www.relaischateaux.fr* ⤳ *35 rooms, 3 suites, 2 apartments* ⚹ *Restaurant, minibars, cable TV, pool, spa, bar, Wi-Fi in rooms, parking (fee), some pets allowed (fee)* ▭ *AE, DC, MC, V* ⊙ *Closed Nov.–mid-Mar.*

$$$–$$$$ ⟦⟧ **Le Mas de Chastelas.** In a lush tropical garden full of mimosas and palms, set back from the main access road into St-Tropez, this 18th-century former silkworm farm offers rooms in a main house as well as a handful of villas clustered around two tree-lined pools. The rooms in the main house are tastefully furnished, sparse and cool, with wonderful tiled floors and colorful touches. The fully equipped independent villas are great for families as they have kitchenettes and small lounge areas. ⊠ *Quartier Bertaud, 83580* ☎ *04–94–56–71–71* 🖷 *04–94–56–71–56* ⊕ *www.chastelas.com* ⤳ *14 rooms, 5 suites, 1 studio, 5 villas* ⚹ *Restaurant, cable TV, 2 tennis courts, 2 pools, outdoor hot tub, Wi-Fi in rooms, some pets allowed* ▭ *AE, DC, MC, V.*

Grimaud

⓫ *10 km (6 mi) west of St-Tropez.*

Once a formidable Grimaldi fiefdom and home to a massive Romanesque château, the hill-village of Grimaud is merely charming today, though the romantic castle ruins that crown its steep streets still command lordly views over the forests and the coast. The labyrinth of cobbled streets is punctuated by pretty fountains, carved doorways, and artisans' gallery-boutiques. Wander along the Gothic arcades of the Rue des Templiers to see the beautifully proportioned Romanesque **Église St-Michel,** built in the 11th century.

$$\text{-}$$$ ✕ **La Ferme du Magnan.** Just 10 km (6 mi) west of St-Tropez and 4 km (2½ mi) south of Grimaud and the village of Cogolin, this bucolic old farmhouse looms on a hillside over forests dense with cork oak and chestnuts. Whether you eat on the terrace or in the rustic dining room, the food tastes and smells of the surrounding country: snails with sharp, garlicky aïoli, mussels grilled on grape leaves, duck simmered with olives, and guinea fowl stewed in Bandol. ✉ *Rte. de la Mole, RN 98, Cogolin* ☎ *04–94–49–57–54* 🖃 *MC, V* ⊗ *Closed Oct.–Easter.*

Port-Grimaud

⑫ *5 km (3 mi) east of Grimaud, 7 km (4½ mi) west of St-Tropez.*

Although much of the coast has been targeted with new construction of extraordinary ugliness, this modern architect's version of a Provençal fishing village works. A true operetta set and only begun in 1966, it has grown gracefully over the years, and offers hope for the pink concrete-scarred coastal landscape. It's worth parking and wandering up the village's Venice-like canals to admire its Old Mediterranean canal-tile roofs and pastel facades, already patinated with age. Even the church, though resolutely modern, feels Romanesque. There is, however, one modern touch some might appreciate: small electric tour boats (get them at Place du Marché) that carry you for a small charge from bar to shop to restaurant throughout the complex of pretty squares and bridges.

Ste-Maxime

⑬ *8 km (5 mi) northeast of Port-Grimaud, 33 km (20 mi) northeast of St-Tropez.*

You may be put off by its heavily built-up waterfront, bristling with parking garage–style apartments and hotels, and its position directly on the waterfront highway, but Ste-Maxime is an affordable family resort with fine, easily accessible, sandy beaches. It even has a sliver of car-free Old Town and a stand of majestic plane trees sheltering the central Place Victor-Hugo. Its main beach, north of town, is the wide and sandy **La Nartelle.**

Where to Eat

$ ✕ **La Maison Bleue.** Cheerful blue-and-white-checked tablecloths and a polished wood façade give this "blue house" on the main pedestrian street a welcoming air that matches the straightforward fresh pasta (tagliatelle, ravioli, or gnocchi) and simple fish dishes, accompanied by well-chosen local wines. ✉ *48 rue Paul Bert* ☎ *04–94–96–51–92* 🖃 *MC, V* ⊗ *Closed Nov.–Dec. 27; Sun. and Tues. Jan.–Mar.; Wed. in Apr. and Oct.*

EN ROUTE As you cling to the coastline on dramatic N98 between Ste-Maxime and Fréjus, you'll see a peculiar mix: pretty beaches and fjordlike *calanques* (rocky coves) dipping in and out of view between luxury villas (and their burglar-wired hedges), trailer-park campsites, and the fast-food stands and beach discos that define much of the Riviera. The **Calanque des Louvans** and the **Calanque du Four à Chaux** are especially scenic, with sand beaches and rocks shaded by windblown pines; watch for signs.

FRÉJUS, ST-RAPHAËL & THE ESTÉREL RESORTS

Though the twin resorts of Fréjus and St-Raphaël have become somewhat overwhelmed by waterfront resort culture, Fréjus still harbors a small but charming enclave that evokes both the Roman and medieval periods. As you then follow the coast east, a massive red-rock wasteland, known as the Massif de l'Estérel, rears up high above the sparkling water. Formed of red volcanic rocks (porphyry) carved by the sea into dreamlike shapes, the harsh landscape is softened by patches of lavender, mimosa, scrub pine, and gorse. At the rocks' base churn azure waters, seething in and out of castaway coves, where a series of gentle resort bays punctuate the coastline. N98 leads to one of the coast's most spectacular drives, the Corniche de l'Estérel. And if you take N7, the mountain route to the north, you can lose yourself in the Estérel's desert landscape, far from the sea. The resorts that cluster at the foot of the Estérel are densely populated pleasure ports, with an agreeable combination of cool sea breezes and escapes into the near-desert behind.

Fréjus

🔟 *19 km (12 mi) northeast of Ste-Maxime, 37 km (23 mi) northeast of St-Tropez.*

Confronted with the gargantuan pink holiday high-rises that crowd the Fréjus–St-Raphaël waterfront, you may be tempted to forge onward. But after a stroll on the sandy curve in tacky, overcommercialized Fréjus-Plage (Fréjus Beach), turn your back on modern times and head uphill to Fréjus-Centre. Here you'll enter a maze of narrow streets lined with butcher shops, patisseries, and neighborhood stores barely touched by the cult of the lavender sachet. The farmers' market at the foot of the cathedral (Monday, Wednesday, and Saturday mornings) is as real and lively as any in Provence, and the cafés encircling the fountains and squares nourish an easygoing social scene.

Fréjus (pronounced fray-*zhooss*) also has the honor of having some of the most important historic monuments on the coast. Founded in 49 BC by Julius Caesar himself and named Forum Julii, this quiet town was once a thriving Roman shipbuilding port of 40,000 citizens. In its heyday, Roman Fréjus had a theater, baths, and an enormous aqueduct that brought water all the way from Mons in the mountains, 45 km (28 mi) north of town. Today you can see the remains: a series of detached arches that follow the main Avenue du Quinzième Corps (leading up to the Old Town).

Just up northbound D37 from the Old Town is the Roman **theater**; its remaining rows of arches are mostly intact and much of its stage works are still visible at its center. The town's more impressive remains, however, are the **Arènes** (often called the *Amphithéâtre*), still used today for concerts and bullfights. To reach the Arènes, follow Avenue du Verdun west of the Old Town toward Puget.

To drink in the atmosphere of Old Fréjus, settle under the shade of the great plane trees and listen to the sound of the fern-heavy fountain at the **Bar du Marché** (✉ 5 pl. Liberté ☎ 04–94–51–29–09). Here a *croque monsieur* (grilled ham and cheese toast), sundae, or apéritif will buy you time to watch the neighborhood putter through its daily rituals.

★ Set 6 km (2½ mi) north of Fréjus on the RN7 is the eccentric **La Chapelle Notre-Dame-de-Jérusalem.** Designed by Jean Cocteau as part of an artists' colony that never happened, it is unusual not only for its octagonal shape, stained glass, and frescos depicting the mythology of the first Crusades, but also because the tongue-in-cheek painting of the apostles above the front door boasts the famous faces of Coco Chanel, Jean Marais, and poet Max Jacob. ✉ *Av. Nicolaï, la Tour de la Mare* ☎ *04–94–53–27–06* 🆓 *Free* ⊙ *Nov.–Mar., daily 2:30–5:30; Apr.-Oct. daily 2–6.*

★ Fréjus is graced with one of the most impressive religious monuments in Provence: the **Groupe Épiscopal,** an enclosed ensemble of cathedral, cloisters, and baptistery. The early Gothic **cathedral** consists of two parallel naves, the narrower one from the 12th century (with barrel vaults) and the broader from the 13th century, with groin vaults supported by heavy pillars. The ensemble is spare and somber, with modern windows. Through the heavy arches of the 15th-century narthex you reach the entrance to the **baptistery,** which dates from the 5th century. This extraordinary structure retains the style of arches and columns that shows just how Roman these early Christians were. The bishop himself baptized them, washing their feet in the small pool to the side, then immersing them in the deep font at the room's center. Outside the baptistery, stairs lead up to the early Gothic **cloister,** redolent of boxwood and framing a stone well. There are two stories of pillared arcades, the lower ones pointed, the upper ones round (an odd effect, yet all were executed during one architectural period). The capitals on the lower pillars are graceful and abstract; the grotesques and caricatures you'd expect appear instead in the unusual and striking wooden roof covering the lower gallery, painted in the 15th century in sepia and earth tones with a phantasmagorical assortment of animals and biblical characters. Off the entrance and gift shop, you can peruse a small museum of archaeological findings from Roman Fréjus, including a complete mosaic and a sculpture of a two-headed Hermes. ✉ *58 rue de Fleury* ☎ *04–94–51–26–30* 🆓 *Cathedral free; cloister, museum, and baptistery €4* ⊙ *Cathedral: daily 8:30–noon and 4–6. Cloister, museum, and baptistery: Apr.–Sept., daily 9–7; Oct.–Mar., Tues.–Sun. 9–noon and 2–5.*

Where to Eat & Stay

$$ ✕🏨 **L'Aréna.** This attractive, bright, ocher hotel located at the edge of the Old Town is surrounded by exotic greenery, blooming geraniums, and an outdoor swimming pool. Breakfast is served under the palm trees out by the pool in the morning. Too bad about the trains zipping below, but the windows are insulated and there is air-conditioning. Duplex rooms have sleeping lofts for the kids, and two rooms on the ground floor have views of the pool. The stylish garden restaurant in deep yellow highlights fresh fish with a Provençal accent, from mullet sautéed with a spicy vinaigrette to roasted sea bass with artichokes *barigoule* (simmered in white wine with bacon). ✉ *Bd. Générale de Gaulle, 83615* ☎ *04–94–17–09–40* 🖨 *04–94–52–01–52* ⊕ *www.arena-hotel.com* ♨ *Restaurant, cable TV, pool, bar, Wi-Fi in rooms, some pets allowed* 🛏 *36 rooms* ▭ *AE, DC, MC, V* ⊙ *Closed 10 days in Jan.*

Sports & the Outdoors

Diving off the calanques between Fréjus and Ste-Maxime gives you interesting underwater insight into the marine life lurking in the rocks. Contact the **Centre International de Plongée** (International Diving Center; ✉ Port Fréjus ☎ 04–94–52–34–99 ⊕ www.cip-frejus.com) for instruction, equipment rental, and guided outings.

The urban **beaches** draped at the foot of Fréjus are backed by a commercial sprawl of brasseries, beach-gear shops, and realtors (for sunstruck visitors who dream of buying a flat on the waterfront). The beaches outside the city, however, are public and wide open, with deep sandy stretches toward St-Aygulf. The calanques just south are particularly wild and pretty, with only tiny sand surfaces.

St-Raphaël

🔟 *3 km (2 mi) east of Fréjus, 30 km (19 mi) southwest of Cannes.*

Right next door to Fréjus, with almost no division between, spreads St-Raphaël, a sprawling resort city with a busy downtown anchored by a casino. It's also a major sailing center, has five golf courses nearby, and draws the weary and indulgent to its seawater-based thalassotherapy. Along with Fréjus, it serves as a rail crossroads, the two being the closest stops to St-Tropez. The port has a rich history: Napoléon landed at St-Raphaël on his triumphant return from Egypt in 1799; it was also from here in 1814 that he cast off in disgrace for Elba. And it was here, too, that the Allied forces landed in their August 1944 offensive against the Germans. Augmenting the Atlantic City vibe of this modern pleasure port is the gingerbread-and-gilt dome of the neo-Byzantine **Église Notre-Dame-de-la-Victoire** (✉ Bd. Félix-Martin), which watches over the yachts and cruise boats sliding into the port. If you wish to gamble, head to **Le Grand Casino** (✉ Bd. de la Libération ☎ 04–98–11–17–77), open daily 11 AM–4 AM, which looks out over the waterfront, catering to the city's many conventioneers.

The reward is worth the bother of penetrating dense city traffic and cutting inland past the train station and into the Vieille Ville (Old Town), a tiny enclave of charm crowned by the 12th-century **Église St-Pierre-des-Templiers** (✉ Rue des Templiers), a miniature-scale Romanesque church.

On the same quiet square as St-Pierre, shaded by an old olive tree, the intimate little **Musée Archéologique Marin** (Marine Archaeology Museum) offers a quirky diversion. Its few rooms contain a concise and fascinating collection of ancient amphorae gleaned from the shoals offshore, where centuries' worth of shipwrecks have accumulated; by studying this chronological progression of jars and the accompanying sketches, you can visualize the coast as it was in its heyday as a Greek and Roman shipping center. The science of exploring these shipwrecks was relatively new when French divers began probing the depths; the underwater Leicas from the 1930s and the early scuba gear from the '50s on display are as fascinating as the spoils they helped to unearth. Upstairs, a few objects—jewelry, spearheads, pottery shards, and skulls—illustrate the Neolithic and Paleolithic eras and remind you of the dense population of Celto-Ligurians who claimed this region long before the Greeks and Phoenicians. A few of their dolmens and menhirs are still visible on the Estérel. ⊠ *Rue des Templiers* ☎ *04–94–19–25–75* 🎫 *€1.50* ⏱ *June–Sept., Tues.–Sat. 9–noon and 3–6:30; Oct.–May, Tues.–Sat. 9–noon and 2–5:30.*

Where to Eat & Stay

$$$ ✕ **La Bouillabaisse.** Enter through the beaded curtain covering the open doorway to a wood-paneled room decked out with starfish and the mounted head of a swordfish. This local institution has a brief, straightforward menu inspired by the fish markets in the neighborhood. Come here for the catch of the day, the classic seafood and saffron paella (served only at lunch), or the rich bouillabaisse, the house specialty. ⊠ *50 pl. Victor-Hugo* ☎ *04–94–95–03–57* 🍴 *AE, MC, V* ⏱ *Closed Mon.*

$$$ 🏨 **Excelsior.** This urban hotel has been under the careful management of one family for three generations. Its combination of straightforward comforts and a waterfront position in the center of town attracts a regular clientele. Rooms are plush and pastel, bathrooms reasonably up-to-date; be sure to request a room with a view of the sea. The café and restaurant attract nonguests for dependable fare and sea views. ⊠ *Next to Le Grand Casino on the Promenade Coty, 83700* ☎ *04–94–95–02–42* 🖨 *04–94–95–33–82* 🌐 *www.excelsior-hotel.com* 🛏 *36 rooms* ⚐ *Restaurant, café, in-room safes, minibars, cable TV, in-room data ports, Wi-Fi in bar, some pets allowed* 🍴 *AE, DC, MC, V.*

★ **¢–$** 🏨 **Le Thimothée.** Philippe and Jean-Claude, the charming owners of this bargain lodging, have thrown themselves wholeheartedly into improving what was an already attractive 19th-century villa. They're incredibly helpful, too: they will rent you a bike, book an excursion, and give you seconds on coffee at the traditional French breakfast (fee) usually served in the garden, where grand palms and pines shade the walkway to a pretty little swimming pool. Be sure to request one of the top-floor rooms with a spectacular view of the sea and air-conditioning during the hot summer months (the two bottom-floor rooms aren't air-conditioned). ⊠ *375 bd. Christian-Lafon, 83700* ☎ *04–94–40–49–49* 🖨 *04–94–19–41–92* 🌐 *www.thimothee.com* 🛏 *12 rooms* ⚐ *Minibars, cable TV, pool, in-room data ports, some pets allowed; no a/c in some rooms* 🍴 *AE, MC, V* ⏱ *Closed Jan.*

Sports & the Outdoors

St-Raphaël's **beaches** form a snaking sliver of sand, starting just east of the port and finally petering out against the red cliffs of the Estérel. From that point on, you'll find tiny calanques and *criques* (coves and finger bays) for swimming and basking on the rocks.

The spectacularly sited 9-hole **Golf de Cap Estérel** (⊠ *RN 98, Saint-Agay* ☎ *04–94–82–55–00*) hovers directly over the sea behind Agay.

St-Raphaël is a serious **sailing and boating** center, with nautical complexes at four different sites along the coast: the Vieux Port, Santa Lucia (by Fréjus-Plage), Le Dramont (at the base of a dramatic little cape below the Estérel), and within Agay's quiet harbor. For information on boat rentals, training sessions, and diving lessons, contact the **Club Nautique St-Raphaël** (☎ 04–94–95–11–66).

To explore the wilds of the Estérel on foot, consider a guided **hike** led by a qualified staffer from the tourist office. Mountain biking is now discouraged in the Estérel for environmental reasons.

The Corniche de l'Estérel

Stay on N98 and you'll find yourself careening along a stunning coastal drive, the Corniche de l'Estérel, which whips past tiny calanques and sheer rock faces that plunge down to the sea. At the dramatic Pointe de Cap Roux, an overlook allows you to pull off the narrow two-lane highway (where high-season sightseers can cause bumper-to-bumper traffic) and contemplate the spectacular view up and down the coast. Train travelers have the good fortune to snake along this cliff side for constant panoramas. It's also a hiker's haven. Some 15 trails strike out from designated parking sites along the way, leading up into the jagged rock peaks for extraordinary sea views. (Don't leave valuables in the car, as the sites are littered with glass from break-ins.) For trail maps, ask at the St-Raphaël tourist office across from the train station. There is also a *sentier du littoral* (waterfront trail), leaving from the St-Raphaël port and following the rocky coast all the way to Agay; you'll see a mix of wild, rocky criques and glamorous villas.

Théoule-sur-Mer

⑯ *21 km (13 mi) northeast of Agay, 2 km (1 mi) south of La Napoule.*

Tucked into a tiny bay on the Golfe de Napoule, Théoule seems far removed from the major resorts around it. A sliver of beach, a few shops and villas, and magnificent views toward Cannes make it a pleasant home base for forays along the coast.

Where to Eat

$ ✕**Nino's.** At the far southeast tip of Théoule's miniature bay, this unpretentious pizzeria serves simple Italian specialties—but, oh, what a setting. A few tables line a wooden "boathouse" porch directly over the lapping water, and at night the whole glittering necklace of Cannes reflects its luxurious glow over the bay. Good wood-oven pizzas and pastas add superfluous pleasure. ✉ *6 chemin Débarcadère* ☎ *04–92–97–61–11* 🖃 *MC, V* ⊗ *Closed Oct.–Mar.*

Mandelieu–La Napoule

⑰ *32 km (20 mi) northeast of St-Raphaël, 8 km (5 mi) southwest of Cannes.*

La Napoule is the small, old-fashioned port village, Mandelieu the big-fish resort town that devoured it. You can visit Mandelieu for a golf-

and-sailing retreat—the town is replete with many sporting facilities and hosts a bevy of sporting events, including sailing regattas, windsurfing contests, and golf championships (there are two major golf courses in Mandelieu right in the center of town by the sea). By the sea, a yacht-crammed harbor sits under the shadow of some high-rise resort hotels. La Napoule, on the other hand, offers the requisite quaintness, ideal for a port-side stroll, casual meal, beach siesta, or visit to its peculiar castle. Unless you're here for the sun and surf, however, these twinned towns mostly serve as a home base for outings to Cannes, Antibes, and the Estérel. In fact, the easternmost beach in Mandelieu dovetails with the first, most democratic beaches of its glamorous neighbor, Cannes.

Fodor'sChoice
★

Set on Pointe des Pendus (Hanged Man's Point), the **Château de la Napoule,** looming over the sea and the port, is a bizarrely wonderful hybrid of Romanesque, Gothic, Moroccan, and Hollywood cooked up by the eccentric American sculptor Henry Clews (1876–1937). Working with his architect-wife, he transformed the 14th-century bastion into something that suited his personal expectations and then filled the place with his own fantastical sculptures. The couple resides in their tombs in the tower crypt, its windows left slightly ajar to permit their souls to escape and allow them to "return at eventide as sprites and dance upon the windowsill." Today the château's stylish and well-funded foundation hosts visiting writers and artists, many of whom are American, who set to work surrounded by Clews's gargoyle-like sculptures. You may visit the gardens from 2:30 to 6, March through October, without the guided castle tour. ⊠ *Av. Henry Clews* ☎ *04–93–49–95–05* ⊕ *www. chateau-lanapoule.com* ⊠ *€6; gardens €3* ⊙ *Feb. 7–Nov. 7, daily 10–6; guided tours at 11:30, 2:30, 3:30, and 4:30. Nov. 8–Feb. 6, weekdays 2–5; guided tours at 2:30 and 3:30; weekends and holidays, 10–5, guided tours at 11:30, 2:30, and 3:30.*

> " Fond of spouting Nietzsche to his titled dinner guests, surrounding himself with footmen, and dedicating his house to Don Quixote (its name is actually "Mancha"), Henry Clews may have had a dubious artistic vision but he certainly enjoyed a vibrant sense of fantasy. "

Where to Eat & Stay

$$$$ ✕ **L'Oasis.** Long famed as a culinary landmark, this Gothic villa by the sea is now home to Stéphane Raimbault, a master of Provençal cuisine and a great connoisseur of Asian techniques and flavorings. The combination creates unexpected collisions—Jabugo ham with anise, lobster, and ginger, or Thai-spiced crayfish with squid-ink ravioli—not all entirely successful. Still, few can quibble with the beauty of the famous garden terrace shadowed by gorgeous palm trees. ⊠ *Rue J. H. Carle* ☎ *04–93–49–95–52* ⊕ *www.oasis-raimbault.com* 🚫 *AE, MC, V* ⊙ *No dinner Sun., no lunch Mon. May–Sept.; closed mid-Jan.–mid-Feb.*

★ $$–$$$ ✕ **Le Boucanier.** The drab, low-ceilinged dining room is upstaged by wrap-around plate-glass views of the marina and château at this waterfront favorite. Locals gather here for mountains of oysters and whole fish, simply grilled and impeccably filleted table-side. The seafood, market-fresh, speaks for itself. No one interferes beyond a drizzle of fruity olive oil, a pinch of rock salt, or a brief flambé in pastis. ⊠ *Port La Napoule* ☎ *04–93–49–80–51* ☐ *MC, V* ⊘ *Closed Thurs. in Nov.–Mar.*

$$$$ ✕⊞ **Royal Hôtel Casino.** As much a resort as a hotel, this modern waterfront complex has deluxe comforts on a grand scale, with a broad beach-terrace, indoor and outdoor pools, and vast conference facilities. Streamlined rooms in soft pastels have balconies and sea views from all sides. At the informal yet glamorous restaurant-grill you can dine on such dishes as artichokes with scampi and lightly grilled *rouget* (red mullet) with kasha while you gaze out over the floodlit swimming pool. ⊠ *605 av. Général-de-Gaulle, 06210* ☎ *04–92–97–70–00* ☐ *04–93–49–51–50* ⊕ *www.sofitel.com* ⇗ *213 rooms* ᗷ *2 restaurants, minibars, cable TV, 2 tennis courts, 2 pools, gym, sauna, bar, casino, in-room data ports, Wi-Fi in some rooms, some pets allowed* ☐ *AE, DC, MC, V.*

¢–$ ⊞ **Villa Parisiana.** In the residential neighborhood of La Napoule, about 500 feet from the waterfront, this impeccably kept hotel offers simple comforts, chenille bedspreads, and a few updated bathrooms. A big balcony-terrace overlooks a jungle of a garden. ⊠ *Rue de l'Argentière, 06210* ☎ *04–93–49–93–02* ☐ *04–93–49–62–32* ⊕ *www.villaparisiana.com* ⇗ *13 rooms* ᗷ *Cable TV, Wi-Fi in rooms, some pets allowed; no a/c* ☐ *AE, DC, MC, V.*

Sports & the Outdoors

★ The **Golf Club de Cannes-Mandelieu** (⊠ Rte. du Golf ☎ 04–93–49–55–39 ⊕ www.golfoldcourse.com) is one of the most beautiful in the south of France, and is famous for its 100-year-old parasol pines that shade the greens. Posh and eccentric, it has a grand clubhouse in half-timber Normandy style and ferries golfers over the River Siagne—between holes. There are two courses—one 18 holes (par 71) and one 9 holes (par 33). The golf club is closed Tuesday except July–August.

Classified as a *station voile* (sailing resort), Mandelieu–La Napoule is a major water-sports center. To rent a boat or charter a fully equipped yacht for one day or more, contact **Cayman Yachting** (☎04–93–93–27–67).

For windsurfing and small sailboats, contact **Centre Nautique** (☎ 04–92–97–07–70). Lessons and supplies for scuba diving are available from **Armand Ferrand Centre de Plongée** (⊠ Port de la Rague ☎ 04–93–49–74–33 ⊕ www.plongee-ferrand.com).

There are two private beaches nestled in between the public beaches, the major difference between public and private being, as it always is, a question of comfort. You can spend the extra euros for a comfortable mattress, an access to shade, and the convenience of a nearby restaurant. On the public beach you have to supply your own comforts. If you have children with you and are on the public beach, keep your eye out for special clubs usually referred to as "Mickey Clubs," set up for young children with games, wading pools, and activities supervised by professionals. **La Voile d'Azur** (☎04–93–49–20–44) rents mattresses for €16, and has beach bar service and a restaurant that serves sandwiches and salads. **Le Sweet** (☎ 04–93–49–87–33) rents mattresses for €16, and has beach bar service and a restaurant that specializes in the catch of the day.

THE HAUT VAR & INTO HAUTE PROVENCE

The hills that back the Côte d'Azur are often called the *arrière-pays,* or backcountry, a catch-all term that applies to the hills and plateaus behind Nice as well. Yet this particular wedge of backcountry—north and west of Fréjus—has a character all its own. If the territory behind Nice has a strong Latin flavor, influenced for centuries by the Grimaldi dynasty and steeped in Italian culture, these westerly hills are deeply, unself-consciously Provençal: wild lavender and thyme sprout on dry, rocky hillsides; the earth under scrub oaks is snuffled by rooting boars; and hilltop villages are so isolated and quiet you can hear pebbles drop in their mossy fountains.

The rocky swells behind Cannes and Fréjus are known as the Haut Var, the highlands of the département called Var. The untamed, beautiful, and sometimes harsh landscape beyond these hills lies over the threshold of Haute Provence—itself loosely defined, more a climate and terrain than a region. The author Jean Giono, born in Manosque, evokes its landscape as windswept and often brutal, directly vulnerable to the mistral and the winds whistling down from the Alps. Its environs include southern bits of the département of Drôme and much of the Alpes-de-Haute-Provence.

It's possible to get a small taste of this backcountry on a day trip out of Fréjus or Cannes. On your way north you may choose to trace the steps of Napoléon himself, who followed what is now N85, today named for him, on his tentative comeback from Elba Island in 1815. But if you give yourself time to wind through the back roads, stop for the views, and linger in shady perched-village squares, you may be tempted to cancel your waterfront plans and settle in for an otherworldly experience.

Fayence

⑱ *35.9 km (23 mi) north of Mandelieu–La Napoule, 27 km (17 mi) west of Grasse, 30 km (19 mi) northwest of Cannes.*

The most touristy of all the hill towns in the Haut Var backcountry, Fayence is easiest to reach from the coast and often filled with busloads of day-trippers. Nonetheless, it has a pretty Old Town at the top, magnificent wraparound views from its 18th-century church down to the Massif des Maures and the Estérel, and a plethora of artisans' galleries and boutiques. If the development—villa-fication, if you will, or perhaps California-fication—that spreads wider each year along its slopes seems off-putting compared to serene Seillans or Bargemon, locals point out that it's a living town, with year-round residents and an active community life that extends well beyond tourism.

Where to Eat & Stay

$$ ✕ **Le Temps des Cerises.** Whether under the trellis at the gaily decked café tables or in the elegant, intimate beamed dining room, you'll find your *bonheur* (happiness) in this stylish, central restaurant. Fresh ravioli, truffled quail, and homemade tarts are served with surprising chic for the middle of a tourist town. Too bad about the trucks and motorcycles roaring past. ✉ *Pl. de la République* ☎ *04–94–76–01–19* ▭ *MC, V* ☉ *Closed Tues.*

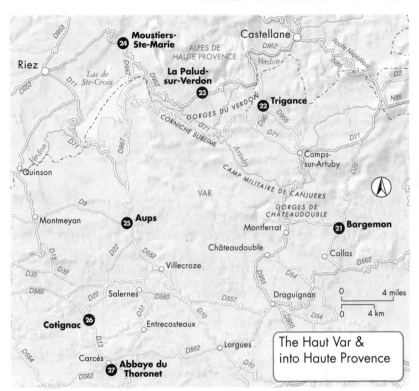

★ **$–$$** ✕🏠 **Moulin de la Camandoule.** On ten acres of stream-side greenery, this noble old olive mill has been turned into a lovely country inn, complete with beams, the original millwheel, and a *pressoir* (olive press) in the middle of the bar. Rooms are fresh and charming with quarry tiles, Persian rugs, and tiled baths. The restaurant serves elegant regional cooking—sea bass roasted in salt crust, quail on herbed fava bean salad, and a beef fillet redolent of black olives. Half-board is obligatory in high season, so you can sightsee in the hill villages, languish by the garden pool, and then dress for your aperitif on the terrace before a memorable evening meal. The relaxed, warm welcome of the Franco-British owners, whose faithful old dogs churn around their ankles, makes this feel like a weekend in a private country home. ⊠ *Rte. de Notre-Dame-des-Cyprés, 83440* ☎ *04–94–76–00–84* 🖷 *04–94–76–10–40* ⊕ *www.camandoule.com* 🛏 *11 rooms* ⌂ *Restaurant, cable TV, pool, bar, Wi-Fi in public areas, some pets allowed; no a/c* ▤ *AE, DC, MC, V.*

★ **¢–$** 🏠 **La Sousto.** Friendly, casual, and accommodating to families and budget travelers, this cozy if spartan little Old Town lodging house offers kitchenettes in every room. Mix-and-match flea-market furniture is backed by whitewashed stucco and polished quarry tiles; some rooms have showers in the kitchen. Rooms 2 and 4 have two large double beds and are perfect for families; Room 5 has a roof terrace overlooking the valley, where you can shower outdoors if you choose. Breakfast (fee) may be served in bed or on the terrace. ⊠ *Pl. du Paty, 83440* ☎ *04–94–76–02–16* ✐ *hotel.sousto@wanadoo.fr* ⇨ *6 rooms* ⚄ *Kitchenettes; no a/c, no room TVs* ⊟ *No credit cards.*

Sports & the Outdoors

Because of its strategic position over the broad valley slope to the sea, Fayence is a hotbed for hang gliders. Anxious to leap into the void yourself? Contact the **Centre de Vol à Voile de Fayence** (Fayence Hang Gliding Center; ⊠ Quai Malvoisin ☎ 04–94–76–00–68 ⊕ www.aapca.net). Also available are rides in glider planes, which are dragged by small prop planes into the heights and then released to free-wheel over the forested hills and valley.

Mons

 15 km (9 mi) north of Fayence, 46 km (28½ mi) west of Grasse, 44 km (27 mi) northwest of Cannes.

Prettier than Fayence but just that much harder to reach, this serene hilltop village stands neatly framed on the flat top of a high plateau. The breadth of its magnificent views contrasts vividly with its tidy, self-contained houses, turned inward on a warp and woof of tiny streets, dipping under arches and through arcades, and tucked into courts and up cobbled steps. It's easy to see how the plague overtook this intimate enclave more than once; and it's just as easy to see why, today, Mons (pronounced *mohnss*) is a popular summer-home retreat, not gentrified but quietly colonized. There are almost no shops and only one restaurant, but be sure to stop into the church to see its fabulous Baroque altarpieces, entirely covered in gold leaf.

Seillans

⑳ *7 km (4½ mi) northwest of Fayence, 36 km (22 mi) northwest of Cannes.*

With its ruined château and ramparts, fountains, flowers, and sunny maze of steeply raked cobblestone streets that suddenly break open over valley views, this is a charming old village that still smacks of the Côte d'Azur. Its church—a Renaissance remake of an 11th-century structure—is the best spot from which to admire the panorama; it's worth a pause to take in the musty Latin atmosphere. There are old-style, competitive bakers here, and an active café life on a miniature scale. The French opera composer Gounod and the surrealist Max Ernst were regulars in Seillans; Ernst retired here.

Just east of town on the Route de Fayence is the Romanesque chapel **Notre-Dame-de-l'Ormeau,** which contains a remarkable altarpiece dating from the 16th century. Sculpted portraits of the wise men and shepherds adoring the Christ child, strikingly real in emotion and gesture, contrast sharply with the simple ex-votos that pepper the walls. ⊠ *Rte. de Fayence* ☉ *Sun. 10:30–6.*

Where to Eat & Stay

★ $ ✕ **La Chirane.** With a handful of parasoled tables perched on the sidewalk high over the Old Town slopes, this small inn looks like any old tourist stop at first glance. But crisp, delicious pizzas, light raviolis, a hefty herring gratin, subtle stewed salt cod, and beef or boar daubes (stews), the latter available during hunting season, show that this little restaurant is worth the stop. Homemade tarts and *omelette norvégienne* (baked alaska) round out an easy, pleasant meal à la Provençal. There's live jazz some Saturday nights. ⊠ *4 rue de l'Hospice* ☎ *04–94–76–96–20* ▤ *MC, V* ⊘ *No lunch Wed. and Nov.–mid-Dec., Jan.–mid-Mar.*

★ $-$$ ✕🖭 **Hôtel des Deux Rocs.** Picture a tiny square with a trickling fountain, venerable plane trees, green valley views, and two massive rocks posing, sculpturelike, where they fell aeons ago. This is a magical place for a hotel. It's almost gilding the lily that the hotel should be small and personal to the point of eccentricity. From the fireplace in the salon to the bright, mixed fabrics in the rooms, to the dainty breakfast, this property exudes Provençal style. All bathrooms have been smartened up with fresh tile and updated fixtures. Ask for Room 10, which has corner views of the idyllic place. Chef Bruno Germanaz whips up hearty dishes such as puff pastry tart with leeks and bacon, wild mushroom terrine with porcini cream, and barbecued meats—for dessert, indulge in the Australian Pavlova (meringue with whipped cream and fruit). You can dine in the romantic stone-and-beam restaurant or under the trees by the fountain. ⊠ *Pl. Font d'Amont, 83440* ☎ *04–94–76–87–32* 🖷 *04–94–76–88–68* ➲ *14 rooms* ⟐ *Restaurant, bar, some pets allowed; no a/c, no room TVs* ▤ *MC, V.*

Bargemon

❷❶ *13 km (8 mi) west of Seillans, 25 km (15½ mi) northeast of Draguignan, 49 km (30 mi) northwest of Cannes.*

By the time you reach this hill village, you'll feel the Côte d'Azur dropping away and the highland winds curling over the mountains: Suddenly you'll stop craving bouillabaisse and start thinking about trout. A few mimosas and orange trees remain, but this is a mountain town, a cold stone bastion of medieval strength surrounded by traces of ramparts. Its ruined château, cobbled streets, and stone arches are softened by the fountains and plane trees of its slow, picturesque modern life. Study the ex-votos and the miraculous Virgin in Notre Dame de Montaigu, just up from the central crossroads. Then

> Settle into a café or restaurant and climb the town's few back-streets, and you'll feel your blood pressure ease back.

step into the imposing Gothic portal of Église St-Etienne, built into the village walls. When your eyes adjust, search out the two exquisite angels at the main altar, sculpted by Marseille artist/architect Pierre Puget.

Where to Eat

$$ ✕ **La Taverne.** Luc and Armelle Nattas are serious about using only fresh regional products; the lamb is from the farm down the road, ditto

CLOSE UP

The Gorges Challenge

TO SEE THE GORGES DU VERDON up close and personal, instead of gawking over its precipices from the safety-railed overlooks, consider tackling the Sentier Martel. But make sure you're in shape before you test your mettle—it's no Sunday-after-lunch promenade. The famous 14 km (9 mi) stretch of the GR4 follows a steep, narrow path flanked on one side by rock wall and the other by nothingness, sometimes passing over loose rubble and sometimes over slick, mossy limestone at a 45-degree rake. And those are the easy parts. One of the trail's many engineered challenges: a series of wrought-iron ladder-stairs (240, count them if you dare) bolted deep into rock cliff and suspended over the chasm below. The grand finale: two womb-dark tunnels through shoe-deep water, one of them 2,198 feet long. Yet, if you're an experienced hiker, you'll be able to take your eyes off your feet and appreciate the magnificence of the setting, one of the grandest canyons in Europe.

Because the Verdon is regulated by two dams, you'll often be confronted with not-so-comforting signs showing a human stick figure running for his life before a tidal wave. This is to warn you to stick to the trail and not to linger on the low, beachlike riverbed when the water is low, as it could rise suddenly at any moment. If you choose to peel off your socks and boots and wade during a much-needed break, keep an escape route in mind. Wandering in to drape yourself over a rock for a quick nap is not recommended, as you may wake to find your retreat cut off by rising, roiling waters. The trail itself stays above the danger line at all times, sometimes so well above it that the risk of drowning seems preferable to the risk of plunging 500 feet into the void.

The Sentier Martel takes anywhere from six to nine hours to complete. Wear good shoes with firm ankle support and textured soles. Carry plenty of water and a flashlight with good batteries; you won't be able to grope your way through the tunnels without it. Dogs and most children under six won't be able to handle the metal ladders. Follow the red-and-white GR marker, and don't leave the trail. You can arrange a taxi pickup at Point Sublime based on a rough estimate of your own abilities, or leave a car at the final destination and ask a taxi to carry you to your take-off point. Most people depart from the Chalet de La Maline, striking out on the long descent and then working their way back up gradually to the Couloir du Samson and the Point Sublime.

The spelunker/explorer Edouard Martel (1859–1938) couldn't arrange a taxi, but first penetrated the Gorges in 1896 with a canvas canoe, an assistant, and two local trout fishermen. Despite repeated attempts, he didn't manage to negotiate the full canyon's length until 1905.

It was in the 1930s that the Touring Club blasted fire-escape-style ladders and catwalks along the precarious rock walls, and drilled two tunnels through solid stone. They added occasional rope railings and steps, and buttressed the trail with rock supports. But much of it crosses rubble slides that shift and change with the years, and steady maintenance can't keep natural erosion from changing the limestone profile over the years. That's why it remains a challenge worthy of its intrepid namesake.

the fresh cheese served with local sweet jams. It's the subtle details that count in this simple restaurant with a stone facade and prominent beams; salads may be seasoned with a local olive oil that's been flavored with blood oranges, the vinegar infused with fig, even the aperitifs come from down the road and are well worth the taste. There are tables under the large plane trees where you can listen to the splashing fountain and chiming church tower as you enjoy the real flavors of Provence. ⊠ *Pl. Philippe-Chauvier* ☎ *04–94–76–62–19* ☰ *MC, V* ⊘ *Closed Mon. Nov. 15–Mar. 15.*

Trigance

❷ *38 km (26 mi) northwest of Bargemon, 90 km (56 mi) northwest of Cannes.*

With a handful of gray-stone houses and a few artists' studios, this infinitesimal hill village between Comps-sur-Artuby and the Gorges du Verdon wouldn't merit more than a glance from the road but for its extraordinary medieval **Château de Trigance.** The castle was restored with a free hand and open purse by Jean-Claude Thomas, who bought it in 1971 and had it rebuilt stone by stone; it functions as a hotel-restaurant today.

Where to Eat & Stay

$$–$$$ ✕▣ **Château de Trigance.** Here's a novelty for honeymooners and romantics: to stay in a restored medieval castle perched on a hilltop in the isolated countryside. Rooms are decked out in a sort of romantic medieval style, with *baldaquin* (four-poster) canopied beds and severe oak furniture. For even more of a fairy-tale feeling, reserve the perfectly round tower room. Dine under a 10th-century stone barrel vault guarded by suits of armor and fleurs-de-lis, or on the broad terrace, wrapped by crenellated walls. The restaurant serves a hefty classic cuisine of smoked duck, oysters, quail, and lamb. It's a Relais & Château property but not in its luxury class—after all, it's hard to find good serfs these days. ⊠ *Off D955, 83840* ☎*04–94–76–91–18* 🖨*04–94–85–68–99* ⊕*www.chateau-de-trigance.fr* 🛏 *8 rooms, 2 apartments* ⚐ *Restaurant, bar, cable TV, in-room data ports, some pets allowed; no a/c* ☰ *AE, DC, MC, V* ⊘ *Closed Nov.–Mar.*

La Palud-sur-Verdon

❷ *14 km (9 mi) northwest of Trigance, 27 km (17 mi) southeast of Moustiers.*

Though several towns bill themselves as *the* gateway to the Gorges du Verdon, this unassuming village stands in its center, on a plateau just north of the gorge's vertiginous drop (to gain the Gorges's southern flank, enter from the elegant village of Moustiers, *below*). It's a hikers' and climbers' town, and—as the Germans and Dutch are more *sportif* than the French—has an international feel. You'll see more beards and Volkswagen vans here than anywhere in France, and you'll probably share a café terrace with backpackers clad in boots and fleece easing off a load of ropes, picks, and cleats. The friendly grocery store sells flashlights and *camping gaz* (cooking propane), and the central intersection flaunts six public telephones, the better to call a taxi to carry you to your hiking departure point.

★ You are here for one reason only: to explore the extraordinary **Gorges du Verdon**, also known as—with only slight exaggeration over another, more famous version—the Grand Canyon. Through the aeons the jewel-green torrent of the Verdon River has chiseled away the limestone plateau and gouged a spectacular gorge lined with steep white cliffs and sloping rock falls carpeted with green forest. The jagged rock bluffs, roaring water, and dense wild boxwood create a savage world of genuinely awe-inspiring beauty, whether viewed from dozens of cliff-top overlooks or explored from the wilderness below.

If you're driving from La Palud, follow the dramatic **Route des Crêtes** circuit (D23), a white-knuckle cliff-hanger not for the faint of heart. When you approach and leave La Palud, you'll do it via D952 between Castellane and Moustiers, with several breathtaking overlooks. The best of these is the **Point Sublime,** at the east end; leave your car by the hotel-restaurant and walk to the edge, holding tight to dogs and children—that's a 2,834 foot drop to the bottom.

If you want to hike, there are several trails that converge in this prime territory. The most spectacular is the branch of the GR4 that follows the bed of the canyon itself, along the **Sentier Martel.** This dramatic trail, beginning at the Chalet de la Maline and ending at the Point Sublime, was created in the 1930s by the Touring-Club de France and named for one of the gorge's first explorers (⇨ Close-Up: The Gorges Challenge, *above*). Easier circuits leave from the Point Sublime on *sentiers de découverte* (trails with commentary) into the gorge known as Couloir Samson.

Where to Eat & Stay

¢–$ ✕🛏 **Le Perroquet Vert.** In a restored house on La Palud's only street, friendly *aventuriers* Michel and Sabine Jordan have created this lovely little sports store-cum-restaurant-cum-B&B complex. Above their sports-equipment shop they have a cozy little restaurant that serves simple, fresh regional dishes with fish brought in from coastal markets, soup with tiny *favouilles* (coastal crabs), basil ravioli, and fresh goat cheese from up the road. They also have rooms to rent of the simple, rustic variety: a room with a large double bed and a duplex with a double bed and three single beds. There is also a small house available for larger families or groups. Don't expect a TV, but rooms are furnished with a lot of good books. To give you an idea of how healthy, natural, and good for you all this is, all rooms are no smoking, virtually unheard of in France, and the yogurt served in the morning is homemade. ⊠ *Rue Grande, 04120* 🕾 *04–92–77–33–39* ⊕ *www.leperroquetvert.com* ↻ *1 room, 1 duplex, 1 house* ⚘ *Restaurant, minibars; no room TVs, no a/c* ☐ *AE, MC, V* ☺ *Closed Nov.–Mar.* �I◯I *BP.*

Moustiers-Ste-Marie

❷ *10 km (7 mi) northwest of La Palud-sur-Verdon.*

Fodor'sChoice
★   At the edge of all this epic wilderness, it's a bit of a shock to find this picture-perfect village tucked into a spectacular cleft in vertical cliffs,

its bluffs laced with bridges, draped with medieval stone houses, and crowned with church steeples. The Verdon gushes out of the rock at the village's heart, and between the two massive rocks that tower over the ensemble, a star swings suspended from a chain.

To most, the name *Moustiers* means faïence, the fine glazed earthenware that has been produced here since the 17th century, when a monk brought in the secret of enamel glazes from Faenza in Umbria. Its brilliant white finish caught the world's fancy, especially when the fashionable grotesques of Jean Berain, decorator to Louis XIV, were imitated and produced in exquisite detail. A colony of ceramists still creates Moustiers faïence today, from large commercial producers to independent artisans. The small but excellent **Musée de la Faïence** has concise audiovisual explanations of the craft and displays a chronology of fine pieces. It is currently housed in a pretty 18th-century *hôtel particulier* (private mansion) with a lovely *salle de mariage* (wedding hall) lined with painted canvas. ⊠ *Pl. du Tricentenaire* ☎ *04–92–74–61–64* ☒ *€2* ☉ *Apr.–Oct., Wed.–Mon. 9–noon and 2–6; Nov.–Dec. and Feb.–Mar., weekends 2–6.*

With all the faïence around, you may end up keeping your nose to the shop windows, where every form (and every quality) of the Moustiers product is for sale. But the walk through town is pretty, too, though it's little more than a double loop along the rushing stream, over a bridge or two, and a peek into the early Gothic church, with its sliver windows in pre-Raphaelite hues.

Moustiers was founded as a monastery in the 5th century, but it was in the Middle Ages that the **Chapelle Notre-Dame-de-Beauvoir** (first known as d'Entreroches, or "between rocks") became an important pilgrimage site. You can still climb the steep cobbled switchbacks, along with pilgrims, passing modern stations-of-the-cross panels in Moustiers faïence. From the porch of the 12th-century church, remodeled in the 16th century, you can look over the roofs of the village to the green valley, a patchwork of olive groves and red-tiled farmhouse roofs. The forefather of the star that swings in the wind over the village was first hung, it is said, by a crusader grateful for his release from Saracen prison.

★ Despite its civilized airs, Moustiers is another gateway to the Gorges du Verdon, providing the best access to the southern bank and the famous drive along D71 called the **Route de la Corniche Sublime.** (You may also approach from the southeast at Comps-sur-Artuby.) Breathtaking views over withering drop-offs punctuate this vertiginous road that's just wide enough for two cars if you all hold your breath. The best of the vistas is called the **Balcons de la Mescla,** with viewpoints built into the cliff face overlooking the torrential whirlpool where the Verdon and Artuby combine.

Where to Eat & Stay

$$$$ ✕◩ **La Bastide de Moustiers.** Gourmands from around the world flock to
Fodor'sChoice this lovely 17th-century *bastide* (country house) transformed by Alain
★ Ducasse into a luxury country retreat surrounded by olive and chestnut trees, cypress, lavender, and trellises filled with the blooms of creeping rose bushes. Individually decorated rooms with evocative names such as *Sun-*

flower, Pumpkin, and *Buttercup*—some with private terrace, some that lead directly into the park—are fresh and comfortable, an unpretentious mixture of antiques and country prints. Young Ducasse protégé Vincent Maillard plans his multicourse menus daily according to nature's abundance, keeping in mind the ripeness of the produce in the vegetable garden and which fresh herbs in the herb garden marry best with the fowl just brought in that morning. It's hard to know which to admire more: the view over the hills from the restaurant terrace or the food itself, such as boned and stuffed rabbit, a cocotte (cast-iron pot) of spring vegetables, and roast pigeon with small artichokes, foie gras, and croutons. Cooking classes can be arranged, as can hot-air balloon rides over the region. Book well in advance, for here no season is low season. ✉ *Chemin de Quinson, 04360* ☎ *04–92–70–47–47* 📠 *04–92–70–47–48* ⊕ *www.bastide-moustiers.com* 🛏️ *6 rooms, 6 suites* ♿ *Restaurant, in-room safes, minibars, cable TV, pool, hot tub, in-room data ports* ▭ *AE, DC, MC, V.*

★ **$$–$$$** 🏨 **La Bouscatière.** Only the most discreet little sign indicates the presence of this exceptional bed-and-breakfast, whose different levels are built down into the rock rather than upwards, offering views of the waterfall and unlikely little terraces (one is accessed through the bathroom). The new owner once worked as a chef on yachts, and his kitchen is so inviting that guests quickly find themselves pitching in when he prepares meals for guests (€30). Most of the furniture is 18th century to match the house, and the cooking is rustic and generous: lamb with honey and rosemary, veal with morel mushroom sauce. ✉ *Chemin Marcel Provence, 04360* ☎ *04–92–74–67–67* 📠 *04–92–74–65–72* ⊕ *www.labouscatiere.com* 🛏️ *5 rooms* ♿ *Dining room, cable TV, Internet room* ▭ *AE, DC, MC, V* ❙◎❙ *BP.*

$$–$$$ 🏨 **La Ferme Rose.** This pretty pink farmhouse, hidden in verdure in a valley outside the village, looks out on Moustier's cliff-top Old Town. Wood-beamed rooms are simply furnished with an easygoing mix of brocante finds and new beds, the bathrooms charmingly tiled. Ask about the large room on the first floor with the king-size bed and its own terrace. The bar downstairs, where you can relax and have your evening aperitif, came from a famous bistro in Marseille and dates from the 1930s. ✉ *04360 Moustiers-Ste-Croix* ☎ *04–92–74–69–47* 📠 *04–92–74–60–76* ⊕ *www.lafermerose.fr.fm* 🛏️ *12 rooms* ♿ *Bar, cable TV, some pets allowed* ▭ *AE, MC, V* ☾ *Closed Nov. 16–Dec. 20.*

$–$$ 🏨 **Le Baldaquin.** This tiny, eccentric little hotel is in a solid 17th-century bastide in Moustiers's old center. Uncharming rooms have frilly cream sateen coverlets on the large double beds and splashes of light blue here and there. They are, however, clean and tidy. As far as decoration goes, the bathrooms fare much better, with brightly decorated all-tile baths. The light and views are serene, and you can hear the water trickling in the *lavoir* (stone laundry fountain) across the street. One room looks out onto roofs and the hill above, another the tiny closed courtyard with a dense cluster of lilacs. Breakfast is served in a charming little kitchen-bar with a whitewashed fireplace. ✉ *Pl. Clérissy, 04360* 📠 *04–92–74–67–28* ☎ *06–08–06–49–95 mobile* 🛏️ *6 rooms* ♿ *Cable TV, in-room data ports; no a/c* ▭ *AE, MC, V* ☾ *Closed Nov.*

Shopping

At **L'Atelier Soleil** (⊠ Chemin Marcel Provence ☎ 04–92–74–63–05 ⊕ www.soleil-deux.fr), next to the Bastide de Moustiers, second-generation potter Franck Scherer makes custom-made plates for Alain Ducasse's auberges—you can visit the workshop and buy pieces with tiny flaws at a reduced price. If you like pottery that's out of the ordinary, seek out the boutique **La Ferme de Milan** (⊠ Rue de la Bourgade ☎ 04–92–77–56–76), where you'll find checkered, polka-dotted, and whimsical butterfly motifs. Hidden away off the main drag is **Saveurs et Nature** (⊠ Rue Scipion ☎ 04–92–74–64–48), where you can brace yourself for the hike up to the town cathedral with a freshly made juice or stock up on local beer, honey, and jam.

4

Aups

㉕ *23 km (14 mi) south of Moustiers.*

Not perched, but rather nestled artfully in a valley of olive groves under imposing pine-covered hills, this village (pronounced *ohpss*) spills in a graceful delta of towers, campaniles, and tile-roofed cubes. Its Old Town, above the modern section, echoes with trickling fountains, and the square, under heavy plane trees, remains undisturbed by tourism. Many noble Old Town houses remain ungentrified, and the backstreets are lined with unpretentious cafés. It has ruins, too, of a 12th-century château-fort with traces of the medieval ramparts that once surrounded it. Aups's claim to fame is the truffle, rooted up from the surrounding forests and sold in a Thursday market from November through April.

Cotignac

㉖ *11 km (7 mi) southwest of Aups, 66 km (41 mi) northwest of St-Raphaël.*

The light changing on the stone bluff, revealing pockets of ancient stairs and dwellings tucked into shadowy hollows, gives this old mountain town, nestled at the foot of a dramatic rock cliff crowned by two medieval towers, a Turner-esque quality. Life in the Old Town below plays out in tones of tinted sepia, in the quiet Renaissance center and along the lazy, deep-shaded Cours Gambetta, where painted storefronts and cafés stand oblivious to time.

Though it's possible to make a running tour of hill villages, popping into churches, perusing the galleries, and drinking a quick one on the squares, Cotignac is a place to stop, stay, listen, and live—even briefly—the rhythm of a Provençal day. It is the place to drink a pastis slowly and practice your French with the couple at the neighboring table; they're likely to live here—and to welcome your attempts. The butcher is proud of his lamb, the bakers compete for your business, and the very few galleries maintain a low profile.

Take time to stroll through the Old Town, an inner sanctum within Baroque gates. On the Place de la Mairie, noble houses from the 16th and 17th centuries encircle a fountain and a lovely ironwork bell tower.

Farther in, Rue Clastre is flanked by medieval houses with shutters painted in muted hues.

If you need a concrete goal, climb up the cliff face into one of the mysterious grottoes; these ancient hollows have served as refuges and lookouts for centuries. From this vantage point you can look down over the plane trees, elms, and red roofs of the otherworldly town.

OFF THE BEATEN PATH

CHÂTEAU D'ENTRECASTEAUX – This long, lean château, on the pretty country roads outside Cotignac (D50 and D31), is a jewel of a sight that offers a change from the stocky medieval style in neighboring villages and deserves a side trip. Built into a forested rock wall, it was first constructed in the 9th century as a fortress, then expanded into its Italian Baroque style in the 16th century. There are vaulted galleries, a grand kitchen and cooks' apartments, a lavoir, and even a small classical garden designed by Le Nôtre (of Versailles fame; it's owned by the commune). The music room is a Baroque gem and in summer may host concerts. At press time, a complete restoration of the Oriental suites was in the works. The most recent owner, Alain Gayral, lives on-site and has been restoring and furnishing it in period-style piece by piece, including paintings, tapestries, and 17th-century furniture. Although the gardens are public, you'll need to take a tour to see the inside of the château and you must phone for a reservation. Nearby there's also a tiny Old Town with a fortified church. ☎ 04-94-04-43-95 🖃 Château: €7; garden: free ⊙ Easter–Nov: garden, daily sunrise–sunset; château, guided tours only.

Where to Stay

★ $ 🖻 **Marie et le Roy.** Tucked away in Cotignac's Old Town, this newly opened *maison d'hôtes* is surprisingly stylish, even hip (a word not often associated with Provençal villages). Eric and Christine greet guests with a friendly aperitif on their rooftop terrace before proudly showing the art displayed in the house (whose main floor hosts temporary exhibitions) and the individually decorated rooms, each of which benefits from Christine's talents as a set designer. Artfully weathered walls, a handpainted headboard, an antique bathtub and another made of cement—this is no ordinary B&B. Homey meals, the domain of Eric, are served either in the kitchen or on the terrace. ⊠ *7 rue Gabriel Philis, 83570* ☎ *04-94-77-74-41* 🖶 *04-94-77-74-41* ⊕ *www.marieetleroy.com* ⏎ *4 rooms* ⚒ *Internet room; no a/c in some rooms, no room phones, TV on request* ⏐⊙⏐ *BP.*

Abbaye du Thoronet

㉗ *13 km (8 mi) southeast of Cotignac.*

This 12th-century Cistercian abbey, an extraordinary example of Romanesque architecture, stands in an austere, isolated valley. The purity of the structure (or severity, if you will) was a reaction in its day to the luxurious extravagance of the abbey Cluny in Burgundy. Study the dense stonework and almost total absence of wooden support, and admire the near-perfect symmetry of the church's ground plan and its gentle forays into Gothic style. The cloister is stark and stolid compared to the delicate cloisters of Fréjus and Arles. ☎ 04-94-60-43-90 💷 €5.50 🕙 Apr.–Sept., Mon.–Sat. 9–7, Sun. 9–noon and 2–7 (3–7 on Catholic holidays); Oct.–Mar., Mon.–Sat. 9:30–1 and 2–5, Sun. 10–noon and 2–5.

WESTERN CÔTE D'AZUR ESSENTIALS

To research prices, get advice from other travelers, and book travel arrangements, visit www.fodors.com.

Transportation

If traveling extensively by public transportation, be sure to load up on information (schedules, the best taxi-for-call companies, etc.) upon arriving at the ticket counter or help desk of the bigger hub stations in the area, such as St-Raphael and Fréjus.

BY BOAT

Considering the congestion buses and cars confront on the road to St-Tropez, the best way to get to that resort is to train to St-Raphaël, then hop on one of the four boats each day (between April and October) that leave from the Gare Maritime de St-Raphaël on Rue Pierre-Auble. The trip take about an hour and costs €9. Transports Maritimes MMG also offers a shuttleboat linking St-Tropez and Ste-Maxime April to October; tickets are €6 and the ride is a half-hour. Once in St-Tropez, stay on the water for a one-hour boat ride tour offered by MMG of the Baie des Cannebiers (nicknamed the "Bay of Stars") to see some celebrity villas.

🚢 Boat Travel Information **Transports Maritimes MMG** ✉ Quai L.-Condroyer, Ste-Maxime ☎ 04-94-96-51-00. **Transports Maritimes Raphaelois** ✉ St-Raphaël ☎ 04-94-95-17-46.

BY BUS

Local buses cover a network of routes along the coast and stop at many out-of-the-way places that can't be reached by train. Timetables are available from tourist offices, train stations, and local bus stations (*gares routières*). Ask for information on commercial bus excursions, too; there are several day-trip tours out of Fréjus and St-Raphaël into the more popular backcountry towns.

St-Tropez's Gare Routière (bus station) is located on Ave. du Général de Gaulle and has bus routes run by Sodetrav to/from St-Raphaël (€9, 1½ hrs, ten daily), the town with the nearest railway station, with stops in Grimaud and Port Grimaud, Ste-Maxime, and Fréjus (€9, 1 hr). Note that in high season, the traffic jam to St-Tropez can lead to 2-plus hour bus rides, so if you arrive in St-Raphaël, it may be best to hop on the shuttle boats that connect the two ports (see By Boat, below). Buses also link up with Ramatuelle and Gassin (both are €4, 25 minutes, 3 daily in peak season). Buses also route over to Toulon (€17, 2½ hrs). St. Raphaël's bus station is on Avenue Victor Hugo next to the train station and has buses linking up with St-Tropez (via Grimaud and Ste-Maxime, €9, 2 hrs), some towns in the Haut Var, and selected stops along the coastal Corniche de l'Estérel, which is also covered by RafaelBus. Fréjus's bus station is on Place Paul-Vernet and Estérel buses have routes to St-Tropez. Some Haut Var towns are serviced by Les Rapides Varois, departing from the train stations at Les Arcs and Draguignan.

🚌 Bus Travel Information **Estérel-Forum Autocars** ☎ 04-94-53-78-46. **RafaelBus** ☎ 04-94-83-87-63. **Les Rapides Varois** ☎ 04-94-47-05-05. **Sodetrav** ☎ 0825/000-650 ⊕ www.sodetrav.fr/.

BY CAR

A8 provides swift, easy access to Fréjus and other towns along the coast. To reach resorts along the Estérel, you must follow the coastal highway N98 east; to get to St-Tropez and the resorts at the foot of the Massif des Maures, follow N98 southwest from Fréjus. To explore the hill towns and the Gorges du Verdon, slow and scenic roads lead north and west from Fréjus and Cannes, including the famous Route Napoléon (D85).

Sailing from Fréjus and St-Raphaël toward Cannes is a breeze on A8, but N98, which connects you to coastal resorts in between, can be extremely slow, though scenic. To the north and east of this region, you break into the country, and the roads are small, pokey, and pretty. If you want to explore any hill towns in depth and at will, a car is indispensable.

BY TRAIN

The main rail crossroads from points north and west are at Fréjus's main station on Rue Martin-Bidoure and St-Raphaël's Gare de St-Raphaël on Rue Waldeck-Rousseau), where the rail route begins its scenic crawl along the coast to Italy, stopping in La Napoule and Cannes. St-Raphaël is the main train hub, on the coastal rail line between Menton and Marseille (it's about 2 hrs from the latter by rail, with hourly trains costing €20). The resort port of Mandelieu–La Napoule is on the main rail line between St-Raphaël and Cannes. There is no rail access to St-Tropez; St-Raphaël and Fréjus are the nearest stops. The train station nearest the Haut Var and the Gorges du Verdon is at Les Arcs, below Draguignan. From there you have to rent a car or take local buses offered by Les Rapides Varois into the hills. The scenic little Chemin de Fer de Provence leads from Nice to Digne and makes a local stop at St-André-les-Alpes, about 20 km (12 mi) north of Castellane, the eastern gateway to the Gorges du Verdon.

The private (it's owned by Vivendi) Provence Railroad network follows the coast from St-Raphaël to Mandelieu, stopping at the coastal resorts. For further sightseeing you have to resort to renting a car or taking a bus excursion.

🚆 Train Information **SNCF** ☎ 08-36-35-35-35 ⊕ www.ter-sncf.com/uk/paca. **TGV** ☎ 877/2TGVMED ⊕ www.tgv.com. **Chemin de Fer de Provence** (Provence Railroad) ✉ 4 rue Alfred Binet, 06100 Nice ☎ 04-97-03-80-80 ⊕ www.trainprovence.com.

Contacts & Resources

CAR RENTAL

If you are planning to rent a car in France, your best bet is to plan ahead by using a national agency you trust from home; they'll not only get you the best rates, they'll save you a lot of hassle. You can, of course, rent a car when you arrive at the airport in Nice, but after a long flight, wouldn't you rather just sign on the dotted line and pick up your car without the long wait? If you take the train to the coast, you'll probably stop in St-Raphaël, where you can always rent a car from a local agency, but beware, the rates will be high.

🚗 Car Rental Agencies **Avis** ☒ 190 pl. Pierre Coullet ☎ 04-94-95-60-42. **Budget** ☒ 40 rue Waldeck ☎ 04-94-82-24-44. **Europcar** ☒ 54 pl. Pierre Coullet ☎ 04-94-95-56-87. **Hertz** ☒ 32 rue Waldeck ☎ 04-94-95-48-68.

EMERGENCIES

For basic information, see this section in the Smart Travel Tips chapter. In most cases, contact the town Comissariat de Police or Gendarmerie.

🚗 Emergencies **Police** ☒ Rue François Sibilli St-Tropez ☎ 17. **Gendarmerie** ☒ Rue de Triberg Fréjus ☎ 17.

INTERNET & MAIL

In smaller towns, ask your hotel concierge if there are any Internet cafés nearby.

🚗 Internet & Mail Information **Kreatik Café** ☒ 17 av. du Général Leclerc, St-Tropez ☎ 04-94-97-40-61. **Cyber Bureau** ☒ 123 rue Waldeck-Rousseau, St-Raphaël ☎ 04-94-95-29-36. **La Poste main post office** ☒ 264 av. Aristide Briand, Fréjus. **La Poste main post office** ☒ Place Celli, St-Tropez.

VISITOR INFORMATION

For information on travel within the Var region—St-Tropez to La Napoule—write to the Comité Départemental du Tourisme du Var. For Cannes and environs, write to the Comité Regional du Tourisme Riviera Côte d'Azur. For the Haute-Provence region between Moustiers and Manosque, contact the Comité Départemental du Tourisme des Alpes de Haute Provence. For the Verdon, contact Verdon Office du Tourisme.

🚗 Local Tourist Offices **Comité Départemental du Tourisme du Var** ☒ 1 bd. Maréchal Foch, 83300 Draguignan ☎ 04-94-50-55-50 🖷 04-94-50-55-51 ⊕ www.tourismevar.com. **Comité Départemental du Tourisme des Alpes de Haute Provence** ☒ 19 rue du Dr. Honnorat, B.P. 170, 04005 Digne-les-Bains ☎ 04-92-31-57-29 🖷 04-92-32-24-84 ⊕ www.alpes-haute-provence.com. **Comité Regional du Tourisme Riviera Côte d'Azur** ☒ 55 promenade des Anglais, B.P. 1602, Nice Cedex 06011 ☎ 04-93-37-78-78 ⊕ www.guideriviera.com. **Fayence** ☒ Pl. Léon-Roux, 83440 Fayence ☎ 04-94-76-20-08 🖷 04-94-84-71-86 ⊕ www.mairedefayence.com. **Fréjus** ☒ 325 rue Jean-Jaurès, B.P. 8, 83601 Fréjus ☎ 04-94-51-83-83 🖷 04-94-51-00-26 ⊕ www.ville-frejus.fr. **Mandelieu-La Napoule** ☒ 340 av. Jean-Monnet, 06210 Mandelieu-La Napoule ☎ 04-92-97-99-27 🖷 04-92-97-99-57 ⊕ www.ot-mandelieu.fr. **Moustiers** ☒ Hôtel-Dieu, 04350 Moustiers ☎ 04-92-74-67-84 🖷 04-92-74-60-65 ⊕ www.ville-moustiers-sainte-marie.fr. **St-Raphaël** ☒ Rue Waldeck-Rousseau, 83700 St-Raphaël ☎ 04-94-19-52-52 🖷 04-94-83-85-40 ⊕ www.saint-raphael.com. **St-Tropez** ☒ Quai Jean-Jaurès, B.P. 183, F-83992 St-Tropez ☎ 04-94-97-45-21 🖷 04-94-97-82-66 ⊕ www.ot-saint-tropez.com. **Verdon Office de Tourisme** ☒ Rue Nationale, 04120 Castellane ☎ 04-92-83-61-14 🖷 04-92-83-76-89.

The Feisty Flora of Provence

ALTHOUGH THE HOTHOUSE CRESCENT of the Côte d'Azur blooms extravagantly with palm and lemon trees and jungle flowers, the rest of Provence has a flora all its own—austere, hardy, and aromatic. The intense heat of the summer sun alternates with the razor-sharp winds of the mistral—a freight train of air blasting down the Rhône Valley. The vegetation battens down and lies low, turning thick, tiny, waxy leaves toward the assault of heat and wind—as if to say, the less surface exposed, the better. Boxwood and holly and dwarf scrub oak cling to the hillsides. Rosemary and lavender send out leaves matchstick thin and wrap themselves in woody bark dense with aromatic resin. Eucalyptus flutters long ribbon strips of aromatic leaves, and olive trees hang clusters of silver ovals, their twisted trunks staked deep into the earth with broad, strong roots. The cork oak develops a thick bark so resistant and watertight it's harvested in sheets. And the pines define the landscape, the tall black-green silhouettes of the *pin d'alep* (a species of Mediterranean pine) tortured into random forms, the mushroom-shape parasol pine spreading a thick, black dome over the earth.

Yet the plane tree is a paradox. Although its brothers tuck in like sumo wrestlers against heat and wind, these *grandes dames* spread glorious branches wide over city squares, their leaves broad and heavy as palms, creating their own deep shade in summer, then shedding all to let in the gentle winter sun.

But the cypress is the symbol of Provence, its tall evergreen spears flanking mansion and *mas* (farmhouse) and symbolizing hospitality. Tradition has it that one cypress symbolizes the proffering of a glass of water to passersby; two means water and a meal; and three means a night's sleep in the barn.

These days, the beautiful flora of Provence and the Côte d'Azur is under assault; brush fires (sometimes set by landowners hoping to develop natural preserves for real estate purposes) have decimated some regions of the coastland in recent years. Happily, notice has been taken, and not only by the international press. Scenes of barefoot, free-spirited environmentalists chanting "Save the Earth" is not what first comes to mind when you think of Cannes, but, believe it or not, the glitzy Riviera resort town has given birth to its own brand of environmentalism.

Seven years ago, for two weeks at the end of May, the city first hosted the Rencontres Nationales de l'Environnement (National Environmental Conference), defying its image of overindulgence. While cynics may be quick to accuse Cannes of jumping on the bandwagon of one of today's trendiest issues, actions do speak for themselves: The city assembled 2,000 students to plant trees and has put money and time into environmental education workshops. These days, the annual conference has moved on—the last was held in Nîmes. But everyone has this on their minds, so don't throw away your bottles anywhere in the south of France.

Nice & the Eastern Côte d'Azur

CANNES, ANTIBES, MONACO & THE HILL TOWNS

Casino, Monte-Carlo, Monaco

WORD OF MOUTH

"In Nice, find a café, drink some wine, wander, get some sun, have a nice dinner, drink more wine, sleep. Repeat for maximum effect."
—tskobo

"You must go to the Villa Ephrussi in Cap Ferrat—think the Isabella Stewart Gardner Museum times 1000, *plus* Mediterranean views."
—Mclaurie

"In Èze, the Château de la Chèvre d'Or is expensive, but worth it for the truly amazing setting—nothing beats lunch there on a sunny day."
—tulips

WELCOME TO NICE & THE EASTERN CÔTE D'AZUR

Le Suquet, Cannes

TOP 5
Reasons to Go

1 **Monaco, toy kingdom:** Yes, Virginia, you can afford to visit Monte-Carlo—that is, if you avoid its casinos and head instead for its magnificent tropical gardens.

2 **Picasso & Company:** Because artists have long loved the Côte d'Azur, it is blessed with superb art museums, including the Fondation Maeght in St-Paul and the Musée Picasso in Antibes.

3 **Èze, island in the sky:** The most perfectly perched of the coast's *villages perchés*, Èze has some of the most breathtaking views this side of a NASA space capsule.

4 **Nice, Queen of the Riviera:** With its bonbon-colored palaces, blue Baie des Anges, time-stained Old Town, and Musée Matisse, this is one of France's most colorful cities.

5 **Sunkissed Cap d'Antibes:** Bordering well-hidden mansions and zillion-dollar hotels, the Sentier Tirepoil is a spectacular footpath along the sea.

St. Paul, Vence & Hill-towns. High in the hills overlooking Nice are the medieval walled villages of **St-Paul** and **Vence**, invaded by waves of artists in the 20th century. Today, you can hardly turn around without bumping into a Calder mobile, and top sights include the famous inn La Colombe d'Or and Matisse's sublime Chapelle du Rosaire.

Cannes. Conspicuous consumption, glamorous fanfare, and a host of wanna-bes characterize the celluloid city of **Cannes** when its May film fest turns it into a global frat party. But the Louis Vuitton set enjoys this city year-round.

Olive-oil tasting

Getting Oriented

Few places in the world have the same pull on the imagination as this stretch of France's fabled Riviera (the Côte d'Azur to the French). Little or no introduction is needed for the ooo-la-la opulence of St-Jean-Cap-Ferrat, the palm-tree-lined promenades of Nice, or the art villages of St-Paul and Vence. But as you get to know this region—which stretches from Cannes to the Italian border—you'll learn it is a land of contrasts and surprises.

5

ITALY

Menton

Peillon

Roquebrune-Cap-Martin

ALPES MARITIMES

La Turbie

Monte-Carlo

Èze

MONACO

Beaulieu

Golfe de St-Hospice

Villefranche-sur-Mer

Nice

St-Jean-Cap-Ferrat

Cagnes-sur-Mer

Baie des Anges

Mediterranean Sea

Monaco and the Corniche Resorts. The 24-karat sun shines most brightly on the fabled glamour ports of **Villefranche-sur-Mer, Beaulieu,** and **St-Jean-Cap-Ferrat**. To the east of glittering Monaco lies **Menton**, an enchanting Italianate resort where winters are so mild that lemon trees bloom in January.

Nice. Walking along the seaside **Promenade des Anglais** is one of the iconic Riviera experiences. Add in top-notch museums, a charming old quarter, scads of ethnic restaurants, and a raging nightlife, and Nice is a must-do.

St-Jean-Cap-Ferrat, Yacht Harbor

Updated by
Rosa Jackson

WITH THE ALPS AND PRE-ALPS playing bodyguard against inland winds, and the sultry Mediterranean warming the sea breezes, the eastern slice of the Côte d'Azur is pampered by a nearly tropical climate that sets it apart from the rest of France's southern coast. This is where the real glamour begins: the dreamland of azure waters and indigo sky; white villas with balustrades edging the blue horizon; evening air perfumed with jasmine and mimosa; palm trees and parasol pines silhouetted against sunsets of apricot and gold. Ideal as a Jazz Age travel poster, this area lives up to the image of the Côte d'Azur, which seems to define happiness itself in the collective mind of the world.

Thus the dream confronts modern reality. On the hills that undulate along the cerulean waters, every cliff, cranny, gully, and plain bristles with hot-pink cement-cube "villas," their balconies skewed toward the sea. Like a rosy rash, they creep and spread, outnumbering the trees and blocking each other's views. Their owners and the renters who stream southward at every school vacation—Easter, Christmas, Carnaval, and All Saints'—choke the tiered highways, and on a hot day in high summer the traffic to the beach—slow going any day—coagulates and blisters in the sun.

There has been a constant march to this prime slice of the Côte d'Azur, going back to the ancient Greeks, who sailed eastward from Marseille to market their goods to the indigenes. From the 18th-century English aristocrats, who claimed it as one vast treatment spa, to the 19th-century Russian nobles who transformed Nice into a tropical St. Petersburg, to the 20th-century American tycoons who cast themselves as sheikhs, the coast beckoned like a dreamscape, a blank slate for their whims. Like the modern vacationers who follow in their footsteps, all have left their mark: Moroccan palaces in Menton, a neo-

Vacationing on the Riviera in the summer only became fashionable after Chanel (whose first shop was on Cannes's Croisette, at No. 5, *mais naturellement*) decreed that suntans were chic in the 1920s.

Greek villa in Beaulieu, the Promenade des Anglais in Nice planted with tropical greenery, to suit English fancies—temples all to fantasy, inspired by the sensual pleasures of sun and sultry sea breezes.

The glamour of the coast, however, is merely skin deep—a veneer of luxury backed by a sharp ascent into relatively ascetic heights. True, the fantasy element spills slightly inland: Day-trippers seeking contrast have transfigured the hills behind the Baie des Anges into something of a Provençal theme park, filled with historic towns and *villages perchés* (perched villages). Towns such as Mougins, where Picasso spent his last years, and Grasse, with its factories that make perfume from the region's abundant flowers, have transformed themselves to fulfill visitors' dreams of backcountry villages, and galleries, souvenir shops, and snack stands crowd the cobblestones of Old St-Paul, Vence, and Èze.

But let's recall that most of the earliest inhabitants of this region were fishermen, and peasants who grew wheat and olives, and grapes for wine. This was not one of those lush regions of France where the living was easy. There were no palaces or gracious châteaux, only small villages, with fortifications here and there for use when Celts, Vandals, Ostrogoths, Saracens, and pirates from Algeria's Barbary Coast were on the rampage. It was only in the middle of the 19th century that a troupe of kings and queens (including Victoria and dozens of her relatives), Russian grand dukes, princelings from obscure Balkan countries, English milords, and a rabble of nouveau riche camp followers began to make prolonged visits here. They had mansions and gardens built; luxury hotels sprung up in imitation of their palaces back home. The newcomers called the coastal strip the French Riviera. The French name for it is *la Côte d'Azur,* the blue—literally, sky-blue—coast. To the French, "Riviera" refers to the Italian coast farther east.

All these rich invaders withdrew to the cooler north for the summer months. No person of quality, and above all no lady of quality, would risk getting tanned like those laboring field hands. Until World War II, in fact, many hotels *closed* at the end of May, reopening in October. Up to that time, sea bathing was shunned by all, except as a drastic medical remedy. Then came the fun revolution. In the 1920s and 1930s people began to like it hot. The peasantry of the West were now pale factory and office workers, and their new badge of leisure and pleasure became the tan that their aristocratic predecessors had so assiduously avoided. Chanel, the famous couturier, made tans the chicest of fashion "accessories." More and more hotels, restaurants, and nightclubs were built. Fun became livelier and more informal. Toplessness, and even bottomlessness, arrived on the beaches. Today, for many travelers, the Côte remains a demi-paradise.

You could drive from Cannes to the Italian border in two hours and see much of the region, so small is this renowned stretch of Mediterranean coast; the swift A8 autoroute allows you to pick and choose your stopoffs. But like the artists and nobles who paved the way before you, you will likely be seduced to linger.

Exploring Nice & the Eastern Côte d'Azur

It's easy to explore this part of the coast, and you can do it in depth without retracing your steps too often. There are parallel roads, especially along the three Corniches between Nice and Menton, that access different towns and reveal different points of view. A8, which runs parallel to the coast, makes zipping back to home base a breeze.

This region is the real heart of the Côte d'Azur. Its waterfront resorts—Cannes, Antibes, Villefranche, and Menton—draw energy from the thriving city of Nice, while jutting tropical peninsulas—Cap Ferrat, Cap Martin—frame the tiny principality of Monaco. Farther inland, medieval villages mushroom out of the nearby hills, offering refugees escaping from the coastal crowds a token taste of Old Provence. Deeper into the backcountry lies a scattering of wild, Latin-accented mountain towns, long cut off from the chic enclaves below. And backing it all,

PLEASURES & PASTIMES

FOR ART'S SAKE. Apart from the sun, 20th-century art is one of the main reasons to come to this region. Renoir, Picasso, Matisse, Chagall, Cocteau, Fernand Léger, and Raoul Dufy all left their marks here; museums devoted to their work are scattered along this section of the coast. Some of these artists threw themselves enthusiastically into the traditions of the region, decorating chapels in intensely personal styles, just as their Gothic predecessors had: Matisse painted one in Vence, Picasso in Vallauris, and Cocteau in Villefranche. Formidable collections of modern masters and contemporary works can be seen in the museums of Nice and at the Fondation Maeght, on a hilltop garden above St-Paul. For a complete run-down, see "Painting Paradise" in this chapter.

SOUVENIRS, RIVIERA STYLE. As the commercialized hilltop villages behind the eastern coast—St-Paul, Vence, and Èze—try to create Provençal atmosphere for day-trippers, the cloyingly sweet smell from the ubiquitous scented-soap shops wafts through the streets (with the exception of Peillon, whose citizens wisely voted to ban boutiques). Other souvenirs include Provençal cottons (which originated around the ancient ports of Arles and Nîmes, farther west), lavender potpourris (harvested from the hills of Haute Provence), and just about anything made of olive wood. All too familiar as these charming souvenirs may be, none of them can claim roots in the coastal region.

Perfume is more this region's forte. In Grasse, bottled scents are made from the flowers on neighboring hillsides, then funneled into industrial-looking vials in its tourist-friendly factories. Arts and crafts are another strong suit. Sculpture, glass, and contemporary art in vivid colors are sold in commercial galleries lining the streets of St-Paul and, to a lesser extent, Vence. But the place to go for artisanal products—sculptures, weavings, paintings—is Tourrettes-sur-Loup, where the artists have made a way of life for themselves on the tiny, raked backstreets of the old village.

Art glass and ceramics dominate the shops in two hill villages outside Antibes: Biot and Vallauris. Biot is where you'll find the extremely popular and sought-after colored glassware that bears its name—La Verrerie de Biot. Its pitchers, goblets, and hurricane lamps are bubbled and pleasantly heavy in form as well as heft. In Vallauris, the streets are lined with ceramicists' studios, and pottery is sold in every form, from useful (if sometimes garish) everyday pieces to works of art.

BAROQUE TO BELLE ÉPOQUE. Despite the view-hogging eyesores sprouting all over the coastal hills, the eastern Côte d'Azur retains many of the Belle Époque villas where wealthy sojourners gave their fantasies free rein. The result is a pleasurable multi-culti aggregation of Moorish-style onion domes and cupolas, Gothic pastiche, glazed-tile roofs in whimsical jewel tones, friezes in Art Nouveau mosaic, and trompe l'oeil frescoes.

These eccentric pleasure domes stand cheek by jowl with the extravagant symmetry of grand waterfront hotels and the classical rigor of broad Italian-style squares. There's Italy in the air, too, in the urban Old Towns, with dark canyonlike alleys flanked by ocher and terra-cotta walls, pastel shutters, and lines of laundry flying like medieval banners.

Baroque churches, some of extraordinary sumptuousness and extravagance of scale, anchor every town; there's one on nearly every corner in Nice's Old Town. Gothic chapels in the medieval hill towns and deep pre-Alpine valleys—such as Vence and Peillon—have a purity of form offset by rich, often simple frescoes; their precedents inspired modern masters to decorate chapels of their own.

LES PLAGES. Despite its reputation as a beach paradise, the eastern Côte d'Azur waterfront is mainly surfaced by stretches of smooth, round rocks the size of your fist; from Cagnes-sur-Mer to Menton, you'll spread your beach blanket or towel over these hard lumps instead of nestling into sand. A thin foam mattress or an inflatable one can make all the difference in a day's stay, as can a pair of slip-on rubber shoes for negotiating the stones. You might consider springing for a private beach, where you can lie on a lounge chair or mattress. All along the coast there are patches of sand between the ports and rocky shoreline, and a few resorts and private beaches farther up the coast have made an effort to haul in sand to cater to the expectations of swimmers. If you're lodging inland and plan to make a day trip to the beach, leave early. Traffic on N98, from which you'll access the waterfront throughout the length of the coast, grinds to a halt as others of like mind flow in from points north, east, and west.

LOOSEN THOSE BELTS. This sunny, sea-warmed area mixes the best of Provençal specialties with fresh Mediterranean fish, including succulent fillets of *rouget* (mullet) and *loup* (sea bass), often served with pungent garlic sauce or grilled with a crunch of anise-perfumed fennel. Along the coast and into the hills, your plate will often be garnished with ratatouille, the garlicky vegetable stew of sun-plumped eggplant, zucchini, and tomato. Zucchini flowers often appear on the table, too, stuffed and fried in batter. As a gateway port intimately allied with Genoa and Liguria and influenced by input from Corsica and North Africa, Nice developed a unique cuisine. In the Old Town off Place Garibaldi, in street stands and *traiteurs* (food shops), you can sample Niçois specialties such as *salade niçoise*, usually a confetti-bright mix of tomatoes, green beans, potatoes, eggs, anchovies or tuna (though true *salade niçoise* contains no cooked vegetables), and the signature tiny, shiny, black, violet, and green olives of Nice. Equally ubiquitous is the *pissaladière*, the father of modern pizza. It's a good picnic takeout, as is a hefty *pan bagnat*, a fat bun stuffed to bursting with tuna, hard-cooked eggs, tomatoes, peppers, and olives. Venture farther to find backstreet exotica: *socca*, a paste of ground chickpeas spread on a griddle and scraped up like a gritty pancake; *petits farcis*, a selection of red peppers, zucchini, and eggplant stuffed with spicy sausage paste and roasted; and sardine *beignets*, fresh, whole sardines fried in a thick puff of spicy batter, eaten crunchy bones and all.

The Three Corniches

The lay of the land east of Nice is nearly vertical, as the coastline is one great cliff, a corniche terraced by three parallel highways—the Corniche Inférieure (sometimes called the Basse Corniche and N98), the Moyenne Corniche (N7), and the Grande Corniche (D2564)—that snake along its graduated crests. The lowest (*inférieure*) is the slowest, following the coast and crawling through the main streets of resorts, including downtown Monte Carlo. Villefranche,

Cap-Ferrat, and Beaulieu are some of the towns located along this 20-mi-long highway. The highest (*grande*) is the fastest, but its panoramic views are blocked by villas, and there are few safe overlooks (this is the highway Grace Kelly roared along in *To Catch a Thief*, and some 27 years later, crashed and died on). The middle (*moyenne*) offers views down over the shoreline and villages and passes through a few picturesque cliff-top towns, including Èze.

looming icy-white on a clear day, rise the Alps, telephoto-close behind the palm trees.

Whether you settle into one coastal home base and make day trips from there or move from resort to city to hill village, this part of the coast has an enormous selection of places to see. It's worth it to visit different resort towns, as each has a distinct personality and its own sights. Even on a short trip, you'll want to make a foray into the hills to see one of the famous perched villages; you can easily visit one or two in a day trip, plus, a night or two in the backcountry offers a pleasant contrast to the seaside. On a longer sojourn, spare at least a day—or a lengthier exploration—to venture into the hills toward the Alps.

Numbers in the text correspond to numbers in the margin and on the Eastern Côte d'Azur, Cannes, Nice, and Monaco maps.

About the Restaurants & Hotels

In these parts, particularly in the bigger cities, you can savor a *salade niçoise* or *soupe de poisson* (fish soup) on a sunny terrace at any time of day. The Niçois, in particular, celebrate snacking, and this city alone in France is famous for its street food. But don't bring high culinary expectations to the top people-watching venues, such as the Cours Saleya in Nice or the Vieux Port in Cannes, though it's a safe bet that the dry local rosé will be well chilled, and the food fresh, if not elaborate. As a rule, restaurants in the Old Towns of Nice, Cannes, or Antibes stick to traditional fare; the more inventive chefs tend to set up shop a little off the beaten path. You'll find these ambitious chefs in picture-perfect hill towns such as Mougins, while the smaller villages of the *arrière-pays* (backcountry) remain bastions of rustic traditional cooking. Here, you're unlikely to find a restaurant that will serve outside conventional mealtimes—entire towns indulge in the afternoon *sieste*.

In this golden stretch you'll see the prices rise, even beyond those of the Estérel. The atmosphere changes, too. In the coastal resorts the major-

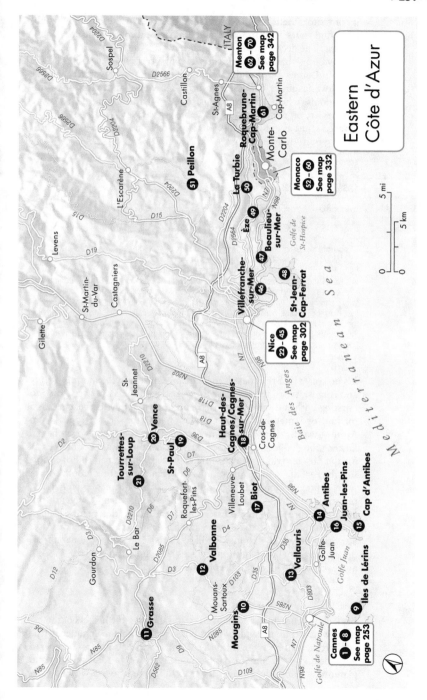

Eastern
Côte d'Azur

ity of visitors seem to value proximity to the sea over cachet, and you'll often find yourself far from the land of Provençal cottons and cozy country inns. The decor here is a peculiar hybrid—vaguely Jazz Age, a little Hollywood—that falls into a loose category known as Côte d'Azur style. In Cannes the grand hotels are big on prestige (waterfront position, awe-inspiring lobbies, high-price sea views) and weak on swimming pools, which are usually just big enough to dip in; their private beaches are on the other side of the busy street, and you'll have to pay for access, just as nonguests do. That said, there are a few treasures worth seeking out—and reserving well in advance.

WHAT IT COSTS In euros					
	$$$$	**$$$**	**$$**	**$**	**¢**
RESTAURANTS	over €30	€23–€29	€18–€22	€12–€17	under €11
HOTELS	over €191	€121–€190	€81–€120	€51–€80	under €50

Restaurant prices are per person for a main course at dinner; note that if a restaurant offers only prix-fixe meals, it has been given the price category that reflects the full set-price. Hotel prices are for a standard double room in high season, including tax (19.6%) and service charge. Assume all hotel rooms have air-conditioning, telephones, TV, and private bath, unless otherwise noted. Hotels operate on the European Plan (EP, with no meal provided) unless we note that they use the Breakfast Plan (BP). Some hotels also offer other meal plan options: *demi-pension* (two meals a day) or *pension complète* (three meals a day); Inquire when booking if these meal plans (which always entail higher rates and are occasionally mandatory in peak season) are available.

Timing

It's no secret that the coast is in its tropical prime in the months of July and August, when the seaside resorts and hill towns are overloaded to bursting with sun-seekers. If you're anxious to enjoy the beaches, aim for June or September, or you could even look for sheltered spots from April onward. Many hotels and restaurants close from November to Easter, though Nice and Monaco thrive year-round. Cannes books early for the film festival in May, so unless you're determined to hover outside the Farfalla with an autograph book, aim for another month (April, June, September, or October). But there are good times, even magical times, all year on the coast. The eastern Côte d'Azur enjoys a gentle microclimate, protected by the Estérel from the mistral that razors through Fréjus and St-Raphaël to the west, and from northern winds by the Alps. So with a little luck you may stroll in shirtsleeves under the palm trees on a winter day (although some places close up during the off-season). and even swim—if you're deeply committed.

CANNES

Backed by gentle hills and flanked to the south by the heights of the Estérel, warmed by dependable sun but kept bearable in summer by the cool breeze that blows in from the Mediterranean, Cannes is pampered with the luxurious climate that has made it one of the most popular and glamorous resorts in Europe. Its graceful curve of wave-washed sand

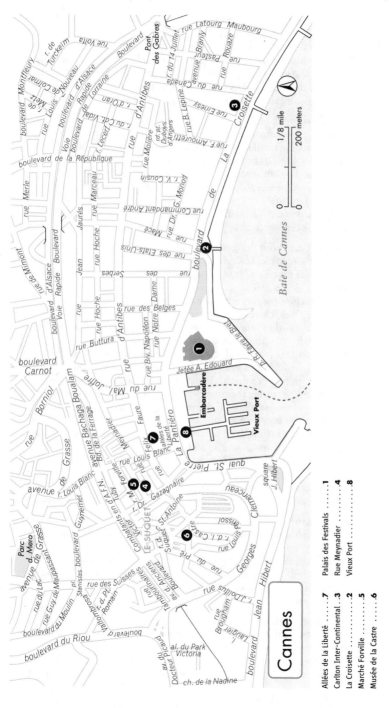

Cannes

Allées de la Liberté **7**	Palais des Festivals **1**
Carlton Inter-Continental ..**3**	Rue Meynadier **4**
La Croisette **2**	Vieux Port **8**
Marché Forville **5**	
Musée de la Castre **6**	

1/8 mile

200 meters

peppered with chic restaurants and prestigious private beaches, its renowned waterfront promenade strewn with palm trees and poseurs, its status-symbol grand hotels vying for the custom of the Louis Vuitton set—this legend is, to many, the heart and soul of the Côte d'Azur. For 150 years the mecca of sun worshippers, it has been further glamorized by the success of its film festival, as famous as (and, in the trade, more respected than) Hollywood's Academy Awards.

Settled first by the Ligurians and then dubbed Cannoïs by the Romans (after the cane that waved in its marshes), Cannes was an important sentinel site for the monks who established themselves on Ile St-Honorat in the Middle Ages. Its bay served as nothing more than a fishing port until in 1834 an English aristocrat, Lord Brougham, fell in love with the site during an emergency stopover with a sick daughter. He had a home built here and returned every winter for a sun cure—a ritual quickly picked up by his peers. A railroad brought even more sunseekers, and by the turn of the century the bay glittered with the gaslight of some 50 hotels.

The most delightful thing to do is to head to the famous mile-long waterfront promenade, **La Croisette,** which starts at the western end by the Palais des Festivals and leads over to the Jardin Alexandre III, and allow the *esprit de Cannes* to take over. This is precisely the sort of place for which the French invented the verb *flâner* (to dawdle, saunter). Stroll past the palm trees and the broad expanse of beaches (almost all private, though open for a fee, each beach marked with between one and four little life buoys, rating their quality and expense) to the glamorous shops and luxurious hotels. With the democratization of modern travel, Cannes has become a tourist and

> "
> A tasteful and expensive breeding ground for the upscale (and those who are already "up"), Cannes is a sybaritic heaven for those who believe that life is short and sin has something to do with the absence of a tan.
> "

convention town, and La Croisette traffic jams now slow up with 20 Twingo compacts for every Rolls-Royce. But glamour—and the perception of glamour—is self-perpetuating, and as long as Cannes enjoys its ravishing climate and location, it will maintain its incomparable panache.

A GOOD WALK

If you arrive by car, abandon it quickly in either the parking garage named La Pantiéro (on the port) or the one under the casino. Then pick up a map at the tourist office in the **Palais des Festivals** ❶, the scene of the famous Festival International du Film, popularly known as the Cannes Film Festival. As you leave the information center, follow the Palais to your right to see the fountains, palm trees, and red-carpeted stairs where the stars ascend every year.

Through the palm trees and flowers and crowds of strolling poseurs (fur coats in tropical weather, mobile phones on Rollerblades, 70-year-olds in white tennis skirts and teetering heels, and sunglasses at night), follow the waterfront promenade known as **La Croisette** ❷ past the broad expanse of private beaches, glamorous shops, and luxurious hotels.

The most famous of these is the wide, white-masonry wedding cake called the **Carlton Inter-Continental** ❸.

After seeing the Carlton—have a drink in its see-and-be-seen terrace brasserie, or even, in season, lunch at one of the seductive beach restaurants—double back and go right on Rue Amouretti, through rondpoint Duboys d'Angers, and left on Rue Molière. Here you'll find glittering big-name designer shops with prices that barely fit on the tag. Cut right up to Rue d'Antibes, Cannes's main shopping street, and window-shop all the way back to Rue du Maréchal Joffre. Turn right and immediately left on **Rue Meynadier** ❹, a lively pedestrian shopping street packed tight with clothing boutiques crammed in with fine food shops. Turn right up Rue Louis Blanc and then make a quick left into the covered **Marché Forville** ❺, scene of the animated morning food market (Tuesday–Sunday, antiques on Monday).

Leave the market via Rue Dr. Gazagnaire, cut right briefly on Rue Meynadier, and climb up Rue St-Antoine into the picturesque Old Town neighborhood known as **Le Suquet**. Wind up the steep and narrow Rue du Suquet and climb the steps of Avenue de la Tour to **Place de la Castre**. Dominating the square is the Romanesque château known as La Castre (from the Latin *castrum*); within its chapel you'll find the **Musée de la Castre** ❻, containing ethnological treasures.

On leaving the museum, angle down Rue Louis Périssol, tiny Rue de la Boucherie, and Rue St-Antoine, and head down to the port, and the broad Provençal-style square called the **Allées de la Liberté** ❼, where there's a flower market every morning except Monday. Across the road the **Vieux Port** ❽ bobs with pleasure boats and grand yachts; here you can buy tickets for boat trips to the Iles de Lérins (⇨ Side Trip from Cannes, *below*).

TIMING You can easily walk this tour in a morning, or make a day of it, window-shopping, watching a pétanque game in the Allées de la Liberté, or studying African masks in the Musée de la Castre. If you have an extra half day, consider the boat trip to one of the Iles de Lérins.

Sights to See

❼ **Allées de la Liberté.** Shaded by plane trees and sheltering a sandy pétanque field (occupied round the clock by distinctly unglamorous grandfathers inured to the scene on La Croisette), this is a little piece of Provence in a big, glitzy resort town. Every morning but Monday a flower market paints the square in vivid colors.

❸ **Carlton Inter-Continental.** Built in 1912, this was the first of the grand hotels to stake out the superb stretch of beach and greenery on La Croisette, and thus is the best positioned. It is here that many of the film festival's grand banquets take place. ⊠ *58 bd. de la Croisette* ☎ *04–93–06–40–06* ⊕ *www.cannes.interconti.com.*

❷ **La Croisette.** For many, this palm-studded promenade along the waterfront, backed by an imposing row of sumptuous apartment houses and hotels, epitomizes the Côte d'Azur. Stretching from the Palais des Festivals to the eastern point that juts into the bay, it's the perfect spot to park on a bench overlooking the Golfe de Napoule, the beach restaurants serving wind-screened meals at the water's edge, and the rows of deck chairs under umbrellas advertising the luxury hotels that own them. If you need a culture fix, check out the modern art and photography exhibitions (varying admission prices) held at the **Malmaison**, a 19th-century mansion that was once part of the Grand Hotel. ☒ *47 La Croisette* ☎ *04–93–06–44–90* ☉ *Sept.–June, Tues.–Sun. 10:30–12:30 and 2–6:30; July–Aug., Tues.–Sun. 10:30–12:30 and 2–7.*

NEED A BREAK?

Head down La Croisette and fight for a spot at **Le 72 Croisette** (☒ 72 La Croisette 04–93–94–18–30). The most feistily French of all La Croisette bars, it offers great ringside seats for watching the rich and famous enter the Martinez hotel next door. It's open 24 hours a day.

⑤ Marché Forville (Forville market). Under the permanent shelter that every morning (except Monday) draws the chefs, connoisseurs, and voyeurs of Cannes, you'll see showy displays of still-flipping fish alongside glossy vegetables piled high, cheeses carried down from the mountains, and sausages, olives, and flower stands. Real farmers sell their fresh local produce here—hand-mixed mesclun, fat asparagus, cherries picked yesterday—but the whole scene gets hosed down by 1 PM, so don't linger too long over breakfast.

⑥ Musée de la Castre (Castle Museum). In the château known as La Castre, built in the 11th century by the monks who inhabited the Iles de Lérins, this small museum is Cannes's token cultural attraction. The front half has been freshly renovated, drawing a large number of local visitors. In the vaulted Gothic chapel and a series of small castle rooms, the collection of 19th-century ethnological treasures—African drums, Asian flutes, and native clothing from America and Peru—seems out of place. But the handful of Impressionist paintings by Provençal artists shows landscapes you may recognize. ☒ *Pl. de la Castre* ☎ *04–93–38–55–26* ☒ *€3* ☉ *June–Aug., Tues.–Sun. 10–1, 2–5; Oct.–Mar., Tues.–Sun. 10–1, 2–6; Apr., May, and Sept., Tues.–Sun. 10–1, 2–6.*

① Palais des Festivals (Festival Palace). This is where it all happens: when the Cannes Film Festival is in town, jostling paparazzi crowd under the palm trees, popping flashbulbs at the glittering movie stars swanning up the broad, red-carpeted stairs to view a colleague's latest performance or creation, or, at last, to find out who has won the Palme d'Or (Golden Palm). Something of a shrine, these stairs are a popular spot for posing for souvenir snapshots. At the foot of the Palais and set into the surrounding pavement, the **Allée des Etoiles** (Stars' Alley) enshrines some 300 autographed imprints of film stars' hands—Dépardieu, Streep, and Stallone among others. ☒ *East of the tourist office on La Croisette.*

④ Rue Meynadier. You may not notice the pretty 18th-century houses that once formed the main street of Cannes, so distracting are the boutiques they now contain. Here inexpensive and trendy clothes alternate with rarified food and wine shops, and some of the best butchers in town. At one end of Rue Meynadier is **Rue d'Antibes**, Cannes's main high-end shopping street.

Le Suquet. On the site of the original Roman *castrum,* this ancient neighborhood seems to cling to the hill overlooking Cannes. Shops proffer crafts and Provençal goods, and the atmospheric theme restaurants give you a chance to catch your breath. Take time to lose yourself awhile on the tiny backstreets, ducking under arches and peeking into courtyards: the pretty pastel shutters, Gothic stonework, and narrow passageways are lovely distractions. At the top is **Place de la Castre**—from behind the square's 16th-century Église Notre-Dame-d'Esperance, take in magnificent views over Cannes and the Ile Ste-Marguerite. The hill is crowned by the 11th-century château, housing the **Musée de la Castre,** and the imposing four-sided **Tour du Suquet** (Suquet Tower), built in 1385 as a lookout against Saracen invasions.

❽ **Vieux Port** (Old Port). Sparkling at the foot of Le Suquet, this narrow, well-protected port harbors a fascinating lineup of grand luxury yachts and slick little pleasure boats that creak and bob beside weathered-blue fishing barques. From the east corner, off La Pantiéro, you can catch a cruise to the Iles de Lérins.

Where to Eat & Stay

★ $$$$ ✕ **La Villa des Lys.** Superstar decorator Jacques Garcia only works for art-collecting billionaires, high-style industrialists, and the most-talked-about restaurants. Into that latter category falls the Villa de Lys, home to the culinary wizard Bruno Oger, who produces stunning menus that leave discerning palates craving more. Inspired by the Belle-Epoque-meets-the-Parthenon style of the Villa Kerylos (up the coast in Beaulieu), Garcia has garnished these luxe rooms with Homeric chandeliers, Mycenean doorways, egg-and-dart moldings, a retractable ceiling, and fabrics that smolder with ancient terra-cotta hues. No matter: Oger's creations take center stage. How can they not with such delights as warm duck foie gras with truffle and peanut tapenade in a braised Jerusalem artichoke (€38, yes for an appetizer); or purple urchin soup with crabmeat, accompanied by a mincemeat crêpe with coral, or turbot marineìre with lemon bread crumbs, confit shallots, and creamy arborio risotto, or Breton lobster with black truffles and creamed macaroni? Save room for dessert: the stuffed orange au supréme caramélisé is a little slice of heaven. ⊠ *10 La Croisette* ☎ *04–92–98–77–41* ⌂ *Reservations essential* ☰ *AE, DC, MC, V* ☻ *Closed Sun., Mon., and mid-Nov.–mid-Dec.*

★ $$$–$$$$ ✕ **Auberge Provençale.** Of the plethora of slightly touristy restaurants lining the long hike up into Le Suquet, this ancient inn is most evocative of Old Provence. This is largely due to its age, as it claims to be the oldest restaurant in town, and the heavy old beams back up the claim. For maximum effect, reserve a table in the room with the stone fireplace that crackles pleasantly on cool days. In summer, terrace tables overlook the sea. Regional specialties dominate, including bouillabaisse, aïoli, *petit farcis* (stuffed tomatoes and peppers with a mixture of meat, olives, tomatoes, and garlic then topped with bread crumbs and roasted), sea bass grilled with fennel, and a rich beef *estouffade* (stew). ⊠ *10 rue St-Antoine* ☎ *04–92–99–27–17* ⊕ *www.auberge-provencale.com* ☰ *AE, DC, MC, V.*

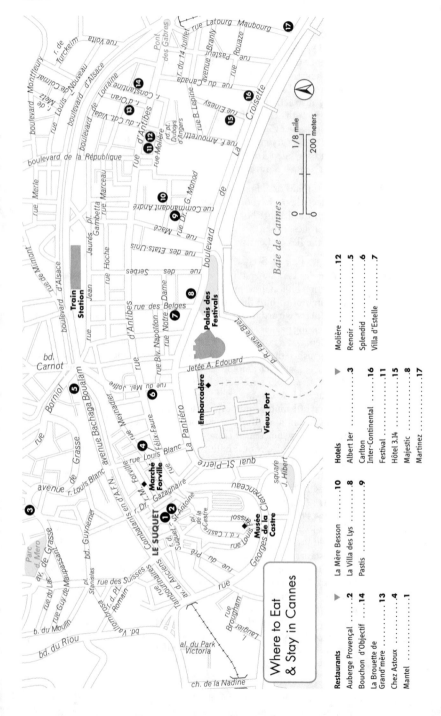

Where to Eat & Stay in Cannes

Restaurants ▶

Auberge Provençal **2**
Bouchon d'Objectif **14**
La Brouette de
Grand'mère **13**
Chez Astoux **4**
Mantel **1**

La Mère Besson **10**
La Villa des lys **8**
Pastis **9**

Hotels ▶

Albert 1er **3**
Carlton **16**
Festival **11**
Hôtel 3.14 ....**15**
Majestic **8**
Martinez **17**

Molière **12**
Renoir **5**
Splendid **6**
Villa d'Estelle **7**

$$–$$$$ ✕ **Chez Astoux.** Open since 1920 and run by the same family for four generations, Astoux is the place to satisfy a craving for oysters or other sea creatures, delivered fresh daily. Tiled tables on the terrace (which is covered and heated in winter) present showy, tiered platters of sparkling-fresh seafood, and bouillabaisse anchors the menu. You can also order seafood platters to go, with the shellfish preopened or not, from the same address (not to be confused with Brun, around the corner, which uses the Astoux name). ⊠ *43 rue Félix-Faure* ☎ *04–93–39–06–22* ⊕ *www. astoux.com* ☐ *AE, DC, MC, V.*

$$$ ✕ **La Brouette de Grand'mère.** Monsieur Bruno's tiny, charming hole-in-the-wall, complete with lace curtains, painted-wood front, fireplace, and old posters, could be a set for one of the Festival's films. Yet it's a true-blue bistro, with a €33, three-course menu to choose from that includes both an aperitif and wine. There's quail roasted in cream, pot-au-feu with beef, pork, and chicken, andouillettes crisped in sweet muscadet, and sharp aged goat cheese. It's only open evenings, and feels especially right in winter. ⊠ *9 rue d'Oran* ☎ *04–93–39–12–10* ☐ *MC, V* ☉ *No lunch. Closed Sun.*

$$–$$$ ✕ **Mantel.** In a city where style often wins out over substance, food lovers Fodor'sChoice treasure this Suquet address, run by former chef and maître d' Noël Man-
★ tel from Les Muscadins in Mougins. Find out for yourself with one of the seasonal prix fixe menus drawing on the finest Mediterranean produce to deliver such simple yet eloquent dishes as pan-fried John Dory, asparagus risotto, and crêpes suzette. ⊠ *22 rue St-Antoine* ☎ *04–93–39–13–10* ☐ *MC, V* ☉ *No lunch Wed. or Thurs. Closed July.*

$$ ✕ **La Mère Besson.** This long-standing favorite continues to please a largely foreign clientele with regional specialties such as sweet-and-sour sardines *à l'escabeche* (marinated in white wine and vinegar), monkfish Provençal (with tomatoes, fennel, and onion), and roast lamb with garlic puree. The formal interior, with damask linens and still-life paintings, is lightened up with clatter from the open kitchen. ⊠ *13 rue des Frères-Pradignac* ☎ *04–93–39–59–24* ☐ *AE, DC, MC, V* ☉ *Closed Sun. No lunch (though during festivals open daily for all meals).*

★ **$–$$** ✕ **Bouchon d'Objectif.** Popular and unpretentious, this tiny, recently renovated bistro serves inexpensive Provençal menus prepared with a sophisticated twist. Watch for its homemade foie gras, rabbit terrine with raisins and pistachios, or a trio of fresh fish with aïoli. An ever-changing gallery display of photography adds a hip touch to the otherwise simple room done in tones of ocher. ⊠ *10 rue Constantine* ☎ *04–93–99–21–76* ☐ *MC, V* ☉ *Closed Mon. and Nov. 20–Dec. 15. No dinner Sun.*

$–$$ ✕ **Pastis.** Just off La Croisette, Pastis looks like a spruced up New York diner but sticks mainly to tried-and-true French fare, though you will find chicken Caesar salad on the menu. The sidewalk terrace is the perfect spot to read the paper and sip a glass of—what else?—the anise-flavored pastis so beloved of southerners. The spot is a local favorite for the aperitif before moving on to Les Coulisses nearby. ⊠ *28 rue du Commandant André* ☎ *04–92–98–95–40* ☐ *MC, V* ☉ *Closed Sun.*

$$$$ ✕🖼 **Majestic.** Classical statuary and tapestries set the aristocratic tone at this La Croisette palace; it's grand but gracious, with a quieter feel than most of its neighbors. The smallish pool is behind a landscaped hillock, so that if you're breakfasting poolside you can't be seen by passersby. Sip a bit of bubbly in the ultrachic brasserie of Parisian fame, "le Fouquet," or dine in the restaurant, Villa des Lys, one of Cannes's gastronomic greats, where wonder-chef Bruno Oger plays with Provençal traditions at refined levels (see above). Though some guest rooms are fussy, most are done in subdued tones of gold and burgundy. Ask for one of the renovated ones, carefully redone in retro style. ⊠ *14 bd. de la Croisette, 06400* ☎ *04–92–98–77–00* 🖷 *04–93–38–97–90* ⊕ *www.lucienbarriere.com* 📞 *305 rooms, 24 apartments* ⚸ *Restaurant, in-room safes, cable TV, pool, hair salon, sauna, bar, Internet, parking (fee)* ⊟ *AE, DC, MC, V* ⊘ *Closed mid-Nov.–Dec.*

$$$$ ✕⊡ **Martinez.** A Hollywood-style face-lift restored the Art Deco Martinez to a theatrical version of its original 1930s glamour, and the refurbished sea-facing rooms on the first and second floors reopened for the Cannes Film Festival in 2005. Renovated rooms have either a splashy neo-Deco or more sober look; avoid those on the interior overlooking the grim parking lot. The Palme d'Or restaurant overlooking La Croisette has a plush, extravagant burled-wood and ebony interior worthy of Napoléon (or Joan Collins). But despite all that, chefs Christian Willer and Christian Sinicropi draw lavish praise for their modern Mediterranean cuisine: red mullet fillets with squid salad and seaweed, pigeon with merguez sausage and Madeira sauce. This excellence carries over to the beach restaurant, considered to be the best of its kind in Cannes. ⊠ *73 bd. de la Croisette, 06400* ☎ *04–92–98–73–00* 🖷 *04–93–39–67–82* ⊕ *www.hotel-martinez.com* 📞 *404 rooms, 11 suites* ⚸ *3 restaurants, pool, beach, bar, in-room data ports, Wi-Fi, some pets allowed (fee)* ⊟ *AE, DC, MC, V.*

★ **$$$$** ⊡ **Carlton Inter-Continental.** This Neoclassical landmark staked out the best position early on, with La Croisette seeming to radiate symmetrically from its figurehead waterfront site. No discreet setback here: the Carlton sits right on the sidewalk—the better for you to be seen on the popular brasserie's terrace, made even more noticeable by the gleaming, renovated facade. Seven new sea-view suites opened in 2005, each named after a film star and decorated in Hollywood style. The main film festival banquets take place in its gilt-and-marble Grand Salon, as do, alas, year-round conferences. Seafront rooms have a retro Laura Ashley look; those in the back compensate with cheery Provençal prints. ⊠ *58 bd. de la Croisette, 06414* ☎ *04–93–06–40–06* 🖷 *04–93–06–40–25* ⊕ *www.cannes.interconti.com* 📞 *338 rooms, 28 suites* ⚸ *2 restaurants, in-room safes, minibars, cable TV, health club, beach, bar, casino* ⊟ *AE, DC, MC, V.*

$$$–$$$$ ⊡ **Hotel 3.14.** The jet-set crowd feels right at home in this new Cannes hotel, whose five floors hop from one continent to the next. The Asian floor radiates Zen while the Americas floor takes a tongue-in-cheek look at the 1970s with bright colors and retro furniture. The rooftop terrace invites you to chill out with its swimming pool, Jacuzzi, and massage room. Past the Bollywood-style lobby decked out in purple velvet, the hotel's restaurant, Mahatma, takes a similarly eclectic approach to food with dishes such as beef spring rolls with truffle or sea bass fillet with coconut dal. ⊠ *5 rue François Einesy, 06400* ☎ *04–92–99–72–00* 🖷 *04–93–68–25–59* ⊕ *www.3-14hotel.com* 📞 *81 rooms, 15 suites* ⚸ *Restaurant, pool, hot tub, in-room data ports, Wi-Fi* ⊟ *AE, DC, MC, V.*

$$$–$$$$ 🏨 **Splendid.** If you covet a waterfront position but can't afford the grand hotels on La Croisette, consider this traditional 1873 palace overlooking La Pantiéro and the Old Port. Maintained in simple comfort, it offers freshly decorated rooms and bathrooms that are impeccably up-to-date, particularly the recently modernized ones facing the sea. Small doubles take in spectacular seaside views; some first-floor rooms have terraces. It's family run and thus full of personal touches: flowers and fruit in rooms, robes and kitchenettes in those with sea views, and pretty Provençal furniture in the breakfast room. ⊠ *Allées de la Liberté, entrance at 4–6 rue Félix-Faure, 06407* ☎ *04–97–06–22–22* 🖷 *04–93–99–55–02* ⊕ *www.splendid-hotel-cannes.fr* ⤳ *60 rooms* ⚿ *In-room safes, kitchenettes, in-room data ports, some pets allowed* ▤ *AE, DC, MC, V* ☾ *Closed 1st 2 wks in Jan.*

$$–$$$ 🏨 **Renoir.** This graceful former mansion is on a quiet backstreet in a residential neighborhood only a few blocks back from the center and beach (some suites even have sea views), but it feels like another world. Highly charged sunflower prints (none of the ubiquitous pink Art Deco), the scent of lavender, and kitchenettes in every suite create a sense of Provence instead of the Côte d'Azur. Sea-view rooms overlook a busier street; for maximum quiet, ask for the backstreet side. ⊠ *7 rue Edith Cavell, 06400* ☎ *04–92–99–62–62* 🖷 *04–92–99–62–82* ⊕ *www.hotel-renoir-cannes.com* ⤳ *10 rooms, 17 suites* ⚿ *Kitchenettes, bar, in-room data ports, some pets allowed* ▤ *AE, DC, MC, V.*

$$–$$$ 🏨 **Villa d'Estelle.** If you long to make the most of the abundant harvest on display at the Forville market, consider renting an apartment with a fully equipped kitchen at this new hotel near the waterfront. The 23 connecting suites combine all the comfort of a hotel stay (daily maid service is an option) with the homeyness of a real apartment, decorated in neutral tones with no detail overlooked. Most spectacular are the duplex penthouse suites with huge terraces overlooking the sea, but there is something for everyone here, from modest studios to four-bedroom extravaganzas worthy of the film stars who descend on Cannes once a year. ⊠ *12–14 rue des Belges, 06400* ☎ *04–92–98–44–48* 🖷 *04–92–98–44–40* ⊕ *www.villadestelle.com* ⤳ *23 connecting suites* ⚿ *Kitchens, satellite TV, in-room data ports, Wi-Fi, pool, some pets allowed* ▤ *AE, DC, MC, V.*

$–$$ 🏨 **Festival.** This small, central property benefits from an owner who is eager to please. Rooms have full marble baths and built-in deco-style ash furnishings; five overlook the neighbor's lovely orange trees and palms. Ask for one of the two roomier doubles on the garden side, and make an appointment for the sauna and whirlpool, scheduled for maximum privacy. In addition to discount packages for long stays and reduced-price entry to several private beaches, the hotel arranges excursions to the islands and nearby attractions. ⊠ *3 rue Molière, 06400* ☎ *04–97–06–64–40* 🖷 *04–97–06–64–45* ⊕ *www.hotel-festival.com* ⤳ *14 rooms* ⚿ *Cable TV, hot tub, sauna, in-room data ports, Wi-Fi, some pets allowed* ▤ *AE, DC, MC, V.*

★ $–$$ 🏨 **Molière.** Plush, intimate, and low-key, this hotel has pretty tile baths and rooms in cool shades of peach with white-waxed oak. Nearly all overlook the vast, enclosed front garden, where palms and cypresses shade terrace tables, and the complimentary breakfast is served in the garden most of the year. ⊠ *5 rue Molière, 06400* ☎ *04–93–38–16–16*

🖷 *04–93–68–29–57* ⊕ *www.hotel-moliere.com* ↩ *24 rooms* ᗐ *Cable TV, in-room data ports, some pets allowed* ⊟ *AE, DC, MC, V* ⊗ *Closed mid-Nov.–late Dec.* ⦿| *BP.*

★ $ 🖭 **Albert Iᵉʳ.** In a quiet residential area above the Forville market—a 10-minute walk uphill from La Croisette and beaches—this neo-Deco mansion has pretty pastel rooms as well as tidy tile baths and an enclosed garden. You can have breakfast on the flowered, shady terrace or in the family-style salon. The hotel has had one owner since 1980, and it shows in the details. ⊠ *68 av. de Grasse, 06400* ☎ *04–93–39–24–04* 🖷 *04–93–38–83–75* ↩ *11 rooms* ᗐ *In-room data ports, some pets allowed; no a/c* ⊟ *AE, DC, MC, V* ⊗ *Closed Nov. 26–Dec. 11* ⦿| *BP.*

Nightlife & the Arts

As befits a glamorous seaside resort, Cannes has two casinos. The famous **Casino Croisette** (⊠ Palais des Festivals ☎ 04–92–98–78–00), which traces its pedigree to 1907, draws more crowds to its slot machines than any other casino in France. The **Carlton Casino Club** (⊠ 58 bd. de la Croisette ☎ 04–93–68–00–33), a relative newcomer to the Cannes nightlife scene, encourages an exclusive feeling in its posh seventh-floor hideaway.

After sipping your aperitif at Pastis, take in the scene at the always-packed **Les Coulisses** (⊠ 29 rue du Commandant André ☎ 04–92–99–17–17). The place to shake your booty until dawn is incontestably the cavernous **Le Baoli** (⊠ Port Pierre Canto ☎ 04–93–43–03–43), where the odd celebrity has been known to alight. **Le Loft** (⊠ 13 rue du Dr Monod), upstairs from the style-conscious Tantra, attracts a youthful, glamorous set.

During the **International Film Festival** the first two weeks in May, Cannes becomes virtually insane with more than 30,000 actors, producers, directors, and other accredited professionals of the seventh art, 4,000 journalists, and 200,000 tourists. It all adds up to crowds, hordes of police, barely suppressed chaos, and a certain manic pushiness from anyone who isn't Sharon Stone—who, incidentally, strolls up those celebrated red-carpeted steps, shoes dangling off her fingers and a large, relaxed smile on her face. But likely you won't be able to catch a glimpse of her; it's impossible unless you're a linebacker, or just plain crazy enough to wait outside with the other hundred-thousand star-struck individuals.

> ### STAR-GAZING?
>
> Remember, the film screenings are *not* open to the public and the stars themselves no longer grace cafés, beaches, or the morning market; they hide in the privacy of the Hôtel du Cap–Eden Roc on the Cap d'Antibes. Your best bets are the red carpet events at the Palais des Festivals.

Sports & the Outdoors

Most of the **beaches** along La Croisette are owned by hotels and/or restaurants, though this doesn't necessarily mean the hotels or restaurants front the beach. It does mean they own a patch of beachfront bearing their name, from which they rent out chaises, mats, and umbrellas to the public and hotel guests (€15–€25 per day). One of the most fashionable is the Carlton Hotel's beach. Other beaches where you must pay a fee include the stretch belonging to the Martinez, which is the largest in Cannes, Long Beach, and Rado Plage. You can easily recognize public beaches by the crowds; they're interspersed between the color-coordinated private-beach umbrellas, and offer simple open showers and basic toilets. To be slightly removed from the city traffic and crowds, head west of town where the open stretches of sand run uninterrupted toward Mandelieu.

Sailboats can be rented—along with the staff and skipper to sail them— at **Locarama Rent a Boat** (⊠ 13 rue Latour Maubourg ☎ 08–92–68–11–85 ⊕ www.cannesboat.com). A wide range of boats are available from **Le Club Nautique La Croisette** (⊠ Plage Pointe Palm-Beach ☎ 04–93–43–09–40). The **Centre Nautique Municipal** (⊠ 9 rue Esprit-Violet ☎ 04–93–47–40–55) has a private windsurfing base off Ile Ste-Marguerite, and organizes diving sorties. The **Majestic Ski Club** (Ponton du Majestic; ⊠ at the Majestic private beach ☎ 04–92–98–77–47) can take you waterskiing, or pull you on a ski-board, an inflatable chair, or up over the water with a parachute.

Bicycles (⊠ Pl. de la Gare) can be rented from the train station for €20.

Shopping

Whether you're window-shopping or splurging on that little Galliano number in the Dior window, you'll find some of the best shopping outside Paris on the streets off La Croisette. For stores carrying designer names, try **Rond-point Duboys-d'Angers** off **Rue Amouretti, Rue des Serbes,** and **Rue des Belges,** all perpendicular to the waterfront. **Rue d'Antibes** is the town's main shopping drag, home base to every kind of clothing and shoe shop, as well as mouthwatering candy, fabric, and home-design stores. **Rue Meynadier** mixes trendy young clothes with high-end food specialties.

You can find almost any item, from moth-eaten uniforms to secondhand gravy boats, at the **brocante market** (⊠ Allées de la Liberté) that springs up every Saturday. The permanent **Marché Forville,** at the foot of Le Suquet, has every kind of fresh and regional food in its picturesque booths every morning but Monday, from 7 AM to 1 PM. On Mondays it fills up with flea-market wares and brocante from 8 to 6. On the first and third Saturday of each month, old books, posters, and postcards are sold at the **Marché du Livre Ancien et des Vieux Papiers** (Antique Books and Paper Market; ⊠ Pl. de la Justice).

Side Trip from Cannes: Iles de Lérins

❾ *15–20 minutes by ferry off the coast of Cannes.*

When you're glutted on glamour and tired of dodging limos, skaters, and the leavings of dyed-to-match poodles, catch a boat from Cannes's Vieux Port to one of the two Iles de Lérins (Lérins Islands). On one of these two lovely getaways you can find car-free peace and lose yourself in a tropical landscape of palms, pines, and tidal pools. Ste-Marguerite Island has more in the way of attractions: a ruined prison-fortress, a museum, and a handful of restaurants. Smaller and wilder, St-Honorat Island is dominated by its active monastery and the ruins of its 10th-century original.

Buy your tickets to Ste-Marguerite island from one of the ferry companies at the booths on Cannes's Vieux Port; look for the **Horizon Company** (✉ Jetée Edouard ☎ 04–92–98–71–36), set back from the street, which has the most comfortable boats. You can also buy tickets at **Estérel Chanteclair** (✉ in front of the Sofitel at Quai St-Pierre ☎ 04–93–39–11–82). Boats to the Ile St-Honorat are run by the monks who inhabit the island and tickets must be purchased from their own company, **Planariain** (✉ in front of the Sofitel at Quai St-Pierre ☎ 04–92–98–71–38).

Allow at least a half day to enjoy either island; you can see both if you get an early start, but might regret the obligation to move on once you've arrived on the first one. Although Ste-Marguerite has some restaurants and snack shops, you would be wise to bring along a picnic and drinks; you'll have to do this if you spend the day on the non-commercial St-Honorat.

It's a 15-minute (€10 round-trip; daily every hour on the hour from 9 AM to 5 PM) to **Ile Ste-Marguerite,** the larger of the Iles de Lérins, which is covered with dense growths of palms, pines, and eucalyptus. On arriving, head left up the tiny main street lined with restaurants and snack shops, or cut uphill and left toward **Fort Royal,** built by Richelieu in the 18th century and improved by Vauban. The views over the ramparts to the rocky island coast and the open sea are as evocative as the prison buildings, one of which supposedly locked up the Man in the Iron Mask. Behind the prison buildings you'll find the **Musée de la Mer** (Marine Museum; ☎ 04–93–43–18–17), with its Roman boat dating from the first century BC and its collection of amphorae and pottery recovered from ancient shipwrecks. The museum's hours are: October through March, Tuesday through Sunday 10:30–12:15 and 2:15–4:30; April through June, Tuesday through Sunday 10:30–12:15 and 2:15–5:30; and July and August, Tuesday through Sunday 10:30–12:15 and 2:15–6:30. Admission is €3. If you have time or prefer nature to history, head right from the port and follow the signs along the coast to the small **bird preserve,** populated by cormorants and talkative gulls, and the quiet beach beyond, a paradise of tidal pools which seethe with marine life at low tide.

Ile St-Honorat can be reached in 20 minutes (€10 round-trip) from the Vieux Port every hour from 8 to noon and at 2, 3, 4:30, and 5:30 (the last boat back is at 6). Smaller and wilder than Ste-Marguerite, it is anchored by its active monastery, which traces its foundation here to the 4th century. That's when St-Honorat sought solitude on this island—and was swiftly followed by devotees also seeking solitude. The large 19th-century structure his heirs inhabit today encloses many older chapels and harbors a shop where the monks sell their herb liqueur, called Lerina. The majority of the island is covered with thick forests of pine and eucalyptus that belong to the monastery, punctuated by small chapels and crisscrossed by public paths. Wild and isolated rock-bound shores surround the island. On the island's southernmost point, just below its modern replacement, the remains of the 10th-century fortified **monastery** send thick walls plunging into the sea; the walls were built to protect the monks from marauding pirates. The monastery's complex of chapels, courtyards, and views from the crenellated rampart is worth the climb.

☎ 04–92–99–54–00 ✉ €2 July–Aug.; free Sept.–June ☉ Sept.–June, Mon.–Sat. 9–4, Sun. 2–4; July–Aug., daily 10–noon and 2:30–4:30.

INTO THE PAYS GRASSOIS

Just behind Cannes, the hills that block the mountain winds rise, sun-bleached and jungle-green. From the well-groomed Provençal village-cum-bedroom community of Mougins to the hill-city of Grasse, the hills are tiled with greenhouses that feed the region's perfume factories. Grasse itself supports modern industry and tourist industry with aplomb, offering a dense Italian-style Old Town as well. Beyond, you can head for the hills of the arrière-pays on the Route Napoléon.

Mougins

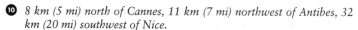 *8 km (5 mi) north of Cannes, 11 km (7 mi) northwest of Antibes, 32 km (20 mi) southwest of Nice.*

Passing through Mougins, a popular summer-house community conven-ient to Cannes and Nice, you may perceive little more than sleek, up-scale suburban sprawl. But in 1961 Picasso found more to admire and settled into a *mas* (farmhouse) that became a mecca for artists and art lovers; he died there in 1973. Despite overbuilding today, Mougins claims extraordinary views over the coast and an Old Town (which is a *zone piétonne,* or pedestrian zone), on a hilltop above the fray, that has retained a pretty, ultragentrified charm. You'll see quite a few off-duty celebrities and any number of wealthy Parisians who have cho-sen this for a Riviera pied-à-terre. Where they go, noted chefs follow, and Mougins is now a byword in gourmet circles.

You can find Picasso's final home and see why of all spots in the world he chose this one, by following D35 to the ancient ecclesiastical site of **Notre-Dame-de-Vie** (✉ Chemin de la Chapelle). This was the hermitage, or monastic retreat, of the Abbey of Lérins, and its 13th-century bell tower and arcaded chapel form a pretty ensemble in a magnificent setting. Ap-proached through an alley of ancient cypress, the house Picasso shared with his wife, Jacqueline, overlooks the broad bowl of the countryside (a bit blighted by modern construction). The estate has, alas, been en-closed in cane fencing by his heirs, who fight to preserve their privacy from art-loving pilgrims. The chapel is only open during Sunday Mass at 9 AM. Elsewhere in town are a small **Musée Municipal,** set in the 17th-century St-Bernardin Chapel, and a huge **Musée de l'Automobiliste,** with 100 vintage cars, in a modern structure on the Aire des Bréguières.

Roger Vergé, mastermind of Provençal sun-kissed cuisine, retired from being a super chef in 2003. He handed over the reins of both his famed Moulin de Mougins (see below) and his **Ecole de Cuisine du Soleil** to Alain Llorca, whose distinct style has been creating waves in gastromic cir-cles since his first stints at the Negresco in Nice. The cooking school, one of the best on the Côte d'Azur, is in Mougins and offers 2-hour courses daily (in the morning and afternoon) for €56 each. The menu changes for each session and students are encouraged to fully participate, includ-ing eating their creations at the end of the course. A booklet of five tickets for five different sessions costs €255. ✉ *Pl. du Commandante Lamy* ☎ *04–93–75–35–70* 🖷 *04–93–90–18–55.*

Where to Eat & Stay

$$$–$$$$ ✕ **Le Bistrot de Mougins.** Set in an old 15th-century stable with high, curved brick ceilings, this is a restaurant that plays up to its historical past. Rustic chairs and flowered tablecloths offer a real picnic-in-the-country feel. Simple, Provençal-style dishes are hard to beat: escargots in butter and herbs, steak with a green peppercorn sauce, or sea bass grilled with fennel are top choices. ✉ *Place du Village* ☎ *04–93–75–78–34* ▭ *AE, MC, V* ⊘ *No lunch Wed. and Sat.*

$$–$$$$ ✕ **Le Feu Follet.** In a beautiful period-house setting with a terrace facing
Fodor'sChoice   the town hall right in the center of the village, reputed chef Jean-Paul
★   Battaglia heads up a battalion of young chefs in an open-plan kitchen. Why so many? Because everything is homemade, from the foie gras to the hand-smoked salmon to mouthwatering basics like roasted scampi with lemon and basil. The best seats are on the enclosed terrace by the quietly tinkling fountain looking out into the mayor's flower garden, but the cozy rooms inside are atmospheric too. The €38 set menu is the best bet in town. Try to save room for dessert—the lavender-infused crème brûlée is truly outstanding. ✉ *Pl. du Commandant Lamy* ☎ *04–93–90–15–78* ▭ *AE, MC, V* ⊘ *Closed Mon. and first three wks of Dec. No dinner Sun.*

$$$$ ✕🖬 **Le Mas Candille.** Nestled in a huge private park, this 18th-century mas has been cleverly transformed into an ultraluxurious hotel. Today, this secluded property with sweeping views over Cannes acts as a magnet for movie stars and politicians. Guest rooms—all cool colors and country chic—are very refined: a profusion of pillows, heated towels, and all the hidden electrical hookups you could possibly need. Antique wallpapers, vintage furniture, and many other high-gloss touches make this place *Elle Decor*–worthy, if not really authentic to the locale. The opulent, saffron-hue restaurant is the well-ordered domain of chef Serge Gouloumes, whose impressive résumé includes stints at Ma Maison in Beverly Hills and the Poisson d'Or in Saint Martin. His succulent menus are causing quite a stir in gastronomic circles; watch for items like wild bass in a rosemary tempura crust or foie gras tatin with Armagnac. In addition to the main house and the gourmet restaurant, there's a bastide (villa) with twenty rooms and a Shiseido spa. Keep in mind that it can be a sleepy here in the off-season. ✉ *Bd. Clément Rebuffel, 06250* ☎ *04–92–28–43–43* 🖷 *04–92–28–43–40* ⊕ *www.lemascandille.com* ⬦ *39 rooms, 1 suite* ⚐ *Restaurant, 2 pools, golf course, spa, sauna, cable TV, in-room data ports, Wi-Fi, some pets allowed* ▭ *AE, DC, MC, V.*

★ **$$$$**   ✕🖬 **Le Moulin de Mougins.** Housed in a 16th-century olive mill on a hill above the coastal fray, this sophisticated inn houses one of the most famous restaurants in the region. Culinary wizard Roger Vergé sold it lock, stock, and barrel to brilliant young chef Alain Llorca in 2004, and the loyal clientele watched in wary anticipation as the proud new owner initiated a radical face-lift for the much-loved institution. They were not disappointed. Local design guru Jaqueline Morabito achieves marvels with white, pink, and plum tones and remarkable silver and gold Baroque chandeliers. Sculptures by César, Arman, and Folon stand beside the signatures of the restaurant's famous guests—Sharon Stone, Liz Taylor—and the chairs are plush comfort. The menu got a full overhaul, too; the result is sun-drenched Mediterranean cuisine that is truly excellent. The menu is divided into classic, contemporary, and light dishes, with a €48 lunch menu that might include Basque ravioli (filled with vegetables and Espelette pepper), the tenderest breast of chicken with lightly cooked summer vegetables, and a rose-flavored macaroon with sorbet. If you're feeling adventurous, order the *ronde des tapas,* which brings 12 surprise dishes. Try the Italian risotto with fresh garden peas, grated truffles, olive oil, and veal, or the Mediterranean sea bass steamed with seaweed, white coco beans, and shellfish. The chocolate-and-orange cake is a slice of heaven. In summer dine outside under the awnings. Guest rooms are elegant; the apartments small but deluxe. ⊠ *Notre-Dame-de-Vie, 06250* ☎ *04–93–75–78–24* 🖷 *04–93–90–18–55* ⊕ *www.moulin-mougins.com* 📑 *3 rooms, 4 apartments* ♻ *Restaurant, cable TV, some pets allowed* 🖃 *AE, DC, MC, V.*

★ **$$–$$$** ✕🖼 **La Terrasse à Mougins.** Perfectly situated, this friendly little hotel offers a decor that is casual, country, and chic. The dapper yellow, white, and pastel blue walls fade into insignificance before the panoramic views that look out on the edge of the Vieille Ville. Up a hillside staircase is La Villa Lombarde, where guest rooms sparkle in a stripped-down country version of Louis Seize. The service is excellent, the restaurant menu varied, although its decor is nothing to write home about and its windows are plate-glass (we are in rural France, are we not?). In any event, an after-dinner drink on the terrace looking out over the valley should constitute a moment of sheer, unadulterated pleasure. ⊠ *1 bd. Courteline, 06250* ☎ *04–92–28–36–20* 🖷 *04–92–28–36–21* ⊕ *www.la-terrasse-a-mougins.com* 📑 *2 rooms, 2 suites* ♻ *Restaurant, minibars, cable TV, some pets allowed (fee)* 🖃 *AE, DC, MC, V.*

$$$$ 🖼 **Le Manoir de l'Etang.** Once a country-style inn, this hilltop hotel with expansive valley views has gone upscale since changing hands in 2004. The Provençal 19th-century manor house is perched over a lotus pond; inside, guest rooms are *vacance*-stylish, most with a light and airy feel, accented with some striking nouvelle-mod pieces. Il Lago, the superb (and pricey) Italian restaurant specializes in easy-to-eat dishes—lovely bruschettas, salads, and pastas. Views of the surrounding countryside are also lovely, as is the simple decor, and the price is gentle considering the competition. Reserve early. ⊠ *Bois de Fond Merle, Rte. d'Antibes, 06250* ☎ *04–92–28–36–00* 🖷 *04–92–28–36–10* ⊕ *www.manoir-de-letang.com* 📑 *16 rooms, 4 suites* ♻ *Restaurant, in-room safes, cable TV, pool, Wi-Fi, some pets allowed* 🖃 *AE, MC, V.*

Grasse

⓫ *10 km (6 mi) northwest of Mougins, 17 km (10½ mi) northwest of Cannes, 22 km (14 mi) northwest of Antibes, 42 km (26 mi) southwest of Nice.*

High on a plateau over the coast, this busy, modern town is usually given wide berth by anyone who isn't interested in its prime tourist industry, the making of perfume. But its unusual art museum featuring works of the 18th-century artist Fragonard and the picturesque backstreets of its very Mediterranean Old Town round out a pleasant day trip from the coast.

It's the Côte d'Azur's hothouse climate, nurturing nearly year-round shows of tropical-hue flowers, that fosters Grasse's perfume industry. The heady, heavy scent of orange blossoms, pittosporum, roses, lavender, jasmine, and mimosa wraps around you like silk in gardens along the coast, especially on a sultry night, and since time immemorial people have tried to capture that seductive scent in a bottle. In the past, perfume makers laid blossoms facedown in a lard-smeared tray, then soaked the essence away in alcohol; nowadays the scents are condensed in vast copper stills. Only the essential oils are kept, and the water thrown away—except rose water and orange water, which find their way into delicately perfumed pastries.

In Paris and on the outskirts of Grasse, these scents are blended by a professional *nez,* or "nose," who must distinguish some 500 distinct scents and may be able to identify 3,000. The products carry the household names of couturiers like Chanel and Dior, perfume houses like Guerlain. The laboratories where these great blends are produced are off-limits to visitors, but to accommodate the crowds of inquisitive scent-seekers, Grasse has set up three factories that create simple blends and demonstrate some of the industry's production techniques. You pass through a boutique of house perfumes on the way back to the bus and . . . well, you get the idea.

> ## SCENTS AND SENSIBILITY
>
> It takes 10,000 flowers to produce 2.2 pounds of jasmine petals and nearly 1 ton of petals to distill 1½ quarts of essence; this helps justify the sky-high cost of perfumes, priced by the proportion of essence their final blend contains.

Fragonard (⊠ Rte. de Cannes "Les 4-Chemins" ☎ 04–93–36–44–65) occupies a factory built in 1782; it displays a small collection of stills, perfume bottles, and "necessaries" for women's—and men's—toilettes. Guided visits are free, just reserve in advance for groups. **Galimard** (⊠ 73 rte. de Cannes ☎ 04–93–09–20–00) offers two-hour "studios des fragrances," during which the house "nose" will coach you in designing your own personally labeled scent (€35, by reservation only). **Molinard** (⊠ 60 bd. Victor-Hugo ☎ 04–93–36–01–62) offers 90-minute workshops where you can blend your own scent (€40 per person, reserve in advance).

The **Musée International de la Parfumerie** (International Museum of Perfume), not to be confused with the small museum in the Fragonard perfume factory that calls itself the Musée de la Parfumerie but feeds directly into the gift shop, traces the 3,000-year history of perfume making. The museum—which is closed for renovations until 2007—has a room equipped with pot-bellied copper stills and old machines, and labels guide you through the steps of production in different eras. It also has a series of displays of exquisite perfume bottles and toiletries. There's even Marie Antoinette's *nécessaire* (travel kit). ⊠ *8 pl. du Cours* ☎ *04–93–36–80–20.*

The **Musée Fragonard** isn't named for the perfume factory, rather, it's the other way around. The grand old Fragonard family of Grasse figured large in the town's 17th-century industry—that of making perfumed leather gloves. (The scents themselves eventually outstripped the gloves in popularity.) The family's most famous son, Jean-Honoré Fragonard (1732–1806), became one of the great French artists of the period, and during the Revolution lived in the family mansion that houses the museum today. The lovely villa, decorated with reproductions of the rococo panels he created (the originals are at the Frick Museum in New York), contains a collection of drawings, engravings, and paintings by the artist, including two graceful self-portraits. Other rooms in the mansion display works by Fragonard's son Alexandre-Evariste and his grandson Théophile. ⊠*23 bd. Fragonard* ☎*04–93–36–93–10* ⬚€*3* ☉*June–Sept., daily 10–7; Oct. and mid-Dec.–May, Wed.–Sun. 10–noon and 2–5.*

The **Musée d'Art et d'Histoire de Provence** (Museum of the Art and History of Provence), just down from the Fragonard perfumery, has a large collection of faïence from the region, including works from Moustiers, Biot, and Vallauris. Also on display in this noble 18th-century mansion are *santons* (terra-cotta figurines), furniture, local paintings, and folk costumes. ⊠*2 rue Mirabeau* ☎*04–93–36–80–20* ⬚€*4* ☉*June–Sept., daily 10–noon and 2–7; Oct. and mid-Dec.–May, Wed.–Sun. 10–noon and 2–5.*

To lose yourself in the dense labyrinth of the **Vieille Ville** (Old Town), follow Rue Ossola down into the steep, narrow streets, enclosed on each side by shuttered houses five and six stories tall. Several little bakeries offer *fougassette à la fleur d'oranger,* a Grasse specialty profiting from the orange water created in its factories; the sweet, briochelike pastry is heavy with orange-blossom perfume.

On a cliff-top overlook at the Old Town's edge, the Romanesque **Cathédrale Notre-Dame-du-Puy** (⊠ Pl. du Petit Puy) contains no fewer than three paintings by Rubens, a triptych by the famed 15th-century Provençal painter Louis Bréa, and *Lavement des Pieds* (*The Washing of the Feet*), by the young Fragonard.

The picturesque **Place aux Aires,** below the central cluster of museums and perfumeries, is lined with 17th- and 18th-century houses and their arcades. Every morning a flower market covers the square in Technicolor hues.

Where to Eat & Stay

$ ✕ **Arnaud.** Just off Place aux Aires, this easygoing corner bistro serves up inventive home cooking under a vaulted ceiling trimmed with grapevine stencils and pretty Provençal prints. Choose from an ambitious and sophisticated menu of à la carte specialties—a nouvelle arrangement of three kinds of fish in garlic sauce and a hearty *confit de canard* (preserved duck). At lunch there's an imaginative fixed-price regional menu, which might include tomato baked with herbed chèvre, veal with pasta, or *pieds et paquets* (pigs' feet and tripe). ⊠ *10 pl. de la Foux* ☎ *04–93–36–44–88* ▭ *MC, V* ☉ *Closed Sun. No lunch Sat.*

$$$$ ✕▥ **La Bastide Saint-Antoine.** The cicadas live better than most humans
Fodor's Choice at this picture-perfect 18th-century estate overlooking the Estéva, once
★ home of an industrialist who hosted Kennedys and Rolling Stones. Now the domain of celebrated chef Jacques Chibois, it welcomes you with old stone walls, shaded walkways, an enormous pool, and a mouthwa-

tering ocher-hue and blue-shutter mansion draped with red trumpet-flower begonia and purple bougainvillea. The guest rooms glossily mix Louis Seize–style chairs, Provençal embroidered bedspreads, and high-tech delights (massaging showers). Although the restaurant is excellent (try the extraordinary truffle, cream, and foie gras soup) and expensive (lobster with a black-olive fondue and beet juice will run you €60), lunch here is a bargain at €53. ⊠ *48 av. Henri-Dunant, 06130* ☎ *04–93–70–94–94* 🖶 *04–93–70–94–95* ⊕ *www.jacques-chibois.com* 🛏 *8 rooms, 3 suites* ⚠ *Restaurant, minibars, cable TV, pool* ▤ *AE, DC, MC, V.*

Route Napoléon

Extends 176 km (109 mi) from Grasse to Sisteron.

One of the most famous and panoramic roads in France, this was the route followed by Napoléon Bonaparte in 1815 after his escape from imprisonment on the Mediterranean island of Elba. Napoléon landed at Golfe-Juan, near Cannes, on March 1 and forged northwest to Grasse, then through dramatic, hilly countryside to Castellane, Digne, and Sisteron. In Napoléon's day, most of this road (now N85) was little more than a winding dirt track. Commemorative plaques bearing the imperial eagle stud the route, inspired by Napoléon's remark, "The eagle will fly from steeple to steeple until it reaches the towers of Notre-Dame." That prediction came true. Napoléon covered the 176 km (109 mi) from the coast to Sisteron in just four days, romped north through Grenoble and Burgundy, and entered Paris in triumph on May 20.

Though the mighty warrior officially started his journey through this region from the coast, the route between Golfe-Juan and Grasse is mostly urban tangle, with the Route Napoléon generally considered to start north of Grasse, when it opens into scenic countryside. Except for the occasional inn with the name Napoléon, there are no historic buildings or monuments, except for the plaques. There are a few lavender-honey stands and souvenir shacks, but they're few and far between. It is the panoramic views as the road winds its way up into the Alps that make this route worth traveling.

Unless you are heading north to Grenoble, you can easily make a circular day trip along the Route Napoléon, starting from the coast at Grasse. Without stopping, you could reach **Sisteron** in 90 minutes, so take your time and stop for a picnic along the way. Sisteron, which is guarded by a medieval citadel perched 1,650 feet above the river, is the gateway between Provence and the Alpine region of Dauphine. It's also famous for its tender lamb, favored by Provençal chefs. If you forge all the way to Sisteron, pick up A51 down to Aix-en-Provence, and then join A6 to return to the Côte d'Azur.

You can make a beeline up the Route Napoléon to Castellane and west to the Gorges du Verdon, the main tourist goal in the region, or take your time winding through the hill towns to the west. The hill towns just east of Grasse—Vence and St-Paul—are much more developed and more frequented by tourists.

Valbonne

⑫ *18 km (11 mi) north of Cannes, 14 km (9 mi) northwest of Antibes.*

A kind of little-England-on-the-Brague (the river that flows through town), this fiercely Provençal hill town has been adopted by the British, especially those working at the nearby high-tech complex Sophia-Antipolis. Thus it exudes a peculiar kind of mixed-country charm, *plus Provençal que les Provençaux,* with a plethora of tasteful restorations. Its principal cachet is the novel layout of the Old Town, designed in a grid system in the 16th century by the monks of Lérins. A checkerboard of ruler-straight *ruelles* (little streets) lies within a sturdy rampart of wraparound houses; at the center, a grand *place* is framed by Renaissance arcades and shady elms.

Where to Eat

★ **\$\$\$** ✕ **Lou Cigalon.** For a taste of the Côte d'Azur at its most creative, visit this wave-making restaurant overseen by chef Alain Parodi, with 27-year-old Sébastien Broda in the kitchen. Fixed-price menus start at €25 at lunch and go up to €90 for the evening tasting menu. Expect the unpredictable, such as langoustines with curry and clementines, or duck foie gras with sesame caramel and saffron, followed by waffle with quince jelly or a prune-and-Armagnac soufflé. The small dining room has old-fashioned charm with stone walls, wooden beams, and pottery by the Niçois artist Emmanuel Bailet. ✉ *4 bd. Carnot* ☎ *04–93–12–27–07* ▭ *AE, MC, V* ☉ *Closed Sun. and Mon.*

BETWEEN CANNES & NICE

The coastline spanning the brief distance from Cannes to Antibes and Nice has a personality all its own, combining some of the most accessible and democratic waterfront resorts (Juan-les-Pins, Villeneuve, and Cagnes) with one of the most elite (Cap d'Antibes). This is vacationland, with a culture of commercial entertainment that smacks of the worst of Florida in the '60s. Hot, poky N98, which goes from Antibes to Cagnes, crawls past a jungle of amusement parks, beach discos, and even a horse-race track. The hill towns of Vallauris and Biot cater to souvenir hunters and lunch sorties. Juan-les-Pins is a party town, its cafés and brasseries thriving into the wee hours. And the glass high-rise monstrosities curving over the waterfront below Cagnes and Villeneuve glow unnaturally bright until dawn. Yet minutes away on a peninsula jutting into the sea, the Cap d'Antibes floats aloof, its mansions and manicured gardens turning their backs on the cheaper real estate on the "mainland."

Everyone visiting this little piece of the Côte d'Azur, whether staying in a villa or a concrete cube, is after the same experience: to sit on a balcony, to listen to the waves washing over the sand, and to watch the sun setting over the oil-painted backdrop of the Alpes de Provence. Wherever you base yourself, you are always just a 20-minute zip from Cannes or Nice, and you can easily wend your way into the hills to visit the ancient villages of St-Paul, Vence, and beyond.

Vallauris

⓭ *6 km (4 mi) northeast of Cannes, 6 km (4 mi) west of Antibes.*

This ancient village in the low hills above the coast, dominated by a blocky Renaissance château, owes its four-square street plan to a form of medieval urban renewal. Ravaged and eventually wiped out by waves of the plague in the 14th century, the village was rebuilt by 70 Genovese families imported by the Abbaye de Lérins in the 16th century to repopulate the abandoned site. They brought with them a taste for Roman planning—hence the grid format in the Old Town—but more important, a knack for pottery making. Their skills and the fine clay of Vallauris were a perfect marriage, and the village thrived as a pottery center for hundreds of years. In the 1940s Picasso found inspiration in the malleable soil and settled here, giving the flagging industry new life. Nowadays, Vallauris has a split personality: the commercial, souvenir-shop tourist section vaunting bins of pottery below, the dense medieval gridwork of the Old Town looming barren and isolated above, with little to see but laundry and cats.

★ During his years here, sequestered in a simple stone house, Picasso created pottery art with a single-minded passion, sometimes dozens of works a day. But he was a painter first and foremost, and he returned to that medium in 1952 to create one of his masterworks in the château's barrel-vaulted Romanesque chapel, the vast multipanel composition called *La Guerre et la Paix* (*War and Peace*)—a difficult and forceful work, created in broad, ruthlessly simplistic strokes in the heat of postwar inspiration. Today the chapel is part of the **Musée National "La Guerre et la Paix,"** where several of Picasso's ceramic pieces are displayed along with a collection of pre-Columbian works. ⊠ *Pl. de la Libération* ☎ *04–93–64–16–05* 🎟 *€3.20* ☉ *Mid-June–mid-Sept., Wed.–Mon. 10–noon and 2–6; mid-Sept.–mid-June, Wed.–Mon. 10–noon and 2–5.*

> **BRING HOME A PICASSO**
>
> Along rue Hoche and throughout the lower village are shops and galleries crammed with bright pottery and ceramic art. Look for the more elegant Galerie Madoura (⊠ rue Suzanne et Georges Ramié ☎ 04–93–64–66–39), owned by the ceramic house with which Picasso worked and still run by descendants of his friends Georges and Suzanne Ramié. You can buy good limited-edition reproductions of his ceramics here.

Antibes

★ **⓮** *11 km (7 mi) northeast of Cannes, 15 km (9 mi) southeast of Nice.*

With its broad stone ramparts scalloping in and out over the waves and backed by blunt medieval towers and a skew of tile roofs, Antibes (pronounced Awn-*teeb*) is one of the most relentlessly romantic old towns on the Mediterranean coast. Stroll Promenade Amiral-de-Grasse along the crest of Vauban's sea walls, watch the cormorants diving off jagged black rock and sleek yachts purring out to sea, and you'll understand why this place inspired Picasso to paint on a panoramic scale. Even more intoxicating, just off the waterfront, is the souklike maze of old streets, its market filled with fresh fish and goat cheese, wild herbs, and exotic spices. This is **Vieil Antibes,** and to our mind these Old Town streets have few peers for their pretty waywardness or achingly lovely charm. Their ambience is nearly Italianate, perhaps no great surprise considering that Antibes's great fort marked the border between Italy and France right up to the 19th century. So if you head to Antibes, be sure to set aside an afternoon to explore these atmospherey streets and, just adjacent to the south, the **Commune Libre du Safranier** (Free Commune of Safranier), a magical little 'hood with a character all its own. Here, not far off the seaside promenade and focused around the Place du Safranier, tiny houses hang heavy with flowers and vines and neighbors carry on conversations from window to window across the stone-stepped Rue du Bas-Castelet. It is said that Place du Safranier was once a tiny fishing port; now it's the scene of this sub-village's festivals.

Fodor's Choice ★

> Wander the back alleys of Vieil Antibes, check out the adorable shops, and chill out at one of the dawdle-and-dine cafés. Old Antibes is absolute beguilement.

Named Antipolis—meaning across from (*anti*) the city (*polis*)—by the Greeks who founded it in the 4th century BC, Antibes has always been the antithesis of Nice, gazing quietly across the harbor at its powerful and vital neighbor. Antibes flourished under the Romans' aristocratic rule, with an amphitheater, aqueducts, and baths. The early Christians established their bishopric here, the site of the region's cathedral until the 13th century. It was in the Middle Ages that the kings of France began fortifying this key port town, an effort that culminated in the recognizable star-shaped ramparts designed by Vauban. The young general Napoléon once headed this stronghold, living with his family in a humble house in the Old Town; his mother washed their clothes in a stream. There's still a *lavoir* (public laundry fountain) in the Old Town where locals, not unlike Signora Bonaparte, rinse their clothes and hang them like garlands over the narrow streets.

Antibes has its glamorous side, too. Whether you approach the waterfront from the train station or park along the Avenue de Verdun, you'll first confront the awesome expanse of luxury yachts in the **Port Vauban.** Some of them stretch as much as 500 feet and swan back and forth at will between Greece, Saudi Arabia, and other ports of call. They won't find a more dramatic spot to anchor, with the tableau of snowy Alps looming behind and the formidable medieval block towers of the **Fort Carré** (Square Fort) guarding entry to the port. This superbly symmetrical island fortress was completed in 1565 and restored in 1967, but can only be admired from afar. Across the Quai Rambaud, which juts into the harbor, a tiny crescent of soft sand beach called **La Gravette** offers swimmers one of the last soft spots on the coast before the famous Riviera pebble beaches begin.

To visit old Antibes, stroll the **Cours Masséna,** where an exotic little sheltered market sells lemons, olives, and hand-stuffed sausages, and the ven-

Continued on page 282

STROKES OF

Matisse, Henri (1869-1954) Blue Nude II, 1952

GENIUS

A kind of artistic Garden of Eden exists in the mind of many painters, a magical place painted in the vivid colors of imagination—a promised land where they can bask in warm sunshine nearly every day of the year, swim in a placid sea of incredible blue, daub flowers so colorful they would challenge even the most riotous palette, and live life as sensually as they sketch it.

This is the dream would-be Adams sought in the late 19th century when, inspired by Impressionist *plein-air* (open-air) painting, artists abandoned the airless studios of Paris for the sunkissed towns of the South of France. By the 1920s, a virtual migration of painters and sculptors heeded the siren call of the Mediterranean muse and began to colonize the Côte d'Azur. Signac made St-Tropez the Riviera's first "Greenwich Village"; Cannes attracted Picasso and Van Dongen; Haut-de-Cagnes and St-Paul-de-Vence lured Renoir, Soutine, and Modigliani; and Matisse and Dufy settled in Nice.

Ceramic Plate by Picasso, Galerie Madoura

A veritable "museum without walls," these locales went on to nurture some of the biggest isms in 20th-century art. Creativity was unleashed, cares forgotten, and *le bonheur de vie* —the happiness of life—became a forceful leitmotiv. The result was an outpouring of art whose exuberance and energy led to the paradise that exists here today: a tightly packed 100-mile stretch of coastline crammed with the houses, gardens, and towns that inspired these artists. Be content to leave their masterpieces to museums scattered around the world, and get ready to savor instead a host of virtual Matisses, 3-D Renoirs, and pop-up Picassos. This rainbow curve of a coast will prove to be an unforgettable road trip through the history of modern art.

THE MODERN ART ROAD

MATISSE Stroll the stone ramparts of medieval **Vence**, then head out to its New Town to exult in the beauty of Matisse's famous Chapelle du Rosaire, created in 1947. Matisse's last testament is a jewel of stained glass and tiled drawings.

SIGNAC, MODIGLIANI, BONNARD Hilltop **St-Paul-de-Vence** was rediscovered in the 1920s when the artists Signac, Modigliani, and Bonnard met at La Colombe d'Or, an inn whose legendary charm remains intact.

RENOIR At the foot of **Haut-de Cagnes** is the Villa "Les Collettes," the last home of Auguste Renoir. He painted his final Impressionist paintings in the two glassed-in studios here, but you can best channel his spirit in the magical garden.

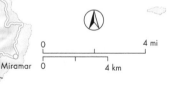

FERNAND LÉGER planned to create a sculpture garden in the medieval village of **Biot**. In 1960, his widow established instead the Musée National Fernand Léger, whose 350 artworks capture the sparkle of this master of Neo-Plasticism.

PICASSO lived or worked on the Riviera for five decades and his presence still resonates through the idyllic backstreets of Old **Antibes**, where he left a striking collection of work at the seaside Château Grimaldi. In **Vallauris**—the "town of a thousand potters"—Picasso's *Man with Sheep* statue anchors the Place du Marché, while nearby is the Musée National Picasso, his vast decorated chapel and "temple of peace" (which rivals *Guernica* for impact). Visit the Galerie Madoura to see the artist's witty ceramic artworks he created between 1947 and 1949.

Musée National Picasso, Vallauris

Peripheral Vision

Journey westward to discover three towns where 20th-century art was first incubated: **Arles,** Vincent van Gogh's promised land (see Chapter 1); **Aix-en-Provence,** Paul Cézanne's hometown (see Chapter 3); **St-Tropez,** where Matisse discovered abstract color (see Chapter 4).

Monte Carlo
MONACO

Beaulieu

Villefranche-
sur-Mer   St-Jean-Cap-Ferrat

Nice

M e d i t e r r a n e a n   S e a

JEAN COCTEAU "The Prince of Poets" covered **Villefranche-sur-Mer**'s Chapelle Saint-Pierre in 1957 with his fanciful curlicues, angels, and eyes, while more of his work can be found up the coast in Menton in the seaside Musée Jean Cocteau and the pretty Marriage Hall of the town Hôtel de Ville.

A banquet of museums entices the art lover to **Nice**, including the Musée Matisse (below), the Musée National Message Biblique Marc Chagall, and the Musée d'Art Moderne, but don't forget to stroll to Matisse's favorite spots—the elegant Promenade des Anglais, Jardin Albert Premier, and enchanting Cours Saleya marketplace.

"The days follow each other here with a beauty which I would describe as insolent." —Nietzsche, writing from Èze, near Beaulieu, 1883

Musée Fernand Léger, Biot

Chapelle du Rosaire, Vence

PICASSO & MATISSE: THE ODD COUPLE

PABLO PICASSO

Born: October 25, 1881, in Málaga, Spain.

Died: April 8, 1973, in Mougins, Côte d'Azur.

Personality Profile: Genius, philosopher-sage, egoist.

Claim to Fame: A one-man history of 20th-century art, Picasso changed styles as often as he did mistresses, but he is best known as the founder of Cubism.

Picasso Peeking: Cane-fencing has been erected around Picasso's last retreat of Notre-Dame-de-Vie in Mougins by his heirs and you are obliged to view his majestic Château de Vauvenargues (where he lies buried) through binoculars.

Picasso Peaking: the Musée Picasso in Antibes and his War and Peace Chapel in Vallauris are top spots to view his masterworks.

Best-Known Works: *Les Demoiselles d'Avignon, Guernica, Au Lapin Agile, Minotauomachy.*

Quote: "You see, I have to paint for the both of us now" (on hearing of Matisse's death).

The "North Pole and South Pole" of 20th century art (to use Picasso's phrase), the two heavyweights of modernism were polar opposites and had a famous push-pull friendship. No matter that Picasso was a structuralist and Matisse a sensualist, or that Picasso was as egocentric and capricious as Matisse was serene and self-effacing—the two masters engaged in a decades-long artistic "game of chess," often played out on the Côte d'Azur, where they were neighbors. It was Matisse's mesmerizingly beautiful paintings created in Nice in the 1930s that probably inspired Picasso's move to the South of France in 1946. He wound up painting in Antibes, sculpting in Vallauris, wooing in Golfe-Juan, and seducing in Mougins. But their ventriloquous dialogue began in 1906 when they first met in the Parisian salon of Gertrude Stein (who lost little time in baiting the artists against each other).

Matisse had already created a revolution in color; Picasso, 12 years younger, was about to create one in form with *Les Demoiselles d'Avignon*—the "first" 20th-century painting, whose cubistic structure was inspired by African sculpture—as it turns out, Matisse's African sculpture, since Picasso had studied his collection of Senegalese totems. When Picasso moves to the Midi in 1946, Matisse presents him with a dove, which inspired Picasso to create his famous poster in homage to France's newly-won peace.

The same year, Picasso is given the keys to Antibes' seaside Chateau Grimaldi, and then bestows on the castle the 30 paintings he created there. Sea-borne light floods canvas after canvas depicting mermaids and minotaurs, satyrs and centaurs, all prancing about in direct homage to Matisse's famously joyous paintings, *La Joie de Vie* and *La Danse.*

Jacqueline. 1960. Coll. Picasso, Mougins

HENRI MATISSE

Born: December 31, 1869, in Le Cateau, Northern France.

Died: November 3, 1954, in Nice, Côte d'Azur.

Personality Profile: Buddha, bon vivant, hedonist.

Claim to Fame: As father of the Fauves—the phrase "wild beast" described their expressive use of shade and hue—his works simplified design and exalted color.

Meeting Matisse: Musée Matisse in Nice, Rosary Chapel in Vence.

Matisse's muse: A decade before Sister Jacques-Marie inspired Matisse's Chapelle du Rosaire, she had been a nurse and model to him.

Best-Known Works: *Luxe, Calme, et Volupté, The Dance, Jazz, The Red Studio, Pink Nude.*

Be Matisse: Rent the Villa Le Rêve, the lovely Vence address he called home for five years. At 261 Avenue Henri Matisse, it is available for $490-$590 weekly (04-93-58-82-68, villalereve@aol.com).

Quote: "Picasso sees everything."

What Tahiti was to Gauguin, Nice was to Matisse. Its flower marketplaces, palaces painted in bonbon pastels, and magnificent palm trees soothed and, together with the constantly changing show of light——so different from the relentless glare of St-Tropez (where, in 1904, he first committed chromatic mayhem with his Fauve "wild beast" masterpiece, *Luxe, Calme, et Volupté*)—inspired him.

By 1919, ailing with bronchitis, he had moved to Nice, where he started to paint images of unrivaled voluptuousness: Semi-nude odalisques skimpily clad in harem pantaloons and swathed in Moroccan fabrics. Their popular success allowed Matisse to relocate, in 1921, to a rooftop apartment at 1 Place Charles Félix, which magnificently overlooked the Cours Saleya flower market and the brilliantly Matissean Place de la Senat Ancien (it is painted a dazzling yellow). To view his art, head for the city's Cimiez suburb and its Musée Ma-

tisse—movingly set next to the Hôtel Regina belle-époque apartments, his last residence until his death—-and the Monastère de Cimiez cemetery, where you'll find his grave.

But to sense his true spirit venture to nearby Vence, where he moved in 1943 when Nice was threatened by World War II. Here he created the sublime Chapelle du Rosaire, his masterpiece ("in spite of all its imperfections") of black-on-white tile drawings and exalted stained-glass windows of emerald, blue, and yellow—best seen, so the artist noted, at 11 o'clock on a winter's morning. The intensely competitive Picasso also saw it, of course, as a challenge. So, in 1952—53 he transformed an empty Romanesque chapel in nearby Vallauris into a "temple of peace" with scenes of *La Guerre* (war) and *La Paix* (peace). Unlike Matisse, however, he designed no liturgical gear, chasubles, or altar, since Picasso remained an avowed atheist.

Matisse's Chapel of the Rosary chasuble

IN LIVING COLOR: LA COLOMBE D'OR

Heading into the hills high above Nice, the road turns and slopes, allowing the full beauty of the rugged coast to be appreciated. A panorama of unexpected charm unfolds upon arriving at St-Paul-de-Vence, a little village perched high on the hills behind its medieval ramparts looking for all the world as if it was a 15th-century Brigadoon. As it turns out, this proved to be one of the cradles of 20th-century art. In the early 1920s, word got out that the owners of its beautiful Colombe d'Or inn would accept paintings and sketches in lieu of payment. Before you knew it, little-known artists were heading to dine and sleep here. The fact that those painters happened to turn out to be Picasso, Matisse, and Braque means that La Colombe d'Or is today one of France's most unique museums—a "museum" you can sleep and dine in. Frankly, if you don't stay or dine here, you simply haven't been to the French Riviera

A "museum" you can sleep and dine in.

If Those Paintings Could Talk

Set just outside the walls of St-Paul—a great location, for summer crowds can easily make you claustrophobic within them—this stone-and-beam auberge occupies a lovely, rose-stone Renaissance-era mansion. Walk into the dining room and you'll do a double take. Yes, those are real Mirós, Bonnards, and Légers on those rustic walls (and yes, they are now nailed down!), indeed given in payment by the artists in hungrier days when this inn was known as the "Café-Restaurant Robinson." It soon became the heart and soul of St-Paul's artistic revival, and the cream of 20th-century France lounged together under its fig trees—Picasso and Chagall, Maeterlinck and Kipling, Yves Montand and Simone Signoret (who met and married here). Off-duty celebs still flock here and it is one of the few places in the world where movie-stars are happy to be recognized.

The Garden Loggia

Choosing the cheese course

STROKES OF GENIUS

5

Under the Fig Trees

Today, the Colombe is now presided over by François and Danielle Roux, the fourth generation in charge, and the famille Roux's extraordinary sense of style would have delighted Pablo, Juan, and Henri. Give in to the green-shaded loveliness of the restaurant terrace and the creamy manners of the waitstaff. Set under timeless fig trees, a luncheon table here is lorded over by a ceramic Léger mural, while the pool is an idyllic garden bower, complete with a Calder stabile, and there's even a Braque by the fireplace in the bar. It is a lesson in self-denial to disregard the famous "*hors d'oeuvres de la Colombe*" (gigantic shrimp, hunks of charcuterie, and other goodies) on the menu. Segue on to the snail casserole, Sisteron lamb, or salmon quenelles, then enjoy the house's signature orange-flavored grappa with dessert while you tune into your neighbor's conversation ("...the Picasso on my yacht dates from...."). No matter the menu prices are as fabulous as the art collection—a meal here is a must.

Mind that Calder!

Head upstairs to your room—you'll have to dodge a Calder mobile (painted red with the artist's permission, to offset it from the white walls)—to be bewitched by Louis XIII armoires, medieval four-posters, wood beams, Provençal borders and painted murals; take a look out your window and you might find yourself staring at a roof of tiles painted every shade of the rainbow. While there are two annexes to the main house, all the guest rooms are flawless in taste (note you can enjoy a dinner or drink here without being a hotel guest). The pool is a dazzler, the bronzed bodies invariably Modigliani–sleek. Henri Matisse once called La Colombe d'Or "a small paradise"—and who are you to argue? Address: Place Général-de-Gaulle, 06570, St-Paul-de-Vence. Phone: 04-93-32-80-02. Fax: 04-93-32-77-78. Web Site: www.la-colombe-dor.com. 15 rooms, 11 apartments. Restaurant, pool, in-room safes, cable TV, bar, some pets allowed. AE, DC, MC, V. Closed Oct. 26-Dec. 20.

Enjoying the pool

Dining under the fig trees

dors take breaks in the shoebox cafés flanking one side. Find the cours by passing through the Porte Marine, an arched gateway in the rampart wall that leads from the port into the town, then follow Rue Aubernon.

★ The **Église de l'Immaculée-Conception,** located between the Cours Masséna and the seafront, served as the region's cathedral until the bishopric was transferred to Grasse in 1244. Its stout medieval watchtower was built in the 11th century with stones "mined" from Roman structures—one reason the town has no amphitheater or ruins today. The church's 18th-century facade, a marvelously Latin mix of classical symmetry and fantasy, has been restored in shades of ocher and cream. Inside you'll find a Baroque altarpiece of the Virgin and Child draping a protective cloak and rosary over the people, humbly underscaled, below; this central composition and the 18 fascinating miniatures that surround it were painted by the Niçois artist Louis Bréa in 1515. A moving *gisant* (full-body death portrait) of Christ, carved in wood in 1447, stands to the altar's right. ✉ *Pl. de la Cathédrale.*

Housing the noted **Musée Picasso,** the medieval **Château Grimaldi** rises on a Roman foundation, in turn constructed on a Greek base. Its square watchtower, along with the bell tower of the neighboring church, defines Antibes's silhouette. The bishops lived here in the church's heyday, and the Grimaldi family until the Revolution. But this fine old castle, high over the water, was little more than a monument until in 1946 its curator offered use of its vast chambers to Picasso, where he was to work with a singular passion against the inspiring backdrop of mountains, village, and sea. Here Picasso experimented with techniques, scale, and mediums, creating vast paintings on wood, canvas, paper, and walls. This extraordinary collection of works, alive with nymphs, fauns, and centaurs, as well as earthy fishermen, forms the core of the Musée Picasso, which closed for several months of renovations in early 2006. A rotating display includes more than 300 works by the artist, as well as pieces by Miró, Calder, and Léger. On the second floor (third story) is a room dedicated to the works of Nicolas de Staël (1914–55), who spent the last winter of his life in Antibes creating more than 300 paintings before throwing himself from a window. These cool, lonely late works offer a marked contrast to Picasso's sunny joie de vivre. Overlooking the blue, blue sea is a sculpture terrace, fetchingly framed by flowers and exotic cacti. ✉ *Pl. du Château* ☎ *04–92–90–54–20* 🖃 *€6 (high season), €5 (low season)* ⊙ *Mid-June–mid-Sept., Tues.–Sun. 10–6, Wed. and Fri. nights until 8 PM in July–Aug.; mid-Sept.–mid-June, Tues.–Sun. 10–noon and 2–6.*

The old **Portail de l'Orme** (Gate of the Elm), built of quarried Roman stone and enlarged in the Middle Ages, leads you from the Cours Masséna and the market toward compelling seaside ramparts. The Promenade Amiral de Grasse—a marvelous spot for pondering the mountains and tides—leads directly to the Bastion St-André, a squat Vauban fortress that now houses the **Musée Archéologique** (Archaeology Museum). In its glory days this 17th-century stronghold sheltered a garrison; the bread oven is still visible in the vaulted central hall. The museum collection focuses on Antibes's classical history, displaying amphorae and sculptures found in local digs as well as in shipwrecks from the harbor.

✉ *Av. Général-Maizières* ☎ *04–93–34–00–39* 💳 *€4* ☉ *Tues.–Sun. 10–noon and 2–6, Wed. and Fri. until 8 in July–Aug.*

From the Commune quarter it's easy to drift farther into the Old Town streets, exploring the mix of shops, galleries, restaurants, and bakeries. Aim to wind up on **Place Nationale,** the site of the Roman forum. It's a pleasant place for a drink under the broad plane trees.

Where to Eat & Stay

$$–$$$ ╳ **Le Brûlot.** One street back from the thriving market, this bistro remains one of the busiest in Antibes. Burly chef Christian Blancheri hoists anything from pigs to apple pies in and out of his roaring wood oven, and it's all delicious. Watch for the sardines *à l'escabèche* (in a tangy sweet-and-sour marinade), sizzling lamb chops, or grilled fresh fish. The interior is rustic and chaotic and the seating so close it's almost unavoidable to become part of one large, unruly crowd. ✉ *3 rue Frédéric Isnard* ☎ *04–93–34–17–76* ⊕ *www.brulot.com* ▭ *AE, MC, V* ☉ *Closed Sun. in Sept.–May; closed 3 wks in Aug. No lunch Mon.–Wed.*

$$–$$$ ╳ **La Jarre.** You can dine under the beams or the century-old fig tree at this lovely little garden hideaway (covered and heated in winter), just off the ramparts and behind the cathedral. Chef Frédéric Ramos serves an ambitious menu of Provençal specialties, many with a Niçois accent: fish soup, deep-fried zucchini flowers, red mullet *socca* (chickpea pancake). Fixed-price menus run from €32 to €40. ✉ *14 rue St-Esprit* ☎ *04–93–34–50–12* ⊕ *www.lajarre.com* ▭ *AE, MC, V* ☉ *Mid-June–Sept., no lunch Sun.–Wed.; Oct.–mid-June, closed Wed., no lunch.*

$ ╳ **Taverne le Safranier.** Part of a tiny Old Town enclave determined to resist the press of tourism, this casual tavern is headquarters for the Commune Libre du Safranier. A handful of tables scattered on the Place Safranier hold locals and visitors relishing spicy fish soup, thick handmade ravioli, and whole *dorade,* a delicate Mediterranean fish that is unceremoniously split, fried, and garnished with lemon. A laid-back staff in shorts and rubber sandals shouts your order into the nautical-decor bar. Blackboard specials are cheap, homemade, and satisfying. ✉ *Pl. Safranier* ☎ *04–93–34–80–50* ▭ *No credit cards* ☉ *Mid-June–Sept., no lunch Mon.; Oct.–mid-June, closed Sun.–Mon.*

$$ ▤ **Le Mas Djoliba.** Tucked into a residential neighborhood on the crest between Antibes and Juan-les-Pins, this cool, cozy inn feels like the private home it once was. Surrounded by greenery and well protected from traffic noise, the swimming pool is a haven if you're too relaxed to hike down to the beach. Rooms, decked in bright colors and floral prints, have either views of the garden or the sea; from the family room on the top that sleeps four, there's a balcony overlooking the Cap d'Antibes. Half-board meals, breakfast and dinner, are included in the price of the room. Friendly, energetic hosts Stephanie and Sylvain prepare fresh regional specialties they serve by the pool. ✉ *29 av. de Provence, 06600* ☎ *04–93–34–02–48* 🖷 *04–93–34–05–81* ⊕ *www.hotel-djoliba.com* ⇌ *13 rooms* ⚒ *Restaurant, cable TV, pool, bar, in-room data ports* ▭ *MC, V* ☉ *Closed Nov.–Jan.*

★ $–$$ ▤ **L'Auberge Provençale.** Overlooking the largest square in Antibes's Old Town, this onetime abbey now has six rooms complete with exposed beams, canopy beds, and lovely antique furniture. The dining room and the arbored garden are informed with the same impeccable taste; the menu allures with fresh seafood inventions such as rascasse (rock fish) sausage with mint, as well as bouillabaisse and duck grilled over wood coals. The restaurant is closed Monday and for Tuesday lunch. ⊠ *61 pl. Nationale, 06600* ☎ *04–93–34–13–24* 🖷 *04–93–34–89–88* ⤶ *7 rooms* ㊂ *Restaurant, cable TV, some pets allowed (fee)* ⊟ *MC, V.*

Festivals & Events

Consider coming to the **Antique Show of Old Antibes** (⊠ Old Port ☎ 04–93–34–65–65 for information) held for two weeks each April. About 30,000 people from all over the world come to view the treasures and pick up a little something for back home; it's one of the largest events of its kind in France. The first week of June, check out the **Voiles d'Antibes** (⊠ Old Port ☎ 04–93–34–42–47 for information), a major meeting of beautiful old teak and brass sailing vessels, metric classes, and maxi-cruisers more than 20 meters long. Don't miss the **Pyromelodic Festival** (☎ 04–92–90–53–00 for information) that takes place once a week in August. Three countries compete for first place in an amazing musical fireworks display that lights up both the water and the sky. Fireworks are set off from boats in Juan-les-Pins; there are great views from the beaches.

Nightlife

If you're ready to party all night, **La Siesta** (⊠ North on Rte. du Bord de Mer ☎ 04–93–33–31–31) is the place; it's enormous, with open-air dance floors, a restaurant, bars, slot machines, and roulette. Laid-back describes the **Colonial Pub and Hop Store Irish Pub** (⊠ 36 bd. d'Aiguillon ☎ 04–93–34–15–33), the haunts of British expats and visitors.

The Outdoors

Antibes and Juan-les-Pins together claim 25 km (15½ mi) of coastline and 48 **beaches** (including Cap d'Antibes). In Antibes you can choose between small sandy inlets, such as **La Gravette,** below the port; the central **Plage du Ponteil;** and **Plage de la Salis** toward the Cap; rocky escarpments around the Old Town; or the vast stretch of sand above the Fort Carré. The Plage de la Salis may be one of the prettiest beach sites on the coast, with the dark pines of the cape on one side and the old stones of Antibes on the other, all against a backdrop of Alpine white. Juan-les-Pins is one big city beach, lined by a boulevard and promenade peppered with cafés and restaurants.

Shopping

At the **market** on Antibes's Cours Masséna, you can buy fruits, vegetables, and a tempting array of other regional products daily until 1 PM. An **antiques and flea market** takes place Thursday and Saturday from 7 to 6 on Place Nationale. You can also find plenty of eclectic little boutiques and gallery shops in the Old Town, especially along Rue Sade and Rue de la République.

Cap d'Antibes

⓯ *2 km (1 mi) south of Antibes.*

For the most part extravagantly idyllic and protected from the concrete plague infecting the mainland coast, this fabled four-mile-long peninsula has been carved up into luxurious estates perched high above the water and shaded by thick, tall pines. Since the 19th century its wild greenery and isolation have drawn a glittering assortment of aristocrats, artists, literati, and the merely fabulously wealthy. Among those claiming the prestigious Cap d'Antibes address over the years: Guy de Maupassant, Anatole France, Claude Monet, the Duke and Duchess of Windsor, the Greek arms tycoon Stavros Niarchos, and the cream of the Lost Generation, including Ernest Hemingway, John Dos Passos, Dorothy Parker, Alice B. Toklas, Gertrude Stein, and Scott and Zelda Fitzgerald. Now the focal point is the famous Hotel Eden Roc, rendezvous and weekend getaway of film stars from Madonna and Robert De Niro to Clint Eastwood and Alain Delon.

★ To fully experience the Riviera's heady hothouse exoticism, head midway out on the Cap to visit the glorious **Jardin Thuret** (Thuret Garden), established by botanist Gustave Thuret in 1856 as a testing ground for subtropical plants and trees. Thuret was responsible for the introduction of the palm tree, forever changing the profile of the Côte d'Azur. On his death the property was left to the Ministry of Agriculture, which continues to dabble in the introduction of exotic species. From the Port du Croûton head up Chemin de l'Aureto, then Chemin du Tamisier, and turn right on the Boulevard du Cap. ⊠ *62 bd. du Cap* ☎ *04–93–67–88–66* ⊕ *jardin-thuret.antibes.inra.fr* ☞ *Free* ⊙ *June–Sept., weekdays 8–6; Oct.–May, weekdays 8:30–5:30.*

At the southwest tip of the peninsula, an ancient battery is home to the **Musée Naval et Napoléonien** (Naval and Napoleonic Museum), where you can peruse a collection of watercolors of Antibes, lead soldiers, and scale models of military ships. ⊠ *Batterie du Grillon, Av. Kennedy* ☎ *04–93–61–45–32* ☞ *€3* ⊙ *June 15–Sept. 15, Tues.–Sat. 10–6; Sept. 15–June 15, Tues.–Sat. 10–4:30.*

You can sample a little of what draws them to the site by walking up the Chemin de Calvaire from the Plage de la Salis in Antibes (about 1.2 km [¾ mi]), and taking in the extraordinary views from the hill that supports the old lighthouse, called the **Phare de la Garoupe** (Garoupe Lighthouse).

Next to the Phare de la Garoupe, the 16th-century double chapel of **Notre-Dame-de-la-Garoupe** contains ex-votos and statues of the Virgin, all in the memory and for the protection of sailors. ⊠ *Follow Bd. du Cap, then follow signs to Phare* ☎ *04–93–67–36–01* ⊙ *Easter–Sept., daily 10–noon and 2:30–7; Oct.–Easter, daily 10–noon and 2:30–5.*

Fodor'sChoice ★ At the very tip of the Cap is the **Villa Eilenroc,** designed by Charles Garnier, who created the Paris Opera—which should give you some idea of its style. The estate commands a vast acreage, threaded with paths and much of it given over to a grand and glamorous garden. Here, in the Roserie you can glimpse the even-grander Château de la Croë, whose shimmering white portico once sheltered the likes of Garbo and Onassis (it was bought in 2005 by a Russian syndicate, whose billionaires' club will now use it as a winter palace, conjuring up the days of the 1920s, when exiled White Russians first colonized the Riviera). You may tour Eilenroc's grounds freely, but during summer months the house remains closed. But from September to June on Wednesdays visitors are allowed to wander through the reception salons, which retain the Louis Seize–Trianon feel of the noble facade. The Winter Salon still has its "1,001 Nights" wall mural painted by Jean Dunand, the famed Art Deco designer; display cases are filled with memorabilia donated by Caroline Groult-Flaubert (Antibes resident and goddaughter of the

> Bring a discreet bag luncheon to enjoy on the terrace chairs overlooking the Bay of Millionaires and give thanks to Mrs. L. D. Beaumont, whose legacy allows us to experience what the Cap was like in its gilded age.

great author); while the boudoir has boiseries from the Marquis de Sévigné's Paris mansion. ⊠ *Near peninsula's tip* ☎ *04–93–67–74–33* ⊕ *www.antibes-juanlespins.com* ✉ *Free* ☉ *Grounds, mid-Sept.–June, Tues.–Wed. 9–5; Sat. 9–noon and 1–7. House, mid-Sept.–June, Wed. 9–5.*

Fodor'sChoice ★ Bordering the Cap's zillion-dollar hotels and fabled estates runs one of the most spectacular walks in the world: the **Sentier Tirepoil**, which runs about 1½ km (1 mi) along the outermost tip of the peninsula. It begins gently enough at the pretty Plage de la Garoupe (where Cole Porter and Gerard Murphy used to hang out), with a paved walkway and dazzling views over the Baie de la Garoupe and the faraway Alps. Round the far end of the cap, however, and the paved promenade soon gives way to a boulder-studded pathway that picks its way along 50-foot cliffs, dizzying switchbacks, and thundering breakers (*Attention Mort*—"Beware: Death"—read the signs, reminding you this path can be very dangerous in stormy weather). On sunny days, with exhilarating winds and spectacular breakers coming in from the sea, you'll have company (families, even), although for most stretches all signs of civilization completely disappear, except for a yacht or two. The walk is long, and takes about two hours to complete, but it may prove two of the more unforgettable hours of your life (especially if you tackle it at sunset).

Where to Eat & Stay

★ $$$$ ✕**Restaurant de Bacon.** Bacon seems a strange name for a restaurant known as *the* spot for seafood on the Côte d'Azur since 1948, a restaurant that prides itself on fish so fresh it's still twitching. The fish-loving Sordello brothers prowl the markets when the boats come, then they simply choose the best. You have to decide whether to have it minced in lemon ceviche, floating in perfect bouillabaisse, or simply grilled with fennel, crisped with hillside herbs, or baked in parchment. Such purity doesn't come cheap, but the warm welcome, discreet service, sunny dining room, and dreamy terrace over the Baie des Anges, with views of the Antibes ramparts, justify extravagance. Fixed-price menus (€50–€75) can help keep the bill down. Meat lovers, don't worry; there's something on the menu for you, too, including a melt-in-your-mouth foie gras. ⊠ *Bd. de Bacon* ☎ *04–93–61–50–02* ⊕ *www.restaurantdebacon.com* ⚑ *Reservations essential* ▤ *AE, DC, MC, V* ☉ *Closed Nov.–Jan. No lunch Mon., Tues.*

★ $$$$ ▣ **La Baie Dorée.** Clinging to the waterfront and skewed toward the open sea, this spiffy inn provides private sea-view terraces off every room.

The exterior gleams with new paint, the rooms are plush and subdued, the ambience discreet to the point of self-effacing, and the reception area is as small as a coat check—yet even the standard doubles feel deluxe when you look out the window. The public grounds and terraces fall in tiers down to the water, from the shaded restaurant and bar to the boat dock to the private beach on the Baie de la Garoupe. ⊠ *579 bd. de la Garoupe, 06160* ☎ *04–93–67–30–67* 🖷 *04–92–93–76–39* ⊕ *www. baiedoree.com* ⇱ *17 rooms* ⚒ *Restaurant, in-room safes, cable TV, beach, bar, Wi-Fi, some pets allowed* ⊟ *AE, MC, V* ⏍ *FAP.*

★ **$$$$** 🏨 **Hôtel du Cap–Eden Roc.** In demand by celebrities from De Niro to Madonna (perhaps understandably, since their bills are picked up by film companies during the Cannes film festival—don't even try to book a room in early May), this extravagantly expensive hotel has long catered to the world's fantasy of a subtropical idyll on the Côte d'Azur. First opened in 1879, the Villa Soleil, as this re-treat for ailing artists was then called, joined forces and facilities with the neighboring Eden Roc tearoom in 1914, and expanded its luxuries to include a swimming pool blasted into seaside bedrock. After the Great War, two stylish American intellec-tuals, Sara and Gerald Murphy, rented the entire complex and in-vited all their friends, a stellar lot ranging from the Windsors to Rudolf Valentino and Marlene Dietrich. Their most frequent guests were Zelda and F. Scott Fitzgerald, who

>
> The pool seems to spill directly into the sea, and a sense of playful indulgence reigns, with trapeze rings suspended over the water, a pontoon swimming dock straight out of summer camp, and a diving board that invites you to jackknife into the indigo sea.

used it as the model for Hôtel des Etrangers in his *Tender is the Night.* Today its broad, sun-drenched rooms, thickly carpeted and furnished with antiques in the main Second Empire mansion, look out on 22 acres of immaculate tropical gardens bordered by rocky shoreline. Down by the water is the Pavillon Eden Roc wing, more modern but with sheer-horizon views. Ultraprivate waterfront cabanas (with surplus rates) with changing rooms, showers, and champagne buckets skew discreetly toward sea views. Everyone dresses stylishly for dinner. Credit cards are not accepted; the hotel can arrange for a bank transfer. And if you're not a celebrity, tip big to keep the staff interested. ⊠ *Bd. Kennedy, 06160* ☎ *04–93–61–39–01* 🖷 *04–93–67–76–04* ⊕ *www.edenroc-hotel.fr* ⇱ *121 rooms, 9 suites* ⚒ *Restaurant, 5 tennis courts, pool, health club, sauna, bar* ⊟ *No credit cards* ⊘ *Closed mid-Oct.–Apr. 1.*

$$–$$$ 🏨 **Castel Garoupe.** Swathed in bougainvillea, Mediterranean in style, and nooked and crannied with antiques, this hotel sits just up the road from the hyperluxe Imperial Garoupe and a few minutes's stroll from the Plage de la Garoupe and the Villa Eilenroc. Long run by the Axa family (who used to be antique dealers from Spain), the hotel has a pretty pool and big tennis court. Guest rooms are traditionally furnished (some come with kitchenettes) and most have balconies to enjoy the umbrella pines and distant cove views. The staff is most friendly, the breakfast yummy, and another plus is a nearby bus stop to help get you to Antibes easily.

✉ *60–74 chemin de la Garoupe, 06160* ☏ *04–92–93–33–33* 🖷 *04–93–67–61–87* ⊕ *www.hotel-lagaroupe-gardiole.com* ➷ *20 rooms* ♨ *Pool, cable TV* ⊟ *AE, MC, V.*

$$ 🏨 **La Garoupe and La Gardiole.** Cool, simple, and accessible to non–movie stars, this pair of partnered hotels offers a chance to sleep on the hallowed peninsula and bike or walk to the pretty Garoupe beach. A sizable pool, framed by high walls and tall pines, offers cool-down time. Rooms are comfortably furnished in both buildings, with the Garoupe offering modern decor and the Gardiole with rustic Provençal design. ✉ *60–74 chemin de la Garoupe, 06160* ☏ *04–92–93–33–33* 🖷 *04–93–67–61–87* ⊕ *www.hotel-lagaroupe-gardiole.com* ➷ *40 rooms* ♨ *Restaurant, in-room safes, minibars, cable TV, pool, Internet* ⊟ *AE, MC, V.*

$–$$ 🏨 **Hôtel La Jabotte.** A few steps from a sandy beach, this adorable guesthouse is built around a central courtyard, where guests relax over a breakfast (included in the room price) of croissants, baguette, fresh juice, and homemade jam. Rooms are tastefully decorated with motifs of birds, flowers or calligraphy, and the owner is as charming as the setting. ✉ *13 av. Max-Maurey, 06160* ☏ *04–93–61–45–89* 🖷 *04–93–67–61–87* ⊕ *www.jabotte.com* ➷ *10 rooms* ♨ *Bar, cable TV in some rooms, Wi-Fi, some pets allowed; no a/c* ⊟ *AE, MC, V* 🍽 *BP.*

Juan-les-Pins

16 *5 km (3 mi) southwest of Antibes.*

From Old Antibes you can jump on a bus over the hill to Juan-les-Pins, the jazzy younger-sister resort town that, with Antibes, bracelets the wrist of the Cap d'Antibes. This stretch of beach was "discovered" by the Jazz Age jet set, who adopted it with a vengeance; F. Scott and Zelda Fitzgerald lived in a seaside villa here in the early 1920s, dividing their idylls between what is now the Hôtel Belle Rives and the mansions on the Cap d'Antibes. Here they experimented with the newfangled fad of waterskiing, still practiced from the docks of the Belle Rives today. Ladies with bobbed hair and beach pajamas exposed lily-white skin to the sun, browning themselves like peasants and flaunting bare, tanned arms. American industrialists had swimming pools introduced to the seaside, and the last of the leisure class, weary of stateside bathtub gin, wallowed in Europe's alcoholic delights. Nowadays, the scene along Juan's waterfront is something to behold, with thousands of international sunseekers flowing up and down the promenade or lying flank to flank on its endless stretch of sand. The **Plage de Juan-les-Pins** is made up of sand, not pebbles, and ranks among the Riviera's best (rent a beach chair from the nearby hotel concessions). Along with these white powder wonders, Juan is famous for the quality—some pundits say quantity—of its nightlife. There are numerous nightclubs where you can do everything but sleep, ranging from casinos to discos to strip clubs. If all this sounds like too much hard work, wait for July's jazz festival—one of Europe's most prestigious—or simply repair to the Juana or Les Belles Rives; if you're lucky enough to be a guest at either hotel, you'll understand why F. Scott Fitzgerald set his *Tender Is the Night* in "Juantibes," as both places retain the golden glamour of the Riviera of yore. These hotels are surrounded by the last remnants of the pine forests that gave Juan its name. Elsewhere, however, Juan-les-Pins suffers from a plastic feel and you might get more out of Antibes.

Where to Eat & Stay

★ **$$$$** ✕⬜ **Juana.** This luxurious landmark retains a Gatsby feel; there are striped awnings, white balustrades, gleaming brass, and ornate Deco ironwork trimming the lobby. Pine trees tower over the grounds and the white-marble pool, and rooms have a cool plain-pastel theme. Though it's two long blocks from the waterfront, the Juana has its own private sand beach there, with changing cabins, bar, and a restaurant that holds live jazz concerts during the Jazz à Juan festival (and has a children's menu). The restaurant La Terrasse has been replaced by Les Pêcheurs, with a luxury yacht theme and exquisite Mediterranean food by chef Francis Chauveau: zucchini flowers stuffed with *pistou* (the local pesto), vegetables, and lobster; Limousin veal with summer truffles and wild mushrooms; and apricots sautéed with rosemary honey are all worth defrauding your heirs for. ⊠ *Av. Georges-Gallice, 06160* ☎ *04–93–61–08–70* 🖷 *04–93–61–76–60* ⊕ *www.hotel-juana.com* 🛏 *45 rooms, 5 suites* ♨ *Restaurant, in-room safes, cable TV, pool, bar* ▭ *AE, MC, V.*

$$$$ ⬜ **Hôtel Les Belles Rives.** If living well is the best revenge, then vacation-
FodorśChoice ers at this landmark hotel should know. Not far from the onetime villa
★ of Gerald and Sara Murphy—those Roaring Twenties millionaires who

devoted their life to proving this maxim—the Belles Rives became the home-away-from-home for literary giant F. Scott Fitzgerald and his wife Zelda (chums of the Murphys). On its docks, the newly invented sport of waterskiing caught on like wildfire, and jazz giants mingled with royalty. Still as exclusive as ever, it now opens its beach and services to some 100 handpicked residents of Antibes. The original Art Deco furniture remains, artfully preserved in an almost museum-like

> ❝
> Lovingly restored to 1930s glamour, this spot pioneered the idea of an inn *pieds dans l'eau* (with its feet in the water), with terraces directly on the waterfront—something that disappointingly few hotels along the Côte d'Azur offer today.
> ❞

neoclassique milieu, though the grand glass doors lead to a vivid and lively waterfront scene. Rooms have fresh, updated fabrics, and sea views are poster-perfect. Cocktails and restaurant meals on the terrace, with the sunset framed over the Estérel, make you want to dress for dinner. There is no pool, but happily the recently renovated private beach is just steps away. ⊠ *Bd. Edouard Baudoin, 06160* ☎ *04–93–61–02–79* 🖷 *04–93–67–43–51* ⊕ *www.bellesrives.com* 🛏 *43 rooms* ♨ *Restaurant, in-room safes, minibars, cable TV, beach, boating, waterskiing, bar, Wi-Fi* ▭ *AE, MC, V* ☉ *Closed Nov. 10–Mar. 10.*

$$–$$$ ⬜ **Hôtel des Mimosas.** This hotel's fabulous setting—in an enclosed hilltop garden studded with tall palms, mimosa, and tropical greenery—makes up for the trafficky hike down to the beach, although most guests lounge around the pool anyway. Rooms are small and modestly decorated in Victorian florals. Ask for one with a functioning balcony: many overlook the garden and pool, which is bigger than most. The lobby and lounge are doily-cozy, with Oriental rugs and bric-a-brac, but you'll probably be drawn to the palm-shaded lawns to relax. ⊠ *Rue Pauline, 06160* ☎ *04–93–61–04–16* 🖷 *04–92–93–06–46* ⊕ *www.hotelmimosas. com* ⤳ *34 rooms* ⚙ *In-room safes, refrigerators, cable TV, pool* ⊟ *AE, MC, V* ⊙ *Closed Oct.–Apr.* ⊚ *MAP.*

Nightlife & the Arts

Every July the **Festival International Jazz à Juan** (☎ 04–92–90–53–00 ⊕ www.antibesjuanlespins.com) challenges Montreux for its stellar lineup and romantic outdoor venue under ancient pines. Tickets may be purchased as early as May and range from €30–€60, depending on the popularity of the artist. There are also a host of exceptional freebies during the festival at various squares throughout town, and a daily marching band that weaves its way through the streets of Antibes. It's one of the oldest festivals in Europe and claims to have had the European debut performances of Miles Davis (pronounce that Meels Dah-*vees*) and Ray Charles. More recent jazz greats gracing the tropical nights include Keith Jarrett, Marcus Miller, and a bluesy Joe Cocker. Though it's a poor heir to the grand casino of Scott-and-Zelda days, the modern glassed-in complex of the **Eden Casino** (⊠ Bd. Baudoin ☎ 04–92–93–71–71) houses restaurants, bars, dance clubs, and a casino, many with sea views. The cavernous **Le Village** (⊠ 1 bd. de la Pinède ☎ 04–92–93–92–00) sets the standard for cool in Juan-les-Pins with thumping music played by the best DJs in town.

The Outdoors

Antibes and Juan-les-Pins together claim 25 km (15½ mi) of coastline and 48 **beaches** (including Cap d'Antibes). Juan-les-Pins is one big city beach, lined by a boulevard and promenade peppered with cafés and restaurants. To study underwater life while circling the cape, contact **Visiobulle** (☎ 04–93–67–02–11), which organizes one-hour cruises (€11 for adults, €5 for children 2–11) in tiny, yellow glass-bottom boats. Boats leave from the Ponton Courbet in Juan-les-Pins three to seven times a day depending on the season; it's best to reserve ahead by phone in summer.

Shopping

Patounet (⊠ Promenade du Soleil ☎ 04–93–61–16–10) is the place for the latest in swimwear from top designers. **Maud** (⊠ 21 rue Dauthville ☎ 04–93–67–11–04) has irresistible summery dresses and casual wear.

Biot

17 *6 km (4 mi) northeast of Antibes, 15 km (9 mi) northeast of Cannes, 18 km (11 mi) southwest of Nice.*

Rising above an ugly commercial-industrial quarter up the coast from Antibes, Biot (pronounced Bee-*otte*) sits neatly on a hilltop, welcoming day-trippers into its self-consciously quaint center. For centuries home to a pottery industry, known for its fine yellow clay that stretched into massive, solid oil jars, it has in recent generations made a name for itself as a glass-art town. Nowadays its cobbled streets are lined with boutiques and galleries, their display windows flashing a staggering collection of goods in vividly colored glass.

Yet despite the commercialism, traces of old Provence remain, especially in the evening after the busloads of shoppers leave and the deep-shaded *placettes* (small squares) under the plane trees fall quiet. Then you can meander around the edges of the Old Town to find the stone arch gates known as the **Porte des Tines** and the **Porte des Migraniers**; they're the last of the 16th-century fortifications that once enclosed Biot. Step into the 15th-century **église**, which contains an early-16th-century altarpiece attributed to Louis Bréa and depicting the Virgin Mary shielding humanity under her cloak; the surrounding portraits are as warmly detailed as the faces and hands in the central panel. **Place des Arcades,** between the tourist office and the church, just behind Rue Barri, has an otherworldly grace, with its Gothic arcades and tall palm trees.

Long a regular on the Côte d'Azur, Fernand Léger fell under Biot's spell and bought a farmhouse here in 1955 to house an unwieldy collection of his sculptures. On his death his wife converted the house to a museum of his works, and in 1967 she donated it to France. The modernized structure of the **Musée National Fernand-Léger** is striking, its facade itself a vast mosaic in his signature style of heavily outlined color fields. Within you can trace the evolution of Léger's technique, from his fascination with the industrial to freewheeling abstractions. The museum reopened following renovations in spring 2006; opening hours and the admission fee were not available at press time (see the museum's Web site for undated information). ⊠ *Chemin du Val de Pomme* ☎ *04–92–91–50–30* ⊕ *www.musee-fernandleger.fr/.*

On the edge of town, follow the pink signs to **La Verrerie de Biot** (Biot Glassworks), which has developed into something of a cult industry since its founding in the 1950s. Here you can observe the glassblowers at work, visit the extensive galleries of museum-quality art glass (which is of much better quality than the kitsch you find in the village shop windows), and start a collection of bubbled-glass goblets, cruets, or pitchers, just as Jackie Kennedy did when the rage first caught hold (she liked cobalt blue). The bubbles come from baking soda applied to the melted glass. Despite the extreme commercialism—there are a souvenir shop, a boutique of home items, audio tours of the glassworks, a bar, and a restaurant—it's a one-of-a-kind artisanal industry, and the product is made before your eyes. ⊠ *5 chemin des Combes* ☎ *04–93–65–03–00* ⊙ *May–Sept., Mon.–Sat. 9:30–8, Sun. 10–1 and 3–7:30; Oct.–Apr., Mon.–Sat. 9:30–6:30, Sun. 10–1 and 2:30–6.*

Marketed under the umbrella title of **Parc de la Mer** (Sea Park), this extremely commercial amusement complex provides parents with bargaining leverage for a day of Picasso and pottery shopping. There's a small **Marineland,** with lively scripted dolphin shows, dancing killer whales, and a Plexiglass walk-through aquarium that allows sharks to swim over your head. Animal lovers may wish to avoid this circus and head instead to the surprisingly deep and fascinating collection of old sea paraphernalia in its museum. Next door is the **Ile Magique aux Oiseaux,** a collection of colorful birds. There's **Aquasplash,** with a wave pool and 12 slides, and beside that, **La Petite Ferme,** a petting zoo. It's only a short distance from Antibes and Biot; take N7 north, then head left at La Brague onto D4, toward Biot. ⊠ *309 rue Mozart* ☎ *04–93–33–49–49* ⊠ *€9–€33 depending on the attraction and the season. Joint-ticket admission and two-day passport for all parks available on request* ☉ *July–Oct., daily 10 AM–midnight for dolphin shows; 10–7 for other attractions. Hours variable in winter.*

Where to Eat & Stay

★ **$–$$** ✕⊡ **Galerie des Arcades.** Tucked away behind the quiet palm-lined Place des Arcades in the Old Town, this combination hotel-restaurant–art gallery draws a chic and loyal clientele. They come to browse in the gallery, enjoy a weekend in one of the extraordinary guest rooms, or dine on the serious, unpretentious, authentic Provençal food: rabbit sautéed in fresh herbs, stuffed sardines, or a Friday *aïoli* (fish and crudités served with garlic mayonnaise). Eat at the checked-cloth-covered tables, either under the arcades or under the cozy beams indoors. Then ask for one of the three *grandes chambres* (large rooms) and revel in antiquity: four-poster beds, stone sinks and fireplaces, beams, and a tapestry-rich color scheme. (The smaller rooms are nothing to write home about.) ⊠ *14 pl. des Arcades, 06410* ☎ *04–93–65–01–04* 🖶 *04–93–65–01–05* 🛏 *12 rooms* ♻ *Restaurant, bar; no a/c* ▭ *AE, DC, MC, V.*

Haut-des-Cagnes

⑱ *14 km (9 mi) southwest of Nice, 10 km (6 mi) north of Antibes.*

Fodor'sChoice ★ Although from N7 you may be tempted to give wide berth to Cagnes-sur Mer—with its congested sprawl of freeway overpasses, tacky tourist-oriented stores, beachfront pizzerias, and train station—follow the brown signs inland touting BOURG MÉDIÉVAL and up into one of the most beautiful *villages perchés* (perched villages) along the Riviera: **Haut-de-Cagnes.** Anyone would find it a pleasure to wander its old byways, some with cobbled steps, others passing under vaulted arches draped with bougainvillea. Many of the pretty residences are dollhouse-sized (especially the hobbit houses on Rue Passebon) and most date from the 14th and 15th centuries. There is nary a shop, so the commercial horrors of

Alice, of Wonderland fame, would adore this steeply cobbled Old Town, honeycombed as it is with tiny piazzas, return-to-your-starting-point-twice alleys, and winding streets that abruptly change to stairways.

Mougins or St-Paul-de-Vence are left far behind. It is little wonder the rich and literate—Soutine, Modigliani, and Simone de Beauvoir, among them—have long kept Haut-de-Cagnes a secret forgetaway. Or almost: enough cars now arrive that a garage (Parking du Planastel) has been excavated out of the hillside, while a free *navette* shuttlebus links Haut-de-Cagnes with the bus station of Cagnes-sur-Mer (about an eight-block walk from the town train station, which lies on the main coastal rail route).

★ Crowning Haut-de-Cagnes is the fat, crenellated **Château-Museé de Cagnes.** Built in 1310 by the Grimaldis and reinforced over the centuries, this imposing fortress lords over the coastline, banners flying from its square watchtower. You are welcomed inside by a grand balustraded stairway and triangular Renaissance courtyard with a triple row of classical arcades infinitely more graceful than the exterior. Filling nearly the entire courtyard is a mammoth, 200-year-old pepper tree—a spectacular sight. Beyond lie vaulted medieval chambers, a vast Renaissance fireplace, and a splendid 17th-century trompe-l'oeil fresco of the fall of Phaëthon from his sun chariot. The château also contains three highly specialized museums: the **Musée de l'Olivier** (Olive Tree Museum), an introduction to the history and cultivation of this Provençal mainstay; the obscure and eccentric **Collection Suzy-Solidor,** a group of portraits of the cabaret chanteuse painted by her artist friends, including Cocteau and Dufy; and the **Musée d'Art Moderne Méditerranéen** (Mediterranean Museum of Modern Art), which contains paintings by some of the 20th-century devotees of the Côte d'Azur, including Chagall, Cocteau, and Dufy. If you've climbed this far, continue to the **tower** and look over the coastline views in the same way that the guards once watched for Saracens. ⊠ *Pl. Grimaldi* ☎ *04-92-02-47-30* ⌨ *€3* ⊘ *Oct.–Apr., Wed.–Sun. 10–noon and 2–5; May–Sept., Wed.–Sun. 10–noon and 2–6. Closed 3 wks in Nov.*

Nearly hidden in the hillside and entered by an obscure side door, the grand **Chapelle Notre-Dame-de-la-Protection,** with its Italianate bell tower, was first built in the 13th century after the fortress had been destroyed; as a hedge against further invasion, they placed this plea for Mary's protection at the village edge. In 1936 the *curé* (priest) discovered traces of fresco under the bubbling plaster; a full stripping revealed every inch of the apse to have been decorated in scenes of the life of the Virgin and Jesus, roughly executed late in the 16th century. From the chapel's porch are sweeping sea views. Be sure to note the trompe-l'oeil "shadows" delightfully painted on the bell tower portal. ⊠ *Rue Hippolyte Guis.*

The beloved Impressionist painter Auguste Renoir (1841–1919) was particularly fond of the Chapelle Notre-Dame-de-la-Protection, and of the whole town as well. After visiting his friend painter Ferdinand de Conchy and falling in love with "la vie Cagnoise," Renoir settled in a house in Les Collettes, an estate set in the town of Cagnes-sur-Mer, just below hilltop Haut-de-Cagnes (from Cagnes's main square, Place de Gaulle, take Avenue Auguste-Renoir right to La Gaude and then to the Chemin des Collettes; Bus 4 from Square Bourdet; or stop Béat-Les Collettes on the Antibes or Nice bus).

> ## LASTING IMPRESSIONS
>
> Famed impressionist Auguste Renoir spent the final 11 years of his life, from 1907 to 1919, at "Les Colettes." He moved here so the sun could heal his arthritis, then so debilitating he taped paintbrushes to his hands and used a scrollable canvas. Eleven last works on view here radiate a bouillabaisse of red, pink, peach, and crimson hues. To quote Renoir: "Look at the light on the olive trees . . . it shines like diamonds. It's pink, it's blue. And the sky which plays across them. It drives you mad."

★ Built by the painter in 1908, Les Collettes is now the **Musée Renoir.** Here he passed the last 12 years of his life, painting the landscape around him, working in bronze, and rolling his wheelchair through the luxuriant garden of olive, lemon, and orange trees. You can view his home and studio as it was preserved by his children, including his bed, his wheelchair, and of course his paintbrushes and easel. You can also view 11 of his last Cagnes Period paintings and a bronze Venus in the garden bearing testimony to his successful ventures into sculpture. On Thursdays in July and August there are English-language guided tours. ⊠ *Av. des Collettes* ☎ *04–93–20–61–07* ⊕ *www.ville-cagnes.fr/* ⊡ *€3* ☉ *June–Sept., Wed.–Mon. 10–noon and 2–6; Oct.–May, Wed.–Mon. 10–noon and 2–5. Closed 3 wks in Nov.*

Where to Eat & Stay

$$$–$$$$
Fodor'sChoice
★

✕⊡ **Hôtel Le Cagnard.** What better way to experience Old Haut-de-Cagnes's grand castle views than to stay in a 13th-century manor perched on the ramparts of the Grimaldi fortress? Maintaining a discreet sense of medieval atmosphere—pastel-rubbed beams, restored murals and vaulting, a few four-poster beds—this enchantingly romantic inn offers regal comfort (bathrooms are ablaze with modern luxe) and storybook allure. Mostly set in adjoining townhouses—although you might find yourself climbing your own private street-staircase or strolling an alley away to find your chamber—most guest rooms look out over the Old Town and on toward the sea. The hub of Le Cagnard is its famous restaurant, where you'll want to enjoy both lunch and dinner. Luncheons are served in a seignorial 14th-century Salle des Gardes, whose vaulted walls were covered by "courtly" paintings by one of Haut-de-Cagnes bohemian residents at the beginning of the 20th century. Dinner is held in an adjacent salon whose remarkable ceiling, covered in Renaissance-style caissons, can be retracted to show off the night sky (cute: they only open it *after* the village birds have eaten and flown over the hill to nest). The lavish menu (no lunch Monday and Tuesday; closed Thursday; reservations essential) lives up to the surrounding splendor with dishes like foie gras cooked with figs, peaches, apricots, and rosemary; an indescribably delcious rouget served tempura-fashion with spring rolls; or the showstopper, second-act curtain, and encore all-in-one: the heavenly black truffle lasagna. Portions are generous, but try to resist and wait for dessert—the caramelized apple pie is amazing, as is everything else that comes out of chef Jean-Yves Johany's kitchen. The word "Cagnard" means "very warm sun" in the Provençal dialect, and we can only say that everyone here will enjoy basking in the warmth of Jean-Marc and Françoise Laroche's welcome. If you are arriving on the town square by the shuttlebus, the hotel's *voiturier* will be sent to pick up your luggage. ⊠ *Rue du Pontis-Long, 06800* ☎*04–93–20–73–21* 🖷*04–93–22–06–39* ⊕*www. le-cagnard.com* ⌨ *24 rooms* ⌕ *Restaurant, cable TV, bar, in-room data ports, some pets allowed* ▭ *AE, DC, MC, V.*

THE HILL TOWNS: ON THE TRAIL OF PICASSO & MATISSE

The hills that back the Côte d'Azur are often called the arrière-pays, or backcountry. This particular wedge of backcountry—behind the coast between Cannes and Antibes—has a character all its own: deeply, unself-consciously Provençal, with undulating fields of lavender watched over by villages perched on golden stone. Many of these villages look as if they do not belong to the last century—but they do, since they played the muse to some of modern art's most famous exemplars, notably Pablo Picasso and Henri Matisse. A highlight here is the Maeght Foundation, in St-Paul-de-Vence, one of France's leading museums of modern art. Its neighbor, Vence, has the Chapelle du Rosaire, entirely designed and decorated by Matisse. It's possible to get a small taste of this backcountry on a day trip out of Fréjus, Cannes, or Antibes; even if you're vacationing along the coast, you may want to settle in for a night or two.

High in the hills these villages loom, parallel to the sea, smelling fragrantly of wild herbs and medieval history . . . and soap shops. So hungry have the hordes that flock to the Riviera become for a taste of Picasso-and-Peter-Mayle that many of the hill towns have been only too happy to oblige. Many of these old stone villages, which once hunkered down against the onslaught of Moors, now open their pale-blue shutters wide to surges of day-trippers from the beach. Stooped stone rowhouses are now galleries and boutiques offering everything from neo–Van Gogh sofa art to assembly-line lavender sachets, and everywhere you'll hear the gentle *breet-breet* of mechanical souvenir *cigales* (cicadas).

As the most conveniently accessible of the famous hill villages, St-Paul and to a slightly lesser degree Vence have become overwhelmingly commercialized, especially in high season. If you're allergic to souvenir shops, artsy-craftsy boutiques, and middle-brow art galleries, aim to visit off-season or after hours, when the stone-paved alleys, backstreets, placettes, and rampart overlooks empty of tourists, and when the scent of strawberry potpourri is washed away by the natural perfume of bougainvillea and jasmine wafting from terra-cotta jars.

St-Paul

 18 km (11 mi) west of Nice.

The medieval village of St-Paul-de-Vence can be seen from afar, standing out like its companion, Vence, against the skyline. In the Middle Ages St-Paul was basically a city-state, and it controlled its own political destiny for centuries. But by the early 20th century St-Paul had faded to oblivion, overshadowed by the growth of Vence and Cagnes—until it was rediscovered in the 1920s when a few penniless artists began paying for their drinks at the local auberge with paintings. Those artists turned out to be Signac,

> Film stars continue to love St-Paul's lazy yet genteel ways, lingering on the garden-bower terrace of the Colombe d'Or and challenging the locals to a game of pétanque under the shade of the plane trees.

Modigliani, and Bonnard, who met at the Auberge de la Colombe d'Or, now a sumptuous inn, where the walls are still covered with their ink sketches and daubs. Nowadays art of a sort still dominates in the myriad tourist traps that take your eyes off the beauty of St-Paul's old stone houses and its rampart views. The most commercially developed of Provence's hilltop villages, St-Paul is nonetheless a magical place when the tourist crowds thin. Artists are still drawn to its light, its pure air, its wraparound views, and its honey-color stone walls, soothingly cool on a hot Provençal afternoon. Even so, you have to work hard to find the timeless aura of St-Paul; get here early in the day to get a jump on the cars and tour buses, which can clog the main D36 highway here by noon, or plan on a stay-over. Either way, be sure to experience a luncheon or dinner beneath the Picassos at the Colombe d'Or, even if the menu prices seem almost as fabulous as the collection.

It won't take you long to "do" St-Paul; a pedestrian circuit leads you inevitably through its Rue-Grande to the *donjon* (fortress tower) and austere Gothic church. But break away and slip into a few mosaic-cobbled backstreets, little more than alleys; door after door, window after niche spill over with potted flowers and orange trees. The shuttered stone houses rear up over the streets, so close you could shake hands from window to window. And no matter which way you turn, you'll suddenly break into the open at the rampart walls; follow along the walkway to see the Tuscan-pretty landscape that quilts over the hills below, backed by an ivory sprawl of Alps. From St-Paul, there is a scenic hiking path to Vence (next to the Chapelle Ste-Claire); the walk takes 1 hour and 20 minutes.

On your way from the overpriced parking garages, you'll pass a Provençal scene played out with cinematic flair yet still authentic: the perpetual game of pétanque outside the **Café de la Place** (⊠ Pl. de Gaulle ☎ 04–93–32–80–03). A sun-weathered pack of men (as for the lack of women playing this game anywhere, you're welcome to your own discussions of sexism) in caps, cardigans, and workers' blues—occasionally joined by a passing professional with tie and rolled-up sleeves—gathers under the massive plane trees and stands serene, silent, and intent to roll metal balls across the dusty square. Until his death, Yves Montand made regular appearances here, participating in this ultimate southern scenario.

One of the world's most famous small museums of modern art is a big reason why many people come to St-Paul. Located a kilometer (½ mi) outside the village, **Fondation Maeght** is a temple of 20th-century art founded in 1964 by celebrated art dealer Aimé Maeght. Set on a wooded cliff top high above the medieval town, the museum is an extraordinary marriage of the arc-and-plane architecture of José Maria Sert; the looming sculptures of Miró and Moore; and its humbling setting of pines, vines, and flowing planes of water. On display is an intriguing and ever-varying collection of the work of modern masters, including the wise and funny late-life masterwork *La Vie* (*Life*) by Chagall. Giacometti's figures stride the courtyards, Miró's *Egg* emerges from the pool, while mobiles by Calder and Arp shift in the breeze. Inside, the multilevel, light-filled museum displays an ever-changing feast of works by Braque, Léger, Dubuffet, and other masters of 20th-century art. In addition, there are temporary exhibitions, artists' studios, a library, cinema, and auditorium (where concerts are held). You can get to the museum using the

Nice-Vence bus. ⊠ *Colline des Gardettes* ☎ *04–93–32–81–63* ⊕ *www. fondation-maeght.com* ☒*€11* ☉ *July–Sept., daily 10–7; Oct.–June, daily 10–12:30 and 2:30–6.*

Where to Eat & Stay

¢–$ ✕ **Le Tilleul Menthe.** Before you plunge into the dense tangle of ruelles in old St-Paul, stop on the ramparts under the century-old lime tree for a light meal or snack at this atmospheric outdoor café-tearoom. Served here are a few hot, plain dishes—roast chicken, pastas, or a hot-goat-cheese salad, for instance—as well as sorbets and fruit tarts served with dollops of whipped cream, and you can idle at a table looking over the stone walls, the valley, and the Alps. ⊠ *Pl. Tilleul* ☎ *04–93–32–80–36* ▭ *No credit cards* ☉ *Closed Jan.*

La Colombe d'Or   **See Page 280**   **5**

★ $$–$$$ ⊞ **Le Hameau.** Less than a mile below tourist-packed St-Paul, with views of the valley and the village, this lovely little inn is a jumble of terraces, trellises, archways, orange trees, olives, and heavy-scented honeysuckle vines. The main hotel, built in 1920, has good-sized rooms and old Provençal furniture; you can also opt for the 18th-century farmhouse, with smaller, more modern rooms but wonderful views. Each room seems to skew toward a private world, several with individual terraces for *grasses matinées* (late, lazy breakfasts). The beautiful pool has hydro-massage and the hotel added a small fitness area with a snack shop in 2005. ⊠ *528 rte. de La Colle, 06570* ☎*04–93–32–80–24* ▤*04–93–32–55–75* ⊕*www. le-hameau.com* ⤴ *13 rooms, 4 suites* ⚷ *In-room safes, cable TV, pool, Wi-Fi, some pets allowed* ▭*AE, MC, V* ☉ *Closed mid-Nov.–mid-Feb.*

★ ¢–$ ⊞ **Hostellerie les Remparts.** This utterly charming medieval inn is the place to stay in St-Paul if you're on a budget. You'll find antique Provençal furniture in the simple, freshly painted rooms, which are free of modern distractions such as television (though some are air-conditioned and in-room data ports are in the works). The restaurant (open for lunch and dinner in summer and only on Fri.–Sat. nights in winter) serves straightforward Provençal cooking—fish soup, spaghetti with pistou, rack of lamb with tapenade—and its enchanting terrace presides over the same sweeping view as those of far pricier places. ⊠ *72 rue Grande, 06570* ☎ *04–93–32–09–88* ▤ *04–93–32–06–91* ⊕ *www.hotel-les-remparts.net* ⤴ *9 rooms* ⚷ *Restaurant, some pets allowed; no a/c in some rooms* ▭ *MC, V.*

Vence

❷⓪ *4 km (2½ mi) north of St-Paul, 22 km (14 mi) north of Nice.*

If you've visited St-Paul first, Vence will come as something of a relief. Just outside the Old Town, its morning food market, though not extensive, attracts genuine producers from the area, and the cafés facing this square feel more down-to-earth than anything in St-Paul. Inside the stone walls of the Cité Historique (Historical City), the newly restored Place du Peyra invites you to linger with its restaurant terraces, relatively tasteful shops selling tablecloths or pottery, and pretty drinking fountain whose water comes directly from the Peyra source. Vence is slightly more conscious of its history than St-Paul—plaques guide you through its historic squares and *portes* (gates). Wander past the pretty Place du Peyra, with its fountains, and Place Clemenceau, with its ocher-color Hôtel-de-Ville (Town Hall), to Place du Frêne, with its ancient ash tree planted in the 16th century, and don't miss the Rue du Marché's old-fashioned food shops, including a butcher, a baker, and a fishmonger.

On Place Godeau, in the Old Town center, the **Cathédrale de la Nativité de la Vierge** (Cathedral of the Birth of the Virgin) was built on the Roman's Champ de Mars (military drilling field) and traces bits and pieces to Carolingian and even Roman times. It's a hybrid of Romanesque and Baroque styles, expanded and altered over the centuries. The carved-wood choir stalls are worth studying (if access to the loft isn't blocked); they were sculpted between 1463 and 1467 by the Grasse cabinetmaker Jacques Bellot, and their detail and characterizations border on the risqué. In the baptistery is a ceramic mosaic of Moses in the bulrushes by Chagall.

On the outskirts of Vence "new town," toward St-Jeannet, it's easy to bypass a humble white chapel below the road, indistinguishable from Fodor'sChoice a home except for its imposing cast-iron cross. But the **Chapelle du Rosaire** (Chapel of the Rosary), decorated with beguiling simplicity and clarity by Matisse between 1947 and 1951, reflects the reductivist style of the era: the walls, floor, and ceiling are gleaming white, with color provided by the light streaming through the small stained-glass windows of green and blue. Stylized biblical characters are roughly sketched in thick black outline; in the annex behind the chapel you can see that earlier versions were more detailed. "Despite its imperfections I think it is my masterpiece . . . the result of a lifetime devoted to the search for truth," wrote Matisse, who designed and dedicated the chapel when he was in his eighties and nearly blind. For more on Matisse, see "Strokes of Genius" in this chapter. ⊠ *Av. Henri-Matisse* ☎ *04–93–58–03–26* ☎ *€2* ☉ *Mon., Wed., Fri., and Sat. 2–5.30, Tues., Thur. 10–11:30 and 2–5.30; closed Fri. during school year.*

Where to Eat & Stay

$$$$ ✕ **Table d'Amis–Jacques Maximin.** Temperamental superchef Jacques Fodor'sChoice Maximin has found peace of mind in a gray-stone farmhouse covered with wisteria and flanked by spikes of cypress—his home and his own country restaurant. Having cut his teeth at La Bonne Auberge in Antibes and become a star at the Chantecler at the Negresco in Nice, he left it all for the arrière-pays. Here he devotes himself to creative country cooking, superbly prepared and unpretentiously priced—shellfish soup with crayfish ravioli, white beans in rich squid ink, Mediterranean fish grilled in rock salt and olive oil, and candied-eggplant sorbet. The yellow dining room is airy and uncluttered, with light pouring through saffron curtains; the garden, sheltered with creamy parasols, is a palm-shaded paradise. ⊠ *689 chemin de la Gaude* ☎ *04–93–58–90–75* ▤ *AE, MC, V* ☉ *Closed Nov. No lunch Mon. and Tues. No dinner Sun. Sept.–Oct. and Dec.–June. No lunch Sun. July–Aug.*

$–$$ ✕ **La Farigoule.** In a long, beamed dining room that opens onto a shady, teak-furnished terrace, this is a fine place to enjoy sophisticated Provençal cooking in an easygoing environment. Watch for tangy *pissaladières* (pizza-like onion-and-anchovy tarts), sardine *beignets* (fritters), fresh scallops with violet artichokes, lamb with olive polenta, and a host of homemade desserts like the lemon soufflé with anise cream. ✉ *15 rue Henri-Isnard* ☎ *04–93–58–01–27* ▤ *MC, V* ⊘ *Closed Oct.–Mar. Closed Tues., no lunch Wed., Sat. in Apr.–Sept. No dinner Sun. in Sept., Apr., May.*

$–$$ ✕ **Le Pigeonnier.** The sight of a lone diner savoring a giant bowl of freshly picked broad beans in their pods sets the tone at this restaurant, which takes pride in its local ingredients. Foie gras terrine, smoked salmon, and fresh pasta are made on the premises, and the *souris d'agneau* (knuckle of lamb) is a specialty, as is an unlikely dish of beef Wellington under its puffy crust. The terrace stretches over a large part of Place du Peyra, and there are dining rooms on two levels indoors. ✉ *3 pl. du Peyra* ☎ *04–93–58–03–00* ▤ *AE, MC, V* ⊘ *Closed Mon. and Jan.–mid-Feb. No dinner Sun., Oct.–May.*

★ $$$$ ✕▤ **Château du Domaine St. Martin.** Exuding an expensive charm, this famous domain occupies the ancient site of a fortress of the Knights Templars. Sitting on a hilltop perch and surrounded by acres of greenery designed by Jean Mus, the huge manor welcomes you with public salons that are light and airy—perhaps too much, as they seem to be overly renovated. All guest rooms are, in fact, junior suites, except for six *bastides* (two- and three-bedroom villas) accented with beautiful antiques. **La Commanderie** restaurant is perhaps the best reason to come here, thanks to its stunning walls adorned with china, chef Philippe Guéin's superb creations, and one of the most panoramic terraces around—the views over Old Vence to the Baie des Anges are eye-popping. ✉ *Av. des Templiers, 06140* ☎ *04–93–58–02–02* 🖷 *04–93–24–08–91* ⊕ *www.chateau-st-martin.com* 🛏 *38 rooms* ⚐ *2 restaurants, minibars, cable TV, 2 tennis courts, pool, bar, Internet, free parking, some pets allowed (fee)* ▤ *AE, MC, V* ⊘ *Closed mid-Oct.–mid-Feb.* ⁝◎⁝ *MAP.*

★ $–$$ ✕▤ **Auberge des Seigneurs.** This extraordinary little inn occupies a wing in an Old Town manor house overlooking the landmark ash tree reputedly planted by François I. Eccentrically decorated with antiques and modern art, it is personally managed by Madame Rodi and her daughter—the third generation. Rooms are spare but manorial, with dark antiques made cheery by Provençal fabrics. The restaurant is formal and a tad stuffy—though it now has a summertime terrace—but the fireplace, spit-roasted rack of lamb, and chicken are legendary. ✉ *Pl. du Frêne, 06140* ☎ *04–93–58–04–24* 🖷 *04–93–24–08–01* 🛏 *6 rooms* ⚐ *Restaurant, bar, some pets allowed* ▤ *AE, DC, MC, V* ⊘ *Closed Nov.–mid-Mar.*

$$–$$$ ▤ **Villa Roseraie.** Although it doesn't have a rose garden, this 100-year-old house has a giant magnolia that spreads its venerable branches over the terrace. Inside, owners Monsieur and Madame Martefon have kept all the charming regional details: mix-and-match old furniture, fine local tiles and fabrics, even homemade bath salts and jams. You can enjoy the generous breakfast on the terrace and lounge by the pool much of the year, and it's a quick walk down to Old Vence. ✉ *51 av. Henri-Giraud, 06140* ☎ *04–93–58–02–20* 🖷 *04–93–58–99–31* 🛏 *14 rooms* ⚐ *In-*

room safes, cable TV, pool, some pets allowed; no a/c in some rooms
▭ *AE, MC, V* ⊗ *Closed mid-Nov.–mid-Feb.*

Tourrettes-sur-Loup

㉑ *5 km (3 mi) west of Vence, 24 km (15 mi) west of Nice.*

More accessible—and thus more touristy—than the little villages on the Route des Crêtes, this steep-sloped old hill town stands over an invisible line that distinguishes it from the day-trip towns of Vence and St-Paul. The wind blows colder, the forest around is dense and arid, and the coast seems hours—and ages—away (though Tourrettes is less than an hour's drive from Nice). From the town square that doubles as a parking lot with an ongoing pétanque game on one side, to the quiet cafés lining it, to the sharply raked, torturously twisted streets snaking down the slopes of the Old Town, this is Old Provence without the stage makeup. Yes, there are dozens of galleries and arts-and-crafts shops, but they're owned and run by real artists and artisans, who have made a life for themselves in this intimate community.

Built in the Middle Ages inside a rampart of stone houses and encircling a 15th-century church, Tourrettes's Old Town crowns a rocky plateau. At its feet the olive orchards are purple with violets in spring, which are cultivated for the perfume industry, candied in Toulouse, or tied into nosegays and sold in flower markets across France.

Where to Stay

$$–$$$ ▦ **La Demeure de Jeanne.** Loyal visitors to this guesthouse come for the rooms in soothing colors with Provençal furniture, private terraces, panoramic views, and a natural breeze that makes air-conditioning unnecessary. But most of all they come for the guest-only tables d'hôte, which take place twice a week in the garden (€50–€60 including drinks). Yolande Cohen-Dichtel's years as a cook in Michelin-starred restaurants show in her selection of dishes: line-caught sea bass with fish coulis, confit knuckle of veal, leg of lamb cooked in hay, turbot with julienne vegetables. She cooks only wild fish and insists on the finest French meats. Come here and you'll have to play by the rules, however: credit cards are not accepted and children under 12 are banned because of the artworks in the house. ⊠ *Rte. de Vence, 06140* ☎ *04–93–59–37–42* ⊕ *www.demeuredejeanne.com* ↬ *4 rooms* ⌂ *Pool, dining room, cable TV* ▭ *No credit cards* ⊗ *Closed Nov.–Feb.*

NICE

As the fifth-largest city in France, sprawling from its waterfront airport to Cap Ferrat, this distended tangle of suburbs, modern apartment buildings, industry, and traffic is often avoided by travelers who expect a more leisurely experience from the south of France. Crawling into town from the airport or stepping off the train at the congested commercial quarter around Gare Nice-Ville, you may be tempted to bolt for the nearest city limit, where signs encircle and slash through the name Nice—as if to say "not Nice."

Flowers, Floats & Fatheads

IF THE WORD CARNIVAL means masked balls in Venice to most, or conjures images of feather-clad dancers writhing rhythmically through the streets of Rio, few people associate Nice with this pre-Lenten festival of excess and droll debauchery. Yet this most Latin of French cities is the capital of Carnaval in France, and transforms itself every February from a relatively sedate seaside metropolis into one vast party. The streets behind the waterfront and around Place Masséna explode in bright lights and color, and parades, masks, and impromptu street celebrations are everyday sights.

It's a tradition that dates back to pagan times, when the Romans fêted the end of winter and the dawning of spring. The festival translated easily into Christian terms, when the Church established the period of partial fasting before Easter. We call it Lent; the French call it Carême; but in Church Latin it was *carne levare* (crudely translated, "take out the meat"), and easily evolved into the word *carnaval*. Thus *mardi gras* (Fat Tuesday) was the last chance to indulge before Ash Wednesday and the deprivations of Lent. It wasn't long, however, before the pleasures of Carnaval outstripped those of Mardi Gras and shook free of their sacred meaning. The festival these days lasts a good two weeks and often takes place smack in the middle of Lent.

Nice's Carnaval is extremely user friendly, with a published calendar of events and easy advance ticket sales for any seated events. There's the presentation of towering effigies of King and Queen Carnaval on Place Masséna, which is transformed into an electric fantasyland of music and blinking lights. There are parades of magnificently crafted *grosses têtes* (literally, "fatheads"), enormous puppetlike personages that make Macy's balloons look like so much rubber. And there are the famous *batailles des fleurs* (flower battles), really full-scale parades complete with marching bands, clowns, and samba troupes. Elaborate floats heaped with Côte d'Azur flowers cruise down the Promenade des Anglais hauling a cargo of spectacularly costumed beauty queens who toss fresh flowers into the crowd. The crowds in the bleachers lining the Promenade des Anglais toss back confetti, wave branches of lemon-yellow mimosa, and cheer for their favorite floats. Weaving between the floats are stilt-walkers, jugglers, and street-theater troupes dressed in phantasmagoric excess who leer at onlookers and tease gawking children. Imagination reigns, and no image is too extreme, too bizarre, too extravagant.

The grand finale of Carnaval, which draws the days and nights of festivity to a close, takes on a solemn air. For the last time the towering dummy-king is paraded down Avenue Jean-Médecin and stands, still and lonely, on the dark pebble beach below the promenade. A parade of torchbearers in friars' robes cuts a glowing swath through the crowd and sets fire to the royal puppet. A silence falls over the crowd, then a cheer—really a primal roar—rises. The flames glow across the water as they engulf the king and, from a boat hovering offshore, fireworks burst in confetti colors over the waterfront. The party's over . . . at least until next year. For dates, schedules, and information, contact ☎ 04-92-14-48-14.

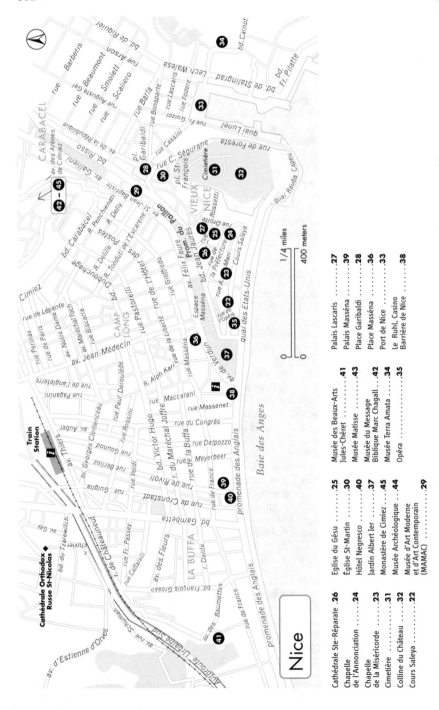

302 <

Nice

They couldn't be more wrong. The vast sprawl of urbanity south of the autoroute pours inevitably toward the sea, and the waterfront, paralleled by the famous Promenade des Anglais and lined by grand hotels and mansions, is one of the noblest in France. It's capped by a dramatic promontory (called "the château") whose slopes plunge almost into the sea and at whose base unfolds a bewitching warren of ancient streets reminiscent of Italy, Greece, or old Sardinia. Work on a new tramway has turned several main thoroughfares, including Avenue Jean Médecin leading up to the train station, into building sites, and it's not scheduled to be completed until 2015. The Old Town, being entirely pedestrian (except for the little garbage "trains" and some outlaw scooters), has been spared the chaos.

It was on the now château-less Colline du Château and at what is now the Plage des Ponchettes, in front of the Old Town, that the Greeks established a market-port and named it Nikaia. Having already established Marseille as early as the 4th century BC, they branched out along the coast soon afterward and founded the city that would become Marseille's chief coastal rival. The Romans established themselves a little later on the hills of Cimiez (Cemenelum), already previously occupied by Ligurians and Celts, and quickly overshadowed the waterfront port. After falling to the Saracen invasions, Nice regained power as an independent state, developing into an important port in the early Middle Ages.

So cocksure did it become that in 1388, Nice, along with the hill towns behind, effectively seceded from the county of Provence, under Louis d'Anjou, and allied itself with Savoie. Thus began its intimate liaison with the House of Savoy, and through it with Piedmont and Sardinia, as the Comté de Nice (Nice County). It was a relationship that lasted some 500 years, tinting the culture, architecture, and dialect in rich Italian hues.

By the 19th century Nice was flourishing commercially, locked in rivalry with the neighboring shipping port of Genoa. Another source of income: the dawning of tourism, as first the English, then the Russian nobility discovered its extraordinary climate and superb waterfront position. A parade of fine stone mansions and hotels closed into a nearly solid wall of masonry, separated from the smooth-round rocks of the beach by the appropriately named Promenade des Anglais (promenade of the English).

Today Nice strikes an engaging balance between Old World grace, porttown exotica, urban energy, whimsy, and—in its extraordinary museums and thriving arts life—high culture (albeit tinged with a soupçon of corruption, a legacy of late mayor Jacques Médecin, who also authored a Niçois cookbook). Thanks to its two universities, there's a healthy dose of the young and hip, too. You could easily spend your vacation here and emerge days or weeks later subtly Latinized, sensually and aesthetically engaged, attuned to Nice's quirks, its rhythms, and its Mediterranean tides.

Vieux Nice

Framed by the "château"—really a rocky promontory—and Cours Saleya, the Old Town of Nice is its strongest drawing point and, should you only be passing through, the best place to capture the city's historic feeling. Its grid of narrow streets, darkened by houses five and six stories high with bright splashes of laundry fluttering overhead and jewel-box Baroque churches on every other corner, creates a magic that seems utterly removed from the Côte d'Azur fast lane.

A GOOD WALK

Begin your exploration on **Cours Saleya** ㉒, preferably in the morning so you can experience the market in full swing. Its cafés, restaurants, and market stalls throng with the sounds, smells, and sights of Old Nice. At its center you'll find the florid Baroque **Chapelle de la Miséricorde** ㉓, worthy of a stop. Then make your way to the far end of the Cours. The tall yellow-stone building at its end, its top floor wrapped around with a balcony, was where Henri Matisse lived from 1921 to 1938; from the apartments on its top floors he took in magnificent views over the sea. Turn left up Rue de la Poissonerie to find the extravagant **Chapelle de l'Annonciation** ㉔. Continue up Poissonerie to Rue de la Place Vieille, then head right to Rue Droite. The **Eglise du Gésù** ㉕ looms large and spare in comparison with neighboring chapels. Turn left on Rue Rossetti and cross the square to the **Cathédrale Ste-Réparate** ㉖, its restored ocher facade an inspired balance of Italianate arcs and lines.

NEED A BREAK?

For fresh, homemade gelato-style ice cream offered in a rainbow of flavors and colors, stop at **Glacier Fenocchio** (✉ 6 rue de la Poissonnerie ☎ 04–93–62–88–80). There's even a choice of locally grown citrus flavors, including blood orange, mandarin, and Menton lemon.

Now take a break from the sacred, doubling back up Rue Rossetti and continuing left up narrow Rue Droite to the magnificent **Palais Lascaris** ㉗, whose broad classical facade squeezed onto this narrow street belies the Baroque extravagance within. Continue up Rue Droite to **Place St-François,** where a fish market holds forth every morning (though some of the fish have traveled a great distance to get here).

Head up Rue Pairolière, but take time to duck left and right up the tiny alleys and steep streets that plunge you into a concentration of popular cafés and restaurants, including the landmark street-food hangout called Chez René/Socca. You'll emerge on Boulevard Jean-Jaurès and empty onto the grand arcaded **Place Garibaldi** ㉘, which would be at home in Milan or Turin. One of its five street-spokes points straight to the **Musée d'Art Moderne et d'Art Contemporain** ㉙, a bold sculpture of a building anchoring a sleek plaza.

From Place Garibaldi and Boulevard Jean-Jaurès, follow Rue Neuve to the **Église St-Martin** ㉚, the oldest church. From here wind your way up Rue de la Providence and Rue Jouane Nicolas to the **Cimetière** ㉛ and ultimately the ruins of the castle, now a park called the **Colline du Château** ㉜, with a wraparound panorama of Nice and the coast. From here you can either follow the switchback steps down or take the *ascenseur* (elevator) to the foot of the fat Tour Bellanda (Bellanda Tower), where the French composer Hector Berlioz once lived.

Next, you can cross Quai des États-Unis to the pebbled beach and rest your weary feet. Or, if you're still feeling energetic, swing left away from the Old Town and hike around the tidy rectangle of the **Port de Nice** ㉝, with its neat rows of pleasure boats, and from its end follow Boulevard Carnot to the **Musée Terra Amata** 🟤, marking the settlement where man first flourished some 400,000 years ago.

TIMING Aim for morning on this walk, so you'll see the markets on Cours Saleya and Place St-François at their liveliest. If you include a visit to the Palais Lascaris and a visit to the Musée Terra Amata, this would make a wonderful full-day's outing.

Sights to See

🟤 **Cathédrale Ste-Réparate.** Named for the 15-year-old Palestinian martyr whose body washed ashore at Nice to become the city's patron saint many centuries ago, this superb ensemble of columns, cupolas, and symmetrical ornaments dominates the Old Town, flanked by its own 18th-century bell tower and capped by a glossy ceramic-tile dome. The cathedral's interior, restored to a bright color palette of ocher golds and rusts, has elaborate plasterwork and decorative frescoes on every surface. Look for the **Chapelle du St-Sacrement** in the north transept, dating from 1707; its twisted marble columns and exuberant sculpture are worthy of Bernini and St. Peter's in Rome. ⊠ *Rue Ste-Réparate.*

🟤 **Chapelle de l'Annonciation.** Also known through typical Nice-lore obfuscation as St-Jaume, St-Giaume, or Ste-Rita, this 17th-century Carmelite chapel is a classic example of pure Niçois Baroque, from its sculpted door to its extravagant marble work and the florid symmetry of its arches and cupolas. The interior concentrates every form of colored faux-stonework, rich marble inlay, gilt, and frescoes—a lot of bombast squeezed into a finite space. Though it's officially dedicated to St. James the Apostle, the people of Nice lavish flowers and candles on the statue of Ste-Rita in the first chapel on the left; having suffered from a leprous sore and a lifetime of isolation in the 14th century, she has come to represent help for the terminally ill. ⊠ *Rue de la Poissonerie.*

★ 🟤 **Chapelle de la Miséricorde.** If you step inside only one Baroque chapel here, this superb 1740 structure on Cours Saleya should be it. A superbly balanced pièce-montée of half-domes and cupolas decorated within an inch of its life with frescoes, faux marble, gilt, and crystal chandeliers, it's the ultimate example of Nice Baroque at its most excessive and successful. A magnificent Bréa altarpiece crowns the ensemble. ⊠ *Cours Saleya.*

🟤 **Cimetière** (Cemetery). This solemn cluster of white tombs looms prominently over the city below, providing a serene or macabre detail of daily life, depending on your mood. Under Nice's blue skies, the gleaming white marble and Italian mix of melodrama and exuberance in the decorations, dedications, photo portraits, and sculptures are somehow oddly life-affirming. There are three sections, to this day segregating Catholics, Protestants, and Jews. ⊠ *Allée François-Aragon.*

🟤 **Colline du Château** (Château Hill). Though nothing remains of this once-massive medieval stronghold but a few ruins left after its 1706 dismantling, the name château still applies to this high plateaulike park, from which you can take in extraordinary views of the Baie des Anges, the length of the Promenade des Anglais, and the red-ocher roofs of the Old Town. Children can let off steam at the playground, which has panoramic views and a bit of shade. ⊠ *At east end of Promenade des Anglais* ⊙ *Daily 7–7.*

22 Cours Saleya. This long pedestrian thoroughfare, half street, half square, is the nerve center of Old Nice, the heart of the Vieille Ville and the stage-set for the daily dramas of marketplace and café life. Framed with 18th-century houses and shaded by plane trees, the long, narrow square bursts into a fireworks-show

Fodor'sChoice ★

> " You don't need to visit the city's famous Musée Matisse to understand this great artist: Simply stand in the doorway of his former apartment (at 1 place Charles Félix) and study the Place de l'Ancien Senat 10 feet away–it's a golden Matisse pumped up to the nth power. "

of color Tuesday through Sunday, when flower-market vendors roll armloads of mimosas, irises, roses, and orange blossoms into *cornets* (paper cones) and thrust them into the arms of shoppers (Tues.–Sat. 6 AM–5:30 PM, Sun. 6–noon). Cafés and restaurants, all more or less touristy, fill outdoor tables with onlookers who bask in the sun. At the far-east end, antiques and *brocante* (collectibles) draw avid junk-hounds every Monday morning. Just beyond, Place Félix seems to lure the most fashionable crowd to see and be seen, perhaps because there are no market stands to get in the way of the most visible café tables, or because it provides clearest access to sun on cool winter days. ⊠ *2 blocks back from the Quai des États-Unis, in the center of the Old Town.*

25 Eglise du Gésù. If Nice's other chapels are jewel boxes, this is a barn. Broad, open, and ringing hollow after the intense concentration of sheer matter in the Miséricorde and Ste-Rita, it seems austere by comparison. That's only because the decoration is spread over a more expansive surface. If it's possible, this 17th-century Baroque chapel is even more theatrical and over-the-top than its peers. Angels throng in plaster and fresco, pillars spill over with extravagantly sculpted capitals, and from the pulpit (to the right, at the front), the crucifix is supported by a disembodied arm. ⊠ *Corner of Rue Droite and Rue Gésù.*

30 Église St-Martin. Also known as St-Augustin, this serene Baroque structure at the foot of the château anchors the oldest church-parish in Nice. Built in 1405, it was here that Martin Luther preached in 1510 and Garibaldi was baptized in 1807. ⊠ *Rue Sincaire.*

29 Musée d'Art Moderne et d'Art Contemporain (MAMAC) (Modern and Contemporary Art Museum). Moored by four marble-front towers, joined by the transparent arcs of pedestrian bridges, and dramatically framing a concourse decked with outdoor sculptures, this building is a bold and emphatic statement of Nice's presence in the modern world. The art collection inside focuses intently and thoroughly on contemporary art from the late 1950s onward, featuring works of the École de Nice (Nice School), the self-dubbed Nouveau Réalistes (New Realists) such as artists César, Bernar Venet, Ben, Yves Klein, Daniel Spoerri, Jean Tinguely, and Niki de Saint-Phalle. The collection includes international acquisitions, too, ranging from Jim Dine and Frank Stella to Miró and Giacometti. Be sure to climb along the rooftop sculpture terrace, a catwalk overlooking the whole of the city. ⊠ *Promenade des Arts* ☎ *04–93–62–61–62* ⊕ *www.mamac-nice.org* ☜ *€4* ⊗ *Tues.–Sun. 10–6.*

㉞ Musée Terra Amata. During the digging for the foundation of a building in 1966, the shovels revealed the remains of a temporary settlement once used by elephant hunters around 380,000 BC. They were perhaps the oldest known inhabitants of Europe. Now the site is a museum reconstructing the ancient beach-camp known as Terra Amata ("beloved land") as it was, lodgings and all—incorporating a real human footprint, calcified in the sand. There are recorded commentaries in English, and films explaining the lifestyle of these earliest Europeans. Don't expect a blockbuster anthropology expo; displays are small-scale and mainly limited to tiny models. ⊠ *25 bd. Carnot* ☎ *04–93–55–59–93* ☜ *€4* ⊗ *Tues.–Sun. 10–6.*

★ ㉗ Palais Lascaris (Lascaris Palace). This aristocratic palace was built in 1648 for Jean-Baptiste Lascaris-Vintimille, marechal to the duke of Savoy, in a manner grand enough to put the neighboring chapels to shame. The magnificent vaulted staircase with its massive stone balustrade and niches filled with classical gods is only surpassed in grandeur by the Flemish tapestries (after Rubens) and the extraordinary trompe-l'oeil fresco of the fall of Phaëthon. On the ground floor an 18th-century pharmacy has been imported from Besançon and reconstructed, complete with built-in wooden cabinets and a lovely collection of faïence jars. There's also a collection of cookware and tools from daily life at the other end of the income scale. Like much of Old Nice, this is a quirky, atmospheric museum, worth a stopover as you explore the backstreets. ⊠ *15 rue Droite* ☎ *04–93–62–72–40* ☜ *Free* ⊗ *Wed.–Mon. 10–6.*

㉘ Place Garibaldi. Encircled by grand vaulted arcades stuccoed in rich yellow, this broad pentagon of a square could have been airlifted out of Turin (though half of the square was ripped up at the time of this writing for work on the tramway). In the center the shrinelike fountain-sculpture of Garibaldi surveys the passersby, who stroll under the arcades and lounge in its cafés. Garibaldi is held in high esteem here: the Italian general fought beside his own sons in the French ranks during the war of 1870.

㉝ Port de Nice. In 1750 the Duke of Savoy ordered a port to be dug into the waterfront to shelter the approach of the freight ships, fishing boats, and yachts that still sail into its safety today. Surrounded in rhythmic symmetry by the ocher facades of 19th-century houses, it makes for a pleasant walk far from the beach crowds.

Along the Promenade des Anglais

Nice takes on a completely different character west of Cours Saleya, with broad city blocks, vast Neoclassical hotels and apartment houses, and a series of inviting parks dense with palm trees, greenery, and splashing fountains. From the Jardin Albert Ier, once the delta of the Paillon River, the famous Promenade des Anglais stretches the length of the city's waterfront.

The original promenade was the brainchild of Lewis Way, an English minister in the growing community of British refugees drawn to Nice's climate. They needed a proper walkway on which to take the sea air, and pooled resources to build a 6½-foot-wide road meandering through an alley of shade trees. Nowadays it's a wide, multilane boulevard thick with traffic—in fact, it's the last gasp of the coastal highway N98. Beside it runs its charming parallel, the wide, sun-washed pedestrian walkway with intermittent steps leading down to the smooth-rock beach; its foundation is a seawall that keeps all but the wildest storms from sloshing waves over the promenade. A daily parade of *promeneurs,* rollerbladers, joggers, and sun-baskers strolls its broad pavement, looking out over the hypnotic blue expanse of the sea. Only in the wee hours is it possible to enjoy the waterfront stroll as the cream of Nice's international society did, when there were nothing more than hoof beats to compete with the roar of the waves.

**A GOOD
WALK**

From the west end of Cours Saleya, walk down Rue St-François-de-Paule past the Belle-Époque **Opéra** ㉟, constructed in classic Italian tiered loggias. Continue up the street, then head right up Rue de l'Opéra to **Place Masséna** ㊱, framed in broad arcades and opening onto the vast, green **Jardin Albert Iᵉʳ** ㊲. Three long blocks past the glamorous **Le Ruhl, Casino Barrière de Nice** ㊳ you'll reach the gates and park of the imposing **Palais Masséna** ㊴; to peruse its eclectic collection of nuggets of Nice history, walk through the grounds to enter from the Rue de France side. Next door, the landmark **Hôtel Negresco** ㊵ expands its colossal facade along the waterfront, crowned at the corner by its signature dome.

Walk along the waterfront for a few blocks, past the busy Boulevard Gambetta, then head inland up tiny Rue Sauvan. Cross Boulevard Grosso and head diagonally up the hill on Avenue des Baumettes. In this quiet, once luxurious neighborhood you'll climb to the **Musée des Beaux-Arts Jules-Chéret** ㊶, built by the Ukrainian princess Kotschoubey in extravagant Italianate style.

TIMING   This walk covers a long stretch of waterfront, so it may take up to an hour to stroll the length of it. Allow a half day if you explore the Palais Masséna or the Musée des Beaux Arts.

Sights to See

㊵ **Hôtel Negresco.** This vast Neoclassical palace hotel dominates a full block of the promenade, and remains, for many, an enduring symbol of Côte d'Azur luxury. Its famous Salon Royal, a broad rotunda at the hotel's center, is classed as a historic monument, with its Gustav Eiffel leaded-glass dome and Baccarat chandelier commissioned by Czar Nicholas II. Like many grand hotels trying to make ends meet these days, it now caters to conferences and tour groups, but of all the hotels in town it remains the most quintessentially Niçois. ⊠ *37 promenade des Anglais* ☎ *04–93–16–64–00.*

㊲ **Jardin Albert Iᵉʳ** (Albert Iᵉʳ Garden). Sandwiched between two busy streets, this garden of tropical greenery stands over the delta of the River Paillon, underground since 1882. Flowers and palm trees are thrown into exotic relief by nighttime illumination, and the wonderful old-fashioned merry-go-round provides a parents' dream photo opportunity.

㊶ Musée des Beaux-Arts Jules-Chéret (Jules-Chéret Fine Arts Museum). While the collection here is impressive, it is the 19th-century Italianate mansion that houses it that remains the showstopper. Originally built for a member of Nice's Old Russian community, the princess Kotschoubey, this was a Belle Époque wedding cake, replete with one of the grandest staircases on the coast, salons decorated with neo-Pompéienne frescoes, an English-style garden, and white columns and balustrades by the dozen. After the *richissime* American James Thompson took over and the last glittering ball was held here, the villa was bought by the municipality as a museum in the 1920s. Unfortunately, much of the period decor was sold but in its place now hang paintings by Degas, Boudin, Monet, Sisley, Dufy, and Jules Chéret, whose posters of winking *damselles* distill all the *joie* of the Belle Époque. ⊠ *33 av. des Baumettes* ☎ *04–92–15–28–28* 💶 *€4* ⊗ *Tues.–Sun. 10–6.*

㉟ Opéra. Demolished by a devastating 1881 fire, the victims of which lie in the cemetery on the hillside of the château, this magnificent Italian-style opera house rose from the ashes in 1885. Charles Garnier, architect of the Paris Opéra, consulted on its design. It's home today to the Opéra de Nice, with a permanent chorus, orchestra, and ballet corps. ⊠ *4 rue St-François-de-Paul* ☎ *04–92–17–40–00.*

★ ㊴ Palais Masséna (Masséna Palace). This handsome Belle Époque villa, to reopen (hopefully) in 2006 after extensive renovations, was built by a grandson of Napoléon's, Marechal Masséna; his great-grandson donated it to Nice under the proviso that it house a museum of the city's history. The resulting **Musée d'Art et d'Histoire** (Museum of Art and History) is a fascinating hodgepodge of private collections reflecting every aspect of Nice's past, from Garibaldi's death sheet to Asian jewelry collected in imperial days to Empress Josephine's tiara, carved entirely in cameo. It also contains extraordinary notebook sketches of Napoléon by Neoclassical painter Louis David, as vivid and natural as snapshots, as well as relief models of Nice in the 1930s and 1954—a desert-island wasteland compared to today's congested overbuilding. There's even a Bréa polyptych of St-Marguerite. It's a must if you love the offbeat, the obscure, and the treasure hunt. ⊠ *Entrance at 65 rue de France* ☎ *04–93–88–11–34* 💶 *€4* ⊗ *Wed.–Mon. 10–noon and 2–6.*

㊱ Place Masséna. As Cours Saleya is the heart of the Old Town, so this broad and noble square is the heart of the city as a whole. It's framed by an ensemble of Italian-style arcaded buildings first built in 1815, their facades stuccoed in rich red ocher. At its center is a heroic fountain in which thick-muscled bronze figures surge from the water. The central activities of the February Carnaval are traditionally held here, though they have been moved to the Promenade des Anglais during work on the tramway. Behind the Place and following the ancient riverbed, stretches the inviting **Escape Masséna**, a long public plaza with fountains, permanent performance spaces, grassy park grounds, and dozens of skateboarders at any given moment.

38 **Le Ruhl, Casino Barrière de Nice.** Recently renovated to the tune of €5 million by the Barrière group, which purchased this casino in 2004, Le Ruhl now lures in the summer vacationers and the winter convention crowd with vivid colors and fiber-optic lighting. Some sign into the hushed gaming room for roulette and blackjack, others try their luck at one of the 300-some slot machines. ⊠ *1 promenade des Anglais* ☎ *04–97–03–12–22* ☉ *Fri.–Sun. 10 AM–5 AM, Mon.–Thurs. 10 AM–4 AM.*

OFF THE BEATEN PATH

CATHÉDRALE ORTHODOXE RUSSE ST-NICOLAS – From the Promenade, hop Bus 7 up Boulevard Gambetta and get off at either the Thiers-Gambetta or Parc Imperial stop, or walk west from the train station to visit this magnificent Russian Orthodox cathedral. Built in 1896 to accommodate the sizable population of Russian aristocrats who had adopted Nice as their winter home, this Byzantine fantasy is the largest of its kind outside the motherland. The church has no fewer than six gold-leaf onion domes, rich ceramic mosaics on its facade, and extraordinary icons framed in silver and jewels. The benefactor was Nicholas II himself, whose family attended the inauguration in 1912. ⊠ *Av. Nicolas II* ☎ *04-93-96-88-02* ☉ *Apr.-Oct., Mon.-Sat. 9-noon and 2:30-6, Sun. 2:30-6; Nov.-Mar., Mon.-Sat. 9:30-noon and 2:30-5, Sun. 2:30-5.*

Cimiez

Once the site of the powerful Roman settlement Cemenelum, the hilltop neighborhood of Cimiez—4 km (2½ mi) north of Cours Saleya—is Nice's most luxurious quarter. Villas seem in competition to outdo each other in opulence, and the combination of important art museums, Roman ruins, and a historic monastery make it worth a day's exploration. To visit Cimiez and nearby museums, you need to combine a bus pass or taxi fare with strong legs and comfortable shoes. If you brave the route by car, arm yourself with a map and a navigator. Bus 15 from Place Masséna or Avenue Jean-Médecin takes you to both the Chagall and Matisse museums; from the latter you can visit the ruins and monastery.

A GOOD WALK

Begin your day at the **Musée du Message Biblique Marc Chagall** ㊷, which houses one of the finest collections of Chagall's works based on biblical themes. Then make the pilgrimage to the center of Cimiez and the **Musée Matisse** ㊸, where an important collection of Matisse's life work is amassed in an Italianate villa. Just behind, the **Musée Archéologique** ㊹ displays a wealth of Roman treasures unearthed on the site of the original colony. Slightly east of the museum is the thriving **Monastère de Cimiez** ㊺, a Franciscan monastery.

TIMING

Between bus connections and long walks from sight to sight, this walk is a half-day commitment at minimum. If you plan to stop into the Chagall Museum, really spend time in the Matisse Museum, and explore the ruins, this could easily be a day's outing.

Sights to See

45 **Monastère de Cimiez** (Cimiez Monastery). High over Nice and its château-bearing hill, this fully functioning monastery, originally established in the 16th century, is worth the pilgrimage. There's a lovely **garden,** re-planted following the original 16th-century lines. There's also the **Musée Franciscain** (Franciscan Museum), a didactic museum tracing the history of the Franciscan order, and a 15th-century **church.** The pretty, single-nave chapel contains three works of remarkable power and elegance by Bréa: the early *Pietà* (1475) flanked by portraits of High Renaissance grace; the *Crucifixion* (1512); and the *Deposition* (1520), with intense suppressed emotion. ⊠ *Pl. du Monastère* ☎ *04–93–81–00–04* 🖃 *Free* ☉ *Mon.–Sat. 10–noon and 3–6.*

44 **Musée Archéologique** (Archaeology Museum). This contemporary building houses a dense and intriguing collection of objects extracted from digs around the Roman city of Cemenelum, which flourished from the 1st to the 5th centuries and dwarfed its waterfront neighbor with a population of 20,000 in its prime. The examples of Greek and Italian treasures—ceramics, jewelry, and coins—attest to the cosmopolitan nature of coastal commerce. Behind the museum, you can wander through the ruins and digs, including the *thermes* (baths) and an early Christian baptistery. Just beyond, the Roman *arènes* (arena) seats 4,000 for the annual jazz festival. ⊠ *160 av. des Arènes-de-Cimiez* ☎ *04–93–81–59–57* 🖃 *€4* ☉ *Wed.–Mon. 10–6.*

43 **Musée Matisse.** In the '60s, the city of Nice bought this lovely, light-bathed
FodorsChoice 17th-century villa, surrounded by the ruins of Roman civilization, and
★ restored it to house a large collection of Henri Matisse's works. Matisse settled in Nice in 1917, seeking a sun cure after a bout with pneumonia, and remained here until his death in 1954. During his years on the Côte d'Azur, Matisse maintained intense friendships and artistic liaisons with Renoir, who lived in Cagnes, and with Picasso, who lived in Mougins and Antibes. Settling first along the waterfront, he eventually moved up to the rarified isolation of Cimiez and took an apartment in the Hotel Regina (now an apartment building), where he lived out the rest of his life. Matisse walked often in the parklands around the Roman remains and was buried in an olive grove outside the Cimiez Cemetery. The collection of artworks includes several pieces donated to the city by the artist himself before his death; the rest was donated by his family. In every medium and context—paintings, gouache cut-outs, engravings, and book illustrations—it represents the evolution of his art, from Cézanne-like still lifes to exuberant dancing paper dolls. Even the furniture and decorations speak of Matisse, from the Chinese vases to the bold-printed fabrics with which he surrounded himself. A series of black-and-white photographs captures the artist at work, surrounded by personal—and telling—details. ⊠ *164 av. des Arènes-de-Cimiez* ☎ *04–93–81–08–08* 🖃 *€4* ☉ *Wed.–Mon. 10–6.*

★ **42** **Musée du Message Biblique Marc Chagall** (Marc Chagall Museum of Biblical Themes). Superbly displayed in a modern structure bathed in light and surrounded by coastal greenery, this is one of the finest permanent collections of the artist's late works. Included here are 17 vast canvases on biblical themes, each in emphatic and joyous color schemes; they celebrate the stories of Adam and Eve, Noah, Abraham, and Moses, and the sensual, mystical Song of Solomon, dedicated to his wife. Preparatory sketches, sculptures, and ceramic pieces enhance the exhibit, as well as a tapestry and, outside, a mosaic. ⊠ *Av. du Dr-Ménard (head up Av. Thiers, then take a left onto Av. Malausséna, cross the railway tracks, and take the first right up Av. de l'Olivetto)* ☎ *04–93–53–87–20* ⊕ *www. musee-chagall.fr* 🎫 *€5.50* ⊙ *July–Sept., Wed.–Mon. 10–6; Oct.–June, Wed.–Mon. 10–5.*

Where to Eat & Stay

★ **$$$$** ✕ **Chantecler.** Long a showplace for Riviera luxury, replete with Régence-fashion salons decked out with 18th-century wood boiserie and Aubusson carpet, the Negresco's main dining room has been playing musical chefs for the past few years. The current chef, the aptly named Bruno Turbot, has grasped what people expect from this kitchen: luxury, as in soft-boiled egg with Iranian caviar toasts, and accessibility, as in a €45 *menu plaisir* at lunchtime (€55 including drinks). From the iced minestrone with clams and basil sorbet, Brittany sole fillets with tiny artichokes and spring onions, and saddle of Sisteron lamb, the menu shows Turbot's ability to draw on Mediterranean ingredients without being a slave to Provençal tradition. ⊠ *Hôtel Negresco, 37 promenade des Anglais* ☎ *04–93–16–64–00* ⊕ *www.hotel-negresco-nice.com* ⌲ *Reservations essential* ⊟ *AE, DC, MC, V* ⊙ *Closed Feb.*

$$–$$$$ ✕ **Jouni.** In a residential street behind the port lurks one of Nice's most talked about restaurants, with a Finnish chef at the helm. Jouni Tormanen worked with the likes of Alain Ducasse and Ferran Adria before opening this shrine to the finest local ingredients. Here he serves a €30 lunch menu and dinner menus at €50 and €70 in the simply decorated dining room and on the sidewalk terrace. The restaurant seats 20, with room for a few more outside. Host Giuseppe Serena will explain to you why the restaurant doesn't serve shrimp on windy days (conditions are wrong for fishing) and talk you through the selection of olive oils on the shelves. Though the cooking is very near flawless, those with hearty appetites might find the portions small and the prices a bit high. ⊠ *10 rue Lascaris, Old Town/Port* ☎ *04–97–08–14–80* ⊙ *Closed Wed. and Dec. 20–Jan. 20.*

$$–$$$ ✕ **Aphrodite.** In a fine old residential neighborhood between the waterfront and the train station, this peculiar little white cube of a restaurant may not look appealing from the outside, but its shape creates a pretty rooftop terrace and a closed terrace, quiet oases where you can enjoy a hearty meal à la Provençal. Specialites include fresh sea bass steamed with mushrooms and braised fowl with potato galettes, all prepared by local chef David Faure. ⊠ *10 bd. Dubouchage, New Town* ☎ *04–93–85–63–53* ⊕ *www.restaurant-aphrodite.com* ⊟ *AE, MC, V* ⊙ *Closed Sun. and Mon.*

$$–$$$ ✕ **Don Camillo.** Don Camillo's formerly staid dining room one street back from the sea and around the corner from the Cours Saleya market now has a youthful, chic new look to go with its chef, Stéphane Viano. He has added a sushi bar with purple walls, white stools, and a Japanese sushi chef, that caters mainly to locals who know it's tucked behind the dining room. The menu otherwise doesn't stray far from the classics of Niçois cooking, from the *borsotti de Mémé Emma* (a family recipe for ravioli) to a variation on the daube theme, made here with lobster in-

Cooking the Niçois Way

Nowhere in France is the food more seductive than along the Côte d'Azur and Provence. No wonder southern French cooking holidays à la Patricia Wells are so popular—yet, except for the most dedicated cooks, a full week can be too big a time and money commitment. That's why longtime food writer and Cordon Bleu–trained cook Rosa Jackson created the home-based cooking school Les Petits Farcis (✉ 7 rue du Jésus, Nice ☎ 06–81–67–41–22 ⊕ www.petitsfarcis.com) in the Vieux Nice neighborhood, a minute's walk from the celebrated Cours Saleya food market. In the yellow-and-burgundy kitchen of her renovated 17th-century apartment, complete with wooden beams and a handmade chandelier of chili peppers and silver cutlery, Jackson teaches students the classics of Niçois cooking: *les petits farcis*, of course (a local stuffed vegetable dish), but also

pissaladière (caramelized onion tart), *poulet à la niçoise* (chicken stewed with tomatoes, bell peppers, and eau de vie), *daube à la provençale* (beef stew with wine and herbs), local fish dishes, and fruit-based desserts. A class always begins with a trip to the market, where Jackson explains the origins of Niçois cooking—Nice belonged to Italy until 1860. After visiting a centuries-old wine cellar and choosing their cheeses at the local *fromagerie* (cheesemonger), students head back to the kitchen for an informal, hands-on class where they learn as much about local culture as cooking techniques. Following a four-course lunch, those who wish can continue with an olive oil tasting and food walk through the Old Town, ending at 6 PM with an ice cream at the legendary glacier Fenocchio. Classes run from €200 to €290.

---

stead of beef and served with gnocchi. There is a daily market menu at €32, but if you really want to splurge, order champagne and ask the staff to open it with the saber that sits in the fireplace. ✉ *5 rue des Ponchettes, Old Town/Port* ☎ *04–93–85–67–95* ⊟ *AE, DC, MC, V* ☉ *No lunch Mon., Thurs., and July–Aug.*

★ $$–$$$ ✕ **Grand Café de Turin/Chez Jo L'Ecailler.** Whether you crowd into a banquette in the dark, low-ceilinged bar or win a coveted (albeit plastic) table under the arcaded porticoes on Place Garibaldi, this is *the* place to go for shellfish in Nice. Order a bottle of something cold, spread butter on the sliced brown bread, and dive into the platters set before you: sea snails, clams, plump *fines de claires* and Mediterranean *bouzigue* oysters, salty snail-like *violets*, and urchins by the dozen, their spines still waving. They've all just been pried open at the refrigerator-counters on the sidewalk, with dripping crates of fresh supplies standing by. It's packed noon and night, and there's a thriving young scene after work. ✉ *5 pl. Garibaldi, Old Town/Port* ☎ *04–93–62–29–52* ⊕ *www. cafedeturin.com* ⊟ *AE, DC, MC, V* ☉ *Closed 3rd wk in Jan.*

★ $$–$$$ ✕ **La Mérenda.** The back-to-bistro boom climaxed here when Dominique Le Stanc retired his crown at the Negresco to take over this tiny, unpretentious landmark of Provençal cuisine. Now he and his wife work in the miniature open kitchen creating the ultimate versions of stuffed sar-

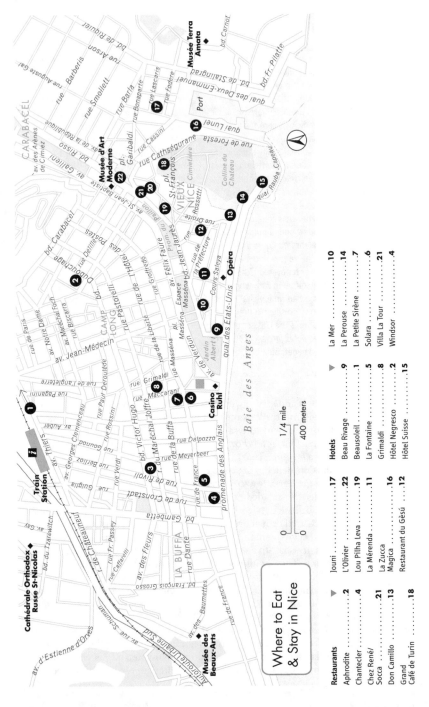

Where to Eat & Stay in Nice

Restaurants
- Aphrodite **2**
- Chantecler **4**
- Chez René/ Socca **21**
- Don Camillo **13**
- Grand Café de Turin **18**
- Jouni **17**
- L'Olivier **22**
- Lou Pilha Leva **19**
- La Mérenda **11**
- La Zucca Magica **16**
- Restaurant du Gesú **12**

Hotels
- Beau Rivage **9**
- Beausoleil **1**
- La Fontaine **5**
- Grimaldi **8**
- Hôtel Negresco **2**
- Hôtel Suisse **15**
- La Mer **10**
- La Perouse **14**
- La Petite Sirène **7**
- Solara **6**
- Villa La Tour **21**
- Windsor **4**

Cathédrale Orthodox Russe St-Nicolas ◆
Musée des Beaux-Arts ◆
Musée d'Art Moderne ◆
Musée Terra Amata ◆
Casino Ruhl
Opéra
Train Station

Baie des Anges

1/4 mile
400 meters

dines, pistou, slow-simmered daubes (beef stews), and the quintessential stockfish (the local lutefisk). It's one man's private mission; stop by in person to reserve entry to the inner sanctum (there are two evening seatings: 7 and 9). ✉ *4 rue de la Terrasse, Old Town/Port* ☎ *No phone* ▬ *No credit cards* ⊘ *Closed weekends, last wk in July, first 2 wks in Aug.*

\$\$–\$\$\$ ✕ **La Zucca Magica.** Tucked in a cozy, rustic shoe box along the port, this vegetarian-Italian bistro, The Magic Pumpkin, is all the rage, thanks to the imaginative cooking of Roman chef Marco Folicaldi. The eat-till-you-drop five-course menu changes daily according to the season, and offers a taste of the rich flavors that the best local markets have to offer: grilled fresh vegetables smothered in smoked cheese, minestrone, cannelloni, stuffed peppers, delicious pizzas, and the justly famous pumpkin-based recipes when autumn arrives. The chef's gruff friendliness, the noisy camaraderie of crowded diners, and the surreal pumpkin art in every form make for a real dining event. ✉ *4 bis quai Papacino, Old Town/Port* ☎ *04–93–56–25–27* ▬ *No credit cards* ⊘ *Closed Sun. and Mon.*

\$–\$\$\$ ✕ **L'Olivier.** In this hole-in-the-wall bistro on Place Garibaldi, two brothers have gone back to their roots, and all of Nice has followed. Frank Musso, trained at the Tour d'Argent in Paris, concentrates his sophisticated gifts on simple dishes: tripe simmered in tomatoes, daubes and pork confits, and crepes with homemade bitter-orange marmalade. His brother Christian provides the cheery welcome. ✉ *2 pl. Garibaldi, Vieux-Nice* ☎ *04–93–26–89–09* 🍴 *Reservations essential* ▬ *AE, DC, MC, V* ⊘ *Closed Sun. and Aug. No dinner Wed.*

¢–\$ ✕ **Restaurant du Gésù.** It's hard to define what makes this restaurant across from the Eglise de Jésus so popular. Is it the cheap yet delicious Niçois food, all made on the premises, from the pizza dough to the ravioli? Is it the gravelly voice of the owner, who won't take reservations but will always find a way to squeeze you in if you're willing to wait a few minutes? Is it the fact that the closely packed tables encourage conversation between strangers? Whatever the reason, the Restaurant du Gésù is packed year-round, turning into a party on summer nights, so try to arrive by 7:30 PM if you want to avoid a wait. ✉ *1 place du Gésù, Old Town/Port* ☎ *04–93–62–26–46* ▬ *No credit cards* ⊘ *Closed Sun.*

¢ ✕ **Chez René/Socca.** This back-alley landmark, where rustic olive-wood tables line the narrow street, is the most popular dive in town for the snack food unique to Nice. Curt waiters splash down your drink order, but you have to get in line for the food and carry it steaming to the table yourself. There's socca, of course, the grainy golden pancake of chickpea flour scraped with a palette knife straight off the griddle; spicy assortments of petits farcis; pissaladières heaped with caramelized onions and shiny black olives; and sweet *tourta de blea,* full of chopped Swiss chard and sprinkled with pine nuts. It's off Place Garibaldi on the edge of the Old Town, across from the *gare routière* (bus station). ✉ *2 rue Miralhetti, Old Town/Port* ☎ *04–93–92–05–73* ▬ *No credit cards* ⊘ *Closed Mon., Jan., and May.*

★ ¢ ✕ **Lou Pilha Leva.** Its name in dialect means "tu prend et tu t'en va" (take and go), but you'll be tempted to stay a while and taste everything here. Not as well known as Chez René but much more serious about the food it serves, this street stand just south of Place St-François offers good, fresh-cooked versions of petits farcis, tourta de blea, and pissaladières as well as full meals of homemade pasta, pizza, *moules-frites* (mussels with fries), soupe au pistou, polenta, stockfish, and fruit tarts, all made on the premises. Order food at the window and drinks at the table. ✉ *10 rue du Collet on Pl. Centrale, Old Town/Port* ☎ *04–93–13–99–08* 🖃 *MC, V.*

$$$$ 🏨 **Hôtel Negresco.** One of those names, like the Pierre or Claridges, that
Fodor'sChoice is synonymous with "Grand Hotel," the Negresco is a wedding-cake,
★ white-stucco slice of old-fashioned Riviera extravagance. Still the icon of Nice and a living monument to the city's golden age of travel, it has hosted everyone from the Beatles to the Burtons, and you'll feel a bit like a V.I.P. just pulling up in front of the entrance as the doorman, in uniformed splendor (knee-breeches and ostrich-plumed tricorn), helps you with your luggage. No other hotel can boast today of quite so many pillars, busts, coffered and painted ceilings, or, indeed, so many acres of white paint and gilding. The place is, in short, the very epitome of La Belle Epoque, justly so since it was built by Henri Negresco in 1912. Yes, the main hall, now denuded of the world's largest Aubusson carpet, is a bit forlorn, but its Gustave Eiffel glass ceiling still awes, as does its *qualité du Louvre* collection of Old Master paintings. Upstairs, each floor is devoted to an era from French history; Napoléon III on the fifth, Louis XV on the third, with some jarring modern notes, like the plastic-glitter bathtubs, the Vasarely Op-art carpet, and the rotating Nikki de Saint Phalle sculpture. Happily, each guest room is decorated differently and even the smallest have been done up with elegance and swank. By the elevators, you'll find a kitty-litter tray, as Madame Augier, the owner, loves her cats (and all animals—you are requested to leave "tips" for humane societies, not the staff). Downstairs, Le Chantecler ranks among the very finest restaurants in France, while the Carrousel Room (complete with merry-go-round horses and Folies Bérgère chandelier) is an over-the-top setting for your breakfast buffet. Never mind if you can't indulge in a room; dress up in your swankiest and have a champagne cocktail in the glorious walnut-and-velour bar, and you'll recapture some of the glamour of the Old Riviera. ✉ *37 promenade des Anglais, Promenade des Anglais, 06000* ☎ *04–93–16–64–00* 🖷 *04–93–88–35–68* ⊕ *www.hotel-negresco-nice. com* 🛏 *145 rooms* ◌ *2 restaurants, cable TV, in-room data ports, beach, bar, some pets allowed* 🖃 *AE, DC, MC, V.*

★ **$$$$** 🏨 **La Pérouse.** Just past the Old Town, at the foot of the château, this antipalace is a secret treasure cut into the cliff (an elevator takes you up to reception). Most rooms have breathtaking views of the Baie des Anges. Some of the best not only overlook the azure sea but also look down into an intimate garden with lemon trees and a cliff-side pool. A sundeck and sauna by the pool, as well as valet parking, add to the sense of private luxury. Most rooms are fairly large; some are decorated in somber plaids, others have painted Provençal furniture. The restaurant serves meals in the candlelit garden May through September. ✉ *11 quai Rauba-Capeau, Old Town/Port, 06300* ☎ *04–93–62–34–63* 🖷 *04–93–62–59–41* ⊕ *www.hroy.com/la-perouse* 🛏 *58 rooms, 4* *apartments* ⚐ *Restaurant, in-room safes, cable TV, pool, exercise equipment, hot tub, sauna, Wi-Fi, some pets allowed* ⊟ *AE, DC, MC, V.*

$$$–$$$$ ⊞ **Beau Rivage.** If you've seen one too many Provençal bedspreads and are tiring of antique furniture, the swishly renovated Beau Rivage might be just the break you need. Recently redecorated by über-designer Jean-Michel Wilmotte in wood, subdued linens, and Persian-style rugs, it compensates for its lack of pool and sea view with the city's largest private beach (which has a restaurant). Matisse lived in this 19th-century building before moving to Cours Saleya and then the hills of Cimiez. ⊠ *24 rue St-François-de-Paule, Old Town/Port, 06000* ☎ *04–92–47–82–82* 🖷 *04–92–47–82–83* ⊕ *www.nicebeaurivage.com* ➲ *118 rooms* ⚐ *Restaurant, beach, cable TV, in-room data ports* ⊟ *AE, DC, MC, V.*

$–$$$ ⊞ **Hôtel Suisse.** Charging modest prices for a spectacular view from the top end of the seafront, where the promenade winds around to the port, the Hôtel Suisse far outclasses most other hotels in this price range. You'll pay a little extra for a balcony with a sea view, but it will be oh-so-worth-it for the sight of the turquoise water glittering below. Recently redecorated by architect J.P. Nuel, the rooms provide all the modern comforts with pleasing cream-and-brown or cream-and-burgundy color schemes, and the lobby/breakfast room has also had been given a hip new look. ⊠ *15 quai Raubà Capéù, Old Town/Port, 06300* ☎ *04–92–17–39–00* 🖷 *04–93–85–30–70* ➲ *42 rooms* ⚐ *Bar, in-room data ports* ⊟ *AE, MC, V.*

$$ ⊞ **La Fontaine.** Downtown and a block from the waterfront, this immaculate, simply designed hotel offers a friendly welcome from its house-proud owners. Rooms are small and comfortable, in cheery blues and yellows and with freshly tiled bathrooms. It even has a pretty little courtyard where breakfast is served. ⊠ *49 rue de France, New Town, 06000* ☎ *04–93–88–30–38* 🖷 *04–93–88–98–11* ⊕ *www.hotel-fontaine. com* ➲ *29 rooms* ⚐ *In-room safes, cable TV, in-room data ports, bar, some pets allowed* ⊟ *AE, DC, MC, V.*

$$ ⊞ **Grimaldi.** Small but stylish, this well-boned little city hotel, halfway between the train station and the waterfront, offers a discreet, personal welcome and a sense of southern charm. Rooms have vivid color schemes and imaginative, old-style bathrooms, and the sleek lobby bar encourages international mingling. Prices are low for this level of comfort. ⊠ *15 rue Grimaldi, New Town, 06000* ☎ *04–93–16–00–24* 🖷 *04–93–87–00–24* ⊕ *www.le-grimaldi.com* ➲ *46 rooms* ⚐ *In-room safes, cable TV, bar, Internet room, Wi-Fi, some pets allowed* ⊟ *AE, DC, MC, V.*

$$ ⊞ **La Petite Sirene.** The central location is key, and its cozy scale helps. Rooms are tidily furnished and plushly carpeted in sleek beige and cream. The restaurant has been transformed into a cocktail bar serving only snacks. ⊠ *8 rue Maccarani, New Town, 06000* ☎ *04–97–03–03–40* 🖷 *04–97–03–03–41* ➲ *16 rooms* ⚐ *Snack bar, cable TV, bar; in-room data ports, Wi-Fi* ⊟ *AE, MC, V.*

★ $–$$ ⊞ **Windsor.** This is a memorably eccentric hotel with a vision: most of its white-on-white rooms either have frescoes of mythical themes or are works of contemporary artists' whimsy. There's also a "relaxation room" on the top floor, where you can exercise, meditate, or have a steam bath and massage. But the real draw of this otherworldly place is its astonishing city-center garden—a tropical delight of lemon, magnolia, and palm trees. Exotic finches flutter through the leaves, and a toucan caws beside the breakfast buffet; a small pool is screened by flowering shrubs. You can breakfast or dine here by candlelight (guests only). Book well ahead to immerse yourself in an exoticism that is particularly Niçois. ⊠ *11 rue Dalpozzo, New Town, 06000* ☎ *04–93–88–59–35* 🖷 *04–93–88–94–57* ⊕ *www.hotelwindsornice.com* ⟲ *57 rooms* ♿ *Dining room, cable TV, pool, steam room, bar, Wi-Fi* ▤ *AE, DC, MC, V* ⦿ *MAP.*

$ 🏨 **Beausoleil.** This big old downtown hotel has a certain urban charm, with French windows, ironwork balconies, and an oak cage elevator that whisks you up to impeccably maintained pink-and-gray rooms. A small bar and a cozy living room with TV make you feel at home. With its location near the train station, this is a convenient home base for day trips by train up and down the coast. The hotel does a brisk business with bus groups, so book ahead. ⊠ *22 rue Assalit, New Town, 06000* ☎ *04–93–85–18–54* 🖷 *04–93–62–49–14* ⊕ *www.beausoleil-hotel.com* ⟲ *53 rooms* ♿ *Cable TV, bar* ▤ *AE, MC, V.*

$ 🏨 **Solara.** One block from the beach and two from the Place Masséna, this tiny budget hotel perches on the fourth and fifth floors, high above the main shopping street. Rooms are fresh and tidy, with bright Provençal fabrics; some have kitchenettes and rooftop views. Don't be put off by the unsavory ground-floor entrance. ⊠ *7 rue de France, New Town, 06000* ☎ *04–93–88–09–96* 🖷 *04–93–88–36–86* ⊕ *www.hotel-solara.net* ⟲ *14 rooms* ♿ *Cable TV, in-room data ports, some pets allowed* ▤ *MC, V.*

★ $ 🏨 **Villa La Tour.** If you want to experience Old Town life, stay at this charming hotel in an 18th-century former convent with a small terrace garden overlooking the neighborhood's slanting rooftops. Each room has been decorated with a romantic personal touch, and some have small balconies or views of the Old Town. Helpful staff complete this perfect budget experience. ⊠ *4 rue de la Tour, Old Town/Port, 06300* ☎ *04–93–80–08–15* 🖷 *04–93–85–10–58* ⟲ *16 rooms* ♿ *Cable TV, in-room data ports* ▤ *AE, MC, V.*

¢–$ 🏨 **La Mer.** Don't be frightened away by the grim street-level entrance; once upstairs, you'll find a warm welcome and rock-bottom prices. Though rooms are spartan, they are freshly renovated, and the location can't be beat: it's right on Place Masséna, near the waterfront and the Old Town. Room rates are budget-friendly, and the staff and owners are downright sweet. Ask for a room away from the square to be sure of a quiet night's sleep. ⊠ *4 pl. Masséna, New Town, 06000* ☎ *04–93–92–09–10* 🖷 *04–93–85–00–64* ⟲ *12 rooms* ♿ *Cable TV* ▤ *AE, MC, V* ⊗ *Closed Jan.*

Nightlife & the Arts

Nice has the most active café society and nightlife on the coast. If you want to explore in-depth, pick up a copy of *Le Pitchoun*, a free, French-language guide to clubs, restaurants, and leisure activities.

The glamorous **Le Ruhl, Casino Barrière de Nice** (⊠ 1 promenade des Anglais ☎ 04–97–03–12–22), gleaming neon-bright and modern, is a sophisticated Riviera landmark that's open daily 10 AM to dawn. If you're all dressed up and have just won big, invest in a drink in the intimate walnut-and-velvet **Bar Le Relais** (✉ 39 promenade des Anglais ☎ 04–93–16–64–00) in the Hôtel Negresco.

L'Ascenseur (✉ 18 bis rue Emmanuel Philibert ☎ 04–93–26–35–30), two blocks east of Place Garibaldi, is the most popular gay and lesbian club in town. Young fans of Brit pop—especially Americans and English—drink and dance at **Wayne's** (✉ 15 rue de la Préfecture ☎ 04–93–13–46–99). **Iguane Café** (✉ 5 quai Deux-Emmanuels ☎ 04–93–56–83–83), along the port, pounds with Latin rhythms and techno until 4 AM. **L'Ambassade** (✉ 18 rue du Congrès ☎ 04–93–88–88–87) draws the crème-de-la-crème of the well-groomed, upscale Niçois young-and-restless. Dress well to get past the sharp-eyed screeners. At **Butterfly** (✉ 67 quai des États-Unis ☎ 04–93–92–27–31), in the Old Town, dance and drink to contemporary pop with a young, laid-back crowd. To stay in touch with friends and family back home, plug into the **Email Café** (✉ 8 rue Saint-Vincent ☎ 04–93–62–68–86) in the Old Town, which offers surf-and-salad options and Qwerty keyboards.

In July, the **Nice Jazz Festival** (☎ 04–92–17–77–77 for information) draws international performers for outdoor concerts in the Parc de Cimiez north of the center, some in the Matisse museum and some in the Roman arena. During past festivals, big-name jazz artists have gathered in the Madisson Lounge of the **Hotel Radisson SAS** (✉ 223 promenade des Anglais ☎ 04–93–37–17–17) for impromptu jam sessions into the wee hours. The **Théâtre de Verdure** (✉ Jardin Albert Ier) is another spot for jazz and pop. Large concerts relocate to the outdoor venue amongst ancient ruins, the **Arènes de Cimiez** (✉ Place de Cimiez) in summer. Classical music and ballet performances take place at Nice's convention center, the **Acropolis** (✉ Palais des Congrès, Esplanade John F. Kennedy ☎ 04–93–92–83–00).

The season at the **Opéra de Nice** (✉ 4 rue St-François-de-Paul ☎ 04–92–17–40–00 ⊕ www.opera-nice.org) runs from September to June. The **Théâtre Municipal Francis-Gag** (✉ 4 rue St-Joseph ☎ 04–93–62–00–03) offers a wide and varied selection of independent theater productions. The **Théâtre National de Nice** (✉ Promenade des Arts ☎ 04–93–13–90–90), headed by stage and screen star Jacques Weber, alternates productions imported from Paris with creative experiments of the Centre National Dramatique Nice Côte d'Azur.

Sports & the Outdoors

Nice's **beaches** extend all along the Baie des Anges, backed full-length by the Promenade des Anglais and a thriving and sophisticated downtown. This leads to the peculiar phenomenon of seeing power-suited executives and secretaries stripping down to a band of Lycra, tanning over the lunch hour, then suiting back up for the afternoon's work a block or two away. The absence of sand (there's nothing but those famous Riviera pebbles) helps maintain that dress-for-success look. The downside of the location: the otherwise stylish streets downtown tend to fill up with underdressed, sunburned tourists caked with salt during beach season.

Posh private beaches have full restaurants and bar service, color-coordinated mattresses and beach umbrellas, and ranks of tanners with phones glued to their ears. Several of the beaches lure clients with waterskiing, parasailing, windsurfing, and jet skiing; if you're looking for a particular sport, signs are posted at the entrance with the restaurant menus. Nice's largest private beach is the **Beau Rivage** (☎ 04–93–80–75—06), across from the Cours Saleya, which has jet skiing and a popular restaurant seating 250 indoors, 150 on the terrace. Here €19 will rent you a cushy lounge chair, an umbrella, and access to a changing room, hot showers, and bar service. At **Ruhl** (☎ 04–93–87–09–70), across from the casino, waterskiing and parasailing boats run steadily all day. Fees for private beaches average €10–€15 for a dressing room and mattress, €3–€4 for a parasol, and €4–€6 for a cabana to call your own. Private beaches alternate with open stretches of public frontage served by free toilets and open "showers" (a cold elevated faucet for rinsing off salt). Enterprising vendors cruise the waterfront, hawking ice cream, slabs of melon, coffee, ice-cold sodas, and beer.

Bicycles (✉ 17 av. Thiers) can be rented at the train station. At Da Vinci parking lots (such as the one under the Cours Saleya) the lending of a bike is included in the cost of parking. The entire Promenade des Anglais is closed to traffic on the first Sunday of every month (except for July and August), making for a terrific 10-km (6-mi) ride along the waterfront.

Shopping

Nice's main shopping street, **Avenue Jean-Médecin,** runs inland from Place Masséna; all needs and most tastes are catered to in its big department stores (Galeries Lafayette, Monoprix, and the split-level Étoile mall). At press time, however, this road was a bit of a nightmare for both cars and pedestrians due to work on the tramway, due to last at least a couple of years. Luxury boutiques, such as Emporio Armani, Kenzo, Chanel, and Sonia Rykiel, line Rue du Paradis, while Rue de France has more accessible shops. The cooking school Les Petits Farcis leads guided half-day gourmet food walks through the Old Town (⊕ www.petitsfarcis.com).

You'll find the best selection of Provençal olive oils in town at **Oliviera** (✉ 8 bis rue du Collet ☎ 04–93–13–06–45 ⊕ www.oliviera.com), run by the passionate Nadim Beyrouti in the Old Town, who also serves simple dishes made with the finest local ingredients.

The venerable **Henri Auer** (✉7 rue St-François-de-Paule ☎04–93–85–77–98) has sold its beautiful selection of crystallized fruit, a Nice specialty once thought to promote fertility, since 1820. Another good, though more commercial, source for crystallized fruit is the **Confiserie Florian du Vieux Nice** (✉ 14 quai Papacino ☎ 04–93–55–43–50), on the west side of the port.

Seafood of all kinds is sold at the **fish market** on Place St-François every morning except Monday; not much of it comes from the local waters, however. At the **market** on Cours Saleya, you can find all kinds of plants and mounds of fruits and vegetables (Tues.–Sat. 6 AM–5:30 PM and Sun. 6–noon).

The **antiques and brocante market** (✉ Pl. Robilante) by the Old Port is held Tuesday through Saturday. For brocante on Monday check out Cours Saleya.

MONACO & THE CORNICHES RESORTS

Purists and hard-core regional historians insist that this final sunny sliver of coast—from Cap Ferrat to the Italian border—is the one and only, true Côte d'Azur. It is certainly the most dramatically endowed, backed by forested mountains and crystalline Alps, with Mediterranean breezes relieving the summer heat and radiant light soothing midwinter days. Banana trees and date palms, cactus and figs luxuriate in the climate, and the hills, bristling with wind-twisted parasol pines, are paved with hothouses where roses and carnations profit from the year-round sun.

Terraced by three parallel, panoramic highways—the Basse Corniche, the Moyenne Corniche, and the Grande Corniche—that snake along its graduated crests, this stretch of the coast is studded with fabled resorts, their names as evocative of luxury and glamour as a haute-couture logo: Cap Ferrat, Beaulieu, and Monte Carlo.

5

Yet it must be said: these pockets of elegance have long since overflowed, and it's a rare stretch of cliff side that hasn't sprouted a cluster of concrete cubes in cloying hues of pineapple, apricot, and Pepto-Bismol pink. The traffic along the corniche routes—especially the Corniche Inférieure that follows the coast—is appalling in peak season (so spare yourself and visit May–June or September–October, or even in the temperate winter, the fashionable season during the 19th century), exacerbated by the manic Italian driving style and self-absorbed luxury roadsters that turn the pavement into a bumper-car battle.

But there are moments. Wrench your car out of the flow, pull over at a rare overlook on the Haute Corniche, and walk to the extremity. Like the ancient Ligurians who first built their settlements here, you can hang over the infinite expanse of teal-blue sea and glittering waves and survey the resorts draped gracefully along the curves of the coast. It was from these cliffs that for 2,500 years castles and towers held watch over the waters, braced against the influx of new peoples—first the Greeks, then the Romans, the Saracens, trade ships from Genoa, battleships under Napoléon, Edwardian cruise ships on the Grand Tour, and the Allies in the Second World War. The influx continues today, of course, in the great waves of vacationers who storm the coast, spring to early fall.

Villefranche-sur-Mer

★ ⑯ *10 km (6 mi) east of Nice.*

Nestled discreetly along the deep scoop of harbor between Nice and Cap Ferrat, this pretty watercolor of a fishing port seems surreal, flanked as it is by the big city of Nice and the assertive wealth of Monaco. The town is a stage set of brightly colored houses—the sort of place where Pagnol's *Fanny* could have been filmed. Genuine fishermen skim up to the docks here in weathered-blue *barques,* and the streets of the Vieille Ville flow directly to the waterfront, much as they did in the 13th century. Some of the prettiest spots in town are around Place de la Paix, Rue du Poilu, and Place du Conseil, which looks out over the water. The deep harbor, in the caldera of a volcano, was once preferred by the likes of Onassis and Niarchos and the royals on their yachts. But the character of the place was subtly shaped by the artists and authors who gathered at the **Hôtel Welcome**—Diaghilev and Stravinsky, taking a break from the Ballet Russe in Monaco; Somerset Maugham and Evelyn Waugh; and, above all, Jean Cocteau, who came here to recover from the excesses of Paris life. Nowadays, its population consists mainly of wealthy retired people, though families do head here to enjoy its sandy (well, gravelly) beach.

> On the outskirts of town, behind towering gates, are the private vacation villas of some of the wealthiest people on earth. The most celebrated is La Leopolda, built in the early 20th century by King Leopold of Belgium for his mistress, and now (newspapers report) the new Riviera pied-à-terre of Bill Gates, who paid a reputed price tag of 75 million euros.

So enamored was Cocteau of this painterly fishing port that he decorated the 14th-century **Chapelle St-Pierre** with images from the life of St. Peter and dedicated it to the village's fishermen. Working in crayon and chalk fixed with paraffin, he covered the walls with earthy, simplistic drawings, heavily outlined and surprisingly—even disappointingly—realistic for this master of the surreal. ⊠ *Pl. Pollanais* ☎ *04–93–76–90–70* 🎫 *€2* 🕙 *Mid-June–mid-Sept., Tues.–Sun. 10–noon and 4–8:30; mid-Sept.–mid-Nov., Tues.–Sun. 9:30–noon and 2–6; end Dec.–Mar., Tues.–Sun. 9:30–noon and 2–5:30; Apr.–mid-June, Tues.–Sun. 9:30–noon and 3–7.*

Villefranche's Old Town is made for wandering, with steeply stepped streets leading up into alleys and passageways arching over the cobbles. The extraordinary 13th-century **Rue Obscure** (literally, "dark street") is entirely covered by vaulted arcades; it sheltered the town's residents when the Germans fired their parting shots—an artillery bombardment—near World War II's end.

The modest Baroque **Église St-Michel** (⊠ Pl. Poullan), just above Rue Obscure, contains a movingly realistic sculpture of Christ carved in fig wood by an anonymous 17th-century convict. Visiting hours are Monday to Saturday from 9 to 6.

The stalwart 16th-century **Citadelle St-Elme,** restored to perfect condition, anchors the harbor with its broad, sloping stone walls. Beyond its drawbridge lie the city's offices and a group of minor gallery-museums. Whether or not you stop into these private collections of local art (all free of charge), you are welcome to stroll around the inner grounds and circle the imposing exterior.

Where to Eat & Stay

$ ✕ **La Grignotière.** Tucked down a narrow side street just a few steps away from the marketplace, this small and friendly local restaurant offers up top quality, inexpensive dishes. The homemade lasagna is excellent, as is the spaghetti pistou. ⊠ *3 rue du Poilu* ☎ *04–93–76–79–83* 🚬 *MC, V* 🕙 *No lunch.*

★ $$–$$$ ✕▣ **Hôtel Welcome.** When Villefranche harbored a community of artists and writers, this waterfront landmark was their adopted headquarters. Somerset Maugham holed up in one of the tiny crow's-nest rooms at the top, and Jean Cocteau moved into one of the corners, with windows opening onto two balconies. Alec and Evelyn Waugh (and later, Liz and Dick) used to tie one on in the bar, and film directors shooting action scenes in the bay sent the guests flowers when special-effects explosions disturbed their repose. The rooms are bright and comfortable—freshly renovated; some in soothing shades of talc-blue with bold striped accessories; some covered in pale flowers. Be sure to request a room with a balcony, it's definitely worth it; and have your aperitif or digestif on the veranda of the wine bar that specializes in *vin du terroir,* wine from local vineyards. ✉ *Quai Courbet, 06230* ☎ *04–93–76–27–62* 🖷 *04–93–76–27–66* 🌐 *www.welcomehotel.com* *37 rooms* *In-room safes, cable TV, bar, in-room data ports, some pets allowed* 💳 *AE, DC, MC, V* ⏲ *Closed mid-Nov.–mid-Dec.*

$–$$ ✕▣ **Hôtel Provençal.** Within walking distance of the port, this inexpensive hotel may not look like much from the outside but is friendly and accommodating. The rooms are large and humbly decorated with deep blue carpets, green velour chairs, and white bedspreads. About half of the rooms have a sea view; the other half look out over colorful rooftops. The Provençal-style restaurant serves up tasty items ranging from freshly grilled fish to hearty soups on a large terrace overflowing with flowers. ✉ *Av. Maréchal Joffre, 06360* ☎ *04–93–76–53–53* 🖷 *04–93–76–96–00* 🌐 *www.hotelprovencal.com* *45 rooms* *Restaurant, minibars, cable TV, bar, some pets allowed* 💳 *MC, V* ⏲ *Closed Nov.–Dec. 24.*

Beaulieu-sur-Mer

47 *4 km (2½ mi) east of Villefranche, 14 km (9 mi) east of Nice.*

With its back pressed hard against the cliffs of the corniche and sheltered between the peninsulas of Cap Ferrat and Cap Roux, this once-grand resort basks in a tropical microclimate that earned its central neighborhood the name "Petite Afrique." The town was the pet of 19th-century society, and its grand hotels welcomed Empress Eugénie, the Prince of Wales, and Russian nobles.

★ One manifestation of its Belle Époque excess is the extravagant **Villa Kerylos,** a mansion built in 1902 in the style of classical Greece. It was the dream house of the amateur archeologist Théodore Reinach, who commissioned an Italian architect to surround him with Grecian delights: cool Carrara marble, alabaster, rare fruitwoods, a mosaic-lined bath/pool worthy of a 1950s toga movie, and a dining room where guests draped themselves on the floor to eat *à la grecque.* ✉ *Rue Gustave-Eiffel* ☎ *04–93–76–44–09* 🌐 *www.villa-kerylos.com* *€7.80* ⏲ *July–Aug., daily 10–7; Sept.–Oct. and Mar.–June, daily 10–6; Nov.–Feb., weekdays 2–6, weekends 10–6.*

Today Beaulieu is usually spoken of in the past tense and has taken on a rather stuffy ambience. But on the **Promenade Maurice-Rouvier,** a paved pedestrian path which begins not far from the Villa Kerylos, you can stroll the waterfront, past grand villas and their tropical gardens, all the way to St-Jean-Cap-Ferrat. The 30-minute-walk winds seaside along the Baie des Fourmis (Bay of Ants), whose name alludes to the black rocks "crawling" up from the sea. The name doesn't quite fit, but the walk will give you great views of the sparkling Mediterranean and surrounding mountains.

Where to Eat & Stay

$$$$ ✕▣ **Métropole.** Affluent travelers have been coming to this palace for more than 100 years, attracted by the heated saltwater pool and beautiful seaside terrace. The Restoration-style furniture and subdued beige and blue-gray tones in the guest rooms offer a welcome change from the Provençal patterns that tyrannize the region. Excellent chef François Blanchet offers up mouthwatering Mediterranean-style cuisine: grilled scallops on balsamic-infused barley, creamed lentil-and-stuffed ravioli soup, or slow-roasted venison are some best bets. ✉ *16 bd. Mar. Leclerc, 06160* ☎ *04–93–01–00–08* 🖶 *04–93–01–18–51* ⊕ *www.le-metropole. com* ⇱ *35 rooms, 5 suites* ⚐ *Restaurant, minibars, cable TV, pool, beach, bar, some pets allowed (fee)* ▤ *AE, DC, MC, V* ☉ *Closed mid-Oct.–mid-Dec.* ❘❑❘ *FAP, MAP.*

St-Jean-Cap-Ferrat

48   *2 km (1 mi) south of Beaulieu on D25.*

The luxuriously sited pleasure port of St-Jean moors the peninsula of Cap Ferrat; from its port-side walkways and crescent of beach you can look over the sparkling blue harbor to the graceful green bulk of the corniches. Yachts purr in and out of port, and their passengers scuttle into cafés for take-out drinks to enjoy on their private decks.

★   Between the port and the mainland, the gaudily beautiful **Villa Ephrussi de Rothschild** stands as a testament to the wealth and worldly taste of the Baroness Ephrussi de Rothschild, who had it built (though she only stayed here a week or two per year). Constructed in 1905 and donated to the Academy of Beaux Arts in 1934, the house was created around the artworks, decorations, and furniture brought to Beatrice de Rothschild's door by eager dealers. Designed in neo-Venetian style (its flamingo-pink facade was thought not to be in the best of taste by the local gentry), the house was baptized "Ile-de-France" in homage to the Baroness Bétrice's favorite ocean liner (her staff used to wear sailing costumes and her ship travel kit is on view in her bedroom). Precious artworks, tapestries, and furniture adorn the salons—in typical Rothschildian fashion, each room is given over to a different *ancièn regime* "époque." On a guided tour of the upstairs, you can see things, things, and more things, including some fine little etchings by Fragonard, but allow yourself time to wander in the gardens. They are one of the few places on the coast where you'll be allowed to experience the lavish pleasures of the Belle Époque Côte d'Azur. There are no less than seven themed gardens (she liked to collect). The extraordinary ensemble reigns over a hilltop at the crest of the peninsula, taking in spectacular, symmetrical views of the coastline. Tea and light lunches are served on a glassed-in porch overlooking the grounds—you can enjoy a truly paradisical moment here. ✉ *Av. Ephrussi* ☎ *04–93–01–33–09* 🖃 *Access to ground*

floor and gardens €8; guided tour in English upstairs €4 extra
☉ *Feb.–June and Sept.–Oct., daily 11–6; July–Aug., daily 10–7; Nov.–Jan., weekdays 2–6, weekends 10–6.*

The signs pointing to all the different walkways in St-Jean are confusing; if you're really at a loss, visit the tourist office at 59 avenue Denis-Sémérria. Otherwise, just go south on the **Promenade Maurice Rouvier,** which runs along the eastern edge of the peninsula. You'll stumble upon reasonably priced cafés, pizzerias, and ice cream parlors on the promenade of the **Plage de St-Jean.** The best swimming is a bit farther south, past the port, at **Plage Paloma.** Keep trekking around the wooded area where a beautiful path (*sentier pédestre*) leads along the outermost edge of Cap-Ferrat. Other than the occasional yacht, all traces of civilization disappear, and the water is a dizzying blue.

The residents of Cap-Ferrat fiercely protect it from curious tourists; its grand old villas are hidden for the most part in the depths of tropical gardens. You can nonetheless try to catch peeks of them from the coastline promenade if you strike out from the port; from the restaurant Capitaine Cook, cut right up Avenue des Fossés, turn right on Avenue Vignon, and follow the Chemin de la Carrière. The 11-km (7-mi) walk passes through rich tropical flora and, on the west side, over white cliffs buffeted by waves. When you've traced the full outline of the peninsula, veer up the Chemin du Roy past the fabulous gardens of the **Villa des Cèdres,** once owned by King Leopold II of Belgium at the turn of the last century. The king owned several opulent estates along the Côte d'Azur, undoubtedly paid for by his enslavement of the Belgian Congo. His African plunder also stocked the private zoo on his villa grounds, today the town's **Parc Zoologique** (✉ Bd. du Général-de-Gaulle). Past the gardens, you'll reach the **Plage de Passable,** from which you cut back across the peninsula's wrist.

A shorter loop takes you from town out to the **Pointe de St-Hospice,** much of the walk shaded by wind-twisted pines. From the port climb Avenue Jean Mermoz to Place Paloma and follow the path closest to the waterfront. At the point are an 18th-century prison tower, a 19th-century chapel, and unobstructed views of Cap Martin.

Where to Eat & Stay

$$$ ✕ **Le Sloop.** Among the touristy cafés and snack shops along the port, this sleek blue-and-white restaurant caters to the yachting crowd and sailors who cruise in to dock for lunch. The focus is fish, of course: *soupe de poisson* (fish soup), St-Pierre (John Dory) steamed with asparagus, or whole sea bass roasted with olives and pistou. Its outdoor tables surround a tiny "garden" of potted palms, and the view of the cliffs and bobbing boats is mesmerizing. ✉ *Port de Plaisance* ☎ *04–93–01–48–63* ⊕ *www.restaurantsloop.com* ⊟ *MC, V* ☉ *Closed Wed. mid-Sept.–mid-Apr. No lunch Tues.–Wed. mid-Apr.–mid-Sept.*

★ $$$$ ⊞ **Le Royal Riviera.** Completely revamped by Parisian designer guru Grace Leo Andrieu, this former *residence hôtelière* for British aristos now invites visitors on an intimate voyage into neo-Hellenic style, complete with an admiring wink at the nearby Villa Kerylos museum. Inside, shades of ocher, wrought-iron, and a judicious mix of contemporary and classic furniture make a striking statement. Rooms in the main building have views of the sea, garden, and/or mountains, while tropical vegetation surrounds L'Orangerie's recently added 16 rooms and suites, which face a vast swimming pool. The Royal Riviera makes a special effort for families: cribs and baby supplies are complimentary, the restaurants have children's menus, and kids' films can be shown on request in a room adjoining the restaurant. Only drawback: the hotel is sited a little too close to the main railway tracks—so request a room away from them. ⌗ *3 av. Jean Monnet, 06230* ☎ *04–93–76–31–00* 🖷 *04–93–01–23–07* ⊕ *www.royal-riviera.com* ⥵ *77 in the main building, 16 in the Orangerie* ♨ *2 restaurants, in-room safes, cable TV, in-room data ports, exercize equipment, pool, beach, spa, bar* ⊟ *AE, DC, MC, V.*

$$$ 🏨 **Brise Marine.** With a glowing Provençal-ocher facade, bright blue shut-
Fodor'sChoice ters, and balustraded sea terrace, this lovely 1878 villa fulfills most de-
★ sires for that perfect, picturesque Cap Ferrat hotel. Though it overlooks one of the cape's many exclusive mansions, complete with vast garden and much-vaunted *chien très méchant* (very nasty dog), *this* little mansion remains unpretentious and accessible, with pretty little pastel guest rooms that feel like bedrooms in a private home—many offer window views of the gorgeous peninsula stunningly framed by statuesque palms. The terraces are shared, the aperitif is a social occasion, and the comforts are first-class. There is also a private three-bedroom villa for rent with access to a swimming pool, perfect for up to six people. ⌗ *58 av. Jean Mermoz, 06230* ☎ *04–93–76–04–36* 🖷 *04–93–76–11–49* ⊕ *www.hotel-brisemarine.com* ⥵ *18 rooms* ♨ *In-room safes, mini-fridges, cable TV, exercise equipment, hot tub, bar, in-room data ports, Wi-Fi* ⊟ *AE, DC, MC, V* ⊘ *Closed Nov.–Jan.*

$$-$$$ 🏨 **Clair Logis.** With soft pastels, antique furniture, and large picture windows, this converted villa is perfectly framed by a sprawling garden park. The main house offers up subtle bourgeois elegance; for the budget-conscious there are simpler, airy rooms scattered over several small buildings. Most have charming balconies looking out over gently swaying palms. There's no pool, but breakfast on the cobblestone terrace is lovely, and it's a good way to gear up for the 15-minute walk down to the beach. ⌗ *12 av. Centrale, Point de St-Jean, 06230* ☎ *04–93–76–51–81* 🖷 *04–93–76–51–82* ⊕ *www.hotel-clair-logis.fr* ⥵ *18 rooms* ♨ *Minibars, cable TV, free parking, some pets allowed (fee)* ⊟ *AE, MC, V.*

Èze

49 *2 km (1 mi) east of Beaulieu, 12 km (7 mi) east of Nice, 7 km (4½ mi)*
Fodor'sChoice *west of Monte Carlo.*
★

Magical, medieval, and magnificent, towering like an eagle's nest above the coast and crowned with ramparts and the ruins of a medieval château, Èze (pronounced *ehz*) is unfortunately the most accessible of all the perched villages. So even during off-season its streets pour with a lava flow of tourists, some not-so-fresh from the beach, and it earns unique status as the only town to post pictorial warnings that say, in effect, "No Shoes, No Shirt, No Service." It is, nonetheless, the most spectacularly sited; if you can manage to shake the crowds and duck off to a quiet overlook, the village casts an extraordinary spell. Its streets are steep and, in places, only for the flamboyantly fit; its time-stained stone houses huddle together in storybook fashion, and its history is remarkable: Colonized milennia ago by the Romans (who may have built a temple here to the Egyptian goddess, Isis—hence the town name), this mountain peak aerie was much coveted by locals fleeing

Consuelo Vanderbilt, when she was tired of being Duchess of Marlborough, traded in Blenheim Palace for a custom-built house in Èze.

from pirating Saracens. By the 19th century, only peasants were left, but when the Riviera became fashionable, Èze's splendid views up and down the coast became one of the draws that lured fabled visitors—lots of crowned heads, Georges Sand, Friedrich Nietzsche.

From the crest-top **Jardin Exotique** (Tropical Garden), full of rare succulents, you can pan your videocam all the way around the hills and waterfront (and then, just a few feet from the entrance, take a time-out lunch at the Nid d'Aigle, an inexpensive eaterie featuring focaccias and salads, quaintly set on stone levels rising up around a tall tree). But if you want a prayer of a chance of enjoying the magnificence of the village's arched passages, stone alleyways, and ancient fountains, come at dawn or after sunset—or (if you have the means) stay the night—but spend the midday elsewhere. The church of **Notre-Dame,** consecrated in 1772, glitters inside with Baroque retables and altarpieces. Èze's tourist office, on Place du Général-de-Gaulle, can direct you to the numerous footpaths—the most famous being the **Sentier Friedrich Nietzsche**—that thread Èze with the coast's three corniche highways. Èze Village is the famous hilltop destination, but Èze extends down to the coastal beach and the township of Èze-sur-Mer; on either side a vast **Grande Corniche Parc** keeps things green and verdant. By car, you should arrive using the Moyenne Corniche, which deposits you near the gateway to Èze Village; buses (from Nice and Monaco) also use this highway. By train, you'll arrive at the station in Èze-sur-Mer, where (most months) a navette shuttlebus takes you up to hilltop Èze, a trip which, with its 1,001 switchbacks up the steep mountainside, takes a full 15 minutes (keep this in mind if you're hiring a taxi to "rush" you down to the train station).

Where to Eat & Stay

$$–$$$$ ✕ **Troubadour.** Amid the clutter and clatter, this is a wonderful find: comfortably relaxed, this old family house proffers pleasant service and excellent dishes like roasted scallops with chicken broth and squab with citrus zest and beef broth. Full-course menus range from €28 to €48. ⊠ *4 rue du Brec* ☎ *04–93–41–19–03* ▤ *AE, DC, MC, V* ☉ *Closed Sun. No lunch Mon.*

¢–$ ✕ **Loumiri.** Classic Provençal and regional seafood dishes are tastily prepared and married with decent, inexpensive wines at this cute little bistro near the entrance to the Vieille Ville. The best bet is to order *à l'ardoise*—that is, from the blackboard listing of daily specials. The lunch menu prix-fixe (€15) is the best deal in town. ⊠ *Av. Jardin Exotique*

☎ 04–93–41–16–42 ▤ MC, V ⊘ *Closed Mon. and mid-Dec.–mid-Jan. No dinner Wed.*

$$$$ ✕▦ **Château de la Chèvre d'Or.** Giving substance to Riviera fairy tales,
Fodor's Choice   this extraordinary xanadu seems to sit just below cloud level in skyhigh
★   Èze. Like a Hilton penthouse, medieval-style, this magnificent conglomerate of weathered-stone houses lets you enjoy "the high life" while turning your back on the world and drinking in unsurpassed sea views. Nearby
are some of the fanciest rooms, little *cabanon* houses built into the cliff
and exquisite in decor: stone boulder walls accented with Louis Seize
torchières, peasant-luxe fireplaces with faux 15th-century panel paintings, chandeliered rock-grotto bathrooms. Nearly all rooms have exposed
stone, arched windows, exposed beams, and brass touches, while even

the cheapest (a pretty penny,
nonetheless) are stylishly done up
and have views over Èze's charming
tile roofs. No fewer than three
restaurants, ranging from the nicely
affordable grill to the *haute gastronomique* grand dining room with
its panoramic view, regale some of
the world's most pampered citizens
(and children, who love the house
special, chicken in Coca-Cola sauce,
which goes for €30). The bar, newly
done up with blazons and suits of
armor in medieval baronial style is
as cozy and luxe a perch as you can
wish. The swimming pool alone,
clinging like a swallow's nest to the

> "
> The "château of the Golden
> Goat" is actually an entire
> stretch of the village, streets and
> all, bordered by gardens that
> cling to the mountainside in
> nearly Babylonian style. Here
> perches the glowing turquoise
> pool that looks as though it's
> dipping into the sky–a beauti-
> ful monochromatic vista that
> has to be seen to be believed.
> "

hillside, may justify the investment, as do the liveried footmen who greet
you at the village entrance to wave you, VIP-style, past the cattle-drive
of tourists. Believe us, it will hard to pack your bags when it's time to
depart this magical realm. ⊠ *Rue du Barri, 06360* ☎ *04–92–10–66–66*
🖷 *04–93–41–06–72* ⊕ *www.chevredor.com* ⇲ *32 rooms* ⌂ *3 restaurants, minibars, cable TV, pool, bar, in-room data ports* ▤ *AE, DC, MC,
V* ⊘ *Closed Nov.–Mar.*

★ **$$$$**   ✕▦ **Château Eza.** Vertiginously perched on the edge of a cliff 3,000 feet
above the crouching tiger of St-Jean-Cap-Ferrat, this former residence
of Prince William of Sweden is one of the most dramatic, romantic, and
expensive inns on the entire Mediterranean coast. Surprisingly, the public salons are cool, sleek, and modern, almost letting you think you're
wandered into Soho. But the guest rooms—there are only ten—are spread
among a cluster of striking Romanesque 13th-century buildings on cobblestone streets too narrow for cars. Most have private entrances and all
are luxed out to the max: canopy beds, costly objets d'art and antiques,
exquisite carpets and tapestries, wood-burning fireplaces, and unbeliev-
able views. If you're not staying the night, the views from the panoramic
restaurant and outdoor terrace (gasp—everyone does) are just as good.
The wine list is one of the best on the Côte, though the food has slipped
a notch. The hotel is nearly at the top of the village's steep alleyways, so
your luggage will need to be picked up by the hotel porters. ⊠ *Rue de*

la Pise, 06360 ☎ *04–93–41–12–24* 🖷 *04–93–41–16–64* ⊕ *www. chateaueza.com* ⇨ *7 rooms, 3 suites* ⚴ *Restaurant, bar, private beach, minibars* 🚭 *AE, DC, MC, V* ⊗ *Closed Oct.–Mar.*

$$ 🏠 **La Bastide aux Camelias.** There are only three bedrooms in this lovely B&B, each individually decorated with softly draped fabrics and polished antiques. Close to Èze Village, set in the nearby Grande Corniche Park, it offers up the usual run of breathtaking views, but also has inviting, less precipitous ones of garden greenery. Have the complimentary breakfast on the picture-perfect veranda, indulge in a cooling drink by the gorgeous pool, or stretch out on the manicured lawn. There's even a spa, hammam, and Jacuzzi included in the price. It's a gentle hospitality that's much in demand, however, so reserve well in advance. ⊠ *Route de l'Adret, 06360* ☎ *04–93–41–13–68* 🖷 *04–93–41–13–68* ⊕ *www.bastide-aux-camelias.fr.st* ⇨ *3 rooms* ⚴ *Minibars, cable TV, pool, hot tubs, free parking, some pets allowed (fee)* ⦿ *BP.*

La Turbie

➄ *5 km (3 mi) northeast of Èze, 7 km (4½ mi) northwest of Monaco.*

Lying directly above Monaco, this village serves as a crossroads for both French and Monagesque commuters stopping for coffee, a pizza, or bread for dinner. A pretty Old Town labyrinth weaves a quiet web just behind the main road, and at its base you can stroll into the Jardin Prince Albert Ier to take in spectacular views over all of Monaco.

★ La Turbie takes its name from its magnificent Roman monument, the Tropea Augusti, or Trophy of Augustus, now known as the **Trophée des Alpes** (Trophy of the Alps). Visible from miles around, this spectacular mass of columned white stone rears above the village, marking the Via Julia Augusta as well as Rome's authority over the alliance of Italy, Gaul, and Germania. It's impressive enough from a distance, but consider visiting it up close. Augustus meant for the trophy to command magnificent views of his turf, and the panorama from its terrace stretches from the Estérel to Bordighera in Italy. There's a film in French on its history and a small museum. ☎ *04–93–41–20–84* 🖾 *€4* ⊗ *July–Sept., daily 9:30–7; Oct.–Mar., Tues.–Sun. 10–5; Apr.–June, daily 9:30–6.*

Peillon

★ **➅** *15 km (9 mi) northeast of Nice via D2204 and D53.*

Perhaps because it's difficult to reach and not on the way to or from anything else, this idyllic village has maintained the magic of its medieval origins. You can hear the bell toll here, walk in silence up its weathered cobblestones, and smell the thyme crunching underfoot if you step past the settlement's minuscule boundaries onto the unspoiled hillsides. And its streets are utterly and completely commerce-free; the citizens have voted to vaccinate themselves against the plague of boutiques, galleries, and cafés that have infected its peers along the coast. There is not much to do here other than bask in the cool mountain air, soak up the views and savor a sophisticated meal on a terrace—the downside of the lack of shops is the accompanying lack of almost any street life.

Where to Eat & Stay

★ **$$–$$$** ✕🏨 **Auberge de la Madone.** This is what you call getting away from it all. Owner Christian Millo and his partner/sister Marie-José come from a traditional farming family with a deep love for this region. Chef Millo and his sous-chef, son Thomas, who studied under Alain Ducasse, are interested in a fresh, organic cuisine using only local products: the cheese served at breakfast comes from a farm down the road; the honey from a local beekeeper; the vegetables are picked fresh from the garden out back; and, to give you an idea of the quality, the olive oil comes from the olives you see hanging on the trees. The cooking itself is a trifle fussy, but there's no disputing the passion that goes into this food. The inn has a tennis court on the slope above, and six little rooms in a village annex called Lou Pourtail, which offers shelter at bargain rates. ✉ *06440 Peillon Village* ☎ *04–93–79–91–17* 🖷 *04–93–79–99–36* 🌐 *www. chateauxhotels.com/madone* ➥*17 rooms, 2 suites in main house; 6 rooms without bath in village annex* ⚒ *Restaurant, tennis court, cable TV in some rooms, in-room data ports; no a/c* ▭ *MC, V* ☉ *Closed Wed., Nov. 2–Dec. 23, Jan. 7–31* 🍴 *MAP.*

Monaco

7 km (4½ mi) east of Èze, 21 km (13 mi) east of Nice.

It's positively feudal, the idea that an ancient dynasty of aristocrats could still hold fast to its patch of coastline, the last scrap of a once-vast domain. But that's just what the Grimaldi family has done, clinging to a few acres of glory and maintaining their own license plates, their own telephone area code (377), and their own highly forgiving tax system. Yet the Principality of Monaco covers just 473 acres and would fit comfortably inside New York's Central Park or a family farm in Iowa. And its 5,000 pampered citizens would fill only a small fraction of the seats in Yankee Stadium.

The present ruler, Prince Albert II (following the death of Prince Rainier III in April 2005), traces his ancestry to Otto Canella, who was born in 1070. The Grimaldi dynasty began with Otto's great-great-great-grandson, Francesco Grimaldi, also known as Frank the Rogue. Expelled from Genoa, Frank and his cronies disguised themselves as monks and in 1297 seized the fortified medieval town known today as Le Rocher (the Rock). Except for a short break under Napoléon, the Grimaldis have been here ever since, which makes them the oldest reigning family in Europe. In the 1850s a Grimaldi named Charles III made a decision that turned the Rock into a giant blue chip. Needing revenue but not wanting to impose additional taxes on his subjects, he contracted with a company to open a gambling facility. The first spin of the roulette wheel was on December 14, 1856. There was no easy way to reach Monaco then—no carriage roads or railroads—so no one came. Between March 15 and March 20, 1857, one person entered the casino—and won two francs. In 1868, however, the railroad reached Monaco, and it was filled with Englishmen who came to escape the London fog. The effects were immediate. Profits were so great that Charles eventually abolished all direct taxes. Almost overnight, a threadbare principality became an elegant watering hole for European society. Dukes (and their mistresses) and duchesses (and their gigolos) danced and dined their way through a world of spinning roulette wheels and bubbling champagne—preening themselves for nights at the opera, where such artists as Vaslav Nijinsky, Sarah Bernhardt, and Enrico Caruso came to perform.

But it's the tax system, not the gambling, that's made Monaco one of the most sought-after addresses in the world—that and its sensational position on a broad, steep peninsula that bulges into the Mediterranean, its harbor sparkling with luxury cruisers, its posh mansions angling awnings toward the nearly perpetual sun. The population explosion here has allowed Monaco to break another French code, that of construction restraints. Thus it bristles with gleaming glass-and-concrete corncob-towers 20 and 30 stories high and with vast apartment complexes, their terraces landscaped like miniature gardens.

> ## GRACE'S KINGDOM
>
> Thanks in part to the pervasive odor of money-to-burn, Monaco remains the playground of royalty, wealthy playboys, and glamorous film stars. One of the loveliest of the latter, in fact, became Monaco's princess when Hollywood darling Grace Kelly married Prince Rainier in 1956; their wedding, marriage, and her tragic death in a car accident—eerily presaged in scenes filmed in Alfred Hitchcock's *To Catch a Thief*—have only added to the mythology of this fairy-tale mini-principality.

The Monagesques themselves add to the sense of flossy, flashy self-contentment. Nearly everything is dyed-to-match here, even the lap dog in the Vuitton bag, and fur coats flourish from September through May. Doormen and policemen dress in ice-cream–colored uniforms worthy of an operetta, and along the port yacht clubs host exclusive birthday parties for little-rich-girls in couture party dresses. Pleasure boats vie with luxury cruisers in their brash beauty and Titanic scale, and teams of handsome young men—themselves dyed blond and tanned to match—scour and polish every gleaming surface. Prince Albert II, who has made the most of his extended bachelorhood, admitted the day after the three-month mourning period following his father's death that he had fathered a child with former air hostess Nicole Coste—his son Alexandre will never become prince as he is not the product of a Catholic marriage, but will inherit part of his €2 billion fortune.

Monaco's gleaming profile is due, for the most part, to an entertainment organization called SBM: the Societé des Bains de Mer. Founders in the 19th century of the original casino, they have burgeoned to reign over a mega-complex of 23 restaurants, 4 hotels, nightclubs, cabarets, and all the casinos in town. In the 1990s they added **Les Thermes Marins de Monte-Carlo** (Sea Baths of Monte-Carlo; ✉ 2 ave. de Monte-Carlo ☎ 377/92–16–40–40), a seawater-therapy treatment center that stretches between the landmark Hôtel de Paris and its sister, the Hermitage. Within its sleek, multilevel complex you can pursue every creature comfort, from underwater massage to seaweed body wraps to light, elegant spa-style lunches—almost all with views over the port.

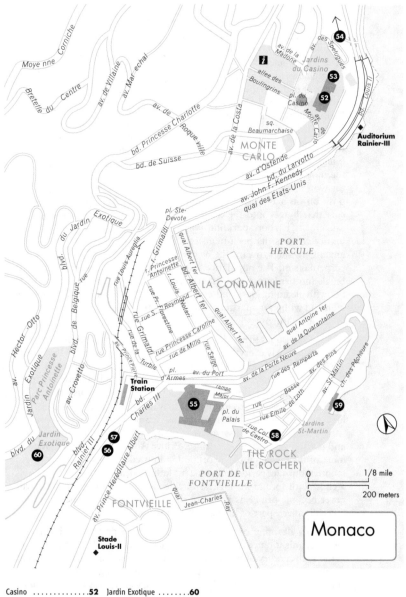

Monaco

You may well gather that Monaco can be intimidating for budget travelers. Eating is expensive, and even the most modest hotels cost more here than in nearby Nice or Menton. As for taxis, they don't even have meters so you are completely at the driver's mercy (expect to pay at least €12 for the shortest possible hop, with prices skyrocketing during events such as the Grand Prix). For the frugal, Monaco is the ultimate day trip, although parking is as coveted as a room with a view.

The harbor district, known as **La Condamine,** connects the new quarter, officially known as **Monte Carlo,** with the Vieille Ville, officially known as **Monaco-Ville** (or Le Rocher), the medieval town on the Rock, topped by the palace, the cathedral, and the Oceanography Museum. Have no fear that you'll need to climb countless steps to get to the Vieille Ville, as there are plenty of elevators and escalators climbing the steep cliffs. But shuttling between the lovely casino grounds of Monte Carlo and Old Monaco, separated by a vast port, is a daunting proposition for ordinary mortals without wings. Before starting off, arm yourself with a map and a bus schedule or an excellent pair of walking shoes and start at the **tourist office** (⊠ 2a bd. des Moulins ☎ 377/92–16–61–66 ⊕ www.monaco-tourisme.com), just north of the casino gardens.

★ ❷ Place du Casino is the center of Monte Carlo and the **Casino** is a must-see, even if you don't bet a sou. Into the gold-leaf splendor of the Casino, where fortunes have been won, shirts lost, and any number of James Bond scenes filmed, the hopeful traipse from tour buses to tempt fate beneath the gilt-edged rococo ceiling.

❸ In the true spirit of the town, it seems that the **Opéra** (⊠ Pl. du Casino ☎ 377/98–06–28–00 ⊕ www.opera.mc), with its 18-ton gilt-bronze chandelier and extravagant frescoes, is part of the casino complex. The designer, Charles Garnier, also built the Paris Opéra, so we are talking one fabulous jewel-box. On show are some of the coast's most significant performances of dance, opera, and orchestral music.

From Place des Moulins there is an escalator down to the Larvotto Beach ❹ complex, artfully created with imported sand, and the **Musée National,** housed in a Garnier villa within a rose garden. There's a beguiling collection of 18th- and 19th-century dolls and mechanical automatons— more than 400 altogether. ⊠ *17 av. Princesse Grace* ☎ 377/93–30–91–26 ⌨ €5 ☉ *Easter–Aug., daily 10–6:30; Sept.–Easter, daily 10–12:15 and 2:30–6:30.*

It's a hike or a ride on bus No. 6 from Monte Carlo to the **port** along Boulevard Albert Ier, where pleasure boats of every shape flash white and blue. It's here that they erect the stands for fans of the Grand Prix. And it's from the far corner of the port that the Institut Océanographique launches research boats to study aquatic life in the Mediterranean, as its late director Jacques Cousteau did for some 30 years.

On the broad plateau known as Le Rocher, or **the Rock,** the majority of Monaco's touristic sights are concentrated with tidy, self-conscious charm. This is the medieval heart of Monaco, and where its cathedral, palace, and the Oceanography Museum can be found. You can either climb up a raked *rampe* from the Place d'Armes, behind the right corner of the port, or approach it by elevator from the seafront at the port's farthest end (past the Yacht Club).

At the center of the Rock's plateau, the broad Place du Palais knots up with crowds at 11:55, when the poker-faded guards—in black in winter, white in summer—change shifts, or, as the French say, relieve themselves. They are protecting hallowed ground: the **Palais Princier,** where the royal family officially "resides" (they have plenty of other houses up and down the coast). You can tell they're home if the family banner flies from the mast above the main tower. A 40-minute guided tour (summer only) of this sumptuous chunk of history, first built in the 13th century and expanded and enhanced over the centuries, reveals an extravagance of 16th- and 17th-century frescoes, as well as tapestries, gilt furniture, and paintings on a grand scale. One wing of the palace, open throughout the year, is taken up by the **Musée Napoléon,** filled with Napoleonic souvenirs—including The Hat and a tricolor scarf—and genealogical charts. (The Grimaldis and the Bonapartes were related, you see.) There is an abundance of military paraphernalia, from uniforms to medals, etchings, and banners, all from the Prince's private collection. ⊠ *Pl. du Palais* ☎ *377/93–25–18–31* ⊕ *www.palais.mc* ≊ *Palace apartments €6; Musée Napoléon €4; joint ticket €8* ☉ *Palace apartments: June–Sept., daily 9:30–6:30; Oct.–Nov. 11, daily 10–5:30. Museum: June–Sept., daily 9:30–6:30; Oct.–mid-Nov., daily 10–5; Dec.–May, Tues.–Sun. 10:30–12:30 and 2–5.*

On the terrasses de Fontvielle are two remarkable sights (opened in 2003): the **Collection des Voitures Anciennes** (Collection of Vintage Cars) and the **Jardin Animalier** (Animal Garden). The former is a collection of Prince Ranier's vintage cars from a De Dion Bouton to a Lambourghini Countach; the latter, a mini-zoo housing Prince Ranier's animal collection—an astonishing array of wild beasts including monkeys and exotic birds. ⊠ *Terrasses de Fontvielle* ☎ *377/92–05–28–56 or 377/93–25–18–31* ≊ *€6 (Voitures); €4 (Animalier)* ☉ *June–Sept., daily 10–6.*

Follow the flow of crowds down the last remaining streets of medieval Monaco to the **Cathédrale de l'Immaculée-Conception** (⊠ Av. St-Martin), an uninspired 19th-century version of Romanesque. It harbors nonetheless some wonderful artworks, including an **altarpiece** painted by Bréa in 1500. Now shielded behind glass at the north transept, it is, perhaps, his masterwork, depicting with tender detail the steady gaze of St-Nicolas; he is flanked by small panels portraying other saints, graceful, chastened, and demure. Despite the humility innate to the work, it's framed with unusual flamboyance in ornate gilt wood. Just beyond the Bréa polyptych, enter the curve of the apse to see the tombs of the Grimaldi clan. The first on entering the apse from the left is simply labeled *Gracia Patricain, Principis Rainerii*; Princess Grace's death date—1982—figures in Roman numerals. It's easy to identify her tomb without reading the inscription; even today it's heaped with fresh flowers.

★ ☾ ❺❾ At the prow of the Rock, the grand **Musée Océanographique** (Oceanography Museum) perches dramatically on a cliff, its many levels plunging dramatically to the sea. The splendid Edwardian structure was built under Prince Albert Ier to house specimens collected on amateur explorations, and evokes the grandeur of the days of imperialist discovery and the old National Geographic Society. Both the museum and its research organization, the Institut Océanographique (Oceanography Institute), were led by Jacques Cousteau (1910–97) from 1957 to 1988. Sumptuously decorated with mosaics of sea life, beveled-oak display cases, and gleaming brass, the museum contains a collection somewhat pared down from its heyday. The main floor displays skeletons and taxidermy of enormous sea creatures, including a 6½-foot-wide Japanese crab, and a magnificent life-scale model of a sperm whale, created from first-hand observation by the museum's conservateur/artist Maurizio Würtz. There are interesting examples of early submarines, diving gear dating from the Middle Ages, and a few interactive science displays. Upstairs you'll find boat models, including a scale miniature of the Titanic sinking. But the reason the throngs pour into this landmark is its famous **aquarium**, a vast complex of backlit tanks at eye level containing every imaginable genus of fish, crab, and eel. The wide-open piranha pond is a crowd pleaser. Watch for interactive programs between visitors and researchers on the open sea, armed with two-way microphones. For a fine view and a restorative drink, take the elevator to the roof terrace. ⊠ *Av. St-Martin* ☎ *377/93–15–36–00* ⊕ *www.oceano.mc* ⊠ *€11* ☉ *July–Aug., daily 9:30–7.30; Sept.–Dec. and Apr.–June, daily 9:30–7; Jan.–Mar. daily 10–6.*

⑥⓪ **Fodor'sChoice** ★ Six hundred varieties of cacti and succulents cling to a sheer rock face at the **Jardin Exotique** (Tropical Garden), a brisk half-hour walk west from the palace. The garden traces its roots to days when Monaco's near-tropical climate nurtured unheard-of exotica, amazing visitors from the northlands as much as any zoo. The plants are of less interest today, especially to Americans familiar with southwestern flora. The views over the Rock and coastline, however, are spectacular. Also on the grounds, or actually under them, are the **Grottes de l'Observatoire**—spectacular grottoes and caves a-drip with stalagmites and spotlit with fairy lights. The largest cavern is called "La Grande Salle" and looks like a Romanesque rock cathedral. Traces of Cro-Magnon civilization have been found here so the grottoes now bear the official name the **Musée d'Anthropologie Préhistorique.** ⊠*Bd. du Jardin Exotique* ☎*377/93–15–29–80* ⊠ *€6.80* ☉ *Daily 9–7 (till dusk in winter).*

Where to Eat & Stay

★ **$$$$** ✕ **Bar & Boeuf.** Jarring slightly with its setting in the futuristic concrete-and-wood structure of the casino and entertainment complex Le Sporting (an expensive cab ride from the center of town), Alain Ducasse's elegant Bar & Boeuf is basking in enduring popularity thanks to the quality of chef Philippe Collino's cooking and the charming, mostly male staff. The menu makes a confusing read: within each of the three categories—sea bass, beef, and "med"—are various headings such as "raw" and "cooked," "wok" and "plancha." Take the advice of the enthusiastic waiters and order the more adventurous dishes—sea bass tartare with a lime and pepper sorbet could prove as much of a revelation as the conversation at the next table ("I have 52 million in my bank account").

✉ *Le Sporting, Av. Princesse Grace* ☎ *377/92–16–60–60* ⚓ *Reservations essential* ⊕ *www.alain-ducasse.com* ⊟ *AE, DC, MC, V* ⊙ *Closed Mon. in Sept.–mid-May. No lunch.*

$$$$ ✕ **Cafe de Paris.** This landmark Belle Époque brasserie across from the casino offers classic dishes: shellfish, steak tartare, matchstick frites, and fish boned table-side. Supercilious, super-pro waiters fawn gracefully over Old World preeners, gentlemen, jet-setters, and tourists alike, serving good hot food until 2 AM. ✉ *Pl. du Casino* ⊕ *www.sbm.mc* ☎ *377/ 92–16–20–20* ⊟ *AE, DC, MC, V.*

$$$$ ✕ **Le Louis XV.** Louis Quinze to the initiated, this extravagantly showy

Fodor'sChoice restaurant stuns with neo-Baroque details, yet it manages to be upstaged

★ by its product: the superb cuisine of Alain Ducasse, one of Europe's most celebrated chefs. With too many tokens on his Monopoly board, Ducasse jets between his other, ever-growing interests leaving the Louis XV kitchen, for the most part, in the more-than-capable hands of chef Franck Cerutti, who draws much of his inspiration from the Cours Saleya market in Nice. His absence is no great loss. Glamorous iced lobster consommé with caviar, and risotto perfumed with Alba white truffles slum happily with stockfish (stewed salt cod) and tripe. There are sole sautéed with tender baby fennel, salt-seared foie gras, milk-fed lamb with hints of cardamom, and dark-chocolate sorbet crunchy with ground coffee beans or hot wild strawberries on an icy mascarpone sorbet—in short, a panoply of delights using the sensual flavors of the Mediterranean. The decor is magnificent—a surfeit of gilt, mirrors, and chandeliers—and the waitstaff seignorial as they proffer a footstool for madame's handbag. In Ducasse fashion, the Baroque clock on the wall is stopped just before twelve. Cinderella should have no fears. ✉ *Hôtel de Paris, Pl. du Casino* ☎ *377/92–16–30–01* ⚓ *Reservations essential* ⊟ *AE, DC, MC, V* ⊙ *Closed Tues. and Wed. (except Wed. dinner mid-June–Aug.), 2 wks in Feb., and late Nov.–late Dec.*

$$$ ✕ **Castelroc.** With its tempting pine-shaded terrace just across from the entrance to the Prince's Palace, you may take this for a tourist chaser, but it's one of the more popular lunch spots in town with locals. The cuisine is a mix of classic and regional flavors, from *anchoïade* (anchovy paste) with olive oil to stuffed artichokes, and garlicky *stocafi* (stockfish) simmered with tomatoes and Provençal herbs. ✉ *Pl. du Palais* ☎ *377/ 93–30–36–68* ⊟ *MC, V* ⊙ *Closed Mon. and Dec. 18–Jan. 26.*

★ **$$$** ✕ **Quai des Artistes.** This warehouse-scale neo-Deco bistro on the port is the chicest of the chic with Monagesque gentry, packing well-heeled diners shoulder-to-shoulder at banquettes lined up for maximum people-watching. Rich brasserie classics (liver and onions, lentils with salt pork) are counterbalanced with high-flavor international experiments (mussels in a red-pepper ceviche, char-grilled salmon served sushi-rare). ✉ *4 quai Antoine Ier* ☎ *377/97–97–97–77* ⊕ *www.quaidesartistes. com* ⚓ *Reservations essential* ⊟ *AE, DC, MC, V.*

★ **$** ✕ **Polpetta.** This popular little trattoria, a favorite with stars and politicos since the 1970s, is close enough to the Italian border to pass for the real thing, and the exuberant Guasco brothers who greet you add to the authenticity. Enjoy a parade of antipasti, seafood risotto, osso buco perfumed with saffron, or the house specialty, *trofie* (skinny Ligurian-style gnocchi) with pesto and tomato sauce. There's a terrific list of Italian wines. ⊠ *2 rue Paradis* ☎ *377/93–50–67–84* ▤ *AE, MC, V* ⊘ *Closed Tues. and 3 wks in June. No lunch Sat.*

$ ✕ **Stars'n'Bars.** This American-style port-side bar/restaurant/entertainment center is such a phenomenal success with the Monagesque that it's worth a stop for the culture shock alone. Fat, juicy burgers, cookie sundaes, real iced tea in thick glasses, and (gasp!) pitchers of ice water draw homesick expats, burrito-starved backpackers—and mobs of locals wallowing in *la cuisine américaine.* Port-side tables are low-key; inside, soft rock, arcade games, and a friendly international bar scene mingle all ages and nationalities.   ⊠ *6 quai Antoine Ier* ☎ *377/97–97–95–95* ⊕ *www.starsnbars.com* ▤ *AE, DC, MC, V* ⊘ *Closed Mon. in Nov.–May.*

★ $$$$ ✕▥ **Hermitage.** They've all been here; the kings, the queens, Pavarotti in jeans. It's otherworld, subdued chic at its best. A riot of frescoes and plaster flourishes embellished with gleaming brass, this landmark 1900 hotel nonetheless maintains a relatively low profile, set back a block from the casino scene. This is where the mink-and-Vuarnets set comes *not* to be seen. Even if you're not staying, walk through the lobby to admire the glass-dome Art Nouveau vestibule, designed by Gustav Eiffel. The best rooms face the sea or angle toward the port. At the formal, sophisticated restaurant Le Vistamar, chef Joël Garault buys his seafood from a local Monagesque fisherman. It's served in a tailored, modern room splashed with cobalt blue. Its broad, broad terrace offers one of the most glamorous dining settings in Monaco. ⊠ *Sq. Beaumarchais, 98005* ☎ *377/92–16–40–00* 🖷 *377/92–16–38–52* ⊕ *www.sbm.mc* ⤳ *80 rooms, 8 suites* ⚐ *Restaurant, in-room safes, pool, sauna, steam room, bar, in-room data ports, some pets allowed* ▤ *AE, DC, MC, V.*

★ $$$$ ✕▥ **Hôtel Métropole Monte-Carlo.** This Belle Epoque hotel, set on land that once belonged to Pope Leon XIII, has pulled out all the stops in its recent renovation—famed Paris designer Jacques Garcia has given the rooms his signature hyper-aristocratic look and the chef is none other than Joël Robuchon (though, since he can't be in Paris, Las Vegas, Tokyo, Monte Carlo and on television at once, Christophe Cussac runs the open kitchen day-to-day). The garden has also been transformed into an urban oasis, now harboring some 3,000 species of plants. Guests can choose from a number of chauffeur-driven half-day and a day trips, plus children's programs and—*mais, oui*—dogs' programs. ⊠ *4 av. de la Madone, 98005* ☎ *377/93–15–15–15* 🖷 *377/93–25–24–44* ⊕ *www. metropole.com* ⤳ *146* ⚐ *Restaurant, in-room safes, pool, spa, bar, in-room data ports, some pets allowed* ▤ *AE, DC, MC, V* ⦿ *MAP.*

$$$$ ▥ **Hôtel Columbus.** Situated on the Fontveille harbor, this super-hip, youthful hotel is a refreshing breath of contemporary air—the farthest thing from stuffy or old-world. A lifestyle hotel opened by the owners of the trendy Malmaison chain, its rooms are luxe, decked out in soft beiges, rich browns, and purples, with metal trim and teakwood accents that would do a *Wallpaper* article proud; the bar is a nighttime favorite amongst Formula One drivers and fans, who are no doubt drawn there by part-owner David Coulthard. ⊠ *23 av. des Papalins, 98000* ☎ *377/ 92–05–90–00* 🖷 *377/92–05–91–67* ⊕ *www.columbushotels.com* ⤳ *153 rooms, 31 suites* ⚐ *Restaurant, minibars, cable TV, bar, Internet, meet-*

ing room, parking (fee), some pets allowed (fee) ☰ *AE, DC, MC, V* ❙❍❙ *MAP.*

$$$$ 🏨 **Monte Carlo Grand Hotel.** *Le dernier cri* in 1960s-chic when it opened, sprawling long and low along the waterfront at Monte Carlo's base, this ultramodern, airport-scale complex is so vast it commands a full-time staff of upholsterers. Bright rooms decked in vivid hues angle onto the open sea. The bars, casino, boutiques, and mall-size lobby easily contain megaconventions, but thanks to the friendly staff, vacationers will feel at home, too. There's a veritable food court of restaurants: the Café de la Mer is coffee-shop comfortable but offers an eclectic choice of seafood and Provençal specialties—at all hours—and the casual rooftop Le Pistou makes the most of the Grand's exclusive position on the open sea. ✉ *12 av. des Spélugues, 98000* 🕾 *377/93–50–65–00* 🖷 *377/93–30–01–57* ⊕ *www.montecarlo.com* ➟ *619 rooms, 69 apartments* ♿ *3 restaurants, in-room safes, minibars, pool, health club, hot tub, bar, casino* ☰ *AE, DC, MC, V* ❙❍❙ *MAP.*

$$$ 🏨 **Alexandra.** The friendly proprietress, Madame Larouquie, makes you feel right at home at this central, comfortable spot just north of the Casino. Though the color schemes clash and the bedrooms are spare, bathrooms are spacious and up to date, and insulated windows keep traffic noise out. Breakfast is included in the price. ✉ *35 bd. Princesse-Charlotte, 98000* 🕾 *377/93–50–63–13* 🖷 *377/92–16–06–48* ➟ *56 rooms* ♿ *Minibars, cable TV* ☰ *AE, DC, MC, V* ❙❍❙ *BP.*

Nightlife & the Arts

The **Living Room** (✉ 7 av. des Spélugues 🕾 377/93–50–80–31) is a popular, crowded piano bar and discotheque open year-round. For a relatively low-key night, try **Sparco Café** (✉ 19 av. Charles-III 🕾 377/93–30–41–06), a piano bar that often attracts good jazz singers. **Tiffany's** (✉ 3 av. des Spélugues) is a year-round hot spot for disco dancing from 11 PM into the wee hours.

Monte Carlo's **Printemps des Arts** (Spring Arts Festival) takes place from early April to mid-May and includes the world's top ballet, operatic, symphonic, and chamber performers. For schedules and information contact the **Direction des Affaires Culturelles** (✉ 4 bd. des Moulins 🕾 377/93–15–85–15). Year-round ballet and classical music can be enjoyed at the **Salle Garnier** (✉ Pl. du Casino 🕾 377/92–16–22–99), the main venue of the Opéra de Monte-Carlo and the Orchestre Philharmonique de Monte-Carlo, both worthy of the magnificent hall. The **Théâtre Princesse Grace** (✉ 12 av. d'Ostende 🕾 377/93–25–32–27) stages a number of plays during the Spring Arts Festival; off-season there's usually a new show each week.

Sports & the Outdoors

The **Monte Carlo Tennis Open** (🕾 377/04–93–41–30–15 for information ⊕ www.masters-series.com/montecarlo) is held in late April in the Monte Carlo Country Club, which lies in the outskirts of Monaco in the French commune of Roquebrune–Cap-Martin.

The **Grand Prix de Monaco** (🕾 377/93–15–26–00 for information ⊕ www.monaco.mc/monaco/gprix) takes place in mid-May. Monaco goes a bit wacky during this car race around the principality in a way that only a

CLOSE UP

Want to Break the Bank?

THERE'S NO NEED TO GO TO BED BEFORE DAWN in Monte Carlo when you can go to the grand casinos. The casinos fix no closing times, but keep the doors open as long as the games are rolling.

The bastion and landmark of Monte Carlo gambling is, of course, the gorgeously ornate Casino de Monte-Carlo. The main gambling hall is the **Salle Européene** (European Room), where for a €8 entry fee you can play roulette, trente et quarante, or blackjack. The slot machines stand apart in the **Salle Blanche** (White Room) and the **Salon Rose** (Pink Salon), where unclad nymphs float about on the ceiling smoking cigarillos.

The **Salles Privées** (Private Rooms) are for high rollers; pay another €15 to play for a minimum stake of €80. Jacket and tie are required in the back rooms, which open at 3 PM. Bring your passport (under-21s not admitted). ⊠ *Pl. du Casino* ☎ *377/92–16–20–00* ⊙ *3 PM–noon.*

Once owned by the rival Loews Hotel (now the Monte Carlo Grand) the Sun Casino has been absorbed by SBM, though its long, low hall remains inside the Monte Carlo Grand hotel and just beside the waterfront convention center. There are no fewer than 435 slot machines here, as well as craps, blackjack, and *roulette américaine.* ⊠ *12 av. des Spélugues* ☎ *377/92–16–21–23* ⊙ *Tables open weekdays at 5 PM and weekends at 4 PM; slot machines open daily at 11 AM.*

Behind the dining room of the Café de Paris you'll find *les jeux américains:* row upon row of slot machines as well as American roulette, craps, and blackjack. ⊠ *Pl. du Casino* ☎ *377/ 92–16–21–24* ⊙ *Tables open daily at 5 PM; slot machines open daily at 10 AM.*

SBM's Le Sporting, a summer-only entertainment complex on the waterfront, has opened the Salle des Palmiers for the full panoply of European games, from English roulette to chemin de fer. Its games are open only at night. ⊠ *Le Sporting, Av. Princess Grace* ☎ *377/ 92–16–21–25* ⊙ *Late June–mid-Sept., tables open daily at 10 PM.*

5

city that prides itself on the outlandish amount of wealth it can display . . . well, outlandishly, can. During the Grand Prix the streets are roped off, the liquor is iced, and the brass is polished, and the enormously wealthy gracefully alight upon the city to lean over balconies—some rented for a mere €10,000 for the two-day stint. The cars fly through the city in a hot blur of Formula One super-speed. It's an exciting event if you can get close enough to the high-priced action.

Roquebrune–Cap-Martin

61 *5 km (3 mi) east of Monaco.*

In the midst of the frenzy of overbuilding that defines this last gasp of the coast before Italy, two twinned havens have survived, each in its own way: the perched Vieille Ville of Roquebrune, which gives its name to the greater area, and Cap-Martin—luxurious, isolated, exclusive, and the once favored retreat of the Empress Eugénie and Winston Churchill. With its lovely tumble of raked tile roofs and twisting streets, fountains, archways, and quiet squares, Roquebrune retains many of the charms of a hilltop village, although it has become heavily gentrified and commercialized. Rue Moncollet is lined with arcaded passageways and a number of medieval houses. Somerset Maugham—who once memorably described these environs as a "sunny place for shady people"—resided in the town's famous Villa Mauresque (still private) for many years.

Roquebrune's main attraction is the **Château Féodal** (Feudal Castle) at the top of the Old Town. Around the remains of a 10th-century tower, the Grimaldis erected an impregnable fortress that was state-of-the-art in the 16th century, with crenellation, watchtowers, and a broad moat. Nowadays this stronghold is besieged by tourists, who invade its restored halls and snap pictures from its wraparound walkway. ☎ 04–93–35–62–87 🖂 €4 ☾ Nov.–Jan., daily 10–12:30 and 2–5:30; Feb., Mar., and Oct., daily 10–12:30 and 2–6; Apr.–Sept., daily 10–12:30 and 3–7:30.

In the **cemetery,** at the far eastern end of the Old Town, Swiss-French architect Le Corbusier lies buried with his wife in a tomb of his own design. He kept a humble *cabanot* (beach bungalow) on the rocky shores of the Cap-Martin, where he drowned while swimming in 1965.

★ You can visit Le Corbusier's stunningly idyllic "cabanon" bungalow and see the glorious flora of the cape by walking the **Promenade Le Corbusier.** It leads over chalk cliffs and through dense Mediterranean flora to his tiny retreat, a modular cube of tiny proportions (3.66 × 3.66 meters) which appealed to his rigorous sense of minimalism. Guided tours can be arranged on Tuesdays or Fridays for €8 through the tourist office. Park at the tip of the cape on Avenue Winston-Churchill and follow the signs.

Where to Eat & Stay

★ $$ ✕🖻 **Les Deux Frères.** Magnificently sited, eccentric, and oozing with charm, this whitewashed 1854 schoolhouse has been transformed into an inn overlooking the sea. Every room is designed with a different theme—African safari, flower power, medieval castle, 1,001 nights—and tied-in videocassettes stand by to back up the mood. It's not as silly as it sounds, but is executed with modern, high-tech style and quality materials. The restaurant (closed Monday, no dinner Sunday, no lunch Tuesday) has set-price menus only (€20 for lunch including wine, €45 for dinner) and offers ambitious and generous French cooking, either indoors by the crackling fireplace or on the terrace *place* overlooking the whole of the Côte d'Azur. Homemade terrines, herbed lamb, and good cheeses draw a local clientele for picturesque culinary excursions. ✉ Above D2254 in Roquebrune village, 06190 ☎ 04–93–28–99–00 🖷 04–93–28–99–10 ⊕ www.lesdeuxfreres.com ⇆ 10 rooms, 2 apartments ⚐ Restaurant, bar, cable TV, Wi-Fi ▭ AE, DC, MC, V ☾ Closed mid-Nov.–mid-Dec., 1 wk in Mar.

Menton

1 km (²⁄₃ mi) east of Roquebrune, 9 km (5½ mi) east of Monaco.

Menton, the most Mediterranean of the French resort towns, rubs shoulders with the Italian border and owes some of its balmy climate to the protective curve of the Ligurian shore. Its Cubist skew of terracotta roofs and yellow-ocher houses, Baroque arabesques capping the church facades, and ceramic tiles glistening on their steeples, all evoke the villages of the Italian coast. Yet there's a whiff of influence from Spain, too, in its fantastical villas, exotic gardens, and whimsical patches of ceramic color, and a soupçon of Morocco, Corsica, and Greece. It is, in fact, the best of all Mediterranean worlds—and humble to boot: Menton is the least pretentious of the Côte d'Azur resorts, and all the more alluring for its modesty.

Its near-tropical climate nurtures orange and lemon trees that hang heavy with fruit in winter. There's another Florida parallel: the warmth attracts flocks of senior citizens who warm their bones far from northern fog and ice. Thus a large population of elderly visitors basks on its waterfront benches and browses its downtown shops. But Menton has a livelier, younger side, too, and the farther you penetrate toward the east, the more intriguing and colorful it becomes.

To get a feel for the territory, start your exploration at the far-east end of the Vieille Ville (Old Town) and walk out to the end of the **Quai Napoléon III,** jutting far out into the water. Above the masts of pleasure boats, all of Menton spreads over the hills, and the mountains of Italy loom behind.

Up a set of grand tiered stairs that lead from the Quai Bonaparte and the Jetée Emperatrice Eugénie the **Parvis St-Michel,** a broad plaza paved in round white and gray stones patterned in the coat of arms of the Grimaldi family. The plaza was created in the 17th century by Prince Honoré II; the letter H is mingled into the design as a kind of signature at the base of his great gift to the city.

62 The majestic, Baroque **Basilique St-Michel** (St-Michel Church), on Parvis St-Michel, dominates the skyline of Menton with its bell tower. A humbler Renaissance church was destroyed by order of the prince to make way for something on a grander scale, and its towering belfry secured its conspicuousness in 1701. Beyond the beautifully proportioned facade—a 19th-century addition—the richly frescoed nave and chapels contain several works by Genovese artists and a splendid 17th-century organ. Visiting hours are daily from 10 to noon and 3 to 5.

63 Just above the Basilique St-Michel, the smaller **Chapelle de Pénitents Blancs** answers with its own pure Baroque beauty, dating from 1687. Between 3 and 5 PM you can slip in to see the graceful trompe l'oeil over the altar and the ornate gilt lanterns the penitents carried in processions.

64 High above the Parvis St-Michel, the **Cimetière du Vieux-Château** (Old Château Cemetery) lies on the terraced plateau where once stood a medieval castle. The Victorian graves here are arranged by nationality, with

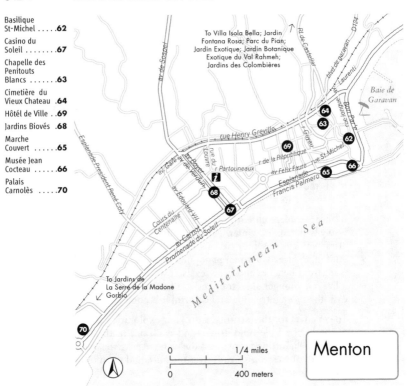

an entire section of Russian royalty. The birth and death dates often attest to the ugly truth: even Menton's balmy climate couldn't reverse the ravages of tuberculosis.

Two blocks below the plaza, **Rue St-Michel** serves as the main commercial artery of the Vieille Ville, lined with shops, cafés, and orange trees. Between the lively pedestrian Rue St-Michel and the waterfront, the marvelous **Marché Couvert** (Covered Market) sums up Menton style with its Belle Époque facade decorated in jewel-tone ceramics. Inside, it's just as appealing, with merchants vaunting chewy bread, mountain cheeses, oils, fruit, and Italian delicacies in Caravaggesque disarray. Outside its walls, other merchants bargain away their garden vegetables and hand-wound bundles of herbs. The market is open daily from 7 AM to 1 PM. Right by the market, the pretty little **Place aux Herbes** is a picturesque spot for a pause on a park bench, a drink, or a meal in the deep shade of the plane trees.

On the waterfront opposite the market, a squat medieval bastion crowned with four tiny watchtowers houses the **Musée Jean-Cocteau**. Built in 1636 to defend the port, the structure was spotted by the artist-poet-filmmaker Jean Cocteau (1889–1963) as the perfect site for a group of his works; he planned and supervised its reconstruction but never saw it finished.

Paradise Found: The Magnificent Gardens of Menton

THE CÔTE D'AZUR was famed for its panoply of grand villas and even grander gardens built by Victorian dukes, Spanish exiles, Belgian royals, and American blue bloods. Although its hothouse crescent blooms everywhere with palm and lemon trees and jungle flowers, nowhere else does it bloom so extravagantly than in Menton, famous for its temperate climes and 24-karat sun.

With a temperate microclimate created by its southeastern and sunny exposure (the Alps were a natural buffer against cold winds), Menton attracted a great share of wealthy hobbyists, including Major Lawrence Johnston, a gentleman gardener best known for his Cotswolds wonderland, Hidcote Manor.

Fair-haired and blue-eyed, this gentle American wound up buying a choice estate in the village of Gorbio—one of the loveliest of all perched seaside villages, set 10 km (6 mi) west of Menton—and spent the 1920s and 1930s making the Serre de la Madone one of the horticultural masterpieces of the coast.

He brought back exotica from his many trips to South Africa, Mexico, and China, and planted them in a series of terraces, accented by little pools, vistas, and stone steps. While most of his creeping plumbago, pink belladona, and night-flowering cacti are now gone, his garden has been reopened by the municipality. It is best to call for a reservation at the Serre de la Madone; car facilities are very limited but the garden can also be reached from Menton via bus No. 7 (get off at Mers et Monts stop).

Back in Menton, green-thumbers will also want to visit the town's Jardin Botanique, the Val Rahmeh Botanical Garden (Av. St-Jacques), planted by Maybud Campbell in the 1910s, much prized by connoisseurs, bursting with rare ornamentals and subtropical plants, and adorned with water-lily pools and fountains.

The tourist office can also give you directions to other gardens around Menton, including the Fontana Rosa, the Villa Maria Serena, and the Villa Les Colombièrs, as well as issue Heritage Passports for select garden visits; log onto www.menton.com. ⊠ *Serre de la Madone: 74 route de Gorbio* ☎ *04-93-57-73-90* ⊕ *www. serredelamadone.com* ✉ *€8 for Serre, €4 for Val Rehmeh* ⊘ *Tours only: Feb. 20–Apr., Fri. 9:30 and Tues.–Sun. 3; May–Oct., Tues.–Sun. 9:30 and 3.*

Outside its walls, a mosaic in round stone (an homage to the Parvis St-Michel) depicts a lizard; the inside floor answers with a salamander mosaic. There are bright, cartoonish pastels of fishermen and wenches in love, and a fantastical assortment of ceramic animals in the wrought-iron windows he designed himself. ⊠ *At the base of Quai Napoléon* ☎ *04–93–57–72–30* ✉ *€3* ⊘ *Wed.–Mon. 10–noon and 2–6.*

Stroll the length of Menton's famous beachfront along the **Promenade du Soleil,** broad, white, and studded with palm trees. The **Casino du Soleil**

(✉ 2 bis av. Félix-Faure ☎ 04–93–10–16–16) stakes out the middle of the promenade that shares its name; it's a modest, approachable, anti–Monte Carlo.

❻❽ Directly behind the casino and perpendicular to the beach, the broad tropical **Jardins Biovès** (Biovès Gardens) stretch the breadth of the center, sandwiched between two avenues. Its symmetrical flower beds and spires of palms are the spiritual heart of town.

❻❾ The 19th-century Italianate **Hôtel de Ville** (City Hall) conceals another Cocteau treasure: he decorated the **Salle des Mariages** (Marriage Room), the room in which civil marriages take place, with vibrant allegorical scenes. ✉ *17 av. de la République* ☎ *04–93–10–50–29* 🎟 *€2* ☉ *Weekdays 8:30–12:30 and 1:30–5.*

❼⓿ At the far west end of town, toward Roquebrune, stands the 18th-century **Palais Carnolès**, in vast gardens luxuriant with orange, lemon, and grapefruit trees. It was once the summer retreat of the princes of Monaco; today it contains a sizable collection of European paintings from the Renaissance to the present day. The halls of the palace themselves are as interesting as the artworks; the **Grand Salon d'Honneur** (Grand Salon of Honor) retains a rich ensemble of Neoclassical grotesques and bas-reliefs. ✉ *3 av. de la Madone* ☎ *04–93–35–49–71* 🎟 *Free* ☉ *Wed.–Mon. 10–noon and 2–6.*

Where to Eat & Stay

$$$–$$$$
Fodor'sChoice
★ ✕▦ **Aiglon.** Sweep down the curving stone stairs to the terrazzo mosaic lobby of this truly lovely 1880 garden villa for a drink or a meal by the pool, or settle onto your little balcony overlooking the grounds and a tiny wedge of sea. There's a room for every whim, all soft-edged, comfortable, and romantic, although you will be loath to leave the grand salon, a picture-perfect confection of 19th-century elegance that wouldn't shame some of the nobler houses in Paris. The poolside restaurant, Le Riaumont, serves candlelit dinners of fresh, local fish lightly steamed and sauced with a Provençal accent; breakfast is served in a shady garden shelter. It's a three-minute walk from the beach. ✉ *7 av. de la Madone, 06502* ☎ *04–93–57–55–55* 🖷 *04–93–35–92–39* ⊕ *www.hotelaiglon.net* 🛏 *25 rooms, 4 apartments* ⚫ *Restaurant, pool, in-room safes, Wi-Fi, bar, some pets allowed* ▭ *AE, DC, MC, V* ☉ *Closed 3 wks in Nov.–Dec.* ⦿ *BP, MAP.*

$$$ ▦ **Royal Westminster.** This Victorian waterfront palace hotel, beautifully restored inside and out in shades of lemon, mint, and robin's-egg blue, usually rents out its light-bathed, sea-view rooms to tour groups of seniors by the week. But you might get lucky on a standby basis, calling to reserve no sooner than 10 days in advance, or even dropping in. Beach mattresses and sun parasols are provided in the rooms. ✉ *1510 promenade du Soleil, 06500* ☎ *04–93–28–69–69* 🖷 *04–92–10–12–30* 🛏 *92 rooms Restaurant, billiards, bar* ▭ *AE, DC, MC, V.*

$$$ ▦ **Hotel de Londres.** This modest, family-run hotel is just a block from the beach and three blocks from the casino. It has an inexpensive traditional restaurant with outdoor tables and a tiny garden bar. Though the building dates from the turn of the 20th century, rooms have been renovated for a fresh clean look; most have big French windows that open over the garden and just a sliver of sea view between the buildings, and a dozen now have air-conditioning. Small back rooms with shower only are a bargain. ⊠ *15 av. Carnot, BP 73, 06502* ☎ *04–93–35–74–62* 🖶 *04–93–41–77–78* ⊕ *www.hotel-de-londres. com* ⌑ *27 rooms* ⚒ *Restaurant, cable TV, in-room data ports, bar; no a/c in some rooms* 🖃 *AE, DC, MC, V* ⊙I *BP.*

Nightlife & the Arts
The **casino** (⊠ Promenade de Soleil ☎ 04–92–10–16–16) has the usual slot machines and roulette tables, as well as a disco and a cabaret in its Club 06. It's open daily 10 AM–3 AM.

In August the **Festival de Musique de Chambre** (Chamber Music Festival) takes place on the stone-paved plaza outside the St-Michel Church. The ★ **Fête du Citron** (Lemon Festival), at the end of February, celebrates the lemon with floats and sculptures, all made of real fruit.

NICE & THE EASTERN CÔTE D'AZUR ESSENTIALS

Transportation

If traveling extensively by public transportation, be sure to load up on information (schedules, the best taxi-for-call companies, etc.) upon arriving at the ticket counter or help desk of the bigger hub stations in the area, such as Cannes, Nice, and Monaco.

BY AIR
The Nice–Côte d'Azur Airport, the second-busiest in France, sits on a peninsula between Antibes and Nice. There are frequent flights between Paris and Nice on the low-cost airline easyJet and Air France, as well as direct flights on Delta Airlines from New York. In the off-season or if you book well in advance you can find a one-way trip from Paris to Nice for a spectacular €30; which definitely beats out both the SNCF and the cost of a rental car. Be sure to compare prices between easyJet and Air France, though Air France is almost always more expensive. The flight time between Paris and Nice is about 1 hour.

A taxi from the airport into Nice proper—say, the train station or the Place Masséna—costs about €25. Sunbus No. 90 from Nice makes the run to and from the train station and the bus station every 30 minutes Monday–Saturday between 6 AM and 9 PM for a more reasonable €4. Regular shuttle buses also serve the main coastal cities (Cannes, Antibes, Monte Carlo, Menton), leaving from both terminals every half hour or so—prices vary depending on the company.

🛈 Air Travel Information **Aéroport International Nice-Côte d'Azur** ⊠ 7 km [4½ mi] from Nice ☎ 04-93-21-30-30 ⊕ www.nice.aeroport.fr.

BY BOAT
The Côte d'Azur is one of the most beautiful coastlines in the world and there are several companies that allow you to drink it all in via boat

and ferry service. Compagnie Maritime Cannoise offers routes between Cannes and Monaco and St-Tropez. Trans Côte d'Azur has routes including the Corniche de l'Estérel, Monaco, Porquerolles, and St-Tropez, plus specialty excursions that feature nighttime dining and glass-bottom boats. Trans Côte d'Azur has routes including the Corniche de l'Estérrel, Monaco, Porquerolles, and St-Tropez. Note that some routes and destinations are only featured March to October.

🚢 Boat Travel Information **Compagnie Maritime Cannoise** (CMC) ✉ 1 Quai Albert Edouard 06400, Cannes ☎ 04-93-38-66-33. ⊕ www.ilesdelerins.co. **Trans Côte d'Azur** ✉ Quai Laubeuf 06400, Cannes ☎ 04-92-98-71-30. ⊕ www.trans-cote-azur.com.

BY BUS

If you want to penetrate deeper into villages and backcountry spots not on the rail line, you can take a bus out of Cannes, Nice, Antibes, or Menton to the most frequented spots. Pick up a schedule for local and commercial excursion buses at the train station, at tourist offices, and at the local *gare routière* (bus station). Note that the quickest way to get around by public transportation is the great coastal train line that connects the main cities and a lot of villages from Cannes to Menton (*see* By Rail, *below*). In addition to town bus stations, you can hook up with buses heading to most destinations in this chapter using the bus station at the Nice airport (next to Terminal 1). Rapides Côte d'Azur runs Bus No. 100, which departs every 15 minutes (between 6 AM and 8 PM and stops at all the villages between Nice and Menton along the Corniche Inférieure. A trip to Beaulieu, for instance, costs €1.80 round-trip and takes 8 minutes from Nice. For the villages set on the Moyenne Corniche, take Bus No. 112, which departs Nice six times a day (three on Sunday). A trip to Èze, for instance, costs €2.50 and takes 20 minutes. Fewer villages are found on the Grande Corniche, the highest highway, but some, such as La Turbie are serviced by Rapides Côte d'Azur No. 116. From Menton's bus station, you can take buses back to Monaco and Nice. Many hotels and excursion companies organize day trips into St-Paul and Vence.

In Cannes, Rapides Côtes d'Azur runs most of the routes out of the central bus station on Place Bernard Gentille, including Nice (€6, 1½ hrs), Mougins (€2, 20 minutes), Grasse (€4, 45 minutes), and Vallauris (€3, 30 minutes). Within Cannes, Bus Azur runs the routes, with a ticket costing €1.30 (a weekly ticket is available). In Nice, the Sunbus is a convenient way to cut across town; a day pass costs €4, and a one-way ticket is €1.35. Get tickets at neighborhood tabacs (tobacconists) or at their ticket office at 10 Avenue Félix Faure or their Station Centrale on Square Général Leclerc. Their main routes include No. 12, from train station to Promenade des Anglais, and No. 30, from train station to Vieux Nice. Monaco's buses help stitch together the principality's widely dispersed neighborhoods. Take a bus from Antibes bus station to Vallauris (€3, every 30 minutes) or one running from the train station in Golfe-Juan. Antibes bus station is by Rue de la République, and has buses connecting with Nice (€5, every half hr), Cagnes-sur-Mer (€2.50, 20 minutes), Biot (€1, 25 minutes), Cannes (€2, 30 minutes). Cagnes-sur-

Mer is one of the coastal towns served by train, but you can easily connect with adjacent St-Paul-de-Vence and Vence using Bus. No. 400, with departures every 30 minutes from Cagnes Ville's bus station on Place du Général de Gaulle. Note that you can take a free navette shuttle bus from here up to the hilltown of Haut-de-Cagnes during June—December. The bus station in Cagnes Ville is about eight blocks away from the train station (but municipal buses can help you make this trip—ask at Cagnes's bus station). Bus drivers give change and hand you a ticket, which must be stamped (*composté*) in the ticket validator.

Bus Information **Cannes Gare Routière (Bus Station)** ⊠ Place Bernard Cornut Gentille ☎04-93-45-20-08. **Nice Gare Routière** ⊠5 blvd. Jean-Jaurès ☎04-93-85-61-81. **Menton Gare Routière** ⊠12 promenade Maréchal Leclerc ☎04-93-28-43-27. **Rhocéens Cars** ⊠ 2 pl. Masséna ☎ 04-93-85-66-61. **Rapides Côte d'Azur** ☎ 04-93-85-64-44 ⊕ www.rca.tm.fr. **Société des Cars Alpes-Littoral** ☎ 04-92-51-06-05. **Sunbus** (Station Centrale) ⊠ Square Général Leclerc ☎ 04-93-13-53-13 ⊕ www.sunbus.com. **Transports Alpes-Maritimes** ☎ 04-93-89-41-45.

BY CAR

A8 flows briskly from Cannes to Antibes to Nice to the resorts on the Grand Corniche; N98 follows the coast more closely along the Corniche Inférieure. The Moyenne Corniche is highway N7. For more info, *see* The Three Corniches Close-Up box *in* this chapter. From Paris, the main southbound artery is A6/A7, known as the Autoroute du Soleil; it passes through Provence and joins the eastbound A8 at Aix-en-Provence.

The best way to explore the secondary sights in this region, especially the deep backcountry, is by car. A car also allows you the freedom to zip along A8 between the coastal resorts and to enjoy the tremendous views from the three Corniches that trace the coast from Nice to the Italian border. A car is, of course, a liability in downtown Cannes and Nice, with parking garages expensive and curbside spots virtually nonexistent. Drive defensively and stay alert. This is one of the most dangerous driving regions in Europe, and the speeds and aggressive Grand-Prix style of some drivers make it impossible to let your guard down. On the A8 toward Italy, tight curves, hills, tunnels, and construction keep things interesting. For English-language traffic reports (as well as BBC news) tune to 86.4 FM.

BY TRAIN

Nice is the major rail crossroads for trains arriving from Paris and other northern cities and from Italy, too. To get from Paris to Nice (with stops in Cannes and other resorts along the coast), you can take the TGV, though it only maintains high speeds to Valence before returning to conventional rails and rates. Night trains arrive at Nice in the morning from Paris, Metz, and Strasbourg.

You can easily move along the coast between Cannes, Nice, and Ventimiglia by train on the slick double-decker Côte d'Azur line, a dramatic and highly tourist-pleasing branch of the SNCF lines that offers panoramic views as it rolls from one famous resort to the next, with more than two dozen trains running a day. This line is called Marseille-Vintimille (Ventimiglia, in Italy) heading east to Italy and Vintimille-Marseille in the west direction. Some main stops on this line are: Antibes (€4, 30 minutes), Cannes (€6, 40 minutes), Menton (€4, 30 minutes), and Monaco (€3, 25 minutes); other stops include Villefranche-sur-Mer, Beaulieu, Cap Martin, St-Jean-Cap-Ferrat, and Èze-sur-Mer. But train travelers will have difficulty getting up to St-Paul, Vence, Peillon, and other backcountry villages; that you must accomplish by bus or car.

🚆 Train Information **Gare Nice Ville** ⊠ Av. Thiers ☎ 08-36-35-35-35. **Gare Cannes Ville** (train station) ⊠ Rue Jean-Jaurès. **SNCF** ☎ 08-36-35-35-35 ⊕ www.ter-sncf.com/uk/paca. **TGV** ☎ 877/2TGVMED ⊕ www.tgv.com. **www.beyond.fr** ⊕ www.beyond.fr.

Contacts & Resources

CAR RENTALS

Most likely you'll want to rent your car at one of the main rail stops, either Cannes, Nice, Monaco, or Menton, or at the airport in Nice, where all major companies are represented.

🚗 Car Rental Information **Avis** ⊠ 69 bd. Croisette, Cannes ☎ 04-93-94-15-86 ⊠ Pl. de la Gare, Cannes ☎ 04-93-39-26-38 ⊠ 2 av. des Phocéens, Nice ☎ 04-93-80-63-52 ⊠ Nice Airport ☎ 04-93-21-36-33 ⊠ 9 av. d'Ostende, Monaco ☎ 377/93-30-17-53. **Budget** ⊠ 160 rue Antibes, Cannes ☎ 04-93-99-44-04 ⊠ 23 rue de Belgique, Nice ☎ 04-93-16-24-16 ⊠ Nice Airport ☎ 04-93-21-36-50. **Europcar Interrent** ⊠ 3 rue Commandant Vidal, Cannes ☎ 04-93-06-26-30 ⊠ 3 av. Gustave, Nice ☎ 04-92-14-44-50 ⊠ Nice Airport ☎ 04-93-21-58-91 ⊠ 9 av. Thiers, Menton ☎ 04-93-28-21-80 ⊠ 47 av. de Grande-Bretagne, Monaco ☎ 377/93-50-74-95. **Hertz** ⊠ Eden Palace II, 147 rue Antibes, Cannes ☎ 04-93-99-04-20 ⊠ 1 promenade des Anglais, Nice ☎ 04-93-87-11-87 ⊠ Nice Airport ☎ 04-93-21-36-72 ⊠ 27 bd. Albert Ier, Monaco ☎ 377/93-50-79-60.

EMERGENCIES

For basic information, see this section in the Smart Travel Tips chapter. In most towns, contact the Comissariat de Police or Gendarmerie.

🚨 Emergencies **Police** ⊠ 1 av. Maréchal Foch, Nice ☎ 04-92-17-22-22. **Police** ⊠ 2 quai Saint-Pierre, Cannes ☎ 04-97-06-42-85.

GUIDED TOURS

The first Tuesday of each month, Antibes offers free guided tours of its Old Town leaving from L'Antiboulenc at 3 PM. Phocéens Voyages organizes bus explorations to Monaco on Thursday for €25, Grasse on Monday for €18, and St-Paul-de-Vence on Tuesday for €18, with English tours by advance request. The Antibes Tourist Office organizes a day-long tour which traces the footsteps of Picasso from Antibes to Mougins. In the morning a private lecturer will accompany you to the museum in Antibes. The afternoon is spent at the photography museum in Mougins. These tours must be reserved in advance with the Tourist Office.

The city of Nice arranges individual guided tours on an à la carte basis, according to your needs. For information, contact the Bureau d'Accueil and specify your dates and language preferences. A small tourist train goes along the waterfront from the Jardin Albert Ier on the Promenade des Anglais, along Cours Saleya, and up to the Château. Santa Azur organizes full- or half-day bus excursions to sights near Nice, including

Monaco and Cannes, either leaving from their offices or from several stops along the Promenade des Anglais, mainly in front of the big hotels. English-language tours are available with advance request. Château de Crémat offers free guided tours of its vineyards with a wine tasting by appointment for €10.

Menton acquaints you with its rich architectural heritage by offering regular *visites du patrimoine* (heritage tours) to its gardens, cemetery, museums, and villas. Details on each visit and points and times of departure are published in the city's free *Programme des manifestations* (events program), published bimonthly by the tourist office. For information, contact the Maison du Patrimonie. Contact the Menton Tourist Office for information on a number of tours, including the *Passeport Menton Côté Charme,* which offers two theme tours to be chosen from the program of excursions along with an outing at sea or a videocassette.

🗋 Guided Tour Information **L'Antiboulenc** ✉ 2 rue Auberman, Arles ☎ 04-93-34-66-07. **Antibes Tourist Office** ✉ 11 pl. de Gaulle, Antibes ☎04-92-90-53-00. **Phocéens Voyages** ✉8 pl. de Gaulle, Antibes ☎04-93-34-15-98. **Bureau d'Accueil** ✉Nice ☎04-93-14-48-00. **Nice tourist train** ☎04-93-92-45-59. **Santa Azur** ✉11 av. Jean-Médecin, Nice ☎04-93-85-46-81. **Château de Crémat** ✉422 chemin de Crémat, northwest of Nice ☎04-92-15-12-15. **Maison du Patrimonie** ✉24 rue St-Michel, Menton ☎04-92-10-97-10.

INTERNET & MAIL

In smaller towns, ask your hotel concierge if there are any Internet cafés nearby.

🗋Internet & Mail Information **Web Center** ✉24 rue Hoche, Cannes ☎04-93-68-72-37. **@CyberPoint** ✉10 ave. Félix-Faure, Nice ☎04-93-92-70-63. **Panini & Web** ✉25 promenade des Anglais, Nice ☎04-93-88-72-75. **La Poste main post office** ✉22 rue Biovouac Napoléon, Cannes. **La Poste main post office** ✉23 av. Thiers, Nice.

VISITOR INFORMATION

The Comité Régional du Tourisme Riviera Côte d'Azur (Regional Tourist Committee) provides information on tourism throughout the département of Alpes-Maritimes, from Cannes to the Italian border.

Local tourist offices are an incredible source of information for last-minute hotel bookings, information on museum passes, tours, festivals, transportation information, and new blips on the local screen. Whatever you do, contact them; they're friendly, bilingual, and only too pleased to help.

🗋 Local Tourist Offices The **Comité Régional du Tourisme Riviera Côte d'Azur** (Regional Tourist Committee) ✉ 55 promenade des Anglais, B.P. 1602, Cedex 01 06011 Nice ☎ 04-93-37-78-78 ⊕ www.crt-riviera.fr. **Antibes/Juan-les-Pins** ✉11 pl. de Gaulle, 06600 Antibes ☎ 04-92-90-53-00 🖷 04-92-90-53-01 ⊕ antibes-juanlespins.com. **Biot** ✉ Pl. de la Chapelle, 06410 Biot ☎ 04-93-65-05-85 ⊕ www.biot-coteazur.com. **Cagnes-sur-Mer** ✉ 6 bd. Maréchal Juin, B.P. 48, 06800 Cagnes-sur-Mer ☎ 04-93-20-61-64 🖷 04-92-20-52-63 ⊕ www.cagnes.com. **Cannes** ✉ Palais des Festivals, Esplanade G. Pompidou, B.P. 272, 06400 Cannes ☎ 04-93-39-01-01 🖷 04-93-99-37-34 ⊕ www.cannes-on-line.com. **Èze** ✉ Pl. de Gaulle, 06130 Èze ☎ 04-93-41-26-00 🖷04-93-41-04-80 ⊕ www.eze-riviera.com. **Grasse** ✉ Palais des Congrés, 22 cours Honoré Cresp, 06130 Grasse ☎ 04-93-36-66-66 🖷 04-93-36-86-36

⊕ www.ville-grasse.com. **Menton** ⊠ Palais de l'Europe, Av. Boyer, 06500 Menton ☎ 04-92-41-76-76 📠 04-92-41-76-78 ⊕ www.villedementon.com. **Monaco** ⊠ 2a bd. des Moulins, 98000 Monte Carlo, Monaco ☎ 377/92-16-61-66 📠 377/92-16-60-00 ⊕ www.monaco-congres.com. **Mougins** ⊠ 15 av. Jean-Charles Mallet, 06251 Mougins ☎ 04-93-75-87-67 📠 04-92-92-04-03 ⊕ www.mougins-cotedazur.org. **Nice** ⊠ 5 promenade des Anglais, 06000 Nice ☎ 04-92-14-48-00 📠 04-92-14-48-03 ⊕ www.nicetourism.com. **Roquebrune-Cap-Martin** ⊠ 20 av. Paul Doumer, 06190 Roquebrune-Cap-Martin ☎ 04-93-35-62-87 📠 04-93-28-57-00. **St-Jean-Cap-Ferrat** ⊠ 59 av. Denis Semeria, 06230 St-Jean-Cap-Ferrat ☎ 04-93-76-08-90 📠 04-93-76-16-67 ⊕ www.-ville-saint-jean-cap-ferrat.fr. **St-Paul** ⊠ 2 rue Grande, 06570 St-Paul ☎ 04-93-32-86-95 📠 04-93-32-60-27. **Vence** ⊠ Pl. du Grand Jardin, 06140 Vence ☎ 04-93-58-06-38 📠 04-93-58-91-81 ⊕ www.ville-vence.fr. **Villefranche-sur-Mer** ⊠ Jardin François-Binon, 06230 Villefranche-sur-Mer ☎ 04-93-01-73-68 📠 04-93-76-63-65 ⊕ www.villefranche-sur-mer.com.

UNDERSTANDING PROVENCE & THE CÔTE D'AZUR

STONE, SUN & SEA: PROVENCE PRIMORDIAL

THE ROASTED RED ROOFS skew downhill at Cubist angles, sun-bleached and mottled with age. Stone and stucco walls emerge from the bedrock all of a hue—amber, saffron, honey. The sky is a prism, scoured to clarity by the juggernaut winds of the mistral; it radiates an azure of palpable intensity and bottomless depth. A rhythm of Romanesque tiles overlaps in sensual snaking rows; they were, after all, mixed from the wet clay and molded over the thighs of women, and like their models are as alike and as varied as the reeds in a panpipe. In the fields behind, white-hot at midday, chill and spare at night, you crunch through an abundance of wild thyme, rosemary, and lavender dried in the arid breeze, their acrid-sweet scent cutting through the crystal air like smelling salts. Sheep bells tinkle behind dry rock walls and churchbells sound across valleys as easily as over the village wall; in the distance is the pulsing roar of the sea. Nowhere in France, and rarely in the Western world, can you touch antiquity with this intimacy—its exoticism, its purity, eternal and alive. Provence and the Côte d'Azur: together they are, as the French say, primordial.

Basking luxuriously along the sunny southern flank of France Provence and its famous coast are bordered to the east by Italy, sheltered to the northeast by the Alps, and lean west and southwest toward its Spanish-influenced neighbors in Languedoc and the Basque country. The Greeks and Phocaeans first brought classical culture to the Celt-like Ligurian natives of the coast in 600 BC when they founded Massilia (Marseille), which thrived as a cosmopolitan colony—the Athens of a nascent Europe—until their alliance with the upstart Romans in Aix turned sour.

Julius Caesar himself claimed Marseille in 49 BC, and thus it came to be Provincia Romana, the first Roman stronghold in Gaul.

The best of Latin culture flourished here until the fall of the Empire, some of it outliving Rome: the theater and triumphal arch in Orange; the amphitheaters in Nîmes and Arles; the magnificent aqueduct bridge called the Pont du Gard; the mausoleum, arch, and village ruins in St-Rémy; the villas and baths in Vaison-le-Romaine—these monuments, still standing today, are considered among the best of their kind in existence, easily rivaling the Colosseum in Rome.

Yet the noble remains of Rome have taken on a patina and given way to the more modest culture of modern Provence, where the village shops shutter down for the *sieste,* matrons pinch melons with the concentration of wine tasters in Bordeaux, and the menfolk hunch earnestly over a milky glass of pastis and size up the angle of a rolling *pétanque* ball with the skepticism and discretion of a federal judge. In this modern province, Provence, the olives blacken at their own pace to onyx, then ebony, and the melons plump with juice drawn deep under the rocky Alpilles; the world moves slowly in the heat.

Until the cell phone rings. Then the "New South" shows its well-tanned profile as one of the most coveted regions for tourism in France—even, no, especially, by the French. Today Provence and its Côte d'Azur imply a lazy, laissez-faire lifestyle, a barefoot idyll, three-hour lunches, sultry terrace nights, and a splash in the Mediterranean . . . but *branché,* plugged in, connected by phones and freeways and airports and the TGV to Paris and the world. Many a pale, embittered northerner has found new lust for life in its chic contemporary pulse, converting old *mas* (farmhouses) into summer homes, and opening restaurants and hotels that out-Provence Provence.

These vacation retreats brim over with Provençal architecture (roughly construed in shades of ocher and pink), Provençal decor (sophisticated country prints, cheery colored pottery, and curves of bronzed iron), and Provençal cuisine (olive oil, garlic, grilled vegetables, and fish). And it doesn't just stop at the borders: the Provence formula is a worldwide fashion now, a panacea of sunshine that brightens the darkest streets of both hemispheres. If the '80s were about Italy, from the dawning of fettuccine Alfredo to Memphis high-tech design to the wholesale invasion of Tuscan villas, the '90s were the Provençal Renaissance—and the fashion shows no sign of abating.

Everyone from Russian princes to American robber barons to writers and thinkers flocked to the southern coast, constructing a fantasy world of gleaming-white villas, turquoise swimming pools, and balustrades framing Technicolor sunsets. The Lost Generation found a new home here under the palms—Hemingway, Zelda and Scott Fitzgerald, nurturing a brood of bitter wits like Dorothy Parker, John Dos Passos, and Gertrude Stein and Alice B. Toklas. And the whole of 20th-century art seemed to bloom under its sun—Picasso, Matisse, Cézanne, Van Gogh, Chagall, Monet, Léger, and Miró. The crystalline light and elemental forms inspired them, and the *volupté* of the Mediterranean saturates their work—sensual fruit, lush flowers, fundamental forms, light and color analyzed, interpreted, transformed, revealed. They, like the literati before them, found in this primeval setting the peace and stimulation to create.

Then came the movie stars, trading the palm trees of Hollywood for the palm trees of the Riviera. Grace Kelly married a prince and led her own tiny principality on a cliff over the sparkling blue waters of Monaco; a tousled and tanned Robert Mitchum was arrested for smoking marijuana and swimming with a topless starlet in Cannes. A teenage Brigitte Bardot moved heaven and earth when she swayed, flat-footed and full-lipped, through *And God Created Woman* in St-Tropez.

And the world followed, blessed with long vacations, easy air travel, and post-war prosperity. Yet caveat emptor—the glamour of the Côte d'Azur has, for the most part, been crowded down to the shoreline and swept out to sea: honky-tonk tourist traps, candy-pink duplexes, and project-like high-rises dominate much of the region, while the wealthy hoard their seaside serenity in private, isolated villas. Only off-season—early spring, late fall, even fine mid-winter days—can you experience the healing balm of the gentle sun, the mesmerizing rhythm of the waves, the squeaky-clean breeze that flows steady and sure from the infinite blue horizon.

To find the grace and antiquity of the region, and the sun if not the seaside, you'll want to retreat to the noble city Old Towns—Nice, Marseille, Aix, and Avignon—and the slow-paced villages, both nestled along the waterfront and rising like ziggurats on stony hilltops behind the coast. Here you'll discover the palpable light, the honeyed hues, the rough-hewn geometry that inspired Van Gogh and Cézanne, Picasso and Matisse. Anywhere in this ancient region you may share their epiphany, whether standing humbled inside the 5th-century baptistery in St-Saveur in Aix; breakfasting on a wrought-iron balcony overlooking turquoise Mediterranean tides; contemplating the orbs and linear perspective of a melon field outside Cavaillon; or sipping the sea-perfumed elixir of a great bouillabaisse (surely the Phocaeans sipped something similar 2,600 years ago) along the docks of Marseille. Evocative, earthy, eternal, primordial—like a woven rope of garlic, Provence and its coast are the essence of Latin France.

— By Nancy Coons

BOOKS & MOVIES

To set the tone for your *séjour* (stay) in the south of France, take time to look into literature and films set in the region. A few choice reads by Lost Generation expatriates include: F. Scott Fitzgerald's *Tender Is the Night,* in which Dick and Nicole Diver wallow in jaded decadence in Juan-les-Pins, and John Dos Passos's *The Best Times,* written in and about Antibes. For some background on the heady 1920s, try Amanda Vaill's *Everybody Was So Young: Gerald and Sara Murphy, a Lost Generation Love Story.* The Murphys were a wealthy American couple who became legendary Riviera hosts to the era's artists and writers. Mary Blume's *Côte d'Azur: Inventing the French Riviera* is a wry, dry history of the region's rebirth as a glamour mecca in the 20th century. Henry Miller wrote to Anaïs Nin in *Letters to Anaïs Nin* of his sojourns on the Riviera.

Peter Mayle put the Luberon on the map with his essays on southern bliss and culture shock in *A Year in Provence, Toujours Provence,* and *Encore Provence. A Dog's Life* tells more Provençal stories from the point of view of his dog. His novels *Chasing Cézanne, Hotel Pastis,* and *Anything Considered* also evoke the region.

Prodigious writer M.F.K. Fisher wonderfully describes her experiences in the south of France; food plays a large role in her evocative work. *Two Towns in Provence* pairs essays on Aix-en-Provence and Marseille. Many of her autobiographical stories also include observations or anecdotes on Provence. In A.S. Byatt's short story collection *Elementals: Stories of Fire and Ice,* several tales take place in Provence. W.S. Merwin's *The Lost Upland* describes the author's life in rural southwestern France; it's out of print, but well worth looking up in a library.

Provence produced several literary stars, from the epic poetry of Frédéric Mistral (*Miranda*), father of the revival of the Provençal language, to the austere novels of Jean Giono—*Regain* and *Jean Le Bleu*—dark with the chill of Haute Provence. Alphonse Daudet wrote folklore and tall tales from his beloved mill in Fontvieille in *Lettres de Mon Moulin.*

Changing hats from playwright to screenwriter to director to novelist to memoirist, Marcel Pagnol was the quintessential raconteur, a great storyteller with a gift for evoking the sensations and smells of Provence as well as the lilting language. The original plays of his Marseille trilogy—*Marius, Fanny,* and *César*—were later developed into films thick with the tried-and-true Midi accent of the Provençal actor Raimu. And there are a dozen other films of equal charm, including his own version of *Manon des Sources (Manon of the Springs)*, with his wife Jacqueline cast as the young goat girl. He wrote four volumes of memoirs, the *Souvenirs d'un Enfance.* Other directors' efforts to evoke his atmospheric stories include Claude Berri's *Jean de Florette* and *Manon des Sources* (1986), filmed in the Luberon.

To recapture the '60s glamour of the Riviera, rent a video of Michael Powell's *The Red Shoes* (1948); Hitchcock's suspense classic *To Catch a Thief* (1955), with Cary Grant and Grace Kelly; Roger Vadim's *And God Created Woman* (1957), which in turn created Brigitte Bardot and St-Tropez; *La Cage aux Folles* (1978), with scenes in the market, port, and old town of St-Tropez; and *Two for the Road* (1967), with Albert Finney and Audrey Hepburn, whose yearly vacation in France—for better, for worse—passes by the south.

FRENCH VOCABULARY

English	French	Pronunciation
Basics		
Yes/no	Oui/non	wee/nohn
Please	S'il vous plaît	seel voo **play**
Thank you	Merci	mair-**see**
You're welcome	De rien	deh ree-**ehn**
That's all right	Il n'y a pas de quoi	eel nee ah pah de **kwah**
Excuse me, sorry	Pardon	pahr-**dohn**
Sorry!	Désolé(e)	day-zoh-**lay**
Good morning/ afternoon	Bonjour	bohn-**zhoor**
Good evening	Bonsoir	bohn-**swahr**
Goodbye	Au revoir	o ruh-**vwahr**
Mr. (Sir)	Monsieur	muh-**syuh**
Mrs. (Ma'am)	Madame	ma-**dam**
Miss	Mademoiselle	mad-mwa-**zel**
Pleased to meet you	Enchanté(e)	ohn-shahn-**tay**
How are you?	Comment ça va?	kuh-mahn-sa-**va**
Very well, thanks	Très bien, merci	tray bee-ehn, mair-**see**
And you?	Et vous?	ay **voo**?
Numbers		
one	un	uhn
two	deux	deuh
three	trois	twah
four	quatre	**kaht**-ruh
five	cinq	sank
six	six	seess
seven	sept	set
eight	huit	wheat
nine	neuf	nuff
ten	dix	deess
eleven	onze	ohnz
twelve	douze	dooz
thirteen	treize	trehz
fourteen	quatorze	kah-**torz**

fifteen	quinze	kanz
sixteen	seize	sez
seventeen	dix-sept	deez-**set**
eighteen	dix-huit	deez-**wheat**
nineteen	dix-neuf	deez-**nuff**
twenty	vingt	vehn
twenty-one	vingt-et-un	vehnt-ay-**uhn**
thirty	trente	trahnt
forty	quarante	ka-**rahnt**
fifty	cinquante	sang-**kahnt**
sixty	soixante	swa-**sahnt**
seventy	soixante-dix	swa-sahnt-**deess**
eighty	quatre-vingts	kaht-ruh-**vehn**
ninety	quatre-vingt-dix	kaht-ruh-vehn-**deess**
one-hundred	cent	sahn
one-thousand	mille	meel

Days of the Week

Sunday	dimanche	**dee**-mahnsh
Monday	lundi	**luhn**-dee
Tuesday	mardi	**mahr**-dee
Wednesday	mercredi	**mair**-kruh-dee
Thursday	jeudi	**zhuh**-dee
Friday	vendredi	**vawn**-druh-dee
Saturday	samedi	**sahm**-dee

Months

January	janvier	**zhahn**-vee-ay
February	février	**feh**-vree-ay
March	mars	marce
April	avril	a-**vreel**
May	mai	meh
June	juin	zhwehn
July	juillet	**zhwee**-ay
August	août	oot
September	septembre	sep-**tahm**-bruh
October	octobre	awk-**to**-bruh
November	novembre	no-**vahm**-bruh
December	décembre	day-**sahm**-bruh

Useful Phrases

Do you speak . . . English?	Parlez-vous . . . anglais?	par-lay **voo** **ahn**-glay
I don't speak . . . French	Je ne parle pas . . . français	zhuh nuh parl **pah** frahn-**say**
I don't understand	Je ne comprends pas	zhuh nuh kohm-prahn **pah**
I understand	Je comprends	zhuh kohm-**prahn**
I don't know	Je ne sais pas	zhuh nuh say **pah**
I'm American/ British	Je suis américain/ anglais	zhuh sweez a-may-ree-**kehn**/ahn-**glay**
What's your name?	Comment vous appelez-vous?	ko-mahn voo za-pell-ay-**voo**
My name is . . .	Je m'appelle . . .	zhuh ma-**pell** . . .
What time is it?	Quelle heure est-il?	kel air eh-**teel**
How?	Comment?	ko-**mahn**
When?	Quand?	kahn
Yesterday	Hier	yair
Today	Aujourd'hui	o-zhoor-**dwee**
Tomorrow	Demain	duh-**mehn**
This morning/ afternoon	Ce matin/cet après-midi	suh ma-**tehn**/set ah-pray-mee-**dee**
Tonight	Ce soir	suh **swahr**
Why?	Pourquoi?	**poor**-kwa
Who?	Qui?	kee
Where is . . .	Où se trouve . . .	oo suh **troov**
the train station?	la gare?	la gar
the subway? station?	la station de? métro?	la sta-**syon** duh may-**tro**
the bus stop?	l'arrêt de bus?	la-**ray** duh **booss**
the airport?	l'aérogare?	lay-ro-**gar**
the post office?	la poste?	la post
the bank?	la banque?	la bahnk
the hotel?	l'hôtel?	lo-**tel**
the store?	le magasin?	luh ma-ga-**zehn**
the elevator?	l'ascenseur?	la-sahn-**seuhr**
the telephone?	le téléphone?	luh tay-lay-**phone**
Where are the rest rooms?	Où sont les toilettes?	oo sohn lay twah-**let**

INDEX

PHOTO CREDITS

Cover Photo (Sunflower field, Provence): *Bryan F. Peterson/Corbis.* F8, *FSG/age fotostock.* F9 (left), *Bruno Morandi/age fotostock.* F9 (right), *Walter Bibikow/viestiphoto.com.* F10, *Kevin O'Hara/age fotostock.* F12 (top), *Peter Bowater/age fotostock.* F12 (bottom), *George Haling/age fotostock.* F13, *Jon Arnold/Agency Jon Arnold Images/age fotostock.* F14, *Walter Bibikow/age fotostock.* F15 (left), *Moulin des Mougins.* F15 (center), *Peres/Ask Images/viestiphoto.com.* F15 (right), *Catherine Hensen/viestiphoto.com.* F16, *Kevin O'Hara/age fotostock.* F17 (left), *Roxane/viestiphoto.com.* F17 (center), *George Haling/age fotostock.* F17 (right), *Walter Bibikow/viestiphoto.com.* **Chapter 1: The Alpilles, Arles & the Camargue:** 1, *Walter Bibikow/ age fotostock.* 2 (top), *Henry Ausloos/age fotostock.* 2 (bottom left), *Corbis.* 2 (bottom right), *Stanislaus Fautre/viestiphoto.com.* 3, *José Fuste Raga/age fotostock.* 18, *Henry Ausloos/age fotostock.* 20, *Roxane/ viestiphoto.com.* 21, *Roxane/viestiphoto.com.* 22 (top), *Stanislaus Fautre/viestiphoto.com.* 22 (bottom), *Roxane/viestiphoto.com.* 23, *Mas de la Fouque.* 28, *Doug Scott/age fotostock.* 29, *SuperStock/age fotostock.* **Chapter 2: The Vaucluse:** 55, *Doug Scott/age fotostock.* 56 (top), *Bruno Morandi/age fotostock.* 56 (bottom),* Johnny Stockshooter/age fotostock.* 57, *Bruno Morandi/age fotostock.* 93 (top), *Chad Ehlers/age fotostock.* 93 (bottom), *Renaud Visage/age fotostock.* 94 (top), *David Barnes/age fotostock.* 94 (bottom left), *David Buffington/age fotostock.* 94 (bottom right), *Craig Lovell/viestiphoto.com.* 95 (left), *Doug Scott/age fotostock.* 95 (right), *Bruno Morandi/age fotostock.* 96 (top), *Susan Jones/age fotostock.* 96 (bottom), *Plus Pix/age fotostock.* 97 (top), *Sergio Cozzi/Ask Images/viestiphoto.com.* 97 (bottom), *Plus Pix/age fotostock.* 98, *Sergio Cozzi/Ask Images/viestiphoto.com.* 99 (top), *P. Cherfils/Ask Images/viestiphoto.com.* 99 (center), *SGM/age fotostock.* 99 (bottom), *Doug Scott/age fotostock.* 100, *L'Occitane en Provence.* **Chapter 3: Aix, Marseille & the Central Coast:** 125, *Doug Scott/age fotostock.* 126 (top), *Walter Bibikow/viestiphoto.com.* 126 (bottom), *Walter Bibikow/age fotostock.* 127, *Erich Lessing/Art Resource, NY.* 142 (top and bottom), *Robert Fisher.* 143 (top), *Erich Lessing/Art Resource, NY.* 143 (bottom), *Robert Fisher.* 164, *Owen Franken.* 165 (top left), *Enrico Bartolucci/Ask Images/viestiphoto.com.* 165 (top right), *Owen Franken.* 165 (bottom), *George Haling/age fotostock.* 166, *Owen Franken.* 167, *Owen Franken.* 168 (top), *Moulin de Mougins.* 168 (bottom), *Christian Etienne.* 169 (top), *Owen Franken.* 169 (bottom), *M. Cristofori/Ask Images/viestiphoto. com.* **Chapter 4: The Western Côte d'Azur:** 199, *Sylvain Grandadam/age fotostock.* 200 (top), *Targa/age fotostock.* 200 (bottom left and right), *Stanislaus Fautre/viestiphoto.com.* **Chapter 5: Nice & the Eastern Côte d'Azur:** 243, *Sergio Pitamitz/age fotostock.* 244 (top), *Walter Bibikow/viestiphoto.com.* 244 (bottom), *Doug Scott/age fotostock.* 245 (left), *Walter Bibikow/viestiphoto.com.* 245 (right), *Moulin de Mougins.* 274, *Matisse, Henri (1869-1954) Blue Nude II, 1952.* © *2006 Succession H. Matisse, Paris / Artists Rights Society (ARS), New York. Musee National d'Art Moderne, Centre Georges Pompidou, Paris, France. Photo Credit : CNAC/MNAM/Dist. Réunion des Musées Nationaux/Art Resource, NY.* 275, © *2006 Estate of Pablo Picasso/Artists Rights Society (ARS), New York. Photo Credit: Galerie Madoura.* 276, © *2006 Estate of Pablo Picasso/Artists Rights Society (ARS), New York. Photo Credit: Walter Bibikow/viestiphoto.com.* 277 (top left), *Walter Bibikow/viestiphoto.com.* 277 (top right), © *2006 Artists Rights Society (ARS), New York/ADAGP, Paris. Photo Credit: SEF/Art Resource, NY.* 277 (bottom left), © *2006 Artists Rights Society (ARS), New York/ADAGP, Paris. Photo Credit: Paul Cherfils/viestiphoto.com.* 277 (bottom right), *Matisse, Henri (1869-*

ABOUT THE AUTHORS

Nancy Coons, who wrote the first edition of *Fodor's Provence and the Côte d'Azur,* could have made up all her reviews by staying home with her family in Lorraine, sipping pastis, watching Pagnol videos, and reading Peter Mayle. But already having put down roots in the land of cigales and plane trees during her years of research for other Fodor's projects (including *Escape to Provence* and *Escape to the Riviera*), she went to the other extreme. She picked grapes in the Var, scuffed shin-deep through ochre dust, rode horseback in the Camargue, set up housekeeping in nine rural gîtes, and trudged 180 km behind 2,500 clamorous sheep. When French vacations allow, her husband and their daughters Elodie and Alice accompany her on the road. Even this can pall: After months of Riviera cuisine, Alice threatened "pesto-cide."

Sarah Fraser left the frozen Canadian tundra with the firm intention of finally finding warmth for her perpetually cold feet. Through a series of chance encounters, she ended up happily—and warmly—ensconced on the Mediterranean Coast, and has not looked back since. *Au contraire,* she found a new home near resplendent Cannes. Further draws? An unmitigated passion for lavender-flavored crème brûlée; the sheer bliss of firewood crackling in a stone fireplace on a summer's night; and a pure delight in the sweet smell of newborn son Raphael. Always in search of the perfect tapenade, Sarah happily tests restaurants and hotels for many travel publications, including Time Out and Fodor's. For this edition, she updated chapters 1 and 4, as well as writing our special features, "Don't

Fence Me In: France's Wild West" and "Blue Gold: The Lavender Route."

Rosa Jackson lived in Paris for ten years before falling in love with a 17th-century apartment in the Vieux Nice, a few steps from the Cours Saleya market. She is now living her dream of teaching Niçois cooking in her home (www.petitsfarcis.com), while seizing every opportunity to explore and write about Provence. For her, the ochre and pink tones of France's most Italian city provide the perfect complement to the more sober elegance of Paris, where she still spends a good part of the year writing about restaurants for Fodor's, Time Out, *Paris Notes,* and *Australian Gourmet Traveller* while designing personalized food itineraries (www.edible-paris.com). Her three-year-old son Sam shows a similar penchant for the good life. For this edition, she updated chapters 2, 4, and 5, as well as writing our special feature, "Cuisine of the Sun."

Editor **Robert I. C. Fisher** would like to thank Louise O'Brien of the French Government Travel Office for allowing him to participate in a press trip to Aix-en-Provence in anticipation of the 2006 Cézanne Year (the 100th anniversary of the great painter's death). As special as that was, his own subsequent tour of the Côte d'Azur was even more magical, as one dinner at the Hôtel de Cagnard in Haut-de-Cagnes proved: While feasting on black-truffle lasagna, he looked up to see the medieval ceiling slide open to reveal the evening sky and his first shooting star. It took him weeks to detox from that trip, but he's ready to "retox" all over again.